800–1000
600–800
400–600
200–400
0–200
Sea Level

Main contours are show
at 61-metre (200-foot) i

——— Generally the
Australian and New Ze
trenches at September

– – – Tracks

——— Roads

Metres

0  100 200 300 400 500 600 700 800 900 1000

Scrubby Knoll

GUN RIDGE

Legge Valley

MORTAR RIDGE

DEAD MAN'S

Pope's
Hill

The Sphinx

Quinn's Post
Courtney's
Post
Steele's Post
German
Officers'
Trench
Wire Gully
Johnston's
Jolly
Owen's Gully
LONE PINE PLATEAU

Rest Gully
Monash Valley
Shrapnel Valley

Plugge's
Plateau
Bridges' Road
Brown's Dip
Artillery Road
BOLTON'S RIDGE

White's Valley
Shell Green

Gully
North Beach
Sap
ARI BURNU
ANZAC  COVE
HELL SPIT
BRIGHTON  BEACH

The Tragedy & Glory of Gallipoli

# ANZAC AND EMPIRE

*Horace Moore-Jones*, Cheshire Ridge, looking west to Table Top and Salt Lake, *1915 (watercolour with pencil, brown pen and ink).*

To the One Who reads this book

I'm not too good at spelling etc. & I've written this under fire most of the time so please excuse mistakes etc

—Diary of Private D. R. Argyle, 6th Battalion AIF, killed in action at Passchendaele, 20 October 1917.

I talked to the Turks, one of whom pointed to the graves. 'That's politics,' he said. Then he pointed to the dead bodies and said: 'That's diplomacy. God pity all of us poor soldiers.'

—Aubrey Herbert, *Mons, Anzac and Kut*, on the armistice at Anzac to bury the dead, 24 May 1915.

The Tragedy & Glory of Gallipoli

# ANZAC AND EMPIRE

Leo Cooper
London

Created and produced by Mead & Beckett Publishing
25 Surrey Street, Darlinghurst 2010 NSW Australia

Text copyright © Estate of John Robertson 1990
Copyright © this edition, Mead & Beckett, 1990

First published in 1990
This edition published by Leo Cooper
Leo Cooper is an independent imprint of the Octopus Publishing Group,
Michelin House, 81 Fulham Road London SW3 6RB

London   Melbourne   Auckland

Designed by Barbara Beckett
Maps by Kate Finnie
Typeset by Asco Trade Typesetting Ltd, Hong Kong
Colour photographs scanned by Bright Arts, Hong Kong
Printed and bound by Kyodo-Shing Loong, Singapore

ISBN 0 85052 6825

# CONTENTS

*Frank Crozier,*
Trench Life at
Anzac. *The distinc-*
*tive experience of*
*Anzac, the constricted*
*battlefield scored with*
*trenches and nowhere*
*out of enemy fire,*
*created strong bonds*
*among those who*
*fought there.*

# _PREFACE_

_T_HIS BOOK is not a tactical history of the Anzac battles. The superlative account is the two-volume official history by the doyen of Australia's military historians, C. E. W. Bean, although there is need for an up-to-date analytical study. Nor does this book seek to cover the same ground or explore the same themes as did Lloyd Robson and Bill Gammage in their famous pioneering works, _The First A.I.F.: A Study of Its Recruitment 1914–1918_ (1970) and _The Broken Years_ (1975), but inevitably there is a little overlap between their books and mine. What I seek to do is to tell a story through the words of Australians who fought at Gallipoli. My aim is to convey the thoughts, attitudes and language of 1915, rather than of the 1980s, which I do not hold to be superior. Nor do I wish to present Anzac in isolation. On the contrary, its fascination increases if it is set in its context of a complex network—of Imperial war strategy (both European and Pacific), of international diplomacy and of British domestic politics. What happened in those arenas helped shape the Gallipoli campaign, including its Anzac component. Indeed, an understanding of the fighting is not possible without knowledge of the wider issues. At the same time, Australia's profound reaction to the events of 1915 shown in its attitude to the official British post-mortem on the campaign helps illustrate the legacies of Anzac, particularly its impact on the Australian psyche. Certain subordinate themes contribute to my picture, such as British appraisals of Australian fighting ability.

I do not seek to exaggerate Australia's role in the Gallipoli campaign, merely to focus strongly on my subject. Not a great deal of space is devoted to the forces of other nations on the peninsula, but this, I hope, will not mislead readers into underestimating their contribution. The Helles battles, for instance, are only lightly touched on, because Australians were heavily involved there only briefly. As a poignant measure of Australia's part in the Gallipoli fighting, note that its dead were slightly less than 7,600, whereas the far larger British forces lost about four times as many killed. French killed totalled 3,706 plus 6,092 missing (who must be presumed killed), making a total of 9,798, nearly all of whom were troops from colonial Africa. The Turks lost some 86,500 men dead, killed in battle, missing or died of diseases contracted in the campaign.

My concentration on a single country needs special mention also in light of this book's title and its main content indicated in the preceding paragraph. It is of course impossible to write a history of the Australians at Gallipoli without frequent references to New Zealanders. Nonetheless, my treatment of New Zealand is strictly limited by several considerations: I lack the specialist knowledge needed to do justice to that country's role in the campaign, the theme I have chosen is substantial enough as it is, and the availability of Christopher Pugsley's very fine _Gallipoli: The New Zealand Story_ removes the need for any further contribution by me.

The Great War is unusual among events in Australian history in that a rich repository of unprinted private and public archives is available to scholars. Official unprinted archives—Department of Defence records, together with AIF war diaries and reports—are voluminous. As well, many senior leaders left private collections which range from good to magnificent. Moreover, many men of much more lowly rank in the AIF, and nurses too, left their own impressions of 'the great adventure' in letters and diaries now deposited in public archives or libraries in Australia or England or held in private hands. The collections naturally vary in size and quality, but nearly all of them have something to offer the scholar, while the best of them give a superb account of how the campaign appeared to the men in the firing line. An obvious corollary of these riches is that, for reasons of space and repetition, it is impossible to present them comprehensively in this one book. Of collections read but not quoted, an occasional one is listed in the notes on sources.

## ACKNOWLEDGEMENTS

*I* AM MOST GRATEFUL to Dr Margot Z. Simington, who read and commented on almost the entire penultimate draft of the book. Professor Alan Gilbert read a draft of the chapter on the Dardanelles Commission, and this and other chapters were read by Dr Robin Prior, Dr Barry Smith and Mr A. J. Hill. I am responsible for any mistakes of fact and infelicities of expression that remain. For expert and friendly assistance, and the provision of fine working facilities, I am indebted to the Australian War Memorial, Canberra; the National Library of Australia; Australian Archives; the Public Record Office, Kew, UK; the Imperial War Museum, London; the National Maritime Museum, Greenwich; the Bodleian Library, Oxford; Churchill College, Cambridge; the Liddell Hart Centre for Military Archives, University of London King's College; the Old War Office Library, Ministry of Defence, London; the India Office Library, London; and Peter Liddle, whose archives when I used them were housed in the Sunderland Polytechnic. The Institute of Commonwealth Studies, University of London, and the Australian Studies Centre kindly provided me with a room and companionship in the first six months of 1982, when I started work on this book—to be followed by a hiatus of three years as I discharged other commitments.

I owe a great debt to Dr J. J. Connors, Dr Terry Gavaghan, their medical helpers and the staff in the Calvary Hospital, ACT, without whose skills I would not have been able to continue working on this book.

The book is dedicated to Margot Simington and to Alec and Patsy Hill, to my sisters and brother, and to other friends and colleagues whose support and sympathy during my recent illness was of such great encouragement to me, in particular Don Beer, Sandra Burchill, Ria de Groot, Peter Dennis, Peter Edwards, Ashley Ekins, Alan Gilbert, Jeffrey Grey, David Horner, Ken and Amirah Inglis, Shirley Lithgow, Brett Lodge, John McCarthy, Robin Prior, John Ritchie, Roslyn Russell, Barry and Ann Smith, Nancy Taylor, Roger Thompson, Gerald Walsh, Wendy Way. . . .

J. R.
January 1989

# Note

John Robertson worked on his manuscript until the day of his death—9 January 1989. He left the task of finalising it for publication in my hands, assisted by Roslyn Russell, who prepared the Biographical Notes. I am very grateful for her help and for that so freely given by others of John's friends, including Alec Hill, Ken Inglis, Chris Coulthard-Clark and Ashley Ekins and by staff at the Australian War Memorial. John's former colleagues in the Department of History at the Australian Defence Force Academy, Canberra, have been a constant support, generously sharing their expertise. Without the department's assistance, it would have been very difficult to have brought this project to a conclusion.

Every effort has been made to document the manuscript comprehensively, but inevitably there are a few sources that cannot be located. I trust readers will understand the difficulties and appreciate that any oversights are inadvertent. On John's behalf, I wish to thank all those who have kindly given him access to material, and allowed quotation from it or reproduction of paintings and photographs over which they hold copyright, including the Trustees of the Australian War Memorial; the National Library of Australia; the Returned Services League of Australia; Mr Peter Liddle for the Liddle Collection at the University of Leeds; the Trustees of the Imperial War Museum; the Trustees of the Liddell Hart Centre for Military Archives, King's College London; the Librarian New College Oxford; the Master, Fellows and Scholars of Churchill College in the University of Cambridge, and the Clerk of Records House of Lords Records Office. Quotation from Crown material in copyright records in the Public Record Office London appears by permission of the Controller of HM Stationery Office.

Despite all our endeavours, it has not been possible to contact every copyright holder.

Margot Simington

# SOLDIERS FOR EMPIRE

$I$N 1900 AUSTRALIAN VOLUNTEERS were fighting for the British Empire in its war against the Boer republics in South Africa. In August the conflict, less than a year old, was in its guerrilla phase. Parties of Boer troops roamed the veldt, eluding larger British forces and attacking their communications and supply depots. One was on a bare hill in the western Transvaal. The Elands River camp was guarded by fewer than five hundred colonial troops, most of them from Australia. It was attacked and heavily shelled by a Boer force of 2,500 to 3,000 men. A nearby British general thought loss of the camp was inevitable, and an Australian newspaper reported the garrison's surrender. The besiegers did proffer an honourable surrender but it was refused. The colonials resisted for twelve days, until relieved by a large force under General Lord Kitchener, who was the deputy commander of Britain's army in South Africa. This was the first time Kitchener came into close contact with Australian troops. Like other British officers he amply praised their resourcefulness and courage in holding the vulnerable post against such odds.[1]

Other features of the siege would have seemed familiar to observers of Australian soldiers in later conflicts. Before the Boers arrived, the Australians were most reluctant to dig protective trenches. After the siege began they dug feverishly at the first opportunity and used much initiative in improving the camp's defences. A relieving force under General Sir Frederick Carrington got to within four kilometres of Elands River and then retreated, for no good reason. Trooper F. W. King, a New South Wales Imperial Bushman under Carrington's command, commented, 'We retired, why I don't know, but I suppose the General does.' Colonel Hore, the British commanding officer at Elands River, forbade night sorties, but Australians disobeyed this order and made many effective night raids. Every morning they hoisted the Union Jack and put it up again whenever the Boers shot it down. After the relief they sold battle souvenirs at a good price to English officers.[2]

Among the British officers who already had seen much of the Australians in South Africa were two generals, Ian Hamilton and E. T. Hutton. Both had Australians under their command as part of Lord Roberts's force, which by June 1900 had occupied the Boer capitals. Hutton had been commandant of the New South Wales military forces from 1893 to 1896 and returned to Australia following the federation of the six colonies in 1901.

Over sixteen thousand Australians served in South Africa, but the army that came into being in March 1901, when the Commonwealth took over the six state forces, existed more in theory than in reality. It was the task of its first commander-in-chief, Hutton, to create a cohesive and more substantial force. Hutton should have found Australia a congenial place in which to serve, for the new nation was remarkably loyal to its 'mother country' and to the Empire. It remained so for years. The ties of empire regularly featured in contemporary literature. Among numerous instances may be mentioned A. Wyatt Tilby's *The English People Overseas*, vol. 5, *Australasia, 1788–1911*, which described how these colonies 'grew into new English nations'. Tilby hoped that, through a selective immigration policy, a new British nation would be built in the south 'better than the old British nation in Europe'. To P. Evans Lewin, librarian of the Royal Colonial Institute in London, as to many Imperial-minded Englishmen, the Australian was 'a Briton modified by his environment. Distance, space and climate [had] played their part in this modification.' *The Oxford Survey of the British Empire* was another of the books which saw Australia primarily as a portion of the greatest empire in the history of the world, 'the empire on which the sun never sets'. On the other hand, at the time of the 1911 census 82 per cent of Australians had been born in the country, and only 13 per cent in the British Isles. Of course the proportion of native-born adults would have been lower than 82 per cent. As well, Australia's population contained a significant Irish element; and the great distance between Australia and Britain was inevitably giving rise to some differences in outlook, not least in questions of foreign policy and strategic issues.[3]

Hutton was determined to work against such 'anti-Imperial' tendencies. He had a 'fervent belief in the British Empire, in which he saw the armies as a force for unity'. His good friend Hamilton told him in January 1902 that he was the only man with the requisite energy and knowledge to carry through this really difficult reorganisation. Hamilton tacitly recognised the existence of Australia's different attitudes in warning Hutton to be deferential and agreeable to Australian cabinet ministers and their wives; he should take care to 'fill them up with champagne' whenever a 'fair opening' arose. But Hutton was an abrasive personality who soon clashed with his ministers, notably over his wish to implement British cabinet ministers' ideas of preparing Australian troops to participate in Imperial wars. Hutton told Hamilton in November 1902, after he had been ten months in his new command, 'Rightly or wrongly Australians have lost confidence in War Office methods and view with something of contempt all that emanates therefrom whether personal or written.'[4]

Nevertheless, there were always British military and political leaders contemplating the help that the colonies could provide in wartime. Hamilton summed up this view in June 1903, the year he became Quartermaster-General. He thought Britain could confidently look to colonies to provide 'great potential resources'. He continued: 'The exact figures our colonies will give us will depend upon the justice of our cause and the military spirit of the nation. As regards your splendid force of Light Horse, I am more sanguine than you are, for I feel sure that, whatever the conditions may be under which they are serving, they will, when the great war to which you refer takes place, very easily be made available for general service.'[5]

A specific, although unofficial, request followed in December 1903. Hamilton asked Hutton if the Australians would be prepared to contribute three thousand to four thousand mounted men to help their Japanese allies (the Anglo-Japanese Alliance had been signed in January 1902) against Russian Cossacks in Manchuria. Hamilton recognised this scheme was 'somewhat visionary'. Indeed it was. The Australian government, under the Liberal leader Alfred Deakin, was not interested in the idea. But Hutton assured Hamilton there was a very strong feeling in Australia to help 'the mother country' in any war in which the general interests of the Empire were involved. Austin Chapman, the Minister for Defence, had already asked Hutton how Australia could help militarily if the current tension between Japan and Russia led to a threat to the British Empire's interests.[6]

Hutton left Australia in 1904, after another row with ministers. The government abolished the post he had held and replaced it with the Military Board. The command of the army was placed substantially in the hands of officers who were

Australian-born or who had had a significant career in Australian forces. This development coincided with a change in the great-power balance in the Pacific.[7]

Japan's victory in the Russo-Japanese War (1904–5) was of great importance in stimulating Australian interest in defence policy. Although the Anglo-Japanese Alliance was renewed in 1905 and again in 1911, many Australians saw Japan as a possible future enemy. They attached new importance to the protection afforded by the British Empire, in particular the Royal Navy. At the same time they paid greater attention to local defence and the distant goal of an Australia independently able to deter an enemy attack.[8]

Partly in response to Japan's rise to power, in 1908 the Australian Labor Party adopted compulsory military training as a central element in its defence policy. Their Liberal opponents also espoused this principle. An amended Defence Act in 1909, sponsored by Deakin's third ('Fusion') ministry, prescribed compulsory military training for boys and youths aged from twelve to twenty, but the legislation did not come into force.

Deakin also invited Lord Kitchener (promoted field marshal in 1909), then nearing the end of his term as commander-in-chief in India, to visit Australia to advise on defence plans. Between 21 December 1909 and 12 February 1910 Kitchener inspected military forces in each state before preparing his report. Because of his reputation and status as the Empire's senior soldier, he was fêted and eulogised almost as a demigod, but a recent scholar has assessed his 'visitation' as of little benefit to the army, apart from his recommendation to set up a military college to train and educate future army officers.[9]

Circumstances surrounding this visit reflected the complex relationship between Australia's loyalty to the Empire and to the nation. Deakin was primarily interested in Australia's national defence, but Kitchener's immediate political superior, R. B. Haldane, the Secretary of State for War, had a different perspective. He wanted to hear from Kitchener what was possible in Australia and New Zealand. 'The constrast with Japan,' he wrote, 'where science has been supreme, ought to be very striking; and yet my impression is that the practical stuff is present in the two British Overseas Dominions if it can only be got together and organised.'[10]

Kitchener saw merit in improving military co-operation between these two dominions, thereby strengthening the Empire. He told Sir Joseph Ward, the Melbourne-born former prime minister of New Zealand, then leader of the Liberal opposition, that the young men of the two dominions, although 'showing markedly different characteristics', were 'splendid material for creating a first-rate fighting machine for the conditions of their country life [were] very similar, producing successful pioneers accustomed to make the land supply the wants of men'. He recommended, 'Uniformity in training and establishment of units, as well as the closest ties of comradeship, in the armed land forces of New Zealand and Australia should be fostered in every way.'[11]

Under the Labor prime ministership of Andrew Fisher, the Royal Military College of Australia opened at Duntroon in 1911; in the same year a system of compulsory military training was implemented. Boys of twelve or thirteen had to do junior cadet training at school. From fourteen to eighteen years they trained as senior cadets. Men aged eighteen to twenty-six could be required to serve in the citizen forces. Despite specific exemptions, notably for those living in sparsely populated areas, this scheme was a major bipartisan commitment to improving Australia's defences.[12]

Both political parties also accelerated the growth of an Australian navy. Fisher's government ordered its first warships in February 1909. The succeeding Deakin 'Fusion' government ordered a dreadnought, then one of the most powerful of warships. Labor, in office again from April 1910 to June 1913, sought the advice of another British officer, Admiral Sir Reginald Henderson, RN, on plans for future naval growth. As a result, on 4 October 1913 the new Liberal Prime Minister, Joseph Cook, welcomed the ships of the Royal Australian Navy when they made a ceremonial entry into Sydney Harbour. Following the flagship, *Australia* (18,800 tons, eight 12-inch guns) were three light cruisers (5,400 tons, 6-inch guns) and three destroyers (700 tons). There was great public rejoicing and an effusion of national pride and Imperial patriotism. Cook hoped the Australian fleet would 'for ever remain . . . the Australian section of the Imperial Navy'. Within a few months two new 725-ton submarines, *AE1* and *AE2*, joined the fleet.[13]

These improvements in defence were appropriate, considering growing world tensions, for Japan's rise to power was only one of several ominous changes which threatened to end the comfortable world of Pax Britannica. Germany's rapid growth in economic and military strength was upsetting established power balances in Europe and beyond. It had acquired an extensive colonial empire and created a large merchant fleet, and it was building a powerful navy. Great potential for disruption centred on the Balkans, where the crumbling Austro-Hungarian Empire confronted rising, and rival, nationalist movements. The Ottoman Empire ('the sick man of Europe') was equally unstable; during the nineteenth century and early in the twentieth it lost much of its territory and therefore power in Europe and elsewhere. This culminated in the Balkan war of 1912–13, when Montenegro, Bulgaria, Greece and Serbia combined to expel the Ottomans from all but a small part of Europe. Such unrest threatened to worsen. There was no guarantee that the European alliance system (basically Germany and Austria-Hungary versus the Triple Entente of Britain, France and Russia), would be able to prevent such local conflicts from drawing the great powers into war. As Australia was legally, emotionally, intellectually and ethnically part of one great power, it could not escape the implications of these growing tensions.

Hence, in another display of the fusion of Imperial and national interests in the formation of defence policy, four years after Kitchener's visit his close associate, General Sir Ian Hamilton, at the request of the Australian government, toured local military establishments to inspect recent progress. Hamilton had been an officer in the British army since 1870. He had shown great courage in various wars of Empire, his left arm having been permanently crippled in action. Promoted to high posts in the British army because of his wide-ranging abilities, he became Inspector-General of Oversea Forces in 1910. He visited every oversea British garrison and forces in South Africa and Canada, finishing a seven-week tour there just seven months before reaching Australia. Hamilton had been a fine marksman; he wrote well and enjoyed poetry and music. He was grandson of a viscount and married to a baronet's daughter. In terms of Imperial style he was not far inferior to Kitchener. He was acclaimed accordingly in Australia.

As the *Otranto* neared Fremantle, Hamilton told his wife he felt 'quite lost in this immense southern ocean'. 'Ye Gods,' he wrote to her, 'what a whirl of travel—banquets—inspections—speeches, work lies before me, stretching right up to May 30th; supposing I last so long.' Next day he was met at Fremantle by numerous civil and military leaders. With Earl Grey, a former governor-general of Canada, who had also travelled on the *Otranto*, he was cordially welcomed at a civic reception in Perth's Town Hall. The *West Australian* celebrated the arrival of 'two such distinguished Imperial citizens' in a leading article. It reported Hamilton's speech at length. After three days of enthusiastic hospitality and adulation, Hamilton wrote to his wife, 'If West Australia is in any way a fair sample of the rest I think I should do all right provided I keep fit and well.' He sailed from Albany on 8 February 1914. As his ship approached Adelaide he complained to his wife about the 'same monstrous line of speeches. One single man, Sir John Forrest, proposed my health four times in four days at Perth.' He continued: 'Ten more weeks of it! I wonder how I shall stand it. And the people are so *common place*. For Heaven's sake keep that to yourself but so far it strikes me so.'[14]

Throughout the land, Hamilton inspected fifty-two thousand army and naval cadets. He had been involved in controversy in England since 1910 through his opposition to conscription, but he explained to Australians that he approved of their system of compulsory military training for boys and youths. He was guest of honour at dinners of veterans of the South African War, where Imperial rhetoric flourished. He was cheered when he expressed hope that cadets being trained in Australia would 'respond to the call of the motherland did she need assistance'.

Hamilton saw almost everything the army had to show. He finished his report, which he predicted would be 'epoch making', late in April as he left Australia *en route* to New Zealand. He was suitably diplomatic in praising Australia and its people in his farewell remarks. Of Australia's young soldier trainees he said, 'Even now the lads are hardy and wiry . . . with a great amount of nervous energy and quickness, . . . it is quite a mistake to think they are not amenable to discipline.' Observers were misled because 'the code of good form in Australia was rather against manifestations of respect'. Hamilton thought that the lads, because they were intelligent, responded 'at once to the direction of a superior in whom they recognise[d] a master of the business in hand'.[15]

While in New Zealand Hamilton predicted that the Pacific might become a battlefield of continents to decide whether Asiatics or Europeans would guide the region's destinies. The comment provoked resentment in the Japanese press and a retort that Japan merely wanted 'equal footing with whites'. Count Shigenobu Okuma, Japan's Prime Minister, called Hamilton a 'disturber of the peace'. The general explained that his comments were purely hypothetical. One could expect a clash of empires as 'nations grew bigger and wars less frequent, but more terrible'. The *Argus* observed that soldiers 'seldom possess the wise caution of the diplomatist' and sympathised with Japanese annoyance at Hamilton's remarks.[16]

While Hamilton was in Australia, Britain's Liberal government, led by H. H. Asquith, announced the appointment of the Scottish parliamentarian Ronald Munro Ferguson as Australia's new Governor-General. Munro Ferguson, from a wealthy aristocratic family with a strong military and political tradition, was associated with the Liberal Imperialists. He reached Australia in May 1914. The Brisbane *Worker* thought him 'cantankerous' and 'retrogressive', but he was received more favourably elsewhere.[17] After two months in the country he wrote to a friend in England: 'You can hardly believe what solidarity of national life there is between Great Britain and Australia, and here all outward expression of loyalty to the Crown is more apparent even than at home. Certainly Australia seems closer to us than any part of the Empire that I know.'[18]

It would soon become clear that 'outward expression of loyalty to the Crown' was not restricted to the Governor-General's social circle. Munro Ferguson was writing during the European diplomatic crisis provoked by the assassination on 28 June at Sarajevo, in the Bosnian province of the Austro-Hungarian empire, of the Archduke Franz Ferdinand, heir to that empire's throne. Would such an event, on the other side of the world, in a town few Australians had heard of, eventually lead to thousands of Australians dying in battle? It did not at first appear likely.

While the handful of men in charge of the diplomacy of Europe's major powers manoeuvred, bargained, and weighed up the risks of war, Australians relied on newspapers for their understanding of what was happening. They were fully aware of the grave European crisis when Austria, holding neighbouring Serbia responsible for the assassination, delivered an ultimatum to that nation on 23 July. But even when, on 28 July, Austria declared war on Serbia, many expected that Sir

Edward Grey, Britain's Foreign Secretary, would mediate and contain the conflict. 'European statemanship will indeed be a poor thing if [the situation] is permitted to develop into a general war,' asserted the Melbourne *Age*. On 31 July, with Belgrade, the Serbian capital, under attack, 'The Dreaded General War' seemed possible. Next day, Australian newspapers still maintained some optimism, but over the weekend the news worsened. On Monday 3 August, with Germany and Austria now at war with Russia, Serbia's would-be protector, headlines proclaimed, 'Great War', 'Greatest War in World's History', 'Armageddon! Europe Ablaze'. British involvement seemed imminent. A wavering Asquith cabinet finally declared war when Germany invaded neutral Belgium seeking a quick victory over France.

Legally, as part of the British Empire, Australia was at war immediately upon the British declaration. That legality reflected the views of most Australians, who were willing to help the mother country in a crisis. Newspapers proclaimed that Australians would support to the 'utmost limit' the Empire within which they had 'grown and prospered for so many years'. At the most fundamental level no conflict was seen between the interests of Australia and of the British Empire. The two coincided: Australia's security depended on a British victory. Leaders of both Labor and Liberal political parties, then engaged in a federal election campaign, were at one on this.

So, with little more than a week's warning of the final crisis, Australia on 4 August entered a state of war with Germany. (The British and Austro-Hungarian Empires were at war from 12 August.) The Adelaide *Advertiser* predicted that this would surpass all previous wars in horror and devastation. There seemed to be an awareness that a major turning-point had been reached in world history. None could have foreseen the full extent of the cataclysm to follow from the disastrous two weeks of European diplomacy; but doubtless most of those ho deplored the execrable diplomacy which had allowed this feared general European war to break out could see that it was important to win the war, for the consequences of defeat would be severe, as the losers found over four years later.[19]

It is easy to understand why many Australians did not want to be involved in European conflicts, which often sprang from bloodthirsty vicious rivalries deeply rooted in history. Perhaps isolationist Australians could be excused for thinking of many European nations as inhabited by unattractive people, not the sort one would willingly choose as allies. Nonetheless, in 1914 such views were overwhelmed by Imperial spirit.

The eminent historians Len Turner and Zara Steiner have convincingly argued that European instability in 1914 did not make war inevitable.[20] Even during the diplomatic crisis of July 1914 the leaders making the fateful decisions could have averted the disaster had they possessed a sufficient fund of wisdom, foresight and decent human qualities such as compassion. In theory, fear or prudence might also have caused restraint; but there were no nuclear weapons to convince political leaders how catastrophic a major war would be.

# CHAPTER 2

# *A SMALL EMPIRE EASILY WON*

$F$OR A NATION of fewer than five million people, Australia's armed services had grown remarkably in the four years to August 1914. Defence expenditure had trebled. The Royal Australian Navy (RAN) had been created, with permanent forces of over 3,600 compared with 400 in 1911. The navy was ready for war. Since 1910 the army had almost doubled to about 3,000 in the permanent forces and 43,000 part-time militia and volunteers.[1] Youths who received military training in the 'boy conscription' scheme, begun in July 1911, were still too young for active service. A military flying school had just been set up at Point Cook, close to Melbourne. The only airmen from the school to fly on active service before the end of 1915 were the four who were to serve in Britain's Mesopotamian campaign.

The doctrine of the military unity of the Empire was widely accepted, especially by those best placed to make or influence decisions. There were disagreements between Australian and British defence planners, each emphasising the dangers in their own region, but defence against local threats was largely seen in Imperial terms. The Empire, it was assumed, would defend its constituent parts wherever and whenever they were threatened. Australia's armed forces were shaped to accord with this concept of Imperial defence, and they were led by Britons or British-trained officers.

The Australian Council of Defence, set up in 1905 to allow government and service leaders to co-ordinate policy, was of no importance during the war, meeting only twice, in February 1915. Imperial Australians, men whose lives had been divided between Australia and other parts of the Empire, dominated membership of both the Naval Board and the Military Board, which were responsible for the efficient administration of their services rather than for matters of policy or strategy. None of the three service members of the Naval Board had been born in Australia, but two, including the 'father' of Australia's navy, Admiral Sir William Creswell, the First Naval Member, had lived in the country for over thirty years and were RAN officers. The other was a Royal Navy officer, as was the commander of the Australian squadron, Admiral Sir George Patey.

From 1910 to 1914 General George Kirkpatrick, a British army officer, occupied the most important post in the Australian army, that of Inspector-General. He was succeeded by Brigadier-General William T. Bridges, who, although Scottish born, had lived for years in Australia. The members of the Military Board were men either of Australian birth or considerable Australian experience. For example, Colonel J. Gordon Legge, who was Chief of the General Staff from 1 August 1914 until May 1915, was born in London but had made his home in Sydney.

Leaders of the opposing political parties pledged their support to Britain. When war came, they were in the midst of an election campaign: in June, Joseph Cook's Liberal government, lacking a majority in the Senate, had obtained from the

Governor-General a double dissolution of parliament. The most famous declaration of Imperial loyalty was the promise by Andrew Fisher, leader of the Labor opposition, that Australians would 'help and defend' Britain to their last man and last shilling. The Cook government, although unsure of re-election, swiftly made decisions consistent with Empire euphoria. Following a cabinet meeting in Melbourne on the afternoon of Monday 3 August, the British government was told that if Britain went to war Australia would be prepared to place RAN vessels under British Admiralty control. Australia was also prepared to send a land force of twenty thousand men 'of any suggested composition to any destination desired by the Home Government'. The force was to be at the complete disposal of the 'Home Government', and Australia would bear the cost of its dispatch and maintenance. Australia would eventually accept the financial liability for keeping a much larger army in the field, in a generous spirit which the British government acknowledged. By 7 August the Admiralty was satisfied that the RAN had been 'effectively placed' under its control.[2] Communications between the Admiralty and the Naval Board were sometimes to take the form of suggestions rather than orders, although by May 1917 an Australian public servant was complaining that the Navy Department regarded itself as 'part and parcel' of the British navy, going to extremes to evade Commonwealth government control. Australia bore the whole cost of RAN activities during the war.[3]

Considering its humble status in world affairs, it was not surprising that Australia had thus promptly surrendered strategic control of its forces to Asquith's Liberal government. This government had gained a famous place in British history through its peacetime work. It was not until much later that W. M. Hughes, Australia's prime minister during most of the war, recorded the judgement that Asquith was 'temperamentally unfitted to lead the Empire in war',[4] a verdict attested to by history and historians.

Britain's full cabinet was too big to discuss war planning effectively, so on 5 August Asquith convened a council of war. It included the service ministers, Field Marshal Lord Kitchener, Britain's senior serving army officer on his first day as Secretary of State for War, and Winston Churchill, First Lord of the Admiralty. Also present was R. B. Haldane, the former Secretary of State for War, now Lord Chancellor.

After deciding to send the British Expeditionary Force to face the German army sweeping through Belgium, the council of war agreed that it needed to reinforce Egypt and, on Kitchener's recommendation, that India be asked to provide the garrison. Then Haldane reported the offers of contingents by Canada, Australia and New Zealand. He said they could best be used to relieve overseas garrisons, although 'this would not be popular in the Dominions'. Asquith said the offers should be accepted—but not for overseas garrison duty: the dominions should decide the strength of their contingents, and they should be sent to England.[5] That day F. G. A. Butler of the Colonial Office, private secretary to Lewis Harcourt, Secretary of State for the Colonies, wrote to a friend in Australia: 'The great feature of the whole crisis has been the magnificent rally of the Dominions.' Butler considered his friend lucky to 'have had the privilege of being in Australia at such a time'. He thought it 'splendid' that Australia was now handing over its own fleet to the Admiralty's unrestricted control, especially as this came hard on the heels of angry objections to Britain's pre-war policy, so forcefully espoused by Churchill, of stationing all the Royal Navy's new battle-cruisers in waters near England, and none in the Pacific. This major divergence of viewpoints—Australia's view of its need for regional defence contrasted with Britain's view of the unity of Imperial defence guaranteed by the Royal Navy's existence inviolate—was swept aside by enthusiastic Australian support for Britain at this critical time.[6] As Munro Ferguson confirmed to Lewis Harcourt, the spirit of the ministers and the people was 'excellent'.[7]

The Asquith government's appreciation of the dominions' response soon led Harcourt to tell Kitchener it was very desirable that contingents from Australia, New Zealand and Canada should march through London on their way to their camps. A public reception 'would have considerable Imperial advantages here'. Kitchener replied that that 'would more naturally come after they had given proof of their prowess in the field...a triumphal march before they had done any fighting would...be a mistake'.[8]

Some Australians, helping to prepare forces to fight at Britain's side, thought the war could be over before their army reached the battlefield. This possibility was ended by the two immense European campaigns then being fought, which decided the shape of the war. Australian newspapers gave their readers an adequate, basically accurate account of the course of those campaigns. Readers followed the German army's sweep through Belgium and its advance on Paris. At Risdon in Tasmania, John Gellibrand, a farmer who in a few years would be a very successful commander of an Australian division, referred sarcastically to the 'usual Belgian victories' in the war news. Australians read of the French cabinet leaving Paris for Bordeaux and understood that 'German strategy assumed a quick, overwhelming victory against France' and that the German repulse at the battle of the Marne (5–9 September) ruined their plans. A map published in the *West Australian* on 12 September showed clearly the territory won and lost in those seven epochal weeks, except that German gains were slightly exaggerated. Newspapers recognised that Germany would offer fierce resistance and conveyed Kitchener's warning of a long struggle. As Private T. J. Richards, of Sydney, in the Australian Medical Corps noted, Germany was very skilled at making war, and the Allies were 'not going to win for a very long time yet'. Australians knew about the enormous size of the rival armies and that warfare on this scale was unprecedented. They also knew about the fearful carnage and slaughter in Belgium and north-eastern France.[9]

They were not quite so well informed on the fighting on the Eastern Front, even though news of Russia's advance into East Prussia soon arrived, and its initial victory at Gumbinnen (20 August) was reported within five days. There was a similar time-lag in the case of the German victory at Tannenberg (25–30 August), but it took longer for Australians to grasp the severity of this massive Russian defeat. It would have been difficult, however, for any Australian to have foreseen the full import for their country of the European campaigns of August and September. Germany's victory on the Eastern Front balanced its reverse on the Western Front, so providing the combination of results most likely to ensure a long war. Germany's eastern victory also shaped the events that led to Australians fighting in Turkey.

Against this background of gigantic European battles, the Cook government began honouring its promise to provide a force of twenty thousand men. Young Robert Antill in Melbourne had written to his parents in England on 3 August: 'Everybody is nearly off their heads here...we have all got the war fever.' He would have loved to be in London for the excitement. In any case, he wanted to be in the fray and have a go at some Germans. He soon joined the thousands of adventurous and patriotic men crowding Australian recruiting offices in those oft-

*Born on 3 January 1901 in the Melbourne suburb of Hawthorn, Jim Martin left school at fourteen and on 12 April 1915 joined the AIF as an eighteen-year-old farmhand. When the transport* Southland, *was torpedoed while on its way from Egypt to Gallipoli, he was injured and spent four hours in the water before rescue. He landed with the 21st Battalion at Gallipoli on 8 September and immediately went into the trenches but soon became ill and died in a hospital ship on 25 October. His two letters from the battle-front mention he had received none of the mail written to him from home.*

described scenes of excitement once enlistment in the Australian Imperial Force (AIF) began on 10 August.[10] A correspondent wrote to Cyril Brudenell White, a regular officer, in August regarding a young acquaintance, a university student who had set his heart on joining the first contingent: 'I admire his courage and enterprise. He is very young and scarcely able to realize the nature of what is before him.' Recruits were sought from the ages of eighteen to forty-five inclusive; parents' written consent was needed for youths under twenty-one. Before long there were no vacancies in some specialist branches of the force. It was stressed that only expert bushmen were required for the light horse, and that the riding test was very severe: it was not enough to have been reared amongst horses.[11]

This was the main force then being recruited in Australia, a force quite separate from the existing citizen army for home service. It was not the only one; nor was it the first to see action. Although Europe's fate was in the balance, Britain did not forget its opportunities and responsibilities in the Pacific. The result was a series of naval and military moves in which Australian forces, at London's behest, followed an Imperial policy which in some cases neglected Australia's strategic interests.

The German empire in the Pacific and 'Far East' stretched from Kiaochow, on China's Shantung Peninsula, to north-eastern New Guinea (Kaiser Wilhelmsland). For thirty years Australians had been concerned about the German presence in territory that shared a border with Australian-administered Papua. Only about 6,500 German nationals lived in this widely scattered empire, but in August 1914 there was a modern German naval squadron in the north-western Pacific. Under the able command of Admiral Maximilian von Spee, it contained two 11,600-ton cruisers, *Gneisenau* and *Scharnhorst*, each with eight 8-inch guns and six 6-inch guns, and three light cruisers, including the *Emden*. It faced Britain's China squadron, and the RAN, whose flagship, HMAS *Australia*, was much more powerful than any British or German ship then in the ocean. As well, Japan with its large navy was allied to Britain and was expected to enter the war against Germany. Although Australian territory was effectively protected from German naval attack, its leaders were conscious of the vulnerability of merchant ships carrying its trade if von Spee's vessels became commerce raiders.[12] In fact, von Spee, afraid of the *Australia*, took the *Scharnhorst* and the *Gneisenau* across the Pacific towards South America. But Australians had no means of knowing this at the time, and uncertainty over the whereabouts of von Spee's squadron dominated some Australian decisions in August and September.

On 5 August the Committee of Imperial Defence, a body that advised the British Prime Minister on imperial defence matters, concluded that the Empire should go onto the offensive in the Pacific. Next day Harcourt cabled Australia asking the government, as a 'great and urgent Imperial service', to seize German wireless stations in New Guinea, on Yap (in the Palau islands) and on Nauru.[13] Ships of the Australian squadron had already gone north to search the German islands for German cruisers, and on 11 August, in response to the British request, Australia began enlisting the Australian Naval and Military Expeditionary Force (ANMEF). Commanded by Colonel William Holmes, a Sydney-born militia officer who had served in the Boer War, it was speedily raised, mainly from New South Wales. The force of 1,764, including an infantry battalion, 500 naval reservists and supporting units, embarked on 18 August aboard the *Berrima*, a commissioned merchant vessel, which would be escorted in convoy by RAN warships.[14]

Meanwhile, Japan was moving towards war. On the day that Harcourt asked Australia to seize the German wireless stations, Sir Edward Grey, the Foreign Secretary, urged Japan to attack German ships in the Pacific. Grey soon had second thoughts, partly out of sensitivity to American fears of Japan's encroachments in the region. Similar Australasian apprehensions were represented by the

Colonial Office. So Grey then tried to keep Japan out of the war or, failing that, to restrain it to only limited acts of war. Churchill disagreed. Because of Britain's naval 'weakness' in home waters, he courted the Japanese and encouraged their navy to help Britain by playing a big role in destroying Germany's power in the Pacific.[15]

There were also differences in Count Shigenobu Okuma's government in Japan, although the 'peace party' was on the defensive. Some thought Japan needed to go to war to honour its alliance with Britain. More importantly, leaders realised that the European war gave Japan its 'one in thousand lucky chance' to enlarge its empire. Okuma was soon convinced by the 'war party' led by Baron Takaaki Kato, the Foreign Minister. On 15 August Japan delivered an ultimatum to Germany, followed by the declaration of war on 23 August.[16]

Britain then asked Australia to extend the scope of its expedition to include occupation of all German territory in the Pacific south of the Equator and of many islands north of that line.[17] That was in accord with Australia's strategic interests as then conceived, but at the same time these interests took second place when Cook's government adopted an Admiralty suggestion that the *Australia* and light cruiser *Melbourne* escort a New Zealand contingent which occupied Samoa on 30 August. Meanwhile, the ANMEF convoy, including the *Berrima*, was delayed to await the return of the *Australia*. The force assembled on 9 September near the Louisiade Archipelago, off the south-eastern tip of New Guinea. It then steamed for Rabaul, seat of the German New Guinea government. After brief fighting, in which six Australians were killed, the force took formal control of Rabaul on 13 September, subsequently occupying outlying administrative or trading posts.

When a report of these events reached London, senior Admiralty and Colonial Office officials assessed it as 'a well described account of a set of operations most efficiently conducted throughout'. The Admiralty thought the story reflected 'great credit' on Patey and on the Naval Board and the Australian government; it suggested Harcourt send a congratulatory message on the RAN's services to the Empire.[18] But whether Admiralty instructions leading to these operations reflected credit on British policy-makers is doubtful. The reaction of Senator E. D. Millen, Australia's Minister for Defence, to Harcourt's cable of 6 August was to express long-established naval doctrine, that the first wartime goal of the Australian squadron should be to seek out and destroy enemy warships in the region—as RAN warships had initially begun to do. Many others have also thought the RAN was given the wrong order of priorities in August and September.[19] The German Pacific territories could do little harm to the Empire cause. Once the German Pacific squadron was defeated—a task within RAN capabilities—they could have been occupied at will with minimum naval escort.

That said, at little cost Australia had gained territory which was of considerable strategic significance and potential economic benefit. It was a startling example of the easy pickings a war can bring. As the *Age* wrote, the European war had opened 'an unexpected path . . . to the furtherance of our ambition . . . [to lay] the foundation of a solid Australian sub-empire in the Pacific Ocean'.[20] Australia had been told on 6 August that any territory taken from the Germans would 'be at the disposal of the Imperial Government for purposes of an ultimate settlement at conclusion of the war'. Nonetheless, after conquering these territories, and administering them, Australia could be expected to try to retain them at the end of a victorious war. In 1919, this objective was to help put Australia for the first time on the world diplomatic stage.

Many Australians were delighted to hear that their nation had taken control of German New Guinea. Among them was Andrew Fisher, a 'long-standing Pacific islands imperialist'. Colonel Holmes regarded his force's victory as being 'of great

importance to the Empire'. He was pleased it would change the map a little.[21] The Colonial Office received copies of his voluminous reports on his expedition's achievement and its initial work in administering the conquered territory.[22]

The German surrender in New Guinea coincided with the swearing-in of a new Labor government, following its comfortable win at the elections on 5 September. Fisher's government held a secure majority in the House of Representatives and thirty-one of the thirty-six Senate seats. Six of the ministers had not held a federal portfolio before, but the other five had had ample experience. Fisher had twice before been prime minister. Born in Scotland, he had lived two decades in Australia. He was as deeply committed to supporting Britain in the war as was Cook. So were the two other most senior men in his cabinet, W. M. Hughes and G. F. Pearce. Hughes, that 'fiery particle' of Welsh parentage,[23] was Attorney-General. While in this office his main contribution to the war was to reorganise the base metals industry so that it was no longer tied by long-term contracts to a small group of German firms but was instead controlled by Empire or Australian interests. Senator George Pearce was Minister for Defence for the rest of the war. Having held that portfolio in 1908–9 and 1910–13, he was familiar with the personalities and problems of Australia's armed services. But the wartime departmental workload proved too much even for his great capacity for work, so in July 1915 a separate Department of the Navy was created, its first minister being J. A. Jensen.

In March 1913 the site for the new nation's capital had been named— Canberra—and the foundation stone laid on grazing land of the Limestone Plains in the Southern Tablelands of New South Wales. For the time being, however, the Commonwealth's administration was centred in Melbourne. Federal parliament met there, as did the Navy Board and the army's General Staff. This was the usual

*Raising and forming the AIF required equipment as well as personnel. Thirty-six 18-pounder light field guns—nearly one-third of Australia's total stock—were used in setting up the Field Artillery Brigade (there were no modern howitzers or heavy artillery in Australia at the time). Another forty 18-pounders would be sent away before the end of 1915. This one was photographed with its crew at Gallipoli.*

venue for federal cabinet meetings. The Governor-General's major residence was also there. In short, Melbourne was the nation's *de facto* capital during the war.

By the time Fisher was sworn in, recruiting and training of the AIF had proceeded so well that the first contingent of twenty thousand Australian troops was ready to embark for Europe. Britain's Army Council, a collective body for the development of army policy and chaired by the Secretary for War, had suggested that the volunteers be organised into four brigades—two infantry, one light horse, and one field artillery. General Bridges was determined to provide a complete division, a formation then numbering approximately nineteen thousand men.[24] Indeed, Australian authorities generally were intent on avoiding the Boer War experience of dispatching small units which would be distributed among various British formations. The War Office was amenable, quickly accepting Australia's preference. As Bridges foresaw, this decision to preserve the separate identity of its force overseas was crucially important for Australia's role in the war. It was also important for the development of Australian nationalism.

Amid sustained enthusiasm, recruiting officers were kept busy enlisting men who were to bring Australia fame. Munro Ferguson told the Colonial Office that the Victorian volunteers were 'good raw material' quickly improving in camp.[25] Colonel H. N. MacLaurin, commander of the 1st Brigade (NSW), was more critical. Hurried enrolment without any forethought, he reported, led to the worst type of men being enlisted while good men from the country came too late for the initial quota. He remarked on 'the exposure of the personnel to the evils of venereal disease' but was glad that 'a constant flow of desertions and discharges, mainly of the criminals and wastrels', had removed the worst elements among those who first enlisted.[26]

The government chose Bridges to organise the expeditionary force and promoted him to major-general. He became commander both of the AIF and of the division, which was organised on the current British model, of three brigades each of four battalions. The 1st Infantry Brigade (1st to 4th battalions) was raised in New South Wales, the 2nd (5th to 8th battalions) in Victoria, and the 3rd in the four less populous states. Each battalion contained about a thousand men, including thirty officers. The artillery and other arms were also organised on a state basis. So was the 1st Light Horse Brigade, comprising three regiments, each of 536 officers and men. So great was the rush of men to enlist that on 3 September another infantry brigade was offered to Britain. The 4th Brigade contained men from each of the six states. As well, by early October two additional light horse brigades had been offered and accepted.[27]

The War Office wanted to know if the 10 per cent 'first reinforcement' of the force would sail with it. (They would sail in the second convoy.) The War Office calculated that further reinforcements, to the extent of 60 per cent of the original force, would be needed to maintain its strength for the first twelve months of the war. The Commonwealth government was asked to arrange for the 'flow of officers and other ranks to replace wastage'. These reinforcements, it thought, would benefit from training in England, and 'their presence so near the theatre of operations would ensure the speedy replacement of wastage.[28]

So ended what was probably the most dramatic seven weeks Australia had yet seen: federal leadership had changed following the first double dissolution election; Australians avidly read news of battles in the greatest war yet to afflict the world; a small empire in the nearby Pacific Islands had been seized; a large military force had been raised, partly equipped and trained, and was now ready to embark. Then came a frustrating delay, as the Australasian governments refused to risk their troops on the high seas with the *Scharnhorst* and *Gneisenau* still at large.

# CHAPTER 3

# ISLANDS FOR JAPAN, SOLDIERS FOR EUROPE

*I*NCEPTION OF Fisher's new Labor ministry coincided with the initial attempts of the opposing armies on the Western Front to outflank each other. Costly fighting resulted in deadlock—trench warfare stretching from the North Sea some six hundred kilometres through Belgium and curving through north-eastern France to the Swiss border. On this front the war of movement was virtually over. Those days decided the destiny of many young Australians: eventually they too would play a role in the deadly stalemate on the Western Front.

The Eastern Front remained a war of manoeuvre. By late September Australia learnt that the Russians had been completely ejected from East Prussia. They also heard of devastating victories by the Russians over the Austrians in Galicia, on the south-eastern front.

Much closer to home, Fisher faced two immediate problems stemming from Germany's presence in the Pacific. These were Japan's moves to expand its empire in the western Pacific and the delay in departure of the first contingent of the AIF because of the threat from German warships.

Having entered the war, Japan moved quickly to take advantage of its 'one in thousand lucky chance'. Sir William Conyngham Greene, Britain's ambassador in Tokyo, on 9 September warned Foreign Secretary Grey that Japan intended to send warships on a four-week cruise around the Marianne Islands (Marianas) to destroy German interests there, and he discussed with Kato, Japan's Foreign Minister, the danger of the cruise being 'misunderstood by the Dominions'.[1]

Lewis Harcourt promptly informed Cook's government of the coming Japanese cruise, which soon developed into an expedition to occupy German islands. Early in October the Japanese occupation of Jaluit, in the Marshall Islands, prompted an official in the Colonial Office, which was usually sensitive to Australian attitudes, to minute that the earlier warnings to the Australian government could hardly have prepared it for Japan to seize German territory so far south. Jaluit was 'not very far from Nauru'. (It was eleven hundred kilometres north of the phosphate-rich island.) He suggested trying to secure from Japan a statement that it did not intend to retain the island after the war. But it was decided on 8 October to take no action until Australia and New Zealand complained.[2]

On 7 October a Japanese force occupied Yap, site of one of the German wireless stations and an international cable station. Japan then asked Britain if Australia still proposed to take over in Yap, as London had originally intended. If so, Japan would withdraw its force. Churchill, at the Admiralty, was happy to leave the Japanese there, but Harcourt at the Colonial Office urged the importance of political considerations and encouraged moves to have the Australians acquire Yap.[3] By 15 October the Japanese navy had completed its task of gaining control of all the other German islands north of the Equator. The news was transmitted to

London on 22 October, on which day the Australian Naval Board discussed details of the expedition requested by the Asquith government, which was to convey a garrison force to take over these islands from the Japanese.[4]

Australia, believing that it was acting in accordance with the Asquith government's wishes, recruited the Tropical Force, under the command of Colonel Samuel Pethebridge, formerly secretary of the Defence Department, to perform this garrison duty. Unfortunately, there was inadequate co-ordination between naval and military authorities, and crucial delays were caused by a lack of escorting warships. Meanwhile, there were riots in Tokyo when news leaked out that Japan might relinquish territory its forces had taken from Germany. Okuma's government thereupon told London it would not hand over the islands. Britain accepted this new development and on 24 November—just as Tropical Force was about to leave Sydney—told the Australian government that it must not occupy German islands north of the Equator. Fisher's cabinet, not expecting such a volte-face, asked for further information. Harcourt's cable of 3 December reiterated that the Japanese should be left in occupation, leaving the question of these islands' future to be settled at the end of the war.[5]

Harcourt did not then tell Australia that on 25 November Greene in Tokyo had cabled Grey that Japan wanted to keep all the German Pacific islands north of the Equator (except for Yap) and would claim them after the war.[6] Instead, on 6 December—a few days after the first AIF contingent landed in Egypt—Harcourt wrote secretly to Munro Ferguson asking him 'in the most gradual and diplomatic way to begin to prepare the mind of [his] Ministers for the possibility that at the end of the war Japan may be left in possession of the Northern Islands and we with everything south of the Equator'.[7]

Britain's volte-face increased Australia's suspicions, harboured since at least 1905, about Japan's ultimate intentions: the useful ally was viewed also as a potential enemy. The Empire's leaders thanked Japan for the way its navy had co-operated with British and Australian fleets in the Pacific. But while Australia thanked the captain, officers and men of the Japanese cruiser *Ibuki* for their services in helping to escort the first AIF contingent through the Indian Ocean, privately on 30 December Admiral Creswell, the RAN's First Naval Member, insisted that Japan's occupation of the northern islands was only temporary, as they were 'definitely and distinctly' surrendered to the Australian force which captured Rabaul. Cabinet agreed with Creswell, stating in February 1915 that it wanted 'the fact . . . thoroughly established that the Japanese [were] only in temporary occupation of the Islands to the north of the Equator so that Australian claims in any final arrangement for their disposal [could] be fully taken into account'. The government wanted to be kept informed of Japanese public opinion about Australia generally, and about the former German islands seized by Japan. British authorities assiduously collected and translated such material and during 1915 sent fat files of relevant information to the departments of the Prime Minister, Defence and External Affairs in Melbourne. In January 1915 Fisher, on a visit to New Zealand, in a move no doubt partly provoked by Britain's volte-face of November, advocated close co-operation between the two dominion navies.[8]

This was about the time Colonel Holmes's force was welcomed home from New Guinea at a march through Sydney. Its combat record might have been small and no spur to national legend, but in strategic terms its achievement was considerable, as many knowledgeable and influential Australians realised. For Australia, one of the great issues of the war was the future control of the Pacific.[9]

Japan's occupation of north Pacific islands led to other differences between Australia and Britain. Japan moved quickly to take commercial advantage of its gains, prompting the British High Commissioner for the Western Pacific to write from

Fiji on 25 February 1915, 'It would . . . be a distinct advantage to the natives in the Gilbert and Ellice Islands if Japanese traders were to compete with Australian firms for the purchase of copra.' This provoked a sharp rejoinder in Australia.[10]

Nor did Britain show itself as a resolute defender of Australia's interests in its dealings with Japan over Yap. In December Okuma's government agreed that an Australian expedition could visit Yap though not the other north Pacific islands, but with Grey and Greene wondering how Australia could occupy Yap in isolation, it seems that this information from Japan was not passed on to Australia. In 1915 relevant dispatches from Greene were relayed to Australia, a Colonial Office official in April thinking that from the latest information it seemed that the British Empire might have had Yap after all. But it was then too late to rectify this. On 29 April—by which time hundreds of Australians had been killed in the Empire's assault on Gallipoli—Harcourt decided that the discussion about Yap should not be reopened unless Australia insisted. Australia did not raise the point, and in July the Colonial Office decided against telling Melbourne that in December 1914 Japan had been waiting to hand over Yap to a relieving Australian force.[11] Also about April, Edwin Montague, Financial Secretary to the Treasury in the British government and Herbert Asquith's former private secretary, told him, 'I would far rather cede Australia to the Japanese than cede to Australia anything that the Japanese want.'

In August and September 1914 Japan could possibly have been forestalled had Australian and British naval authorities given a higher priority to occupying the northern Pacific islands. Perhaps the Australian administration later in 1914 and 1915 was a little lax in neglecting an opportunity to reopen the issue of Yap. However, it is hard to imagine Japan, after the war, permitting Australia to retain groups of islands stretching thousands of miles across the Pacific. On the other hand the doctrine of the Empire's diplomatic unity implied that London should act resolutely on behalf of its overseas dominions. As we have seen, this did not happen.

Defence Minister Pearce and Colonel Legge, Chief of the General Staff, saw that it would have been difficult and expensive for Australia to hold these northern islands. Sir William Irvine, formerly Cook's attorney-general, was not anxious for an Australian occupation, although he did not want the Japanese there. A fairly general acceptance of such realistic considerations made it easy for Munro Ferguson to implement Harcourt's instructions to prepare his ministers' minds for Japan's post-war hold on the islands. Not that the reality was pleasant. What was a feather in the hands of the Germans would in due course become a sword in the hands of the Japanese. The full import of this unfortunate by-product of the European war was seen late in 1941 and early in 1942 when Japan made efficient use of these gains, particularly its naval base at Truk in the Carolines, in its devastating southern drive towards Australia.[12]

While Australia's interests in the Western Pacific were being compromised and its future security in the region jeopardised, its soldiers for distant battlefields were ready for embarkation. But sailing had to be delayed for four weeks. In the Indian Ocean the light cruiser *Emden* had begun its spectacular career as a commerce raider. Moreover, the *Gneisenau* and *Scharnhorst* on 14 September appeared off Apia, capital of Samoa, before vanishing over the horizon. The big cruisers could have reached New Zealand or Australian waters within a few days. The New Zealand government was particularly worried, as there was no strong escort for its troops on their impending voyage across the Tasman Sea to join the Australian contingent.

Shipping arrangements had to be altered and warships diverted in response to the potential danger, although opinions differed about the degree of caution needed. King George V's deep concern was conveyed to the Colonial Office. Any accident to the convoys 'would be disastrous in the respective Dominions'. Munro Ferguson cabled Lord Liverpool, Governor of New Zealand, stressing the risks of an unescorted voyage to Australia. Harcourt rebuked Munro Ferguson for acting on his own initiative; but the sailing was delayed.[13]

On 30 September news arrived that the *Scharnhorst* and *Gneisenau* had been at Tahiti, 3,200 kilometres from New Zealand, on the 22nd. It now seemed clear that these warships were heading east to South America, and Admiralty and Australian authorities were prepared to allow the troopships to sail. The Admiralty was becoming irritated that the transports and cruisers were lying idle in Australian waters, and it wanted to hasten the 'arrival of these valuable military forces to the scene of active operations'. New Zealand, however, was very cautious and would not allow its troops to sail until they had adequate escorts, to remove the slightest risk of a disaster at the hands of the German cruisers. Churchill prepared a response to a report that New Zealand women were anxious about the fate of the troopships should they sail. Fortunately his message went through the normal channels for transmission; in the Colonial Office it was deemed truculent, inaccurate and unjust, giving no weight to the fact that the contingents were 'being sent to help us in Europe, and [were] not being used for the direct and selfish purposes of the Dominions'. Churchill agreed to changes in the cable before it was sent.[14]

It was not until 16 October that the New Zealand convoy sailed, with four warships as escorts. Two days later the Australian troopships began to make their way, independently, to the assembly point in King George Sound, off Albany, Western Australia. The month's delay probably determined the destination of the first contingent, for had the original timetable been adhered to the Australians might have sailed on to England as first intended, arriving before Turkey entered the war.

Von Spee's squadron steamed on to destruction in the battle of the Falkland Islands on 8 December. By this time—apart from sporadic commerce raiding—German naval power in the Pacific and Indian oceans had ceased to exist for the remainder of the war. But Australian authorities were critical of the way in which the Admiralty had used the Australian squadron during these early wartime weeks. Against strong Australian wishes the Admiralty had ignored the maxim that the squadron's first wartime task should have been to find and destroy enemy warships. Because these enemy cruisers remained at large, the Admiralty felt more dependent upon Japan for help and thus provided Japan with a diplomatic framework for its occupation of the islands north of the Equator. The long delay in the departure of the first convoy was a direct result of the failure to destroy the threat from the German warships. Munro Ferguson told the British government of Australia's doubts about the wisdom of the Admiralty's attitude. He thought its performance was such that Australia was sure to demand a 'large measure of local autonomy' when the war ended.[15]

The recruiting figures conceal thousands of human dramas as men left families and settled routine for the hazards of war. There would have been many anxious family discussions. Doubtless, some young men gave long and serious thought to their decision, but probably many did not analyse carefully the precise reasons for volunteering beyond recognising it as an instinctive personal reaction to the needs of the time. It is not likely that any assessment of motives for enlisting will improve on what is already available.[16]

One recruit, possibly typical of many others, earned more money in the AIF than he had ever seen before. After nearly two months of observing his fellows in Egypt, another wrote, 'I don't know about succeeding contingents, but in this one [the first] there are many men to whom this was a real Godsend, men who've never been better dressed nor earned so much money before in their life.' On the other hand, Robert Antill left a good job as a cabinet-maker to volunteer. He 'tried for the light horse but . . . the riding test was a little too good' for him. W. L. (Dick) Fowler of Innisfail left his banking job and his active sporting life because it was his 'bounden duty as a single man' to offer his services 'towards the upholding of the glorious traditions and the everlasting supremacy of the good old British Empire'. O. S. (Sam) Blows, in the Western Australian bush, heard about the war a few days after it began and was one of those who wanted to get in quickly before the British army entered Berlin.[17]

One of the more atypical recruits was Ellis Silas of Perth, an artist whose work on a large canvas was interrupted by the war. He often broke camp to work on his painting, which he hoped to finish before sailing. He found conditions 'terrible' and did not care for 'life in camp and the uncongenial society of rough Bushmen'. Nevertheless, he noted, 'They are good fellows and seem to think a lot of me.' He thought he knew how bad the war would be, although his comrades were very despondent at the thought that it would soon end. His absences at his studio were deemed to merit discharge. But despite this, and having an undersized chest, he wangled his way back into the army. He was moved from the 11th to the 16th Battalion, entailing a voyage to Melbourne. He could not stand the noise of rifle fire (although he did quite well on the range), thought Broadmeadows camp 'rotten' and soon 'tired of being filthy'. Visits to Melbourne's art gallery and a short friendship with a married lady consoled him.[18]

Australasian troops had to go through many distinct stages before reaching the front. Doubtless many would have agreed with Ellis Silas that initial training—at Blackboy Hill, Enoggera, Liverpool and other camps—was not very glamorous. It could be marked by unpleasant discipline. On 7 September at Blackboy Hill, for instance, the whole battalion was paraded to see the discharge of about a dozen 'not wanteds' who had absented themselves for some days after being paid. They were 'stripped of their uniform and put into dungarees and marched out of the camp lines'. On the other hand, unit marches through the streets of nearby cities were a festive occasion. Officers tried 'to make order out of chaos'; one of them— Lieutenant-Colonel Alfred Sutton of Brisbane, commanding the 3rd Field Ambulance—lamented: 'O Australia! how can you expect us to make war successfully when all the times of peace you scoff at war and make no preparations.'[19]

Great emotion surrounded the departure of the first troops. From ports as far north as Townsville, men of the AIF left camp on their way to their ships. Queenslanders leaving Enoggera on 25 September were cheered at every station. Embarkation went smoothly, watched by huge, cheering crowds. 'It was very pretty to see the hundreds of paper streamers of all colours held by men on the ship and women and girls on shore,' wrote Sutton. At 12.40 p.m. his ship, the *Rangatira*, cast off. It reached Melbourne on 28 September, where it was held up for weeks. The next battalion raised in Queensland, the 15th, went by train on 24–26 November, to join the 4th Brigade at Broadmeadows.

'The man with the donkey', Private John Simpson Kirkpatrick, on this occasion with a skeleton. Private A. J. Currie is on the left. As part of the 3rd Australian Field Ambulance, they were doing a training course at Blackboy Hill, WA, before leaving Australia.

Once the threat from von Spee's squadron disappeared, the final stages of assembling the first contingent in Western Australian waters could begin. Men began boarding their ships in Sydney on 20 October. A mass of people on the pier in Melbourne gave the *Orvieto* an enthusiastic send-off, with much bunting and waving of handkerchiefs. From Adelaide the *Ascanius* sailed with the 10th Battalion. One of its soldiers, twenty-year-old Lance-Corporal George Mitchell, a clerk before the war, wrote, 'We are going into the biggest thing that has hit civilization,... civilization means being able to kill and wound a lot of men in a short time.... The Tenth Infantry is highly civilized.... There will be no turning back until the might of the German Empire is tumbled to the dust.'

By this time a host of personal relationships, of varying degrees of friendliness and friction, had developed within the AIF's units and sub-units. There was much horseplay as the ships crossed the Great Australian Bight. A subaltern commented that he was very happy with conditions on board and his busy work day, from six o'clock in the morning to ten at night.[20]

All but two ships went to King George Sound. Sutton was enthralled at the spectacle as his ship approached Albany, 'the prettiest town' he had seen in Australia. But it was 'a forbidden Paradise', as no shore leave was granted except to some who were ill. Some others were discharged because they refused to be inoculated against typhoid. In the mid-morning of 28 October the Australian contingent was joined by four warships, including the Japanese cruiser *Ibuki*, escorting ten transports carrying the New Zealand contingent. Sutton had 'never before seen so thrilling a sight for they steamed in in perfect order'.[21]

While some forty ships swung at anchor, a short-lived change in plans was discussed. In South Africa, some Afrikaners were in revolt against the pro-British war policy of Louis Botha's government. Britain wanted the Australasian contingent to sail via the Cape to help suppress the rebellion if need be. Munro Ferguson discussed this prospect with Fisher one night, along with accompanying requests for up to twenty thousand rifles and five to ten million rounds of ammunition. Fisher was 'quite pleased' to think that Australia could help in these 'anxious' circumstances. He felt that an appearance by the Australians at the Cape would soon restore order. Munro Ferguson told Fisher that the Australians had fought too well 'in the last war' to be very popular with the 'Dutch'.[22] In the event, Australia sent ten million rounds of rifle ammunition but could not spare any rifles. In any case, Botha's government was able to deal with the rebellion, so before the convoy left Albany, the original plan of going via the Suez Canal was reinstated. Munro Ferguson told Harcourt that Fisher's cabinet was amenable to these changes of plan, adding wryly that there would probably be a mutiny if 'our heroes' were turned out to fight Arabs instead of Germans.[23]

Two of the Australian transports, the *Ascanius* and the *Medic*, called in to Fremantle to embark the Western Australians. George Mitchell, of the 10th Battalion, disliked Fremantle and roundly criticised Perth. To the men from Adelaide, the suburban train between port and capital seemed quite inferior. But Perth had attractions for his company, three-quarters of whom became 'fighting drunk' when they went ashore. Mitchell approved of the 'Sandgroper troops' when they came on board on the 31st. 'They are a fine hefty body of men, and very decent chaps—though fairly tough.' With over two thousand on board, the men thought they were 'packed just like sardines'. A friend told Mitchell that 'the moral tone of the mess' was 'a little lower than a shearing shed'.[24]

On the morning of 1 November (precisely one month after the first Canadian contingent of thirty-three thousand men had sailed for England) the thirty-six transports and three escorting warships steamed out of King George Sound into the open sea three abreast. Sutton described the glorious sight viewed by the soldiers lining the decks and reflected, 'Our magnificent fleet with 30,000 men moves on to—the unknown.' On the same day the *Ascanius* and the *Medic*, escorted by the *Ibuki* and a small British cruiser, left Fremantle. 'Boatloads of excursionists came out all day long' to the ships at rest about two kilometres off the port, 'and girls kept shrieking to their respective Willies, Daves and Alfies, "Goodbye, and mind you come back safely."' Two days later, well out to sea, men on the ships from Fremantle saw a grand spectacle as the main convoy appeared over the horizon. The *Ascanius* and the *Medic* took station near the head of the convoy for the voyage across the Indian Ocean to Suez.[25]

The convoy passengers took with them the fervent best wishes of all Australians, as exemplified when the new parliament had first met on 8 October. The Empire's 'splendid devotion to the role of duty' dominated Munro Ferguson's short speech. In later debates, Liberal Senator T. J. K. Bakhap from Tasmania forecast future problems; in spite of the hell and misery, he said, the war had to be won properly and not ended by a patched-up peace that would allow it to break out anew. Statements by men on the left of the political spectrum showed the extent and depth of this devotion to the Empire. James Mathews, the Labor member for Melbourne Ports, agreed with 'the Jingo Tories' that 'the Empire was one and . . . in a war it did not matter for the ultimate good that certain sections of the Empire should suffer, so long as the head centre survived the fight, seeing that afterwards we could re-create' what had been temporarily lost. Even Frank Anstey, often thought of as being on the left of the Labor Party, held that the issue was whether Australia could retain its membership of the Empire with the same king and the same flag. It was Australia's duty to furnish all the aid it could in arms and men. He thought that all parliamentarians recognised that the fight for possession of Australia was already taking place on the European battlefields. However, class ideology rather than Imperial-national sentiment guided his voting as one of a minority of five against donating a hundred thousand pounds to Belgium. Anstey's tirade against the Belgian king's atrocities in the Congo pointed out that the king and many of the 'moneyed classes' had scuttled like rabbits from the Germans to the safety of Britain. He feared that it was most unlikely that the money would reach the people who deserved it, the suffering, needy Belgians still in their occupied homeland. He also asserted that no funds should be sent abroad until Australia had devised a scheme to relieve misery, poverty and unemployment at home.[26]

At about the same time, linchpins of the legislative framework for running the war, the War Precautions Act and the Trading with the Enemy Act, became law after brief discussion and no opposition.[27] Hatred of Germany, intensified by its invasion of Belgium, was nourished by events such as the burning of the centre of Louvain, including its valuable library, in August. Naturally, the British government was anxious to make best political use of 'all cases of outrage' by German troops. It wanted Australian troops to be ready to provide information on German atrocities, although only if such cases could be well established on unimpeachable evidence.[28]

# CHAPTER 4

# *THE VOYAGE*

$O$N THE DAY AFTER leaving Albany Lieutenant-Colonel Sutton noted in his diary that England had declared war on Turkey. Technically, he was three days premature, for the legal state of war began on 5 November, although there had been warlike acts between the two nations on the 1st and 2nd. Men on board promptly speculated on the likelihood of disembarking in Egypt, while in London the War Council discussed possible moves against Turkey, including Churchill's suggestion for a landing at or near the Dardanelles.

Some of the Australians found the trip monotonous, with inadequate opportunity for recreation on crowded ships. The heat in the tropics was stifling. Nine soldiers died during the voyage: four times in the first eleven days out of Albany men lined the deck rails to watch the sombre ceremony of a burial at sea. Pneumonia was rife on some of the ships.

To Private Murray Aitken, a romantic 'homesick and mother sick' lad, who would sit entranced watching a glorious sunset, the spectacle of 'lines and lines of big ships right back as far as the skyline' was ample compensation for physical discomfort. 'I never tire of gazing at our wonderful fleet,' he wrote. 'Isn't it a grand performance for Australia?' He was sure such a magnificent sight would never be seen again in Australian waters. In the moonlight he thought the convoy looked 'a veritable fairyland' with 'twinkling fairy lights disappearing and reappearing as the waves came between'.[1]

The convoy should not have been so well lit, for it was at some risk from the *Emden*, which had been enjoying great success in attacking British merchant ships in the Bay of Bengal and northern Indian Ocean. Its exploits alarmed British patriots, one of whom, in London, exclaimed, 'It is a pity our Navy cannot capture or destroy this little beast.' On Monday 9 November, at the Cocos Islands, the *Emden*'s path approached that of the first contingent, resulting in its being beached on North Keeling Island after a battle with the newer and more powerful *Sydney*. Lieutenant William Henry Dawkins, of Ferntree Gully, Victoria, aged twenty-two and number ten on the list of those enrolling at Duntroon, was proud of this achievement. 'It is wonderful the power of Britain at sea. This huge convoy just proceeds uninterruptedly on its own course in its own time.' Many other 1st Division men exulted that Australia had 'the honour of wiping out the *Emden*'. They hoped 'the glorious news' would cheer them up at 'home'. It did that, and also brought joy in Britain, not least at Lloyds. Andrew Fisher hoped this triumph would end local criticism of the Australian navy; Liberal and Labor politicians each claimed the major share of the credit for the RAN's existence. Munro Ferguson told Harcourt on 10 November that the most common comment in Sydney was 'I'm glad it wasn't the "Melbourne"'.[2]

After the *Emden* fight, the next break in shipboard routine was the ceremony of crossing the line, with its licence for wild, rough horseplay. 'It was great fun to the men ducking the Colonel,' wrote Sutton. Two days later he enjoyed the privileges of rank, strolling around Colombo, but thinking that for 99.9 per cent of the contingent it was 'so hard to be so near and yet not see the place'. Perhaps it was as well, he reflected, that the men were not allowed on shore, and that the convoy stayed only briefly in this exotic setting, for he feared that 'the lazy joys of Colombo would ruin the "grittiest" man on earth'. At Aden, which Sutton thought lacked the charm of Albany and Colombo, boats carrying local hawkers were driven away from the ships, to the disappointment of the troops. Sutton commented, 'I do not approve of this over discipline, it seems to me the men are unnecessarily harshly dealt with, treated more like naughty schoolboys than men.' Private Richards referred to the *Euripides* as a 'convict ship'; but he was enthralled by a glorious golden sunset. Second lieutenant H. J. F. Coe mentioned another deprivation: 'We have not spoken to a white girl for five weeks. The Sisters don't count.'[3]

The convoy had reached the Red Sea before being told, on 28 November, that nearly all the troops would disembark in Egypt. The news got a mixed response. Some were surprised, others gloomy at losing the chance to 'reach the Old Country by Christmas'. Many cheered, delighted at the prospect of exchanging monotony for work in an agreeable climate. Lieutenant Dawkins was one of these; there would be more daylight than 'at home', by which he meant Britain. He thought it would be wonderful to have a few months' experience in the land of the Sphinx before going on to Europe. He thought that having a large body of Australasian troops in Egypt would have a good influence on the natives and help secure the Suez Canal against Turkish attack. All troops realised that the new destination signified a great change in their plans.[4]

The Empire's high command had decided on the change of destination ten days before the men on the convoy were told. Early in October an Australian army officer who visited the camp site at Salisbury Plain found nothing had been done towards building huts for the troops from the antipodes. An army doctor then reported that to 'house Australian troops in tents in mid-winter on this windswept area after [a] long voyage in troopships passing through tropics and sub-tropics would be criminal'. Colonel Harry Chauvel, the Australian representative at the War Office, visited the plain and endorsed this advice. Sir George Reid, the Australian High Commissioner, took up the issue and promptly saw Kitchener, who urged that the convoy not proceed to England. On 17 November Reid cabled this news to the Australian cabinet. It was impossible to assure proper accommodation at any other site in England for the troops on arrival. The effect on the Canadians already at Salisbury Plain was 'serious, especially as regards discipline'. Kitchener said that the suggested change of plan was not prompted by any shortage in Egypt, where there already were large numbers of British troops.[5]

Within a few hours Fisher's cabinet cabled its approval of the change. Despite Kitchener's assurance, it seems likely that Britain's leaders were pleased to have Australasian troops strengthen the British garrison in Egypt, which was open to attack following Turkey's entry into the war. Harcourt's advice to Munro Ferguson explicitly noted the men were to assist in the defence of Egypt. Major Thomas Blamey, then on the General Staff of the 1st Division and a future field marshal, linked Britain's change in plan with the trouble threatening from Syria.[6] Moreover, there was some fear that anti-British and pro-German and pro-Turkish feeling in Egypt was strong enough to cause serious local disturbances unless the garrison was strengthened. Men on the convoy heard rumours to this effect, but many assumed that the Australian army's presence would knock any such ideas out of Egyptian heads.[7] Thus, there was a coincidence of Imperial needs and the perceived interests of the troops in the first contingent. Kitchener pledged to 'send them to Europe to fight beside British troops' when they completed their training.[8]

Fisher's cabinet many have thought there could be some disappointment in

*Mena camp, near Cairo, probably taken in late 1915, showing the 'flaming desert' across which many grinding route marches with pack on back were conducted.*

Australia at the change in destination. When Pearce told parliament on 3 December—a little prematurely—that the troops had disembarked in Egypt, he conveyed Harcourt's advice that they were to help defend Egypt and complete their training, which gave both national and Imperial reasons for the change. He said that it had been made on Kitchener's strong recommendation.[9]

So the men passing through the Suez Canal knew they were having a first glimpse of their temporary home. 'The pretty little railway stations, with their Indian guards, the dredges, the small camps on the banks all are very fine', wrote Sutton, 'and inspire one with respect for the might of England.' Private C. H. Copp from Melbourne, no doubt expressing the thoughts of many in the convoy, wrote, 'What a glorious thing it is to be British, one begins to realize the huge expanse of the Empire on a trip like this.'[10] The sense of participation in a great enterprise was intensified at Port Said, where ships carrying English, Indian and French soldiers and sailors were at anchor when the Australians began to arrive. Round after round of 'great cheering . . . went up from all the various ships'.

From Port Said the convoy steamed west through the Mediterranean, hugging the Egyptian coast some 250 kilometres to Alexandria. Disembarkation took several days. The troops' first experience ashore in Egypt brought them more of the army life's tantalising mixture of hardship and glamour. Conditions were so cramped in the open cattle trucks that some of the troops made noises like cattle or sheep to emphasise that they were being treated like animals. Murray Aitken ruefully told his mother, 'Of course, it was just our luck to travel in the night and miss everything interesting.'[11]

The Australians were taken past Cairo, fifteen kilometres south-west to the edge of the desert, and there shown their camp at Mena. 'And what a hole it is,' complained Aitken. The British Empire had not prepared for them. All they had at first was the sand for a bed, the sky for a roof, such comforts as they had carried with them, and the Sphinx and the Pyramids to admire. One man felt that these ancient sights had moved him back several thousand years. Another revelled in seeing 'the Great Pyramids in the moonlight, a most awe inspiring sight'. Some who reached Mena when it was too cold to sleep walked up to the Pyramids. So they whetted their sense of history and then strolled back to the camp where they would soon resume their training to fit them for their own niche in history.[12]

# CHAPTER 5

# THE AIF BUILD-UP IN EGYPT

$B$RITAIN HAD BEEN in effective control of Egypt since 1882, although nominally the country was under Turkish suzerainty as part of the Ottoman Empire. With Turkey now an enemy, Britain moved to resolve the anomaly of its legally undefined position in Egypt. On 18 December 1914 it declared a protectorate over Egypt, dethroned the Khedive on the ground that he supported Britain's enemies, and installed the pro-British Prince Hussein as Sultan. Australians were among the Empire troops who lined Cairo streets to ensure there was no protest at Britain strengthening its hold on Egypt. This display of might was effective. C. E. W. Bean, Australia's official war correspondent who had arrived with the convoy and would later become official war historian, told Australia of an Egyptian view that Britain was a kinder overlord than Turkey.[1]

The Suez Canal was of crucial importance to Britain, especially for its communications with India. By the same token it was an obvious target for Turkey, whose territory adjoined Egypt in the Sinai Peninsula, two hundred kilometres east of the canal. Accordingly, Britain's primary concern at this stage was to put Egypt's defences on a wartime footing. At the same time, however, Britain also mounted a few minor, sporadic attacks at widely scattered points on the periphery of the Ottoman Empire—at Smyrna, Akaba, Basra, Alexandretta and, on 3 November, at the Dardanelles, where the outer forts were briefly bombarded. Indeed, the Asquith government considered various other moves too, including a landing at or near the Dardanelles which Churchill suggested would be the best way of defending the Suez Canal.[2] But Britain had made no firm decisions about a Mediterranean strategy when the first AIF contingent reached Egypt.

At the end of August, Kitchener selected Lieutenant-General Sir John Maxwell as commander-in-chief of British forces in Egypt. Maxwell had spent nearly thirty years of his military life in that country. To secure British control against both Turkey and a possible Egyptian nationalist uprising, Maxwell had at his disposal from mid-December the equivalent of about four divisions of troops stationed in or near Cairo. By mid February he had well over seventy thousand men. It was an Imperial garrison. Australians, New Zealanders (including Maoris), Indians, colonial British of the Ceylon Planters' Rifles, and 'Terriers'* of the 42nd (East Lancashire) Territorial Division mingled with Egyptians and Sudanese in Cairo's streets and shops, bringing local traders a bountiful tourist season.

Before the first contingent finished its transit of the Suez Canal, Kitchener decided that Australian and New Zealand troops in Egypt were to be formed into a corps.[3] As its commander, he chose Lieutenant-General William Birdwood, one of his favourites and supporters in the British army's senior officer corps who as an

* The name given to men in Britain's volunteer Territorial army, a weekend army of part-time soldiers, as distinct from the full-time professional aramy.

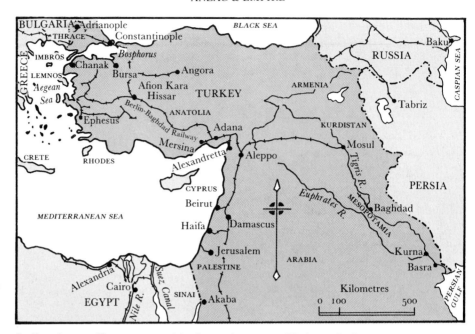

*The Ottoman Empire in August 1914.*

Indian Army officer was outside the mainstream. Birdwood's force was named the Australian and New Zealand Army Corps, comprising two divisions: one was Bridges'; the other was a composite New Zealand and Australian (NZ and A) Division, eventually to contain the New Zealand Infantry Brigade, two mounted brigades (the 1st Australian Light Horse and the New Zealand Mounted Rifles) and the 4th Australian Infantry Brigade, which as part of the second contingent from Australia was disembarking at Alexandria on 1 February. This second division was led by Major-General Sir Alexander Godley, an unpopular British army officer who had commanded New Zealand's forces since 1910 and was to lead the New Zealand Expeditionary Force throughout the war.

Sir William Riddell Birdwood, 'a neat little man with cheery face', was a very different style of man from Godley. Born in India, he had a general for a grandfather, and his father was under-secretary to the government of Bombay. He was educated in England and commissioned from Sandhurst; in 1894 he married a baron's daughter. A successful officer of assured social status, Birdwood had been in India and South Africa since 1885, with a total of nine years on Kitchener's staff, seven in India. He had had a happy association with Australasian troops during the Boer War,[4] and this, together with his wide-ranging experience outside England and his pleasant personality, possibly influenced Kitchener's choice.

The first convoy was in the Red Sea when news arrived that it was to be formed into a corps under Birdwood. The men then knew little about him except that he was a 'Kitchener man'. He was holding high office in the government of India when appointed to his new command. Sailing from Bombay on 12 December, he exchanged flowery greetings with the Fisher government but told General Sir Henry Rawlinson, then commanding a formation on the Western Front, 'I fancy I shall find a real difficult job before me as I go to troops and staff I do not know and who do not know each other.' He expected to 'remain in Egypt with his Colonials for some little time' before joining the British army in France and Belgium.[5] Birdwood landed at Suez on 21 December and set up his headquarters in the famous Shepheard's Hotel. Shortly afterwards he told Kitchener, 'Bridges and Godley I both like very much' and there is 'good material' in the men.[6]

He soon developed a reasonably good rapport with Australian soldiers. He was one of the few English generals to be liked and admired by men of the AIF, his

*Lieutenant-General William Birdwood, 'a neat little man with cheery face', outside his dugout at Anzac.*

popularity resting not on his skills as a commander and tactician but on his friendly approach. He recognised them as civilians in uniform, and they in return would grow to respect him for his cheerfulness, courage and example at Anzac. A report that another general was piqued at Birdwood getting this command prompted him to tell Kitchener in mid-January that that individual 'would have been absolutely useless here, as with his manner and side, he would never have got these Australians to do anything for him. . . . I may be useless at anything else, but I think I have been able to make them work happily for me.'[7]

Before the first contingent sailed from Australia, volunteering had been heavy enough to ensure that further units would follow. Almost 53,000 Australians had enlisted by the end of 1914, and the rate slackened very little during the first three months of 1915. The second contingent, 10,500 Australians and 2,000 New Zealanders, sailed in late December. It included the 4th Infantry Brigade, commanded by the able citizen soldier and cultured engineer, Colonel John Monash, whom Munro Ferguson characterised as a 'competent Jew'. Also on board were the 2nd Light Horse Brigade and the first reinforcements for both contingents. The Governor-General, who whenever possible visited troops at embarkation, thought these men from the country the best yet recruited. They 'looked more like veterans, being older men, than new levies'.[8]

The Army Council had already notified Australia that three months experience of war (on the Western Front) showed the rate of reinforcements 'to replace wastage' would have to be higher than previously stated. The council asked whether Australia could provide reinforcements at the rate of 10 per cent a month for cavalry and 15 per cent a month for infantry. On 27 February 1915, following arrival of the second contingent, Bridges in similar vein advised that Australia could best increase its help by sending reinforcements to keep existing units up to war establishment. The 'first reinforcement' for his division of 10 per cent had been largely absorbed in 'repairing peace wastage'.[9] Reinforcements at an increased rate, some 3,200 monthly for the AIF as then constituted, were thenceforth dispatched.

But so many men were volunteering that, in addition to providing ample reinforcements for existing units, the Fisher government was able to offer Britain further new units. Australia had to prompt London for a response about how they were to be organised. Lewis Harcourt asked the Colonial Office to 'stir the appropriate people up', at which the War Office duly accepted the offer: it preferred infantry, for which demands were exceptionally heavy, and saw little need for more units of mounted soldiers.[10]

The third convoy disembarking in Egypt on 21 March 1915 brought to approximately thirty-one thousand the number of Australian soldiers who had made the voyage. A 3rd Light Horse Brigade, raised in Australia in October 1914, formed part of this third convoy and was the last Australian formation to reach Egypt early enough to serve in the main Anzac battles. Three new infantry brigades (5th, 6th and 7th) and the 4th Light Horse Brigade, offered to London by 1 April, reached Egypt in June and July.

Every week from April to December 1915, two or three ships carrying a total of about twenty-five hundred AIF personnel, which included nurses, reached Egypt from Australia. The only naval escort for the second convoy had been the RAN submarine *AE2*, towed by the troopship *Berrima*. With German naval power swept from the Indian Ocean, thenceforth no naval escort was needed; after the third convoy, troopships were permitted to sail singly, which greatly eased the problem of carrying the AIF to the war theatre.

No later sailing from Australia rivalled the spectacle of the first contingent. Nevertheless, individual soldiers throughout 1915 found the voyage just as great an adventure. Many volunteers had travelled a great distance within Australia to reach the embarkation point. This was particularly true of the 4th Brigade, whose men came from most parts of the country and had to be concentrated for training at the cordially disliked Broadmeadows camp outside Melbourne.

Dick Fowler, who became a corporal in the 15th Battalion, made the long journey from Innisfail to Broadmeadows. He often visited cousins in Melbourne, but felt 'a stranger in a strange land'. Ellis Silas, an immigrant who had been in Australia for seven years and who was grateful to the land that had given him his 'great chance in life', was worried about the voyage. 'How will I stand being cooped up with all these rough men in such a confined space. There are 3,000 of us on board; nowhere quiet where I can go away to think.' Silas soon found that these tough men were not inconsiderate. 'At mess to-day,' he wrote early in the trip, 'a youth is rather rude to me—my vis-à-vis, a rough bushman, turns to the youth and says "'Aven't you got an 'eart, mate; can't you see 'e ain't used to this kind of life like we are?" Though rough, the boys were very kind to me.'[11]

At various ports men disobeyed orders and went ashore. Whether at Fremantle or Colombo, whenever an AIF troopship was in the harbour one could expect numbers of soldiers to take their own leave by sliding down ropes to rowing boats. At Colombo men from the second contingent 'sneaked ashore in all kinds of undress and were to be seen rushing about the streets drunk, hatless and coatless and singing songs at the tops of their voices'; by contrast, the New Zealanders in Colombo behaved impeccably. 'There was a disgraceful scene at the Galle Face Hotel where scores of drunken troops were brawling in a perfectly nude condition. They had got it into their heads that if they did not wear uniform they could not be taken by the picquet.' As punishment these defaulters were given the task of coal trimming. Non-commissioned officers were court-martialled and lost their stripes. In the case of voyages by single ships, officers not surprisingly seemed more prepared to have their men go ashore. From one troopship reaching Colombo after sailing north from Brisbane and through the Torres Strait, the men were taken on a route march through the city.[12]

Many soldiers thought the voyage very comfortable and carefully planned. For others the Suez Canal compensated for the rigours and unpleasantness of the journey. What they saw in that Imperial artery made them 'realize more than ever the greatness of the British Empire'. Slow progress through the Canal gave all men on deck good views of Empire troops manning the banks. Major Iven Mackay, very critical of the men's behaviour during the voyage, noted they were 'smarter and more soldierly already'. Hostile surroundings, he thought, would do more than anything else 'to weld them into a disciplined company'.[13]

Love of Empire went hand in hand with disrespect for some of its army officers. The monocled English officer, now commonly ridiculed by some Australasians, was in December 1914 described at some length by Stanley Natusch, a young New Zealand private. 'Two English . . . lieutenants, and one with a monocle which never in the course of a long day dropped from that well set eye were the centre of attraction. The monocle exercised a fascination on our men, more so, I think, as our identification discs of about the size of a penny had been served out only a day or so before, and many emulations of the "Haw Haw" Englishmen have been walking about our decks. However I do not think anything occurred to offend that officer's dignity.'[14]

By the end of 1915, 116,986 Australian soldiers (3,879 officers and 113,107 other ranks) had made this voyage and landed in Egypt,[15] resulting in a large build-up there of the AIF. The initial division, which Bridges with military method designated '1st' rather than 'Australian', was, like those to follow, drawn from all six states—a representative Australian formation. It was remarkably homogeneous: 72 per cent of the division had been born in Australia and almost all the rest had been born elsewhere in the Empire. They were predominantly single—nearly 90 per cent. As regards age, 21 per cent of the men were under twenty-one, another 36 per cent under twenty-five, and 42 per cent in the twenty-six-to-forty range. Officers as a group were a little older, only 9 per cent being under twenty-one and 53 per cent being in the twenty-five-to-forty age group, and more of them were married. A greater proportion of this division than its successors had had military training: of over seventeen thousand men, nearly eleven thousand had served in the home force and 96 per cent of officers had had previous militia service, some 16 per cent with previous war service. Reflecting more specialised recruitment criteria, 1st Light Horse Brigade officers and men were slightly older than the 1st Division, a higher proportion were born in Australia (79 per cent), and 56 per cent (compared with 37 per cent) were first-, second- and third-class marksmen.[16]

War inexorably would reach more deeply into the Australian population and somewhat modify these patterns, most obviously by drawing in more men from the youngest age range with less or no citizen force experience, though to what degree cannot yet be said with confidence.[17]

From mid-September 1914, Bridges, the first Australian given powers constituting 'national command', had dual responsibility for the burgeoning Australian force—as General Officer Commanding (GOC) the whole AIF, including the 1st Light Horse Brigade, and as GOC 1st Division. But this national commander was an Imperial Australian; it was Bridges who created the distinctive name for the force which blended the 'Imperial' with the Australian theme. He had only administrative and not operational control over troops outside his own division, such as the Australian half of Godley's division and the 2nd and 3rd light horse brigades; these units on arrival were assigned to neither division but made responsible directly to Birdwood as corps commander. This limited the extent of his 'national' command. Moreover, in eschewing administrative matters as much as possible, Bridges retreated from, rather than fully exercised, the national character of his appointment. He recognised that the unexpected decision to land in Egypt required an alternative in the Middle East to the planned London base organisation for handling the multifarious needs of Australian soldiers, but none was established until 15 January 1915. The intermediate base depot eventually established within Maxwell's headquarters was run by Colonel V. C. M. Sellheim, transferred from Bridges' headquarters. Godley would later comment that Bridges 'came out tremendously and commanded his division real well', referring no doubt to his battlefield rather than his administrative record.[18]

On Bridges' death in May, the Australian government replaced him with the professional soldier Legge, then still Chief of the General Staff in Melbourne. Although London-born, Legge had reached Australia as a teenager and had an Australian viewpoint, together with a reputation for quarrelling with his peers. He was junior in service to the AIF brigade commanders and without front-line experience at Gallipoli, but the government deemed him to be both competent and the best available officer. The British commander, Sir Ian Hamilton, influenced by angry Australian brigadiers and unaware that the War Office was not objecting, on 19 May asked Kitchener to 'prevent the appointment'. He later gracefully admitted the 'Australian Government seems to have been right, and I quite wrong' about Legge.[19] Indeed, the government was very firm about inserting Legge into the AIF at Gallipoli; it was actively concerned that competent Australians command their own troops. But a more practical arrangement evolved after Legge left Gallipoli for Egypt in late July 1915 to form the three new 5th, 6th and 7th infantry brigades into the 2nd Australian Division. The government concurred in (and later confirmed) Birdwood's assumption of the AIF command but would continue to press for Australians instead of British officers to be appointed to important AIF field commands. Years later Sir Frederick Shedden, long-time secretary of the Defence Department, credited just two of the Labor ministers with this active policy—Hughes and, especially, Pearce.[20]

In the administrative area, Sellheim's work with the constantly arriving Australian units and reinforcement troops was recognised as valuable. However, Maxwell was 'undoubtedly a strong man and held in great esteem in Egypt by the Australians'. Sellheim's intermediate base was not permitted to control AIF medical arrangements (see chapters 31 and 32) or the training and discipline of reinforcements, which were conducted by a British general dispatched for the purpose by Kitchener. Coping with residual areas of ordnance, records and finance still necessitated considerable expansion of Sellheim's staff, and while less than half those Australians who reached Egypt during 1914–15—about fifty thousand—served on Gallipoli, detailed records of the precise numbers who did so are unavailable.[21] This is not surprising considering the number of men involved, the hasty planning, the fact that many men made the voyage to Lemnos several times, and the chaotic administrative arrangements for landing the sick and wounded. Late in 1915, the Australian government would recognise the urgent need for national control of the AIF's support structure and move to reorganise the base so all aspects of Australian administration would come under that single authority.

But this is moving ahead of our story. The fate, if not the immediate comfort, of Australian soldiers early in 1915 depended less on this administrative structure than on the transition they would make on the wharves of Alexandria—from the jurisdiction of Maxwell's British army into that of Hamilton's Mediterranean Expeditionary Force (see chapter 7). And at this stage, Australians in Egypt believed they were completing their training preparatory to fighting on the Western Front.

As we shall shortly see, Australian troops drawn from across a country of erstwhile rival colonies, recently federated, quickly displayed a distinctive, common identity, transcending the somewhat unwieldy command and administrative arrangements. A name for them and the New Zealand soldiers was already at hand, though not widely known before they went into action. In early 1915 headquarters staff at Shepheard's Hotel struck a stamp abbreviating the cumbersome corps title to 'A&NZAC'. This soon became known as the 'Anzac' stamp, and Birdwood adopted 'Anzac' as the official code name for the corps.

# CHAPTER 6

# 'PAINTING CAIRO VERY RED'

*T*HE AUSTRALIANS IN EGYPT were camped at three main locations close to Cairo. The 1st Division was in the desert at Mena, by the Pyramids. In due course the light-horsemen were camped beside the 'pleasant oasis' of Maadi, six kilometres south of Cairo, on the east bank of the Nile, and the 4th Infantry Brigade was placed with its division (the NZ and A) at Heliopolis, on Cairo's north-eastern outskirts.

Facilities to receive the Australian contingent in Egypt were little better than those so narrowly avoided on Salisbury Plain. Although there were barracks built for the climate, Imperial soldiers occupied them, so throughout their stay in Egypt the Australians were in camps. Maxwell did not know that the first contingent had no tents, so none were ready for them. The men had to sleep on the sand under the stars, which, except for the cold, was no hardship for hardy young soldiers during rainless, balmy nights. Within a week, however, it rained furiously for hours one night, drenching them. Next day many 'built cunning little tents constructed with blankets and rifles'. Proper tents eventually came from England, and within three weeks all troops were under cover. The camp then seemed 'like a small city especially when lit up at night time'.[1]

It was a month before the men's comfort was 'greatly increased' by the building of dining huts and the arrival of tables and seats. Lighting was then installed in these huts, which, General Bridges wrote, would improve conditions in camp. Late in February he reported another great improvement: the provision of shower baths, whose absence some had regarded as the camp's major defect. Numerous shops and stalls, set up by 'native enterprise' in or near the camps, and several cinemas also helped improve conditions. But there was a shortage of clothing, and sickness was a problem.

In the eyes of many Cairenes the AIF's problem was not ill-health but excessive good health, or at least boisterousness. Thousands of healthy, high-spirited young soldiers confined to ships for a voyage of six weeks had been deposited on the edge of a desert with few comforts beyond what they carried in their kits. Small wonder that while their conduct in camp was usually good, their behaviour in Cairo often left much to be desired. Bridges admitted there was some excuse at first, owing to the absence of satisfactory accommodation in the Mena camp. The men could not all be expected to behave genteelly in town.[2]

Within a few days of landing in Egypt the Australians had begun to make an impression. Ronald Storrs, on the staff of the British Agency in Cairo, on 5 December told Lieutenant-Colonel Oswald FitzGerald, Kitchener's personal military secretary, that the Australians seemed 'a roughish lot. I am told they are inclined to knock the Egyptians about.' Maxwell was disturbed at the Australians 'painting Cairo very red' and complained to Birdwood soon after his arrival about the drunkenness in the streets. Birdwood appealed to his troops to prove their fighting qualities and give Australia a good name.[3]

They did not always listen. Birdwood told Kitchener on Christmas Day, 'The men are perfectly without discipline, and Cairo has been a perfect pandemonium.' Although they were not camped very near to Cairo, this did 'not prevent them coming in in droves every evening and large numbers [were] constantly rolling about the streets drunk.'[4] 'What with Christmas, women and drink,' Maxwell told FitzGerald, 'the Australians have been rather naughty but they are settling down again—they have far too much money. The officers have very little control over their men, and NCOs none, but they will improve in time.' Richard Gardiner Casey, a young officer from Victoria and a future governor-general of Australia, thought the men were 'amenable to proper discipline but the majority of officers both junior and senior [had] little notion of the proper attitude to take towards them'.[5]

*Opposite: AIF tourists in Egypt on New Year's Day 1915. At Mena camp there were no leisure facilities. A few of the soldier tourists met their death scaling the nearby pyramids. Many others, given liberal leave, flocked to Cairo. Their comparative affluence (six shillings a day) duly served the official policy of encouraging Australian spending in Egypt and contributed to a bountiful season for local traders.*

Many Australians would have largely agreed with Maxwell's strictures. Leave to visit Cairo was generally readily available, and permitted leave was often exceeded. The journalist Oliver Hogue ('Trooper Bluegum'), a second lieutenant in the 6th Light Horse Regiment, told readers at home, 'Cairo, with its crowded, narrow thoroughfares, polyglot population, quaintly costumed, and weird cacophony of itinerant hawkers, donkeymen, and dragomen, was an entirely new sensation for the Australians.'[6] 'Marvellous' Cairo was giving a 'vast and varied' education to the men, agreed Lieutenant Dawkins. Second Lieutenant Howard Elder of the 5th Battalion contrasted the city's 'awful slums' with 'the magnificent homes of the wealthier classes'. For those seeking innocent pleasures, Cairo had its beauties, but it was 'a hotbed of vice'. Some disliked its chaos and the sights of 'the native quarters'. 'When any native passes within 15 yards of you, you know it, Phough.'[7] Others noted the 'crude slow methods and the laziness of the population' and wondered how Egypt was so prosperous: 'a white man could make a small fortune on this land'.[8] 'Terriers' might show Australians around some of the city's busy parts, but, on earnings of a shilling a day, they soon complained that the Australasians had spoilt the town, pushing up prices because of their comparative affluence. Monash, who later noted the 'hard, tough look of the Australians and New Zealanders', contrasted these men with the Lancashire Territorials who spoke 'in an almost foreign dialect and [were] a wonder and a puzzle to our Australians'.[9]

One Australian diarist was delighted to find a Sydney-like restaurant in Cairo: 'Determined to stay over night and break leave. Hotels wouldn't accept us without night pass. At last dug out place—wanted charge 5/- for room. Beat them to 2/6. Had first sleep in bed since at home with vaccination. Stayed till 9.30 next morning and then had brekker brought up. Had hot bath filled brimful. I lay in it and smoked for one hour and nearly fell asleep. Niggers much amused. Went to church. Treat to see some English girls again and to hear pretty organ music. Everyone in town much amused to see us in as Australians don't get morning leave. Psalm music identical with St. Andrews.'[10] Then followed a glowing description of Cairo mosques.

At Mena, in off-duty hours, men rode donkeys and camels and shouted their few Egyptian words. 'Hundreds' of asses, mules and other animals roamed near by, and men watched 'all kinds of peculiar people' with 'the most peculiar customs imaginable'. There were also some familiar animals, for Mena soon boasted some pet kangaroos. Tourist activities naturally included climbing the Pyramids. When several Terriers and Australians were killed falling from these heights, Private Copp astutely decided that he had better climb them quickly before they were placed out of bounds. He found the climb tiring but safe and, in company with the twenty AIF men he met at the top, enthused over the magnificent panorama of the Nile Valley and the surrounding countryside, as did many other men of the AIF. Lieutenant Dawkins, for one, found his stay in Egypt so rich and interesting that he told his mother he was in danger of forgetting that there was 'a place called Australia where one once lived'.[11]

The 1st Division enjoyed its first Christmas. Lieutenant Dawkins had a six-course dinner. 'We all dined sumptuously at Dinner,' wrote Sergeant J. S. Hagan. 'Plently of pudding, preserved fruit and wine, beer and smokes. Everyone has plenty of everything. Seven or eight brass bands performing simultaneously so the air was full of music. . . . Most of the men have imbibed too freely.' He went into Cairo for another great meal of 'roast turkey etc'. Here, Christmas excesses were more evident. 'Everywhere you looked was half drunken chaps having a musical evening on their own. The Australians are notorious characters when let loose and

on this occasion they completely ran amuck.' On Boxing Day Hagan was back at training—digging trenches.[12]

Hagan was in the 3rd Battalion. New South Welshmen seem to have been in a particularly riotous mood then, for another 1st Brigade man wrote: 'Our brigade . . . ran amok on Friday last and did not settle down again till Sunday night. The "clink" is full of prisoners as a consequence.' About sixty prisoners were in it, mainly for being absent from the camp.[13] George Mitchell, now a sergeant, might have found the 1st Brigade's behaviour rather mild, for he thought a group of South Australians from his battalion 'the worst set of men [he had] ever . . . struck'. 'Many hard cases are in our clink, most of them have lambasted the red caps [the British military police]. . . . They have put the fear of death into their hearts.'[14] A non-drinking soldier could still have a 'marvellous' Christmas. Harry Coe did so, enlivening it with some buckjumping.[15]

The camp, rather than Cairo, seemed to bear the brunt of the Australians' New Year's Eve revelry. That evening, wrote Lieutenant-Colonel Sutton, 'pandemonium reigned throughout the whole camp, bands played everywhere supplemented by tin cans, bugles blew and the pipes screamed, the men serenaded their officers, sang Auld Lang Syne and For he's a jolly good fellow and so ended the year 1914.' There was no rest that night, complained Murray Aitken, as 'roisterers, many drunk, were parading making night hideous, letting down tents, and such pranks, and being nuisances generally'. As Sergeant Hagan remarked, 'the whole camp appeared similar to civil life'.[16]

Extensive coverage in Australian newspapers about the activities of 'our men in Egypt' sometimes featured the roistering. Articles by Bean and Hogue were informative on certain aspects of their daily life. Bean was rather too informative for some soldiers, who greatly resented his complaints about their behaviour. Indeed, he risked some physical abuse. Philip Schuler, a journalist with the Melbourne *Age*, later wrote a vivid, sympathetic account of the 'wild, shouting' Australians on leave in Cairo in *Australia in Arms*. Aitken complained that the papers were wrong to say the contingent was just having a good time. 'This is a hellish hole; the last two days we have existed in one continual sand storm.' He thought the hardship would toughen him up, and a fortnight later, at seventy-eight kilograms and approaching his twenty-fifth birthday, he declared himself 'as hard as nails'.[17]

Training had resumed fairly soon after the men reached Mena. Much of it was of the strenuous, rudimentary kind, aimed at toughening the men after the comparative sloth of the long voyage. Much drill consisted of 'rushing up hills with fixed bayonets with . . . full packs on'. Some found an excess of 'the inevitable short sharp rush business' too tiring, while others loved the busy days filled with work and felt fitter and prouder of wearing uniform than ever before. Lieutenant Dawkins thought the training was 'absolutely as strenuous as it could possibly be. The limit of what the men can do has been reached and under most adverse circumstances', for example, marching in sand 'six to twelve inches thick'.[18]

These early exercises had their limitations. When he reached Cairo, Birdwood was 'rather alarmed' to learn how little training his corps had had, even in the case of officers as senior as brigadiers. He told Kitchener on 25 December that the Australians had done no bayonet fighting, no digging and very little musketry. Their artillery was 'very indifferent'. But Egypt's climate of 'lovely days' was suited to uninterrupted training, and Birdwood also told Kitchener how glad his officers were that he had saved them from the rain and mud of Salisbury Plain. Birdwood emphasised long marches. He wanted his soldiers, when they reached France, to be allowed 'as long a march as possible' from Marseilles to the front. 'The march discipline will do my troops all the good in the world,' he told Kitchener. Birdwood frequently returned to his dream of a march through France, but this was one ordeal his troops were to escape. More usefully, specialist training—for example, for artillerymen and signallers—began before Christmas. By early January Dawkins was practising sapping, mining and other engineering work, and within two months he was building bridges and pontoons and tackling challenging and interesting engineering problems faced by an army in the field.[19]

The unexpected decision to land in Egypt had, as we have seen, pre-empted the plans made for a base organisation in England. Sir George Reid sought guidance from the War Office. With Sir Thomas Mackenzie, the New Zealand High Commissioner and former prime minister, Reid reached Egypt on Christmas Eve to meet the commanders, inspect the troops, speak to them and make it clear that the Australian government was not losing its direct interest in their welfare. One listener thought Reid 'spoke admirably', but many troops, of course, were too far away to hear what he said. They could look forward to reading his speech later. One who had been in the march past commented that he would have liked to share Reid's lifestyle. 'As he reclined (gracefully!!!) in his motor he looked a veritable bloated bag of hidden things, I'll bet he'd go well cooked.'[20]

For some, New Year's Day was a time for reappraisal: '1915 with its hidden adventure, the great year for us, has dawned,' wrote George Mitchell. A year earlier, he reflected, he did not imagine that in twelve months' time he would be in Egypt 'waiting to be tipped into The Scrap'. Lieutenant-Colonel Sutton wrote, 'Well here's for a Happy New Year and plenty of fight, we need this idea to carry us on through our strenuous training. May we show that we are worthy of the trust imposed on us by Australia.'[21]

Colonel James M'Cay gave a 'very straight talk' to his men in the 2nd Brigade, Charles Copp noted in his diary, 'comparing the absolutely rotten behaviour and discipline of our men with the hardships and work being done in the fighting line and saying that we are less fit to go now, than when we left Australia. He urged every man to try and see his duty and endeavour to get fit as soon as possible instead of drinking and other things. The lecturing impressed most chaps.' John

Gellibrand agreed with M'Cay, telling his brother Walter, 'There is no denying that we left Australia with a lot of men that were useless to God or man and that we are in [the] process of getting rid of them.' He was writing of cases of misconduct and poor health.[22]

Murray Aitken, who assured his mother he was looking after himself, blamed the 'unwitting foolishness' of the authorities for much of the AIF's troubles. 'There are hundreds of cases of venereal disease in camp, some very serious.' He thought the papers were right to say that 'the conduct of many of the troops [was] very deplorable; but they're paying for it, both physically and financially'. He was having 'a lifelong object lesson' and 'had seen too much to allow [himself] to descend to the common level'. He considered it a great pity that the division was not quartered well away from any town and thought that Australia had been given 'a very poor advertisement' by its troops at Mena.[23]

Senator Pearce's response to the argument and press controversy in Australia was to explain that the force had been assembled so hurriedly that there was inadequate time to 'weed out wasters'. This weeding process would continue. The worst-behaved men were returned to Australia. On 3 February one diarist noted, 'Undesirables and others bound for Australia... were marched out of camp today.'[24] About 120 of them left on the *Kyarra* that day. Pearce was sorry these 'wasters' had misbehaved but approved of their discharge. The *Kyarra* reached Melbourne in mid-March. As a routine measure the names were published of those discharged for disciplinary reasons. The Defence Department said that the number of venereal disease cases on the *Kyarra* was small. Later, other groups of 'bad conduct cases' returned to Australia. There seemed to be no argument that such men should be discharged, but there was some dispute about the conduct of the AIF generally. For example, the *Sydney Morning Herald* published a long letter from James Green, senior Methodist chaplain with the 1st Brigade, who vigorously defended the general good bearing of the Australians in Egypt. A soldier claimed that it was unfair that men cheerfully suffering the hardships of Egypt and 'doing their level best for their country' should be criticised by stay-at-homes.[25]

It certainly was asking a great deal to expect angelic behaviour from thousands of adventurous young men, half a world away from their families, with little opportunity for polite female company, and spending what was for many the last months of their lives on exhausting military training. Some of the criticisms no doubt made inadequate allowance for the pressures on the soldiers.

A. E. Pfeifer, a Queenslander, was typical of many who enjoyed Cairo without behaving too badly. At the age of eighteen and a half he volunteered and joined the 15th Battalion. He would be wounded on Gallipoli and survive to serve in France. In a typical diary entry he recorded on Saturday 13 February: 'Went to Cairo with the bhoys. Had good time. Returned home stony broke and very merry.' On the 27th he wrote, 'Arrived in camp 11.30. Merry as usual.' When another soldier, Private Frank Morrish (B Company, 1st Battalion), died of wounds on 25 April, his stepfather was told, 'His character was exemplary and he was one of the few men of the Company who could boast of a clean conduct sheet.'[26]

In March, nineteen-year old William Fairbairn, a New Zealand gunner, devoted a large part of a letter to his mother to a joke he had heard about a guard at one of the camps. 'He heard someone coming one night and challenged him—

*'Halt! Who goes there?'*
*'Ceylon Planters Rifle Club.'*
*Sentry—'Pass, friend.'*
*A little later—'Halt! Who goes there?'*
*Answer—'Auckland Mounted Rifles.'*

['*Pass, friend.*']

*As the next person arrives*—'*Halt! Who goes there?*'

*Answer*—'*What the ——— has that got to do with you?*'

*Sentry*—'*Pass, Australian.*'

The identical joke was related, five months later, by Lady Godley to her husband as 'a lovely story'.[27]

Private A. E. Joyce of the 9th Battalion (Queensland) was typical of other Australians. On a January Saturday he was taken 'around the dreadful spot known as the Wassa Bayoux which is beyond description. Hundreds of women of all nationalities on the globe dancing around one, or sat at the door of these hovels. . . . horrid music of the Arabs who parade up and down the filthy Alleys trying to sell sham antiques. . . . it is a sight one would never tolerate at home in a British city and I was jolly glad when we found ourselves out in the street again, when we took a Carriage home to Camp.' Next day Joyce went to church.[28]

Perhaps there were more clean-living sober Christians among the AIF in Egypt than is sometimes realised. New Zealander Stanley Natusch, a self-styled 'soldier of the Empire', was 'disgusted' at hearing so many reports of Australian drunkenness. He was surprised 'at the little drunkenness there has been'. The liberal politician and judge Henry Bournes Higgins was proud of the 'Australian boys in khaki' he saw in Cairo in March and April and tolerated the misbehaviour of the few, attributing it partly to the lack of 'home influences' and partly to Cairo's licensing laws and the consequent sale of 'filthy and poisonous' liquor. The small number of 'undesirables' who returned to Australia had a far easier time than the thousands who remained in Egypt to undergo 'a rigorous course of military training' which made the 'work at Blackboy Hill' seem like 'mere child's play'.[29]

In the new year, battalions were reorganised into four companies, each holding 240 officers and men. Training became more serious, and gradually more interesting, although grinding route-marches through the desert 'with pack on back' continued. A 'Galloping Major' once led his men five kilometres out into the desert 'at breakneck speed', so 'that about two companies of men were overcome by the heat and dust and had to drop out'. Another soldier, one of six thousand who marched fifteen kilometres, mainly passing through Arab villages, did not complain about the experience. In fact, he was 'feeling splendid' except for 'being a little tired in consequence of [his] trips to Cairo'.[30]

Shortage of ammunition for guns and rifles posed problems. The War Office ration was seventy-five practice rounds per rifle and thirty shells per gun. During training, diarists noted the 'usual parades', time spent on firing rifles, fatigues and digging trenches—or the construction of field defences. Men 'trudged off to the Valley of Despair for shooting practice on short ranges'.[31] Late in January Private Joyce found bayonet drill a pleasant change from musketry. After individual training, the men were taught how to function as a military unit, as members of a battalion, then of a brigade, then of a division. Joyce practised night assaults 'with the steel'. Just when battalion drill was 'getting simply rotten', in mid-February, he began brigade drill. Murray Aitken told his mother, 'It's good to see such a large number of men working together.' However, he damned as 'a pure farce and an insult to our intelligence' a very strange performance when troops in the desert were ordered to practise billeting in an imaginary French village. The sight of officers and NCOs knocking on imaginary doors, talking to non-existent French villagers and avoiding imaginary obstructions might have persuaded any onlooking Egyptian that the days of British rule were numbered.[32] Such bizarre amusements might have been useful antidotes to news from the front. A man in the 1st Battalion remarked that many of his comrades, with families in England, had had one, two or even three brothers killed at Mons, Ypres or other places. He looked forward to the eventual advance on Berlin, adding, 'Our captain's face will make the Germans retreat.'[33]

For the people at home, Charles Bean described divisional manoeuvres of Bridges' 1st Division on the sandy Sahara or Libyan Desert, and of Godley's New Zealand and Australian Division on the stonier Arabian Desert, like the gibber plains of central Australia. From a small hill he had a superb view of a division practising the art of retaining its cohesion and maintaining its supply procedure while on the move and on the attack.[34] Detailed battle instructions were prepared for formation exercises so as to give fighting troops and staff officers added verisimilitude to battle conditions. Monash prided himself that his 4th Brigade was the best trained in the AIF.[35]

One of the little dots on the desert that Bean could see was Private Joyce. He was in a bad mood when he wrote, 'All the Brass hats as we call them were out on their nags and camels to witness our ordeal in the sand. Of course they could not think of walking under such circumstances. I would just like to see the old Colonel do a double up hill with a pack on . . . it would break his spine.' Joyce once had 'a terrible march back into camp, the day being a scorcher'. Another soldier wrote, 'Marching over that flaming desert was getting on our nerves.' At another time Joyce noted how a series of night marches tired most of the 9th Battalion troops. One night he went to bed early, glad to get his boots off after three days. The artistic Ellis Silas thought it was wonderful 'after the hell of camp life' to enjoy an elegant dinner with refined women. 'Getting killed is, to my friend and myself, the least terrible part of soldiering.'[36]

Some officers needed to improve their skills. In one training incident the 9th Battalion 'made a terrible mess of a mock attack' on the 11th Battalion, when an officer mistook a command. The men charged with bayonets only and 'were wiped out by machine gun fire'. One wonders why this lesson was not always remembered on Gallipoli. The Queenslanders returned to Mena covered in snow-white dust as if they had been dumped in flour. Incidents like this gave rise to some criticism of officers, 'the damn toffs' who 'mess us about in various ways', as one soldier put it.[37] References to the incompetence or officiousness of officers did not, however, constitute a major theme in the writings of the AIF in Egypt.

The benefits from all the torment of training soon became obvious. Joyce noted, 'We are getting as fit as fiddles.' Bridges told the Minister for Defence of the steady improvement in the men's skills. Birdwood commented on his artillerymen: 'To me it is wonderful how they have worked and got to master the complicated details they have.' A week later Birdwood wrote, 'The men are absolutely a magnificent lot, very keen, intelligent and meaning such absolute business in the killing Germans line that I am sure they will give a real good account of themselves when the time comes.' Men noted with satisfaction in their diaries advice from their commanders that their units were ready for war.[38]

A Turkish attack on the Suez Canal provided a break for some from the training routine. As early as 28 December one soldier noted the news that Turks were coming from Palestine to try to retake Egypt from Great Britain.[39] A force of twelve thousand crossed the Sinai desert by an inland route in a skilful operation and launched an assault on 3 February. It was easily repulsed, mainly by Indian troops. Australian and New Zealand soldiers moved to the Canal, with 'great cheering' as the 7th and 8th battalions marched out of Mena. Although no Australian infantry took part in the battle, men of the 3rd Field Company of Australian Engineers came under fire and were praised by their British superior officers for having 'comported themselves' well. Birdwood was convinced that they were 'very disappointed' that their 'highest hopes of fighting' were dashed.[40]

Arduous training continued. By late January 'everyone' was getting sick of
Mena. Men tired of the 'terrific sandstorms' which were 'almost blinding'.
Although the nights remained bitterly cold, by mid-January the days were becoming really hot for a few hours in the early afternoon. By late February summer was
coming, the heat in the tents could be stifling, and even Western Australians complained of the blistering heat and the glare of the sun.[41]

Many had the consolation of discovering they liked soldiering. Lieutenant Dawkins was one. 'I was made to be a soldier,' he wrote to his mother, and I like this
life, as I told Generals Birdwood and Bridges recently.' He thought those who did
not volunteer were ' a despicable crowd', denounced these second-raters' dalliance
with girls at home while the real men were in the AIF, and thought there would be
troubles in Australia after the war when men who had bravely fought 'in the
greatest world struggle of all time' confronted those who had remained 'safely and
snugly at home'. He urged his younger brother to volunteer. (He did so, but did
not serve at Gallipoli.) In a charming postcard to his little sisters, he wrote, 'I hope
you think sometimes of your brother Will and all the Australian soldier boys in
Egypt and that you are still working at school for the Expeditionary Force.' The
young girls were disappointed that he did not send them kisses in his letters, an
omission he promptly rectified.

To some, the nearby city was now becoming boring. By mid-February Private
Joyce was 'getting fed up with Cairo'. He had seen all there was to see, and the
famous cosmopolitan capital, redolent of history, was 'getting stale'. So he consoled himself, as did 'thousands of lithe and lanky antipodeans', by climbing over
the Pyramids. Another drew solace from the 'good brawls' in Cairo, or in having
very exciting bare-knuckle fights with men in his company, the outcome of one of
those old arguments to which soldiers are prone. At church parades—'not compulsory, but you have to go'—men might listen to a powerful harangue on the use of
bad language and profanity. 'The intention was good,' wrote one listener, 'but the
matter rather poorly put.'[42]

Bean reported a general impatience to get to the front. He told of a cartoon in
one of the Mena messes showing old men—the volunteers of 1914—shuffling away
from Egypt on their crutches in the year 2000. As an 11th Battalion man put it:
'[We] have rather outstayed our welcome here; the natives are no longer fulsome
in their admiration now that our money is gone. . . . The Pyramids and the Sphinx
no longer charm us; the niggers and their beasts are only a nuisance. We fall back
on civilization and amuse ourselves with picture shows and music-halls of which
we have four in camp.'[43] Men spoke of being 'as keen as mustard' to fight the
Turks before going on to Europe and hoped that in combat Australian soldierly
qualities would come to the fore. A Queenslander told his sister that he was 'too
safe for [his] liking, worse luck'. He was to be killed at Anzac on the first day.[44]
Murray Aitken told his mother, 'I don't think I'll be afraid of danger, Mother, I'm
schooling myself to be cool in everything, to never be taken by surprise, to always
be ready, and to take things philosophically; it's the best way, a soldier's life is
hard, but oh! I feel a man and I'm afraid of nothing.'[45] To those who wondered
when they would get to the fighting, Birdwood replied that there was no hurry:
'They may fully count on bellies full of fighting in their turn.'[46] This was being
planned for them in London and Constantinople.

# CHAPTER 7

# THE GALLIPOLI ENTERPRISE

$A$USTRALIANS TRAINING IN EGYPT had grown up while Germany and Britain were vying with each other for influence over Turkey, or, more correctly, the Ottoman Empire. On the eve of the war, following the territorial losses recently suffered, this empire, which had reached its zenith in 1555 and had been in intermittent decline ever since, was reduced to a mere eighteen thousand square kilometres in Europe, in the south-east of the Balkan Peninsula. This was a small part of a still large empire, with an area of over 1.7 million square kilometres, a frontier of twelve thousand kilometres and a coastline of eight thousand kilometres, of extraordinary diversity in geography, climate, culture, economic standards, race, religion and traditions, stretching through Asia Minor to Persia in the south and, nominally, to Egypt in the west. Ancient and famed Constantinople, the empire's capital and biggest city, straddled Europe and Asia at the Bosphorus. The heartland of the empire and national home of the Turks was Anatolia. The territory over which Constantinople exercised suzerainty was largely backward, road and rail transport being rudimentary and education and literacy deficient.

No census had been taken (the first modern professional one was in 1927). One informed guess at the empire's population on the war's eve was a total of twenty-one million inhabitants, of whom seven million were Turks and nine million Arabs, with Armenians, Greeks and Kurds each totalling a million and a half. Smaller numbers of Jews, Druses and a variety of other tribes, races and ethnic groupings such as Georgians comprised about half a million. Other guesses put the population several million higher, assessing miscellaneous groups at two million and the Turks at nine or ten million. The ruling Turks thus constituted only a third of this fragile empire; they were the only willing bearers of the military task and so carried the burden of maintaining the empire's integrity. Other groups, infected by nationalism, as Arnold Toynbee put it, were either indifferent to the fate of the Ottoman Empire or were its enemies who in wartime saw the Entente powers (France, Britain and Russia) as their possible deliverers. These powers, especially Russia, had territorial ambitions in the unstable empire.

In 1908 army mutineers joined with long-standing revolutionary groups, commonly known as the Young Turks, to wrest control of government from the Sultan Abdul Hamid II, whose rule since 1876 had been that of an inefficient autocracy. The sultan was deposed in 1909, and the self-appointed leaders of the Young Turks set up the Committee of Union and Progress (CUP), which became the new government, or Sublime Porte, controlling the empire (with one or two short intervals) until it collapsed under the shock of military defeat in 1918. By 1914 Mehmed Talaat Pasha, Enver Pasha, and Ahmed Djemal Pasha were prominent leaders of the CUP and, with their immediate colleagues, largely determined the issue of peace and war in their empire.

The shaky new government needed friends. The rulers of the empire's most important traditional ally, Britain (despite its revulsion against the Bulgarian atrocities of the 1870s), gradually became disillusioned with the new regime as the prospect of constitutional government ended and a military despotism emerged. Nonetheless, Britain retained important links with, and influence on, Constantinople, in particular through its naval mission, led from 1912 to 1914 by Rear-Admiral A. H. Limpus. At the same time, Constantinople could not regard Britain with unalloyed cordiality: since 1882 Britain had occupied Egypt, nominally part of the Ottoman Empire. France, too, had designs on Arabian areas of the empire. Neighbouring Russia, Turkey's traditional enemy, wanted nothing less than Constantinople and the area bordering the Bosphorus and the Dardanelles and the northern littoral of the Sea of Marmara. A vigorous advocacy of these well-known aims appeared in a book by Vladimir Jabotinsky, *Turkey and the War*, in 1917. The author was a war correspondent for a Moscow newspaper. He ardently defended Russian territorial claims on grounds of economic necessity, virtually declaring them an inalienable Russian right. His other justification was that Russian plans only aimed at what he regarded as 'non-Turkish' lands substantially occupied by subject races. Russia did not plan the destruction of the Turks' national home in Anatolia.[1]

Under these circumstances it was hardly surprising that the Sublime Porte welcomed support from Germany, which had no territorial designs upon Ottoman territory. Since the 1880s Abdul Hamid II had cultivated German friendship. This well suited expansionary Germany, with its policy of *Drang nach Osten* and its dream of a Berlin-Baghdad railway. The German general Colmar von der Goltz was in charge of reorganising the Ottoman army from 1883 until 1895 and again from 1908 to 1911. Other instances of Germany's close ties with Turkey abounded, including growing trade and commercial links; they were symbolised by important visits in 1889 and 1898 by the Kaiser, who valued Turkish friendship.

The Young Turks dramatically expanded Abdul Hamid's policy of cultivating Germany. As Djemal explained in his memoirs,[2] Mahmud Shevket Pasha, as Grand Vizier, decided early in 1913 that Turkey would speedily have to reorganise its army on the German model. Germany promptly complied with his request for a training mission on 'the grand scale'; General Liman von Sanders arrived in December as the head of a group of some seventy officers.[3] He was made Inspector-General of the Ottoman army and soon began revitalising it, although naturally this was not a short-term task.

To have one's army trained by officers from the best army in the world was one thing; to enter into a diplomatic alliance with that power was another. In his post-war memoirs, Djemal, who occupied a series of important posts from 1913, justified the recourse to Germany as the only option on the ground that France and Britain rebuffed Constantinople's overtures and it was necessary to escape 'the iron claws of Russia'.[4] Germany was anxious for an alliance to strengthen its position in Europe, and negotiations began before the war, ending in the signing of an agreement on 2 August 1914. Initially its existence was known only to three Turkish plotters at the nerve centre of the Ottoman government—Enver, the dashing Young Turk promoted to general and since January 1914 the Minister for War; Talaat, Minister of the Interior; and Mehmed Said Halim Pasha, the new Grand Vizier and Minister for Foreign Affairs. Djemal, who was not a party to the successful negotiations, still tended to favour the Entente powers for a time; but Enver's success soon converted him, for the thought of a powerful European state offering an alliance, on the apparent basis of equality, with the backward, despised Ottoman Empire, was too attractive a bait. Nonetheless, outside the ruling junta, and despite the long-standing ties with Germany, there was strong opposition, both in the government and among the population, to entering the war on its side. For three months, those who stood for peace were in constant struggle with those in favour of war. There was no doubt that, despite von Sanders' reforms, the army was not ready for war, which also helps to explain the three months' delay. Turkish critics of Enver also pointed out that, since a German victory could not be guaranteed, the alliance could end in disaster for the Ottomans, which of course is what duly eventuated.

A combination of strong German pressure and unsympathetic British diplomacy eventually forced a hesitant Constantinople into war. London helped the German cause by its seizure of two battleships, the *Sultan Osman* and the *Reschadich*, whose construction in Britain had been paid for by contributions from the Turkish population. Germany's influence in Constantinople was measurably increased when its battle-cruiser *Goeben* and light cruiser *Breslau* avoided British warships in the Mediterranean and safely reached the Golden Horn, to become virtually integrated with Ottoman naval power.

The issue of peace or war was virtually settled by a *coup de main* by the German Rear-Admiral Wilhelm Souchon, who in September replaced Admiral Limpus and became commander-in-chief of the Turkish navy. On 29 October the *Goeben* and *Breslau*, under Souchon's command but flying the Turkish flag, bombarded several Russian Black Sea ports. This was done with the connivance of Enver's war party in the CUP. The peace party, outraged at this high-handed action, advocated abrogation of the German alliance. But under the pressure of events it was impossible for this group to counter the arguments of Enver and his associates. By this stage, war was virtually inevitable. Various further hostilities occurred before Turkey and Britain entered into a formal state of war on 5 November.

An observer could be tempted to agree with scholars such as Ahmed Emin who assert that in 1914 the Entente powers, especially Britain, gravely miscalculated in not making resolute attempts to secure Turkish neutrality.[5] The situation in Constantinople was so evenly balanced that such an outcome seems to have been possible had the Entente made the effort. Clearly, the Entente lacked the will to do so. Russia wanted to occupy the Ottoman Empire's capital and adjacent territory of crucial strategic significance; France and Britain placed a higher value on Russia's friendship than on Turkish neutrality, and both had their own important territorial designs on the sprawling empire. But no doubt it is going too far to take the cynical view that London's decision-makers preferred Turkish enmity to its neutrality, as the former provided a golden opportunity to take some of its lands.

This sympathetic judgement on London's attitude is not vitiated by the fact that, for almost a decade before the war, as Germany gained greater influence at Constantinople, Britain had had to consider the possibility that it would find itself at war with its quondam friend. If this happened, what military action could it take? Contingency planning was absolutely essential. The General Staff studied this problem and gave their opinions in a succinct paper, dated 19 December 1906, for the Committee of Imperial Defence (CID). Wise and experienced officers, they produced an excellent paper, showing the risks involved in alienating Turkey and coming very close to stating that Britain could not mount a successful attack on it. There were no suitable objectives, and the Sultan's army was vastly bigger than any force Britain could bring against it. The committee thought the least unpromising route for an offensive was north from the Sinai, through the Palestinian and Syrian regions of the Ottoman Empire.

The dangers facing a joint naval and military expedition against the Dardanelles were so great that the General Staff would not recommend it. If it is decided, they wrote with prescience, 'to attempt a joint naval and military attack upon the Gallipoli Peninsula by an expeditionary force dispatched from the United Kingdom, with all the inevitable publicity of preparation for such an undertaking, it is as certain as anything can be in war that, however much our arrangements are veiled in mystery, however much we feint and dissemble, and wherever we fix our first rendezvous—be it Egypt or elsewhere—a powerful force, possibly even 100,000, will be found ready to receive the joint expedition when it appears off the coast'. That would be enough to doom a landing, because, as the committee stated, to succeed, the supporting fleet would have to guarantee that the men, horses and vehicles of the landing force should reach the shore unmolested. Then they would need an adequate area free from hostile fire to enable them to form up for battle on suitable ground. The Director of Naval Intelligence, Captain Charles L. Ottley, was slightly less pessimistic than the General Staff, thinking there was some chance that British military might could overcome the great obstacles.[6]

In September 1914 this expert view was still accepted by the decision-makers in London.[7] But its wisdom was overlooked in the crisis of the following months. Stalemate on the Western Front provided strong stimulus for Britain to use its maritime power to open an alternative theatre of war. As well, Russia was in difficulties and probably needed help: a Russian collapse could have been disastrous for the Entente powers, as Germany could then have concentrated all its forces on the Western Front. Also, Britain's position in the Middle East would have been put at risk. These, then, were ingredients for a continuing and lengthy disagreement over strategy between 'Easterners' and 'Westerners' in the British cabinet.

The Asquith government's serious consideration of an attack on the Dardanelles began on 2 January 1915, when Russia, following a defeat by Turkish forces in the Caucasus, appealed to Britain to help relieve Turkish pressure. Britain had to attach great weight to this request, but the immediate sequel was baffling: Russia's successful reversal of the position in the Caucasus, with a crushing victory at Sary-kamysh a few days later, was virtually ignored in subsequent arguments in Asquith's cabinet.[8]

Churchill's belief that the best point at which to attack Turkey was at the Dardanelles led to a raging controversy among British policy-makers throughout 1915 and beyond. Although it is an oft-told story, some of its key features must be repeated to put the AIF's role in context.[9] A 'meeting place of Asia and Europe', the Dardanelles strait, about seventy kilometres long, was well guarded by forts from its Aegean Sea entrance to the Narrows at Chanak (Çanakkale). Its southern, or Asian, shore did not figure prominently in Britain's military planning. On its northern or European shore lay the Gallipoli Peninsula, running in a north-easterly direction from its tip at Cape Helles. The town of Gallipoli (Gelibolu) is on the coast where the strait begins to open out into the Sea of Marmara. There are some plains on the Gallipoli Peninsula—such as at its south-western tip and between Maidos (present-day Eceabat) and the Aegean coast—but much of it is rugged and most is hilly, providing a series of far better natural defensive positions than on the British (northern) sector of the Western Front, for example. About seventy kilometres from its tip the peninsula narrows to a neck, five kilometres wide, where there is another potentially strong defensive position, the Bulair line. If any invading troops, with the navy on their right, fought their way off the peninsula and past Bulair, they would still have had to fight through rolling hills, which provided a succession of good defensive locations, before they reached the Chatalja Lines, Constantinople's last major line of defence, about thirty-five kilometres west of the capital. Small wonder that the CID paper of 1906 warned against attacking at the Dardanelles.

In Asquith's War Council of senior ministers and their advisers there was inadequate appreciation of the rugged nature of the Gallipoli Peninsula. Although

*The alternative war zones discussed in January 1915.*

Lieutenant-Colonel Maurice Hankey, secretary to the CID and secretary to the War Council and its immediate successors, had sailed through the Dardanelles, he had not landed on the peninsula. No cabinet minister had examined the area, although Churchill had visited Turkey. In any case, the geography and topography of the peninsula did not at first concern Asquith's ministers, for it was believed that the Royal Navy would be able to force its way through the Dardanelles without any help from the army. As political ruler of the world's greatest navy, the young, ambitious Churchill doubtless saw a great opportunity to use his glittering weapon for a strategic master-stroke whose success would bring him international fame as the inspired leader who dramatically altered the course of the war.

In the course of the arguments within Asquith's administration about an attack on Turkey, Churchill conjured up visions of alluring rewards for a bold master-stroke. With a successful thrust at Turkey's 'heart' through the Dardanelles, Constantinople could be occupied, Turkey would surrender, the Mediterranean route to Russia could be opened and a Balkan front established against the Central Powers, which, surrounded on three sides, might be forced into an early surrender.[10]

As Churchill wrote on 9 March, Constantinople was 'only a means to an end, and that end [was] the marching against Austria of the five re-united Balkan states'.[11] It was a breathtaking concept: Balkan national and racial hatreds were to be conveniently submerged in the interests of the Entente powers. The idea was chimerical. The notion that mutually antagonistic Balkan states—Greece, Bulgaria, Romania, Serbia and Albania—should join in a common cause coinciding with British interests might seem so far-fetched as to be hardly worth considering. But most Balkan states wanted to join whichever side seemed assured of victory, so there was a belief in London that the far-fetched goal might be attained through an impressive British military victory in the region.

Britain was enjoying no success in its Balkans diplomacy. Greece, a traditional enemy of Turkey, showed some sympathy for Britain's cause and for a time half-heartedly considered offering a force to attack at the Dardanelles. This alarmed the Russian government, which early in March insisted that Greeks should not take part in such a campaign, for that would conflict with its designs on Constantinople and the two crucial straits. Britain, by a secret treaty later in March, agreed to Russia's wishes.[12] So, in a sense, the Australians on Gallipoli would be fighting to win the area for Russia, although none of them knew so at the time.

Although some of its homeland was occupied by the German army, France's interests in the eastern Mediterranean were such that it looked askance at an all-British expedition there. France was determined to be involved in any military or naval operations in the region, and this further complicated the diplomatic framework of the strategy governing the deployment of the AIF in 1915. In January French warships were sent to join the Royal Navy in bombarding the Dardanelles forts.

These vessels would be able to test a new theory about the value of ships' guns in a duel with forts. Since the CID study of 1906, advances in the technology of naval guns had led to claims that their long-standing inferiority to fortress guns no longer applied. Britain's newest battleship, the *Queen Elizabeth*, carried 15-inch guns. Surely these could pulverise the Dardanelles forts. British optimists said that after this was done the Allied fleet would steam through the strait and the Sea of Marmara and then, as Kitchener said, 'overawe Constantinople'.[13] Churchill and others sanguinely claimed that the fleet's appearance off the Golden Horn would cause Turkey to capitulate, with the consequential benefits already mentioned.

*Winston Churchill, first Lord of the Admiralty from 1911 to 1915 and prominent advocate of the strategy for a combined naval and military assault on the Dardanelles, with his fiery First Sea Lord, Admiral John ('Jackie') Fisher, in Whitehall.*

Well-placed contemporaries and learned historians have disagreed about whether the appearance of British warships off the Golden Horn would have led to a popular uprising and the replacement of the pro-German government with one friendly to the Entente. Henry Morgenthau, United States ambassador to the Sublime Porte from 1913 to 1916, thought the government would topple, a point of view he vigorously elaborated in a memoir, *Ambassador Morganthau's Story* (1919).[14] Lieutenant-Colonel R. H. Williams, the United States military attaché in Constantinople, typified a different view. He later claimed he had always thought that the Gallipoli operation was futile in conception and that the arrival of the fleet off the Golden Horn in March 1915 would have had no effect at all.[15]

Even if British warships steamed through the Sea of Marmara past the Topkapi Palace and took station outside the Golden Horn, what were they then supposed to do? They could not bombard mosques, palaces and residential areas without inflaming Moslem opinion in the British Empire and without Britain appearing in the eyes of the world, including of the United States, to be on a par with Germany for barbarism. Morgenthau thought of this. At a stage of the Entente's naval attack when most people in Constantinople—including Baron von Wangenheim, the German ambassador, and most German officers on the spot, but not Enver— assumed the Allied fleet was on the point of breaking through the Dardanelles, the ambassador spent some time seeking the warring governments' agreement to delineate certain areas of the capital which were legitimate targets for naval bombardment; other areas, including residential districts, were to be safe.[16]

The Turkish government was frightened enough to begin moving its records and necessary administrative paraphernalia to a safer place in the interior. The Allied fleet could have destroyed the munitions factories near Constantinople, although Germany could, with some difficulty, have supplied most of the deficiency because Romania and Bulgaria allowedGermany to transport ammunition through their territory. As well, if Constantinople 'fell' to the fleet it would still need to be garrisoned, even if Turkey sued for peace.

Testing of the hopeful theories began on 19 February when British warships began an intermittent bombardment of the Dardanelles' outer forts. This made modest progress over subsequent days. However, the main defences were in the throat, not the mouth of the strait and they included mobile howitzers and minefields in support of the forts.

Australian involvement in the Dardanelles gamble began a few days before this naval bombardment opened, although no Australian had a hand in initiating it.

*The great new battleship,* Queen Elizabeth, *steams off Cape Helles while Turkish shells burst near by. First of its type and the most powerful ship afloat, it carried eight 15-inch guns but did little serious damage to Dardanelles forts in March 1915. When attempts to capture the forts were finally abandoned in mid-May, the vessel was recalled from the Mediterranean.*

The six men present at the British War Council meeting of 16 February decided that, if necessary, units in Birdwood's corps should be moved to Lemnos, a Greek island about sixty-five kilometres west of the mouth of the Dardanelles.[17] At that stage it was envisaged that the troops would be needed only in a subsidiary role, to occupy ground and forts from which the naval guns had driven the Turks. Two thousand British marines had already been sent to Lemnos, and some eight thousand more of the Royal Naval Division and a French division of eighteen thousand had been earmarked for such a role.[18] More troops were needed, to take advantage of any success gained by the Royal Navy in its major attack planned for March. On 24 February Asquith asked if the Australasians 'were good enough' for an important operation of war. Kitchener replied that 'they were quite good enough if a cruise in the Sea of Marmora was all that was contemplated'.[19] Two days later he told the War Council that the eight thousand Australasian mounted troops in Egypt 'were very good soldiers', and could reinforce the Gallipoli Peninsula.[20] When ordered to provide troops for the move to Lemnos, Bridges chose the 3rd Brigade, which began to reach Lemnos on 4 March.

The Allied fleet's attempt to force its way through the Dardanelles was well reported in newspapers throughout the world, including Australia. By early March the Australian public knew that an expedition would be landed at the Dardanelles. People could read about the Turks hurrying forward to reinforce the threatened area, and about alarm or panic in Constantinople. Newspapers published informed analyses of the awesome obstacles confronting an army that sought to march on the city.[21]

Asquith's government was not breaking faith with the Australian government in deciding, without consulting Melbourne, to prepare to commit Bridges' troops to the peninsula. The Australian offer had been made on the explicit understanding that the government in London would decide on the deployment of the AIF, an undertaking explicitly repeated when the 4th Brigade (second convoy) left Australia.[22] This was quite natural, considering Australia's constitutional and emotional links with Britain.

During early March, as British and French warships continued an intermittent, inconclusive bombardment of the Dardanelles forts, opinions still differed in London on the likelihood of the fleet being able to force its way through the strait. A growing belief that it would not be able to do so unaided meant that a bigger role would have to be given to the army. The War Council became convinced that any army landing on the Gallipoli Peninsula would need to be strengthened by a formation of experienced soldiers. After much argument and vacillation, it decided on 10 March that the 29th Division, containing regular, long-service soldiers, should sail from England to assist in the Dardanelles campaign.[23]

This expansion in the army role meant that, to his disappointment, Birdwood was to have a more senior general placed over him.[24] Kitchener chose Sir Ian Hamilton. Probably Kitchener himself was the only serving British general better known to Australians. The charming Hamilton had known Birdwood for thirty years and was a good friend of Churchill. Asquith thought he had 'too much feather in his brain'. Fêted and honoured in Australia in 1914, Hamilton in 1915 would suffer an ignominious end to an illustrious career, although it may be doubted whether any other British general available could have triumphed under the circumstances he inherited. As Lieutenant-Colonel Charles Repington, military correspondent of *The Times* during the war, would write in 1919, 'Hamilton must often have made longer or better preparation for a week's covert shooting than he was enabled to make for the Dardanelles.' At the outset, before leaving London on 13 March, Hamilton showed caution by altering the name of his command, replacing the first word of Constantinople Expeditionary Force with 'Mediterranean'.[25]

Racked by argument, Asquith's government was drifting further into a substantial commitment at the Dardanelles, one from which it was becoming difficult to withdraw, politically speaking. And the Australians training in the Middle East were unwitting victims of this imbroglio.

*General Sir Ian Hamilton (second from right) with Commodore Roger Keyes, chief of staff of the Eastern Mediterranean Squadron (far left), Vice-Admiral John de Robeck, commander of the Allied fleet, and Major-General Walter Braithwaite, Hamilton's chief of staff.*

# CHAPTER 8

# 'THE WILD COLONIAL CORPS HAS LEFT CAIRO'

$A$s a result of the War Council's decision to move a force of Australians to Lemnos, the 3rd Brigade was paraded on Sunday 21 February to be told they would leave Egypt in a week's time. 'The boys cheered like billyho and got quite merry about it,' wrote Charles Copp. Men were proud and wildly excited and the officers 'highly jubilant' that their brigade had received the 'great compliment' of being the first chosen. Murray Aitken was 'overjoyed at the prospect of leaving this God-forsaken place of sacred filth and glaring sand'. Although it was still over two months before the landing on Gallipoli, he, like many others, was already expecting hard work and a 'hot reception' as his brigade would 'be the first to land in the dark'. Many men in the other brigades were not sure where the 3rd was going; 'probably France', some guessed.[1] Both Richard Casey and John Monash claimed they had no idea where the brigade went; as late as the end of March its location remained a complete mystery to Monash. Others thought Turkey was the destination but suggested Smyrna or Alexandretta as the most likely landing spots. Soldiers contentedly paid farewell visits to familiar training areas, such as the 11th Battalion's 'old Tiger's Tooth, one of our little pet hillocks where we have often shot, skirmished and drilled by day, and dug and watched and shivered by night'.[2]

On 28 February Private Joyce of the 9th Battalion was one of the thousands who bade farewell to that stretch of desert at the Pyramids which had been home for three months. There were farewell lunches. Then the battalions marched off as bands played, and the remaining troops cheered lustily. 'The 3rd Brigade were very very much envied,' George Mitchell noted. 'A striking part about the men now that we are up against the Big Thing is that they take everything stoically and growl at nothing.' Aitken told his mother that he was now starting on 'the third period in [his] quest of manhood. . . . it has every promise of being an epoch in the history of Australia, and incidentally of being a great factor in the forming of my future life'.[3]

Tommies were interested observers of the men's march through Cairo. Some officers took the opportunity to have a last elegant lunch. Private Joyce was so tired that he slept on the overnight train to Alexandria. Here the 9th and 10th battalions were tightly packed in the *Ionian*, which reached Lemnos on 4 March. They travelled 'fairly well sardined' in a 'tub' that was 'in a filthy condition'. But while steaming through the Greek archipelago one of their number, a wandering ex-student of Melbourne University, Private V. Finch, was 'thinking hard about the old Greek and Latin poets and what they had to say' about the region he was traversing.[4] The 9th Battalion bivouacked on shore, but Lemnos lacked enough facilities for the entire brigade, so the 11th Battalion stayed on its crowded ship. Perhaps it was lucky. It rained heavily on Joyce's second night ashore, and at daylight the soldiers 'rolled out . . . like wet rats'.[5]

*The 3rd Brigade was the first AIF unit to move to Lemnos, arriving on 4 March, a month ahead of the other brigades. Training continued at Lemnos. A new element was a lot of practice at 'getting down rope ladders into ship's boats with full equipment and landing on the beach'.*

The 3rd Brigade spent a month on Lemnos before being rejoined by the remainder of the division. The island—which had joined the Greek kingdom after the Balkan Wars of 1912–13—would be a significant staging base for the coming campaign. Its main advantages were its proximity to the Dardanelles and its large natural harbour, Mudros. It had few other advantages. Brigadier-General A. J. de Lotbinière, the Chief Engineer of Birdwood's corps, thought Mudros the worst base that could have been selected because it lacked landing facilities.[6] One Royal Navy officer firmly agreed; the selection of Lemnos as a base shook his confidence in the expedition. It was quite unsuitable, barren and unattractive and lacking wharves and piers; water was scarce. But to many Australians it was 'very picturesque', even idyllic, and greatly appreciated after Egypt. Many also liked Mudros and thought that Castro (population fifteen hundred), fifteen kilometres away, was 'a fine quaint town'. The local Greeks were 'a fine lot', thought Lieutenant-Colonel Sutton, 'and the children behave very nicely, so unlike the Egyptians, they are shy but not stupid and are quite trustful and soon make friends and *do not beg*.'[7]

During March the 3rd Brigade endured cold, rainy weather and boisterous winds. Men complained that the weather was 'as bad as Melbourne'. They had no leave at all and the troops felt like 'a lot of convicts on an island'. Their training was no less vigorous than in Egypt. 'Whenever the colonel sighted a very steep hill, he led up it at top speed. This sort of thing gets monotonous.' There was a lot of practice at 'getting down rope ladders into ship's boats with full equipment and landing on the beach at Lemnos'. An unforeseen delay in training during a wet night provoked a philosophical comment: 'So we lay down in the rain, awaiting the dawn, singing "I want to be a soldier" . . . but as we were quite wet we were quite happy.' The men had the 'treat of their lives' on 1 April when 120 bags of mail arrived. We 'jump at our letters like children', wrote Sutton. 'Cooped up as we are it is a great pleasure to get news from home.' They were inspected by generals and became aware that the task facing them was becoming tougher. 'Rumour says that the Turks and Germans are strongly entrenched on the Dardanelles,' wrote Aitken on 10 March. A British sailor told an Australian private that Turkish mines in the strait were as 'thick as sea-gulls'; they picked up ninety in one night. The general prediction was that the covering force would lose 80 per cent of its men.[8]

The Australians saw the steady growth of Allied forces in Mudros harbour as more troops and warships arrived. Sutton enjoyed the bustling cosmopolitan scenes in Mudros: The French expeditionary force uniforms were 'very gaudy, the blue coat and crimson trousers are very swagger, and the Zouaves are a sight to see.' He also enjoyed sailing around the harbour looking at 'the warships with marks of Battle on them'. He was able to see all over the vast *Queen Elizabeth* and thought this the experience of a lifetime.[9]

Then news reached the 3rd Brigade of a British naval disaster at the Dardanelles. Hamilton had reached the Mediterranean in time to see the great naval battle of 18 March, when the combined British and French fleets made their most determined effort to overcome the forts and steam through the Dardanelles. The Turks, under expert German guidance, had used the several months' warning to excellent purpose to turn the Dardanelles Narrows into a virtually impregnable section of the strait. A mere three German officers and 160 German soldiers, with enthusiastic Turkish co-operation, were enough to place the guns scientifically and to repair the ancient but very sturdy forts, most of which had earthen defences, which were quite effective against the shells from the Allied fleet. Moreover, a minefield was skilfully laid, protected by the guns of the forts and by mobile field artillery, in such a way as to make it virtually impossible for the Allied minesweepers to dispose of the mines. As well, the Germans succeeded in rejuvenating a Turkish shell-making factory near Constantinople, to help supply their guns.[10] German experts would have welcomed an Allied attack on the strait, feeling sure it could only lead to a Turkish victory. Admiral Limpus, who from 1912 until September 1914 had been Britain's naval counterpart in Turkey to army adviser Liman von Sanders and knew the Dardanelles well, said that the attack should never have been made, because the Turkish defences were so strong.[11]

Despite an impressive display of naval might, the ships failed and sustained heavy losses from the mines. Of the four French battleships in the attack, one was sunk and another badly damaged. Of the six British capital ships, two were sunk and one disabled. British naval officers in the action thought it was 'a bit of a disaster' and that it now seemed impossible to force the Narrows by ships alone. One complained about politicians who thought they were 'born strategists' and who put ill-informed pressure on naval commanders. A gunner on the *Albion* thanked God for bringing him 'safely out of one of the hottest fights of modern times'.[12] Vice-Admiral John M. de Robeck, who had just assumed command of the Allied fleet, refused to resume the attack. The claim that he was close to victory because the Turkish forts were running out of ammunition has been effectively rebutted by Robin Prior in *Churchill's 'World Crisis' as History*.[13] The Turks knew they had achieved a great victory, one that is still kept before travellers in the region.[14] Even the *Queen Elizabeth*'s 15-inch guns had their limitations when used against land targets, as Hamilton indicated to Kitchener on 18 March: 'At the first tremendous surprise caused by the Queen Elizabeth's shells, there no doubt was a panic, and the Admiral thinks that 5,000 men could at that time have marched from Cape Helles right up to the Bulair Lines. But that phase very quickly passed, and now the Germans have taken hold of the situation.'[15] Events had proved that ships were still at a disadvantage when pitted against forts, at least when supported by mobile artillery.

Failure of the naval attack revolutionised the nature of the Dardanelles-Gallipoli campaign, but not, by forcing a return to Egypt, as some feared. Asquith's government, partly for reasons of prestige, decided that it had to persist with the venture. This meant the main burden would now fall upon soldiers, who would have to be landed on the Gallipoli Peninsula in order to capture the forts and open the way for the fleet to pass through the Dardanelles. Many more troops would have to be committed, including the Australian and New Zealand units still based in Egypt. The role of the 3rd Brigade on Lemnos changed dramatically. Instead of being poised to secure shattered forts abandoned by demoralised Turks, it would be given one of the hardest of military tasks—to spearhead a landing against a fortified coast held by alerted troops defending their own country.

Hamilton, too, was given a very difficult task. At short notice, and with limited help from the War Office, he was ordered to prepare a major, complex operation of war, against an enemy that was taking good advantage of the warnings it had been given of likely invasion; Turkey was busily reinforcing the peninsula and fortifying it with trenches, wire barriers, machine-guns and artillery emplacements.[16]

One of Hamilton's duties was to inspect his troops, including the Australians. The men of the 3rd Brigade did not know of his reaction when he inspected them. Some might have been surprised to learn that he told the British Prime Minister they were 'as wild as hawks but splendid men', who would do well in combat. They were sturdy, healthy, seemingly 'in excellent fettle', and full of self-confidence. They thought they could 'beat any troops existing in the world'. It was just as important 'from the point of view of morale' to inspect the Australians in Egypt, and Hamilton stayed there an extra day to do this. On 29 March he 'saw the whole of Birdwood's crowd . . . including the latest reinforcements, amounting in all to some 30,000 men. The physique of the rank and file could not be improved upon, and officers and men have learnt in the past four or five months at least the rudiments of discipline—I mean, they understand now that an order is something more than a mild suggestion to be acted upon or not as they think proper. They are all as keen as possible and will, I am certain, render a very good account of themselves if the conditions encountered give them a fair chance.' To Bridges, he remarked on the improvement in the troops and their equipment since his inspection in Australia in early 1914.[17]

In Egypt, the men's training was becoming repetitive. They were now accustomed to marching through sandstorms and occasionally through a great cloud of locusts. Attacks were practised on a brigade scale. R. G. Casey complained of some 'perfectly rotten fire control', and commented on a brigade exercise: 'The day was characterized by wild fighting in the open. The disregard of cover and the advancing in face of a strong fire in the open will have to be remedied—or our troops will very soon be wiped out.' Looking back much later, one soldier claimed that 'the long and severe training in Egypt . . . though wearisome and trying at the time, [was] the finest preparation for our campaign [on Gallipoli] which we could have had'.[18] Their training, which consisted of long advances across the desert based on British experience in South Africa, scarcely prepared them for trench warfare on precipitous scrubby slopes at Gallipoli. But at least they were fit. This explained why they were able to last so well despite their great privations at Anzac.

Nonetheless, since leaving Australia the contingent had never been entirely free from measles or influenza developing into pneumonia, diseases which, Bridges reported, had caused most of the AIF's deaths from illness. The AIF's first death had occurred in Adelaide on 28 September 1914. Before the Gallipoli landing, forty-three members of the force had died in Australia, fifteen from various forms of pneumonia, two from typhoid and ten from other diseases, thirteen from accidents (including four drownings), one from heat stroke and one from delirium tremens, while one died insane. By 24 April, twenty-four men had died on the journey to Egypt, nine of them in the first contingent. The first AIF death in Egypt occurred on 13 December. By the end of February, Monash's brigade had a sickness rate of about 20 per cent; by the end of March, deaths from 'ordinary causes' in his brigade occurred at the rate of one or two a week.[19] Before the landing, eighty-six members of the force had been buried in various Egyptian cemeteries: Heliopolis, Cairo, Mena, Alexandria, Abassia, Port Said, Maadi and Ismailia. Pneumonia had killed fifty-four, meningitis five, and smallpox three; two had committed suicide, six had been killed in accidents. Ten other diseases had claimed one or two lives each. All told, 153 men of the force had died before it took part in any fighting.[20]

Some attributed sickness at Mena to the bad water supply. Cairo prostitutes were another source of disease. About two hundred men with venereal disease left Mudros for Cairo before the landing.[21] As John Gellibrand wrote, the men were 'aflames pour les femmes', and into the brothels they went and later into hospital. In March the *Argus* expressed concern about the number of deaths in the AIF,[22] and the health of the force was debated in the House of Representatives in April, when Labor Party backbencher Frank Anstey claimed that ill men were returning 'in droves' because they were overworked and underfed. Charles Bean claimed that those who had returned ill were the victims of their own hard work, enthusiasm and dedication. The men's ration scale in Egypt was less than Australian men had been accustomed to eat, and some army officers thought the troops suffered through having to do too much strenuous activity during hot days while getting insufficient protection against the cool night air of the desert.[23]

Men were eclectic in their entertainments and in their condign punishments. Private R. L. Donkin of the 1st Battalion beat up a corporal in a fight and a few days later went on a very enjoyable genteel tour of Cairo, including a visit to the Opera House. He lost a day's pay as punishment. He was also irked by the rapacious Egyptian donkey-owners who sidetracked with their fares, going to all their relatives at stalls with things to sell. After the 2nd Battalion sports were over, Private D. J. C. Anderson wrote, 'I don't think there were 3 sober officers or 100 sober men.' Even signaller Ellis Silas was punished 'for refusing to attend that farcical absurdity Church Parade'. He noted wryly, 'All the camp are delighted to hear that Silas has C. B. [he was confined to barracks for three days]—the lads are immensely amused and come along to see me do it.'[24]

By early March, men in the 1st, 2nd and 4th brigades expected to be leaving soon for the Dardanelles. Some became apprehensive about how they would feel under fire or when facing real hardships. Ellis Silas hoped he would not 'blow out' before he had 'at least done a little'. Robert Antill, proud to be in a machine-gun section, frankly told his parents of the dangers of this position and said he wanted to kill at least one German before he died. Harry Coe, second lieutenant at the age of twenty, was more sanguine about his future: 'What tales I will have to tell later on.'[25]

Despite all the previous well-founded rumours, the order to the 1st and 2nd brigades to move to Lemnos came rather unexpectedly on Thursday 1 April. No one in Birdwood's command could have doubted that they were 'to go to the Dardanelles and have a smack at the Turks'.[26] Some Australian and New Zealand soldiers reasoned that they now had their last chance to wreak vengeance on the prostitutes and brothel-owners of the Wassa district, who were thought to have been dishonest in their dealings with Australian clients and to have infected some troops with venereal disease. Next day, Good Friday, there occurred the 'wretched affair' of the notorious riot, sometimes termed 'the battle of the Wassa' (also Wasser or Wazzir). Only a small proportion of the Australians were involved, but their excesses naturally attracted much attention.

The generals commanding the first two British divisions which were to land on Gallipoli commented somewhat philosophically on this fracas. The tall, big-framed Major-General Aylmer Hunter-Weston ('Hunter-Bunter' to fellow generals), commanding the 29th Division, who struck one observer as the epitome of a British professional officer, described how Australians, 'mostly drunk', threw furniture into the street and set fire to it. He went on benignly: 'They are a fine body of men, but undisciplined in peace. I think they will be grand fighters. Grand physique, intelligent looking and, I should judge, with plenty of grit.' Major-

General Archibald Paris, who commanded the Royal Naval Division, a creation of Churchill's (which contained about twelve thousand men, compared with the 29th Division's eighteen to nineteen thousand), thought the Wassa episode did not 'really give one much confidence' about Australian troops. However, he added, 'I daresay they will fight well enough.'[27]

Among others who did not join in the riot, opinions differed. Stanley Natusch partly excused the troops involved, saying that 'English military police had not always acted with discretion'. A fellow New Zealander, the young artilleryman William Fairbairn, told his mother, 'A description would not be very edifying.' No doubt the judicious and practical approach of Corporal Alf Clennett, a Tasmanian farmer turned artilleryman, would have been typical of thousands of the Australians in Egypt: 'It is a great pity it happened, it will get us a bad name all over the world, but they have been bottled up here so long and were rather excited at the prospect of getting away, still that does not excuse them.'[28] Lieutenant Will Dawkins saw a lot of the riot, as he was in town making his last purchases, and he helped to clear the streets afterwards. He thought, 'No one would suffer if 7/8th of Cairo was burnt out. It's as low as it could possibly be—incredibly so. . . . The New Zealanders were prominent in the whole affair. . . . those who don't quite understand what our troops have put up with in Egypt are apt to paint [the riot] blacker than it really is.' Major Stanley S. Argyle, a future premier of Victoria, partially explained the riot by saying the troops were becoming very restless: 'It is high time that our boys were given some serious work to do.' Other Australians commented more scathingly, being 'absolutely disgusted' at these 'disgraceful scenes' and regretting the unenviable reputation their country would earn.[29]

Lancashire Territorials had to be used to quell the riot. One of them, Corporal T. Valentine, who had spent twenty-four years in the British army, recorded his feelings: 'Rioting in Cairo today with the Australians and New Zealanders and Maoris and the natives. . . . Australians gone mad going into houses and throwing furniture in the street and setting it on fire. Fire brigade turns out, hose pipe cut. They are a disgrace to the Army, nothing but an undisciplined mob. We had to turn picquets out with fixed bayonets to clear the streets. 3rd April. The row in Cairo is still going on. Lasted all through the night and we are all confined to Barracks through them. They are all mad drunk having their Easter holidays but we dare not do as they do, they do as they like. 4th April. The Colonials have quietened down again and they are ashamed of themselves now.'[30] Compensation of £4,000 was claimed for damage by the rioters. Army authorities cut the figure to £1,700, and the governments in Melbourne and Wellington were presented with the bill.[31]

With the riot over, the troops could concentrate on packing up the camp. Bean had told his readers that the men were bored with training and were looking forward to moving to the front. Alf Clennett expressed this view, telling his mother on 4 April: 'Nearly all are glad to leave as we've had enough of Mena and Cairo—except for a few who have got cold feet at the thought of being so near to the first engagement. I think we're going to the Dardanelles. I don't think we will have much trouble to beat the Turks.'[32]

The men's cheerfulness at leaving was no doubt nourished by the khamsin, which was blowing more ferociously than before. At the station one officer boasted that the railway officials were 'rather surprised' the entraining took only twenty minutes instead of the expected two hours. For several days the succession of troop trains travelled the 210 kilometres from Cairo to Alexandria. 'Being accommodated in the 3rd class nigger carriages,' wrote Charles Copp, 'things were naturally somewhat cramped and stuffy.' General Paris commented, 'the wild Colonial Corps has left Cairo.'[33]

Lady Elizabeth Rochdale, who moved in British governing circles in Cairo and was daughter and wife of British army officers, had noted in January that the Australians all seemed very rich and free-spending; she found it 'really quite a blessing to be rid of them, they are too undisciplined to be in a place like Cairo.' A month or so later nearly all the wounded soldiers she was tending were Australians. She then found them cheerful and very polite, longing for something to read, and she reflected: 'Certainly the Australians have done well—but at what cost of life and limb!'[34]

Alexandria harbour was packed with troopships. Captain Orlo C. Williams, one of Hamilton's staff officers, marvelled at the truly wonderful sight at the docks. 'Transports crowded side by side and troops and baggage embarking the whole time. To think that few know where they are going and where they will, so many of them, meet their fate.' Arrangements were not always perfect. Food was not always readily available for the men. The conditions on ships varied, from fine cabins for officers to cramped sleeping space (60 centimetres by 180 centimetres each) for men. Some ships were clean; another was 'dirty stinking and unsavoury . . . [a] blackhole of Calcutta', full of vermin and filth on the lower deck. Men who boarded first had to wait a few days in harbour until later units were embarked.[35]

The ships carrying the 1st and 2nd brigades sailed on calm seas. Nearing Lemnos, they passed many islands with snow-topped mountains. It was very pretty indeed, one man later remembered, 'just perfect scenery for oil paintings'. The 1st and 2nd brigades reached Mudros in the second week of April, at about the time the 4th Brigade began its move from Egypt. Corporal Valentine watched some of these men leaving Heliopolis. He noted that they were 'spoiling for a fight and they are singing their favourite song, Australia will be there, as they are marching to the station'. They travelled in third-class carriages, too crowded to allow men to sleep, save for a few who lay on the floor.[36]

In the morning of 14 April, troops of the 4th Brigade reached Mudros, to marvel at the 'magnificent sight' of great numbers of ships in the harbour and to join their fellow Australian soldiers of the 'rather undisciplined' 3rd Brigade, and the 1st and 2nd brigades, in helping to swell the large force of Empire and French troops preparing to land on the Gallipoli Peninsula.[37]

# CHAPTER 9

# PREPARING FOR A LANDING

$M$UDROS HARBOUR was now 'covered with ships', most of them double-banked—that is, tied together to save space. The vile weather continued, as howling winds, the cold, and pouring rain gave men a bad time. Private Willie Harris of the recently arrived 16th Battalion complained, 'We all long for a decent feed as we are getting tired of bully beef and biscuits. Several fellows have broken teeth over the biscuits.' He also noted that the two hundred rounds of ammunition issued to each man were very heavy to carry. Spending nights cooped up on crowded ships was 'pretty rough', but for some there were pleasant interludes. Murray Aitken was fascinated when thoroughly inspecting the *London*, an old but still 'wonderful' battleship which was to carry him to Gallipoli. Lieutenant-Colonel Sutton found that his French lessons had been valuable when he visited the French hospital ship *Canada* and was shown around by a service doctor who spoke very little English.[1]

The Australians' reputation as potentially good soldiers was spreading, both at the heart of Empire and amid less eminent Britons who observed them. Birdwood and his headquarters staff travelled from Alexandria to Lemnos on the *Minnewaska*, which was also carrying the 1st Battalion, raised in Sydney. He told Kitchener: 'Really the spirit is magnificent. Every single man means real business and I have no doubt whatever about their fighting qualities—they will all fight like tigers and go at anything. I am only a little afraid of them losing heavily by wanting to go too bald-headedly at hopeless obstacles. If only we can get to close quarters with either Germans or Turks I can confidently answer for results.'[2] Two weeks later General Hunter-Weston told Major Clive Wigram, private secretary to the King, 'The Australians and New Zealanders impress me as magnificent troops.' Major Duncan Glasfurd and Captain Guy Dawnay, two British army officers associated with the AIF, similarly praised the 'magnificent men' in Bridges' division.[3] The Reverend W. F. Scott, a Royal Navy chaplain, was impressed on meeting 'some Australians who also seem nice but appallingly casual. . . . however they will fight well which is the main show.' At Mudros, as A Company, 11th Battalion, boarded some of the *London*'s boats to practise for the landing, Charles Drage, an eighteen-year-old Royal Navy midshipman, remarked on the 'lines of long, lean Australians in their broad brimmed hats and Britishers . . . looking rather puny beside the Colonials'. Ellis Ashmead-Bartlett, that most experienced English war correspondent, first met Australian troops on a transport on 8 April. 'Their physique is remarkable,' he wrote. 'We seldom see such a high standard in our own army, except in Guards Battalions.'[4]

Meanwhile, Asquith's administration continued its extended, indecisive and at times benighted wrangling over the future conduct of the campaign. This involved much intricate diplomacy of which Australia was virtually ignorant. Although the precipitating cause of this great war had been an assassination in the Balkans,

Australians, with many large issues to worry about, tended not to give much thought to Serbia, even though the AIF was assigned to that general region. Australian compassion for a small nation unjustly invaded by a great power was bestowed on Belgium. It is completely unrealistic to expect Australia to have developed by 1915 any diplomatic expertise or even much informed interest in dealings with Balkan nations. For the time being Australia was content to let London decide these strategic issues.

In the early stages of the bombardment of the Gallipoli forts, Major-General Charles Callwell, Director of Military Operations at the War Office, believed that the Turks would 'drift off out of the Gallipoli Peninsula'. Its occupation would then 'be a fairly simple matter and well within the competence' of forty thousand men.[5] This tendency to underestimate the Turkish army was widespread in London's highest planning circles.

Men in high places tended to ignore the more accurate information available from junior British officers. In 1906, as a subaltern in the Grenadier Guards, H. Charles Woods, acting under orders from Britain's military attaché at Constantinople, had skilfully reconnoitred the defences of the Gallipoli Peninsula. On this topic he became one of Britain's leading experts. As well, he made himself reasonably proficient in Turkish. In his opinion, between February and April in 1915 the Turks made the peninsula almost impregnable. In February 1917 he was to claim that the decision-makers made no effort to use his expertise or to consult two generals who were familiar with his information.[6] Perhaps his views were resented partly because, although educated at Harrow and Sandhurst and having served in the South African war, he had left the army in 1907. He then became a military and diplomatic correspondent, specialising in the Balkans region. He travelled extensively and by 1917 had written five books on the relationship of the Balkans problem to the European war.

Captain W. Maxwell, who was in the War Office early in 1915 before becoming Chief Censor in Hamilton's force, had spent a great deal of time in Turkey and among the subject peoples of the Ottoman Empire. He had formed a fairly high opinion of the fighting capacity of the Turkish soldier and was amazed at the intelligence staff's ill-informed low opinion of Constantinople's ability to defend the peninsula.[7] In the AIF there was at least one officer with similar knowledge. Lieutenant-Colonel Charles Ryan, a surgeon born in Victoria in 1853, had spent two years in the Turkish army and had served at Plevna during the tenacious, though unsuccessful, defence against Russian forces in 1877. Ryan was known as 'Turkish Charlie' and was 'covered with' Turkish decorations. He spent some time on the Gallipoli Peninsula and in 1917 expressed a view typical of those who knew Turkish troops: 'I had a high opinion of their fighting qualities, especially in trenches.' In the light of his knowledge of the quality of the opposition, on the eve of the Gallipoli landings he told a friend that Hamilton's force was embarking on one of the most dangerous enterprises in military annals.[8]

It is not clear if Asquith's War Council was aware of a balanced analysis by the War Office in March 1915 which stated that, since the Balkan wars, Turkey's army had been reorganised and its officers effectively trained by the von Sanders mission. The British army's handbook, *Notes on the Turkish Army*, was a sensible, well-informed document which the British War Council should have taken into consideration before making a hasty decision to land at Gallipoli. However, the Turkish army, liberally estimated at 1,250,000 men, was not rated equally with European armies.[9] Churchill and others were no doubt greatly influenced by Turkey's humiliating disasters in the recent Balkan wars. Churchill might also have made too much of an incident at Alexandretta on 18–20 December 1914 when Ottoman troops had not shown themselves to be serious opponents. Furthermore, the War Council seemed to regard the failed Turkish attack on the Suez Canal in February as a sign of weakness. Although a failure, the attack displayed a commendable degree of competence considering the awesome natural difficulties that were overcome.[10] All available comments by Britons who knew the Turkish soldier before 1915 agree that while his army's organisational skills might put him at a disadvantage in a mobile war, he was a courageous soldier who could shoot straight, ideally suited to defensive, trench warfare. Churchill's idea of going straight for the heart played right to Turkey's strength.

Hamilton, in a letter to Kitchener on his arrival in the theatre, indicated the gap between London's perceptions and the reality of the Dardanelles: 'Here, at present, Gallipoli looks a much tougher nut to crack than it did over the map in my office. The increases to the garrison, the new lines of trenches nightly being excavated, the number of concealed field guns, the rapidity of the current, are all brought forward when assessing military operations.' In a remarkable example of wishful thinking, he added, 'The very numbers of the enemy may prove detrimental to him on so small a space of ground for deployment.'[11]

Although Asquith's government underestimated the Turks' fighting capacity, the army had good information on the number of troops defending the Gallipoli Peninsula. The War Office estimated late in 1914 that there were probably 200,000 Ottoman troops in the area from Constantinople to the Dardanelles, a distance of roughly 260 kilometres. Kitchener on 24 February gave the War Council an estimate of 40,000 on the peninsula. On 10 March he raised this to 60,000, with possibly another 120,000 defending the capital.[12] It was Kitchener's awareness that a landing would be a difficult undertaking, with severe fighting, that made him insist that the invasion be delayed until the 29th Division arrived, bringing troops available to about 67,000.[13] Unfortunately, the Turks could reinforce the peninsula more quickly than Britain could reinforce the Mediterranean Expeditionary Force (MEF). In any case, in March 1915 the greater part of the Ottoman army was stationed near Constantinople or on or close to the Gallipoli Peninsula.

British commanders on the spot became pessimistic as AIF and British intelligence reports indicated how strongly the Turks were reinforcing and fortifying the peninsula. By early March Birdwood had enough information to realise that the landing would be a tough job. By the 23rd the reports showed five Turkish divisions—or a hundred thousand troops of good quality—in the area, although the true figure probably was sixty-two thousand. Major Aubrey Herbert, a British parliamentarian attached to Godley's division, mainly as an interpreter for intelligence work, had many discussions with military and naval officers who wished the landing would take place at Alexandretta rather than on the Gallipoli Peninsula. These officers thought they would 'get a very bad knock' on the peninsula.[14]

Turkey formed the 5th Army to defend the peninsula and on 24 March put General Liman von Sanders in command. The War Office knew this within a week. Hunter-Weston on 25 March thought that the landing did not have a reasonable chance of success. He added, 'To attempt a landing and then fail to secure a passage through the Dardanelles would be a disaster to the Empire.'[15] British reconnaissance constantly detected new trenches and wire entanglements sited to command possible landing beaches.

On 12 April, in one of those actions which kept the Turks fully aware of Britain's intentions, the *Queen Elizabeth* steamed up and down the peninsula's west coast, about three kilometres offshore, to enable Hamilton, several of his staff, and other officers, including 'a lot of Australians', to get a good idea of the coast, the landing beaches and the hinterland. Bridges could clearly see the trenches north of Gaba Tepe, where his division was scheduled to land.[16]

In early April Birdwood told Kitchener that the Turks had so strengthened the peninsula's defences that what had once seemed feasible now seemed doubtful. Privately, Major-General Callwell wrote that he was 'very anxious' about the Dardanelles: 'A landing in face of opposition is under modern conditions the most difficult and dangerous operation in war.' H. A. Gwynne, editor of the London *Morning Post*, to whom Calwell wrote, was one of those favouring abandonment of the scheme and put his views to Asquith. Another was Lord Charles Beresford, a former fierce critic of Fisher's policy of building dreadnoughts to the detriment of smaller warships, who thought that Hamilton should never have been given such an important command. Many of the generals thought that on military grounds the expedition should have been abandoned, but by this stage it had a momentum of its own. Anglo-French prestige was involved, and Asquith's government was committed to the venture.[17]

So Hamilton and his staff were not in the most optimistic frame of mind as they planned for amphibious operations on a scale greater than any previous similar undertaking. The peninsula had few beaches suitable for landings, and they were small. Lieutenant-Commander G. K. Rylands must have represented much naval opinion; he related that when he and his fellow officers received their operational orders they were amazed to find that the army had decided to land at nearly all the places he had reported as being either difficult or impossible. He was convinced that if the landing succeeded it would be at the expense of heavy casualties.[18]

As the immediate objective of the expedition was to silence or capture the guns overlooking the strait, Hamilton had to restrict his main landings to the south-western tip of the peninsula. The Royal Naval Division would carry out a feint at Bulair, and the French division another at Kum Kale, on the Asiatic shore at the mouth of the Dardanelles. The 29th Division was to land at five beaches at the toe of the peninsula and then move eight kilometres to gain the ridge of Achi Baba on the first day.

Birdwood's corps was to land north of Gaba Tepe. From there a plain stretched to the Narrows, eight kilometres distant. To the south the plain was overlooked by the Kilid Bahr plateau, which commanded the forts at the Narrows. To the north it was bordered by the rugged Sari Bair range. As it seemed a likely landing place, the Turks had strong defences on the stretch of beach north of Gaba Tepe. The plan was for Birdwood's troops to advance seven kilometres across the peninsula to a line running from Boghali to Mal Tepe, a south-western spur of the Sari Bair range, so cutting the road running down the peninsula to its tip.

Birdwood had told Kitchener in February that although the Australians remained as 'keen as mustard' for a fight, they were untried in warfare and their officers had much to learn. He warned, 'My Australians will be children at first at anything like this mountain warfare.' So he wanted to have the 29th Indian Brigade, then in Egypt, allotted to his command in exchange for two light horse brigades. As he told Kitchener, 'A good Indian Battalion on either flank would be most useful . . . if only to show [the Australians] how the game is played at the start.' He was now quite pessimistic, expecting 'a lot of hard fighting for a *long* time to come'.[19]

On 11 April Captain H. G. Carter, on the *Minnewaska*, learned of the plan for the march on Constantinople. It would be hard but interesting, he commented. Captain John Corbin, a medical officer on the staff of No. 1 Australian Stationary Hospital, was less sanguine on 17 April when he learnt that the 3rd Brigade was to be the covering force, the first ashore north of Gaba Tepe. 'We may be shelled all the way from the boats to the beach. If the troops make good their position, we shall land the rest of our men and staff, and establish a proper clearing Hospital. The whole job looks like being extremely dangerous and quite unlike any of our expectations.' Aubrey Herbert thought this landing could 'set the war back a year, besides producing an indefinite amount of trouble in the East'. Officers' awareness of the prospects did not always extend to the troops. Corbin and Herbert lacked the serene confidence of Private Willie Harris, who, sharing the understanding of unknown numbers of his fellow soldiers, on 20 April wrote, 'We land at the Gallipoli Peninsula, march 140 miles over the desert and attack Constantinople.' Kitchener's warning was sombre in a message telling the men that they were to attack an almost impregnable position. 'I pray God', wrote Ellis Silas, 'that I shall not be wanting when we are under fire.'[20]

Thomas Blamey told his mother, 'Soon young Australia will have tasted battle. . . . we are about to undertake . . . a historic [operation] for its great and experimental interest.' He gave quite a low rating to the Turks' fighting ability, and thought they were 'sure to be kicked out of Europe. But it was never dreamed', he continued, 'that an Australian force would do most of the kicking. The oddest thing is that the Turk likes the English and on the whole we rather like him.' Monash, who as early as 25 March expected to be soon occupying Constantinople, wrote of the coming 'great events, which will stir the whole world, and will go down in history . . . to the eternal glory of Australia, and all who have participated'. Richard Casey agreed that the Australians were on the eve of 'the greatest landing of History'.[21]

The Australian submarine AE2 in Mudros harbour. On 25 April the AE2, in a daring operation to support the landings, dived through and under minefields to enter the Sea of Marmara, where it attacked enemy shipping. On 30 April the submarine went out of control and sank. Its crew became prisoners of war. Australia thereby had lost both its new submarines, the AE1 having disappeared without trace in September 1914 during operations for the capture of German New Guinea.

The landings were scheduled for St George's Day, 23 April, but bad weather forced two postponements. The delay possibly meant that more men had time to realise the difficulty of the task facing them. George Mitchell did not think the covering force had much chance of survival. It was 'going to strike a hot corner imported straight from hell'. Major Fred Biddle expected to land under fire, adding, 'We shall have had some experiences to talk about before we finish.' 'We are going to have a real hard and rough time of it,' wrote Private Copp. Still, he expected success. He noted Birdwood's message in his diary: 'We are about to undertake one of the most difficult tasks any soldier can be called on to perform.'[22]

Senior officers had to maintain that the first day's objectives were reasonable. General Hunter-Weston announced on the night of 24 April that he would be on the top of Achi Baba next day. Captain R. W. Chambers of the 2nd Australian Field Ambulance was told that the landing force would probably be right across the peninsula by the end of the first day, or at least by the next day. Using the code name for the corps, Birdwood told Kitchener brightly about his plans for taking various ridges at 'Anzac'.[23]

To outward appearances the soldiers on 24 April behaved during leisure time as on any previous day, some playing gambling games, or reading, or yarning about the war. But it was no ordinary day, for Lemnos was 'enjoying real Australian sunshine'. The ships could sail that night. 'It is strange and interesting to be in the midst of it and to notice the bearing of the officers and men,' wrote John Corbin. 'The latter do not for a minute grasp fully the desperate work ahead of them. They are for the most part as unconcerned as if on a pleasure trip, going about their duties as if they were still in Australia, playing cards, joking and generally appearing absolutely unconcerned.' He could not 'help thinking of those in Australia most acutely'. Monash was astonished at how light-hearted everybody was, 'whistling, singing and cracking jokes, and indulging in all sorts of horse-play and fun'.[24]

People back home knew that great events were imminent. If the Australian

*Men of the 9th Battalion aboard the destroyer HMS* Beagle *en route to the Dardanelles.*

troops in Egypt take part in the Dardanelles expedition under Hamilton, wrote the *Sydney Morning Herald* on 24 April, they will exchange the dull routine of camp life for 'exciting and perilous adventures'. Harry Coe looked forward to battles in 'good fighting country' and stressed the historic significance of the coming landing in Turkey: 'We get our chance of proving ourselves.' Private C. J. Lawless, a member of an ambulance unit, noted Kitchener's warning in his diary. 'I don't know my own feelings,' he wrote on the 24th. 'I don't think I am afraid at any rate. It is just a mixture of excitement and wondering what it will all be like.' Charles Bean on 24 April expected to 'be in a devil of a funk tomorrow'. He hoped, like others with similar feelings, that he would not show it.[25]

As troops for the landing left Mudros that day, a British diarist noted that the Australians could easily be distinguished from other Empire troops 'by their Wallaby Call'. Ashmead-Bartlett, the British war correspondent, noted how busy the 11th Battalion was kept, practising disembarkation and landing from the battleship *London*. They were now using wooden ladders, instead of the original rope ladders which were found to sag. This amphibious operation was in many ways a marvellous feat of organisation. But in war a few mistakes can lead to disaster, and so it was to prove with the landings of 25 April.[26]

On the eve of leaving Lemnos, Bean noted that 'some people' were 'a little thoughtful'. By nightfall the ships carrying the 3rd Brigade were steaming through the Aegean Sea, near Imbros. As dawn approached, Ellis Silas thought, 'I do not feel the least fear, only a sincere hope that I may not fail at the critical moment.' They slipped east through the calm, moonlit water while, as George Mitchell wrote, 'many eyes gleaming with lust of adventure were turned to that scowling line of hills, rising out of the mirror . . . sphinxlike, holding the mysteries of life and death.'[27]

# CHAPTER 10

# 'THE REAL MEANING OF WAR'

Opposite. Above: *Looking north along the very narrow Anzac Cove.* Below: *Looking down on the cove at its southern end near Hell Spit, which provided some protection from Gaba Tepe for troops landing on 25 April 1915. These photographs were taken by the author in June 1986.*

*T*HE ROYAL NAVY brought more than thirty thousand soldiers of the Empire to the Gallipoli Peninsula on 25 April. Many of them died before they landed. At Helles the 29th Division lost heavily and gained only one-third of its first day's objective. Hamilton's feints helped to confuse the enemy command for a time; then most of these troops were moved to the Helles front. But the Turks were able to confine the invaders to a small piece of land at the peninsula's tip. This was despite the excellent reputation of the 29th Division, formed in Britain after the war began out of experienced troops drawn from battalions serving in India.

North of Gaba Tepe the covering force, the 3rd Australian Infantry Brigade, containing men of the four so-called outer states, began landing at 4.30 a.m. A great deal went wrong that day. As the Turkish coast loomed up, every eye was on 'that grim looking line of hills . . . so shapeless yet so menacing in the semi darkness'. Then the captain of the destroyer *Foxhound*, in 'a very disturbed voice', told Major Frank Beevor of the 10th Battalion, 'We are going to land you at the wrong place.' Second Lieutenant Henderson Smith (11th Battalion) was one of those who came under heavy rifle and machine-gun fire while rowing the last few yards to the shore. 'Our feelings under the circumstances may be better imagined than described,' he told his father.[1]

Because the landing was made in the wrong place, about two kilometres north of the intended spot, the men faced a narrow beach and steep cliffs and a hinterland of tangled hills and gullies instead of the open plain or gentle slopes they had expected. The navy's tows, each of from three to six troop-laden picket-boats, became mixed up, so that units were not landed in their proper order. Much staff work—specifying precisely where supplies were to be stacked—was completely wasted by the navy's mistake. Not surprisingly, Colonel E. G. Sinclair-MacLagan, commanding the 3rd Brigade, 'was very disturbed' at this.[2] Five days later, Lieutenant R. G. Casey surveyed the Turks' defensive wire entanglements and trenches at the intended landing place and thought it providential that the navy had made a mistake.[3] Many, from Birdwood (who accepted the blame for the mistake, because he had insisted on landing before daylight) to private soldiers, later agreed that the Australians would have suffered far heavier casualties had they landed where planned.

Nonetheless, the botched-up landing placed a tremendous and unexpected burden on the troops. As their boats grounded, some men were cursing and others were singing 'This bit of the world belongs to us.'[4] Private R. A. Nicholas described how 'our boys had to jump over the side of boats into the water, in some places up to the armpits . . . men killed in the boats and in the water. . . . Hell was loosed in all its furies. . . . stopping to think meant certain Death. . . . looking down at the bottom of the sea, you could see a carpet of dead men who were shot getting

out of the boats.' A wave of cold fear swept over George Mitchell when he 'realised the meaning of those terrible cries which arose at short intervals all round'. Corporal J. R. Keast described men of his battalion (the 11th) 'shouting and hurraying and calling the Turks all the rude names they could think of'. Captain Dixon Hearder relates that the men near him in the 3rd Brigade did not waste their breath cheering but forced the Turks to flee with a wild bayonet charge. Private W. M. Clark (10th Battalion) noted, 'I cannot explain the feeling a man gets under fire the first time but I felt damned queer.'[5]

Murray Aitken 'quite forgot to be frightened'. Instead he 'got quite annoyed' as, in 'great disorder and high excitement', the men made the mad rush from the beach up the cliff and up the first hill beyond, later known as Plugge's Plateau. 'Everybody was taking leave of their senses,' wrote Sergeant H. A. Cheney of the 10th Battalion. 'Although I knew well enough what fear is, it left me completely in that charge. Straight up that rugged, rocky precipice we went.' He thought it was simply bluff that carried them through. Another man said that later on, when they had spare time to retrace their steps, the men themselves were astonished to see

*Australians landing from crowded rowing boats at Gallipoli on 25 April 1915. Their full packs contained rations for three days, and they carried two hundred to three hundred rounds of ammunition. Steamboat 'tows' stand off shore.*

the route they had taken.[6] This amazement was shared by Australasian soldiers in later waves of landing troops, one of whom in mid-November wrote, 'The more I see of this inhospitable place, the more I marvel that any [of the 1st Division] survived. The original men must have been a combination of mule, goat and lion, to have succeeded as they did.' Thus, in the first hour of the landing these men from the 'outer states' had set standards which Victorians and New South Welshmen later emulated. A 2nd Battalion man, after landing, fixing his bayonet, letting out a yell and rushing inland, did not remember what happened. 'And I don't think I wish to,' he went on. 'I must have gone mad [until] I came to my senses with face and hands bleeding from scrambling in the bushes.'[7]

George Mitchell's introduction to shrapnel caused a shock to his system. There 'was a weird shrieking note somewhere in the air, which increased in volume every fraction of a second. It culminated in a deafening report and a cloud of smoke some thirty yards on my right, and thirty feet high. Simultaneously there was the swishing sound as the bullets beat down bushes and swept the earth and a devilish scream. The scream was caused by large pieces of the case [of the shell], as they spun through the air.'[8]

Because of the faulty landing and the rugged hinterland, it was impossible for units to retain cohesion. Instead, groups of men dashed or struggled inland as best they could. Many men's versions agreed with Murray Aitken's assessment: 'With the exception of a few isolated examples, we were not led by our officers; the men acted on their own initiative, and by taking the whole affair into their own hands, so saved a very critical situation.'[9]

Although the individual front-line soldier had only a confused impression of that day's battle, he was aware that it was not going well. To be successful, a landing force generally needs substantial numerical superiority over its opponents in the locality, and while the first Australians to land were opposed by a single battalion, this fortunate state of affairs lasted only a few hours. Turkish reinforcements were hurried to the landing spot, and the Australians soon faced a division and a regiment—from ten thousand to twelve thousand men compared with the sixteen thousand Australasians landed by midnight. The Turkish division was the 19th, led by a brilliant, very energetic commander, Mustafa Kemal, a politically active professional army officer whose fame in defending the peninsula would eventually lead to his becoming, as Atatürk, the founder of the republic of Turkey and its first president in 1920. Kemal's division was close to the landing beach and ready for almost immediate combat. There were some delays in landing reinforcements for Birdwood's troops. The 1st Division landed in the morning, but the 4th Brigade did not arrive until nightfall.

Early in the morning some men of the 3rd Brigade penetrated about one-third of the distance to the impossibly optimistic first day's objective, the line from Mal Tepe to Boghali, more than six kilometres inland. They forced their way through the thick shrubs and undergrowth which covered the tangled ridges and spurs and densely filled the gullies. After heavy fighting, in which Turkish artillery was very effective, the Australians lost control of two important hills which dominated the gullies and ridges falling away westward to the sea: Baby 700, at the north-eastern corner of their perimeter, and the 400 Plateau, at the south-eastern corner. The fierce Turkish resistance and the heavy casualties put the landing force in a perilous position, and during the night the commanders discussed evacuation. Precisely what effect that would have had on Australian opinion is hard to imagine. Hamilton gave his order to dig in[10]—something the men could do once darkness protected them from Turkish bullets and shells—and the firing line at nightfall would develop into the beachhead's front line for months.

It was a day of military failure which almost became a disaster. As one observer put it, 'The landing arrangements seem to me to have been very badly thought out and to make no allowance for any enemy being there to oppose.' A participant who had won a Victoria Cross in South Africa thought that if the Turks 'had not funked when he and his men charged with the bayonet' the Australians could never have held that beach. 'Had British or Germans manned the trenches,' he thought, 'everyone would have been killed.'[11]

So that night the Australians dug in along a roughly semicircular perimeter. At their farthest point inland the Australians held the first ridge, about one-sixth of the distance towards their first day's objective. Nearly every Australian who got past the first ridge on that day was killed. Among the numerous Australians who described their role in helping to hold on to that vulnerable beachhead on 25 April was a soldier of the 3rd Brigade whose account was written shortly after the event:

*I can assure you that we put in a trying time, sitting jammed together like sardines in the boats, while the Turks blazed away merrily at us from the top of a big hill just skirting the shore. . . . My battalion being the first to reach land, we quickly filed out along the beach, fixed bayonets, and dashed up the hill at the Turks strongly entrenched on the top; the lads cheered every inch of the way, which I really believe helped to dishearten the Turks, for when we got near the top, they jumped out of their trenches and ran like old Harry to their second line of trenches, a distance of half a mile or more. . . . after taking a breather on the top and collecting what was left of the Battalion we made for their second line of defence. . . . we were not wrong in our surmise that the Turks would counter-attack, for between eleven and twelve o'clock, being strongly reinforced, they commenced a desperate counter attack, supported by artillery and machine guns, and having our range to a nicety, they gave us the hottest time of our lives, but we had to do as the Indians do, grin and bear it till our supports came up.*[12]

Private J. H. Reid described his activities that day in a letter to fellow teachers of Mosman Superior Public School.

*We . . . took up a position on the right flank of the firing line which we reached about 10 a.m. We had to lie in the open facing an open stretch covered with low scrub and bushes which rather favoured the Turks. Our cover consisted of plants scarcely a foot high and we were exposed to a terrific fire all day. I shall never forget it. Shrapnel shells screeched over our heads and bursting with a loud report scattered their contents with dull thuds all round us. It seemed that every*

*Men of the 7th Bat-
talion machine-gun
section—Privates
A. J. Walker and K.
Muirson and Lance-
Corporal H. A.
Barker—take a break
in a dugout behind
Courtney's Post late on
26 April 1915.*

*square foot of country was hit. The machine guns would rattle out a hail of lead that swept our
position and the bullets seemed to fairly whistle around our ears. . . . For a time we could get no
glimpse of the Turks. . . . In the afternoon the navy began a heavy bombardment and added
thunder-like peals to the noise of the battle. . . . Later in the afternoon an Indian mountain
battery came into action and the fighting began to be more even. . . . difficulty [was] being
experienced in getting the wounded away. Men were being hit around me all the afternoon, the
uncertainty of when my own turn would come was almost unbearable. It seemed as if the sun
would never set.*[13]

A bullet passed through Reid's boot and a 'poor fellow' beside him was fatally
wounded. Reid himself was badly wounded in the head a day or two later and was
evacuated to Alexandria, where he wrote his letter.

Captain H. G. Carter 'was thoroughly scared at first but managed to rally the
men when they twice started to retire in disorder'. Private Ray Baker, however,
wrote, 'Many of our officers were shot down and most of the time we got no orders
at all but had to rely on ourselves to do the best we could. Whenever we did
happen to see an officer the order was always the same: "Get ahead lads and stick
it into them." Many a poor fellow died urging his mates onward with his last
breath.' 'The hail of bullets was simply awful,' thought Baker, 'and shrapnel shells
were bursting around us all the time.' George Mitchell, 'after climbing what was
virtually a precipice, . . . came upon the real meaning of war. A sturdy Australian
lay on his face, congealing blood from a ghastly wound in the head streaking his
face and forming a crimson pool.' Mitchell 'did not regard death in a spiritual
light, but rather as a painful shutting out of all life's promise'.[14]

Corporal C. Alwynne (2nd Battalion) noticed that 'as a Turk gets hit he lets out
a mournful howl of Allah Allah Allah and judging by the noises they make you
would think that the whole population of Turkey was wounded'. Alwynne wrote of
'bullets spattering all around us like rain', some 'hitting that close that the dirt flies
all over you. The sensation is very queer, all sorts of thoughts running through

your head.' The noise of battle was so loud that a man's voice could not carry twenty metres. Private Donkin, a 24-year-old labourer from Maitland, New South Wales, thought the first shell headed in his direction 'sounded like the Moree Mail coming'. He was completely unnerved by that day's fighting and could not do what he knew he should do—return to the firing line. But within a day he was lying out in the front line, among dead and wounded, until he himself was hit. Ray Baker thought that the noise of machine-gun bullets coming thick and fast 'was for all the world like the buzz of an electric fan'.[15]

Mitchell made a short advance under fire. 'A scramble, a rapid pounding of heavy boots and clattering of equipment, a startled yell and a crumpling body which has to be leaped over, a succession of slithering thuds, and we are down in the bushes forty yards ahead. . . . In this little advance Alec Gilpin has been fatally wounded in the stomach. All day he begged to be shot.' Mitchell expected to be hit any second, as men next to him were killed. A soldier who rushed up to join him did not last long. 'He fired a few shots and again I heard the sickening thud of a bullet. I looked at him in horror. The bullet had fearfully smashed his face and gone down his throat rendering him dumb. But his eyes were dreadful to behold. And how he squirmed in his agony. There was nothing I could do for him but to pray that he might die swiftly. It took him about twenty minutes to accomplish this, and by that time he had tangled his legs in mine, and stiffened. I saw the waxy colour creep over his cheek and breathed freer.'[16]

At about 5.30 p.m. Sergeant Hagan and his mates, holding an exposed position in the front line, beat off the most ferocious massed attack they had faced all day. Then they 'worked strenuously all night' digging pits and trenches. 'Thus ended one of the worst days I have ever witnessed,' wrote Hagan.[17]

Private Ernest Skinner of the 4th Brigade knew he would never forget his first night at Anzac. 'The first sensation is the worst. After that you don't notice so much.' Private I. A. McCowan noticed that Turks had 'a singular dislike for the cold steel'. He commented on the 'hot time' with shrapnel, and on the 27th noted, 'What a hell of a mess. . . . I can hardly stand the stench of dead bodies on our front. Burial party goes out. Turks give them a warm time.' Private V. E. Smythe from Narrandera did not like his baptism of fire. Years after 25 April 1915 he recalled, 'That night I was devastatingly frightened that enemy troops would come flooding down on top of me and my section—I fervently wished that I had not left home.' He was soon commissioned as a second lieutenant in charge of a signal section. Captain C. R. Duke later recalled, 'Many of the best officers and men were killed and wounded in the early days on Anzac through being too game—they just scorned to take the necessary cover.'[18]

Birdwood's staff expected a counter-attack on the second day. In fact, Kemal wanted to drive all the Australians into the sea before they had time to consolidate their hold on their tiny beachhead. But the Turks had been so badly mauled on the 25th that they could not mount an all-out assault; nevertheless, they were able to make life very difficult for the Australians. Because there were gaps in the Australian front line, 'snipers were very troublesome and did for a large number of men'. Turkish snipers in Australian uniform operating within the beachhead got no mercy when caught, just the bayonet. A private who thought Turks 'the cruellest race', liable to bayonet wounded Australians, refused to spare the life of a prisoner he captured. Later, an officer intervened to prevent another prisoner from sharing the same fate.[19]

After three days of fighting, George Mitchell wrote of the 'same old programme, bullets, bullets, bullets. Dead and dying everywhere.' Private Richards of the ambulance unit met a party from the 3rd Brigade and was shaken at how worn-out they looked—'a glassy stare in their eyes and a quite ghastly colour'. Willie Harris thought the heavy firing was 'like a thousand whips cracking at once'. 'All along the route', wrote Ellis Silas, running messages in the beachhead, 'I keep coming across bodies of the poor chaps who have been less fortunate than I.' But sometimes groups of Australians were saved from a tight position. Charles Copp described one such incident: 'It seemed to us the end and we kissed ourselves good night but coo-eed for reinforcements. That "Coo-ee" and the call for "Australians" was magnificent, men began to rush across the valley to our aid, a lot got across and we were soon 110 strong.' That was enough to deter the Turks from making their threatened attack in that locality.[20]

At first the Australians lacked artillery support, a serious deficiency. When that was rectified, men in the front line felt more secure. Naval guns, also, sometimes saved groups of Australians from annihilation. John Corbin found that the 'shock of the big 15-inch guns of the "Queen Elizabeth" firing from there miles out [was] like a physical blow on one's body.' He thought the attendant noise and concussion almost unbearable. But in the front line this noise was 'sweet music'. Murray Aitken described another of the navy's valuable roles. 'All through the night the ships play searchlights, like great unblinking eyes, on the danger spots [reminding] me of nothing so much as long, uncanny, ghost fingers, fine tooth-combing the country for danger.' The ships also created havoc in towns such as Maidos, scarcely leaving a building unscathed.[21]

Four days of almost constant fighting in the firing line left the survivors desperately exhausted and in urgent need of relief. This was arranged. A Victorian describes how he benefited on Wednesday the 28th, the third day after the landing. 'The 5th collected and scuttled down the valley, non stop, fell all over the place, slid down on our trousers; and dog tired reached the back of a hill where we were to have a few days spell and sleep.' He dug in and settled down and managed to sleep a few hours, his first sleep since Saturday night.[22]

During these first days, when the beachhead was being secured, news of the fighting did not reach Australia. People at home had to wait some days to learn with what panache their men in uniform had brought Australian history into its new era. Although the 1st Division's landing was marked by chaos and by some instances of cowardice and irresolution, and even though the objective was not gained, the day was redeemed in Australian eyes because of the reputation its troops created for bravery in adversity. As Private Richards put it, the day separated the wasters from the brave men.[23]

*General Bridges' first headquarters at Anzac during lunch on 3 May.* Left to right: *General Bridges (in dugout), Lieutenant L. G. Riches, Private A. H. Wicks (batman to General Bridges), Captain Foster, ADC, Major John Gellibrand, Colonel Neville Howse, Major T. A. Blamey, Lieutenant-Colonel C. B. White, and Major Wagstaffe. Like every other position at Anzac, theirs was exposed to shrapnel fire; Major Gellibrand was wounded there.*

It would be difficult to exaggerate the dangers and difficulties of the landing at what came to be called Anzac Cove. As an illustration, take the landing in 1982 of a brigade of top-class professional soldiers at Port San Carlos on East Falkland Island. They landed unopposed in daylight, with good maps, at exactly the intended spot. The navy landed the units in the planned order; behind the beach was a gentle slope and then flat boggy country. But the landing turned into a shambles, with units mixed up. The brigade had to sort itself out before it could move inland. On 25 April 1915 the landing force, in wooden boats, for a time were sitting ducks for the guns and rifles of an invisible enemy. Today such an operation would be regarded as suicidal. At the Suvla Bay landing in August, troops were taken ashore much more quickly and safely in steel-plated self-powered 'beetles', or barges, forerunners of modern landing-craft, with a long ramp forward which enabled soldiers to land dryshod, and which also made it easier to land guns.[24] Small wonder that Ellis Silas, under heavy fire even though the 16th Battalion landed very late on 25 April, hated 'the feeling of utter helplessness' while packed tightly in the boats.[25] Like thousands of his compatriots, he was that day subject to an ordeal that has never been imposed on any other substantial body of Australian troops.

To land in the wrong place, to face unexpected cliffs, to have units landed in jumbled confusion, to have carefully laid plans for distributing supplies ruined— all this constituted a series of calamities which might have led to a complete disaster even for an experienced professional force. Indeed, it is sometimes suggested that the Australians partially retrieved the situation precisely because they were not regular soldiers but 'civilians in uniform', or 'camouflaged civilians', as they sometimes described themselves.[26] Notwithstanding that view, the Australians' achievement was in fact the more meritorious because few of them had been under fire before the landing, and it is often thought advisable for units to begin their battle experience with comparatively easy tasks.

Royal Navy officers who watched men of the 3rd Brigade charge up the hills were unstinting in their praise. 'It was awe inspiring', wrote Harry T. Bennett, a

*The southern end of a narrow beach just north of Ari Burnu, on the day after the landing; a working party on the skyline is probably under shrapnel fire, near the knoll from which during the landing troops came under enfilading fire. The photograph was taken by the official war correspondent, C. E. W. Bean. As there was no official AIF photographer until November 1916, the photographic record of the AIF at Anzac is largely dependent on those provided by Bean and by ordinary soldiers who were able to have cameras because the order against private photographers was not enforced at Gallipoli.*

navigating lieutenant on the battleship *Canopus*, 'to watch the brave attacks made by the Australians to take what was obviously a very difficult, in fact almost impregnable position. We could see what a fight they had had for it by the dead and wounded ashore on the beach.' Lieutenant-Commander R. W. Wilkinson, commanding the destroyer *Ribble*, which brought in 430 men of the 12th Battalion (Tasmanians, Western Australians and South Australians), in his praise for his passengers depicted their inexperienced enthusiasm. The 12th was the last of the 3rd Brigade battalions to land. The men 'pulled in singing a song "Australia will be there"'. Many lost their rifles in their eagerness to jump out of the boats and I could see them scaling the cliffs waving their bayonets and hear them "cooeeing" like mad. Unfortunately in threes and fours they pursued Turks well inland, only to be cut off.' Midshipman Drage wrote of the Australians, 'of whose doings in Cairo we had heard the most disquieting rumours', carrying 'the beach and the ridge behind it in one magnificent rush'. They 'ever displayed a perfect obedience coupled with an intelligent readiness to help, which though equalled by our own troops could be surpassed by none'.[27]

Royal Navy praise was echoed by other officers. Captain K. M. Gresson, 1st Canterbury Regiment, admired the Australians' 'impetuous rushes' and their 'wild course inland'. The intelligent, sensitive young British captain, Guy Dawnay, on Hamilton's staff, and a friend of the Royal family and the Asquiths, told his wife that 'regardless of losses' the Australians 'stormed their way up the first hills'. He went to their positions on the 28th, 'and it seemed almost incredible that any troops could have done it. . . . How they got up fully armed and equipped over the rough, scrub-clad hillsides one can hardly imagine.' Back on the beach, on the 26th, Harry Bennett thought it 'strange to see the absolute coolness with which the Australian troops took the whole thing. During the afternoon some of them were even bathing for amusement while all this rattle and roar was going on. Their engineer section constructed a road very quickly and it was marvellous to watch them working under what I should have thought were very difficult circumstances indeed.' Next day, he wrote, in 'a fine piece of work' Australian artillerymen of the 3rd Artillery Brigade brought up their guns 'by the most impossible track one could possibly imagine'. Over the next three days he noted: 'The way the Australians held the position was simply too wonderful for words. . . . The Australians are most certainly extraordinarily brave, and have achieved a marvellous feat in landing where they did and firmly establishing themselves.' Captain C. K. Brampton, RN, agreed: 'These Australians have courage and are full of fight.' Stanley Natusch's comment indicates the typical New Zealander's assessment: 'All honour and glory to the Australians, especially the men of the 3rd Brigade, who bore the brunt of the attack.'[28]

This reputation was quickly endorsed by the highest-ranking officers at the landing. Birdwood and Bridges were proud of what their men had done. Hamilton told Kitchener of Australians who 'did wonders'. Godley told his wife that the 'untrained (or rather irregular) troops . . . landed with the most wonderful dash and carried everything before them, though many were killed and wounded. They then scaled the most impossible heights . . . and got all hopelessly intermingled and lost, and those who went too far . . . were, of course, either killed or taken prisoner.' In fact, very few Australians were taken prisoner during the first days. For 'four days', Godley told his wife, 'some of the men have had no sleep, little food and practically no water, and how they have stuck it I don't know.'[29]

Admiral C. F. Thursby, in command of the naval force supporting the landing at Gaba Tepe, could not speak too highly of the extraordinary gallantry and dash shown by the soldiers in the covering force. Praise came too from Commodore Roger Keyes, Chief of Staff of the Eastern Mediterranean Squadron. The Allied

fleet commander, Vice-Admiral de Robeck, both in his official report and privately, spoke 'absolutely glowingly of the splendid behaviour' of the forces landing at all the beaches. He could not understand, on 28 April, why the widespread praise for them was not publicised in Britain and Australia.[30]

In the House of Commons on 5 May, Colonial Secretary Lewis Harcourt was asked if the Australians and New Zealanders had been congratulated on their bravery. In fact, on 28 April the War Office had said there was no further military objection to the two antipodean governments publicising the landings. Harcourt immediately sent a congratulatory cable which said in part: 'You have proved that Australians are worthy of the race immortalised at Mons. . . . We are following the doings of your force with keen interest and looking forward eagerly to the time when you will enter Constantinople.' Next day, news that Australians had landed at the Dardanelles was posted in front of newspaper offices. Congratulatory messages from the King, and Churchill, on the Australians' 'brilliant achievement' soon arrived. So did the suggestion that the landing had been mishandled, made in parliament by Lord Charles Beresford, probably Britain's best-known retired admiral and a genial polemicist.[31]

On 8 and 9 May appeared the first lengthy accounts of Australian heroism during the AIF's 'glorious entry into the war', when much prominence was given to the reports by the war correspondent Ellis Ashmead-Bartlett. Near these 'thrilling narratives' of the 'amazing dash' of 'our men on Gallipoli' were long lists of names of wounded soldiers. Charles Bean's report, under more modest headlines, telling of the Australians winning 'imperishable fame', appeared a week later.[32] To his annoyance, it had been delayed by the censors.

Mingled pride and sorrow swept the nation, exemplified in the letter Senator Pearce wrote to General Bridges (on the day after Bridges had been mortally wounded, congratulating him on 'the brilliant work' of his division 'in effecting a landing'. 'Well General the work of yourself, staff, officers and rank and file has simply sent Australia wild with joy; tempered of course by the sadness caused by the thought of so many gallant fellows who have fallen. You have indeed *made good*.'[33]

They 'made good' only by a very narrow margin. In the more secure days of June, Monash wrote of the terrible ordeal, excessive dangers, great anxiety and gradual consolidation of the beachhead during the first five days. A Turkish breakthrough, with dire consequences, was prevented only by 'the magnificent quality of our troops' who 'dug like demons'. He was surprised by the quality of the young AIF officers and rated the troops as better than British regulars, a theme to which he returned later. 'For physique, dash, enterprise and sublime courage,' he claimed, 'the Australians are head and shoulders above all others', a fact, Monash said, that was readily admitted by British officers.[34]

In Australia the pride, and censorship, for weeks obscured the fact that the landing had failed. All the bravery was lavished on a landing that was strategically a defeat. At the Dardanelles, failure was evident by the night of the 25th and soon openly commented on. L. S. Amery, an officer chosen by General Callwell to visit the Balkans to study the best route for Hamilton's army to take into Hungary once the Dardanelles had been forced, wrote on the 27th from Lemnos to Lord Milner, Conservative politician and former Imperial pro-consul, 'The whole of the business out here will have been a gigantic mistake unless it is done properly.'[35] Among the desiderata were six more divisions, immediately, for Hamilton. Within the first few days commanders lamented the plight of the force and fumed at the contributory mistakes. Godley did not know what was going to be done. Birdwood expected nothing better than very slow progress. Hamilton told Kitchener: 'The campaign so far has borne no resemblance to any other in the world that I have ever heard of. Everything has to be improvised to meet conditions quite unexampled.' He thought the only sound procedure was to hammer away until the enemy got demoralised. Kitchener told cabinet he wanted to withdraw from the Dardanelles but regretted that that could not be done. He warned Maxwell to do his best to prevent rumours of difficulties in the Dardanelles getting about in Egypt; but the torrent of wounded would have made Egyptians aware of the disaster.[36]

Some Australians at first feared that the AIF's role might attract little attention because it was being wasted on a minor campaign. Canadian troops had just earned renown in their first battle of the war by dogged resistance after the Germans' first use of gas on the Western Front, at Ypres, created a wide gap in the line. While applauding the Canadian role, the *Sydney Morning Herald* stressed that readers 'need not admit that the services of the Australians in Turkey are less worthy of a place in the history of the war'.[37] It emphasised the strategic significance of the campaign. A less apologetic tone soon developed. The landing was compared to Wolfe's capture of the Heights of Abraham, although the comparison was thought unjust to the 'current generation' who had had to face 'murderous fire'. Despite its strategic failure, the unique nature of the campaign engaged the sentiments of observers and the people 'back home'. Its remoteness, at first regarded as a blow to aspirations for national recognition, quickly had the opposite effect. The beachhead, almost immediately known as Anzac and invested with a distinctive identity, developed an aura which set it apart from the Western Front and commanded a remarkable amount of publicity for a relatively small force of two divisions.

CHAPTER 11

# 'THIS NEWLY DISCOVERED SEASIDE RESORT'

Despite their valour, the Australians could not break out of their beachhead at Anzac. They tried hard in a series of costly local battles early in May, but once both sides had begun to dig trenches the power of the defence greatly increased.

The value of fieldworks dug on the spot had been proved in many wars, including the Russo-Turkish war of 1877–78, where the Turks at Plevna held up the Russians for five months, inflicting heavy casualties on their enemy. For decades, professional soldiers had been perplexed by the problem confronting infantry advancing against a well-entrenched enemy. The attackers first had to pass through a belt of effective gunfire, and then could have as much as eighteen hundred metres to cross where they could be mown down by an invisible enemy's rifle fire. Whether the topography was rugged or flat, the problem facing advancing troops seemed much the same. Recent battles on the Western Front confirmed the existence of this long-recognised problem, but the lessons, including the need for better artillery/infantry co-ordination, were ignored by army commanders. Australians and Turks on the Gallipoli Peninsula were thereby condemned to endure a horrific series of battles.

'The country here is nothing but steep hills, valleys and ravines,' wrote Ernest Skinner. It reminded Private Richards of the Blue Mountains in New South Wales.[1] The Empire troops held a roughly semicircular position, based on a stretch of 2,560 metres of coastline. But because the Turks held surrounding vantage points, including Gaba Tepe, where they had guns and which they used throughout the campaign as an artillery observation post, the force could only be supplied through Anzac Cove, the name officially used from early May to designate the small inlet between Ari Burnu and Hell Spit.[2] Walker's Ridge, in many places a 'knife-edge' ridge where a step backwards would mean hurtling down to instant death, marked the northern boundary of the beachhead, and Bolton's Ridge the southern. There were 'trenches hundreds of feet up in the air', wrote Richard Casey, 'precipices all over the place. . . . What a country to fight in!' The artery of the Anzac position was Shrapnel and Monash valleys, running from below Hell Spit up to the front line, which everywhere was less than a kilometre and a half from the beach. Today one can stand on Hell Spit and look straight up Monash Valley to see on the skyline the cemetery at Quinn's Post, one of the amazing positions constituting the Anzac inland perimeter along a ridge on which a series of posts—including Pope's, Courtney's and Steele's—was dug. At Quinn's, the Turkish trenches were only ten metres or so from the Australians.

Quinn's was the most vulnerable part of the perimeter, recognised as 'really the key of the whole position'. It was the most advanced post, jutting out in front of all the others. Here, 'there was no back to the Australian trenches, just the cliff'.[3] The Turks had only to advance twenty metres to be able to look right down Shrapnel

*Turkish snipers 'make us more nervy than anything else,' commented Private Willie Harris. 'We show them little mercy.' This camouflaged Turk, shown in an official Admiralty photograph, perhaps considered himself lucky to have been brought in.*

and Monash valleys. As the Anzac beachhead really depended on Quinn's being held, trenches there were constantly packed, with troops close in reserve, to counter a surprise Turkish attack. 'All day and night mining and counter mining, bombing and sharp shooting, go on without ceasing.' For much of the time Quinn's was held by troops in Godley's division (New Zealand and Australian); but it was June before he visited it. 'I am glad to have seen it myself,' he told his wife, 'as it makes it easier to give orders to other people about it. . . . The bombing is so bad there, that it is almost impossible to get men to occupy this forward trench and one can only have sentries with loaded and cocked rifles at the sap heads and ends, ready to shoot the first Turk that appears—and if they get into the trenches, then try to turn them out again with the bayonet. It is a very unsatisfactory state of affairs.'[4] Roger Keyes, visiting some of these trenches, passed through a 'very rough' Western Australian miners' battalion. He thought them wonderful diggers but remarked on their appalling language. At the end of July, on an afternoon that stood out in his memory long afterwards, he saw Quinn's—'*the* sight of Anzac'. A soldier threw a bomb to show how the Turks reacted with machine-gun fire. Keyes asked the men how they liked it. 'Better than fatigues,' they replied.[5]

Anzac was so small that almost every part of it was dangerous, the beach as much as the front line—and, of course, far more vulnerable to artillery fire. Hamilton described the setting to Kitchener on 3 June: 'There is not a square inch of the ground [the Australasians] hold which is really safe from shell and rifle fire, unless . . . you absolutely sit in a dug-out. The reserves and supports are, in fact, almost as much in the battle as the front line, except for the bomb throwing.' When walking along a path leading up a deep valley to the trenches, he explained, 'you find notices stuck up warning you to keep to the right or left of the track. Extraordinary, one half of the road being comparatively safe, the other most dangerous. If the Turks were twenty yards nearer the edge of the cliff they would look right down into the valley.'[6]

After three months at Anzac, Godley was to complain to General Sir Henry Rawlinson, commander of the 4th British Army on the Western Front: 'We are in a most annoying, not to say humiliating, position here now. We have only a cheesebite out of the cliffs—and little more than two miles along, with a perimeter of defence of $2\frac{3}{4}$ miles and a depth in its widest part of $\frac{3}{4}$ mile. . . . Within this we are daily and nightly and perpetually shelled and sniped and it is a dog's life. . . . We trudge around the trenches daily and return hot, dusty, weary and footsore to the old dug-outs.'

At Anzac a commander was in almost as much danger as his troops. The various headquarters were much closer to the front line than was the case on the Western Front, the distances being as follows: battalion, fifty yards; brigade, two hundred yards; division, three hundred yards; corps, a thousand yards. The sharing of dangers and privations—although officers naturally enjoyed some of the privileges of rank or responsibility—encouraged friendship between officers and men and promoted the sense of comradeship in the AIF. So far as rank was concerned, 'things [got] rather slack in the firing line', where it did 'not count so much as when on ceremonial parade'. Second Lieutenant Harry Coe, on reaching Anzac, carried ammunition under appalling conditions for eighteen hours, including all night. 'On a job like this, the men always do better if the officer helps. It was cruel work.' It left them exhausted for several days.[7]

All too often men had occasion to comment on the death or wounding of an officer. After the first day at Anzac George Mitchell wrote of the death that night of 'our beloved Lieutenant [Byrne] with the same happy little smile that he always wore'. Following a tragic mistake by a sentry one night, a 2nd Battalion man wrote: 'Our old Colonel [Braund] shot dead last night hard luck for us just as we had got to like him we lose him. He was worrying too much lately.' A few days later, when a 'much beloved lieutenant' was killed by a shell, Sapper G. Colin Grove, at the night interment, thought of the burial of Sir John Moore, the British lieutenant-general killed in 1809 in the Peninsular War at the end of the retreat to Corunna. Groves's companions 'felt like lost sheep without a shepherd'. Of course, front line officers had their lapses. One soldier, on 8 May, described a lieutenant taking his men into a trap and then turning away 'to find cover for himself'; but George Mitchell knew of only one case of an Australian officer who 'turned cur'.[8] So many officers and non-commissioned officers were killed or wounded that promotion from the ranks was rapid for many survivors. One such was fascinated at the 'gradually enlarging field of vision' as he rose up the army's ranks. Another, no doubt representative of many, refused promotion, saying he had enough to do looking after himself without having to look after others.[9]

From his elevated position a member of a gun crew watched the ever-changing aspects of the gully beneath: now a string of stretcher bearers, now a company of men hauling a howitzer, perhaps a mule train of ammunition or a detachment of soldiers freshly landed. After being among the first to land at dawn on Sunday 25 April, Murray Aitken had gone inland. On the Tuesday he returned to the beach and then wrote: 'I was amazed at the spectacle which confronted me, in place of the bare beach we had landed on; men, like ants, were busy in every direction with stacks of stores and ammunition; guns were being rapidly prepared for action; mules and donkeys were being hurried to the front with water and supplies; a wireless station was in full working order; a telephone station, with wires stretching to every part of the firing line; in fact, the metamorphosis almost took my breath and one could not imagine a more thrilling sight than this to realize the power of England's military authorities.' Godley told his wife, 'The beach is like Margate! Crammed with stores, donkeys, mules, marines, Jew Mule Corps men, Australians, New Zealanders, Indians and all sorts.' In the steep cliffs behind the narrow beach 'we live in our holes.'[10]

The beachhead remained predominantly Australian, with smaller numbers of New Zealanders. Units from the Royal Naval Division (RND) gave some aid in the front line for a fortnight from late April. But of the 27,182 men landed at Anzac by 1 May, at least 17,326 were in the AIF and at least 4,290 in New Zealand units.[11] The proportion of Australasians increased during mid-May when men of the first three light horse brigades and the New Zealand Mounted Rifles, all fighting as infantrymen, arrived at Anzac, and the men in the RND moved to

*A view of crowded Anzac, which reminded General Godley of Margate, whereas one Australian thought of the scrub around Sydney's Maroubra beach. Indeed, it was typical of the Anzac summer scene that so many men were swimming. Bathing was their only real leisure activity; it was also a necessary one, with water too short to allow normal washing and with the droves of flies, the dust and the oppressive heat of the trenches. All ranks participated, which contributed to an egalitarianism among Australian troops.*

Helles. No Australians were fighting and dying anywhere else in the world, so it was not surprising that the attention of people at home focused on this small tongue of wildly tangled hills in a remote and scarcely inhabited part of a country few Australians would have thought very much about before 1915.

To a woman friend, Private Finch described 'this newly discovered seaside resort'. 'No more charming spot in the world could be chosen for a holiday,' wrote Lieutenant-Colonel Sutton, 'and now it is a veritable hell.' General Hamilton thought that there had never been 'anything quite like the strain' undergone by the defenders at Anzac. George Mitchell thought that a fraction of what he had seen, if described, 'could turn the most hardened sick with horror.' At his beach hospital, the first days seemed to John Corbin, now a major, 'like a hideous nightmare. I shall never forget the incessant stream of wounded, the courage. . .of the men. . .the racking tiredness of limbs, body and mind. . . .the loss of sleep was the hardest thing to bear. . . . One blanket and an oilcloth sheet on a pebbly beach was cold and uncomfortable.' The first few nights without a sleeping bag were frightful, but once he had got one it was a godsend to him. The 'cursed Battery' at Gaba Tepe was the devil. Corbin complained about the delays in building shrapnel-proof shelters for his patients. 'It is absurd that wounded men, Doctors and Dressers should be exposed to death when a few hours work would make it comparatively safe. Of course the Engineers have been very busy and most of [the] timber and bags have been needed to protect men in [the] firing line.' However, by mid-June the engineers told Corbin that they could not make the hospital safe.[12]

The small beachhead was exposed to fire from both flanks as well as the front, analogous to a situation in which the AIF would find itself again, over a year later, at Pozières. Private V. E. Frankcombe (12th Battalion) and his mates had shrapnel showering down over them all day on 1 May, when there was a particularly heavy Turkish bombardment. 'A terrible cannonade was opened at daybreak by the enemy,' wrote Private F. W. Johnston, and tons of shrapnel and high explosive were hurled into our lines. So severe was this shelling that no man ventured to leave his dug-out, not even to make tea or to go for food.' The bombardment lasted all day with little or no reply from the Anzac land batteries. 'The ships however sent a never ceasing stream of shells over and at dusk we could see from out our dugout the flame lit sea as each gun flashed.' When his gun crew was moved from Anzac, Johnston and his mates tried to imagine that all that they had experienced 'was but a dream'—however, they were moved to Helles.[13]

Among the attacks aimed at strengthening the beachhead's position, that of the night of 2–3 May was particularly significant. The aim was to seize the heights at the head of Monash Valley, from Quinn's Post to Baby 700. As Ellis Silas noted, the situation was 'so critical that at all costs the enemy must be shifted from the Ridge'.[14] From Constantinople and the Asiatic shore, the enemy had strongly reinforced what they knew as the Ari Burnu front and by 1 May had twenty-eight battalions (eighteen thousand combatants) there. On 2 May these Turks were hammered by an extraordinarily violent fire, before the infantry attack.

That attack was made by Royal Marines, two battalions of New Zealanders, and Monash's 4th Brigade, the brunt of the fighting falling on the 16th Battalion. Two of its members have left accounts of this attack on Bloody Angle, between Quinn's and Pope's. Ernest Skinner recalled before the assault: 'Looking around . . . one could feel something one couldn't explain everybody appeared very quiet and yet in a way excited. I remember passing remarks to several of the boys they most of them seemed oppressed and although I felt inwardly something myself was quite determined not to show it to the others and thought if it were possible to cheer them up in any way it was my duty to do so. I thank God I was able to feel and do as I did then for although knowing we were in for a stiff proposition yet in

*Looking from Walker's Ridge across Mule Gully along Russell's Top to the Sphinx. Photographed by John Robertson in 1986.*

myself somehow felt confident I should come through. At the same time I felt quite resigned to whatever might through God's will happen.'[15] 'Just as the sun was setting,' Ellis Silas wrote, 'throwing its rich colour o'er all the landscape, we formed up for the final march off for the attack—it was difficult going, crawling through the gully which skirted the foot of the hill we were to attack.' At seven o'clock Lieutenant Geddes looked at his watch and said 'Come on, lads, at 'em.' 'Up we rushed—God, it was frightful,' Silas recalled, '—the screams of the wounded, bursting of the shells, and the ear-splitting crackling of the rifles. In a very few minutes the gully at the foot of the hill was filled with dead and wounded. . . . It rained men in the gully; all round could be seen the sparks where the bullets were striking. Amidst this Hell of writhing, mangled men and hail of bullets', survivors struggled up the steep slope. It 'was like going up the side of a house,' wrote Skinner. Silas was ordered to carry a message to the rear. On his way he went through gullies 'choked with wounded'; all along the route he kept coming across 'poor shattered things crawling along in their agony'. 'The horrors of this night have been too much for me,' he wrote. 'I cannot get used to the frightful sights with which I am always surrounded.' Dawn revealed, along the edge of the ridge, bodies 'hanging in all sorts of grotesque and apparently impossible attitudes.'[16]

Dawn also confirmed that the assault was a complete and costly failure. The 16th Battalion now mustered nine officers and 290 men compared with seventeen officers and 620 men who entered the attack. Private Lawless, stretcher-bearer, had extra work to do that night. 'This is the eighth day of the battle,' he wrote, 'and it is raging as fiercely as ever yet. . . . My God, what a time it has been. I hardly know what day it is.' He described the 16th Battalion 'fighting like madmen', but losing heavily, and mentioned a wounded man 'glad to get out of it as his nerve is going'. The Turkish official account estimates their losses at Ari Burnu from the landing until 4 May as 199 officers and 13,955 men, with the invaders' losses being 8,000.[17]

In his report on this action, Monash wrote, 'If the Marines had been in a position of readiness . . . and if the accidental shattering of the right of our line by our artillery had not occurred, I feel sure that this Brigade could have made good and held the line gained; but it could not . . . have been possible with the troops available, to carry out the original plan to seize and hold Knoll 700 and the line thence to Quinn's Post.'[18]

Birdwood could not often repeat such methods without squandering too many troops. There was no respite, however, in the constant warfare on a smaller scale.

*Two 11-inch shells from the new German battle-cruiser* Goeben *in the Narrows thirteen kilometres away land in the sea near Anzac Cove. The* Goeben *had been virtually integrated into the Turkish navy in mid-August 1914. Several British battleships were sunk in May and June by the Turkish and German navies, a boost to enemy morale.*

133

Sergeant Alwynne described how he was to be in a party of eight men, led by a lieutenant, which would cross no man's land, armed 'with hand Grenades which we are to drop in the sap that the Turks are digging towards us. We are to have a tot of rum before we go out. I am not in favour of this. I will have mine when I get back (if I do). One wants to have his brain clear not muddled in a job like this.' The bomb attack 'was carried out with great success,' Alwynne noted the following day, '[and we] had our Rum as soon as we got back.'[19]

Nor was there much respite in the constant attrition of the beachhead's force from Turkish rifle and artillery fire. When one first hears shells flying around, commented Private E. A. Moor, 'I can tell you, it puts a funny feeling through one. . . . the shells come screaming like a thousand demons through the air [and] you start wondering if it is going to hit you.' To Murray Aitken, shrapnel bursts looked like 'balls of harmless cotton-wool floating in the air or like a pretty cloud effect'. It was a messenger of death which had 'but one redeeming feature, it gives a shriek of warning before bursting; which warning, needless to say we take.'[20]

Sapper Grove described dodging six-inch high-explosive shells. In the late afternoon of 11 May his dugout became the target for them.

*At intervals of about one-quarter of a minute we got shell after shell poured into us. During this first few minutes we were anxiously waiting crouched behind some earthworks expecting every next shell to cut us all to pieces. We could hear the explosion of the gun, a few seconds later the whistle of the shell and then the explosion of the shell as it came into the dugouts. After about three shells had come we decided that it was no place for us so directly we heard the fourth shell explode we made a dash for it; how we escaped I don't know but as we ran we heard the gun again and a second or so later it burst all around us throwing up a whole suit of web equipment and overcoats tobacco shaving gear water bottles and goodness knows what else. Boots went up into the air and into the sea, bits of rifles flew in every direction and then we were round the gully under cover of the banks . . . to our astonishment not one of us of about forty had been even touched.*[21]

Private Lawless thought lyddite shells were 'hell-made things. They are all over our head, and the shriek of them and the air vibrating overhead is nerve-wracking.'[22]

Naturally, everyone was anxious to push on to Constantinople and so shorten the war. But an officer gloomily reflected, 'We seem to have come to a stand-still and it looks as if this trench war is going on just as in Flanders.' Richard Casey lamented the failure to secure Baby 700 on the first day. If troops had been landed quickly enough they might even have been able to hold Hill 971. 'As it is,' he went on, '971 dominates us and is a constant menace to our progress.' He was depressed, concluding that the force would be 'stuck at Anzac until the southern landing made good. . . . We have gaily waded into this show with too few men.'[23]

General Hamilton reasoned similarly, as did Private Richards, who said it seemed practically impossible for one side to push the other back once they were dug in and protected by wire entanglements. He was surprised that British aeroplanes were not 'kept watching the enemy's movements a little more thoroughly'. Then he mused, 'How stupid it seems for me to be thinking of improving what these great war authorities are doing.' By mid-May John Gellibrand was 'puzzled at the probable historical value of the show'. After a great deal of intense fighting, there was very little change, except for casualties. 'We have of course established a claim for fighting qualities and the like and yet that seems on the inadequate side.' He thought there might have been a 'miscalculation' in the way the campaign was organised.[24]

Trying to break the deadlock, Hamilton decided on another massive offensive at Helles. To reinforce this he ordered the Victorian brigade (the 2nd) there from 3 to

16 May. So it took part in another of the campaign's horrible, costly and unsuccessful attacks in a foredoomed advance towards Krithia. This was the only occasion when Australian units fought at Helles. Apart from some gullies, the Anglo-
French position there was a flat plain, with the opposing front lines some distance
apart. Captain Chambers found 'it was a great change being in such open country
compared with Anzac and where we could walk about without fear of being
sniped'. The story of the advance, in the late afternoon of 8 May, which cost 182
Victorians killed, 335 missing and 539 wounded, is fully told by Bean. One of the
participants, Private McCowan of the 5th Battalion, noted, 'The whole of our line
to the rear is now lined with graves of our fellows.' The battleground was 'now a
regular slaughter house'. Clearing the wounded was an immensely difficult task.
Men lay out in the open, calling for water or crying, 'Have you forgotten me
Cobbers'.[25]

Someone in authority realised that Australians had soldierly skills which could
be more usefully employed than in walking across a plain in the face of machine-
gun fire. So McCowan enjoyed a new experience, which he described in his diary:
'[10 May] 6.45 p.m. I am going out to try my hand as a sniper as I am reconed a
very tidy shot. [11 May] I have been sniping . . . and had some very good sport.
[12 May] 8 p.m. I am out again sniping it is an exciting game far more than
football. [15 May] I have had the first decent sleep for 10 days. Still no mail. . . . It
is surprising how callous men can become.'[26] Next day McCowan, and the other
members of the brigade, were shipped back to Anzac.

CHAPTER 12

# 'BEARING THEIR GRIEF NOBLY'

I<small>T WAS SOME TIME</small> after the landing before Australians at home became aware of the tactical situation on the Gallipoli Peninsula. With its reputation at stake, the British government for weeks concealed the truth from parliament. In May Lord Northcliffe, owner of the *Evening News*, *Daily Mail*, *Daily Mirror* and *The Times*, declared that the Press Bureau, a government agency set up to guide British newspaper coverage of wartime stories, was 'keeping the truth from the people'. He was very critical of the 'cable-butchering' censorship. In fact, censorship of opinion, as distinct from news, was very mild. From May Northcliffe waged a powerful campaign against Kitchener, so much so that the Services Club of Pall Mall banished *The Times* and the *Daily Mail* from its precincts.[1]

Meanwhile, the government continued to mislead parliament and the public. On 6 May Asquith declared that the operations were pressing ahead under 'highly satisfactory conditions'. Twelve days later Kitchener told the House of Lords the same, although he admitted that progress was necessarily slow because the country was so difficult. Lord Lansdowne, Conservative leader in the House of Lords, complained that the information released by the government was so vague that it had little value. That situation obtained for about four weeks, while Australian newspapers published falsely optimistic reports about desperate Turks hemmed in with the Allies converging as fighting continued far inland from Gaba Tepe. The *Sydney Morning Herald* had a mysterious source in Athens which variously reported that the British had captured Maidos, the heights dominating the Kilid Bahr Plateau, and Krithia, localities which the Turks held throughout the campaign. In mid-July Monash told a correspondent in Australia not to take the slightest notice of any news coming from Athens, because in the past it had been 'ridiculously inaccurate'. An optimistic member of the House of Commons, R. L. Outhwaite—a Tasmanian-born Liberal who had entered parliament in the 1906 landslide—asked Foreign Secretary Sir Edward Grey if Australia and New Zealand would be consulted about the disposal of Constantinople in accordance with the pledges given.[2]

Munro Ferguson was glad that Australians ignored the mismanagement of the campaign and generally regarded it 'as one of orderly and continuous progress'. The War Office wished to encourage this impression, stating on 13 May: 'The advance of our . . . troops is being slowly but surely pushed forward. . . . The Australian and New Zealand troops are strongly entrenched.' A few days earlier Godley had told a colleague that he did not suppose 'anything so utterly mismanaged by the British Government will ever be recorded'.[3]

Suspicion that the landings were not proceeding well became stronger in the third week of May, with news that Achi Baba had not been captured. People began to realise that the Australians were probably going through an experience quite unlike anything they imagined when leaving Australia. It was now clear the Turks were fighting bravely, which reminded some observers of their reputation as fine defensive soldiers. Australia could not expect a quick move across the peninsula to the Narrows; but an eventual advance to Constantinople was still expected. In a departure from previous practice, the Turkish attack of 19 May (see chapter 13) was reported briefly, but fairly, in Australian newspapers within a week. Readers would have found some difficulty in reconciling that account with what they had previously read about the campaign's tactical situation.

Munro Ferguson eventually became so dissatisfied with the trickle of news that he asked London for more information. An official in the Colonial Office minuted, 'What information we get—and we don't get it daily—is telegraphed out pretty fully.' But the Governor-General's prompting brought results. On 26 May the Colonial Office cabled a six-page dispatch for publication. It was terse but reasonably accurate, mentioning Australian reverses although tending to play down the problems facing the men. With the publication of this cable on 28 May, Australians were first made clearly aware of how little ground had been gained. The report brought worried public reflections about the progress of the Australian forces in the Dardanelles. 'How much longer must we wait for decisive news of the forcing of the straits and the release of Russia's immense stores of grain and other produce . . . ?' Late in June, Munro Ferguson told the Colonial Office that there was 'no complaining,' though even ministers had begun 'to express anxiety as to the outcome' of the campaign.[4]

There were also delays in informing the Australian public of the scale of casualties. In the first week of fighting, the 1st Australian Division lost about half of its infantry, killed, wounded or missing. Worst hit was the 3rd Brigade, which after three days at Anzac retained only 25 per cent of its effective fighting strength. News of the terrible casualty rate at both Anzac and Helles reached the War Office on 28 April. On 6 May Asquith told the House of Commons that losses had been heavy, and the Colonial Office reported this to Australia, where the first list of casualties was published on 3 May, accompanied by a message from Prime Minister Andrew Fisher conveying sympathy to the bereaved along with pride in the soldiers' valour and skills. This list contained the names of eighteen killed and thirty-seven wounded. Photographs of casualties appeared in a *Sydney Morning Herald* tableau headed 'Heroes of the Dardanelles'. Brief biographical details were also printed. At the same time Senator Pearce, the Minister for Defence, released a frank statement explaining why 'the awful conditions set up by war' often caused a long, 'very distressing' delay in notifying casualties. He appealed to 'the national dignity of Australia [to] enable her people to suffer their private grief without adding to the difficulties . . . of our men on active service'.[5]

By the second week of May, very long lists of wounded men were being published in newspapers. The great disparity between the large numbers of wounded and the relatively small numbers reported killed or missing created suspicion and unease, and Munro Ferguson told Colonial Secretary Lewis Harcourt that Australians were 'much agitated' over the campaign and impatient at the lack of details on the fighting and the delay in providing casualty lists. He made an issue of this with the Colonial Office, on 14 June listing eight of his cables since 17 May which had complained about the delays in obtaining the lists, delays that created a 'most painful impression' in Australia. He asked that figures on British casualties should also be telegraphed, so Australians knew that the sacrifice was being shared. When a 'further long list' arrived he was worried that he could not match this loss of life with news of a military triumph. Nonetheless, he told Harcourt, 'We are full of pride over the achievements of our troops in the Dardanelles.'[6]

There was a good reason why lists of wounded reached Australia generally much more quickly than lists of dead. The former lists were compiled either when the relevant ship reached Alexandria or from hospital returns. This allowed speedy notification. Deaths of prominent officers were also publicised fairly quickly. In the first four weeks the 1st Division lost its commander, General Bridges, and the commanding officers of the 1st Brigade and of three of its battalions. News of these fatalities was made public within three to nine days.

It was often much harder to ascertain whether a private had been killed. This was because of the initial mixing of the units, the fact that the Turks held much of the ground where many of the first day's casualties were sustained, and because in the early fighting identification tags were often buried with dead men. Monash was sure there would be 'much wailing and outcry in Australia about the slowness of news about our killed and wounded', but it was 'quite unavoidable'. He added,

*Members of the 1st Australian Signal Company in May 1915 wearing motley Anzac*

'Even within my own Brigade I have the greatest difficulty in getting the daily casualty lists.' He explained the general problem of obtaining accurate casualty records during the first ten days of heavy fighting, pointed out that many wounded were shipped from Anzac to various destinations without their names being recorded, and forecast that it would take 'weeks if not months' to complete an accurate list.[7]

To make matters worse, there was an administrative bungle, which Harcourt excused as the result of continuous fighting. Some missing returns, which left Gallipoli on 5 May, did not reach Alexandria until 7 June. Probably about five hundred Australians died in the first twenty-four hours at Anzac, but by 20 May the deaths of only eighty-one officers and 211 other ranks had been publicly notified. It was 29 May before the total of deaths published in the press reached five hundred.

Late in June, Munro Ferguson was still complaining to London about delays in the casualty lists, but by this time procedures were being speeded up, which meant

*garb. Expecting to reach Constantinople quickly, officers in the unit agreed not to shave until they got there. They changed their minds when it proved impossible to advance. In the centre is Lieutenant S. H. Watson, responsible for the pier at Anzac Cove which bore his name.*

*Horace Moore Jones, View of Anzac from the southern point of Anzac Cove, 1915 (watercolour, 14 × 22 cm). Anzac terrain and colours put one Australian at Gallipoli in mind of the Blue Mountains of New South Wales.*

that large numbers of deaths were being notified. The impact upon a family of the death of a loved one was of course devastating. The grief tended to be a private matter. On the wider stage the sacrifice was viewed as a tragic but inescapable consequence of Australia's decision to fight for what it regarded as a righteous cause. As Louis Roth of Katanning, Western Australia, wrote to his relative John Monash on 19 May, 'Australia is beginning to feel the loss of so many men, but this can't be helped as we must win, at all costs.'[8]

Andrew Fisher wanted to know if the British government was inquiring into the fate of Australian soldiers reported missing, and whether any information obtained would be telegraphed to Australia. R. H. Muirhead Collins, official secretary in the High Commissioner's Office in London and former secretary of the Department of Defence, wrote to Pearce of the 'good deal of sad feeling in Australia'. He went on: 'All other wars seem to be insignificant compared to this titanic struggle.' Pearce told Godley, 'We are now all aware of the grim business you are engaged upon.' Six weeks earlier, when the AIF had incurred only a small fraction of its eventual total casualties, he had told Bridges: 'Public are taking the big list of casualties well. There is no hysteria, but a deep feeling that though it is a heavy price to pay Australia is determined to pay it without complaining. Relatives of the fallen are bearing their grief nobly, feeling that their loved ones have fallen in a noble cause.'[9]

The noble cause was not prospering. Throughout May British commanders, and some observers, commented on the forlorn hopes of the Dardanelles expedition. General Paris feared it was proving a grave strategic error in which a hundred thousand Allied troops were being wasted on a sideshow which had gained nothing more than a small strip of barren land. Lord Curzon, one of the Conservative political leaders and a former viceroy of India, was told that the expedition, 'lightly undertaken', was in danger of being completely destroyed. Hamilton had similar terrifying fears, although he could console himself: 'Anyway we are not yet driven into the sea.'[10]

The military stalemate did not affect the Australian government's stability. It had had no hand in planning or running the campaign, and few Australians questioned its value. By contrast, the expedition's failure helped provoke a political crisis in London. In mid-May the Liberal government fell and was replaced by a coalition cabinet, Asquith remaining Prime Minister. A. J. Balfour succeeded Churchill at the Admiralty, and Andrew Bonar Law, the Conservative leader, replaced Harcourt as Colonial Secretary. News that Churchill was leaving the Admiralty was 'an awful blow' to Hamilton and some others on the Gallipoli Peninsula: his eclipse projected 'a black shadow' over the Dardanelles. Godley did not think that Churchill could survive the upheaval. He was largely right, for Churchill was demoted to the junior post of Chancellor of the Duchy of Lancaster. Hamilton wrote to him, 'If only by the mercy of God I can succeed here it will vindicate you.'[11]

Under the coalition, the War Council became the Dardanelles Committee, a striking illustration of the importance in war planning of the argument over the Gallipoli campaign. Churchill was a member. The committee had to decide whether to reinforce Hamilton, evacuate his force, or leave it to wither away in the sun. There was a small avalanche of reports and memoranda on various possible courses of action, with Churchill strenuously urging a large-scale assault. At Hamilton's and Birdwood's headquarters, planning to break the deadlock at Anzac began. They could afford this luxury only because the Australians had just defeated a furious Turkish onslaught aimed at driving them into the sea.

*During the landing, units became mixed up any many men acted on their initiative with no officer to lead them. At the same time, officer casualties were high. Lieutenant A. P. Derham, Staff Captain 2nd Brigade, who won the Military Cross for service during the first three days, was wounded three times.*

# CHAPTER 13

# 'A VERITABLE INFERNO'

*W*HILE THE 2ND BRIGADE was at Helles, General Birdwood made some more costly attempts to strengthen the vulnerable beachhead. So, on the night of 9–10 May, men of the 4th Brigade were once again ordered to assault from Quinn's Post. This attack was as fruitless as that a week earlier. A soldier 'who managed to get through several bayonet charges' reckoned 'the most severe' was that at midnight on Sunday 9 May: 'It's a matter one cannot describe—the only thing is for a person to go through one to find out exactly what it is like.' After the charge, Private J. C. Lennie of an ambulance unit sadly noted that only about 160 of the 16th Battalion were left. 'The Roll is called,' wrote Ellis Silas, 'how heart-breaking it is—name after name is called; the reply a deep silence which can be felt.' What was left was 'just a thin line of weary, ashen-faced men'. The loss of life had been to no avail. Richard Casey, lucky enough to be able to get to the *Minnewaska* for a clean-up, when looking at the scene from the ship realised more forcibly than before how very small was the Australasian hold on the peninsula: 'It is as though we were hanging on by our teeth.' At times he became severely depressed at being so cooped up, 'plastered with shells from well concealed positions—no freedom of manoeuvre and no getting on'.[1]

'Oh they are horrible,' wrote one soldier of the Turkish heavy guns which shelled Anzac relentlessly. 'The shell can be seen from the time it comes over the horizon and where they hit they dig enormous holes in the ground.' Many a man had stories to tell of near misses. A shell burst in the air 'within three feet' of two men. It shattered the adjacent cliff. 'Both of us—dazed, confused, deafened, covered with dust—felt ourselves over for wounds and cowered down while shell after shell came into this narrow gully.' After this, Lieutenant-Colonel Sutton, wet, worn and dirty, wrote ironically in his diary, 'War is very glorious.' That night he was too tired to be kept awake even by the noise of heavy guns firing.[2]

Murray Aitken described his narrowest escape, which left him unhurt but destroyed the breakfast he was cooking. The Turkish habit of shelling at mealtime gave rise to the expression 'duck for dinner'. Robert Antill cheerfully told his English parents, 'As you see I am still alive but I can't tell you hardly how it is, for I have had some of the most marvellous escapes a fellow could have.' Another private reassured his mother on 15 May. 'I am still safe and sound. Haven't got a scratch yet. I seem to be bullet proof. The bullets whizz all round but do not touch me.' His commanding officer was not so fortunate, for it was on that day that General Bridges was mortally wounded. It was said that the sniper responsible was soon killed by a sergeant in the 1st Light Horse Regiment. At about the same spot, four days later, perhaps the best-known of all the men at Anzac, Private Simpson (Kirkpatrick)—'the man with the donkey'—was shot through the heart. No longer would wounded men be helped by this man who 'talked to the donkeys

92

as they plodded slowly along, in a strange mixture of English, Arabic profanity, and Australian slang' and who 'had won the V. C. fifty times over', according to a Newfoundlander at Gallipoli. Simpson's fame was widespread.[3]

As well as the dangers from shells and bullets, there were discomforts. It rained all night on 11–12 May and, so one 15th Battalion private put it, 'it is not very pleasant in a wet dugout with only an oilskin sheet and overcoat'. The rain turned the trenches into mud, which made conditions worse than before. For several weeks the men had to endure the cold nights without blankets. Men began to wear their trousers inside out to help thwart lice. But many a man learned to accept the rough conditions, and many became 'rather a dabster at cooking'. Continually, the men were 'digging, ever digging . . . we pick and shovel like navvies'. They learnt the art of good trench construction—to localise the effect of shellfire, for example. After three weeks at Anzac it occurred to Murray Aitken that 'our advent will be a veritable Godsend to the papers'. He speculated on the headlines and would have liked, then and there, to be reading some of the accounts. He hoped his mother was saving them for him.[4]

Australian losses were so heavy that light horse units were being brought to Anzac to fight as infantry. All was excitement at Heliopolis on 8 May when men in the 1st and 2nd regiments were issued with ammunition and rations for embarkation. Within a week they were at Quinn's. An infantryman noted in his diary that the light horse had 'brought a prisoner in, a thing never known in the infantry'. Men from the 2nd Light Horse Regiment were soon (15 May) used in an attack at Quinn's which, like previous assaults, failed to improve the situation. One infantryman thought this showed that the light-horsemen were not such good fighters. Private Fred Robson of the 15th Battalion saw a friend, Ted, who had been in this charge. 'He seemed broken up and said home would do him. I do not think he is fit for fighting. The Light Horse fellows were growling about being sent to a place like this. Wait until they have done as much fighting as we have but I do not think they could stand it.' Other infantry naturally derived some amusement from watching the light horse, deprived of their glory, 'sweating up and down hill under the weight of an infantry pack. Our fellows chaff them a lot and are always ragging them about their horses.'[5]

One soldier who knew he had reached his limit was Ellis Silas; but he could not face the prospect of leaving his mates. 'I do wish I could get wounded so that the matter could be decided for me.' His captain decided the issue. 'You're not cut out for this kind of thing,' he said; and Silas left Anzac that night, 17 May. He was soon in hospital at Heliopolis, an 'exquisite sensation' after the horrors of Anzac. He concluded his war diary affirming that his dead comrades 'in the greatness of their souls have handed to future generations a fuller, deeper meaning of the word Patriotism'.[6]

Silas left just before the beachhead withstood its biggest attack. Its position was so confined and seemed so precarious that the German general Liman von Sanders, Essad Pasha, the Anzac zone commander, and Lieutenant-Colonel Mustafa Kemal, his leading divisional commander, agreed that a massive attack might well overrun it and drive the invader into the sea. The task was given to four divisions and a regiment, under Kemal. The Turks committed 42,000 men; the Anzacs had 17,000 men, of whom about 12,500 were in the front lines. The attack was timed for 3.30 a.m. on 19 May. Fortunately, a British reconnaissance aircraft on the 18th detected the Turkish reinforcements. The Australians were ready and repulsed the attack, inflicting heavy losses at comparatively slight cost to themselves. The Turks admit to losing ten thousand men; about three thousand of them were dead. Lewis Einstein, on the staff of the United States Embassy in Constantinople, claimed that on 19 May three transports full of Turkish wounded reached the Golden Horn. Birdwood estimated that the Australians fired about 950,000 rounds during the attack. It was at Courtney's Post, during this furious fighting, that Albert Jacka, a Victorian in the 14th Battalion, won the AIF's first Victoria Cross. He quickly became a national hero.[7]

This battle of 19 May was a crucial stage in the history of Anzac, for it confirmed that the beachhead could be held, at least until there was a major change of circumstances. Some of the Australians said this was 'the best bit of sport they ever had'. A fortnight later some told newly arrived light-horsemen that the assault was 'better than a wallaby drive'. Murray Aitken's feelings were more ambivalent. His platoon was in support and so should not have been in the firing line. 'But do you think they could keep us out?' he wrote. 'We got up to all sorts of dodges to get in and into all sorts of positions to have a shot. I forgot to take cover and did not notice the shrapnel while the blood-lust was on me, and . . . I'll admit to a certain savage pleasure in firing to kill.' Nonetheless, 'it was pitiful to see it all' as the Turks kept coming on 'despite the dreadful slaughter. . . . For a time it was a veritable inferno. . . . I'm perfectly satisfied now that the Turk is a fanatic.'[8]

Private W. W. Paterson, one of the 3rd Brigade men who had pushed inland on 25 April, was in a machine-gun crew on outpost duty at dawn on 19 May. He was 'pretty nervy' but survived to describe the massed attack. Admiral de Robeck, commanding the expedition's naval support, commented, 'The Australians have been doing big things lately and been fairly giving the Turks hell.' Hamilton, despite his anxiety about the beachhead, was glad when the enemy attacked, for it

*Ellis Silas, The roll call 10 May 1915, 1920 (oil on canvas, 101.5 × 152.5 cm). The 16th Battalion suffered heavy casualties at Quinn's Post on 9 May. After roll call the following morning, Ellis Silas wrote: 'How heartbreaking it is . . . there are few of us left to answer to our names—just a thin line of weary, ashen-faced men, behind us a mass of silent forms, once our comrades.'*

provided 'a real opportunity to punish them'. The journalist Ashmead-Bartlett told Asquith that this was the most successful engagement so far in the campaign. It had had an excellent effect on the spirits of the colonials, who, 'being a highly intelligent and superior lot of men, had become somewhat discouraged by the failure to achieve any definite success and extremely bored with sitting day after day in trenches'. Birdwood was keenly conscious that von Sanders' forces had outnumbered his three to one. Had von Sanders concentrated his attack at one point, Birdwood noted, 'he might well have come near driving me into the sea. . . . As it was, he . . . made several disjointed attacks which my boys had no difficulty in defeating.' A price was being paid, apart from the casualties. Monash commented, 'Everybody exhausted with want of sleep and heavy mental strain.'[9]

Some troops of the 3rd Light Horse Brigade reached Anzac three days after the Turkish attack. They have left a record of what was by now becoming a routine procedure for reinforcements. As they approached the beach they noted:

*Between the roaring of the artillery and the guns of the cruisers, we could hear the sharp crackle of rifle fire and the splutter of machine guns. We passed close to the stern of a cruiser at anchor and then hove to waiting for the pinnaces and barges to take us ashore. . . . from the destroyers we jumped aboard the barges—great unwieldy things like those used on the canals in England and France, but drawing very little water—threw in our packs, rifles, tools and baggage, and then with hearts beating faster than usual waited for the pinnaces to move shorewards. We never knew what was in front of us, but ahead we could see a crescent shaped cove, called 'Anzac Cove', [and behind] a narrow strip of shingly beach the land rose at a steep angle to Plugges Plateau, the slopes being pitted with dugouts. . . .*

*It did not take us long to reach the small pier formed of stones, sandbags and barges, and out of the best part of a thousand men not a single one was hit coming ashore. We could not understand why the naval officers were in such a desperate hurry to get us off the barges and away from the beach, but we had landed in daylight in full view of the Turks and it was a wonder that we were not severely shelled on our way to and on shore. It was a providential escape, as shortly afterwards it meant almost certain destruction to land troops during daylight and it was often difficult to land stores. . . .*

*Next morning we continued our digging-in operations, and it was fortunate for us that we did so, as in the afternoon we got our first taste of shelling. The Turks from their observation posts away to the North had spotted us and about tea time we heard a low boom, followed by a ripping tearing scream, and then the crash of the exploding shell. A shrapnel shell had exploded further up the slope amongst the 8th Light Horse and was shortly followed by several more. . . .*

*. . . the Brigadier had a look-out man posted on Plugges Plateau who sounded a whistle whenever the smoke [from a Turkish gun firing] was seen, giving us four or five seconds to dash for cover.*

*It was really laughable when we came to think of it later on the way we used to duck for shelter. Instinctively when we heard a shell coming—usually a small howitzer—I have often seen men—and I've done it myself—crouch behind a bush that might happen to be close by, and which would afford no cover whatsoever, while one day I tried to hide myself among some mail as a shell from Beachy Bill roared by a couple of feet above my head.*

*The noises made by bullets and shells are wonderful in their variety. The nickel casing of the bullets used by the Turks is extremely thin and bursts when it ricochets off ground or a sand-bag, and then as it sped along we could hear it humming or whistling. Sometimes a bullet high overhead would be heard like a boy whistling, starting on a low note, getting higher and higher, then gradually sinking lower and lower until it died away. Others would be like the droning of a bee, the whimper of a whipped dog, the crack of a whip, or a faint zipp as a sniper's bullet flew close by one's head. When a '75' burst the pieces flew through the air at a terrific velocity humming louder and louder as they approached and hit the ground with a dull thud or growing fainter as the fragment went out into space.[10]*

*A blindfolded Turkish envoy is led along the beach to corps head-quarters on 22 May for negotiations to arrange an armistice to bury the dead. Of ten thousand Turkish casualties from their furious attack of 19 May, more than three thousand lay dead in front of Australian trenches, posing a serious health problem. The talks spread over two days, and the armistice was held on 24 May.*

*Soldiers move freely about a strangely quiet battlefield during the armistice of 24 May. Australian and Turkish troops worked together digging communal graves and later exchanged badges and cigarettes. This photograph was taken by Lieutenant-Colonel Charles Ryan of the Australian Army Medical Corps.*

By the time these light-horsemen arrived, a serious health problem had developed because of the thousands of bodies in no man's land. A truce to bury them was arranged for 24 May. Sapper Grove thought it 'seemed very queer all day with everything so quiet no firing or anything all the time. Our men and Turks were exchanging cigarettes.' At 4.30, with the bodies buried, the truce ended. Then it was 'like Hell let loose' as rifles and guns added to the 'Dante's Inferno'.[11] Some shrewd observation by Turkish and German officers during this truce apparently strengthened their belief that a carefully planned assault on Quinn's Post might be successful.

The attack duly came early in the morning of 29 May. The defenders were men of Monash's 4th Brigade, with a few light-horsemen. 'For a while it was hell,' wrote one of them. 'The enemy had blown up our first line of trenches and before anyone had time to do anything they were in it in dozens. They got into our bomb proofs which commanded the main road to the trenches and for some time held up all the reinforcements which were pouring up from the valley.'[12] The crisis passed, after savage fighting, with the Turks who got into the trenches being killed or captured.

The Australians' ability as fighters continued to impress Britons who worked with them. In May 1915 S. S. Butler, an officer in the British army who later became a general, was placed in command of the Intelligence Section at Birdwood's headquarters, so beginning a two-and-a-half year stay with the AIF. In his memoirs he summed up the Australians and New Zealanders in these words: 'A gallanter body of men never existed. They were simply superb, scorning danger and death. Physically, they were such a splendid lot of men that at the end of a long and terrible battle for a position which they had won, they still had the physical strength and nerve to beat off a counter attack.' Once they got to know a British army officer, continued Butler, they were 'the most loyal and pleasant friends and comrades'. Their battle discipline, thanks to their very high standard of intelligence, was very good. They responded readily and wholeheartedly to

orders. They were a little wild at first, and rank meant little to them, but all this righted itself as time went on. The stories of the gallantry of these men, he said, would fill many a book.[13]

General Cunliffe Owen, a British army officer in command of Birdwood's artillery, thought that at Anzac the Australians became 'as well trained as an amateur army composed of magnificent and intelligent material could be'. However, at that stage he thought the officers generally were 'the weakest spot'. He had high praise for the wonderful improvement in shooting by the artillerymen as experience came at Anzac. The Reverend W. F. Scott, a Royal Navy clergyman who saw many 'harrowing things', wrote: 'It takes a good deal out of one to visit strong men in mortal pain. I feel it particularly with the Colonials and Territorials. The former are such fine big men . . . fine fellows—have come all this way to fight our battles

*Looking up Monash Valley to Quinn's Post, as seen and photographed by John Robertson in 1986. It was vital to the whole Anzac beachhead that Quinn's Post be held.*

*The 4th Brigade massed in Reserve Gully, where the troops were addressed by General Godley. Before being relieved at the beginning of June, the 4th, the only brigade drawn from all six Australian states, had for one month endured the strain of holding Quinn's and Courtney's posts.*

for us and quite voluntarily. They are extremely brave and cheery and say how awfully glad they are to be able to fight for the Old Country.'[14]

Such praise came as the Australians were transforming themselves into skilled, professional soldiers. Naturally, in their first days at Anzac they had shown some inexperience. Birdwood had had to order them to stop wasting ammunition on non-existent targets. Hamilton told Kitchener that the Australians had reacted worse than the British troops in their initial disappointment at being checked by the Turks instead of pursuing them through open countryside, as they had expected. Hamilton was at that stage convinced about the Australians' dash in attack but unsure of their reliability in defence. His doubts were short-lived, for he soon thought the Australians recovered quickly once they saw their first need was to hold what they had, rather than march on to Constantinople.[15] They settled down to face more weeks of dogged defence while their political masters in London discussed reinforcing them and Hamilton's staff devised plans aimed at breaking the stalemate.

# CHAPTER 14

# 'AN ANTHEAP OF KHAKI ANTS'

Aᴛᴛᴇʀ Mᴀʏ the Anzac beachhead, having survived its greatest crises, seemed relatively secure, although, as Hamilton told Kitchener, theoretically it would be considered impossible to hold, as the situation there was so extraordinary. In a few weeks it had become one of the Empire's wonders, a scene without precedent in the belief of those best qualified to judge. Thousands of soldiers lived on the slopes and precipitous hillsides, their front-line trenches in many places overlooked by the Turks holding the higher ground. Ellis Ashmead-Bartlett, in a memorandum read by Asquith to the Dardanelles Committee in June, claimed, 'The Australians at Anzac hold the most extraordinary position in which an army has ever found itself, clinging as they are to the face of the cliffs.'[1]

Visitors were astonished at what they saw. Orlo Williams, the chief cipher officer on Hamilton's staff, chose an excellent day to visit—24 May. He wrote in his diary: 'The only thing to be said about the Anzac position is that it is amazing. To imagine it if one had not seen it would be impossible. The first impression from a boat is that of seeing the cave dwellings of a large and prosperous tribe of savages who live on the extremely steep slopes of broken sandy bluffs covered with scrub which go up from a very narrow sandy beach to a height of 300 feet. . . . the place is in perpetual motion like an antheap of khaki ants. It is almost inconceivable that a whole Army Corps, headquarters and all, should be holding such a position, the whole exposed to shellfire. . . . In fact it is an extremely strong position to hold, though a very difficult one to advance from. They have got all their guns up the steep hill, which in itself is a wonderful feat.'[2] Williams 'took several photographs' but remarked: 'Nothing could reproduce the ensemble, together with the activity animating it. All here agree that it is the most amazing thing they ever saw.'

Hamilton urged Kitchener to come out to the peninsula and take a look at the 'many things of extraordinary interest'. Hamilton knew what he was talking about. Private McCowan of the 5th Battalion noted that when Hamilton went through the trenches he was 'fairly quick in picking out things'. The later renowned writer Compton Mackenzie visited Anzac on the same day as Orlo Williams, 24 May. One view dominated his memories. 'The impression which that scene from . . . Quinn's Post made on my mind has obliterated all the rest of the time at Anzac,' he wrote years later. 'I cannot recall a single incident on the way back down the valley. I only know that nothing could cleanse the smell of death from the nostrils for a fortnight afterwards. There was no herb so aromatic but it reeked of carrion, not thyme nor lavender, not even rosemary.' But the victims of the assault of 19 May were soon hygienically buried, and when Major C. J. L. Allanson, of the Indian regular army, arrived at Anzac in August, he was impressed at how 'beautifully clean and well kept' the Australians' trench system was: 'As a wonderful bit of work which sort of put itself together, it is remarkable.' Maurice Hankey,

*The corps signal office at Anzac showing something of the cave-like existence which astonished visitors to Anzac. The steam engine on the left may have been used to light corps headquarters.*

secretary to Asquith's cabinet and the Dardanelles Committee, visiting Anzac late in July was as amazed as Williams at the spectacle.[3]

The beachhead had been made strong partly through a great deal of hard work in digging an effective trench system. 'We are of course extraordinarily lucky in having among our men a really fine lot of miners who are tigers at such work,' Birdwood wrote. He proudly showed visitors over the trench system and extolled its wonders to London. Australian troops gained a reputation as experts in mining and tunnelling, and some went to Helles to instruct British troops there in the finer points of the art, such as construction to localise the effect of shellfire. Later, it would be claimed—and vigorously refuted—that the term *digger* for the ordinary Australian soldier originated at Anzac. The term seems to have gained currency during 1916 in France. Its great popularity would lead one foreign visitor to Australia in 1934 to see soldiers liking *digger* because it identified them with gold-miners rather than convicts.[4]

The risks of digging, like mining, were high. Men were entombed when Turks blew up one Australian tunnel. Birdwood told Kitchener how the Turks gave Anzac 'the devil of a shelling', and men wrote of the 'terrible sensation' caused by a

shell bursting at close quarters. In that hilly beachhead men could be in danger from their own artillery. One 4.7-inch gun was placed on the side of a hill and fired over the next hill on the reverse slope of which a brigade headquarters was dug in. When the gun was about to fire a man came out in front and blew a whistle, on hearing which everyone in the line of fire would dart for cover. One round killed eight Australians. The brigade headquarters used scarce sandbags to protect itself not against enemy fire but against this 'friendly' fire.[5]

The Turks, of course, were also continually strengthening their entrenchments. Every morning new lines of Turkish trenches appeared. Von Sanders later explained that the Turks dug trenches close to Australian lines to protect themselves from Royal Navy gunfire. On 2 July Hamilton told Kitchener of the problems all this posed for his generalship. 'The old battle tactics have clean vanished. I have only quite lately realised the new conditions. . . . you may hold one half of a straight trench and the enemy may hold the other half, and this situation may endure for weeks. The only thing is by cunning or surprise, or skill, or tremendous expenditure of high explosives, or great expenditure of good troops, to win some small tactical position which the enemy may be bound, perhaps for military or

*Troops watch the unloading of a gun from a barge at Anzac Cove, with Watson's Pier in the distance and the ubiquitous swimmers.*

perhaps for political reasons, to attack. Then you can begin to kill them pretty fast. To attack all along the line is perfect nonsense—madness.' Small-scale trench warfare thus became part of the Anzac pattern, so that Guy Dawnay, when telling his wife that some Australian troops had taken seventy yards of Turkish trenches which they had held for some hours, could comment: 'It must have been a fine effort—but they are fine fellows. What a war!'[6]

As no part of Anzac was out of range of Turkish gunfire, which could be heard at any time of the day or night, religious services were conducted in unusual circumstances. A Royal Navy chaplain who held a communion service in a dressing station told his mother, 'The Turks were shelling some lines behind us and to hear their shells going overhead and bursting close by, while the service was going on, was novel, to say the least of it.' Fortunately, the Turks had serious problems of supply and so had only enough guns and ammunition for intermittent shrapnel fire on the beach. Had it been much more consistent, the beach would have been uninhabitable. As it was, Roger Keyes thought it quite extraordinary that men were bathing on the beach all day, even though there had been a great many casualties as a result.[7]

Many, perhaps most, of the troops thought that the campaign was made tolerable only by the excellent bathing. As one Australian put it, swimming was 'not funny' because of the shells, but it was highly necessary because the water shortage meant there was no other way of washing. It was also virtually the only pastime open to soldiers during their rare 'leisure hours'. The smells of dead horses, mules and donkeys added to the unpleasantness of the beach. Alf Clennett explained to his mother, 'When one sees a couple of hundred chaps playing in the water like a lot of school boys it is hard to realize they are soldiers just out of the firing line, for a swim is great after poking about in dusty trenches all day in the heat and getting about a handful of dust down ones neck every time the old pea shooter fires.'[8]

Swimming in Anzac Cove led to familiarity which British generals recounted with relish. One well-known story, variously told of Birdwood and of the more corpulent 'old Braithwaite' (Lieutenant-Colonel W. G. Braithwaite, Godley's chief of staff), had an Anzac saying: 'My bloody oath mate, you 'ave been among the biscuits.' It was about this time—on the day of the armistice—that another piece of AIF folklore was born, with an Australian soldier allegedly butting into a conversation between high-ranking Allied and Turkish officers to ask, 'Heh! Have any of you muckers pinched my kettle?'[9] The average, less informal Australian soldier, after his swim, if not returning to the front line usually did fatigue duty, such as carrying or digging.

Brief, hazardous frolics in the waters of Anzac Cove were hardly sybaritic consolation for other privations. Hamilton told Kitchener on 3 June that only recently had the soldiers even had a blanket; a comfortable square meal and a sound, uninterrupted sleep were things they had forgotten existed. There was no canteen where the troops could buy some modest luxuries not included in their rations. Birdwood and others quickly recognised this lack, but it was the end of August before their requests brought results. Hamilton reserved the first shipment of the longed-for stores, worth six thousand pounds, for the New Zealanders and Australians, as they had had the hardest time. They were virtually sold out in an hour or two. There were also many complaints about slow delivery of mail and non-arrival of parcels from Australia.

As the weather got hotter, Australians shed many of their clothes, cut trouser legs off above the knee, and lived and fought in shorts and boots and 'not even stockings'. Some had canvas shoes, others went barefoot. English visitors to Anzac remarked on the extraordinary sight of these half-clad sunburnt men. Keyes thought the men looked very quaint when bathing, their bodies banded with white and dark brown skin. By early August newspapers as far away as New York were telling their readers of the Australians' 'huge frames and gaunt limbs . . . burnt by the sun to a dull brick-red'. John de Vitre, a Royal Navy chaplain, told his relatives that 'a chap' came to his ambulance section 'and sat down to feed and I really thought he was a Maori or a black man: he only had on his boots and shorts and his body was almost quite black . . . but . . . he was really a white man. . . . he certainly was an extraordinary colour, quite the blackest white man I have ever seen.' Doctors saw an advantage in the paucity of clothing: if a man were wounded there was less chance of the bullet carrying cloth into the body.[10]

With the heat came the flies. They always become a nuisance at Anzac from about early June, when the weather warms up. But they were particularly bad in 1915, because of the lack of sanitation and the putrefying bodies. Complaints were legion. One Western Australian countryman thought the flies at Anzac were as bad as at home. Another wrote, 'Some of them must have tin-openers on their feet: they bite that hard.' Monash found the flies 'dreadful'.[11]

Operations in June and July were on a small scale compared with what had been and what was to come. During these months, Anzac warfare took the form of sniping, mining, tunnelling and bomb-throwing, with occasional relatively small trench raids, all against the continual backdrop of shellfire. Bomb-throwing could last throughout the night at Quinn's Post.[12] It was at this time that the periscope rifle, invented by Lance-Corporal W. C. B. Beech of the 2nd Battalion, came into widespread use, 'with astounding results'. Birdwood told Kitchener, 'We've been able to dominate the enemy's snipers.' The future author Ion Idriess described this 'invention of ingenious simplicity' whereby two small looking-glasses attached to the rifle-butt enabled the firer to observe over the trench when his head was safely below the sandbags. Birdwood told Hamilton of a Queensland light-horseman named Billy Sing, 'a great marksman' who lived 'in a little hole on the extreme right of the line', with a companion with a telescope to spot. Sing claimed a phenomenally large number of victims. Hamilton relayed the story to Kitchener. The sniper's mates were just as impressed. Lieutenant Oliver Hogue of the light horse claimed that officers had checked Sing's record of over 150 Turks. For a time Idriess 'spotted' for Sing, known as the Murderer, 'a little chap, very dark . . . a picturesque looking mankiller'.[13]

Difficulties in arranging proper burials had unpleasant side effects. Digging saps

*Improvised 'bombs' being made from jam-tins with fragments of Turkish shell, cut-up barbed wire, stones, nails, and the like serving as shrapnel; the explosive could be gun-cotton, and the contraption would be completed with a detonator and fuse. The Anzacs on arrival at Gallipoli possessed neither hand grenades nor experience in using them, whereas the Turks had stocks of factory-made 'bombs' and, on Liman von Sanders' orders, had had some training. Bomb-throwing could last all night at Quinn's.*

or widening trenches often meant unearthing bodies. 'Many times', wrote Private A. W. Skinner, 'I stumbled over boots sticking up in the ground and felt the earth give way as I trod on a dead body.'

Despite all, Second Lieutenant Smythe thought life at Anzac not unduly unpleasant, except that the food was uninteresting. As Alf Clennett put it, they were stationed on a hill where the ground was very dry, so it was quite healthy living like rabbits in dugouts. On the other hand, G. A. Radnell experienced both hell and heaven on the same day. Hell was Anzac with its dirt, flies, lice, water shortage, never undressing except when swimming, mother earth for a bed and the Turks to contend with. After being wounded he found heaven in being washed, having a clean bed, good food and Australian nurses 'to contend with'.[14]

Above them the soldiers sometimes saw aircraft, forerunners of a new type of warfare which in a few years would make beachheads like Anzac absolutely untenable. Aerial reconnaissance was useful to both sides, but Godley, for one, thought it galling that nothing could be done about German aeroplanes. Britain, 'the richest nation on earth', 'ought to have dozens' to drive away enemy aircraft. Frank Howitt, a twenty-year-old British lieutenant on Gallipoli, could not imagine why every nation did not possess hundreds of aircraft. Apart from the material damage they could do, they added yet more strain to the horrors of war. 'The effect of these aerial bombs is much more stupefying than an ordinary shell, as you can see them coming, without the slightest chance of getting out of their way.' For much the same reason Private Paterson was 'in mortal dread' of aeroplane bombs.[15]

Monash had time to complain about the laurels which the 1st Division, and especially the 3rd Brigade, had been receiving at the expense of his own 4th Brigade. At the end of May he said that the public would not hear much about his brigade's work as 'Charley Bean rarely comes our way'. He continued: 'Bean seems to write nothing but about the Australian Division; his boosting of the 3rd Brigade on the first two days is simply ridiculous. My Brigade had a far worse time (see the casualty list) and made more ground than any other Brigade.' In a passage unique amongst all comment on the landing, in which he was guilty of a few factual errors, Monash termed it 'a mere nothing compared with what followed'. He did not state, although he may have thought, that his own brigade would have been more effective in the first few hours of 25 April. He stressed that for five weeks his brigade was in the front trenches—with men spending forty-eight hours in the firing line and then having forty-eight hours relief—and that the formation had been 'fighting particularly hard the whole time'. He 'gave Bean a good talking about it' and hoped he would mend his ways. An alternative publicity outlet presented itself in the person of C. P. Smith, a journalist for the Melbourne *Argus*, who spent intermittent periods with the brigade and whom Monash found far more agreeable.[16]

Amidst all the 'unstinted praise' which 'the home forces' gave the Australians and New Zealanders for their 'magnificent' work, there remained some reservations. One was expressed by Private Richards of the Army Medical Corps: 'There is no doubt that our men are hard and even cruel. They are willing to bayonet helpless Turks when they could have spared them.' But the circumstances, he believed, made men 'restless and revengeful'. The Australians were 'good at fighting but not at much else,' was one blunt comment. Frank Howitt, at a rest camp on Imbros Island in July, was in a bivouac next to some Australians. These colonials had left such an extraordinarily bad name in their wake that Howitt's curiosity was roused. Certainly, he noted, their patriotism to the Mother Country was astonishing, 'and as fighting men they had no peers, and that was what they had come for; but with that one could say no more.' Roger Keyes thought the Australians and New Zealanders 'extraordinary people. . . . The men, or 90% of them, never salute—seldom say "sir".' By September, Major Allanson still thought the Australians magnificent soldiers but added 'their idea of discipline is ludicrous'. Allanson had in mind the 'discipline' of cleanliness or sanitation. The Australians' habits, he wrote, 'are just too disgusting and filthy for words. With the result that we all suffer and flies are worse than one could imagine possible. [The] number of unnecessary cases of sickness brought on by gross want of care is terrible.'[17]

When one considers the enormous strain of life at Anzac, and the scale of casualties—by 4 June, for example, Godley's division had sustained a casualty rate of over 50 per cent—it is not surprising that there were cases of self-inflicted wounds or that there were numerous offences leading to courts-martial. Some offenders, even junior officers, were drunk in the front line, but a rum issue to the

*A sergeant demonstrates a Japanese trench mortar mounted on an improvised platform. Four of these were issued at Anzac in mid-May, two to each division. They were an improvement on the primitive Garland mortar, the most commonly used mortar at Anzac, which was never very effective.*

front-line troops was standard procedure at times of particular stress. To fall asleep while on sentry duty was an extremely serious military offence, but in terms of human physiology it was explicable, as men under constant fire for weeks or months were exhausted, ill, and generally not very well fed.[18]

The commanders saw no prospect of a quick victory for their men. Birdwood told Kitchener that the Turks, although not well trained, were 'most formidable when in trenches and give me a terrible warm reception when I attack—so much so, that I really often wonder how I am ever to get a move on from here, when Achi Baba has been taken'.[19] Birdwood frequently put such pessimisic thoughts on paper, but even the assumption that Achi Baba would be taken proved optimistic. Hamilton agreed that the Turks 'would stick it out as long as, or longer than, most', as 'this cursed trench warfare' developed, until 'this infernal place' became 'a regular fortress'. Previous standards did not apply, and gains that used to be deemed hardly worth a few dozen casualties were now considered worth far heavier losses. 'There is no strategy, no tactics,' Hamilton commented; 'all that is wanted is a high courage . . . and a clear determination not to let loss of life stand in the way of gaining a few yards of ground.' He thought it very hard to weigh the chances of taking the all-important Kilid Bahr Plateau, overlooking the Turkish forts on the Narrows.[20]

Hamilton thought the Turks had plenty of ammunition and apparently no lack of reinforcements. At the end of May the British high command estimated that the Turkish force at the Dardanelles, despite heavy losses, had grown from 75,000 in April to 125,000, approximately equal to Hamilton's force. Hamilton was worried about his own supplies, especially after the loss in May of three old battleships to German submarines hampered sea transport and weakened his naval support. He was especially worried about his future water supply. Birdwood had 'many sleep-less nights' worrying that the Turks might attack Anzac at a weak point. On the other hand, he hoped that they might expend themselves on a big frontal attack. Godley thought the worst the enemy could do was to bring up heavy howitzers.[21]

A landing by reinforcements at Bulair was considered. There was some wishful thinking that Greece and Bulgaria might enter the war on the Allied side. Italy 'joined in the argument' on 23 May but gave no help at the Dardanelles because of Russian objections. Birdwood employed various ruses—like having his troops cheering or showing bayonets above the parapet—to trick the Turks into thinking an attack was imminent and so induce them to waste ammunition. The prospect of a winter campaign was already a nightmare, and to many the chances of a success-ful evacuation seemed slim.[22]

So the Australians were reduced to holding on for months in appalling condi-tions. Even though it was a matter of self-preservation, they added a reputation for steadfastness to their renown for reckless dash. They 'displayed greater qualities of endurance' than Colonel Brudenell White had ever expected. They were cheerful and patient and lavished colossal labour on their defensive works. Hamilton told Asquith of his order of merit among the troops in his command. 'These New Zealanders and Australians and, best of all, the Australian Light Horse and the New Zealand Mounted Rifles, and above all the last named, are the flower of our troops or of any other troops in the world.' Godley was 'very proud to command such splendid men as these are' and told General Rawlinson on the Western Front that they were splendid fellows who had fought like tigers. Kitchener early in June told Edmund Barton, the former Australian prime minister, how greatly he appreciated the work of the Australasians, adding, 'I can't have too many of them.' Writing from London, Barton told Andrew Fisher, 'This community looks upon Australia with a fervency of gratitude and affection which no pen can describe.'[23]

# CHAPTER 15

# *REINFORCEMENTS FROM AUSTRALIA*

$O$N THE Australian home front, one prompt response to the news from Gallipoli was a marked, sustained increase in enlistments, which reached its zenith in the great Victorian recruiting drive of July. In the first four months of 1915, 33,758 men volunteered; in the following four months, 85,320. Munro Ferguson told Bonar Law that this 'eclipsed the most sanguine expectations'. The news was passed, by way of Hamilton, to the Australians on Gallipoli. John Alexander (Alec) Raws was one of the thousands in Victoria who enlisted in July. Born in Manchester in 1883 and educated in South Australia, he was a sportsman who had worked on newspapers since 1902. When he enlisted he was leader of the *Argus* reporting staff; his brother, Robert , formerly a warehouseman, had already left Australia in May as a second lieutenant. Alec told his father, the Reverend John G. Raws, who lived in Malvern, Adelaide, why he was enlisting. 'I do not think that I was ever a great man for heroics but . . . I curse . . . the hideous fraud of a civilisation, which permits this dreadful welter of blood and suffering to have enveloped the world. . . . And yet I go to join in it, believing that the only hope for the salvation of the world is a speedy victory for the Allies.'[1] A Melbourne correspondent told Monash that everything in the city was connected with the war and that new training camps were being set up in the country. A relative in camp at the Ballarat Show Ground told him the animal pens had been floored and the recruits slept on the boards and that the new recruits in his company of 161 were 'simply splendid. They all work like ones possessed. Keen as mustard and every one up to standard intelligence—includes civil engineers, architects, accountants, commissioners for taking affidavits, telegraphists, bank managers, etc.' Meanwhile, Melbourne was giving a great deal of help to returned sick and wounded soldiers, while donations to comforts funds greatly exceeded Sydney's. From Katanning, Louis Roth told Monash that all country businesses had great difficulty carrying on, as nearly all of their clerical staff had volunteered. In mid-September Roth was still anxiously awaiting the fall of Constantinople, rumours of which sometimes circulated.[2]

Alec Raws would not reach Gallipoli, unlike Robert whose 23rd Battalion became part of the 2nd Division, formed in Egypt out of the 5th, 6th and 7th brigades. Meanwhile the 8th Brigade was being raised in Australia. As well, some specific units were created at Britain's request. For example, early in July the Army Council asked if Australia could provide a battery of four 5-inch howitzers for Gallipoli. Immediately, the government said it could, although administrative problems followed and the unit did not reach Egypt until late September. In that month the Commonwealth government offered a mining corps of up to a thousand men to serve in the Dardanelles or elsewhere. The Army Council greatly appreciated the offer, saying the corps would be most valuable in the form of tunnelling companies.[3]

Munro Ferguson told Bonar Law, early in his term as Colonial Secretary, that although there were 'doubtless faults in method and some lack of foresight' in Australia's war effort, there was 'also wonderful vitality and adaptability in facing hard facts'. Already the Defence Department had equipped and embarked an impressive number of men. He thought Pearce was 'the best man available' as Minister for Defence, although he lacked initiative and was 'too much in the hands of his military advisers'. The Governor-General thought that some of the administrative failings during the great recruiting boom occurred because nearly all the best officers were at the front. For this reason the government refused to allow Lieutenant-Colonel Thomas H. Dodds, the Adjutant-General, to go to Egypt in July to join the 2nd Division. Munro Ferguson was also worried about the inadequate supply of rifles from the War Office, which he thought hampered recruiting.[4] Training might have suffered, but the whole of the expeditionary forces were provided with 'rifles of the latest pattern', 25 per cent of which were made at the Commonwealth Small Arms Factory at Lithgow, which had begun production as the AIF began recruiting.[5]

The newspapers remained full of news from Gallipoli, Bean's reports being read far and wide. Local papers published lists of men from the district who had been passed fit to join the AIF, doing 'such gallant service for the Empire' at the Dardanelles. The press emphasised the heroism of the troops, but this was realistically grounded in an awareness of the hardships and horrors endured. The meaning of the casualty lists was clear enough. Descriptions of bomb-throwing at ten metres, of attacks on sections of trenches and generally of life at Anzac meant that civilians broadly understood the nature of the fighting. Most, too, would have comprehended the difference between 'understanding' and experiencing. Letters from the front did not always protect the reader from the worst. Information from letters was passed around by word of mouth, and many were published, although these tended to be the less horrific ones. The first wounded were arriving back in Australia in July too.[6]

*An Australian soldier displays one of the British Maxim guns used by the Anzacs on Gallipoli. When the AIF left Australia, men had not been specifically recruited for machine-gun work, and there were only two Maxim guns per battalion. By about August 1915, as the techniques of trench warfare were being learnt, the allotment of machine-guns was doubled.*

On 4 August parliament marked the first anniversary of the war's outbreak by affirming Australia's resolve to fight on to victory and for the 'ideals of liberty and justice which are the common and sacred cause of the Allied nations'. One aspect of Australia's commitment to the war was summarised a week later in Prime Minister Andrew Fisher's budget speech. He estimated that the Commonwealth's expenditure for 1915–16 would be twice that of 1914–15, that is, £70 million compared with £35 million. Four-fifths of that increase was accounted for by greater war expenditure. At this time forty thousand men were doing their initial training in Australia, while seventy-six thousand had sailed overseas. Also, twenty-four thousand horses had been sent away with the AIF. Captain Cyril Seelenmayer, a veterinary officer, told Monash there were more horses in Egypt than the military authorities knew what to do with. He found it discouraging to care for horses which seemed not to be wanted.[7]

Henry Stead, an Englishman visiting Melbourne, sent Lewis Harcourt an impression of the pride which in Australia helped assuage the grief. Australia, Stead explained, was so far away from the rest of the world that its people had the most

*Horse teams of the 5th Field Battery leave Anzac in mid-May for return with all the other artillery teams to Alexandria. Few positions at Anzac were suitable for field guns. Such field artillery as was retained at Anzac was manoeuvred up the hills by the soldiers themselves—most artillery horse teams stayed on ship off shore. Those of the 5th Battery, however, had been landed.*

distorted idea of what was possible. He gave one illustration which he said was typical of hundreds. When the light horse paraded through the streets, the remark was heard everywhere; 'Ah, just wait till these fellows get to the front, then things will begin to move.' 'And they actually did believe,' Stead continued, '. . . that the few thousand lighthorsemen . . . would be the means of defeating the Germans! Quite otherwise sane business men insisted that this would be the case. Many people refuse to believe that there are any troops but Australians on Gallipoli and when one proves that there are many more British they say "Oh well our fellows are doing all the fighting anyway."'[8] It had taken less than four months for the Australians on Gallipoli to create this deeply ingrained belief among the folk back home.

Such insouciance was linked with continuing almost total faith, on the part of the government, that Britons knew best how to run the military and diplomatic affairs of Empire. British leaders had the experience, and they were on the spot. How could their superior expertise be challenged by politicians in Australia who knew very little of the theatre in which the AIF was employed? For this reason, and because of loyalty to and trust in the revered leaders of the British Empire, there was less controversy in Australia over the conduct of the campaign than in Britain or on the peninsula itself. Munro Ferguson thought that Australians understood the 'preliminary naval bungling' of the campaign. They took it very well, he told London. 'The absence of all carping here over the premature bombardment, and postponed lists of heavy casualties, is above all praise.' 'No grievance', he wrote in mid-July, could 'affect the war-like enthusiasm of Australia, which steadily increases.'[9]

At Westminster, Asquith's coalition government kept a tight clamp on the Dardanelles issue. On 30 June the House of Commons held its first, short, debate on the campaign. Its most noteworthy feature was the complaint by Sir Henry Dalziel, a hard-headed Scot and clever parliamentary debater who became a newspaper proprietor, turning *Reynolds's Weekly Newspaper* into a prosperous Liberal Party journal. An ally of Lloyd George, he was no admirer of Asquith. He pressed his grievance that thus far the government had given no real information. However, some of the truth was now emerging, from German press reports, and as men returned from the Dardanelles. A noteworthy example was Lieutenant-Colonel

Lord Rochdale, who commanded the 126th Brigade, part of the British 42nd Division, at Helles. He thought casualties were excessive and avoidable and conditions at Helles harsh. As a member of the House of Lords he thought it his duty to tell leading ministers of the problems facing the Mediterranean Expeditionary Force. He visited England during the summer, reporting to Kitchener, Bonar Law, Balfour and others.[10]

The British press was not muzzled. Lord Northcliffe, who believed the hushing up of the Dardanelles difficulty was 'a fatal blunder', criticised Kitchener in his newspapers. Hamilton told Kitchener the press baron was 'a dirty dog'; he would 'gladly put a bullet into him', as he thought him a traitor. Birdwood was delighted that the *Daily Mail*'s offices were wrecked because it had attacked Kitchener.[11]

On the Gallipoli Peninsula, criticism abounded over conduct of the campaign. Orlo Williams noted that even among generals much fault was found in Hamilton's headquarters and in its conduct of operations. Major Allanson was appalled at the conditions on Gallipoli, felt sick at the horrifying loss of life, and noted that everyone regarded it as 'criminal: one of the greatest crimes in history'. In June, Kitchener was told that Hamilton was 'physically incapable of standing the racket of this show'; that Major-General W. P. Braithwaite, his chief of staff, was an obstinate, dangerous fool; and that both men should be recalled, for the expedition was being badly handled as chaos engulfed the army's affairs. Even Birdwood told Colonel FitzGerald, Kitchener's personal military secretary, of unhappiness on Hamilton's staff and of Braithwaite's unpopularity.[12]

The contrast between living conditions at Anzac and on the *Aragon*, which housed line-of-communication staff, and the *Arcadian*, that 'magnificent pleasure steamer', as Monash termed it in May, which for a time housed Hamilton's headquarters, became a byword on the peninsula, giving rise to ill-feeling. The contrast was not entirely one of rank; General Godley and his wife, who was in Egypt organising convalescent homes for New Zealanders, expressed views that could have come from a private in the firing line—had he been able to see the luxury aboard the *Aragon*, which was 'like an Enchanted Isle'. Lady Godley told her husband of two colonels who were full of abuse of the staff officers on the ship, who, they said, knew nothing, did nothing and cared less, and who ought to be put in the trenches for a bit to learn to be civil. Three weeks later Lady Godley wrote to her husband, 'I had heard that some bombs had been dropped on Sir Ian's camp at Mudros—it would have been better if they had been plumped on the "Aragon".' In January 1916 a British subaltern visiting the *Aragon* was to complain that he was 'treated with the usual insolence and rudeness meted out to strangers. . . . One comes on board into tremendous luxury, but one immediately feels that one is an interloper, and has no business there among the beautifully turned out permanent Staff.'[13]

In Australia little or nothing was known of these recriminations on the peninsula. Australians had realised for some time that the campaign was going badly, but indicative of the largely inescapable limitations under which the Commonwealth government worked was its request, in mid-June, for a supply of large-scale maps of the Dardanelles. Fifty copies of the War Office map of the peninsula, on the scale of one inch to one mile, were sent to High Commissioner Sir George Reid to be forwarded to Australia, and more detailed maps were to follow. The bundle of fifty reached Melbourne early in September. Munro Ferguson kept five copies and sent forty-five to the Prime Minister's Department.[14] At this late stage of the campaign there was no chance that they might help the Australian government exert some influence over the conduct of operations at Anzac.

The great increase in recruiting encouraged Melbourne and London to agree to double the flow of reinforcements leaving Australia from 5,263 a month to 10,526. This was in addition to supplementary drafts for the new units previously mentioned. Every week from May to August two or more ships would reach Egypt, carrying Australian troops. The embarkations were not always carried out correctly. One example was the departure of the *Euripides* from Melbourne on 8 May, carrying the 24th Battalion with sixty more men than it should have had. During ensuing months the Military Board spent some time examining this most unsatisfactory occurrence, along with lengthy discussions on the errors in the nominal rolls of embarking units. It recorded that because of 'the irresponsible manner in which troops have been embarked at the port of Melbourne' it was impossible to do justice to the dependants of the soldiers embarked. 'An exposure . . . would be considered a public scandal', and it was thought better to keep the matter out of public scrutiny, especially as there was no evidence that similar laxity existed at other embarkation ports.[15]

The AIF base in Cairo complained that contingents reaching Egypt were not as fully equipped as desirable. The situation steadily improved as Australia made many articles not previously produced in the country—for example, heliographs, enamelled water bottles, bits, stirrups, spurs and shovels. However, the AIF in Egypt still had to rely on Britain to supply deficiencies.[16]

There were no threats from enemy warships, but the typical voyage was not without hazards and upsets. Deaths at sea, for example from pneumonia, were still too numerous. When the Victorians of the 6th Brigade reached Colombo, two battalions were allowed ashore but the 23rd was not. Some of its members decided to defy orders and rushed the guard on the gangway. In the mêlée, men got black eyes or broken noses or were knocked unconscious. Such scenes were not repeated at Suez, for the ships anchored well away from the wharves. The men did not see the town. On another ship, a lieutenant was annoyed that men who were denied shore leave at Bombay were 'treated and spoken to like naughty children'.[17]

The ships from Australia were now arriving in Cairo's summer, when training was virtually impossible from 9 a.m. until 5 p.m. Even to a young Western Australian, accustomed to a hot climate, Cairo's heat was almost unbearable. This sandgroper's diary contained constant references to 'Hellish hot weather', 'Weather hot as blazes', 'Hell with the lid off', and similar heartfelt, and no doubt sweaty, complaints. The temperature in one officer's tent averaged 115 to 118 degrees Fahrenheit each day for a week—and that was a double Bell tent sprayed at intervals with water. He believed that in the men's tents the mercury rose to 132 degrees. Major E. T. Brind told his mother of the extreme heat in Cairo, with 'a wind blowing like fury off the desert'. The weather was adversely affecting health, and Brind was anxious to avoid Cairo because of its unpleasant smells in the heat, and for other reasons. 'The whole place is rotten. Sodom and Gomorrah must have been quite decent in comparison. . . . the rottenness of the whole thing is appalling. It's a cruel shame to put troops in such close proximity to it.' Despite all, great numbers of Australian soldiers still thronged Cairo's streets. Tensions between them and English soldiers persisted. H. T. C. Alcock told his brother that they could not 'get on together at all'. 'They don't look at each other in the street. I think the reason is that the Tommies get only 1/6d per day and the Australians get 6/-.'[18]

The city's outskirts could bring disillusionment. Lieutenant J. T. H. Aram, lawyer, schoolteacher and accountant from St Kilda, Victoria, told his mother: 'I don't think I can sing the "Bedouin's Love Song" and "Dervish Vigil" with such feeling as I once put into it. The reason being that I see Bedouin camps almost daily, and such dirt and squalor you could never imagine.'[19]

Sir John Maxwell, British commander-in-chief in Egypt, thought that some of the Australian soldiers were behaving badly because they were 'full of fight' and wanted to get to the front where they would train on better than in Cairo. Here they questioned things (for example, discipline and orders), whereas at the front they would see the need for battle discipline. Some Australians rioted on Saturday 31 July, burning down a few brothels. Second Lieutenant W. H. Bertwistle, who saw it, told his family thousands were involved, but Robert Raws said that only thirty were responsible for causing destruction. He stressed the trying conditions in the high summer and claimed that apart from nurses and British officers' families, '99 out of every 100 white women' in Cairo were prostitutes.[20]

Colonel Victor Sellheim, commandant of the AIF's administrative headquarters in Egypt, regretfully told his government that it would have to pay another bill for the damage done—and this time Wellington would not share the bill as there were no New Zealanders among the rioters. Robert Muirhead Collins, the English-born official representative in the High Commissioner's Office in London, commented to Senator Pearce on the latest riot: 'It is really dreadful reading. The Egyptians must think they would be just as well off to have Germans there as to have Australians.' He thought more drastic action by the responsible officers was needed and that the sale of liquor to Australian soldiers in Egypt should be stopped. Maxwell complained that he had 'no end of complaints of brutalities committed by unidentified men. It is a thousand pities they do these things,' he went on, 'but their officers cannot restrain them and once they are in the town, their numbers alone paralyse civil police, military police, and picquets so the blackguards remain unidentified, and from a false idea of loyalty to each other, the good name earned so worthily by the Australians is covered with dirt in Egypt. It is sad that amongst the finest body of men I have ever seen, there should be a few—quite a few—that would bring disgrace on any Community.'[21]

For all their faults, and with all their hot-headedness, Australians could be cool when it counted in battle. 'What heroes our chaps have been,' the recently arrived Lieutenant Aram, writing from his camp at Heliopolis, told his mother. 'They are worshipped by the Indians who call them the White Ghurkas.' The relationship between Ghurkas and Australians was very friendly, although they understood little of each others' language. The Ghurkas sometimes called themselves 'Black Australians'. The mettle of the Australians—and Ghurkas and others—at Anzac would soon be tested again, for by mid-July at the beachhead there were constant rumours of a big move which, it was hoped, would soon 'resolve itself into a rout of the Turk'.[22]

*An Indian mountain battery at Gallipoli. Two mounted batteries arrived at Anzac with the landing, each having six small 10-pounder guns, manoeuvrable on muleback. There was Indian infantry at Anzac too, including Sikhs and Gurkhas. Warmth developed between them and Australians, particularly with the Gurkhas, as reflected in such terms as 'Black Australians' and 'White Gurkhas'.*

# CHAPTER 16

# 'ON THE BRINK OF THE UNKNOWN'

$I$N LONDON and at Hamilton's headquarters there were lengthy discussions about a new offensive. In mid-May the Liberal government, in its last days, had decided to send another division from Britain to Helles, this being the 52nd, comprising Territorials from the Scottish Lowlands. It arrived on 6 June. Lord Selborne expressed what was no doubt a prevailing view among the Conservative ministers who joined Asquith's coalition government: 'We are in complete agreement about the colossal blundering of our predecessors. But we could not withdraw when we took office; nor can we now.' This was for reasons of national prestige and influence in Persia, Egypt and the Balkans. Selborne even thought withdrawal would mean rebellion in India. Kitchener feared 'a rising in the Moslem world' if Gallipoli were abandoned.[1]

Churchill, despite his lesser portfolio, was on the Dardanelles Committee and annoyed many by maintaining his pressure for reinforcing Hamilton's army. Like Hamilton, he remained optimistic about the eventual outcome of the campaign. On 5 June, in an oratorical extravaganza delivered to his constituents in Dundee, Churchill, desperately anxious to justify his Dardanelles strategy, appeared intoxicated by optimism. He fantasised about 'the fall of a world-famous capital', beyond 'those few miles of ridge and scrub' currently the home of Hamilton's force. He spoke of 'a brilliant and formidable' victory, 'shortening the duration of the war' and leading 'to a triumphant peace'. Unusually for Churchill at this time, he painted an entrancing picture of Empire loyalty. 'See Australia and New Zealand smiting down in the last and finest crusade the combined barbarism of Prussia and of Turkey. (Cheers.) General Louis Botha holding South Africa for the King. (Cheers.) See Canada defending to the death the last few miles of shattered Belgium. Look further, and, across the smoke and carnage of the immense battlefield, look forward to the vision of a united British Empire on the calm background of a liberated Europe.'[2]

Bonar Law, the new Secretary of State for the Colonies, thought the Dardanelles operation could not be abandoned, but he was most pessimistic about its prospects, believing that the Turks would not succumb even if Hamilton were heavily reinforced. But evacuation, as well as being politically undesirable, seemed militarily impossible, a view endorsed by much professional opinion, including generals on the spot. Kitchener had a nightmare vision of the slaughter on the helpless, departing boats. These considerations prevailed over the views of 'Westerners' like Sir Douglas Haig, who in December was to become commander-in-chief of the British Expeditionary Force on the Western Front, and Sir Henry Wilson, chief liaison officer with the French army, both of whom wanted 'to clear out of the place [Gallipoli]' before becoming hopelessly involved and thus crippling the Allies on the Western Front. After yet another round of discussions, by

*The Turkish Zone commander, Essad Pasha, holds a conference with his staff, including Mustafa Kemal (standing on his right) at a point overlooking the battlefields. Essad's headquarters were almost directly in line with Anzac and about a kilometre and a half east from the Australian front line, near Scrubby Knoll. From within a few metres of this spot, a constant look-out could be maintained on the Anzac sector from Courtney's Post to Lone Pine.*

the end of July the new government had decided to send Hamilton a further six divisions from Britain: three (10th, 11th, 13th,) from Kitchener's New Army of wartime volunteers, two Territorial formations (53rd and 54th) and a Mounted Yeomanry Division—which of course was to fight on Gallipoli as an infantry division. All but the last of these reinforcement divisions had already sailed. Their arrival made it clear to the men at Anzac that a new offensive was in the offing. On 17 July an AIF sapper wrote in his diary, 'I heard there were 25,000 troops on Imbros waiting for the move so that they can attack Hill 971.'[3]

The cabinet was also anxious to get some first-hand information on what was actually happening at the front. In mid-July it decided that Churchill should pay a visit. He was delighted, but the news caused 'a perfect furore' at Gallipoli. Godley wondered how 'these Colonials' would react to seeing Churchill on the peninsula. Major Allanson caustically observed, 'I believe he would be scragged alive.' Many in the Dardanelles theatre held Churchill 'responsible for many thousand lives.' In Cairo both Maxwell and Sir Henry McMahon, the High Commissioner, blamed him for the Gallipoli failure. In the event, cabinet decided it would be better if Churchill did not go. Instead, Maurice Hankey, the cabinet secretary, would go. This news perturbed Hamilton, who had very little success to show for several months of bloodshed on the peninsula and who knew that Hankey had the ear of cabinet, and especially of Asquith. Hamilton wanted Hankey kept under tight control while he was in the theatre, so that his feet were set 'firmly in the right path'. He told Admiral de Robeck, 'My idea would be to give him a shake down in the sand together with a few centipedes and flies. Then to send him in charge of a trusty staff officer to Anzac and Helles to be shelled, and then he will be anxious to get back as quickly as he can without hearing too much naval and military irresponsible gossip.'[4]

The reinforcements just mentioned were significantly larger than the force originally allocated to Hamilton. They were dispatched following new War Office and Admiralty assessments, drawing on reports from commanders at the Dardanelles, which analysed the chances of a new offensive being successful. At Helles, a series of attacks, drawing to a conclusion in June, produced heavy casualties and slight gains. By the middle of the month Birdwood decided, and Hamilton agreed, that the next main offensive would be based on Anzac, with the aim of breaking out of the beachhead and gaining the heights of the Sari Bair range, which overlooked

Anzac and also the Dardanelles. For weeks the launching of this great operation occupied the minds 'waking or sleeping' of the men on Hamilton's and Birdwood's staffs. 'The Sari Bair hills', Guy Dawnay told his wife in August, 'are a huge knot of hills nearly 1000 feet high at the highest point. Very big and rough, and intersected with huge ravines down which the watercourses (now dry) run.' Mustafa Kemal expected a British outflanking move through this country. Major Richard Casey, who three months earlier had ruefully admitted that Hill 971, at the peak of the Sari Bair range, dominated the Anzac beachhead and was a constant menace to progress, had over subsequent weeks frequently discussed in his diary possible ways to approach that menacing feature.[5]

The new plan led to what has often been called the battle of Sari Bair. Much of the responsibility for the detailed planning for the advance on the Sari Bair ridge lay with Birdwood and his chief of staff, Lieutenant-Colonel Andrew Skeen. Its genesis can be traced back to the first half of May. North of the Anzac perimeter the Turks, despite Kemal's foresight, were defending the country only lightly. This provided some opportunity for a surprise advance aimed at capturing the crest of the Sari Bair range before the Turks could put a large force there. As it eventually evolved, the Anzac offensive was to begin on the evening of 6 August with a major feint on the southern flank at Lone Pine. This was designed to hold Turkish forces in that sector and would begin a few hours before the start of the main offensive from the Anzac beachhead. This was to be a 'left hook', a breakout through Anzac's

*Horace Moore-Jones, North Side of the Sphinx, 1915 (watercolour, 24.9 × 34.1 cm).*

northern perimeter, to begin with an overnight march through extremely rugged country—worse than the Anzac beachhead itself. The aim was to capture the undefended crests of the Sari Bair range—Hill 971, Hill Q and Chunuk Bair— before the Turks realised what was afoot and moved troops there. With the crest securely held, the British, it was hoped, could dominate the Turkish guns barring the strait, prevent the Turks using the waterway, and render the Turkish positions on the peninsula untenable. At dawn on 7 August, New Zealand troops, having taken Chunuk Bair during the night, would move down the slope to the rear of the Turkish lines on Baby 700. At the same time the 3rd Light Horse Brigade would make a frontal assault, across the Nek, against the same Turkish lines, which would thus be caught in a pincer movement. Of the three main attacking columns which composed the 'left hook', the New Zealanders would have the shortest distance to march. The 29th Indian Brigade was to take Hill Q. John Monash's 4th Brigade was given the hardest task, to take Hill 971. Monash's left flank was to be protected by British reinforcements. Some of these were landed at Anzac, but most were in Lieutenant-General F. W. Stopford's 9th Corps, which would land at Suvla Bay, about five kilometres north of Anzac.[6]

Since mid-July Monash had been considering his plans for his brigade's role in the offensive. By early August he was having a series of conferences which went exhaustively into all the details. He took Stopford on a walk through Monash Valley and busily pored over maps of the route his men would take on their night march.[7]

The commanders displayed varied and fluctuating degrees of optimism about the success of the coming offensive. Stopford made many criticisms of the roles planned for his corps. Birdwood had long foreseen that an advance would be 'a most difficult operation'. The Turks would 'hold their trenches like the devil and cause us very heavy casualties'. The crests of Sari Bair seemed awesomely formidable. 'The hill I must tackle', he told Kitchener, 'is really very much more difficult than what I had to take the day we landed, as it is so terribly precipitous and cut up with ravines.' Even the most difficult country, he regretfully noted, was 'trenched to a very great extent'. Despite many doubts, he still thought there was some chance of success.[8] Godley was similarly cautious, although he trusted that 'Freddy Stopford's re-inforcements' would enable the British 'to make a significant push to get the Fleet through the Narrows, at last'. On the day he first saw Anzac, Hankey told Kitchener, 'The great hope as regards the next push lies in the fact that the Australians are to be used.' Major-General F. C. Shaw, commanding the 13th Division, thought the plan of operations quite sound; but Major Allanson, commanding the 1/6th Gurkhas, a unit in the 29th Indian Brigade, did not like his march plan for the night of 6 August, thinking that any subaltern at a promotion examination who made such a proposal would not be praised. Hamilton on 5 August told Asquith that his force was 'on the brink of the unknown sure only that big events are coming up'. Hamilton's tension explains why he impressed one visitor then 'as being cold, formal and non-communicative'. Next day Birdwood told de Robeck, 'I feel sure my boys will shove through.'[9] At no stage does any commander seem to have thought of using the Australian light horse, in their proper role as mounted infantry, to help speed up the advance on the Suvla plain, in terrain that would have held not the slightest terrors for these skilled, hardy horsemen.

Ellis Ashmead-Bartlett later claimed that he was 'filled with alarm' when he heard of the plan on 9 July. 'To me it is an utterly impracticable operation of war... which will only lead to fresh reverses and enormous losses. I have never heard of troops being asked to perform such a strange feat of arms before. . . . How can the Australians successfully debouch from . . . Anzac and storm these hills?'

*Before the attack at Lone Pine, the 2nd Battalion war diary for 5 August read: 'All bayonets being sharpened by armourer . . . for attack tomorrow.'*

'How', he asked on 5 August, 'can the landing at Suvla possibly succeed?' Compton Mackenzie lunched with Stopford in his mess on 5 August, assessing him as 'a man of great kindliness and personal charm, whose conversation . . . left me . . . without hope of victory at Suvla.' It is only fair to add that Hamilton had tried without success to obtain more effective corps commanders from the Western Front. A brigadier-general sitting opposite Stopford held forth truculently about the folly of the plan which the 9th Corps was meant to implement.[10]

The 2nd Battalion War Diary noted on the 5th: 'All bayonets being sharpened by armourer . . . for attack tomorrow.' Men in Godley's division to go in the night march were told that none but urgent casualties would be evacuated before daylight, and that the first night of the operation would be sleepless, and the second probably so. As the hour came nearer, Birdwood wrote to Roger Keyes, 'We are on for a real big thing tonight, and I hope that humanly speaking everything possible to be done to ensure success has been seen to, and I have every hope that my boys will carry all before them, but it will be an anxious time.' Major Stanley Argyle, on the staff of No. 1 Australian General Hospital, was more sanguine. On 22 July he expected the capture of the Dardanelles within four weeks. 'If the Russians hold Warsaw and we get Constantinople,' he continued, 'the end will be in sight.'[11]

# CHAPTER 17

# 'WE FELT LIKE WILD BEASTS'

$A$UGUST 1915 was not an encouraging month for the Entente powers. On the Western Front there was a comparative lull in the fighting which during the year saw them suffer heavy casualties for minute territorial gains. On the Eastern Front success attended the great triple offensive of the Central Powers. Day after day Australian newspapers featured bad news for the Allies. In early August the Russians lost Warsaw, and by the 27th the Germans had taken Brest-Litovsk, the advance of two hundred kilometres contrasting with the stalemate which had lasted three-and-a-half months on Gallipoli. This steady and costly Russian retreat continued until a north–south line through Pinsk was reached at the end of September. This eastern disaster allowed Turkey to concentrate a large proportion of its army against Hamilton's force.

It has been estimated that on 1 August there were twenty-seven thousand Turkish troops on the Anzac front (the 9th, 16th and 19th divisions, and two regiments), thirty-six thousand at Helles and thirty-seven thousand in reserve on the Gallipoli Peninsula. As well, within easy reach of the front line there were twelve thousand troops on the Asiatic side of the Dardanelles, while forty-five thousand were at Kesan, some ninety kilometres from Anzac. They were well placed to reinforce Liman von Sanders' troops in an emergency. By 19 August the number of Turkish divisions on the peninsula had risen to sixteen. One estimate is that in August half of the Turkish army was on the peninsula, including the best units stiffened by German officers and men.[1]

Hamilton's August offensive was a bigger operation than the April landings. The British landed four divisions (10th, 11th, 53rd and 54th) at Suvla Bay from 6 to 11 August, by which time there were thirteen Allied divisions on the peninsula, compared with five at the end of April.

The oft-told story of the Sari Bair battle must be summarised here before accounts by participants and eye-witnesses are presented. On the afternoon of 6 August there was a feint at Helles, as planned. At 5.30 that afternoon the 1st Brigade of the AIF launched its attack—the feint at Lone Pine. This was successful, but only at terrible cost after ferocious fighting and amid appalling scenes of agony, blood and slaughter. The night advance in the 'left hook' from Anzac's northern perimeter soon slipped behind schedule. Monash's 4th Brigade, with the hardest task, was stopped by the Turks on the 8th, about fourteen hundred metres short of its objective, Hill 971. At daybreak that day—twenty-four hours later than planned—some New Zealand troops gained their objective, the crest of Chunuk Bair, from where they could see both the Aegean Sea and the Dardanelles. These troops lost heavily and had to be relieved by British and Indian soldiers. The Turks moved much greater numbers of their troops to this critical point, and at daybreak on 10 August they launched a massive, ferocious charge, so forcing the

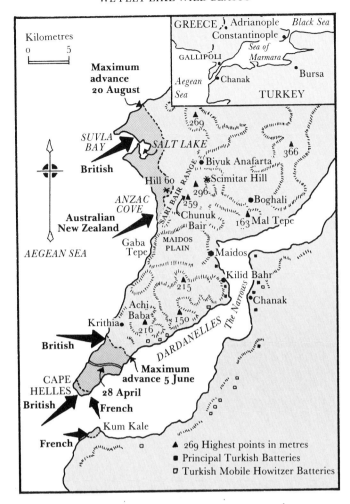

Kilometres
0    5

Maximum
advance
20 August

*SUVLA BAY*
SALT LAKE
British

269

GREECE · Adrianople    *Black Sea*
· Constantinople
*Sea of Marmara*
GALLIPOLI
*Aegean Sea* · Chanak    · Bursa
TURKEY

366

· Biyuk Anafarta
Hill 60    ✳ Scimitar Hill
296
*ANZAC COVE*    259
Chunuk    Bair    163 Mal Tepe
· Boghali

*AEGEAN SEA*
Australian
New Zealand

Gaba
Tepe    *MAIDOS PLAIN*    · Maidos

· Kilid Bahr
215

Achi
Baba    150    · Chanak
Krithia ·    216

British    *DARDANELLES*    *The Narrows*

Maximum
advance 5 June
CAPE
HELLES    28 April
British    French
Kum Kale
French

▲ 269 Highest points in metres
● Principal Turkish Batteries
□ Turkish Mobile Howitzer Batteries

*Helles, Anzac and
Suvla, 1915*

Empire troops off the crest and sealing the fate of the August offensive. As Godley
rather breathlessly explained to his wife, 'We didn't get to the Heights—almost
did so—we got a precarious footing only, almost at the top.'[2]

The troops that were landed at Suvla failed to gain their objectives, or else
gained them later than planned, under controversial circumstances which on 15
August led to Hamilton relieving Stopford and two of his divisional generals of
their commands. He also dismissed Stopford's chief of staff, Brigadier-General
H. L. Reed, of whom Roger Keyes, de Robeck's chief of staff, said 'a bigger rotter
never held an important position in the Army'.

Those who watched the August battle while being fortunate enough not to be
involved saw an awesome display of gunfire. Men on ships anchored off the Anzac
coast could see almost the entire battle. The spectacle must have been as close as
any impressionable observer had come to watching *Götterdämmerung*, as the
amphitheatre-battlefield seemed covered in smoke and fire under a never-ceasing
thunder. George Drewry, as a midshipman on the troopship *River Clyde*, had been
one of its five crew members to win the Victoria Cross during the April landings at
Helles. On the night of 6 August his ship passed Anzac on its way to land soldiers
at Suvla. 'It was a remarkable sight from the sea,' he wrote. 'One large space of
hillside lit up brilliantly by the destroyer searchlights and exploding shells and star
lights, at sea nothing to be seen except the numerous hospital ships anchored off
Anzac with their band of red and green lights and yet the sea teamed with life.'[3] A
young soldier on land, although deafened by the 'incessantly reverberating roar'

and dazzled by intense lights, thought the pandemonium was grand.[4] 'All forms of death, and of the engines that scattered it broadcast, were concealed in every copse and under every shrub,' wrote Lieutenant J. W. McPherson. His ship was shaken from stem to stern as shells from 14-inch guns on Royal Navy monitors rushed over his head. At night the 'naval guns lit up the Peninsula with star shells, and red and white rockets went up on shore from the Turkish lines, whilst muskets and machine guns kept up a continuous rattle, which increased enormously every time a star shell or rocket lit up its objective.' In too short a time a thousand wounded men were attended to by the staff on McPherson's ship. Three hundred lightly wounded 'were bandaged and sent back to try their luck again'. When the ship reached Imbros, one stretcher-bearer who had worked very hard died in his sleep.[5]

Drewry had to make several trips to Anzac in charge of a motor lighter carrying Indian labour troops, supplies, mules and horses from Suvla. On his first trip, on the 8th, he ran inshore just south of Ari Burnu—that is, just inside Anzac Cove. He found the beach 'almost choked with sunken lighters and boats a little offshore and towards Hell Spit was the masts and funnel showing above water. The beach was deserted except for our natives. . . . It was unhealthy.' Within five minutes a Turkish gun with high-explosive shells started at Hell Spit and 'worked right along the beach towards us, one fell just short and we got splinters on board, next one just over and then as far as Ari Burnu and back again. . . . Our shelter of 3/8" steel seemed very thin when H.E. was flying about.'

On his second trip, Drewry reached Anzac Cove after dark that night. 'Now Anzac beach is not nice during day,' he told his father, 'but its awful at night. About half a mile out, feeling our way in, bullets began to hit us and became thick as we got closer, ones from the trenches, almost spent that make a nasty sighing sound as they come. There was only the coxsin and myself on deck and I had to go right forward to see where we were going. I had no cover and felt most funky. The beach itself was not so bad only a few bullets falling here and there. The beach party at Anzac are fatalists—they are sure to be killed or wounded, everyone has so far except Goodbun [a friend of Drewry's] and he has been scratched twice.' As Drewry brought his lighter in to the shore he noticed that there were few stretches of water clear of wreckage.[6]

When Drewry brought supplies to Anzac Cove, the great battle was undecided, although even then the advantage lay with the Turks. The most successful phase of the offensive was the 1st Brigade's feint at Lone Pine. Many who saw that charge, and doubtless most survivors who were in it, wrote about it. On the night of 5–6 August, Private A.L. de Vine and his companions had their best night's sleep for a very long time. At 4.30 p.m. on the 6th, as the British bombardment started, with 'shells everywhere, ours screaming incessantly overhead', rum was issued to the men who were to charge. De Vine was among the first troops to leave the trenches at 5.30 p.m.[7] Second Lieutenant J. L. Merivale took part in the action. 'They went like a pack of forwards charging down a field after a football and in an instant hundreds of rifles turned upon them and shells (both shrapnel and high explosive) and those awful hoses of lead, the machine guns—they fell in tens but the remainder dashed on, and in half an hours fierce fighting hand to hand, turned the Turks out.' Private Albert E. Dowse was one who did not enjoy being in that charge. 'It is very trying on the nerves when you have to charge a turks trench and about four machine-guns [are] waiting for you. I have a particular dread of machine-guns they will fairly cut a man in halves if they get properly on him the bullets come that fast.' Merivale died after this attack.[8]

Corporal J. Neal, of the 2nd Battalion, also in that charge, told a young woman in Burwood (Sydney) that her ring had kept him safe 'through that terrible battle between the 6th and 12th of August'. On getting the order to charge the

Turks' trenches 150 metres away, Neal had raced across, seeing men falling with a groan and others blown to pieces. 'I glanced upwards,' he related, 'to see nothing but a sheet of fire or smoke caused by bursting shells of all sorts and machine gun fire. The next moment I felt a bump and my rifle fell to pieces in my hand.' He was soon in hand-to-hand fighting in the Turkish trenches. When Private John K. Gammage charged, after watching the biggest bombardment he had ever seen, he 'fell over a lump of barb wire when half way across' but got up again. He recalled: 'The machine [gun] bullets were falling around me like rain but lucky again. . . . On reaching Jacko's first trench I jumped on to a wounded Turk. . . . the moans of our own poor fellows . . . was awful.' As bombs flew thick and fast in the Turkish counter-attack, he said, 'we had no time to think of our wounded . . . their pleads for mercy were not heeded . . . some poor fellows lay for 30 hours waiting for help and many died still waiting. . . . [Next morning] it looked almost impossible to hold the place but we would have sooner died than retreat.'9

Private Stan Jury, a lad from Ashfield (Sydney), wrote to his mother from St George's Hospital, Malta, 'I would have wrote before only we have been to busy fighting.' He was in the charge at Lone Pine. 'It was terrible hard fighting. . . . [a] living hell dead laying five and six days in the trenches in fact you could not walk without treading on the dead when you put your foot down you feel the body quiver under your feet it was horrible. . . . I was very lucky I was hit on the shoulder both feet and stomach thank God it was not serious I expect to be back at the turk in a month time as long as septic dont set in.' Corporal Robert Antill viewed his convalescence very differently. At about 2 p.m. on the 7th he received a bullet wound in the right thigh. For seven hours it would have been death to move; the burning sun nearly drove him mad. Being taken home to 'dear old London', close to his parents was some compensation.10

Private A. J. Mychael, a driver from Moonan Flat near Scone, New South Wales, slipped away from Alexandria and, without orders, went to Anzac. He got only seven hours' sleep in his first 102 hours at Anzac, but he was glad he had come and 'had the chance of being in a charge', even though it was just a living hell with a rain of bullets bombs and shells'. 'One doesn't feel afraid,' he explained; 'you dash in just the same as on a football field.' But it was 'terribly lonely now such a lot of old mates gone', for 'the Scone lads had a very bad time', many being killed. One soldier at Lone Pine, during the repulse of the counter-attacks, said some 6th Battalion reinforcements 'were mere boys and they fought like old soldiers but few of them came out of Lone Pine alive.'11

Entries in the War Diary of the 2nd Battalion, which was raised in northern New South Wales, tersely indicate the scenes, and the attendant problems:

6 August—2130 . . . Our wounded lying all over the trenches, and are hampering movement. Effort being made to evacuate them. . . . Enemy's dead everywhere and we can't avoid walking on them, as they are so thick. . . .

8 August . . . A start made to clear the trenches of dead, which in some trenches are lying three deep, some being Australians . . . and some being Turks. . . .

10 August . . . A start made in cleaning up. . . . Dead bodies in a very bad state of decomposition. Men can only work by using respirators.12

Holding on at Lone Pine involved fighting no less severe than during the assault, for the Turks launched a series of ferocious counter-attacks. Men 'had to make a barricade of bodies and so keep the Turks off,' explained Private de Vine, 'and so we managed to hold what we had won.' With his mates he blocked off 'with dead men' a communication trench leading to the Turks. Private Gammage was relieved one evening after fifty hours of solid fighting. After seven hours off, at 3 a.m. on the 9th, he had to rush back to the firing line to help beat off yet another

On 10 August there was satisfaction on the faces of Australians who captured Turkish trenches at Lone Pine. Howitzer shells had been effective in penetrating this well-reinforced Turkish position.

Turkish attack. 'We felt like wild beasts,' he wrote, 'but were calm and never fired reckless but deliberate.' He hoped that the repulse of the charge increased the Turkish casualties 'to perhaps equal the Australians'. At one stage the 4th Battalion was using bombs only, because rifle fire was of no use 'owing to position of trenches'. De Vine, amidst descriptions of heavy attacks and shelling, commnted, 'This was the tightest corner that I have ever been in. Marvellous how I managed to get out without a scratch.' Private Donkin, who on 25 April had been so unnerved by the fighting that he could not, for a time, return to the firing line, now described men hanging 'over the parapets with the rifle still in their hands, their friend in death even'. His last diary entry read: 'This job is one of the most costly ones this war has seen.' He was killed by a shell on 15 August when, after others had left, he tried to man a gun and hold a position alone.[13]

For a few days all the food that Private Gammage had was taken from dead comrades' haversacks. 'But its all for a good cause,' he observed. 'Rum and tea is served out pretty freely,' noted de Private de Vine on the 9th, 'which is practically all the nourishment we have received for the last three days.' Shortly afterwards he got a little rice, his first solid food since the 6th. Private F. W. Bennett, one of the relieving troops who took over in Lone Pine at a later stage of the battle, months later recalled, 'The smell of the Turkish dead was awful and we had to eat our meals and sleep among the smell for 48 hours.' The 12th Battalion, in reserve to the 1st Brigade, soon had the task of helping the stretcher-bearers remove the large numbers of wounded, under heavy fire. An anonymous writer, recalling that the captors of Lone Pine had been consistently fighting for four months and were thin and worn, accounted for their 'sang froid . . . because they are so jolly tired that they don't care if a shell bursts a yard from them or not'. All and sundry obeyed their orders, which were to take Lone Pine and hold on. One who was evacuated to Mudros had a restless first night there, fighting Turks all the time. These captured trenches were held for the remainder of the Anzac campaign. Although Ashmead-Bartlett later questioned the value of the attack, the men who won this local triumph did not seem to do so.[14]

On 10 August Private de Vine listed in his diary eight names, including his own—one corporal and seven privates—who were all that remained in C Company, 4th Battalion, of the original two hundred who had left Sydney in October 1914. The battalion, he wrote, was for the time being quite unfit for any further service.[15]

The main assault from Anzac, the breakout to the north, was a very different operation. Corporal E. H. Kitson was with his men of the 4th Field Ambulance at Anzac on the night of 6 August as the 4th Brigade marched past to begin its advance. 'It was a great and impressing sight to see an army marching along the beach at night, so quietly and stealthily without any undue excitement. As we stood there with stretchers ready we saw company after company and battalion after battalion pass silently by no-one speaking above a whisper. We soon got on the march, following on in the rear of the Infantry.'[16]

A hardy veteran of Gallipoli thought that 'the strain and the sights along the way [of the 16th Battalion's advance towards Hill 971] were enough to break the strongest of men down'. He was thankful that he had 'stood it very well' and wondered how many escapes he had had while 'other poor fellows [were] going down'. Major Allanson, leading his Gurkhas behind the Australian vanguard, found the country 'covered with dead and dying, many in great pain, and throwing themselves about: one began to know again what war was.'[17] Lieutenant J. R. Bell wrote to his mother, 'If you could see the headless bodies and stiff cold hands that one is daily in touch with.' A private who carried wounded to medical attention lamented that the quiet peaceful seashore north of Anzac was turned in a few moments into 'one of the roughest places on God's Earth'. A corporal in the 13th Division, who was a dispatch rider, saw many 'absolutely awful sights' and a continual procession of the Empire's wounded, 'groaning terrible'. On the morning of 11 August he went some way up the Aghyl Dere (the valley leading from the coast up to Chunuk Bair), remarking, 'Smells and sights up these gullies terrible.' At noon he passed dreadful groaning rows of wounded on stretchers, waiting to be taken off the beach.[18]

The failure of the 4th Brigade to attain its objectives reflected no discredit upon the men, a fact attested to by commentators at the time and historians such as Peter Pedersen seven decades later. On 15 August 1915 Guy Dawnay told his wife: 'It was on the lower spurs of the southern part of these hills [the Sari Bair range] that the old Australian position has been ever since the end of April. The main ridge is a tremendous climb, and the dry watercourses up which the troops went are indescribably rough, steep and winding. Up they went, however, led by the New Zealanders, quite undaunted and meeting more and more opposition as they climbed. All in the pitch dark too—no moon. How they ever did the march alone—leaving the opposition out of account—is almost a miracle.'[19]

Hamilton's force suffered heavy casualties in losing this complex battle. Of fifty thousand troops involved in the fighting, one-third became casualties in four days of combat. Roger Keyes told his wife on the 16th: 'Since the 6th we have had 26,000 wounded—and I suppose 6000 or 7000 killed—that the Turks have lost as many doesn't make up for it. I hate it and I feel all the time that we could stop it all and win that great prize—I simply can't bear it.'[20] Keyes was here referring to his belief that the Royal Navy could break the deadlock if given another opportunity to force a passage through the Dardanelles.

Two days after the failure of the offensive was confirmed on 10 August by the terrible Turkish charge on Chunuk Bair, Godley accepted defeat. He told his wife the force would have to try again, soon; and he had the awful thought that it might be on the peninsula for the winter. Keyes wondered how much would leak out 'about the failure of this last business on which the Army and Government built so much'. In a short letter to Senator Pearce on the 14th, Godley emphasised the courage and skill of the officers and men in his division and the overwhelming force

*Looking back from Lone Pine to the jumping-off trench from where on 6 August 1915 the 1st Brigade began the attack on Lone Pine.*

arrayed against them. He mentioned the heavy casualties and the gains—'the acquisition of about seven hundred more acres of Turkey' in front of his division, and the linking up with the forces that had landed at Suvla. Hamilton summed up the gains of the August battles by telling London that the Anzacs had been extricated from a theoretically untenable position and their borders enlarged. Also, they had been entirely released from shelling on the northern flank. Ashmead-Bartlett told readers in Australia that there was no longer 'a stifled feeling among the troops' previously cramped in at Anzac; but the incomplete success had left 'an awful scene of desolation between the lines'. Bonar Law told Munro Ferguson that he was not as sanguine as Hamilton about prospects on the peninsula. Letters from Gallipoli reached men on the Dardanelles Committee urging Hamilton's recall and claiming that he had made 'a terrible mess and massacre' of the expedition from the start. 'The tasks units were ordered to perform were . . . nothing but bloody murder.' By the end of August Birdwood saw no prospect of another big advance. He sadly admitted that he could 'no longer see light' as he had in April. A British lieutenant agreed with Turkish prisoners he interviewed that the campaign had become 'fatuous'.[21] It was a stalemate. The Turks could not eject the Empire troops, and the British could not move on.

*Major L. J. Morshead of the 2nd Battalion in a captured Lone Pine trench. One of the dead was probably Australian: in battle, the white armband was one means of distinguishing AIF from the enemy, whose uniforms were much the same colour.*

# 'THE NEK ATTACK: SOME CONFLICTING VERSIONS

$A$LL OBSERVERS and commentators agree that heroism abounded among the Australians and New Zealanders who vainly sought victory in those terrible, bright, hot, sunny days of early August. In the four days of intense fighting at Lone Pine, seven Victoria Crosses were won and more no doubt deserved. But one small, discrete part of Birdwood's operations especially epitomises the horrifying chasm between the bravery of the front-line troops and command failings—the infantry charge by men of the 3rd Australian Light Horse Brigade at the Nek in the early morning light of 7 August. Among those familiar with the Gallipoli campaign, this charge is usually singled out as the example *par excellence* of sacrificial bravery against hopeless odds.[1] It is instructive to note the differences between contrasting accounts of this tragedy, as generals sought to conceal their mistakes.

Initial orders for the charge came from Birdwood and Lieutenant-Colonel Skeen, his chief of staff, to Godley, in the planning stages of the operation. From Godley and his chief of staff, Lieutenant-Colonel W. G. Braithwaite, the orders went to Brigadier-General F. G. Hughes, a militia officer aged fifty-eight and brigade commander. He was told that his brigade was to charge from trenches at Russell's Top a distance of about fifty metres along the Nek, a ridge less than a hundred metres wide with cliffs falling away on either side, to take the strongly held Turkish trench system on Baby 700 and the Chessboard, a labyrinth of Turkish trenches stretching south from Baby 700. The attacking force was to advance even further 'if and when the situation admits'. The assault was to be made in four lines, each of 150 men. The 8th Light Horse Regiment, from Victoria, would provide the first two lines, and the 10th, from Western Australia, the last two. Troops were to be rested as much as possible during the night. If the charge were postponed, the soldiers were to 'remain in readiness to attack at half an hour's notice'.

There was some vagueness about the purpose of this charge in the overall battle. Was it to be a feint? Birdwood and Skeen recognised that an unaided attack would be 'almost hopeless'.[2] So it was planned that this assault would be made in conjunction with an attack on the enemy's rear by New Zealanders advancing downhill from Chunuk Bair. Under such circumstances the 3rd Light Horse attack might make a valuable contribution to breaking the Turkish lines. On the other hand, if Chunuk Bair were not won, the light-horse attack would be suicidal and of no benefit to the general British plan.

Late in the afternoon of 6 August, troops on Russell's Top could see, a kilometre and a half to the south, the 1st Infantry Brigade attacking at Lone Pine. During the night they had no means of knowing how much success was attending the 'left hook'. As the hour approached for the light-horsemen's charge, none of the hoped-for conditions had been met. In particular, the New Zealanders had not gained the heights of Chunuk Bair, and the 6th Battalion, at Steele's Post, had not been able to capture German Officers' Trench, where Turkish machine-guns en-

filaded the Nek. Nevertheless, Birdwood and Skeen decided to proceed with the attack. Most accounts state that a premature cessation of the supporting artillery bombardment enabled the Turks to strengthen their front line at the crucial time. Other versions do not mention the premature cessation but stress that the artillery bombardment was ineffective. As Maurice Hankey explained, 'It is a fact that at Anzac and Suvla the artillery has hitherto been insufficient to prepare for our attacks' because no suitable positions could be found for more guns.[3]

The massacre of the first two lines—the 8th Light Horse Regiment—so effectively described by Bean, was tersely summed up by the regiment's war diarist: 'Owing to a deadly machine gun fire the attack failed to get home.' The diarist of the 10th Light Horse Regiment gave a much fuller account of its role in the tragedy. On 6 August he noted: 'Very heavy shelling by both sides. All ranks fully 45% physically below their normal standard.' The next day's diary entry began:

*All ranks to arms at 4 a.m. as usual and in their position preparatory to launching assault. The artillery were to smash enemy machine guns and trenches preparatory to our assault. This was not done. The destroyer opened fire in the direction of the Nek at 4 a.m. and continued to 4.30 a.m. and almost immediately and before the first line of ours had left our trenches, enemy rifle and machine gun fire opened on our parapets. First and second lines, who were in the firing trenches, then sprang forward to the assault and were mown down. Before allowing the third and fourth lines to assault, position was discussed with Brigade H.Q., but the 10th Regiment were ordered to immediately carry out orders to push on and carry enemy's trenches. Our third line was then ordered to assault and was mown down in a similar manner, with the exception of those on our left who were sheltering in some dead ground. Before launching fourth line the position was again brought before brigade H.Q., but again this line was ordered to carry out orders, and the fourth line rose over the parapets and assaulted, but with same result as the previous three lines. Major Love . . . proceeded to left of line, where some 80 to 100 of all ranks were lying, . . . and decided that it was impossible for men to move forward a yard and live, under such a hail of well aimed and distributed rifle and machine gun fire.*

*George Lambert*, The charge of the 3rd Light Horse Brigade at the Nek, 7 August 1915, *1924 (oil on canvas, 152.5 × 305.3 cm). George Lambert was an official war artist with the light horse in the Palestine campaign in 1918, and then a member of a group which Bean, as official historian, led to Gallipoli in 1919. They spent six weeks there. At Gallipoli, Lambert for the first time was struck by the tragic side of war. Bean later said Lambert was 'more sensitive than the rest of us to the tragedy—or at any rate the horror—of Anzac.'*

Major Love returned and 'placed position before Brigade H. Q. and then received orders to withdraw'.[4]

The brigade headquarters' diarist noted laconically, 'No response from our leading troops who were unable to make ground all being killed.' He continued: 'The position assaulted . . . was absolutely impossible to take by frontal attack. . . . There was no hesitation or faltering amongst our officers and men, especially of the 8th L. H. Regiment who were practically wiped out.'[5]

In three reports Godley, the divisional commander, gave several versions of this assault. They differed slightly from one another, but not as much as they differed from what had happened. In all three he did not mention the 10th Regiment and claimed that the 8th had occupied and cleared out the Turkish trenches but had then had to withdraw to its own lines. In one report he claimed that from 4 a.m. to 4.30 a.m. 'an exceptionally heavy bombardment' of the Turkish trenches took place, by 'all available guns, assisted by guns of H. M. Ships'. Godley admitted to heavy casualties but claimed that surviving members of the brigade 'rendered signal service, in containing large numbers of Turks in the trenches in front of them, by demonstrations and ruses of every kind, and much enterprise in the way of rifle fire and bomb throwing'. The assault 'undoubtedly' helped in inflict severe losses on the enemy (in fact it seems that not one Turk was killed during the charges). Godley claimed that this and nearby assaults 'fulfilled their object of engaging the enemy's attention and preventing him from detaching troops to other portions of the line'.

Birdwood mentioned the Nek charge in his autobiography. He wrote that the 'position was too strongly held to be taken, and both regiments lost many fine men. Nevertheless, this attack had been of value in pinning the Turks to the spot and preventing them from sending reinforcements to their right.' About the same time as the tragedy of the Nek, a like fate was met by the first line of a charge by the 2nd Light Horse Regiment at Quinn's Post. There, the officers prevented any further slaughter by cancelling the remaining planned charges. Godley approved of this, saying they had 'exercised what was probably a wise discretion'.[6]

Hamilton, in his telegram to Kitchener of 8 August, referred briefly to the Nek thus: 'In the left sector of the Anzac position two minor operations were attempted during the night of 6th–7th August in order to occupy the Turks on that front, but owing to the intricate nature of the Turkish positions and the heavy machine-gun fire brought against us, these were not successful.' He added a little in his official report, published in January 1916. He did not mention the 10th Light Horse Regiment, but said that the 8th 'only accepted their repulse after losing three-fourths of that devoted band who so bravely sallied forth from Russell's Top. Some of the [Turks'] works were carried, but in these cases the enemy's concealed machine-guns made it impossible to hold on.' Nonetheless, he regarded these attacks as justified in that all day they pinned down Turkish reserves which might otherwise have been moved to confront the 'main enterprise' on Sari Bair. He did not mention the Nek incident in his *Gallipoli Diary,* published in 1920, and is surprisingly brief in his account here of the Lone Pine attack and the 'left hook' from Anzac.[7]

Brigadier-General Hughes and Colonel J. M. Antill, the brigade major, were the officers who could have overridden orders and cancelled the suicidal charges. Antill, 'the main influence in the command of the brigade,'[8] was a regular army officer from New South Wales. In 1914 the Military Board had called on him to show cause why his services should not be dispensed with, in view of the findings of a court of inquiry into his role in serious problems of indiscipline at Liverpool camp. He wrote at length in his defence but did not exonerate himself in the board's view. Nevertheless, he held a crucial position on 7 August 1915 and later wrote of the charges, 'It was pitiful, but would have been worth while, perhaps, had the people at Suvla done their job.' He also blamed the headquarters staff for bad advice that the Turks were only lightly defending the Nek, and complained, 'Our piffling bombardment did no damage to their trenches.' Both Birdwood and Hamilton had been told of Andrew Fisher's wish that 'any incompetent officer would be sent back at once, the safety of the men being always the first considera- tion'. Nevertheless, Antill later was to command the 2nd Infantry Brigade at Ypres and on the Somme and to retire in 1924 with the rank of honorary Major-General. In February 1916 he noted that of the 3rd Light Horse Brigade's ninety officers he was the only one who went right through its period on Gallipoli.[9]

It took a few weeks for the story of the disaster at the Nek to unfold in Australia. By 26 August reports were circulating that the 8th and 10th Light Horse regiments had been practically wiped out earlier that month. This prompted the Defence Department to publish a table showing total casualties in the ten light horse regi- ments. The figures made very sad reading, with 196 dead in the 8th and 102 in the 10th. A fortnight later the *Argus* published its first lengthy report, by Bean, on the charge at the Nek. This account had taken about six weeks to reach the Australian public; a week later extracts were published in the *New York Times*. Bean's report falsely claimed the losses in the charge were justified by Turkish losses at least as great. Two weeks later still, another long report on the tragedy was published, from a special correspondent. This included a story on the death of Lieutenant- Colonel A. H. White, the commanding officer of the 8th Regiment, who perished leading his troops whereas he might have been better advised to have stayed in the trench and added his authority to those officers trying to have the subsequent charges cancelled.[10]

These newspaper stories, which first made Australians aware of the slaughter of their compatriots on a small stony segment of a far-away ridge, contained sig- nificant factual errors and some misconceptions, but the general impression conveyed was accurate. The charge, depicted as 'sheer self-sacrificing heroism', was unsurpassed in history, claimed Bean. A survivor told him that the Turkish trenches were crammed with troops. He could see the bayonets of the front row of Turks above the parapet, and behind them appeared to be two further rows, stand- ing waist-high above the parapet, and firing their rifles as quickly as possible. The

*The view from Baby 700, as photographed by John Robertson in 1986, showing the commanding view this important position had of the Nek. A white Turkish memorial, situated on what was the Turkish front trench line, can be seen. The Australian memo- rial behind it (not visi- ble) is on the Austra- lian line.*

second, longer account explained: 'There was as nearly as possible a wall of flying missiles blocking the zone over which the Victorians had to pass. But orders were definite and precise, and the men never had a thought of flinching. . . . no one dreamt of shirking.' Then broad daylight came 'in all its glory to look upon a band of men who had gone down to save their mates'. 'Lying out there in the scrub' in no man's land, Bean wrote, were 'a number of tumbled little heaps of that pea-soup coloured Australian khaki'.

On 20 October the *Age* published a letter from a private who had been in the second line when the 8th Light Horse charged at the Nek. He said that only a few men reached the Turkish trenches, and they were blown to pieces by bombs. Those who fell wounded were very lucky if they could get back into the trench, because otherwise they mostly were blown to pieces by bombs. He was lucky enough to fall back into the trench. In this letter there was no concealing the heavy casualties and the dreadful consequences of that charge.

The 1981 film *Gallipoli* contrasted the self-sacrifice of these light-horsemen with the lackadaisical dallying of British troops on the shores of Suvla Bay. More to the point, their bravery served no tactical purpose. The *threat* of an attack would have been enough to tie the Turks to that part of their line. Lieutenant-Colonel Noel M. Brazier, commanding the 10th Light Horse Regiment, whose pleas to stop the senseless attacks were overruled, summed up the tactical issues accurately in the final paragraph of his report: 'The attack seemed premature and in view of the heavy machine gun fire, should have been held up, as by demonstrations the Turk would have been held to his position and many valuable lives saved, until the operations on our left had progressed further or the trenches in front were reduced by guns.'[11]

One soldier wrote a week later of the massacre of the light horse: 'Turkey is paying for it. It won't be long now before we will have them well settled.' Within a few days the smell of the Australian corpses on the Nek was dreadful. 'Nothing can compare with decomposed human flesh for horror.' The bodies could not be removed, and the process of decomposition continued, within view of the living. Three months later a soldier 'had a long look over the parapet at that terrible place where the Light Horse were so fearfully cut up when attacking on 7th August. One can see many of the men still lying out there in the "No Man's Land" with packs on their backs and water bottles complete; the bodies, though, are now mere skeletons.'[12] Four months after the charge an Australian, Major John J. Walker, perhaps unaware that much of the responsibility for the fiasco at the Nek lay with AIF officers, wrote bitterly of British generals who 'sent out these fearless Australians to a certain death'. He saw the bodies lying out between the trenches 'as a grim reminder of the ruthless incompetence and cold blooded decision of a monocled blighter. May his conscience drive him out of the Empire.'[13]

H. W. Nevinson, author of one of the best early histories of the Dardanelles campaign, compared the Nek to the famous suicidal charge at Balaclava. He provided a good, honest account without criticising its strategy. Ashmead-Bartlett was far more forthright. It was an 'utterly futile frontal attack. . . murderous . . . which the merest tyro could perceive had no possible chance of succeeding'.[14]

# CHAPTER 19

# 'STORIES... UTTERLY FALSE AND MISLEADING'

$I$T TOOK SOME WEEKS for a reasonably truthful account of the August offensive to reach Australia. The fact that new landings had been made was kept from the public at home longer than in the case of the April landings. By the time the veil was lifted—11 August in *The Times*, next day in Australia—the generals on the spot had recognised that the offensive had failed. On the 13th, Australians were told that fifty thousand more men had landed at the Dardanelles and that the area held at Anzac had trebled. For a fortnight, sparse details of heavy fighting trickled through to the Australian public. The death of four Australian colonels was reported twelve days after they had been killed at Gallipoli. Reports hinted at success and told of a rapid advance by the Australians. Brief extracts from Turkish communiqués were published. They indicated the state of the battle reasonably accurately but perhaps were not accepted as truthful by Australian newspaper readers.

News that the Suvla landings had failed was revealed in Britain more quickly than in the case of the April landings, but some Australians, including editors of major newspapers, were slower to accept defeat. On 20 August *The Times* announced that the newly landed force had sustained heavy losses and was at a standstill. Details followed fairly quickly.

Australia's first big story on the Suvla landing, published on 24 August, originated from the Athens correspondent of the English *Daily Chronicle*. The landing was termed a 'splendid feat', 'the most brilliant work yet carried out since the war began'. It was 'a complete and staggering surprise' which 'brought out all that was best in the fighting qualities of the British troops'. Within twenty-four hours, it was stated, the leading troops had marched six miles inland. (In fact, the total advance from the coast averaged less than three miles.) The Suvla and Anzac fighting was so successful, Australians read, that Turkish communications down the peninsula to the Helles front were 'seriously threatened'. Next to this account, some Australian newspapers printed a terse, truthful Turkish communiqué stating that the British offensive had failed.

Over the following few days Australians could read other accounts which did not reveal the truth. The Adelaide *Advertiser* wrote of 'a wonderfully successful operation'; the *Argus* believed the landing would 'redound to the lasting glory of British arms'. The Turks would now realise that Britain was determined to win. Next day this paper printed the first dispatches from Bean on this offensive. Dated 9 and 11 August, they were detailed but not frank. He termed the 3rd Light Horse Brigade's charge 'a most gallant and desperate attack', but did not mention it was a complete failure. In the two weeks from the 25th there followed a series of reports, by Ashmead-Bartlett and Bean, and from Reuters, which, under headlines proclaiming that Australians were 'Devils for Fighting', described the AIF's further deeds of glory in the most flattering fashion. Reports emphasised the bravery of the Lone Pine attack and claimed that the 4th Brigade's night march would 'live in history', without mentioning that the brigade had failed to gain its objective. Ashmead-Bartlett, in a detailed report published on 27 August, claimed that the operations at Suvla 'were being carried out splendidly'. The planning for the landing was so careful, he said, that 'every officer and man knew the exact role he had to play'.[1]

Not everyone was fooled. Some newspaper editorial comment was cautious. Reports from Greece were 'chronically unreliable'. It was clear that the 'turning' movement aimed at in the offensive was not yet in progress. E. F. Allan, who contributed occasional articles to the *Argus* in which he reviewed the progress of Allied aims, was not optimistic about the prospects for the August offensive, and he pointed out the difficulties faced by Hamilton's force.[2] A week later, with the publication of a long account by Ashmead-Bartlett of the Australian role in the attack of 21 August on Hill 60 (see next chapter), it should have become generally obvious that the great offensive had failed.

The *Kalgoorlie Miner*, whose patriotic coverage of the war could scarcely have been exceeded, was one of the many Australian newspapers that printed at length the carefully worded dispatches from Bean and Ashmead-Bartlett which described fighting but did not mention victory or defeat. The *Miner*'s editorial on 28 August titled 'A Long Way to Constantinople', claimed that, although it was a difficult task, the Allies would eventually occupy the Turkish capital. The grievous losses during the month, it asserted, were justified by the issues at stake.

It was about six weeks before it became obvious in Australia that the offensive had failed. The *Sydney Morning Herald* printed local, independent commentary on the state of the war. On 18 September the writer of this column, headed 'War Notes', commented, 'Looking back on the earlier stories every one can now realise how utterly false and misleading they were.' The comment was provoked by the announcement in the British House of Commons of the Allies' casualty figures at the Dardanelles, which from 28 July to 21 August numbered 38,392. If these London figures were accurate, said the 'War Notes' writer, the setback to the British armies 'in the Anafarta region was even greater than appeared from the cabled reports'. During those twenty-four days the British army suffered more casualties in the Gallipoli fighting than in all its fighting on other fronts and almost as many as in the previous three months of 'intermittently heavy fighting' on the peninsula. 'War Notes' again warned readers not to accept reports that the Turkish force on Gallipoli was short of munitions and supplies and approaching demoralisation.

There were ample indications that progress was unsatisfactory on the Gallipoli beachheads. No victories were being reported, although some people might have gained a little comfort from the limited advances in late August. On 15 October, under the heading 'The Position at Gallipoli. A Soldier's Criticism', the *Age* published a letter which was unusual in that writer and recipient were not identified. 'The Turks are very fair opponents, and are tough fighters,' ran the letter, composed in the trenches on 16 August by a man who had been at Anzac since April. 'We have come to the conclusion here that we have a heavy task in hand, and in our present worn-out and weary state we are unable to put up our best fighting.' He thought that they could win, given more fresh troops. Three days later, as total reported British casualties at the Dardanelles neared 97,000, the *Age* printed Ashmead-Bartlett's judgement that the results of the campaign were 'wholly unfavourable' to the British Empire and published extracts from London evening newspapers which forthrightly criticised the conduct of the campaign. Doubtless the inconsistencies in the celebrated war correspondent's opinions stemmed from censorship changes. By 1 November the *Argus* was accepting that the Suvla landing was very badly executed; it printed criticism by Lord Milner, active Tory dissident and future minister in Lloyd George's cabinet, that 'blunder after blunder' had been committed.

Throughout September and the first half of October Australian newspapers published lengthy accounts of particular episodes in the August fighting sent by Bean, Oliver Hogue ('Trooper Bluegum'), Ashmead-Bartlett and the Reuters correspondent. Stories by and letters from participants were also soon being printed in the newspapers. Interspersed with accounts of the August battles were items on the routine of life in the Anzac firing line before that offensive, or else describing earlier tragedies, such as the slaughter of the men on the *River Clyde* at Helles on 25 April.

Censorship was naturally a continuing feature of the Gallipoli campaign. Overall, the expedition's main censorship problem was not that there was too much but that there was too little. The announcements to the world, before 25 April, of the coming landings—so condemning more men to die—were unforgivable.[3] Once the footholds had been gained on the peninsula, censorship was quite effective in denying useful information to the enemy. For example, the August offensive largely caught the Turks unawares. The evacuation in December was to be an even clearer instance of successful concealment of intentions. Soldiers' letters were censored by officers, and the men acted as self-censors.[4] They did not write letters giving away military secrets which would jeopardise their safety and their likelihood of victory. If necessary, an extra security safeguard could be imposed by delaying the dispatch of all letters for a stipulated time.

After the landings, one of the two most contentious aspects of censorship was its use to protect the British government and the commanders by concealing the extent of the failure. It has been shown precisely how effective that was, in delaying but not preventing the emergence of the truth. The second contentious area was its use to delay publicity about some of the bungling by the authorities in areas such as the return of wounded to hospitals in Egypt (see chapters 31 and 32).

Censorship did not prevent Australians from obtaining an accurate impression of the horrors of the fighting, for newspapers published many stories about battlefields strewn with dead Australian soldiers and of men meeting ghastly deaths. Moreover, there was no suppression of the casualty lists, although there were inescapable delays in their publication. The lists from the August fighting began to be published in September. Figures published on the 7th and 18th showed a rise from 16,478 to 21,728 in total casualties, and from 4,334 to 5,764 in dead and missing.[5] Although there was a time-lag of some weeks, the Australians of 1915 had an excellent general understanding of what was happening at the Anzac beachhead.

*Ellis Ashmead-Bartlett, the British newspaper correspondent whose reports of battles and conditions at Gallipoli were also published in Australia and New Zealand.*

# CHAPTER 20

# 'THAT SUVLA BUSINESS'

$F$OR TWO DAYS after its landing at Suvla on the night of 6–7 August Stopford's 9th Corps was opposed 'by a mere four battalions'. But it did not push resolutely inland, across topography the very opposite of the tangled terrain surrounding Anzac Cove, to gain its objective some kilometres from the coast.[1]

In its distinctive way, Suvla was as much a potential death trap as was Anzac for a landing force. From the bay there stretches an extensive plain, almost flat except for a few slight rises. But about 270 degrees of the horizon is ringed by a brooding range of hills. One glance at the terrain is enough to confirm that it was crucial for a landing force to occupy the high ground as quickly as possible. But four divisions would not have been enough to control even the inner circle of hills. It would have been virtually impossible for Stopford's troops to have prevented the Turks from occupying much of the range, with its commanding view of Suvla Bay.

The Australians on 25 April showed they had the qualities that were lacking, yet so greatly in demand, at Suvla during the first twelve hours or so after the landing. Roger Keyes, in the course of a long description to his wife of the infuriating and 'maddening' delays while opportunities were being missed, asserted: 'The 29th Division or the ANZAC's would have been on every hill top—I am sure. . . . It ought to have been a glorious success.' Readers of *The Times* were told much the same. In a long account of the four-day battle at Suvla, Ashmead-Bartlett stated that dominion troops failed in their attempt to hold a crest largely because another corps did not make good its position. In later weeks troops in the 9th Corps displayed ample reserves of bravery, suggesting that the disastrous inaction of the first few days after their landing was probably attributable to failures in leadership at various levels or perhaps to inadequate training.[2]

Rear-Admiral H. T. England, in a submission of 14 December 1916 to the Dardanelles Commission, affirmed that before the landing he had agreed with Skeen that the troops had to advance immediately so as to be well up Anafarta Valley by daybreak on 7 August. He blamed lack of leadership at the top, and poor staff work, for the Suvla failure, a bitter disappointment 'to us at Anzac'. After discussions with officers involved in the landing, he decided that the organisation and preparation of the troops fell very far short of the standard attained by Birdwood's corps on 25 April. General de Lotbinière, chief engineer at Anzac, later ascribed the Suvla fiasco to the failure to use the experienced Anzac staff.[3] A British subaltern on Gallipoli and Ashmead-Bartlett were two who later claimed that the Australians being slaughtered at Lone Pine and elsewhere in 'Old' Anzac should have been put ashore at Suvla. Ivone Kirkpatrick, a subaltern in the 10th Division, severely wounded at Suvla, said later he had no idea where he was or what he was supposed to do after landing. One specific instance of poor staff work, later to become the subject of controversy and intense questioning in the Dardanelles Commission, was the failure in arrangements to supply water to the troops.[4]

The weight of opinion at the time blamed Stopford's 9th Corps for the overall failure of the August offensive. Many harsh words circulated about both commander and troops because they did not take advantage of the wonderful opportunities for easy advances. Stopford's indecision was perhaps partly excusable as there was some confusion in his orders, which did not stress clearly enough the need to occupy the inland hills quickly, partly in order to help the 'left hook' from Anzac. He also had new troops which were asked to 'do a lot' (although not nearly so much as the Australians in April). However, even if blame properly rested with Hamilton and his planning staff, Stopford's New Army troops acquired an unenviable reputation. There was no gainsaying that Suvla was an 'all-British show' and an embarrassing defeat. All the criticisms for its mismanagement had to be accepted by Britons of one rank or another.[5]

For our purposes, a crucial result of the Suvla campaign was the establishment of a firm belief that the soldiers from the antipodes were better than those from Britain. At the April landings Australians had felt honoured to be compared on roughly equal terms with the 29th Division, whose heroism was widely acknowledged in the Mediterranean Expeditionary Force. The post-Suvla view was summed up in the tart comment of Private Stanley Natusch, the young New Zealander who a year earlier had proudly classed himself as a 'soldier of the Empire'. One hundred thousand Australasians, led by 'our own officers', would have won the campaign on Gallipoli by this time, he asserted. He told his mother to put the value of colonial troops at twice that 'of their English fellows.'[6]

Many at high command levels saw good reason for this conceit. Keyes related a story told to him by Godley, who from one vantage point could see both Anzac and Suvla. 'You can imagine my feelings when I watched my men fighting like Tigers doing practically the impossible, and at the same time could watch within three miles the 10th and 11th divisions loafing and bathing.' In December a Victorian officer was to refer to 'those rotten troops that muddled up the Suvla landing'. He thought that a newspaper article containing a 'terrific criticism of the English section of the army' at Gallipoli was quite true.[7]

British diarists reported rumours circulating among antipodean troops of soldiers from the United Kingdom turning tail. About 10 August Lieutenant McPherson heard a story—about Irish troops running in a demoralising incident—'from Colonial troops as a tale they could hardly believe'; later he heard the same story from other sources. Sergeant Edney Moore, serving in the Australian Army Medical Corps, noted on 8 August: 'The Tommies here are not making a good impression on Australians and there is no doubt they are not the same stamp of fellows as the Australians and New Zealanders. They haven't the stamina . . . and they certainly won't or can't fight like our fellows.' A specific instance of the Suvla troops relying upon Australian expertise was mentioned by Lieutenant-Colonel W. J. K. Rettie. At Suvla some Turkish snipers remained behind the British lines, painting their hands and faces green to conceal themselves better in the foliage of the trees. Australians 'with a knowledge of bush-whacking were eventually sent over to us and they went off into the bush to deal with this nuisance'. Rettie said it was a job after their own hearts, which they carried out effectively.[8]

Monash privately wrote a series of savage criticisms of English soldiers. 'There is now no longer any question that our Australian troops are in every way superior to the British and Indian regulars,' he wrote on 18 August. A month later he became irate at overhearing two British staff officers denigrating the Australians' capacity for 'real soldiering'—'yet those are the blighters we've been fighting for, and for whom Australia has been shedding her good red blood'. He thought it high time that people asked why Australian troops were 'being sacrificed in such large numbers'. Formerly an admirer of Hamilton's control, he now joined the critics of

*Chunuk Bair, held briefly by New Zealanders during the August offensives, offers a panoramic view. From here, Suvla Bay operations could easily have been seen to the northwest; 180 degrees the other way, across yet more of those serried ridges, was the tantalising but unreachable blue of the Dardanelles. (Photo: John Robertson)*

Stopford's 9th Corps and castigated Britain's running of the campaign since early April. He was also furious at the 'red tape run mad' on Lemnos, and the occasional 'prize fool' of a British staff officer who did nothing to cope with problems. He also damned the gross mismanagement and incapacity of English military hospitals.[9]

Britons both in England and at the front freely denounced the performance of Stopford's corps. The more Keyes heard of 'that SUVLA business' the more maddening and awful it was to contemplate. Hamilton and officers on his staff formed the same opinion, which led to the dismissals previously mentioned. 'People coming back from Gallipoli,' Lady Godley told her husband in late October, 'all say that the Suvla landing and fighting was an absolute disgace to our army and organization.' The Welsh Division (the 53rd), Hamilton told Kitchener on 19 August, had fallen 'utterly to pieces', and the Lowland Division (the 52nd) did not have 'a good spirit in it'. As well, the 10th, 11th, 53rd and 54th divisions earned a bad reputation on Hamilton's staff and further afield. General Sir Henry Sclater, the Adjutant-General at the War Office, later claimed that Kitchener deliberately chose the three weakest available Territorial divisions to go to Gallipoli.[10]

Maurice Hankey was frank in his assessments. Asquith on 20 August told Kitchener that he had read enough of Hankey's long, interesting letter to be satisfied that the generals and staff engaged in the 'Suvla part of the business' ought to be court-martialled and dismissed from the army. Almost three months later R. A. Sanders, a British officer serving on Gallipoli, wrote to Lord Edmund Talbot: 'The worst feature is the rottenness of a lot of the troops. Battalions lost all their officers and half their men at the start and have been filled up with raw drafts. They are now absolutely rotten either for fighting or working, and the officers are very junior and ignorant. The stories one hears here of the Suvla landing are enough to make one wonder how our army ever succeeds in anything. It seems to have been an absolute example of everything staff work ought not to be.' By early September the United States' Embassy in Constantinople had heard that the British officers in charge of the Suvla landing were ignorant and incompetent and had produced a muddle 'beyond description', although for twenty-four hours they saw virtually no Turkish troops.[11]

Years later, when C. F. Aspinall-Oglander was writing the British official history of this campaign, one correspondent, asked to comment on his chapters on

Suvla, replied: 'I think the English language is hardly adequate to describe the state of affairs which existed at Suvla on 9th August, 1915, when the 153rd Brigade landed there. Your picture is good as far as it goes but it still does not convey the atmosphere of indifference, laissez-faire and chaos into which we plunged.'[12] General Callwell, in his earlier study of the campaign, despite his extreme reluctance to make critical comments, did point out that Stopford's corps 'failed to move' on 9 August, that it could have relieved the pressure on Godley's troops, and that Birdwood had every reason to expect at least some indirect help from that quarter during his corps' desperate attempt to secure Sari Bair.[13]

While Britons were embarrassed by the performance of Stopford's corps, the reputation of the Australians and New Zealanders was enhanced during the August battles. Hamilton was now referring to the troops under Birdwood as 'that famous Corps'. These troops, he told Kitchener, 'cannot be praised too highly'. He spoke of 'their magnificent night march' over rugged country, and 'their dash and vigour in attack'. The Australians' gallant capture and defence of Lone Pine 'are exploits which will live in history'. Birdwood was equally glowing in his assessments, claiming that no other troops in the world would have been thought good enough to be given the task of making the breakout through the rugged country on Anzac's northern flank. Another British general wrote, 'The spirit shown by the Colonials is wonderful, and ought to put some millions of men in this country to shame.' 'The Anzac people are simply splendid and there is no other word for them,' wrote Keyes, speaking for others as well as himself. Similar sentiments were conveyed to readers of *The Times* by Ashmead-Bartlett when he wrote that at Lone Pine the Australians 'rushed forward to the assault with the fury of fanatics'. The August offensive 'was a combat of giants in a giant country and, if one point stands out more than other, it is the marvellous hardihood, tenacity, and reckless courage shown by the Australians and New Zealanders'.[14]

A few comments, widely separated geographically but concentrated into five days, underline the extent of the Australasian troops' reputation. In London, in his submission of 30 August to cabinet, Hankey wrote: 'The Australians and New Zealanders have a splendid *morale* and their discipline, if unorthodox, appears to produce satisfactory results.' Hankey's praises were echoed by many other Britons. From Cairo on 28 August, General Maxwell observed to Hamilton that in his mixed force 'the Australians and New Zealanders seem hard to stop, once they get launched, the others seem easier to stop than to launch!!' On Gallipoli, Birdwood told de Robeck how magnificently his troops had done in such terrible country.[15]

Turkish prisoners, some wounded, await embarkation on Watson's Pier on 9 August. Both sides took prisoners during the August attacks, but throughout the campaign the Allies took many more than the Turks. Note the bales of hay for mules and horses and the prohibition on swimming without permission.

# CHAPTER 21

# THE 2ND DIVISION REACHES ANZAC

O N 12 AUGUST Hamilton told London that the great offensive had failed. He asked for more reinforcements. He was sent forty-seven thousand, enough to hold his ground and undertake several operations with limited objectives. The most significant new formations sent to him were five thousand British yeomanry of the 2nd Mounted Division, serving without horses, and the 2nd Australian division.

The move of this division to Anzac was spread over several weeks, the 5th Brigade (17th to 20th battalions), from New South Wales, being the first to leave Egypt. They went eagerly. A Victorian onlooker wrote: 'It is wonderful to see the spirit of the lads who are going away with the 5th Brigade. All day yesterday . . . they were singing shouting and cheering, yet every day they see thousands of their Comrades walking around the streets wounded.' He mentioned the praise for his countrymen and added, 'Thank God I'm Australian.' The spirits of the 5th Brigade were nourished by this reputation. As one wrote, 'Although have heard a lot of nasty things about we Australians still it is recognized by everyone that they can fight. [An Indian] reckons our boys are just it with the bayonet.' To Private Douglas Argyle, a 6th Battalion reinforcement, who left Heliopolis on 11 August, the men were behaving as if they were off to a sports meeting. They were happy as they 'started on a journey that [they had been] waiting for six months'. Three days later he saw the torpedoed *Royal Edward* sink, with the loss of over a thousand British soldiers. At Mudros nurses commonly gave the name 'the evening sacrifice' to the shiploads of troops they saw leaving at dusk for Gallipoli.[1]

Men from the 5th Brigade reached Gallipoli in time for some to take part in two attacks on the Suvla Plain near the junction of old Anzac and the Suvla beachhead, in the sector from Scimitar Hill to Hill 60. Here, the front line at one point was only a kilometre and a half inland from the sea. Hamilton wanted to strengthen the link between Anzac and Suvla by pushing that line further inland. The resulting battle was fought on 21–22 August. At first the attackers—British, Indians, New Zealanders and Australians—were mainly experienced but tired and ill veterans. Then at short notice at dawn on 22 August the newly arrived 18th Battalion was ordered to attack Hill 60. Half of this brave but inexperienced battalion became casualties, almost two hundred men being killed. At excessive cost, small gains were made, including the lower slopes of the gentle rise known as Hill 60.

Within a few days Birdwood decided to try again to strengthen the line by seizing the summit of Hill 60. The attack was made from 27 to 29 August, mainly by tired veterans, reinforced by the 17th and 18th battalions. The Turks lost some more of the lower slopes and trenches but retained control of the summit. The junction between the two beachheads was made reasonably secure, at high cost in men's lives. During the fierce fighting on 29 August Lieutenant Hugo Throssell, a farmer from Cowcowing, Western Australia, in the 10th Light Horse, won the Victoria Cross. The attacks of late August showed no improvement in tactics compared with earlier assaults. Monash wrote, 'The whole was a rotten, badly-organized show—and those who planned it are responsible for a heavy loss.' He was extremely worried about the unsatisfactory condition of his brigade. The battle coincided with conclusive proof reaching the American Embassy in Constantinople that the Suvla landing had 'accomplished nothing save to extend the line'.[2]

This fact, stressed by later historians, was commented on forcefully by participants lucky enough to survive. A British subaltern complained about the MEF's bombastic, over-confident staff. 'It is the whole story over again,' he wrote of the horrors of 21 August. 'Until we have learned that we are not the only nation the Almighty has planted on the face of the earth, and that such people as the Turks, though uncivilized and unchristian, are as brave as many and braver than most, until a very different spirit is infused into our general command, such costly failures as that of to-day must inevitably continue.' 'The whole place [the approaches to Hill 60] is strewn with bodies,' wrote Major Allanson, '—Gurkhas, Australians, Connaught Rangers . . . the sights [are] revolting and disgusting.'[3]

John J. Walker was one of the New South Welshmen who had his 'baptism of shrapnel on August 22'. He was knocked down by an exploding shell as he crossed the open plain towards the Turkish trenches. He thought the attack 'was a terrible blunder [by] our heads. . . . It was madness to cross this place in daylight.' For the benefit of his siblings he analysed modern trench warface, which was 'totally opposed to anything taught in military works'. After the bombardment the tactics were: Charge with fixed bayonets and lose about half of your men. Bomb the enemy out of his back trenches with hand grenades, etc. Connect his trench with your own. Result gained 60 yards of ground, 120 yards of trench. Lost 1000 men. No Good.' As he pointed out, the Australians were only 1,200 yards from the 'original historic landing of the ANZAC'. He described the hell of the attack on Hill 60, which produced 'the most horrid monument of war's destructiveness' he ever wanted to see. He described the piles of bodies in 'about 12 acres. Men were there dead in all positions. Some holding their heads as if distracted, others in praying attitude.' 'Of course,' he added, 'in every action many of the wounded died between the trenches because the Army Medical Corps cannot reach them'. And so he closed 'this horrid tale of war' to his siblings.[4]

Hamilton told Kitchener that the fighting of 27–29 August, which resulted in a further four hundred acres of Turkish territory being wrested from the enemy, 'was almost entirely hand-to-hand and of a very severe nature'.[5] Accounts by Bean and Ashmead-Bartlett were appearing in the Australian press from 6 September.

These were the last attacks of any size launched by the Mediterranean Expeditionary Force. It did comparatively little fighting after August. The rate of battle casualties mercifully fell, although the force still sustained losses from Turkish fire on its confined territory. Disease continued to ravage the force. This was partly in reaction to the August failure, but even newly arrived units suffered. For example, 350 men of the 23rd Battalion were sick during its fourteen weeks at Anzac. Robert Raws, now a lieutenant, reached Anzac on 3 September and stayed until the end; the most important military manoeuvre he saw on Gallipoli was the evacuation.[6]

The 6th and 7th brigades were thus spared the ordeal of a set-piece attack at Gallipoli. Not that they realised their good fortune as they prepared to join the leading brigade in their division. As H. F. Curnow of the 22nd Battalion put it, 'We are all so glad to feel that at last we're off to the front. No doubt many of us will be back in hospital in a week or so and others less fortunate will pass out but we are all living cheerfully a day at a time.' He went on to say, 'I want to write to a few more pals while I've got life, a right hand, good eyesight, etc etc.' Robert Raws had felt sure that his brother, Alec, would have to enlist in due course: 'the call

*Horace Moore-Jones, Yeomanry Camp, Imbros Harbour, GHQ, 1915 (watercolour with pencil, 19.3 × 28.2 cm). During the Gallipoli landings, Hamilton and his general staff were aboard the* Queen Elizabeth, *but he eventually set up headquarters on Imbros. It was 24 kilometres from Gallipoli, though within earshot of Anzac gunfire. The island also served as a staging post for some of the troops used in General Stopford's Suvla operation, including the 2nd Mounted, or Yeomanry, Division.*

becomes more urgent.' He added, 'The extraordinary advance of the Germans into Russia has been occupying our minds all week.'[7]

The voyage to Mudros was more hazardous than it had been in April. On 30 August the 21st Battalion boarded the *Southland* at Alexandria; the ship was on its way to Gallipoli for its first experience of war. A company of the 23rd Battalion and some other soldiers were also on board, making a total of fifty-three officers and 1,315 men. Three days later a German submarine torpedoed the ship, about sixty-five kilometres south of Mudros Bay. The men had had no boat drill, despite the loss of the *Triumph* and *Royal Edward*. When the boats were lowered 'one was swamped by a rush of stokers' as soon as it touched the water. The soldiers calmly waited their turn to enter the boats as the ship seemed to be sinking. It then became apparent that it was not so badly damaged as at first thought and that there was a chance of nursing it to Mudros. Seventeen Australians and a British officer (of the 29th Division) volunteered to stoke the *Southland*'s fires, and the ship, looking a strange sight as it lumbered through the water at an awkward angle, reached Mudros that evening. Lieutenant Aram was one of those who stayed on board. He told his mother that he was too scared to get into one of the small boats, as he was not a very good swimmer.[8]

Thirty-three men—twenty-nine of them Australians—had died because of the torpedo attack. The Australian government at first wanted to delay publication of news of the incident because of the possible impact upon civilian morale. Then the British government requested that the news be withheld. Possibly the aim was to deny useful information to the enemy; but could some British authorities have been sensitive about the inability of the Royal Navy to protect troops bound for the battle area? In any case, letters describing the incident soon reached Australia, and a danger developed of exaggerated rumours. By early November Australian ministers were seeking approval from Britain to publish the truth. The War Office and the Admiralty now agreed, but the Colonial Office was slow to pass on this agreement to Australia, not doing so until a further request had arrived from Melbourne, eleven weeks after the torpedo struck. Joseph Cook, leader of the opposition, said that no outsider could understand why the authorities withheld this statement for so long, as all the details were well known.[9]

The 2nd Division men were brought ashore in Anzac Cove, where the 3rd Brigade had landed. This gave them all the chance to experience some of the natural obstacles faced on 25 April. Although troops now landed in the dark, there were dangers. One occupant of a barge which was almost sunk by a shell had recurring visions, for fifty years, of the menacing column of water rising alongside the barge and threatening to engulf it.[10]

The last AIF brigade to reach Anzac was the 7th, comprising the 25th to 28th battalions from the four least populous states. The 25th Battalion had marched through Brisbane on 29 May but did not sail from Sydney until 7 July. It reached Suez on 2 August. With the 26th (Queensland and Tasmania) it disembarked at Anzac on 11 September, two days later than the 28th, from Western Australia.

To Anzac veterans the new diamond shoulder patches of the 2nd Division men made a very welcome sight. 'The wearers, radiant with good health, looked like a different race of men and made us realise our wasted and worn-out condition.' The British commanding generals were as impressed by the physique of the men in this formation as they had been by that of the first Australian soldiers they had seen. The generals differed in their first impressions of the quality of the officers and non-commissioned officers, although Hamilton and Birdwood agreed they were inferior. The latter hoped Australia would not raise further units, as he feared it would be almost impossible to provide enough good officers.[11]

The new arrivals walked in awe on the ground hallowed by the earlier contingents. They had to prove themselves worthy of the traditions so quickly created by the Anzac veterans; and they were soon recording their impressions of the beachhead, the lifestyle and the fighting. One noted in a letter, 'Those brave fellows made history'; another entered in his diary, 'All round us [near the landing-place] were the last resting places of the brave lads who had done their duty, helped to pave the way for us, and laid down their life for their country.'

Almost two hundred men of the 18th Battalion saw little of Anzac—those who landed on 19 August and died in the Hill 60 attack on the 22nd. When the new units took over from the veterans, the 7th Brigade, for example, relieved the NZ and A Division in its sector on the north of 'old' Anzac. That division had fewer

*Piles of equipment and clothing collected at Anzac after the August battles. In the foreground are mules carrying rations to the trenches.*

*The 'cookhouse' at which these men are queuing is likely to have been a very basic affair. There was no catering corps—only some army bakers and butchers on Imbros. It was up to individual units to organise any cooking of the rations provided. The infantry generally cooked for themselves, another activity to share with friends. The diet was predominantly bully beef, hard biscuits, a little cheese and bacon.*

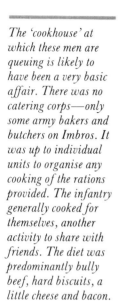

men capable of fighting than did the brigade that took over its length of line.

'It won't be long before I'm a kind of wild man,' wrote Private Argyle, 'we don't wash take off our clothes or sleep much at this game the tucker is bad. . . . I smacked a chap in the eye tonight for talking about steak and eggs . . . carrying tea from the cookhouse to the trenches up a steep Hill men over here do the work that a horse does at home.' A few days later he 'was half buried in a fall of earth'. He did not mind the bullets but hated the shells. Even so, after two weeks at Anzac he could sleep through the terrible noise of gunfire. Lieutenant Frank Coen told his mother that he looked a real villain after seven days of this style of living; it was a wonderful sensation to take off his boots after seven days. During his stay in the front line, under fire the whole time, the men's lives had been 'saved' by the first rum issue. Men had to subsist for twenty-four hours on one biscuit and a pint of water. Coen got a splitting headache from the noise and shock of the shells going overhead. Like so many others he quickly realised, 'Things happen with remarkable suddenness here.' One minute he was talking to a man who was dead the next minute.[12]

John Walker, who had been so critical of the Hill 60 attack, was resilient. 'Our life is hard,' he told his parents, 'but we don't mind. Plenty of work, little sleep, good food and few washes makes a strange mixture. But I am pleased to be here and would not have missed it for anything.' Staff Sergeant A. E. Leane had similar feelings. He had had a desk job with good quarters at base in Egypt, but he gave that up as he had come to the war to go to the front and did not want to return home to say that he had never been under fire. He was aware that sons' attitudes might not be shared by mothers. News that a family friend had probably been killed would, he thought, kill the bereaved mother. The missing soldier was an only child, and his parents 'went on their knees to him not to go'.[13]

Lieutenant Aram had spells of homesickness, increased by the natural beauties at Anzac—the beautiful sea view, the sunsets, perfect moonlight nights. 'You couldn't imagine anything so beautiful!' he told his mother. He commented on the number of old friends and acquaintances he met on the beachhead, 'particularly lads whom [he had] taught'. He reckoned that the men were 'quite fed up with having to live like rabbits' and that it was 'taking the officers all they [knew] to keep [them] from jumping the parapets and having a real good go at old "Abdul"', but such a thing would be madness and suicide'. Aram's appraisal of Australian bravery had not changed. On the other hand a recently arrived Australian sergeant had doubts about the fighting qualities of some of the men. He thought highly of his own platoon but told his mother, 'I think some of them [men in other platoons] will be dirtying their trousers when they get the order to charge.'[14]

Although it did not take part in a major operation on Gallipoli, the 7th Brigade suffered casualties from rifle and machine-gun fire and from 'plenty of shrapnel buzzing around'. On 22 September, a 'dark day' for the 28th Battalion, it lost thirteen men killed, or wounded, all from shrapnel. The flies were still terrible, especially at meals. Many dead men remained lying in front of all positions, and Sam Blows noted, 'Jacko takes the boots off any near his line.' The new brigade also provided some entertainment for the 'old hands'. Alf Clennett told his mother about veterans laughing at how the new men in the 26th Battalion dodged the shells and bullets.[15]

The 2nd Australian Division reached Anzac just in time to give survivors of the 1st Division an essential rest. A schedule was established whereby units spent some weeks recuperating on Lemnos. It was not before time, as many veterans thought they had 'earned a decent spell'. There was disappointment at some delays in the schedule. The 4th Battalion suffered because it took longer than expected to embark the 1st and 3rd battalions. The men were moved to the beach on 12 September. They waited from 2 a.m. until 6 a.m. and then were told to go back to their previous position. According to one soldier, the 'language of the men

*Men of the 2nd Australian Division were reaching Anzac in early September. Some of them are shown here in trenches at Lone Pine. Note the variety of headgear and the district loyalties: one hatband has 'COLAC' (a town in Victoria) inscribed on it in indelible pencil.*

*Men of the 7th Battalion returning to Anzac after a short break at Lemnos. Arrival of the 2nd Division enabled some relief for 1st Division veterans.*

turned the air blue'.[16]

Men who found it a welcome change to get away from the shells and bullets took stock of what had happened to their comrades. Private Albert E. Dowse reflected: 'I am the only one left out of the lot that used to be in the tent with me at old Kenso. I have had a few slight cracks but nothing serious.' Private Henry Daniels added up the number of originals left in the first four platoons of the 16th Battalion. 'No. 1 2 left; No. 2 0 left; No. 3 4 left out of 51; No. 4 2 left.' Murray Aitken told his mother that of the original 11th Battalion of over a thousand men who had landed on 25 April, there were only sixty-nine survivors, who had never left the peninsula except on duty.[17]

To many of the soldiers Lemnos looked attractive in its autumn colours, even though the weather turned cold, a keen wind often blew, and the rain fell. There was insufficient accommodation, so some men had to sleep in the mud all night. Relatively short drills, including bomb-throwing and route marches, helped to keep the men occupied. Sports were organised. Men could ride horses, donkeys or mules around the island. There was a daily issue of beer and better and more varied food, the latter sometimes having untoward results. The sudden change to good food at Sarpi camp at first caused indigestion. In time the better food brought benefits, as did the general rest on Lemnos. J. Fitzmaurice, a member of the 10th Light Horse who had filed into the trenches an hour before daybreak on 7 August, left for Lemnos on 10 November. Three days later he wrote: 'Feel as if we are in a new world. Cannot sleep at night as there is no noise.' Five weeks later he felt 'a new man', being 'as fit as a fiddle'.[18] The men's time on Lemnos was limited, and eventually they embarked for the short overnight trip to the familiar Anzac beachhead, which to some men no doubt appeared almost homely.

# CHAPTER 22

# 'WAITING FOR THE TURKS TO GROW TOO OLD TO FIGHT'

*T*HE CAMPAIGN must be 'one of the most colossal blunders we have ever made,' reflected Major Allanson. 'All we poor devils have to pay the penalty. There is no doubt that to have to advance against modern weapons is a most awful task and a most terribly costly one.' The commanders came to realise this, so after August there were no more offensives. By 9 September—a little belatedly—Monash saw that Hamilton's overall plan had failed. That had overshadowed the many minor successes of Australasian troops, especially those in the 4th Brigade. He admitted the Turks had 'fought with the greatest bravery and skill: A few days later, when he and Godley visited the Aghyl Dere,' Monash remarked, 'Godley funked going to the foremost point.'[1]

Troops at Anzac settled into a slightly revised routine. Towering three hundred metres above them was the range on which some of their fellows had briefly held out early in August. Anzac was only marginally enlarged by the offensive and remained a very cramped lodgement. The Turks, on the higher ground, still dominated the beachhead, which was almost as vulnerable as ever to enemy fire. Movement of supplies still had to be concentrated into the night hours. At dusk the strings of mules and mule-carts would begin carrying ammunition, rations, water, bombs and other supplies to the front line. By September the whole of Anzac beach was strewn with wrecks of lighters and boats.

One difference from earlier months was that gunfire was now interspersed by periods of silence; men could 'wonder if the war was on'. 'Barring a few small skirmishes,' one veteran wrote, 'very little doing. Must be waiting for the Turks to grow too old to fight it looks like.' The 'sit down' style of warfare was different from what the newcomers had expected. 'Trench warfare is no good to our boys,' wrote one. 'God help Abdul if we get him on the desert. He won't be able to trench and it will be right in our hands.'[2] Others agreed: 'In ordinary country we should go through them like a hot knife through butter, but this is far from ordinary country.' Some Australians still remained optimistic about their chances of making a break-through and then pushing on. Others, well aware of the wider issues—although they had to concentrate on the immediate issue of survival—were reduced to hoping against hope that the Dardanelles would be forced. Birdwood told Kitchener that his men would soon be in Constantinople if all could match the performance of Sing, his 'pet sniper', who by the end of October was said to have the phenomenal 'bag' of two hundred enemy victims to his credit. Robert Raws might have been a soldier at heart, for he found 'the technical situation . . . exceedingly interesting'.[3]

One soldier told his mother what this 'sit down' warfare entailed. He wrote of the system of forty-eight hours in the firing line, followed by a forty-eight-hour spell. 'We are glad of the spells,' he said. 'It is of course a big strain while we are in and every day we have some casualties, as . . . bombs continually fly over both ways. When a Turk gets hit he makes a deuce of a row about it and calls "Allah Allah" innumerable times. None of our chaps have made a whimper when they have been hit and they have some of them had some horrible wounds, but they never make a sound. It's just great the way they behave.' He told a relative about the rum issue the men got after they had done their forty-eight hours in the trenches. 'It puts a different aspect on life altogether, and you see smiles where before only gloom reigned supreme.' Private Abbott from Victoria described how he had to go down a sap about four metres towards the Turkish trenches and lie there for an hour holding a revolver to a loophole in some sandbags. 'Our engineers blew up this sap when they met the Turks,' he wrote, 'so now it has to be guarded. Felt a bit shaky going down at first but soon got used to it. Had to.' He was given a worse job in November being rostered to guard a tunnel running towards the enemy lines. 'No one liked been on guard in it as it was that small you had to crawl to get along it.' Sergeant P. W. Chapman had some different tasks: he liked patrol work because it gave him scope for freedom of thought and action.[4]

If they were not to advance, the Australians could at least make their beachhead more secure by adding to their already intricate trench system. A British subaltern who first visited Anzac late in September thought 'it would take up pages' to describe the trenches, which were 'a perfect marvel and a regular maze to a person who does not know his way about'. Two weeks later he was still enthusing over them as 'a perfect eye-opener, and . . . simply magnificent. They are certainly the most wonderful thing I have seen on the Peninsula. There is a wonderful system of subterranean passages being bore right up to the Turks' lines.' 'What really awful underground warfare modern fighting has become.' However, the trenches were 'spotlessly clean'. Murray Aitken, a front-line soldier who had hardly left Anzac since 25 April, still thought it worth while to describe the trench system to his mother. He compared it with the Kalgoorlie he knew so well. It was a 'system of short jerks and horns', reminding him of 'what would happen if some thousands of miners and prospectors got mad drunk and attempted to dig their individual ways around the world, and not any one going in the same direction as any other'. He explained that this apparent confusion restricted losses from shrapnel hits.[5]

By 8 September Major Allanson was commenting on the awful strain of being under constant fire for five weeks. Many Australians, of course, had been under such strain for much longer, and their privations scarcely lessened after the August offensive. In late September a British soldier who had been at all the beachheads wrote from Malta, where he was ill: 'I see the British Press is getting restive on the Dardanelles question. No one who has not been present can conceive the bravery and hardships of the troops, especially the Colonials, and no one better than they can see the awful extent of the blunder.'[6] High-ranking British officers agreed. A General Wallace, a 'nice fat man' whom Lady Godley met at dinner, had spent a few minutes at Anzac, thought it was awful, and could not imagine how anyone endured it. Major-General C. G. A. Egerton, commander of the 52nd Division, said that a few months at Helles was enough to kill any man and that conditions were far worse at Anzac. An artillery officer, recently arrived from France, was struck by the 'different show' on the peninsula—no nice farm house to billet in with French bread and wines, mails regular every day or so'. Despite the gains of August, the 'tremendous difference between Helles and Suvla and Anzac' still impressed visitors. There was 'room to move about at the first, none at the other two'. Lady Godley told her husband that some of the men from Anzac whom she saw in convalescent depots in Cairo needed a long rest, even though they had not been wounded. They were 'just done and their nerves utterly upset'.[7]

Sam Blows wrote. 'It is peculiar to see us in our little dugouts, and it is a pity a few rabbits are not here, as then a fellow could crawl down their holes, and thus save us from much digging. It is terribly hilly and unclimbable in most places. . . . Had to be careful when digging our dugout here, for fear of finding something we do not wish to see or think about.' But it was good to see 'our warships' and to hear them fire. Within a week of arriving, Blows and his mates had dug themselves in well—'and don't we scuttle into [our dugout] when shrapnel comes our way'. 'We are always very very thirsty,' he noted. Alf Clennett told his mother that he did not want any of his letters to go into the newspapers. He would have liked to tell her more about the war, but he was on his honour, so had to refrain. This hardened veteran could derive wry amusement from a distinctive pleasure which only a battlefield could provide. He met someone he knew from home, who was 'boots and rousabout for an officer', and did not have to go into the trenches. He said he had not come to fight, he did not believe in getting hit, and he was dead scared when some bullets whistled over the dugout where he was talking to Alf. 'I was wishing', Alf told his mother, 'the Turks would start shelling us to have some fun with him.'[8]

Private H. A. Fildes, on his return to Anzac after being wounded, told his mother about his food and accommodation. Bread was a luxury the soldiers rarely saw, but they had rice, biscuits, bully beef and jam, and bacon for breakfast every day or so. He had good fresh water for drinking and cooking, but it was 'criminal to wash in it'. Private Angus washed twice in his first six weeks at Anzac. Lieutenant Eric Edgerton of the 24th Battalion had his first all-over wash in three weeks in less than a pint of water. 'We are all as lousy as a bandicoot,' wrote Private Argyle. 'The vermin are a dam sight worse than the Turks to fight. . . . My mate tells me if my mother saw me she would put me to bed for three weeks.' Life in dugouts, thought Private Fildes, was like prehistoric days: every man had his dugout where he could eat, sleep and shelter.[9]

Army rations could sometimes be supplemented by extras bought at the beach from enterprising sailors. Private H. Paull mentioned that eggs, milk, tea, chocolate, cake and so on were snapped up by men who were 'so glad to get a change' that they paid the inflated prices.[10] Lieutenant Aram praised the variety of the food and sent his mother a rosy picture of Anzac conditions. 'By way of a change today, each man was given two eggs each to eat with his bacon and yet they call it war. They couldn't be doing better if they were living in an hotel.' Even a private could be satisfied that he had been 'getting excellent tucker'.[11] From time to time men received from home parcels which might contain sweets or similar foodstuffs, along with cigarettes, matches, socks and other useful items.

*After the anticlimax of the August offensives, the health of men at Anzac deteriorated alarmingly. Appetites faded, and enfeebled men in agony with dysentery spread by the millions of flies slept overnight by latrines. These men of 8th Battalion Signal Section show the effects of emaciation.*

Nevertheless, these were only palliatives. With the anticlimax after the August offensive, the health of the men at Anzac deteriorated alarmingly. Birdwood frequently told Hamilton of this. Hamilton recognised the need for more variety in food and expected some improvement with the arrival of canteen ship later in August. 'You find a fine big Australian,' he told Kitchener, 'who will tell you he is as weak as a cat and, although his spirit is all for fighting the Turk, he cannot. . . climb up a hill.' By the end of the month the prolonged strain in the trenches had led to the daily evacuation from Anzac of about two hundred cases of sickness.[12]

Early in September one correspondent clearly encapsulated the health problem in an assessment which eventually reached Lord Curzon, one of the highest ranking Conservative ministers in the coalition cabinet and a member of the Dardanelles Committee: 'Our men both at Helles and [Gaba] Tepe are becoming very stale and tired and in many cases disheartened by heavy losses in their officers and best men. There is no real rest camp in either place. . . . Continuous shell fire even if only for some hours daily becomes very trying to men's nerves. The troops here want a complete rest for some days together.'[13]

Birdwood could 'not have believed to what an extraordinary extent really strong men can get run down merely by an enervating climate and ordinary sickness'. His doctors assured him that the men could 'do little more than lean against the parapets and fire over them, as they were absolutely done'. In early October Birdwood's senior medical adviser emphasised the seriousness of the situation. The physical condition of troops at Anzac was 'very serious', he wrote. 'Many of them, who have been here for some months, are extremely feeble, suffering from rapid pulse, shortness of breath on slight exertion, great loss of weight, anaemia, and "dysenteric diarrhoea". . . . At present efforts are being made to patch up hundreds of men, who are being treated by the [Regimental Medical Officers] in the line. . . . nearly all these cases will have to be evacuated on the onset of bad weather. . . . I view with great apprehension the approaching winter owing to the weakened state of the men.'[14] One of the ill men suffering from dysentery was Private Paull: 'Have a nasty touch of dysentery again,' he wrote; 'it is a hellish complaint and bothers a man so at night spoiling his sleep.' A few days later, to his great regret, he had to leave Anzac. 'I have been almost in agony at times lately with this complaint.'[15]

As early as the end of August one Australian soldier noted, 'The nights are gradually getting colder now and we shall soon need extra blankets.' Within a few weeks Murray Aitken was preparing for a possible long stay. 'I've got iron on my roof, lined the dug-out with blankets, built my bed up from the floor with the aid of biscuit boxes, and generally made it as safe and comfortable as possible under the circumstances; have got a rain screen in the front, too and also pictures of pretty girls on the walls. The best I can do.' Others, however, complained that they lacked shelter and materials even though the authorities had had five months to supply these needs.[16]

Despite the stalemate and the approach of winter, 'the cheeriness of the men' was 'a great contrast to Suvla', thought Lieutenant A. M. McGrigor, Birdwood's aide-de-camp. Two other British officers, Major Allanson and General Paris, at Suvla, no doubt would have agreed. Allanson told his brother, 'I shall never leave this peninsula alive I am convinced.' Paris wrote in late September, 'Things are rotten out here and it's difficult to keep cheerful, merry and bright.' Meanwhile, Birdwood was telling Hankey, 'We all at "Anzac" are full of cheeriness and confidence in the future, which rather makes one think that in time to come we will have created geography as well as history, as I think the word "Anzac" will have to appear in all future maps.'[17]

Lieutenant Aram presented a cheerful face to his family. 'Talk about the horrors of war. The humours far outweigh them.' So magnificent did the Aegean appear from his dugout that he called it 'Seaview'. He was enthralled by the gorgeous sunsets. 'Never are there two alike. Old Sol sits in glorious splendour behind the Islands made famous in Grecian Mythology.' He interrupted his lyrical description of this timeless beauty to ask his mother to be sure to arrange his membership of the Melbourne Cricket Club. Sergeant William Alabaster told his family that he was 'having a fairly good time, [finding] life full of interest—these are interesting times are they not? But Brigadier-General Granville Ryrie, commander of the 2nd Light Horse Brigade, told his wife to tell his daughters on no account to marry a soldier; 'it is the rottenest profession of the lot, nothing but absolute slavery, and no soldier has a shilling to bless himself with. . . . I have had enough fighting to last me for the rest of my life and I wish I was on my way home now.'[18]

On 2 September Private Argyle, writing about a friend, said, 'He reckons this is a cranky game he says the Turks are fair fighters and it's madness to be shooting at one another.' Others had a well-developed sense of duty and the wider implications of their role in the war. Robert Raws told his nephew that all young people must do what they could, after the war, to see there was no repetition of the catastrophe. Frank Coen told his family he was grateful to have been spared so far 'for the continuance of that supreme duty' he owed to them, his country, and himself.[19] For many, mateship had the same effect as duty. Some soldiers, glad to get a minor wound which took them from the beachhead, were reluctant to return to the fighting. But there is no way of knowing how many thought like this, and how many convalescents were anxious to get back to Anzac to share its dangers with their mates. There were plenty, fretting in Alexandria, wanting to return to the trenches 'for another go at Johnny Turk'. 'Would rather be at Gallipoli,' wrote a soldier in an Alexandria hospital; 'it gets on your nerves loafing here.'[20]

The Australians' tenacity and cheerfulness were sustained by their pride in their achievements. Murray Aitken ascribed their ability to the fact that they were 'born fighters', each with 'his separate individuality and his priceless initiative which made him . . . infinitely better than the clockwork soldier'. Aitken had been in

*Troops make preparations in Rest Gully before the August offensives. Major Bill Brind observed to his mother on 2 November 1915, 'The name "Rest Trenches" is given in sarcasm as the men do anything but rest when they go into them.' Much the same might have been said of Rest Gully, even though John Walker found to go there away from the trenches 'still a rest'.*

many bayonet charges, and he told his mother he enjoyed them. 'When the position was made safe and there was time for a breather men shook hands with one another seemingly as long-lost friends re-united; and, finally, . . . when the excitement had worn down it was reckoned to be all in the days work.'[21]

With such spirit displayed by men after four months in the thick of the fighting, little wonder Britons in contact with them were warm in their praise. Birdwood told Kitchener on 6 September that the 54th Division, a Territorial division from East Anglia, were 'an extraordinarily young lot of boys, and seem almost children compared with most of my Australians, a great many of whom look as if they could eat up any two of them'. Birdwood soon declared himself 'so completely an Australian' that he identified with them; but others without his attachments and affection for them made similar assessments.[22]

One person who commented was an old boy of Harrow, the Reverend W. F. Scott, RN. On Lemnos at the end of September he visited Themina, the only spot on the island where beer was available. The place was full of Australians, drinking their first beer for 'centuries'. 'The Australians are no respectors of persons, and express themselves very freely indeed about certain units of the New Army, which joined them at Suvla. But they are real men and appreciate the right stuff when they do see it—as they have done with the famous 29th Division.'[23]

High and low, the praises circulated. In mid-September Bonar Law told Munro Ferguson, 'I can only say again what I have written you more than once—how deep has been the impression made upon the people of this country by the splendid qualities shown by the Australians and New Zealanders.' A Royal Navy man who had been stationed off Anzac since the landing thought 'our Anzacs' were 'toppers, nothing stops them'. Roger Keyes while at Mudros told his wife a story about twelve British Army Service Corps men, 'lazy devils who sat doing nothing all day'; they would not help him pitch a tent, but a young Australian officer who happened to be near by begged to help and did the task.[24]

In July Hamilton had charged Lieutenant-General Sir Edward Altham with the job of improving conditions at Mudros, which was a badly disorganised base. In late September Altham told Hamilton, 'I am sorry to say we are having a little trouble with the Australians trying to paint red Greek villages and bistros, but I am taking disciplinary measures to stop it.' Hamilton did not let such misbehaviour affect his assessment of the AIF when he later wrote to Lord Stamfordham, George V's private secretary. The Australians, 'although hopeless from our point of view as regards punctilio etc etc, and although also having, to put it mildly, a very good opinion of themselves, yet . . . are indubitably splendid fighting stuff under such trials as we have been experiencing here'.[25]

Imperial officers still commented on less appealing Australian characteristics. Some complained that luxuries had to be well guarded or 'they [got] stolen by the Australians in the most scandalous way'. They stole boxes of food 'on every possible occasion' and said that they did 'very well as they [had] efficient "Foraging officers"'. Guy Dawnay was impressed by the contrast between the Australians in Cairo and at the front. 'The Australians are a most lawless, turbulent and undisciplined crowd, who really break out and commit fearful atrocities! But it is wonderful what good fighting men they turn out when they get up to Gallipoli.' Royal Navy chaplain John de Vitre told with approval a 'quaint yarn' about Australians at Anzac, tired of paying 'fabulous' prices to a sailor-entrepreneur who sold goods on the beach, taking all the man's stores one night and distributing them among some dugouts. A British army officer at Anzac told of a fellow officer who had just reached the beachhead: 'He was a real old campaigner. The first thing he did was to land six enormous cases from Fortnum and Mason's and set an armed guard over them. He had heard tell of the Australians.'[26]

# CHAPTER 23

# LONDON STALEMATE; BALKANS DISASTER

*W*HILE THE MEN at Anzac improved their accommodation for a long stay, strategic issues were being hotly contested in the heart of the Empire and between London and Hamilton's headquarters. Quite properly, the argument resumed with a new intensity as soon as the main August offensive failed. That failure caused serious concern among the officers on Hamilton's staff, several of whom were becoming increasingly critical of his leadership and of his refusal to tell the government precisely what was happening. Orlo Williams despaired at 'the shallow optimism of an obstinate man' who thought it 'unsoldierly to tell unpleasant truths' and who was no strategist.[1] As early as 13 August Hamilton's staff officer, Major Guy Dawnay, thought that Anzac and Suvla should be evacuated. Some of his fellow officers agreed. Surgeon-Admiral Sir James Porter, who on 28 July had arrived in the theatre as Principal Hospital Transport Officer, told his wife that Hamilton's dispatches were 'readable journalism and remarkable chiefly in that they *give no indication* of the truth. . . . His immediate staff is said to be glaringly incompetent. To my mind the situation is criminal—and no good will be done till they are removed. The position on that dreadful Gallipoli peninsula is worse today than at the start—and they could not get the men off it if they would without dreadful slaughter.' Malta and Alexandria, he added, were choked to the utmost with between thirty thousand and forty thousand sick and wounded. 'It is positively wicked,' he commented.[2]

On 19 August an acrimonious discussion in the Dardanelles Committee, Britain's supreme body to decide war policy, set the tone for the long, inconclusive argument. Next day Kitchener said he would be glad if Britain could rid itself of the Gallipoli problem, while Churchill produced figures showing that the 'wastage' of recent attacks could readily be replaced by Australians and others who had recovered from wounds or illness and by the Australians who had recently reached Egypt from their homeland. In the course of a long minute to Kitchener on 23 August, Churchill summed up the dangers in a typically vigorous passage. 'The scale, the dangers and the importance of the operations have increased beyond all expectations. The windy weather is approaching. The possibility of the German armies overawing Rumania, crushing Servia, and seducing Bulgaria comes nearer every day. The difficulty of maintaining the army on the peninsula during the winter will be extreme and the wastage very great. Should the Germans obtain free transit for ammunition and heavy guns to Turkey the position of the army may be rendered untenable and a catastrophe fatal and final will ensue.' To obviate this catastrophe, Churchill urged the prompt launching of a renewed major naval attack. Roger Keyes, also, was constantly urging that a forceful resumption of the naval attack would bring victory, but Admiral de Robeck was unimpressed. He could 'only see disaster'.[3]

Churchill's views received significant endorsement in a memorandum circulated by Hankey on 30 August. He stressed 'the tremendous tactical difficulties of a withdrawal' and said that, with further reinforcements, Hamilton could gain 'another success in the Anzac region'. This advice would have been influential. Hankey's opinions and expertise were respected, and he was the only man close to the Empire's high command who had inspected Gallipoli. Churchill's advocacy worried Sir Edward Carson, the Ulster Unionist leader in the House of Commons, who was among the foremost critics of the Gallipoli venture on the Dardanelles Committee. He feared a new move was about to be made on the peninsula without proper preparation. He doubted if anything good would come of the campaign and whether creation of the coalition government had brought any improvement.[4]

By mid-September there were 125,000 Allied soldiers on the Gallipoli Peninsula. Hamilton's total forces of 200,000 also included 37,000 men in Egypt or at other Mediterranean bases; and over 37,000 reinforcements for various of his fifteen divisions were either on the way or under orders to sail to the Dardanelles.[5] Any chance that Hamilton might receive further reinforcements was receding, as on the Dardanelles Committee opinion strengthened that no more lives should be wasted on what increasingly seemed to be a hopeless venture. As well, disquieting reports were arriving about Hamilton. These included an anonymous letter, from someone with special knowledge of the 10th Division, fiercely denouncing Hamilton's 'bad generalship and inadequate arrangements [for] causing [the] fiasco of Suvla'. This letter was printed as a cabinet document in mid-September.[6]

On 10 September Guy Dawnay arrived in London on an extraordinary mission. He travelled, of course, with Hamilton's permission; but Hamilton did not know that Dawnay's object was to warn the Dardanelles Committee of the desperate situation on the peninsula and to stress Hamilton's failings. Dawnay stayed for three weeks, speaking to Kitchener, Churchill and other ministers. Nearly all were impressed by his clear warnings 'that the situation was grave, and even desperate.' However, Churchill's belief that the expedition had not yet failed was reinforced by what Dawnay told him.[7]

Just as there was stalemate at Gallipoli, so there was in the Dardanelles Committee. There was to be neither a further offensive nor any evacuation, at least for

*Using the Kaiser as a target for the Turks— a macabre touch which might also encourage the enemy to expose himself to the sniper, or at least to waste ammunition.*

*Tracks like these became slippery in the bad weather that came with the onset of winter. This photograph dates from just before the August offensives, when Australian fatigue parties were forming ledges or terraces in broken road to accommodate newly arriving troops.*

the time being. After six weeks for wrangling, and voluminous memoranda, on 23 September the Dardanelles Committee, at a meeting attended by six Conservative and five Liberal ministers, agreed it was important to prepare for a winter campaign. Kitchener telegraphed Hamilton: 'I need hardly say there is no intention of abandoning the Dardanelles.' Officers in the Admiralty and War Office studied the problems of a winter campaign. At Anzac Major John Corbin warned of the coming 'terrible, stormy weather', and General Godley commented, 'It will be a job getting up and down these steep hills when the rain really comes. It was getting very slippery this morning.'[8]

On one of the few occasions when the Asquith government allowed a parliamentary debate on the campaign, one of its inveterate critics, the Liberal newspaper owner Sir Henry Dalziel, declared there had been 'colossal blundering' in the Dardanelles, which had cost thousands of lives. Sir Arthur Markham, another Liberal member approaching fifty and a former subaltern in the British army, condemned the government for keeping the House in ignorance of what was happening at the Dardanelles.[9]

The spectacularly disastrous collapse of Britain's Balkans policy gave a new urgency to the Dardanelles Committee's consideration of the fate of the Mediterranean Expeditionary Force. No success had attended the Asquith ministry's hopes of manipulating the governments of south-eastern European nations in order to create a united Balkans front against the Central Powers. It was reasonable to suppose that military success against Turkey would persuade some of the Balkan states to enter the war on the Entente's side, but Britain's diplomatic aims were frustrated because Hamilton's force did not produce the necessary victory. Worse, the failure of the August offensive helped persuade the long-undecided Bulgaria to join the Central Powers; on 6 September it signed a convention whereby it undertook to declare war on Serbia. Faced with the prospect of being overrun, Serbia turned to Britain and France for help. It had been Serbia's integrity as a sovereign state which precipitated the outbreak of the war. Britain and France were now under moral obligation to help the threatened nation, despite the difficulties.

The trend of Balkan politics continued to run against Britain. On 21 September Bulgaria mobilised. Ever the optimist, Hamilton hoped he would live 'to see Ferdinand [King of Bulgaria] transfixed by an Australian bayonet.' Reality was far different. After much discussion between London and Paris it was decided to send an Anglo-French force to Salonika, the nearest Greek port to the Serbian frontier. The first two divisions for this force were moved from Gallipoli on 30 September, a French division taken from Helles and the 10th (Irish) Division from Suvla. They began to disembark on 3 October, a few days before Austrian and German forces, and later Bulgarian, invaded Serbia. The Allied force, under the French general Maurice Sarrail, advanced into Serbia but was repulsed by Bulgarian troops and fell back on Salonika. There, for the time being, it stayed.[10]

Birdwood had good reason to regret 'this appalling Balkan tangle'. As a correspondent observed to Lord Curzon, 'Apparently our diplomacy in the Balkans has been as bad as the strategy that took us to the Dardanelles.' Carson told Bonar Law on 23 October: 'I imagine it is all up with Serbia or will be in a day or two. Take care you are not too late at Gallipoli.' From Melbourne, Munro Ferguson remarked on the 'inexplicable failure of our diplomacy in the Balkans, the naval and military muddles at the Dardanelles, the sacrifice of Servia'.[11]

The Balkan disaster had another ominous implication for the men of Gallipoli. The ultimate German objective in this Balkans offensive was to open a direct route to Turkey to ensure it remained in the war.[12] On 11 October Lloyd George expressed concern that the Germans would have reached Gallipoli by the third week in November. The immediate sufferers would be the men of the Mediterranean Expeditionary Force. It had long been recognised that the position at Anzac (and to a lesser extent at Suvla and Helles) would be rendered untenable if the Turks were able to bombard it with high explosive shells from heavy artillery. With Bulgaria an ally, and Serbia in the process of being overrun, Germany now had unimpeded land access to Constantinople. It was only a question of time before the Turks on the peninsula received significant reinforcements in equipment and ammunition, if not in troops.

This disastrous turn of events in the Balkans meant another agonising reappraisal in London of the Gallipoli enterprise. Obviously, with the opening of the Salonika front, Gallipoli had lost its pre-eminent position in the Entente powers' Balkans strategy. Concomitantly, Allied military pressure on Turkey had been reduced. Members of the Dardanelles Committee, and their military advisers, prepared and considered yet another series of memoranda and reports on the Dardanelles. Grey, on 11 October, reconsidered evacuation, but Kitchener said this would cost about twenty-five thousand men and 'would be the most disastrous event in the history of the Empire'.[13] The wrangling continued, with ministers who favoured evacuation contemplating resignation if their views were not endorsed.

# CHAPTER 24

# KEITH MURDOCH'S LETTER

*W*HILE THE RULERS of Empire argued, their goals frustrated by minor Balkan powers, there arrived in London a young Australian journalist who was to have some impact on the course of Imperial history. Keith Murdoch was a thrusting, capable young journalist on the Melbourne *Age*. As a parliamentary reporter in 1912 he established an acquaintance with Fisher, Hughes, Pearce and other Labor ministers. He addressed his letters to Pearce 'Dear George', a rare familiarity among that reserved minister's correspondents. He was a founding member of the Australian Journalists' Association in 1910, and in September 1914 he was narrowly beaten by C. E. W. Bean in the journalists' pool which chose the official Australian war correspondent. In 1915 his employer transferred him to London as managing editor of the United Cable Service.[1]

*Journalist and future newspaper tycoon Keith Murdoch with the Australian Prime Minister, W. M. Hughes, in 1918. Murdoch's letter to Hughes's predecessor, Andrew Fisher, was a damning indictment of General Hamilton and his tactics at Gallipoli.*

Despite the Fisher government's acceptance of Britain's conduct of the Gallipoli campaign, it was unhappy over some aspects of the facilities accorded the troops, including their mail deliveries, so much so that it wanted the deficiencies investigated. Fisher therefore asked Murdoch to break his journey in Egypt and to report on delays in mail services to the troops. Murdoch reached Egypt in August, and from Cairo on 15 September he told Pearce: 'The men value their letters next to their lives, and they can get few or no letters after they have left the firing line. In hospital the present mail arrangements have collapsed.' He cabled that the only remedy was a big change in Australian methods. He also suggested changes in the cable system, in particular as it affected information about the wounded. He thought it inexcusable that authorities in the Defence Department in Melbourne were so slow to react to his suggestions. As well, he damned Colonel Sellheim, in charge of the AIF's base in Egypt, telling Pearce, '[He] has messed up everything he has touched and just clings on to his job here.'[2]

Murdoch's criticism of the British was more significant. Lloyd George came to suspect that the Fisher government had sent the journalist 'to report on the position of the Australian troops' on the peninsula. That suspicion might have been well founded. Late in August Murdoch obtained Hamilton's permission to visit Anzac. He asserted that it was natural for a journalist to want to see the beachhead which his countrymen had made famous. Hamilton at first thought Murdoch 'seemed a sensible man', although he was uncomfortable with his 'elaborate explanation of why his duty to Australia could be better done with a pen than with a

rifle'. He claimed he spent about four days on the peninsula; they were very instructive days.[3]

Murdoch later explained to the Dardanelles Commission, which was set up in 1916 to inquire into the origin and conduct of the Dardanelles campaign, that he reached Gallipoli with the conventional idea that it was only a matter of time before the Allies would hold the whole peninsula. But after talking to people on the spot he decided that the expedition had wholly failed, that it was in a parlous position, and that London was not giving the situation proper attention. After much persuasion he told the commissioners that the senior officers who had conveyed these gloomy impressions to him were White, Walker, Legge, Chauvel, Smyth (an Englishman who commanded the 1st Brigade at the Lone Pine attack), Ryrie, Godley and Monash. Appalled by the mismanagement he saw, Murdoch told Pearce that some AIF brigadiers had cost many lives 'through their ignorance and unadaptability to these extraordinary conditions'. He talked long, he said, with Hamilton and Birdwood, and he met Ashmead-Bartlett, who was by now bitterly critical of the conduct of the campaign. Murdoch agreed to carry a letter from Ashmead-Bartlett addressed to Asquith. However, at Marseilles Murdoch was forced to hand it over to a British army officer acting under orders from the War Office. Eighteen months later, during a sitting of the Dardanelles Commission, Fisher was to tell a witness, Sir Edward Carson: 'I have a strong and growing feeling that it was not a friendly action on the part of the Government here to send a military officer to seize Mr. Murdoch's belongings and examine them while he carried the credentials of the Prime Minister and the Minister of Defence on a mission on which he had been despatched because we could not get any information. Now, that feeling is growing daily, and I feel that when a communication of a Dominion Government entrusted to a man who is a native of the country has been treated in the way in which it was, it is an insult and an affront.'[4]

Murdoch wrote a letter of eight thousand words, which on 23 September 1915 he sent to Fisher from London. This letter, despite some errors, forcefully described the bungles at Gallipoli and alleged that the British staff and command

generally were unequal to their task. It characterised Hamilton's tactics as 'murder through incapacity'. Through his press contacts Murdoch soon met Asquith government leaders. His assessment of the campaign strengthened the resolve of those cabinet ministers—for example, Carson—opposed to its continuation. Lloyd George was impressed by Murdoch at their meeting on 24 September and found his account of the Dardanelles impasse the more disquieting. He urged Bonar Law to see Murdoch, who was asserting that it was impossible to make any significant advance at Anzac. Murdoch also met Foreign Secretary Sir Edward Grey, Home Secretary Reginald McKenna, Carson, Hankey, Churchill and Balfour. When Asquith read Murdoch's letter he quickly ordered it printed as a cabinet paper and discussed it with his friend Guy Dawnay. On 6 October the letter of the thirty-year-old Australian journalist was discussed at a meeting of the Dardanelles Committee. Lloyd George spoke approvingly, asserting that its essence— although not its style—corresponded fairly closely to Hankey's judicious report of 30 August. Bonar Law said that, despite its errors and exaggerations, Murdoch's letter contained 'a substratum of truth'.[5]

That was a strong statement to make about a report that included violent denunciations of British generalship. In subsequent days comments by the Empire's war leaders on Murdoch's letter were voluminous. Hamilton naturally felt that Murdoch had betrayed him and had behaved in a most ungentlemanly way. He defended himself as best he could. On 14 October he wrote to Kitchener: 'I would give six months pay if I could only have had you with me in those Australian trenches. Everything there, the friendliness and cheeriness of the officers and men gives so absolutely the lie to what was said by Mr. Murdoch the correspondent.'[6]

Lloyd George was certain that Murdoch's letter would 'create a sensation' when it reached Australia. Unless the Dardanelles Committee reconsidered Gallipoli, he told Bonar Law on 25 September, its members would be held personally responsible for the disaster. Although Asquith was sorry that the letter—which might 'do mischief in Australia'—had been sent to Fisher, he decided he could do nothing about it. Lloyd George also thought it inadvisable to send a copy of Hankey's report to Fisher, although Asquith said he would not in the least mind this being done.[7]

The British leaders need not have worried. It is impossible to detect any impact made by Murdoch's letter in Australia. This is perhaps largely explained by the replacement of Fisher as Prime Minister by W. M. Hughes on 27 October. Pearce, who continued as Minister for Defence, also was disinclined to rock the Imperial boat, and he might have been instrumental in ensuring that the letter did not create a sensation in Australia. The Hughes government thought Hamilton had erred in allowing Murdoch to visit Gallipoli and in November asked Britain to ensure that in future no Australian press representative be allowed to visit the front without prior approval by the Australian government.[8]

So the Commonwealth government ensured that Murdoch's letter did not embarrass the British government. But Murdoch's allegations had further weakened Hamilton's reputation among British ministers.

CHAPTER 25

# HOME FRONT

M URDOCH'S MISSION was the closest the Australian government came in those
months to intervening in the conduct of operations at Anzac. A few days after the
journalist left Gallipoli, Pearce again showed his uncritical attitude in a letter to
Godley: 'From reports that are coming in, you have been having some pretty hard
fighting over there lately; the problem is a very difficult one but we trust that
complete success will in good time crown the efforts so ably being put forth.'[1]

The information, both public and private, which Pearce was receiving from
London and Gallipoli was inconsistent, but it contained warnings which ought to
have been enough to dampen any spirit of optimism about the likely outcome.
Kitchener made a discreet statement on Gallipoli in the House of Lords on 15
September, the day on which Sir Henry Dalziel condemned the 'colossal blundering' which he said was common knowledge. Two days later Bonar Law wrote to
Munro Ferguson: 'I am sure that you and Australians generally understand pretty
well what the position in the Dardanelles is. There is no immediate prospect of
success but everything is being done to strengthen the position there and what
further steps will be taken must depend on the western front in the near future.'[2]
This message was scarcely sanguine, but gloomier assessments followed.

In October Pearce received a long description of the dispositions at Anzac from
Major-General Legge, commander of the 2nd Division. He included a sketch map
which had an arrow pointing to Lone Pine with the caption 'This projection cost
1,000 men.' 'Failing some great international developments,' wrote Legge, 'I cannot see that we shall do anything here, except to hang on till the spring, and lose
men all the time from exposure. Our policy and plans here have been too uncertain
and without definite purpose—very much like a bungle.' He expected to be at
Gallipoli over winter, when his men would 'do a great deal of mining work', but he
saw no signs of the materials needed to build satisfactory winter quarters. While
some subsequent letters from Legge and Birdwood were not pessimistic, there was
no concealing the casualty lists, which showed 'a great wastage'. Bonar Law
cabled Munro Ferguson about a winter campaign, and the latter discussed that
grim prospect with Pearce.[3]

Pearce got a clear impression of the Gallipoli disaster from Captain Muirhead
Collins, who wrote several letters in September and October strongly criticising
the London government's war policy and Asquith's capacity as a war leader. He
condemned the 'strategical incapacity' of those running the Gallipoli operations
and claimed that the Dardanelles campaign had been marked by blunders from its
beginning. He believed the Australian government had a very direct interest in this
issue because its men had suffered so much as a result.[4]

Any important speech by a British cabinet minister on the Dardanelles campaign and the wider ramifications of Balkans policy was reported at length in the
Australian press. One Sydney response to Kitchener's statement of 15 September

was that it could tell the British public—and German eavesdroppers—nothing it did not already know.

Australian newspapers kept their readers informed of developments on the Eastern Front, the most active area of fighting during these weeks. That news was almost consistently bad, as the German army advanced deeper into Russia. These German and Austrian successes had a serious effect on the Entente's position in the Balkans, a deteriorating situation not checked by Italy's declaration of war against the Ottoman Empire, which was to have negligible military consequences. The Italian government believed Turkey would collapse under the strain of the Dardanelles campaign. It wanted to benefit from this expected collapse but not contribute to it. In any case, Russia did not want Italy taking an interest in the Dardanelles, and General Joffre, the French commander, wanted the Allied military effort concentrated more heavily on the Western Front. So the Allies' commitment to the Balkans theatre had almost reached its apogee as the Central Powers were preparing a new offensive there. By mid-September Australians knew that a German attack on Serbia was imminent, while news about Bulgaria's attitude was 'not altogether reassuring'. The *Sydney Morning Herald* wrote despairingly of the Balkans maze, and a leading article criticised Allied diplomacy in the region.[5]

On 6 October Austrian and German forces invaded Serbia. A Bulgarian attack promptly followed. Australian newspapers described how the gallant 'Servians' were resisting this onslaught on three sides. But the odds were too great, and within a few weeks Serbia was overwhelmed. Survivors of its army were forced into a retreat through Albania to the Adriatic coast, a retreat which produced further horrors duly recorded in the Australian press.

The long-term prospects for the Anzac beachhead looked gloomy; its need for reinforcements seemed great. In recognition of this, day after day more men joined the Australian Imperial Force. Newspapers published daily tallies of men offering and accepted at various recruiting depots. One man abandoned his job on railway construction works at Hamilton to walk over three hundred kilometres to Melbourne, where he was glad he was accepted to fight the enemy. A group of men marched from Gilgandra to Sydney, attracting recruits along the way. Mrs J. McRae of Warracknabeal got a letter from Buckingham Palace because she had five sons at the front. That story prompted a reader to tell the *Argus* that Mr and Mrs John Neyland of Birchip had seven sons in the AIF. By 13 October enlistments had brought the Australian army for active service to a strength of almost 166,000 men, 70,000 of whom were training in Australia.[6]

Even more men were needed. It had long been realised that spectacular events, such as a march by soldiers, aided recruiting. In Sydney early in September 425 recruits from the tramways marched through city streets to Victoria Barracks. Spectators who thronged Melbourne streets during one lunch hour in late October cheered lustily when a mile-long column of about two thousand khaki-clad trainees marched four abreast from Ascot Vale camp. They equalled about one-twelfth of the total casualties thus far sustained by the Australians on Gallipoli. The Fisher government also instituted a war census, to ascertain the nation's resources for the conflict. 'Personal' cards had to be filled in by all males aged eighteen to sixty, and 'wealth and income' cards by anyone over seventeen who earned an income, owned property, or helped to administer the property of a company, club or similar association. Completed cards had to be submitted to the Commonwealth Statistician, Melbourne, by 15 September. The Fisher government stepped up its recruiting campaign. The *Sydney Morning Herald* appealed to the young men of Australia to enlist in 'The Great Adventure'. But with harvest approaching and a record area under crop in New South Wales, a rural labour shortage was in prospect, as so many patriotic volunteers from the country had joined up.

Similar considerations led the chairman of the State War Council in Victoria and the chairman of the state's Parliamentary Recruiting Committee to decide that it would be premature to hold another recruiting campaign.[7]

Despite the rush of men to enlist, some people thought conscription would eventually be necessary. The Tasmanian Liberal Senator Thomas Bakhap had said this in April and in June. In parliament he submitted a motion for conscription, which was debated in August. Growing support for this policy was given more substance by the formation in Sydney in September of the Universal Service League. Led by prominent citizens, including politicians, among them W. A. Holman, the Labor Premier of New South Wales, the league soon had branches in all states and speedily issued a manifesto urging conscription. Debate on its objective began to flourish, and newspapers were soon giving almost daily airing to advocates of conscription, although Fisher's implacable opposition was well known.[8]

Opponents of conscription were numerous, and there was even some questioning of the voluntary system. Late in August Fisher rebuked one of his backbenchers from Victoria, Frank Brennan—a law graduate, son of Irish immigrants and an early critic of the war—for some comments which he interpreted as a reflection on the soldiers who were defending Australia. In an explanatory statement in parliament Brennan allowed some merit in Australia's involvement in the war and praised Australia's soldiers, although he thought they should not be enlisted as young as eighteen.[9]

Every few days a ship would reach Australia carrying sick or wounded soldiers. They were usually, and appropriately, referred to in the press as wounded heroes. They were given a warm welcome by the general public and civic authorities as well as by families and friends. Some of their stories of battle were printed in the daily press. One of the returning wounded was Private Willie Harris, who in April had been expecting to march on to Constantinople. Instead, he was wounded and by July was in Egypt. As a convalescent he attended a church service with the strangest congregation he had seen. 'Men were clad in full uniform, pyjamas, etc, etc. . . . There are a big crowd of fellows going home and one could see slings and bandages every where.' On 15 August he left Egypt on the *Themistocles*, carrying wounded to Australia. 'Everyone happy and keenly excited at the prospect of seeing home in a few weeks.' Although a South Australian, he was deluged 'with flowers fruits sweets girls etc' when he reached Melbourne on 9 September. On the 12th his parents and brothers, along with hosts of pals shouting welcome, met him at Adelaide.[10] Some people were already worried about the difficult adjustment to

*Benign Australian faces as an enemy wounded is carried out of 1st Australian Field Ambulance dressing station suggest the respect which developed in the trenches for 'Johnny Turk'.*

civilian life confronting returned soldiers. The *Barrier Miner*, for example, suggested that they needed some help.[11]

Newspapers publicised the growing number of awards and honours for men in the AIF. On 18 October the *Age* featured seven Australians and a New Zealander who had won Victoria Crosses. The Australians, including Captains A. J. Shout and F. H. Tubb, Lieutenant W. J. Symons and Private John Hamilton, had won this honour at Lone Pine. A twenty-year-old clerk from Ballarat, Corporal William Dunstan, also won a VC in that battle. Wounded, now a sergeant-major, and somewhat embarrassed at being the centre of so much attention, he was hugged and kissed by women at the Ballarat railway station. The *Age* described at length the city's civic reception in his honour, attended by over seven thousand people.[12]

Every few days further casualty lists would appear, becoming longer and more frequent as information about the August offensive reached Australia. People realised that the scale of fighting was increasing: by 20 August, 2,739 deaths had been notified; two months later the total had reached 4,751. Relatives provided newspapers with photographs and brief biographical details of dead soldiers. The *Sydney Morning Herald*'s photographic display of the 'Heroes of the Dardanelles' and the *Age*'s 'Australia's Roll of Honour' became bigger—as many as thirty photographs on one day—but 'limits of space' prevented immediate use of all the photographs and short biographies supplied by grieving relatives. One issue of the *Sydney Morning Herald* printed photographs of three brothers—two had died of wounds and the other was missing. A fourth brother was in camp at Liverpool. A fortnight later appeared a family photograph of a soldier killed at the Dardanelles, the father of eight children of whom the eldest was ten. Parents, friends, brothers, nieces and nephews of dead soldiers inserted death notices in newspapers' 'On Active Service' sections. A notice might declare that a loved one had died 'bravely fighting for home and Empire', or that he had 'played the game', or had 'died for his country gloriously'. Other notices merely mentioned the place and date of death, and the relationship to those who had inserted the notice. Families that knew a son had been killed were in some ways less unfortunate than those who suffered the agonising uncertainty of having a son listed as missing. Mrs Scott of Wallsend, New South Wales, was one such mother. She wrote to Hamilton, asking if he could help her find her son, reported missing since 22 August. Her son, she told the general, always spoke of him in the highest terms.[13] Mrs Wallace-Crabbe of St Kilda, another bereaved mother, wrote to Monash about her son, a lieutenant in the 14th Battalion, who had landed on 'that glorious first day': 'I know thousands of other mothers are suffering with me, but it does not make the individual case any lighter.' Monash's sympathetic reply led Mr Wallace-Crabbe to thank him for giving comfort to his wife. Another correspondent wrote to Monash: 'If this beastly war could only end how thankful millions of people would be—it seems such a barbarous way to decide things.' In September Joseph Cook, leader of the opposition, was a principal speaker at a memorial service organised by the Salvation Army and held in the Sydney Town Hall for Australian heroes who had fallen at Gallipoli.[14]

The losses underlined the need for continued declarations of what Australians were fighting for. The issue at stake still seemed crucial to most people. The *West Australian* posed stark alternatives: 'We are in this war to win, or to go under as a people.' Most Australians were confirmed in their belief that they were fighting in a righteous cause by new enemy atrocities. When the *Lusitania* was sunk on 7 May, J. H. Scullin, then editor of a Labor evening daily in Ballarat and soon to be a leading anti-conscriptionist, had written, 'The soul of humanity grows sick with horror at the awful crime.' When the White Star liner *Arabic* was sunk on 19 August, fewer lost their lives, but the *Age* thought this torpedoing an even 'more detestable act of cold-blooded piracy'. This outrage was frequently mentioned in the press in later weeks, as was the anger of the United States over the loss of more American lives to German submarines. Most Australians were reassured that they were fighting the 'wild beast of nations' on hearing in October that the Germans had executed Nurse Edith Cavell, 'an English lady who conducted a nursing establishment in Belgium'. She was shot because she had harboured French and English soldiers, helping some to escape. Australian newspapers naturally gave much publicity to the execution. It was termed 'the bloodiest outrage'. Most Australians no doubt would have agreed that this demonstrated once again that Germans were 'unspeakable monsters'. 'Neither chivalry nor courtesy has for fourteen and a half months past been expected from anyone imbued with the Prussian spirit; but the military murdering of women in cold blood has intensified the loathing of a world already sick with German barbarities.' The *Argus* published many readers' letters on this shooting. Long accounts appeared in the Australian press of Miss Cavell's memorial service in St Paul's, London, at the end of October. A few days later a similar service was held in St Paul's, Melbourne. The Colonial Office sent the Australian government copies of correspondence relating to this case.[15] The image of a line of German soldiers shooting a nurse was horrifying to the Australians of 1915 and emphasised a contrast between good and evil so stark and easy to understand that even schoolchildren could absorb its message about the wickedness of Germans. Such images sustained many Australians in their belief in the justice of what they were fighting for.

Although Germany seemed adept at giving its foes potent material for propaganda, it had not yet adopted techniques of mass murder of civilians. Rather, it was the Ottoman Empire that had seen such appalling atrocities. Among its suffering minorities were Christian Armenians, many of whom had been massacred by Turkish troops shortly before the war. Many Armenians were sympathetic to the Allied cause, and some had helped Russia. This gave Talaat Pasha, the leader of the CUP parliamentary party and the Minister for the Interior, and Enver Pasha, the Minister for War, the excuse, if not a genuine reason, to resume massacres on a horrifying scale in 1915. They totalled perhaps three hundred thousand, although much higher estimates were made then and later. Lord Bryce, a former British ambassador to the United States, appealed to the United States in September to protest against the wholesale slaughter. The American Embassy in Constantinople was horrified at what was happening. One of its staff members, Lewis Einstein, by early July heard of 'revolting tales of cruelty' coming from the interior. These stories of massacre and cruelty increased. Of Talaat, the main instigator, he wrote, 'Power has brought out cruelty in this son of a gipsy.' He specified many details of death marches, crucifixions and the like—many came flowing in from consular officials in Anatolia—and criticised Germany for doing nothing to stop these horrors, 'terrible in their grim tragedy'. Henry Morgenthau, the Ambassador, if anything, was more appalled at what the Turks were doing with German connivance. 'The great massacres and persecutions of the past . . . seem almost insignificant when compared with the sufferings of the Armenian race in 1915.' Morgenthau tried without success to prevent Talaat from persisting in his brutalities. His horror at these cruelties was partly what led him to ask for a premature end to his posting in 1916.[16]

Until the end of the Gallipoli campaign the Australian press printed news of these atrocities. One story from an eyewitness of revolting cruelty came from Bean. The *Age* realised that the numbers of those who perished were being exaggerated but was in no doubt as to the general veracity of these stories of 'wholesale butcheries of the hapless Armenians'.[17] Although Australian civilians knew that the men of the AIF respected 'Johnny Turk' as a fair fighter, newspaper readers knew what sort of barbaric regime the Australians were fighting against.

# CHAPTER 26

# 'A CHOICE OF DISASTERS'

*D*URING OCTOBER, as the comparative lull in fighting on Gallipoli continued, in London the raging controversy over the campaign intensified. There were long, wearisome wrangles in the Dardanelles Committee and, after 6 November, in its successor, the Cabinet War Committee.

The Australian public was kept generally aware of tensions in the British government over war policy. Key extracts from British press criticisms of the Gallipoli campaign were reprinted in the Australian press, as was Ashmead-Bartlett's judgement that the results on the peninsula were 'wholly unfavourable' to the Empire's cause. In mid-October it was reported that some Liberal members of the House of Commons wanted a committee appointed to inquire into the initiation, conduct and current position of the Dardanelles campaign.[1]

The agonising in Britain produced a flurry of public statements and decisions. On 12 October Sir Edward Carson resigned from cabinet partly because he opposed holding on at Gallipoli. Two days later Asquith's cabinet decided to recall Hamilton, sending this news to him on the 16th. On the 14th the House of Lords heard two of its members—Ribblesdale and Milner—urge that the peninsula be evacuated to avoid 'complete disaster'. Ribblesdale, aged sixty-one and a large landowner who in 1886 had retired from the army as a major, spoke infrequently on Imperial issues, whereas Milner was one of the most famous servants of the Empire. Both speeches attracted wide publicity. The *New York Times* promptly speculated on the possible abandonment of the campaign. The reaction in Australia to Milner's and Ribblesdale's speeches was commented on by some British newspapers, the *Daily Mail* claiming that colonial circles were perturbed at the possibility that the true situation in the Dardanelles was worse than had been publicly admitted.[2]

In Britain Milner's speech provoked numerous letters. Next day Hankey told Asquith that the military leaders with whom he had discussed the issue agreed 'the only way to minimise losses in a withdrawal is to ensure absolute surprise. . . . If a withdrawal from Gallipoli (supposing it should ever be decided on) is to be preceded by a popular clamour, and speeches by people of Lord Milner's eminence, it can only result in an unparalleled disaster. This speech alone is quite sufficient to place the Turks on the look out for it.' He added, 'It is difficult to conceive a more unfortunate pronouncement at the present moment.' One correspondent condemned Milner for his insult to 'our magnificent Colonial troops', adding, 'Australia is already dismayed and angry.' On the other hand, Lord Sydenham, a former governor of Victoria and Bombay who had served on the Committee of Imperial Defence, congratulated him: 'Neither the Antwerp nor the Dardanelles fiascos could have been possible if any competent soldier had been able to speak out before the Council.' Among the other correspondents who expressed strong views

about Milner's speech was an elderly history schoolmaster, congratulating him on criticising a 'huge disaster' which was madness from the start. 'Oh! The poor Australians and New Zealanders—lives thrown away by incapacity and muddle. The Government it seems to me are either blind themselves or they are blinding the people.'[3]

Another who worried about Gallipoli's impact on Empire relations was L. J. Maxse, owner of the *National Review* and a firm Imperialist who styled himself 'a mere man in the street' when writing to Bonar Law on 15 October:

*General Hamilton at Imbros upon his dismissal, flanked by MEF headquarters staff before leaving for England. Hamilton, who once described himself as optimistic, would continue optimistically to defend his handling of the campaign.*

[*This*] *deplorable adventure in the Gallipoli Peninsula, which has steadily gone from bad to worse and has never at any stage held out the faintest prospect of achievement, is inflicting incalculable harm upon the relations between the Commonwealth of Australia and the Dominion of New Zealand, and the Mother country. The one and only thing for us to do lest worse befall us is to clear out bag and baggage at the earliest possible moment, because the sole alternative is that we be kicked out with the loss of all our forces, with the utmost ignominy by a combination of Turks, Bulgars and Germans. The man in the street is normally a very docile person, much too docile, prepared to endure almost anything, but he is getting fed up with the ghastly ineptitude displayed through this Gallipoli campaign, and he demands that the curtain should be rung down upon it.*[4]

On 19 October the Colonial Office cabled the news of Hamilton's recall to the two Australasian governors-general, Munro Ferguson and Lord Liverpool. They were told that the Asquith government had chosen Lieutenant-General Sir Charles Monro, who had commanded the Third Army in France, to visit Gallipoli to report as quickly as possible on the prospects of the Mediterranean Expeditionary Force. The government would then 'without delay decide on the course to be adopted'. The prime ministers could be told this information confidentially.[5]

On 20 October the Australian public heard of both Carson's resignation and of Hamilton's replacement by Monro. Some remarked that Carson's departure emphasised the difficulties for a democracy in waging a great war. Rumours of even further dissension in Asquith's cabinet led the *Sydney Morning Herald* to chastise Englishmen who showed 'their patriotism by denouncing their leader and belittling the efforts of their countrymen'. If Britain were to win, it had to revitalise the spirit which, under Pitt and Castlereagh, 'carried her through the Napoleonic war'. Other newspapers adopted a similar attitude. Those in 'positions of supreme trust', wrote the Sydney *Daily Telegraph*, had a 'patriotic duty' to do or say nothing that would embarrass the war minister and his colleagues in carrying out their duties. The Adelaide *Advertiser* was puzzled that 'men so intelligent as [Carson] should choose the present, of all moments, for treating [the drive on Constantinople] as a minor operation that might better be abandoned.'[6]

Carson received unsympathetic treatment from the *Age*, which thought it unpatriotic to criticise the policy of a British government which best knew 'the precise military exigencies of the nation at any fighting line'. It went on to say:

*Australia has a particular grievance against these British agitators, inasmuch as they have been industriously endeavouring to represent Australian sentiment as bitterly dissatisfied with the prosecution and progress of the Gallipoli campaign. Now, it would be quite fair to state that the people of the Commonwealth are disappointed that, after so great a sacrifice of blood and treasure, our brave boys, and the forces with which they are co-operating, have not yet . . . made a path to Constantinople. But when we say that we say all. The people of Australia are not so stupid or so besottedly arrogant as to suppose they are better able to direct the Empire's fight against the Turk than Lord Kitchener and the expert executive officers under his command. Some of us may believe that the expedition was erroneously conceived, and pressed to an issue with insufficient reason. But, as we are fully aware that we are not competent to pronounce judgement, even this section has the grace to hold its tongue.*[7]

The decision whether or not to abandon Gallipoli properly rested with the British government, and Australia would 'not whine nor raise a foolish outcry' if it were decided to leave.

Hamilton's recall provoked more comment, but initially it was ill-informed, for it was not immediately obvious to those uninitiated in such matters that he had been relieved of his command. When this became clear, many Australian newspapers, taking their cue from Britain's press, assumed this indicated that the campaign would be pursued with a new vigour. When the reason for the recall became clear, some regretted that a general who had created a fine reputation by long and sterling work was now going back to England a failure.[8]

The recall caused consternation in the MEF's command. Orlo Williams talked of the 'bombshell'; others on Hamilton's staff, and some generals, were also surprised. Godley wondered if the government was dissatisfied with Hamilton's performance or if he was being moved to another command. In fact, Hamilton's days of soldiering had finished. Both Godley and Paris thought, correctly, that Hamilton could have saved himself had he been prepared to sacrifice his chief of staff, General Braithwaite, his 'evil genius', who 'lacked the necessary brains for the job'. Within a fortnight Godley realised that Murdoch had had a hand in Hamilton's downfall. He had been 'damning us all', Godley told his wife, and she could 'expect to hear of *us* [himself and Birdwood] being kicked out next'. Murdoch was later to say that it had been absolutely essential to have a fresh mind at the Dardanelles.[9]

Hamilton's dismissal was a step towards evacuation, which was being more widely discussed behind the scenes as well as in public. Lieutenant-Colonel Fitz-Gerald, Kitchener's personal military secretary, was told that numerous people at Gallipoli, from all ranks, thought there was not the slightest chance of victory and that it was a useless waste of life to send more troops. One of Hamilton's staff, Lieutenant-Colonel C. F. Aspinall, wrote a paper on the issue, and rumours circulated about a possible evacuation. Some experts realised that the situation at

Suvla, let alone Anzac, would be untenable if the Turks used really heavy German artillery. But the Empire's war leaders could not agree. Evacuation seemed too risky, and too much loss of prestige would be involved. It did not yet seem absolutely necessary. Ministers, such as Churchill, opposed to evacuation were still too numerous and influential on the Dardanelles Committee.[10]

In the British army there were officers who were much more critical of the campaign than were Australian public figures. One example was Brigadier-General Horatio Mends, retired since 1908, who on 19 October wrote to General Hutton, Australia's former army commander: 'I hardly like to touch on the Dardanelles tragedy, but could almost have foretold it. No plan of campaign, no proper staff, muddle and gasconade from the beginning. It is awful to think of the life recklessly, and to my mind, criminally thrown away, and after nearly 100,000 casualties we are where we started! The military part of the fiasco well matches the Diplomatic.' It was not until 22 October that the Australian public was told that the officer who commanded the troops landing at Suvla (Stopford's name was not mentioned) no longer held any command.[11]

The spate of disconcerting news from London naturally provoked a press reassessment of the Gallipoli campaign. On the one hand there was need for more informed Australian press comment. On the other hand, with the opening of the Salonika campaign, the military and diplomatic ramifications of Gallipoli became more complex, making it more difficult for Australian newspapers to make relevant, knowledgeable comments. A gloomy remark by the *West Australian* indicates these difficulties: 'We are so completely in the dark as to the number and composition of the Allied troops in the Balkans . . . that no opinion of value can be expressed as to the issue of the campaign. . . . Bulgaria, a racial outpost of Russia, is against us; Greece, which was brought into being as a modern state by Britain, France, and Russia, now thwarted those powers and Roumania, a Latin nation surrounded by Slavs, is hesitating.' The *Argus* saw virtue in necessity: 'God forbid that either pressmen or politicians should ever be allowed to determine questions of military strategy.' It then criticised Lord Northcliffe for trying to 'control' strategy in the Dardanelles; this probably stemmed from 'a spirit of self-advertisement'.[12]

Australian newspapers were now canvassing the merits of evacuation, only to reject that move. To the *Newcastle Morning Herald* Bulgaria's entry into the war made it more important for Turkey to be kept occupied in the Dardanelles. But the writer of a very patriotic independent column in this daily discussed the pros and cons of abandoning the beachheads in an open manner. An 'old cobber' wrote to Monash from Australia, 'Now we are hearing that it's a mistake our being on Gallipoli and talk of our retiring, and all this after expecting every day to hear that the top of Achi Baba was blown off' and the Turks retreating to Constantinople. Turkish confidence that they could hold the Allies in the Suvla region was reported, as was the fact that the Turkish forces in the region outnumbered the Allies by some eighty thousand. Perhaps some optimists, reared on stories of the Royal Navy's successes against lesser powers, thought this adverse balance might be overturned by the arrival at the Dardanelles of slow-moving, torpedo-proof monitors, carrying 14-inch guns.[13]

The *Ballarat Courier* considered the conundrum in a long editorial. It accepted Ashmead-Bartlett's criticisms and chastised the authorities who had made 'every conceivable blunder' but opposed evacuation as threatening a heavy loss of life. The Turks would harass the Australians down to the water's edge. Many others in Australia opposed evacuation because they did not want to admit defeat. They did not want to please Germany by giving up a beachhead which the Turks could not overrun. Like Verdun in 1916, Anzac had taken on a symbolic importance of its own, divorced from its intrinsic strategic significance. Sir Joseph Carruthers, a member of the New South Wales Legislative Council and formerly premier of the state, was cheered when, at a recruiting meeting in Sydney, he opposed giving up Gallipoli because it was 'sanctified by the graves of thousands of our best'. To suggest abandonment was to be 'a traitor to our hopes'.[14]

Since August, and possibly earlier, it had been considered a certainty in federal political circles that Andrew Fisher, tiring of leading a restive parliamentary party, would soon succeed Sir George Reid as High Commissioner, with W. M. Hughes, the Attorney-General, to become the new prime minister. That duly happened when parliament resumed sitting on 27 October. Munro Ferguson cabled the news to the Colonial Office on the 29th, along with Hughes's assurance that there would would be no change in the policy of prosecuting the war to the utmost until victory was gained. The Governor-General hoped that Hughes, like Louis Botha, might prove himself 'an Imperial asset', and told Bonar Law that the new leader was more suited than Fisher to war conditions. He also thought that Fisher, although likeable, and possessing many sterling qualities, would not be as effective a high commissioner as Reid. Fisher was to be given every facility to visit Australian troops in Egypt and on Gallipoli, but he did not leave Melbourne until 22 December, just after the last Australians left Gallipoli.[15]

Shortly before resigning, Fisher was told that Bonar Law had announced in the House of Commons that he would welcome full and confidential discussions with dominion prime ministers if they visited London. The invitation was repeated to Hughes on 5 November. Six days later he accepted this opportunity for a 'frank interchange of views'. He planned to leave in January. There is nothing to suggest that his decision was influenced by Murdoch's letter of 23 September.[16]

Hughes became prime minister when Australians were becoming more aware of public criticism in London of the Gallipoli campaign. Ashmead-Bartlett gave a lecture to some 2,500 people in which he recounted the mistakes and claimed that success at Suvla would not have meant an entry into Constantinople, because the Turks had other formidable fortifications to overcome. Lord Brassey, a former governor of the colony of Victoria, had toured the Dardanelles and claimed that all the officers he had met thought the enterprise a huge mistake.[17]

Following Ashmead-Bartlett's remarks, Hughes took the opportunity to expound his government's attitude. On 29 October, in a parliamentary question, J. H. Catts, a Labor backbencher, said: 'It seems that the sending of our men to Gallipoli means sending them to useless slaughter. Is it not time for a debate on the subject?' Hughes replied that his government was not responsible for directing the campaign. 'Our business is to carry out the instructions of the Imperial Government, and to give that Government our hearty and enthusiastic support.' He admitted he did not 'understand the situation in the Dardanelles', but he knew his government's duty, which was to mind its own business, to refrain from criticising the British government, to provide the quota of men which London thought necessary, and to have as many soldiers as possible efficiently led, fed and equipped for service with the British. Bonar Law told Munro Ferguson he was 'greatly pleased' to see this response by Hughes.[18]

Defence Minister George Pearce was as robust as Hughes. In a message to Birdwood, which included what may have been an oblique reference to Murdoch's letter, he said: 'We are all naturally keenly interested in the progress of events at the Dardanelles, there has been much criticism of late, but very little of it has emanated from Australia; such references as are made to Australia are by people at Home who appear to have set themselves up as interpreters of our opinion. I feel sure that I am but speaking for the vast majority, when I say that we are content to entrust the conduct of such affairs to our Military Advisers.'[19]

Sir Charles Monro, Hamilton's successor, was a 'Westerner' who had been fighting on the Western Front since the start of the war. He approached Gallipoli with a sceptical mind. On 28 October he told Kitchener that he was 'very favourably impressed' by the Australasian units he had just inspected at Mudros. After briefly visiting the Gallipoli beachheads, he decided that the Anzacs, as he called them, were the only troops on the peninsula who could soon be ready for a further offensive. On 31 October he telegraphed London recommending evacuation. Churchill's jibe about Monro—'He came, he saw, he capitulated'—is often quoted.[20] Monro, unlike Churchill, had at least seen the beachheads.

On 2 November British parliamentarians made their most sustained criticism thus far of the Dardanelles venture, criticism the more pointed because members of the House of Commons were becoming aware of the danger that Bulgaria's entry into the war might allow Germany to bring heavy artillery to the Gallipoli front. The debate followed Asquith's statement on the general war situation. As Prime Minister he accepted the main responsibility for British forces being on the peninsula. But most members knew that Gallipoli was Churchill's brainchild.[21]

In the parliamentary debate the elderly Admiral Lord Charles Beresford and Sir Henry Dalziel, long-standing critics of the campaign, renewed their attack. Beresford described the condition of the troops as 'shocking'. Dalziel, in criticising the continual muddle, said an explanation was needed 'when the Colonies send their best blood to be destroyed by machine guns which were there waiting for them'. Sir Edward Carson, three weeks after he had resigned from cabinet, termed the campaign Britain's worst disaster of the war, a miscalculation 'which has hung round our necks like a millstone throughout the whole of these recent months'.[22]

In the House of Lords men lamented the suffering caused by the 'terrible story' of the 'impossible venture'. Lord Milner, on the 8th, again called for evacuation. Lord Ponsonby, a pacifist throughout the war, complained, 'There is now disastrous indecision as to the right course to pursue.' Naturally, the debate and Asquith's speech were extensively reported in the Australian press. The Brisbane *Courier* ingenuously commented, 'It is particularly gratifying to note that Mr Asquith did not join in the rather popular chorus of condemnation of the Dardanelles operations as so much entirely lost effort.'[23]

While British leaders dithered, soldiers on Gallipoli endured the familiar routine of death and mutilation amid the eternal noise of guns and 'overs'. Even to get away from Anzac for two days was a relief. It made a subaltern feel a self-

*In the words of Second Lieutenant Norman Hart, a 'good bag' of generals and staff officers: Lord Kitchener, Birdwood on his left and Brigadier White on his right at Walker's Ridge on 13 November, possibly looking towards the Nek. Suvla Bay is in the distance.*

respecting human being again to walk about above ground without bothering to think of cover. Second Lieutenant Norman Hart, who served with the 1/6th Gurkha Rifles, part of the 29th Indian Infantry Brigade, once walked eleven to twelve kilometres from Anzac to Suvla. He noted that the Suvla firing line was five kilometres inland, so that, unlike Anzac, the base was not often shelled. A captain who had been wounded and was now back at Anzac—and at Quinn's Post, moreover, where the opposing trenches were twenty metres apart—told a woman in his home state of New South Wales, 'It is rotten being under artillery fire when you can't return it and all you have to do is to try and dodge the shells.' He had no grudge against the Turks, except that they were between the Australians and their objective. It would be a different matter if they were opposing Germans.[24]

On 15 November, in a letter to his mother, Hart mentioned Kitchener's visit to Anzac. He went up to look at Walker's Ridge. It was a good thing, wrote Hart, that the Turks did not start strafing the pier with high-explosive shells when they could have had 'a good bag' of three generals and some staff officers.[25]

Conceivably, some of Kitchener's cabinet colleagues would have thought it not altogether inconvenient had he been killed at Gallipoli. His visit was linked with the deepening crisis in Asquith's government, as well as with the wish for another high-level judgement on Monro's recommendation to evacuate. The Dardanelles Committee met for the last time on 6 November. The Cabinet War Committee, which replaced it, nominally comprised five members, including Lloyd George and Bonar Law, the two leading advocates of abandoning Gallipoli. Neither Churchill nor Kitchener were members, although the latter did attend meetings after his return from his trip to the East. The two service chiefs were also present.[26]

The struggle over the fate of the Mediterranean Expeditionary Force had thus entered a new phase in which the opponents of evacuation were on the defensive. Hamilton, back in London, still vigorously urged the decision-makers not to evacuate, but his views now carried little weight. Another consistently strong opponent of evacuation, Roger Keyes, visited London at this time to argue that a renewed naval offensive would end the impasse. Birdwood hated the idea of evacuating and claimed that with two more divisions he could 'get through the Turks'. Godley opposed evacuation because, among other things, the Allied forces on the peninsula tied down Turkish forces which could be used elsewhere. This argument was frequently used by Australian newspapers. Major-General Callwell also saw merit in this: hanging on at Gallipoli meant Britain did not have to worry about Egypt. Acting Vice-Admiral Wemyss, who in November replaced de Robeck as commander-in-chief of naval forces, also opposed evacuation. Maurice Hankey found the military arguments for and against evacuation fairly evenly balanced but thought the political arguments heavily favoured remaining. So on 6 November he told Bonar Law, 'It is a choice of disasters, but on the whole the greater and more certain disaster would appear to be evacuation.' He went on to say that 'the consequences in Australia and New Zealand' of an evacuation would 'also be very bad'. For Austen Chamberlain, the Conservative Secretary of State for India who had joined the coalition in May, the choice between the disasters seemed to be determined by the impossibility of maintaining the force on the peninsula.[27]

In the cabinet some, like A. J. Balfour and Lord Crewe, were inclined against evacuation, partly because of the 'loss of prestige' and the 'humiliation' of admitting a failure, but also because of their horror at the prospect of a heavy loss of life during any evacuation. Cabinet ministers spoke of the likely loss of from twenty thousand to forty thousand men in the evacuation and imagined fearful scenes of frightful slaughter on the beaches and in the boats. L. S. Amery mentioned another alternative—for the troops to hang on as long as possible until they were forced to surrender. Small wonder that Asquith's cabinet had long, exhausting wrangles as it vacillated on the issue. Balfour and Bonar Law, both on the Cabinet War Committee, received trenchant views from Leopold Maxse, who was appalled at the prospect of Monro's being discarded: 'Mr Asquith's amour propre apparently demands that another 100,000 men shall be sacrificed in this insane enterprise rather than its authors admit their fallibility.' Balfour needed persuading, but Bonar Law on 8 November told Asquith he would resign were evacuation much longer delayed.[28]

Bonar Law did not feel free to be frank with Melbourne. On 9 November he told Munro Ferguson that the Dardanelles situation was 'all very serious'. He went on:

*You know the feeling I have long had—that it is extremely desirable to give your Government more information than it has been possible to supply hitherto but it is very difficult. . . . You speak of this expedition as a fiasco and I am afraid it is not too hard a word but if I remember rightly Clausewitz said a mistake once made in strategy can never be repaired. In this case it certainly cannot be repaired except at a great cost. It is really impossible for me to write more but I think you will be able to read between the lines that we are considering every aspect of this situation and I trust that your Ministers realise this also.*

On the day after writing this letter, Bonar Law tried to convince the wavering Balfour of the need to leave the peninsula. Similar opinions were often put on paper in those weeks, whether it be by a convinced 'Westerner' like General Sir Henry Wilson, chief liaison officer with the French army, or by a Conservative backbencher like Henry Bentinck, who thought that even if the heights overlooking the Narrows were wrested from the Turks, that would only be the start of a Herculean struggle against the Turkish army.[29]

Kitchener's journey to the Eastern theatre was reported in the Australian press from 8 November, with almost daily announcements of his whereabouts, but not, of course, of his advice to London. The *Argus* wondered if the journey portended a grand concerted offensive. It was 15 November before London officially informed the Hughes government of Kitchener's journey. After three days inspecting the beachheads, he cabled Asquith: 'To gain what we hold has been a most remarkable feat of arms. The country is much more difficult than I imagined and the Turkish positions at Achi Baba and Kilid Bahr are natural fortresses of the most formidable nature.' Next day, in the House of Lords, Lord Ribblesdale announced it was common knowledge that Monro had reported in favour of evacuating the Dardanelles. The speech caused anger among many who had the interests of the troops at heart, for it threatened to give the Turks ample warning of what to expect.[30]

Meanwhile, Churchill's response to his demotion—when the Dardanelles Committee was replaced by the Cabinet War Committee—was to resign from cabinet. He did not mention Australia or New Zealand when defending his handling of the Dardanelles campaign in his resignation speech in the House of Commons on 15 November. In the extensive Australian press coverage of these developments and of some of Asquith's speeches at the time, Churchill attracted some criticism, even from the strongly Imperial *Age*, as the minister 'chiefly responsible for the ill-fated Gallipoli enterprise'. Defects in his policies and his ambitious temperament were mentioned. A week later Ashmead-Bartlett wrote a long letter to *The Times*, strongly critical of Churchill's version of the Gallipoli saga. Major Australian newspapers printed the gist of this letter.[31]

Perhaps partly under the influence of Monro and Kitchener, by 17 November Birdwood was reported as saying that Anzac could be evacuated without much loss. On the 22nd Kitchener, after days of hesitation, advised firmly in favour of leaving Suvla and Anzac, but not Helles. Keyes was furious at what he saw as Kitchener's *volte-face*, denouncing him in private as 'a vacillating old villain'.[32]

# CHAPTER 27

# 'NOT DEAD YET YOU SEE'

$O$NLY A HANDFUL of the most senior officers at Anzac had any glimmering of the high-level discussions on the expedition's future. For nearly all the men, the weeks after Hamilton's recall were occupied with patrolling or improving the beachhead and trying to reduce casualties from Turkish fire. As John Gellibrand put it, 'Tactically we mine and they countermine or they mine and we counter-mine—they shell and we retaliate; they bomb and we endeavour to return two for one.' These weeks of comparative calm, less demanding than the April and August offensives, were in their own way also a test of character.[1]

Maintaining morale was one major goal. 'The outlook is pretty gloomy here,' wrote Robert Raws, 'but we keep cheerful.' Doubtless, some men's cheeriness stemmed from ill-founded optimism about the military situation. 'I think Abdhul is nearly played out and will soon sling in the towel,' Gunner E. Burgess, a recent arrival with the 2nd Division, told his sister. Lieutenant Aram was more prescient. He thought the war might be won on other fronts while the Anzacs were still sitting at the beachhead. 'Won't that be a rotten job . . . [to] be shipped off home from here without moving any "forrader".' He was amused 'to hear the different ideas going the rounds' on how and when the war would end. 'Everyone declares it is not going to last long now,' he wrote, 'yet everybody is preparing for a long stay; and old Johnny Turk appears to be well keeping his end up.'[2]

The Australians put a good face on things. Lieutenant McGrigor, Birdwood's aide-de-camp, talked to a lot of them as he walked through the trenches, and he found them 'very cheery'. They seemed always to be short of reading material, and so they were very grateful when he took up lots of newspapers. Things were often so quiet that Lieutenant Keith Chambers at times found it hard to believe that he was in the very front trench. 'You might as well be in George Street,' he told his parents, although he admitted there were casualties each day. After a few weeks without writing, Sergeant D. W. Caldwell dashed off from Russell's Top a letter beginning 'Dear Mum, Not dead yet you see'.[3]

Letters helped morale. Gunner Burgess, writing when he was sitting behind the parapet of the firing line, told his 'very dear Father and Mother': 'It is hard for you to realize how we build our hopes on maildays out here. It is next best to seeing you all, and seems to carry me right back to dear old Geelong and Melbourne.' Robert Raws complained about the paucity of writing material; ink was 'the greatest of luxuries'. Despite Keith Murdoch's endeavours, there still were fre-quent complaints about inadequate postal deliveries and suspicions that some par-cels intended for the front-line troops were being stolen *en route*. Most parcels got through, however, and when a group of soldiers in a dugout opened several parcels they could behave 'like overgrown schoolboys'.[4] A warrant officer, while grateful to his family for a parcel, told them not to waste their money on him. 'I have every-thing I can possibly want,' he wrote. Disaster struck at Anzac's Christmas mail, for most of the outward mail posted between 12 and 20 November was lost at sea in a storm, while 160 bags of Australian mail was lost when a troopship was torpedoed on its way from Alexandria to Lemnos.[5]

Men at Anzac used the mails to reassure their families and to tell them how comfortable they had made their dugouts. A seventeen-year-old told his parents that life in the trenches suited him. Lieutenant E. R. Cavanagh described his 'cosy and snug' dugout to his family. 'I have a string fixed along one side of the Dugout and a few Post Cards and photoes I have had sent to me hung on it.' He had 'things hanging on Turkish bayonets stuck in the wall', and his rifle was hanging under the picture gallery. For Raws it was luxury to move from the front line, where he never saw the light of a candle at night, to a dugout where he could have a candle every night. He also had bread and meat every other day and milk every day. Fred Biddle celebrated his birthday in great style with a 'meal of gluttony'— tomato soup, 'sardines etc etc', ginger nuts and sweets. Murray Aitken was content being the host in his dugout for many evenings to three sergeant-majors who made up a bridge four. 'It's quite like old times. . . . The dugout just holds us and we illuminate with slush lamps, fat lamps, or candles, whichever luck trots along.' He also got 'a double issue of rum to commemorate six months on the Peninsula'.[6]

The awe felt by reinforcements on reaching Anzac led some to describe the scenes in detail. Private B. W. Champion, for example, saw a monitor as his ship approached the cove. 'These monitors are funny-looking boats, more like flat barges only with a huge gun in front. They draw very little water and can stand in close to shore where the warships cannot go.' His first morning in the lines was a time for renewing acquaintanceships.

*Soon we were the centre of an animated group. New arrivals meeting old friends and making new ones. Surely these men were not the spic and span soldiers we had seen leaving Australia a year before! Nearly all had beards or had not shaved for weeks; all were dirty, their breeches hacked off at the knees, and few were wearing puttees. But they were happy, cheerful and full of jokes, and they had developed a jargon of their own, which took us, new arrivals, some time to under-*

*The Lone Pine garrison files through White's Valley after being relieved. The cheerfulness of Australian troops in comparison with those at Suvla impressed Birdwood's aide-de-camp, Lieutenant McGrigor.*

*stand. New words for everyday things and new words for new war terms. Grouped together, they*
*had a sameness which I had never realised before. There was a definite Australian character,*
*which is hard to explain, but which was present in every one of them.[7]*

By this time many soldiers had taken up the practice of writing the name of the
town they came from on their hats with indelible pencil. Within ten days the new
arrivals were 'as dirty as the old hands and as lousy, too'. 'We are a rough looking
crowd here,' wrote another recent arrival—'everyone looks weary worn and dirty,
and every day we do the usual "insect" hunt.'[8]

By this time most of the survivors who had served since April at Anzac had had
a spell on Lemnos. Murray Aitken, now a sergeant, thought it 'a vast camping
ground'. Beer was issued, and Aitken 'saw some real girls, nurses, and heard a
band playing'. The weather could be shocking. 'The sand nearly cut my eyes out,'
he wrote, 'and I can't face the wind at any price.' He thought Kalgoorlie weather
was 'a King to this'. The spectacle of ships in Mudros Bay, especially when lit up
at night, was a beautiful compensation for the 'pig of a place' he sometimes
thought Lemnos to be. He had been very glad to leave the peninsula; but within a
few days at Lemnos he was anxious to be back at Anzac. 'Camp-life with its rules
and regulations, red tape, and ceremony is very distasteful after having been thro'
the real fighting.' Private Guy Arnold also was glad to be back on the 'Old Peninsula again after two months holiday', having returned feeling really well. Many
other soldiers might have felt like Aitken and Arnold, but one medical officer with
the 1st Brigade on Lemnos thought that not many 'candidly wanted to go back
again'.[9]

New arrivals, not entitled to a period on Lemnos, might be given a week's
spell in Monash Valley. Although it was only about one hundred metres from the
trenches, it was still 'a rest', as John J. Walker assured his parents. And some men
treated their wounds lightly. Lieutenant Aram wrote of a sergeant in a machine-
gun section who had a deep furrow cut across the top of his head. He had the
wound dressed but refused to go to hospital.[10]

Like their predecessors, the new arrivals described the various sounds made by
shells from different types of gun. They also noted that the sound varied according
to the listener's position in the hills. The delayed 'swish' from a captured French

*Playing two-up in Brown's Dip, an open depression not far from Lone Pine. It was a double gamble given the shell bursting near by. Five minutes after this photograph was taken, another shell killed four of the men.*

'75' would put 'the fear of God into one's heart'. Another shell burst 'with a most heart-breaking wail'. The most terrifying noise, thought Aram, was made by one of their bomb-throwing mortars. 'Have you ever seen a hail storm in the summer when all the country is covered with dust?' Lieutenant Cavanagh asked his family, who lived near Horsham in Victoria. 'You will have noticed little spurts of dust rising every few inches. Well that is what the ground looks like when the shrapnel is making a curtain of lead to shield the advancing troops.'[11]

Fears that the Turks might use gas led to the issue of gas helmets, 'guaranteed to give one a headache for a whole week if used for an hour'. A religious interlude could still provide a brief respite of a sort from the prospect of death or injury. 'Came down from trench for church service and enjoyed it,' wrote Sergeant L. S. Horder, a light-horseman; 'held by a new minister, not a very good preacher but earnest, at times could not hear what he was saying because of bursting shells.'[12]

Men looked forward to the day when they could get a 'good solid bath' to get rid of dirt that was 'daily, hourly accumulating'. They sometimes regretted that war souvenirs were becoming difficult to collect and retain, wondered which horse had won the Melbourne Cup, and became angry at being denied promotion. There was pride in being chosen as a permanent bomb thrower, a task reserved for the bravest and best.[13]

Ominously, on 19 November the Turks heavily bombarded Anzac. Veterans said it was the worst morning since the landing. At home, such rigours were fully understood through the many detailed, vivid, precise and realistic—though often long-delayed—accounts from participants printed in newspapers. It was not unknown for two long columns of letters from the trenches to appear in one issue. Occasionally a long article generalising on fighting conditions at Anzac could be characterised by bravado, for instance, by beginning with the statement 'No one feels afraid before battle.' But the great majority of the multitude of reports from the front spoke, as did Sergeant Hector Dinning, a Queensland journalist, not of 'the pride and pomp of glorious war', but of 'the hard graft, dirt, sweat and peril'. It remained routine to print Turkish communiqués on the situation at the Dardanelles. There was still plenty of praise for British troops when due. Australian newspapers on 1 November published a dispatch from Ashmead-Bartlett on the heroism of the 'gallant 29th Division' at Helles and Suvla. The *Barrier Miner*

*Fears that gas might be used at Gallipoli led to issue of primitive gas masks and the occasional practice of gas drill.*

printed a special war issue on Sunday 24 October with a wide variety of articles on aspects of the fighting and accounts of the troops' impatience, in Cairo in early 1915, to go to the front. There were also more stories about the riot of 2 April.[14]

The *Argus* reported pessimism among some it termed 'intellectuals', despondent people who saw little hope of Britain and its allies winning the war. Certainly, the recent military failures of the Entente powers on several fronts made it clear that substantial further reinforcements would be needed. On 22 October King George V sent his message addressed to all subjects of the Empire: 'I ask you men of all classes to come forward voluntarily and take your share in the fight.' At the time, enlistments were falling off. Some recruiting authorities correctly predicted that volunteering would pick up after the harvest. Meanwhile, on Monday 8 November a special recruiting week began in Brisbane, climaxing with a rally in Exhibition Hall and a march through the city of 3,600 troops.[15]

One Labor backbencher from Victoria, James Fenton, thought the recruiting campaign was too successful with young men, or lads. If aged under twenty-one they were supposed to obtain their parents' consent before enlisting. But, Fenton complained, 'we have many youths whom no restraint will keep from going to the front.' Lads would run away to another state and swear they had attained their majority. 'The number of young fellows who seem to have caught the war fever is amazing, and it is a difficult matter to deal with them.' A woman correspondent told Monash, 'My little son is just 13 years to-day and he has war fever.' Sometimes fathers would reluctantly consent to their sons enlisting rather than have them run away from home.[16]

As Fenton spoke, the first of the remarkable marches of recruits from country towns in New South Wales and Queensland was in progress. The 'Coo-ees', who left Gilgandra in October, 30 strong, attracted more recruits at the country towns they passed through on their way to Sydney, which they reached, numbering 263, after a march of thirty-five days. Similar marches from other country towns in the summer of 1915–16 were to bring 1,545 hardy country men to city recruiting halls.[17]

The information collected through the war census cards was published late in November. This showed that there were six hundred thousand 'fit' men aged from eighteen to forty-four who had not volunteered. It was thought that many of these might be induced to enlist. So the government expanded its recruiting organisation and decreed that no males of military age (eighteen to forty-five) would in future be allowed to leave Australia without a passport. No passport was to be issued unless 'satisfactory reasons' were given. A personal appeal from Hughes to enlist was sent to eligible men.[18]

At the end of November Hughes offered Britain fifty thousand additional troops, in excess of the monthly quota of 9,500 reinforcements. The fifty thousand troops were to be trained and partly equipped before embarkation, but Britain would have to supply rifles and machine-guns for them as Australia did not have enough. London promptly welcomed 'this fresh proof of [the] wholehearted determination of the people of the Commonwealth to hasten [the] victorious issue of the war'. Planning went ahead for the creation of new units which Australia would provide under this additional offer.[19]

Hughes, anxious for more recruits, on 4 December told Pearce: 'If this recruiting campaign is to be successful—and it must be if we are to avoid a very serious alternative—it is essential that the public mind should not be disturbed by complaints about hospital treatment, camp troubles or news of the war or opinions in regard thereto like those for example of Ashmead-Bartlett or Lord Ribblesdale. I think therefore you should issue instructions to the Censors accordingly.' Pearce was soon able to assure Hughes that he had instructed the censors to keep a watchful eye on such criticisms.[20]

On 15 December Hughes issued a 'Call to Arms'. He claimed the state of the war 'imperatively' demanded 'exercise of the full strength of the empire and its Allies'. This was followed by a questionnaire to eligible men, seeking their response to enlisting; they were asked to reply to their local recruiting committee within seven days. Major newspapers aided the campaign. Not that recruiting figures until that time were unimpressive. By November over 170,000 men had volunteered. Most had already sailed, and, as noted in chapter 5, by the end of 1915 more than 116,000 of them had disembarked in Egypt.[21]

The friends and relatives of these distant soldiers wanted to make their Christmas as happy as possible. In late October a shipment of forty tons of mail left Melbourne for the troops. It contained over two hundred thousand parcels, of an average weight of nearly three kilograms. Other large shipments were sent to the soldiers, and under a voluntary but organised scheme Australians in every state packed 'Christmas billies' with useful gifts for their soldiers in the far away trenches. Perhaps both sentiment and practicality led the voluntary helpers to dispatch the Christmas gifts in billies, a traditional camp-fire cooking utensil useful, among other things, for making tea.

# CHAPTER 28

# ANZAC-SUVLA TO BE ABANDONED

$C$LIMATIC CONDITIONS during the height of summer had imposed added strain on the troops at Anzac. There followed a pleasant autumn. 'The days and nights continue to be gorgeous,' Lieutenant Aram told his mother on 11 November. Soldiers wrote lyrical descriptions of the magnificent scene as the sun set behind mountainous Imbros Island, enveloped in a purple haze. Some cool, overcast days in October were comfortable; and flies were not as bad as before.[1]

Nonetheless, Australians were already apprehensive about winter snows and blizzards. 'We shall suffer very much,' noted Sam Blows. Monash foresaw heavy work preparing for 'a much more formidable enemy than the Turk, viz—the winter weather'. Two weeks later, as winter set in at the time of Kitchener's visit, men on the peninsula were beginning to complain about the generally appalling weather. An English officer wrote: 'I suppose this place must have the most variable climate in existence. Three weeks ago it was hot, really hot and the sun never vanished during the day for one second—now it is cold—really cold even for England and we haven't seen the sun for five days.' The troops had to endure a freezing wind 'fresh from Siberia'. Heavy rain made the tracks up the hills very slippery. A series of storms blew barges and boats ashore. On 17 November the worst windstorm so far prevented outside work. Men just had to sit in their dugouts, Lieutenant McGrigor said, as he watched the piers being gradually washed away.[2]

*A devastated Watson's Pier after the violent gales in November.*

*These men of the 9th Battery, a Tasmanian unit, had probably seen snow before, but for many Australians late November 1915 was their first experience.*

All this was a prelude to the violent blizzard of 26–29 November. Birdwood, writing as the storm raged, told Kitchener, 'Hands so cold I can hardly write!!' Robert Raws settled down to a night in his 'cosy little dugout' while the storm raged, only to be called out to lead a party in an unsuccessful attempt to save a barge banging against a pier.[3] Lieutenant McGrigor was on Imbros for the storm. He knew there was a lot of damage in Mudros harbour and felt very sorry for the men on the peninsula. One soldier vowed that never in his life would he forget the awful discomfort the troops went through. His own bedding was frozen as stiff as a board, and he stood it on end while cleaning debris from the storm out of his dugout. English officers who had suffered frostbite in Flanders' trenches in the previous winter agreed that conditions were worse during the storm at Anzac–Suvla. One, writing to his mother, compared the storm to Napoleon's retreat from Moscow. Australian newspapers printed an American correspondent's comment: 'Never since the Crimea have British troops endured such an ordeal.' The blizzard caused a sevenfold increase in the rate of evacuations because of illness: 4,211 frostbite cases were taken from the peninsula. Suvla, with 7,750 evacuees, and nearly all of the 280 deaths from exposure, was by far the worst affected of the beachheads. 'I never thought any place could be so cold,' wrote General Ryrie; 'all water was frozen into blocks of ice.' Private Gammage became 'almost mad with thirst'. Ryrie pointed out, 'We must expect even worse than we have had and I don't know how we are to stand it.' Despite the hardships, some Australians commented on the beauty of the scene, with snow blanketing the hills and bushes. A few days later at sunset the snow turned rose pink. Some snowballed with zest; others were pleased at the snow hiding 'all the ugliness of war'.[4]

While the troops on Gallipoli suffered, Asquith's government still vacillated. On 23 November the cabinet, following Kitchener's advice, agreed to evacuate the peninsula. The decision was promptly suspended, but its sense was conveyed to the command at Anzac, which decided to begin preparing for possible departure. So Brigadier-General Brudenell White, who had become Birdwood's chief of staff following the evacuation of Skeen with enteric fever, instituted the scheme termed the 'silent stunt', in order 'to teach the enemy that silence along the firing line did not mean withdrawal'. Orders were issued that Turks were only to be fired on under exceptional circumstances, for example if they attacked. For three days the troops chafed under this 'silent stunt', the significance of which few could fathom. Soldiers' diaries are sprinkled with puzzled or angry comment about this veto on firing. Sergeant Horder, machine-gunner, thought the order 'extremely mad'. Private Champion found the silence uncanny. The 'stunt' ended at midnight on 27–28 November, as the storm intensified.[5]

When the storm ended, the Turks, on the 29th, launched a particularly heavy bombardment. Sergeant T. P. Ahern, a recent arrival from Victoria, wrote: 'It was awful. . . . They buried a lot of our men alive. . . . we were digging them out for three days. I hope I never have the same experience again.' The bombardment smashed the front-line trenches, so that much of the work of recent weeks had to be redone. For some time, work had been in progress at Anzac to prepare for a winter stay. Trenches and dugouts—now sometimes called 'funk-holes'—were deepened, strengthened and improved to cope with both winter conditions and fire from German or Austrian heavy-calibre siege guns. Reports concerning the increase in artillery fire reached Britain and Australia, adding to the anxiety felt by so many at home for their menfolk so precariously placed.[6]

Coinciding with the height of the storm, Bonar Law advised Munro Ferguson that Kitchener's and Monro's reports showed Anzac was so vulnerable that Kitchener's return in a few days might result in Asquith's cabinet deciding upon evacuation. Law warned that the leaking of this information would lead to serious loss of life. Hughes alone was to be told of the situation. Law wanted to know how Australia and New Zealand would react to evacuation. Munro Ferguson replied that although evacuation would be a rebuff it would have 'no moral effect' in Australia. A loss of life because of a neglect of expert military advice would have a disastrous effect, judging from the 'uneasiness' caused by Ribblesdale's disclosures. New Zealand's Governor, Lord Liverpool, hoped that the censors would pass no further 'mischievous criticisms' such as had recently been appearing in the press.[7]

As the men from Gilgandra marched along dusty roads, through the sun-filled, lengthening days towards Sydney and enlistment, in London controversy intensified over the immediate fate of their compatriots in the 1st and 2nd divisions. In the British cabinet five men—Lords Curzon, Selborne, Crewe and Lansdowne, and Sir Frederick Smith—fought as hard as they could in a last-ditch attempt to keep the troops on the peninsula. Maurice Hankey, who sympathised with their viewpoint, thought a paper produced on 26 November by Curzon one of the most able he had ever read. Four years later Orlo Williams saw Curzon as an evil influence who was a reason why evacuation was delayed. Ashmead-Bartlett later was eloquent on the terrible contrast between Curzon, sitting comfortably in his study in Carlton House Terrace, giving academic reasons for holding on at Gallipoli, while the troops there endured the dreadful blizzard. Some navy and army officers still supported these five cabinet ministers. Hamilton to the end opposed evacuation. On 6 December he told Curzon, 'I ought to go back if they have the nerve to nail their colours to the mast and see the thing through.' The persistent Keyes still thought evacuation was 'too horrible to think of' and kept on trying to convince the decision-makers to renew the offensive, led by the navy. Like everyone else who knew the beachheads, he was very worried about the risks of evacuation. He added, 'I don't believe the Australians and New Zealanders will stand it and I can well imagine the fury which will be aroused in those Colonies at such a ghastly sacrifice.' In later years it was 'torment' to Keyes to think of what the fleet might have achieved at the Dardanelles had it been energetically and skilfully led.[8]

Supposed colonial wishes were invoked by both sides in the closing stages of the tortured cabinet debate about Gallipoli. Those wanting the force to remain cited repercussions in Australia and New Zealand if it had to be admitted that all the sacrifice had been in vain. Churchill, for example, used this argument, along with numerous others. Curzon stressed the risks in running away from an Asiatic enemy and claimed that evacuation would arouse 'a feeling of exasperation' in the dominions; their confidence in Britain's resolution would be shaken. They might even say that they would provide no more soldiers and do no more fighting for the Empire. He added that the spirit of the Australian troops would be entirely opposed to evacuation and argued that a new offensive could be launched if the eleven thousand Australians convalescing in England returned to Gallipoli, with proper logistic support.[9] Such arguments were not necessarily specious, as much Australian opinion, at Anzac and at home, was opposed to leaving Gallipoli.

As London and Paris were 'buzzing with rumours' about the Allied force leaving Gallipoli, on 1 December Bonar Law prematurely told Munro Ferguson and Lord Liverpool that Asquith's government had decided to evacuate Anzac and Suvla. Munro Ferguson relayed this news to Hughes, who duly destroyed the letter after noting it. The Governor-General was 'much affected' by the news. He worried about the bad effect on public opinion if there were a disaster or a total evacuation from the Near East without adequate explanation. Law responded blandly that operations in the Near East were under the supreme command of Monro, in whom the British government had complete confidence.[10]

Kitchener's report of 2 December to cabinet on his Eastern mission initiated the final phase of the governmental argument over what to do at Gallipoli. Cabinet was probably not surprised to be presented with a mixture of contradictory opinions in which romantic sentiment jostled with military good sense. Birdwood, for example, agreed with Monro's military judgement but declared he 'would prefer to leave his bones at Anzac than give it up in view of the vast political reasons for retaining it.' Kitchener asserted that regret about leaving was 'greatly intensified because we were most anxious, if possible, to leave Anzac in the hands of the Australians who had so gallantly defended it'. However, there was agreement that Anzac and Suvla were now interdependent. Even Birdwood thought it was asking too much to expect the Australians and New Zealanders to hold on to the original area of Anzac through the winter. Kitchener was sure that the Empire's troops faced 'long odds' if they stayed. Suvla, he said, could not hold out against German artillery, and this involved giving up Anzac. Like Birdwood, he was less pessimistic than previously on the risks of an evacuation. Even so, there was a current saying that optimists expected the loss rate at Suvla (where a secret evacuation would be only slightly less challenging a task than at Anzac) to be at least 15 per cent, whereas pessimists expected 40 per cent.[11]

The long, acrimonious debate finally ended on 7 December when Asquith's cabinet made its irrevocable decision to evacuate Anzac and Suvla. Governments of the four dominions were told that, after discussing the issue with the French for several days, Britain had decided for the present to hold on to the Salonika beachhead.[12]

On the day the Asquith cabinet finally decided to abandon Anzac, Lieutenant John J. Bourke, a Victorian farmer turned artilleryman, told his father, '"Abdul" has consolidated his position so well that I think our opportunity of taking the Peninsula has been lost; we have the men to go through anything but lack competent leaders.' He was sure the Allies would win the war, mainly because of Russian help, but it would 'probably be some years yet'. Major H. H. Page summed up a gloomy stalemate for the benefit of his brother, Dr Earle Page, 'We . . . still have the methods that prevailed in times of the old Greeks and other ancients in almost all departments.' A breakthrough would require at least fifty thousand troops, and Kitchener's army would 'not do it if they had 100,000', Robert Raws wrote. 'So this curious kind of warfare goes on, and many of us wonder how it will all end.'[13]

Soldiers took comfort in the prospect of their Christmas billies, often a topic of discussion. One wary man warned: 'There will be just ructions if they don't turn up. It will be like the old pillow slips we used to hang up at home at Xmastime.'[14]

# CHAPTER 29

# 'THE TURKS HAVE BEATEN US. WE HAD TO GO'

Awareness that a big move was pending gradually spread among those most personally affected by London's decision. Lieutenant-Colonel Chambers, a medical officer on Lemnos, on 19 November mentioned a rumour about possible evacuation. After the departure, Lieutenant Hart was to tell his mother that he first suspected something was afoot when he was on Imbros about 20 November. A few days later, during the 'silent stunt', Lieutenant Bertwistle thought it likely the troops would go. However, as late as 11 December Lieutenant Aram was 'flabbergasted' when told of the impending move, and next day a gun crew wondered what was in the air and speculated on their chances of being relieved. Sergeant E. G. Lawrence did not believe the rumours until 13 December; Corporal Hubert Billings was not completely convinced until the 15th. Even as high-ranking an officer as Monash was caught unawares. On 10 December he knew Monro had recommended evacuation but assumed that Birdwood's rejoinder to Kitchener meant that the last had been heard of that proposal. The Anzacs opposed it. Two days later he heard the 'stupendous and paralysing' news, 'like a thunderbolt from a clear blue sky' of impending departure.[1]

When it became clear they were to leave, reactions among the Australians varied. It is almost certain that sentiment against leaving was stronger at Anzac than at Suvla. Sergeant Lawrence described the 'great consternation and indignation on Anzac' at rumours it was to be abandoned. Robert Raws said the news hit the officers quite hard. They were filled 'with a strange feeling'. Murray Aitken, then on Lemnos, worried that the move would be a morale boost for the enemy. The men were gloomy that 'the heartbreaking time' they had had, sustaining heavy losses, was to end this way.[2] Captain H. E. S. Armitage of the 10th Battalion saw 'at least two hardened soldiers (Boer war men too) weeping over the news. We all feel extreme disgust at the weakness of Kitchener's army—who bungled up the "Sari Bahr" action, and . . . Suvla Bay'. Private Richards reflected, 'What an awful bungling mess these short-sighted damned fool Englishmen have made of this business.' Lieutenant Chapman was sorry to leave because he felt at home at the front. He enjoyed jobs that others disliked. 'I like the work here and it agrees with me. I am fitter than I have been for years which does not speak much for the hardships of campaigning, does it?' John Walker was very anxious to leave. Many writers expressed what was probably the dominant thought: it was sad, hurtful, a bitter disappointment to leave, but there was no chance of success. 'The Turks have beaten us,' wrote Lieutenant H. E. Moody. 'We had to go.' Private de Vine thought 'the whole business' had been 'a very sorry mess up and a sheer waste of men and material'. 'It is bitter to leave so many of our dead heroes in their lonely graves in this foreign soil,' wrote Frank Coen. 'The story of their heroism shall be told to Australians for generations to come; they gave all for their country, let us trust their country will accept the gift with gratitude.'[3]

Major Allanson, a British officer who knew Anzac well, had no sentimental attachment to the beachhead; he thought Britain should have left Gallipoli in September, to concentrate on holding Egypt. Many Australians, then and since, saw the issue much as Allanson did. Half a century later a veteran of the 11th Battalion, who as a lance-corporal was present at the landing and who stayed to the end, still regarded the opposition to evacuation as 'sheer lunacy', as the troops on the peninsula lacked clothing, fuel and other materials needed for a winter occupation.[4]

One advantage of the Asquith cabinet's long procrastination was that the high command at Gallipoli had time to think about the problems of an evacuation and to do some contingency planning. Some preparations had been made since November. The story of planning and executing the departure has been told before. Monash, for example, knowing that organisation meant the difference between success and failure, promptly began working out carefully planned fine details for the 4th Brigade. Medical authorities were told to prepare for heavy casualties.[5]

Birdwood, upset at having to leave his 'beloved Anzac', told Hamilton on 12 December: 'I was almost crying when going through my old Anzac trenches yesterday. Neither officers nor men had any idea of the immediate withdrawal, and they were showing me with such pride how they had wholeheartedly done all they could to carry out my wishes and make themselves shell proof. . . . I feel . . . that Anzac at least could stand out against anything, so you can imagine how bitterly I felt going. It is like deserting one's child, and the irony of it, that I who have so wanted to stay on am the one who had to conduct the withdrawal.'[6]

Birdwood's message to his troops expressed the gist of their final operation at

*The bleak scene at North Beach in late November looking towards Suvla, where with the onset of the harsh Turkish winter British soldiers were drowning and freezing to death in trenches. Australian soldiers too were suffering from frostbite and other effects of exposure.*

Anzac. He trusted to their 'discretion and high soldierly qualities to carry out a task, the success of which will largely depend on their individual efforts'. The message continued, 'If every man makes up his mind that he will leave the trenches quietly when his turn comes and see that everybody else does the same, and that up to that time he will carry on as usual, there will be no difficulty of any kind.' Birdwood expressed confidence that his troops, if attacked during the withdrawal, would 'hold their ground with the same valour and steadfastness as heretofore, however small in numbers they may be.' As Frank Coen put it, 'A simple blunder may imperil the whole force.'[7]

In the preliminary stage of evacuation, from 22 November to 8 December, the number of troops at Anzac was reduced from 41,724 to 36,011. Over the ten succeeding nights, the intermediate stage, the force was reduced to 20,277. These remaining men had to be withdrawn on the last two nights, 18–19 and 19–20 December. Ryrie thought it would be impossible to deceive the Turks, but every effort was made. Stratagems employed have passed into Australia's military folklore: the game of cricket on Shell Green on 17 December; the men detailed to loiter in the enemy's view to suggest the area was still crowded; the contrivances to ensure the firing of some rifles after the troops had gone. All food stores were thrown open to the men, who had a feast. Great quantities of other stores were destroyed. Never before had Lieutenant Chapman 'realised how wasteful war can be'.[8]

Captain S. L. Milligan, on the staff of the 1st Brigade, was one of those with an important subordinate role during the planning for departure. On the 15th he supervised blowing up a 4.7-inch gun. Next morning at 5.30, when it was very dark, he showed NCOs the route to the beach. 'I have about 3/4 million rounds of small arms ammunition to dispose of,' he noted, 'and propose to bury half a million tomorrow. Everything seems to be cut and dried and operation should be successful. Strength of Brigade now reduced to 3642.' He was detailed for traffic control on the last two nights. He thought the staff work 'most thorough'. 'Every provision has been made,' he observed. Half of those remaining at Anzac were taken off without mishap on the night of 18th–19th.[9]

Milligan described the competition among the men to be in the final party, the rearguard. The most active, gallant, fittest and alert men were chosen for this role—to delay the enemy if he followed up too closely. Brudenell White, the officer primarily responsible for the meticulous planning, wrote of men asking their commanding officers to be put in the last party to embark. 'And they had no doubt in

*Turkey fought five major campaigns during the Great War and eventually lost them all except for Gallipoli. Here, Turkish soldiers mark their victory standing on an Australian defensive position after the withdrawal.*

their minds', he wrote, 'that if the Turk came after them they could beat him and still get away!!' Private D. W. Lechte's lieutenant was told that his platoon was to be among the last to leave. 'He was very nice about it and told us that probably the Turks would find out and most likely we would be dead or taken prisoner before the third night.' The men were given the option of leaving early, but of course they all said they would stay to the end.[10]

On the last afternoon on Gallipoli, Milligan made a final tour through the brigade's whole firing line. He noted that enemy action was normal and the men cheerful and confident, even though the line was thin. 'A walk through the back trenches now gave one the creeps,' wrote Lieutenant Aram, for where before there were hundreds of men now there were only ones and twos and these were scattered far apart.' Private Lechte recalled, 'We spent the day running round the almost empty trenches firing off rifles making out things were as usual.' In the last few hours, wrote Lieutenant Chapman, seventy-five of them were holding what was formerly held by fifteen hundred.[11]

When darkness came the various parties had to move at the appointed times to embarkation piers. Hubert Billings, in a group to leave that night, wrote in his diary: 'Everyone doing his best to keep quiet. All talking done in whispers, and a lot of us had stockings over our feet. Anyone who dared let a mess tin rattle was greeted with "sssh" and told off. Arrangements at the Piers were excellent . . . and it was universally agreed reflect the greatest credit on those responsible.' Private de Vine was in one of the last groups to leave. It was guided by lighted candles 'under a tin, in which small holes [had] been punched arrow shape, indicating the route. All other tracks, trenches, etc [had] been filled up with barbed wire and barred with sentries posted on each.' De Vine's party blocked up the track as they left it. Then, he claimed, there was no AIF man left in the trenches, support or reserve lines.[12]

'We were very doubtful', Lieutenant Aram told his mother, that the men could leave without the Turks discovering what was happening. As Monash wrote, the last hours at Anzac 'were tense and exciting in the extreme'. Guy Dawnay, at the scene, saw how fears of disaster gradually evaporated. 'As the night wore on one could hardly believe one's eyes when report after report came in saying that everything was going on without a hitch and with the Turks still apparently quite unconscious of it. . . . It really was the most wonderful operation ever heard of—most wonderfully arranged and carried out to an unimaginably successful conclusion.' At 4.20 a.m. Captain Milligan went aboard his 'beetle' (the embarkation barge), and by 11 a.m. he was safe at Mudros Bay. After Monash reached Mudros at 4 a.m. on the 20th, he reflected on the perfect staff work, the most perfect discipline, and the 'miracle of organization and good luck' marking the evacuation.[13]

Then followed, for many, a weary march to the camp, where the first task was to pitch tents. 'Fourteen of us turned in together and were soon asleep. The wind was blowing hard and early in the morning our tent blew down and we had to turn out in the rain and peg it again.' The soldiers were dealing with such prosaic nuisances while leader writers throughout the Empire were about to compose their paeans of praise. Having helped bring renown to his country, having created a legend, Gunner R. J. Brownell smugly noted that he was able to indulge in another hot salt water bath 'before the new mob found out the bathroom'. Even a new unit like the 28th Battalion, which had not suffered particularly in thirteen weeks at Anzac—it still had 650 men left out of 1,000—obviously needed a rest. 'We did look a forlorn looking rabble in dirty and odd looking uniforms each going his own pace, we were too weak to march in any semblance of order.' To Monash, 'hopeless muddle' marked Britain's running of the Mudros base; but he realised he had to be discreet about this.[14]

So began the process of recuperation. Lieutenant Aram described his men's improvement: 'The first night we landed here the men were very tired, next night they began to get their spirits, and so on, a little more each night, and now as I write they are laughing joking and singing. . . . And during the little time they are on parade they enter into their work with vim and zeal, glad to be out of the narrow, cramping trenches and to breathe fresh air and live a wholesome life again.' Private Lechte was amazed to see how, under the influence of good food, hot baths, shaves and haircuts, the men soon 'all looked like soldiers again'. To Robert Raws, Lemnos was 'heaven after Gallipoli'. Captain Armitage, especially enterprising, and favoured, visited a ship for a hot bath. He felt strange to have a 'clean body, clean clothes, and no vermin'. On the first night the absence of his 'constant companions' kept him from sleeping.[15]

Men took donkey rides to Castro, the principal town on the island, prettily situated on the coast about thirteen kilometres from Sarpi, where they were camped. Murray Aitken, who would be promoted to lieutenant early in the new year, was still possessed by his 'old fascination for a battleship'. He went aboard the *Swiftsure*, where his group was 'treated like toffs'. A craze spread for beautifying the tent camps at Sarpi. 'Every tent is surrounded by borders of stones very neatly arranged,' one soldier noted. The Australian coat of arms was worked out in pebbles before one tent; another group did it in bits of coloured glass. Men made all sorts of designs, including one of typical mine scenes at Broken Hill.'[16]

The men got their billies at Christmas, with their varied and wonderful collections. They were greatly welcomed. 'Could the people of Australia but have seen the happy result of their thoughtful kindness, their own Xmas would indeed have been happy,' wrote Frank Coen. 'The billies were an immeasurable success.' 'You should have seen all their faces when the billy-cans were distributed,' Lieutenant G. G. Allardyce told his father. 'The fellows were all like children opening them and taking one thing out after another just like kiddies.' Some would have preferred their billies to have come from their own state but nonetheless gratefully wrote thank-you letters to the senders. One was wryly amused to find a container with an illustration of a kangaroo kicking the Turk off Gallipoli, the caption reading 'This bit of the world now belongs to us.'[17]

The men were, of course, particularly homesick at the time. This aside, they were probably as content with their Christmas as were the eleven thousand Australians convalescing in England, for whom the 'most complete arrangements' included lavish fare, with 'only sunshine missing'.

In contrast to the Mena bacchanalia twelve months earlier, New Year's Eve celebrations at Sarpi 'passed off very quietly'. The men displayed their distinctive enterprise three days earlier when they heard of 'a mail floating about the Bay aimlessly'. There had been stories of gross incompetence in mail deliveries, of bags having been taken to Anzac and then returned to Egypt. The men did not want a similar disaster to befall the consignment in Mudros harbour. So they 'collected' and distributed it. The recipients were talking, reading and opening parcels all night long; they were too busy to sleep.[18]

As men regained their health and energy, some looked forward to the coming battles. Stirring band music made a man's blood rush 'to his head and he feels like fight,' wrote Captain Armitage. 'You don't know what a "March Past" is', he told his parents, of a parade that was addressed by Brigadier-General Chauvel, 'until you are with a platoon that has done solid service—and your massed Brigade band is playing our Regimental March—one literally treads on air then.' His brigade, the 3rd, was rapidly getting its punch back. He wanted another stunt, a real fight, 'not a trench affair'. 'Jacko has given most of us an appetite. . . . We'll make our names stand out in Hunnish blood.'[19]

# CHAPTER 30

# 'ANZAC IS NOW FAMOUS THROUGH-OUT THE EMPIRE'

$I$N THE SPACE of three days during the intermediate stage of the evacuation, the *West Australian* published three disturbing reports. Heavy German howitzers, of the type that had been so successful in battering down the forts of Liège and Antwerp, had reached the Gallipoli Peninsula. More than a column of extracts were printed from *What of the Dardanelles?*, by a United States officer, Captain Granville Fortescue, containing very astute criticisms of failures in the campaign. And a letter from Trooper Keenan, of the 10th Light Horse, to his father, told how he was wounded in attacking Hill 60 on 29 August: two hundred charged, eighty-one were killed, seventy-nine wounded, and forty were 'let off'.[1]

Most of the Australian public stoically accepted this steady stream of bad news. The War Office, however, was worried lest garbled stories or 'mendacious accounts' from German sources about Australians driven into the sea cause a painful impression if not forestalled with prompt official news of the evacuation. But British and French troops were still at Helles, and nothing could be published that might prejudice their safety.[2]

As soon as possible the news was released, appearing in Australian newspapers on 21 December. Asquith's government should have been satisfied at Australia's public response. Hughes, like Pearce, did not criticise but made an extremely patriotic statement. The evacuation served 'but as a spur to our resolute purpose'; Australian soldiers' glory would 'for ever remain on the soil soaked with their heroic blood'; Australia's 'brave soldiers' would uphold their reputation on other battlefields. Munro Ferguson had good reason to tell Bonar Law that the evacuation had been 'well taken', although 'the whole affair [was] a terrible disappointment for Australia had come to look upon Gallipoli as her special job'.[3]

The main dailies of course endorsed Hughes's attitude. The *Age*, for example, in an editorial partly intended to help recruiting, claimed the evacuation ranked 'among the greatest naval and military achievements of all time'. A German professional opinion at the time agreed, asserting that the event would 'stand before the eyes of all strategists of retreat as a hitherto quite unobtained masterpiece'. The *Daily Post* of Hobart wrote of this 'military miracle', a product of 'the minutest time table of arrangements'. The *Age* had lavish praise for 'the heroes of Anzac' who had 'incurred tremendous sacrifices' but 'won immortal fame'. They had 'always been specifically exempted from blame for the failure of the Allied operations'. The paper was not in the mood to blame anyone for the failure as it also lauded the 'unrivalled skill of Sir Charles Monro and his naval coadjutors' and 'the diplomatic genius of the British Government and Lord Kitchener'.

A headline in the *Newcastle Morning Herald* announced: 'Anzac Given Up'. Its accompanying editoral emphasised regret, even sorrow, at leaving a beachhead where Australian soldiers had 'won the title of being among the most intrepid fighters in the world'. The fame and pride were recalled, and also the suffering and the bereavements. 'Anzac, with its rows of graves, roughly but lovingly marked by sorrowing comrades with crosses and inscriptions, will for ever be a sacred spot in Australian eyes.'

Other dailies, while naturally agreeing with most of the *Age*'s sentiments, were more critical. The *West Australian*'s leader writer anticipated later scholars' views. He was not completely surprised by the departure, for the campaign had failed strategically. He thought the fault lay not with Australian soldiers, who would suffer no loss of prestige, but with those in command. He severely criticised the stupidly criminal mistakes and falsely optimistic reports of the first weeks. The total casualties at Gallipoli were a 'stupendous price to pay for failure'. He hoped 'that in the inner circle of military officialdom some of the calamitous misfits who have cost the nation and the Allies so dearly have been rendered impotent for further mischief'. This was leader-writing fit for a British journal railing against the Gallipoli venture and its perpetrators.

The *Barrier Miner* emphasised the relief—shared by 'everyone who has a sincere interest in the welfare of our soldiers'—that the force had been extricated from a perilous position. For some time, in the tightly knit community of Broken Hill, there had been widespread knowledge of the judgement of officers returned to the town from Anzac, who said that evacuation would not be possible without a loss of at least five thousand men in the rearguard. For a long time, wrote the *Miner*, it had been obvious that the original object of the campaign, the forcing of the Dardanelles, could not be achieved. Since the failure of the August offensive the MEF had not been an efficient use of the Empire's military resources. There was a sprinkling of enemy reports that the Turks had driven the Australians in confusion into the sea; they were saved from utter disaster by fog. One assumes no one in Australia believed these falsehoods.

Many newspapers with smaller circulations, or directed at special publics, took the same attitude as the main dailies, sometimes with a distinctive edge to their assessments. The Labor *Daily Standard* of Brisbane regretted the loss of 'the Ledge of Death', as it called Anzac, and joined the praise of the men's fighting qualities. The Brisbane *Worker* acclaimed the military adroitness of all concerned in carrying out the evacuation successfully, and later printed many remarks by defenders of Churchill's strategy. The *Australian Worker* (Sydney) made no editorial comment but, like the dailies, published relevant extracts from British newspapers. The Ballarat *Evening Echo*, a Labor daily edited by J. H. Scullin, later to be Australia's first Catholic prime minister, wrote of 'glory', 'incredible valor', pathos, and of great pride as 'our men almost did the impossible'. More nationalist than the Imperial-minded *Age*, the *Echo* saw great benefit in the enviable military tradition that Australians had created. This would help to deter any potential enemy thinking of invading Australia.

*Labor Call* (Melbourne) was less 'patriotic', simply printing a few brief, caustic comments on the evacuation. Other Labor or left-wing journals, such as the *Socialist* (Melbourne) or the *Westralian Worker*, said nothing or virtually nothing about the evacuation. The Sydney *Truth* used the most violent language in protesting against the sacrifice of 'our brave boys' on the altar of Imperial military incompetence. The whole campaign, it said, 'seems to have been carried out as if those, politically, most responsible for it were the inmates of a madhouse'. It launched a vicious attack on Churchill and called for an inquiry to clear up the mystery of the bungling. The Melbourne *Tribune* also complained of inexcusable blunders by the command on Gallipoli, and rated the English 'Tommy' as a poor soldier. For the Melbourne *Advocate*, a journal for Australia's Irish community, the Anzac battlefield had 'been consecrated by the many brave sons of our soil'. Those who died did so 'in a noble cause'; 'our place in the sun was gained at Anzac'. It denied that the campaign was 'a monumental failure'. It had hoped 'the whole course of the war' would have been changed when the Cross replaced the Crescent on Sancta Sophia. It marvelled at the successful evacuation, supported Hughes, and criticised the tirade by the Northcliffe press against the campaign.

In the House of Commons Asquith paid gracious tribute to Britain's Australasian kinsmen, and Sir Henry Dalziel asked, 'How many lives have been wasted by the stupidity of the War Office?' Sir Arthur Markham criticised Hamilton and the 'gross incompetence' which had caused so many deaths. Sir Edward Carson condemned the scandal of the Government's silence on the fiasco of the August landings and asked why the men were 'left in a kind of hell' for months while the authorities were trying to make up their minds what to do. Headlines in a special article in the *New York Times Magazine* proclaimed, 'The Gallipoli Campaign, Just Closed, Proved the Greatest and Costliest Military Blunder of the War'. Always, Australia could derive consolation from the generous British press praise for the Australian soldiers. *The Times* of London was comparatively restrained in pointing out: 'Anzac is now famous throughout the Empire.'[4]

Among British officers, relief at the safe departure was widely expressed. Although Birdwood told one correspondent that he hated leaving the beachheads, he told Kitchener they had left just in time, just before a 'real south-westerly gale

*An aerial photograph of the Anzac beachhead. After leaving Anzac, Birdwood saw two of these aerial photographs. They confirmed his belief that it 'was really . . . rather marvellous that we should have been able to carry on as we did'.*

sprang up', which would have made embarkation of large numbers of men almost impossible. Moreover, the enemy had just started firing big howitzers. The 'Westerner' General Douglas Haig warmly congratulated Kitchener on this success. Lord Milner was pleased to hear 'a bit of good news at last'. Guy Dawnay described to his wife this perfect evacuation. 'And so ended what so much had been endured for—so much blood shed for. No "end" about it really of course—the story is deathless. But it is also very sad. No question of its being the right thing to do. We would have done no more there'.[5]

After leaving Anzac, Birdwood saw two aerial photographs of the beachhead. He thought they gave a better idea of what was held than did any photographs taken on land. They confirmed his belief that it was 'really . . . rather marvellous that we should have been able to carry on as we did'.[6]

After the initial disappointment at having to admit defeat lessened, Australians at home would have been greatly relieved that their soldiers were spared the threatening perils of a hard-pressed, shell-blasted winter at Anzac. They would have hoped that their British commanders would assign the AIF more attainable objectives on its next battlefield. Meanwhile, and with good reason, they basked in the reflected glory of widespread recognition for a great feat of arms.

A few weeks reflection brought no change in Pearce's attitude. 'It was a grand attempt,' he told Godley, 'and, though it failed in its direct objective . . . [it] kept busy a number of Turks and Germans who could have done infinite mischief elsewhere. In fact I think we gave the Russians breathing space' and helped contribute to the recent 'turn of the tide' on the Eastern Front. The government, he assured Godley, had 'complete confidence in [its] military leaders.' Godley's response was a natural one. Writing from Egypt, shortly before he was to be given command of the Second Anzac Corps, he told Pearce that his comments should 'be framed in letters of gold and hung in the offices of all critics and pessimists, and it is delightful to get a letter from one in your position expressing such sentiments, when all round one hears such quantities of irresponsible criticism.'[7]

Indeed, comparatively speaking, there was probably more bitterness in Britain than in Australia about the loss of life caused by the 'hare-brained excursion' to Gallipoli. Australia's reaction to withdrawal from Gallipoli was affected by events on the battlefield which were now already legend, an Anzac legend celebrating pride in Australian military achievement. In the contemporary parlance, Anzac 'blooded' the young nation for its 'place in the sun'—equality within a great Empire.[8] And along with pride in the nation's military deeds and a sense of national self-esteem went pride in traits identified by Australians and Britons alike as distinctive to those who won glory: the initiative, comradeship and egalitarianism of the ordinary Australian soldier.

Opposite, above: *Frank Crozier,* The beach at Anzac, *1919 (oil on canvas, 123.3 × 184.2 cm). A clerk from Maryborough in Victoria, Crozier had attended the National Gallery School in Melbourne for two years. He joined the 22nd Battalion in March 1915 and at Gallipoli worked on* The Anzac Book, *edited by C. E. W. Bean and published in 1916. He was an official war artist from September 1918 to June 1920. This painting reflects the pride Australians took in the achievement of their troops at Anzac.*

Opposite, below: *A graveyard at Shell Green overlooking the sea and Gaba Tepe. It was initially used only for the 9th Battalion, but later other units filled up all the spare ground seen in the picture.*

# CHAPTER 31

# 'THE SUFFERINGS OF THE WOUNDED': APRIL–JULY 1915

$T$HE SUFFERINGS of the Gallipoli wounded make a sad story. British and Australian soldiers endured alike much hardship; there was no discrimination by British authorities against the Australians. But few could maintain that the Royal Army Medical Corps (RAMC) performed meritoriously in its duty of succouring wounded soldiers on Gallipoli.

The Australian government had promised that sick and wounded members of the AIF would get the best nursing and medical treatment possible. The performance did not match the promise, partly because of the ill-defined boundary of Australian and British responsibilities. Australian authorities thought all arrangements for moving AIF sick and wounded from the front would be made by the War Office, with Australia later paying the bill. This was a reasonable assumption, as Australians had no part in the higher planning of the AIF campaigns. Australia would provide such medical staff and facilities as it could, with Britain to make good any deficiencies. But relying on Imperial good will proved a disaster for Australian wounded. While much was achieved through good-natured ad hoc Imperial co-operation, the anomalous relationship often meant 'the medical problems of the Australian force were not the recognised business of anyone in particular'.[1]

Almost certainly, these problems were much worse because the AIF did not go to France in 1915 as was originally expected. The change in destination to Egypt hampered planning for the force's medical services. Despite its long occupation, Britain faced significant obstacles in providing adequate hospitals and convalescent homes in Egypt. Evacuation of wounded from the front line in France was eased by a highly developed land transport network. If need be, a voyage of a few hours across the English Channel followed. By contrast, many soldiers wounded at Anzac had to endure a voyage of 1,140 kilometres, normally lasting two to three days, to Alexandria, before receiving significant medical help.

The combination of 'hesitancy and haste' which ruined prospects for the assault on Gallipoli was also disastrous for medical arrangements. Late in December 1914 the War Office appointed Surgeon-General R. W. Ford as Director of Medical Services for the Empire's force in Eygpt. In September 1915 Lieutenant-Colonel Richard H. J. Fetherston, while acting DMS of the Australian Army Medical Services, summed Ford up as 'an old man (much older than his years), overworked and consequently with a bad memory . . . a weak administrator [who] always gave in to anyone who chose to resist or fight'.[2] Ford's responsibilities were not extended to cover the landing; after the Mediterranean Expeditionary Force was formed, Surgeon-General W. G. Birrell was appointed as its Director of Medical Services—that is, the chief medical officer in Hamilton's command. Birrell did not reach Egypt until 1 April. Whether Birrell and Ford co-ordinated their roles properly is doubtful. Compton Mackenzie termed him 'poor old muddled-headed General Birrell' and told a story of his anger one night at 2 a.m. at being awakened to make a decision about replacing a full hospital ship which had just left Anzac. Ashmead-Bartlett, the experienced war journalist, wrote, 'As usual, with the start of all British expeditions, the medical arrangements were totally inadequate.'

By this time the Australians had their own significant medical problems, ranging from their top-level management to the health of the troops. The AIF's first Director of Medical Services was Australia's only regular army medical officer, Colonel (honorary Surgeon-General) W. D. C. Williams, aged fifty-eight. He had run an army hospital in the Boer War competently but was now a 'large Fat gentleman' in indifferent health and with an outlook 'self-contained, and restricted by his immersion in the past'. Monash was kinder, referring to Williams 'in all his stately bulk'.[3] His incapacity helped ensure that Ford did not give him the respect his position warranted, with unfortunate results soon to be mentioned.

After Williams sailed with the first contingent, Fetherston, a militia officer, held the army's senior medical post in Australia. In November 1914 he wrote to Surgeon-General Sir Alfred Keogh, the director-general of Great Britain's Army Medical Service, explaining what Australia had done and could do to provide medical services for the AIF. Already, 150 medical officers were serving with the force. Many others would come forward if the Imperial government needed them; and Australia could provide hundreds of fully trained female nurses and one thousand men trained in ambulance work.

Numbers 1 and 2 Australian General Hospitals reached Egypt in January. These were major units each of 520 beds, comparable to a large civilian hospital. No. 1 AGH occupied the magnificent Heliopolis Palace Hotel on the north-eastern outskirts of Cairo, about six and a half kilometres from the city, and No. 2 went to Mena, by the 1st Division's camp. Dr Stanley Argyle, on the staff of the hospital at Heliopolis, was ecstatic that it would 'take up its abode' in the 'gorgeous building in an oasis in the desert'. He continued: 'All I had heard, and I had heard a great deal, had not given me the faintest idea of the magnificence of the Palace. I have never seen nor even dreamed of such a building. . . . The only thing I fear is want of sufficient work to keep us busy.' Subsidiary units included numbers 1 and 2 Stationary Hospitals, each of two hundred beds, a casualty clearing station and field ambulance units. Until August 1915 the only military ambulance transport in Egypt—for use by all Empire troops—was provided by Australia and New Zealand.[4]

J. W. Barrett, an eye and ear specialist and registrar of No. 1 AGH, was a forceful personality who took the initiative in expanding hospital facilities for Australian troops in Cairo. He arranged to take over various buildings—clubs, hotels, a skating rink (Luna Park)—for a network of auxiliary hospitals. His fifty-two-bed hospital thereby grew to a 10,600-bed organisation. This expedient was unorthodox. Moreover, Barrett's growing stature, and his brusque manner, annoyed many of his Australian colleagues. He clashed with his equally strong-willed principal matron, Jane Bell. Barrett's other bitter enemies included his fellow-Victorian, Argyle, who vilified him as the 'octopus of Heliopolis'. Monash summed up Barrett: 'In spite of his great abilities and industry and splendid work, [he] always contrives to antagonize people. He has as many enemies as friends.'[5]

Dissension among the managers of No. 1 AGH was only one of the problems for the AIF's medical services in Egypt. According to AIF doctors in Egypt, medical examination of the first volunteers was not always of a high standard. Many unfit men, it was asserted, sailed with the first contingent. Authorities in Australia were advised to improve their medical testing. Certainly, there was an unexpectedly high rate of illness in the force. In its first four months in Egypt its rate of disease was much the same as that of the Canadian contingent in England, which, although it had to contend with the cold, damp Salisbury Plain, had the benefit of better medical facilities. Excessively rigorous training perhaps contributed to the 1st Division's ill health. Infectious diseases, including measles, hospitalised many men. Before the landing, over two thousand Australian soldiers were incapacitated by venereal disease, 3 per cent of the force being sick with this ailment at any one time. A special hospital was set up at Abassia to treat them; 1,350 of the worst affected were returned to Australia in 1915.[6]

Various other problems arose, or loomed on the horizon. An administrative bungle surrounding the return to Australia of sick men on board the *Kyarra* eventually led to a departmental inquiry. As the weather warmed, Argyle had second thoughts about the suitability of the Heliopolis Palace Hotel. He believed that by April it would be too hot for use as a hospital. The temporary appointment of a British officer to a post in the Australian medical hierarchy in Cairo illustrated the blurred demarcation line between Australian and British responsibilities. There was some Australian feeling that its medical arrangements there were 'rather amateurish'. Unexpectedly large numbers of sick troops were returned from Egypt. Munro Ferguson commented on the inadequate standard of the troops' hospital accommodation in Australia.[7]

On 28 April James Mathews, Labor member for Melbourne Ports, moved a formal adjournment motion in the House of Representatives to express concern over AIF health issues. Like some other members of parliament, he had received letters complaining of the treatment accorded sick men in Egypt. He thought this amounted to 'a terrible indictment' of the AIF's health administration there; as 'the cream of Australia' was in the camps, the death rate should be very low or non-existent. Sir Robert Best, opposition member for Kooyong, mindful of the impact on recruiting, joined in support of Mathews. The Labor radical Frank Anstey queried why the death rate among officers was less than that for men. The Fisher government did not want a long debate and allowed the motion to lapse.[8]

Had Mathews and Anstey known how AIF wounded were at that very time being treated at Anzac Cove their anger would have turned to apoplexy. Birrell's arrival in Egypt on 1 April left little time to organise the MEF's medical facilities. Planning for care of the wounded was low in Hamilton's order of priorities. On 18 April, five days before the landing was due, Birrell warned that without some improvement it would be 'impossible from a medical point of view to commence serious operations'. Storms which postponed the landing for two days allowed some emergency steps to be taken, and it was not until 24 April that Birrell issued his orders to those under his control. Three weeks later a British admiral was telling a colleague that the 'military medical arrangements' at Gallipoli 'were entirely inadequate and that Birrell was 'absolutely incompetent to deal with the situation'. Two years late Neville Howse, then the AIF's Director of Medical Services, said the same to the Dardanelles Commissioners. A very competent man in Birrell's position would have been able to ensure some improvements in the plans, but the problem was essentially one of inadequate time and resources, and lack of foresight at a level higher than Birrell.[9]

For the Anzac landing, Birrell allotted one hospital ship, the superbly equipped *Gascon*, designed for up to three hundred 'serious cases'. It was not meant to receive lightly wounded men. The transports *Clan MacGillivray* and *Seang Choon*, after unloading their troops, were to be used as hospital ships, to take 'light cases'. Godley complained to Birdwood that all wounded and sick, even if only slightly affected, were to be returned all the way to Alexandria. He wanted 'light cases' to be treated at Lemnos, where an Australian hospital could accommodate at least four hundred patients. That hospital was intended to move to Gallipoli after the

invaders had gained enough territory. It waited four weeks, unused, ready to move, but it could not go forward as planned, because the Anzacs did not gain enough space for such a hospital; after that, Lemnos was used as an intermediate base for sick and wounded.[10]

Arrangements for clearing the wounded from Anzac during the first days were inadequate to cope with the reality of an appalling torrent of casualties. The corps' failure to gain its first day's objective caused frightful difficulties for the medical services. The beachhead was too small and vulnerable to accommodate medical facilities normally provided immediately behind the front line. These facilities remained on board ship, and too great a strain was thrown on shore-to-ship communication. It was the evening of the 26th before the first wounded sailed from Anzac. On the 29th four shiploads reached Alexandria. Within a few days Australian hospitals in Cairo were taxed to the utmost.

Some of those who helped to clear the wounded from Anzac at the landing have told their stories. E. Bidder Clark, a midshipman on HMS *Prince of Wales*, was in charge of the ship's pinnace which on 25 April collected wounded from the beach at Anzac. He found no proper landing place to take off the wounded, who had to walk up 'wobbly planks' to the pinnace. He could have taken more had there been a proper landing place. 'It was terrible having to refuse so many wounded lying there who begged to be taken,' he told his mother. After filling the pinnace, he recalled, 'we went a dreary round of the transports until we found one who had some room for our wounded. She had 400 already and only 2 Doctors and no dressings.' By that night 'the whole 600 yards of beach [at Anzac] was strewn with wounded . . . all in one continuous tangle'. They had to lie on stones. Light rain began to fall about 2 a.m., adding to their discomfort, as the medical staff had little or nothing to cover them with. Eight years later a fleet surgeon remembered with admiration the 'uncomplaining body of men' waiting patiently for transport to the ships.[11]

*Wounded AIF lie unattended amongst a confusion of people and equipment on cramped Anzac beach on 25 April 1915. Plans to clear wounded from Anzac after the landing could not cope with the appalling torrent of casualties. Because the beachhead was so small and vulnerable, medical facilities remained on board ship. Not until the following evening did the first wounded sail from Anzac, and many received no surgical aid until reaching Alexandria.*

Major Corbin's medical unit of five men landed at 11.30 a.m. on the 25th. Within three days his group, 'one of whom did practically nothing', handled about 3,300 casualties. 'The continuous succession of hideous wounds and the difficulty of doing as much as one would wish for them makes the work distressing as well as arduous,' Corbin wrote. Four days after the landing, a Royal Navy captain at Anzac wrote of the 'poor fellows waiting hours on the beach in scorching sun'. The shortage of staff meant it was often impossible to give anaesthetics. There was nowhere safe to put hospital cases at Anzac. Wounded lying on the beach were wounded again. A story told by Charles Drage, midshipman on the *London*, illustrates the danger. On the 27th, off Anzac, he was told to persuade about a hundred stretcher-bearers to move to the beach from the shelter of an iron tug. They refused to go. A stoker, an Australian and 'the worst character in the ship', disappeared into the stretcher-bearers' haven, the tug's deckhouse. There came the sound of blows and 'a babel of truly awe-inspiring language, followed by a torrent of stretcher bearers, tumbling over each other in their eagerness to escape from the gigantic and turbulent figure in their rear'.[12]

For six days, until the *Gascon* returned from Alexandria, there was no hospital ship at Anzac, so thousands of wounded soldiers, including Australians, were carried from Gallipoli to Alexandria in 'black ships'. These were transports which had brought troops, and in many cases horses, to the peninsula. Some were British ships; others were captured German ships; others had come from the Levant or wherever the British government could hire them. With little or no modification apart from flying the British flag, they were urgently pressed into service as an emergency makeshift to carry wounded from the peninsula. Unlike hospital ships, which were marked and entitled to protection under the Geneva Convention, these 'black ships' were simply military transports and thus highly vulnerable to attack by German submarines. Ashmead-Bartlett was sure that the lack of adequate hospital ships meant 'many succumbed who might otherwise have been saved'. Charles Drage commented: 'The wounded in all these transports must be dying like flies, with few doctors, no nurses and practically no convenience of any kind. I hope someone hangs for it.' Almost every such ship used to evacuate wounded in the first days was 'full of horses'. It had been planned to land these horses on the peninsula. Instead, because of the failure to make good ground at Anzac, they spent some time on the ships before returning to Egypt.[13]

It took months for news of this bungling to reach Australia and England. The

*AIF wounded aboard the transport* Mashobra, *one of the 'black ships' hastily improvised to carry wounded from Gallipoli. Sanitary arrangements were rudimentary, and in many cases the vessels had carried horses or mules to Gallipoli. The* Mashobra, *indeed, still had 240 horses on board but was still considered one of the more salubrious of the 'black ships' used during the landing.*

303

scandal had a delayed result in the importance attached to the medical arrangements in the inquiries conducted by the Dardanelles Commission. Many of its witnesses recalled the horrors of those first days. Neville Howse told Andrew Fisher that the plans made for handling Australian wounded 'were so inadequate that they amounted to criminal negligence'.[14] He thought 'the suffering and loss of life that was entailed upon the troops was very serious'. It appeared to him that the authorities 'really did not expect wounded, but they got them'. Many Australian wounded received no surgical aid until reaching Alexandria. Ashmead-Bartlett also told the commission 'nothing could have been more deplorable than the sufferings of the wounded' at the Anzac landing. Barges carrying wounded went from one ship to another, seeking one that had suitable space. P. C. Fenwick, a senior New Zealand medical officer at the landing, said the *Lutzow* had horses on board and though not in the least prepared to take wounded, took five hundred. In March 1919 Lieutenant-Colonel Charles Ryan—'Turkish Charlie', by then an honorary surgeon-general—who had been on the *Lutzow*, told A. G. Butler, official historian of the AIF's medical saga, that it was 'the dirtiest and nastiest boat' he had ever seen. Why it should ever have been chosen to carry wounded men passed his comprehension. The captain was a German, and the crew Levantines, Greeks, Italians and Turks. 'The row kicked up by [the] frantic horses kept everybody from sleeping.' On this ship carrying seven hundred to eight hundred wounded there was no bedpan and no paper. On another ship, men coming out of anaesthesia and those with broken jaws were given bully-beef and biscuits. When the *Itonus* reached Alexandria after a 'simply awful' voyage, it was after midday on 1 May before the last of the wounded had been unloaded, yet many of these men had been wounded on 25 April. On 12 May Stanley Argyle noted that it routinely took six days to get to Heliopolis after being wounded in the firing line. Little wonder that many limbs were amputated and lives lost which might have been saved.[15] Similar chaos prevailed at Helles beaches.

At the Dardanelles Commission, John Corbin, by then a lieutenant-colonel, testified that the problems of shore-to-ship transport of the wounded at Anzac far outlasted the chaos of the landing. As medical officer of the 1st Australian Casualty Clearing Station he was at Anzac from the landing until 21 August. He commented on the shortcomings of the temporary piers and on the shortage and unsuitability of boats for the wounded. Horse barges were used, but it was hard to get them clean. For only a fortnight did his unit have the use of boats especially provided for sick and wounded. In the emergency times, he said, 'one would have a load of mules coming in which had perhaps been in these barges for many hours, the mules would be unloaded and we would load wounded into these barges. They have mats for the mules to stand on the iron floor and they are usually saturated with the urine and excreta of the mules, and from the point of view of asepsis or anything of that sort were not at all satisfactory.' Corbin was not relying solely on his memory for this evidence, as he recorded much of what he saw in his diary. In May 1915, when arrangements were deplorable, he thought that the Royal Army Medical Corps men were 'all scared stiff of offending someone higher up. . . . Should have our own barges and our own towage and man it ourselves.'[16]

Surgeon-General Birrell was allowed to defend himself as a witness before the Dardanelles Commission. He disputed some of Howse's evidence and questioned his fitness to make sound judgements on the matter. Some witnesses defended Birrell's arrangements. One was Albert Jacka, who said that volunteers from the infantry battalions were continually helping to clear the beach of wounded. Even when prompted by the commissioners, Jacka made no complaints about their treatment, although he admitted he could not see much at first hand, as he was in the firing line by 26 April. A New Zealand officer, Major Ross Cairns, an artilleryman who landed on the 25th, claimed there were enough small boats to take the wounded to the ships. Admiral Sir William May, one of the commissioners, remarked that it was quite singular that there should be such a clash of evidence between these two soldiers and so many other witnesses.[17] Among other British medical officers the commissioners also heard Surgeon-General Ford, Colonel Alfred Keble, Birrell's deputy, and the Director-General of Britain's Army Medical Service, Surgeon-General Sir Alfred Keogh.[18]

Some of the most damaging evidence to the Dardanelles Commission about the 'black ships' came from the Dowager Countess of Carnarvon, a benevolent and also redoubtable lady. She reached Egypt in April 1915, intending to stay two weeks, but remained for about thirteen months. 'All the wounded were coming in such quantities and there was such a terrible state of things,' she recalled. She had no commission and no official status, and she visited hospitals without permission. She was very critical of medical arrangements, but the British army had to endure her interference lest she cause them more trouble if thwarted. Lady Elizabeth Rochdale thought Lady Carnarvon was having a beneficial effect in Alexandria; she seemed 'to have a private large supply of nurses'. She met wounded men coming down the gangway and gave them cigarettes and sweets and also showed 'many kindnesses' to the bearers and other medical workers. Her role in history did not end with her leaving Egypt. In 1917 she led the list in the Commonwealth government's recommendations for the award of the OBE, in recognition of her untiring devotion to the AIF in Egypt. She later told the Dardanelles Commissioners that the 'black ships' were especially bad and remained so throughout the campaign. One was 'a dreadful cattle ship'; on another, nine fit sisters and five fit medical men had to cope with 983 bedridden patients. 'Men were crying out when I got on the ship. I got them the morphia and some other things they wanted.' The cries were dreadful on one ship, she said. 'There were no washing appliances, the sanitary arrangements were horrible.'[19]

Evidence was also given by Lieutenant-Colonel Ryan, who had been Assistant Director of Medical Services for the 1st Australian Division before transferring to Birdwood's staff as principal medical adviser to the corps commander at Anzac. He described conditions on the *Luxoor*, a ship taken over from the Germans and used to carry wounded although it was no way equipped as a hospital ship. It had about seven hundred wounded on board, and there were no bedpans. 'In about two or three days all the paper on the ship was used, and the men . . . were messing in their trousers all over the place.' It was a 'beastly boat' with a 'scratch crew of Levantines and the riffraff of Alexandria. For six weeks it also carried about two hundred horses, and they were kicking and making a great noise at night. Despite these conditions, Ryan did not think a great many lives would have been saved had there been more hospital ships. Of the 7,156 men embarked on the first thirteen shiploads of casualties from Anzac, 273 died before reaching Alexandria. Most of those severely wounded did not survive long enough to reach a ship. Two other witnesses, both medical officers at Anzac, Lieutenant-Colonel John Gordon and Colonel C. M. Begg, a New Zealander, told the commission that almost every ship used to evacuate wounded in the first instance was 'full of horses'.[20]

The shiploads of wounded from Gallipoli severely taxed the Empire's hospital facilities in Egypt. Hospital trains from Alexandria brought wounded 'in appalling numbers' to Cairo. These were the least severely wounded, those judged fit enough to survive the train journey. The worst cases were taken to British hospitals in Alexandria. Initially the AIF had no hospitals there, but some medicos soon realised that the port would have been a better location for the force's main concentration of hospitals. It was too late, however, for a major relocation as medical staff were fully occupied coping with the flood of wounded, many covered with muck or

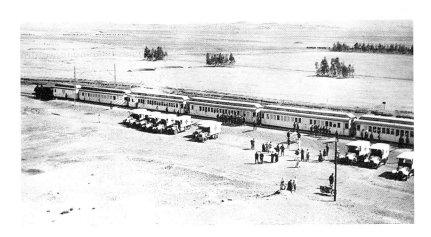

Hospital trains from Alexandria brought wounded in appalling numbers to the 'Palace', No. 1 Australian General Hospital, Heliopolis. Ambulances in the photograph are probably Australian; until August 1915 the only military ambulance transport in Egypt was Australian and New Zealand.

suffering from gangrene if their wound had not been dressed for days. Sister E. H. Cuthbert described a typical reaction to the arrival of 'so many more than we expected or than we had provided for'. Many 'badly wounded would arrive only half clad, and the whole situation was so new to us, that many a Sister when the badly wounded first arrived, had at times suddenly disappeared into the pantry to control her feelings for these poor suffering boys; and their wonderful patience and endurance, and kindly sympathy and care for each other, really seemed to make it harder for the women to bear.'[21]

Lady Godley, who organised three convalescent homes for New Zealanders in Egypt, kept her husband informed of her views on the local hospital scene. She criticised Australian medical authorities and some New Zealand medicos but was just as scathing in commenting on General Maxwell and other Britons in authority. She was appalled at 'the great unpreparedness of all the medical arrangements'; 'if it was not for the civilian energy, I don't know what would have happened. . . . The W.O. and the Headquarters here ought to be hung. They should have known what would happen and should have taken advantage of all the help that was offered them, instead of refusing it.' Even after the 'frightful business' of dealing with the rush of thousands of wounded, there were still shortages of medical and nursing staff, and summer had come. It was 116 degrees Fahrenheit in the shade in Cairo, Lady Godley told her husband, 'which is very hard and cruel for the poor patients with bad wounds'. The skating rink at Luna Park, when packed with wounded, was just awful, she said. 'I have never seen anything like the pandemonium it is. Seven hundred beds in the awful heat and the tin roof. All the patients seem cheery, but how anyone can get well in such a place is past belief.'[22]

One of the wounded Australians brought to Egypt was Private Willie Harris. He was hit on 2 May: 'Suddenly got a bang like a sledge hammer. Glancing round I saw the blood rushing from my left arm.' He thought his life had been saved because his diary deflected the bullet. He could place his thumb in the hole in the muscle of his arm. His pals bound up the wound as quickly as possible, but he lost a great deal of blood and felt giddy. He was taken to a temporary dressing station and then boarded a ship, in great pain. 'Cannot get into easy position for long. Arm is aching all over and I cannot bend it or move it much.' At Alexandria his arm was re-dressed. It was rotten and smelt like decayed fish. Men near his bed in hospital were dying of their wounds. Willie, despite the terrific heat, the flies which nearly drove him silly, sleepless nights and other discomforts, gradually recovered. By late May he recorded a significant triumph when he was able to get his coat on over both arms. At this time John Gellibrand told his brother what it felt like to be wounded by shrapnel in the shoulder. 'If you will get Brother T. W. to hit you hard on the shoulder with a cricket stump, then wind you in the lower chest, lay you flat out and cut your clothes off you would have a very fair representation of my experience.'[23]

Wounded Australians taken to Malta or England praised the treatment they received. On 19 May H. F. Nelson of Buderim, Queensland, was badly wounded in the face, his right eye being shot away. He praised conditions on the hospital ship *Soudan* and at Malta. He had virtually no complaints about English hospitals, although he 'felt very much at home' when he moved to an Australian hospital at Harefield Park. This hospital in Middlesex, set in a hundred hectares, had been provided by a patriotic Australian as a convalescent home. By midsummer there were five hundred beds there, and a few months later it was transformed into a general hospital. For another wounded AIF man, Dick Fowler, England was home, even though his parents lived in Toowoomba. Wounded on 29 May, during one of the Turks' attacks on Quinn's Post, he lay for twelve hours, having 'a pretty bad time near the firing line' until a stretcher-bearer reached him. He was in a good deal of pain. 'Whilst lying on the ground the scenes of home came through my thoughts very very often.' Four weeks later, 'after years of longing to see dear old England—my desire came at last'.[24]

Ray Baker, wounded on 25 April, counted himself extremely fortunate to be taken to Malta instead of Egypt. He was very comfortable on the island, enjoying the marvellous views of the harbour and 'electric light, water handy and all other conveniences'. He was also pleased at the good relations with local schoolchildren, who regarded the poor maimed Australians as great heroes. This contrasted with the attitude of the Cairenes, groups of whom 'jeered and rejoiced' as Empire wounded were taken through the streets.[25]

Most Australian sick and wounded went to Egypt, where conditions remained bad. A month after the landing, an AIF medico wrote: 'Medical arrangements have been shocking. Surely someone ought to be hanged if ever there is an enquiry.' Stanley Argyle became convinced that his hospital was too far away from the firing line to get the best results. 'Many wounded are septic,' he noted; 'that would not be so bad had they been attended to regularly and promptly.'[26]

After fighting subsided at Anzac in May, illness rather than wounding became a major problem among soldiers holding the beachhead. Water shortage did not help. Cramped, insanitary conditions produced great clouds of flies which carried disease through the corps by way of latrines and dixies. A cholera outbreak was feared, but inoculation forestalled this. Although the trenches were kept clean, by the end of July gastro-intestinal diseases were out of control, latrine poles were perpetually thronged by men, and many were killed or wounded at latrines exposed to Turkish fire. Still there were men so stricken by dysentery that at night they took their blankets and slept alongside the latrines. The corps was diseased and unfit, and some of the worst affected had to be shipped to Egypt. Yet men had enough resilience to be capable of responding briefly to the demands of an offensive.[27]

By mid-1915 some publicity had been given in Britain's press and parliament to reports of poor treatment meted out to wounded from the Dardanelles. The authorities, of course, professed to see it otherwise. Birrell on 10 June told Sir Alfred Keogh, 'All goes well [with] medical arrangements and health of the troops.'[28] On 23 June 1915 H. J. Tennant, the Prime Minister's brother-in-law and Undersecretary of State for War, told a questioner in the House of Commons there had been deficiencies in May in caring for the wounded, but matters had since been put right. Tennant and Birrell were wrong, as the case of the *Saturnia* indicated. At the end of June, after heavy fighting at Helles, this black ship sailed to Alexandria, packed with maggoty wounded. An Australian surgeon on board was doing his best but could not cope. A New Zealand medical officer later told the Dardanelles Commission that he 'boiled with indignation' when he went from the *Saturnia* to the nearby *Aragon*, where staff officers lived a very comfortable, elegant existence. Field Marshal Nicholson, one of the commissioners, asked how such an appalling journey as that of the *Saturnia* could have been made two months after the landing? 'It fills one with amazement. Is it not a case of neglect of the very grossest nature?' On behalf of the British Red Cross, Sir Frederick Treves visited the theatre in May and June. Treves had been a consulting physician to British forces in the field during the Boer War and had been created a baronet following his world-wide fame after operating successfully on an acutely ill Edward VII. He served in the War Office from 1914 to 1918. On 9 July *The Times* published his 'reassuring' letter stating that hospital arrangements were adequate for reception of the Gallipoli sick and wounded. Lady Godley told her husband that 'everyone' was very angry with Treves for 'telling such lies'; he had got on by toadying. In 1917, before the Dardanelles Commission, Treves explained that in his letter to *The Times* he had not dealt with serious medical problems. He had not thought he was 'called upon to raise matters that would only give distress to the people in England'. He then criticised officers on the *Aragon* for their ignorance of the condition of the wounded, and he gave the commissioners damning evidence about the shipment of the wounded from Gallipoli to the hospitals in Egypt, Malta and Lemnos.[29]

In Australia initally there was little public reaction to the scandalous handling of the wounded, a silence no doubt helped by effective censorship. As Lady Godley explained, 'Some press men who came lately from Australia wrote about it, but their letters weren't allowed to pass the censor. So now they say they will travel back to Australia and publish the facts there and that there will be a most awful row.' She mentioned an Australian Salvation Army man who had seen all Cairo's military hospitals and 'was quite horrified at Luna Park'. He must have been Isaac Unsworth, who in July visited Luna Park, at Maxwell's request, and later commented, 'The sight of these 1,400 men lying there crowded together in this terrible heat with the flies pestering them was awful.' He angrily blamed Maxwell for allowing this crisis to develop.[30]

The Australian public furore over the AIF's medical arrangements centred on the increasing tension between its senior officers in Egypt. The situation became so bad partly because there were no clear, firm precepts to define the relationship between the Australian and British medical services, and partly because Colonel Williams was too old, unwell and inadequate to be a satisfactory head of the AIF's medical staff. His appointment had been approved by Bridges, who soon realised the mistake. Within a few weeks of Bridges' death, Imperial authorities effectively ended Williams's power. Senator Pearce meekly acquiesced, leaving the Australian medical service in Egypt without a head, its interests subordinated to those of Britain's set-up. To the fury of his enemies, Barrett, the registrar of No. 1 AGH, was able to ingratiate himself with Surgeon-General Ford, who took it upon himself, without informing Australian authorities, to elevate Barrett to be his Australian adviser.[31]

By early June friction on the staff of No. 1 AGH was so bad that it was becoming widely known in Australia. Keogh and Sir George Reid advised the Fisher government that an inquiry was needed. Pearce agreed, and the War Office acted quickly. The Army Council heard much conflicting evidence and then recommended that Barrett devote himself entirely to Red Cross work and that two of his main opponents—Lieutenant-Colonel William Ramsay Smith and Matron Jane Bell—be recalled to Australia. Pearce agreed. He would have preferred Barrett's return also, but the latter had an amazing capacity to persuade Imperial authorities of his worth. Both Maxwell and Sir Henry McMahon, the British High Commissioner in Egypt, strongly urged Barrett's case. Pearce was unimpressed, but Ford intervened and Barrett stayed in Egypt with the AIF until in February 1916 he obtained an appointment in the Royal Army Medical Corps. After the war he went on to a further thirty years of some prominence in Victoria's public life. In October 1915 both Bell and Ramsay Smith asked the Defence Department for a full inquiry into the circumstances of their recall. Fetherston supported this, but Lieutenant-Colonel T. H. Dodds, the Adjutant-General, objected, so the matter lapsed.[32]

The tangled skein of Anglo-Australian relations in Egypt and the MEF saw another serious row when ill-feeling developed between Australian and Imperial authorities following reports to Australia in May and June 1915 by Lieutenant-Colonel C. A. K. Johnston that a great many Australian soldiers in the British convalescent camp at Mustapha, on Alexandria's outskirts, were complaining they were not being properly looked after. Men had 'to go about in rags', and some said they were 'being treated as if they had committed a crime in being wounded'. The whole camp was 'frothing with discontent'. Amongst a thousand Empire soldiers in Mustapha were about thirty-five Australians. Willie Harris was one of them. He was not happy with conditions and was one who gave evidence when Johnston heard complaints.[33] Lieutenant-Colonel A. R. Tweedie, commanding the convalescent camp, deeply resented this 'most gross and unjust reflection on the personnel and work' of his unit, writing several firm letters in this vein in June.

Brigadier-General C. McGrigor, the British commandant of the base, visited the convalescent camp without notice and told Johnston his complaints were 'most unwarranted and an unjust reflection on the work' of the British personnel at Mustapha. He refused Johnston's request for a court of inquiry. Johnston went higher and had a tense meeting with Sir John Maxwell, who supported McGrigor. Maxwell told Johnston he should never have made such criticisms and that the convalescent camp was no affair of his, even though he was in command of the 1st Australian Division's Overseas Base. Maxwell warned Johnston that 'if he could not attend to his own affairs, and made mischief,' he 'would be obliged to return him to Australia'. He also told McGrigor that Johnston 'was out for trouble and self-aggrandisement. He is a hopeless fellow, an obstructionist who quarrels with others and does not work the right way to help Australian interests.' Maxwell did not want news of this imbroglio to reach Melbourne, but Johnston wrote to the Defence Department on 8 June.[34]

Maxwell was obliged to write to Pearce about this incident. He claimed that 'everything humanly possible' was being done for the welfare of sick and wounded Australians. Johnston's report and copies of his correspondence with British officers about the affair aroused considerable resentment in the Australian defence hierarchy. Dodds, who had served in the South African War, saw it as a clear clash between Imperial and Australian jurisdiction. In a minute to M. L. Shepherd, secretary of the Defence Department, he wrote of a 'scandalous state of affairs'. He was sure that a haughty Maxwell had dismissed Johnston's complaints as coming from 'a damn'd colonial officer'. Pearce agreed with Dodds and so did the cabinet. The government told London it took 'strong exception ' to Maxwell's attitude and, at Dodds's suggestion, requested the Army Council to set up a court of inquiry into Johnston's allegations. Despite the difficulties, the Army Council did make inquiries, eventually concluding that Johnston had exaggerated and made insufficient allowance for the intractable problems facing Maxwell and his medical authorities. In any case, from September 1915 few Australians remained at Mustapha. One of those who left was Willie Harris. Although he thought Alexandria 'much cleaner and more European than Cairo', he was delighted, late in July, to

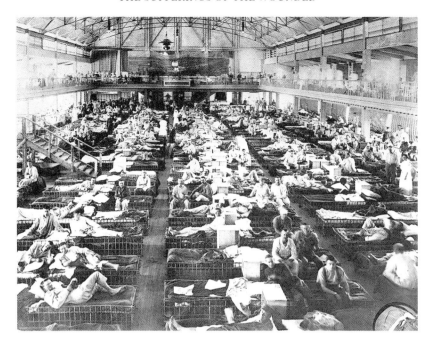

No. 1 Australian
General Hospital,
Heliopolis, grew to
10,600 beds to handle
the great flood of
casualties. Auxiliary
establishments used for
the lighter cases in-
cluded this one, which
is probably Luna
Park, with its in-
famous tin roof.

leave the 'awful hole' after eleven weeks and move to Luna Park, Cairo. Here their food was splendid, and they 'were made quite a fuss of', receiving 'a real Australian welcome'. The Australian nurses seemed anxious to do all they could to help. He was glad to 'have done with English doctors and orderlies', and pleased not to have to perform any of the menial tasks required of him at Mustapha.[35]

In May, reports of bad treatment of the Gallipoli wounded led the War Office and the Admiralty each to choose a high-ranking officer to go to the theatre to set things right. Surgeon-General W. Babtie was selected for the new post of Principal Director of Medical Services, throughout Malta, Egypt and the Dardanelles. The Admiralty brought out of retirement the 64-year-old Vice-Admiral Sir James Porter as Principal Hospital Transport Officer, controlling movement by sea of Gallipoli wounded. The War Office told Hamilton it had been assured that Porter would do everything possible to meet Babtie's requests. Porter would be able to represent Babtie's needs to Admiral de Robeck, the naval commander, much better than the general could.[36] Birrell, who estimated almost exactly the number of casualties to be produced by the August offensive, came under Babtie's command until he was recalled in September.

Babtie arrived in the theatre on 15 June, Porter not until 28 July, which suggests certain Admiralty shortcomings. Both men received some high praise from medical and support staff, but there was also disagreement whether Porter's advent brought immediate improvement. As soon as he reached Cairo, Babtie found fault with some Australasian medical arrangements. For example, he condemned Barrett's decision to turn the Luna Park skating rink into a hospital. Nonetheless, Luna Park was to remain in use for another year, its patients enjoying a very good recovery record. The same was generally true of Cairo's other Australian hospitals. Conditions were uncomfortable, but few patients died, a record helped by the fact, already mentioned, that the seriously wounded men who reached Egypt were treated in British army hospitals in Alexandria. Nonetheless, both Maxwell and Babtie told the War Office that their hospitals in Egypt and Malta were crowded with sick and wounded, and that they needed more hospital ships to move some patients to England or Australia. These worries about unsatisfactory medical arrangements continued throughout the lull in fighting at Anzac in June and

July.[37] Would the medicos cope better if there were another major battle at that cove?

Many other disturbing reports reached Australia, leading Munro Ferguson on 10 August to cable London: 'I have very bad accounts up to June 26th from private sources of medical attendance on Hospital transports between the Dardanelles and Alexandria and of the consequent suffering and condition of wounded. Scandal would be great if [,] after all Australia has done [,] for wounded there were avoidable neglect or mismanagement.' This cable was repeated to Maxwell,[38] and Munro Ferguson was assured that the War Office complied with all requests from the theatre for medical personnel and equipment. The Secretary of State cabled on 15 August: 'War Office state that they are advised that everything is being done, so far as circumstances will permit, to make passage of the wounded on ships from Dardanelles as little trying as possible. Army Council are assured that all transports have adequate medical and nursing personnel and sufficient equipment.'[39] This assurance could hardly have been further from the truth.

Fisher's cabinet had already decided it wanted more accurate information on the treatment of Australian wounded. To this end it decided in July that Lieutenant-Colonel Fetherston, who had been the Australian army's acting Director of Medical Services since Williams had taken up his post on Bridges' staff, should visit the Mediterranean.[40] The *Argus* could see no reason for Fetherston's visit. It thought he was being sent to do the job Surgeon-General Williams was supposed to be doing. Fetherston did not sail until 24 August, by which time nearly all the heavy fighting at Anzac had ceased. It remained to be seen what story of horrors Fetherston unearthed, and whether he could influence improvements.

*George Coates, Arrival of first Australian wounded from Gallipoli at Wandsworth Hospital, London 1921 (oil on canvas 154.4 × 128.6 cm). Coates, born in Melbourne, was apprenticed to a stained-glass manufacturer and later studied at the National Gallery School and taught art but had moved to England in 1900. From April 1915 to April 1919 he served with the Royal Army Medical Corps at Wandsworth together with other artists, including Arthur Streeton, so he was there when overflow casualties from the landing and invalids from Malta and Egypt began reaching British hospitals in June 1915.*

# CHAPTER 32

# THE AIF'S SICK AND WOUNDED: AUGUST– DECEMBER 1915

$W$ITH EXPERIENCE of the April landing as a guide, authorities could have made better plans to evacuate casualties of the August offensives. A larger force was involved, in a complex operation, so a commensurately larger number of casualties should have been expected. Hamilton would not give a firm forecast, but mentioned possibly twenty thousand. He thought this an alarming figure but not extravagant considering previous Dardanelles fighting. Thirty transports would have to be converted into temporary hospital ships. The War Office could not provide and fit so many and at the same time maintain the supply of reinforcements and stores.[1] So the story of the wounded and their treatment following the August offensive echoed many of the tragic themes of April and May, although by this time the seriously alarmed Australian government was beginning to take some interest in developments.

New hospitals were set up on Imbros, twenty-four kilometres from Anzac, and greatly expanded on Lemnos. Some extra ships and small craft arrived, but not enough to cope satisfactorily. As in April, Hamilton's headquarters gave medical preparations a low priority in planning. Officers concerned were not given enough time and resources to evolve a satisfactory system of moving wounded to hospitals. Neville Howse, the AIF's senior medical officer at Anzac, told Birdwood of his misgivings on 29 July. In the event, from 7 August to 8 September the Empire's ships moved 51,867 casualties from the peninsula. Of these, 23,686 were from the Anzac front. Little wonder that Admiral Porter wrote: 'I have not met a soldier or sailor with confidence in Ian Hamilton. They do not see the reasons for these frontal attacks on prepared death traps.'[2]

Despite 'a good deal of outcry' about the handling of wounded at Anzac on the night of 6 August, a reasonably satisfactory job was made of moving to the beach wounded survivors of the attacks from the original Anzac front line, on the sector from the Nek to Lone Pine. Some of the credit for this rests with Howse, who was becoming increasingly disillusioned at the failure of Imperial authorities to make adequate preparations.

Far more harrowing was the fate of men wounded in the 'left hook' aimed at Sari Bair. Monash's 4th Brigade, on its impossible task, suffered from deplorable medical arrangements. When it retreated on 8 August it had to leave many of its wounded in the scrub. Monash's divisional commander, General Godley, told his wife, 'The difficulties of getting the wounded out of that awful country have been ghastly.' In 1917 before the Dardanelles Commission, Lieutenant-Colonel Ryan gave a glimpse of the fate of those lucky enough to be rescued. Some wounded, clothes saturated in blood, lay out unattended for days, because the country was so rough. When they finally reached a ship, their clothes, stinking with blood and flies, had to be cut off, although usually no replacements were available.[3]

At 'new' and 'old' Anzac alike, as at the original landing, arrangements to move wounded from the beach to a ship and then to a hospital proved inadequate, mainly because there were not enough small craft or hospital ships. The beaches were full of wounded. Under intermittent shellfire they lay during the day in the broiling sun and at night suffered in severe cold. There was not enough drinking water for them, and many died through lack of attention. 'Arrangements about hospital ships is awful,' wrote Edney Moore of the Australian Army Medical Corps. 'Two ships are quickly filled up and we have no more. It is awful to see poor fellows who it is impossible to help here whereas if they could be got to a hospital ship no doubt many lives could be saved. Naturally with a rush like this it is hard to have everything working smoothly.'⁴ Walking wounded had a much better chance of reaching a hospital ship than did seriously wounded stretcher cases.

Although the Admiralty did not have enough ships to meet requirements, with proper estimates it could have done better. As it was, it took months after the August offensive to restore an effective transport system. The voyage to a hospital was often little better than a typical journey in April. For example, the *Clan Mac-Gillivray* was used on at least one trip as a hospital ship, although it had no beds and no operating room. The hospital ship *Delta* left the peninsula on Sunday 8 August carrying 1,161 patients, twice its supposed capacity; 47 of its patients died before it reached Alexandria early on Wednesday. Brigadier-General H. Haggard, who commanded a brigade in the 11th Division, on 7 August sustained a thigh wound which became putrid. 'The smell of a dead Turk was nothing to what I was,' he told the Dardanelles Commission. Admiral Sir William May, one of the Commissioners, said that if a general could get into such a state it showed that many men must have suffered terribly on 'black ships', just as they had done after the April landings.⁵

A medical officer told of his reaction to receiving Australians, British and Gurkhas wounded in the August battles.

*We knew a great fight was going on . . . yet it was a shock to me when four lighters pulled up alongside and we saw the poor shattered figures, with bloody bandages, grimy faces and dirty clothes who were crowded together below us. . . . men were dying every minute, and one [medical officer] was utterly lost amongst the multitude needing his care.' [The ship was badly overcrowded] but lighters kept coming alongside with their burden of suffering humanity and the man in charge would shout— 'For God's sake take this lot on, we've been going about from ship to ship and no one will have us, and more men are dying.' We worked, one and all, until we could no longer tell what we were seeing or doing, all day and all night, picking out the cases where the dreaded gangrene had set in, and where immediate and high amputation was the only hope of saving life. Even the clean open decks stank with the horrid smell of gangrenous flesh. . . . The operating room . . . was a stinking, bloody shambles [where amputations were carried out in a couple of minutes], the limb thrown into a basket with many others, awaiting incineration—[so producing another] poor victim, a maimed testimonial to his life's end of the brutality and savagery of war . . . . The whole voyage was a nightmare.⁶*

Although Admiral Porter resolutely defended himself before the Dardanelles Commission, in August 1915 he had told his wife that he could not 'bear to think over much about' the large number of casualties on his hospital and black ships. One of his makeshift hospital ships embarked 180 wounded, nearly all Australians, to take them to Imbros. 'Several died on the way there—fine cheery uncomplaining brave men all. They have had a severe handling . . . but no lack of determination.' Almost two decades later, in his old age, Porter recorded that some wounded made the voyage to Egypt in conditions that later aroused the strongest indignation in England and Australia. Had Hamilton or 'the authorities in England' begun their planning earlier, 'a very great deal of avoidable suffering' would have been prevented. This also would have minimised sights that were 'highly detrimental to the morale of the troops'.[7]

Despite some expansion, hospital facilities on Lemnos could not cope with the numbers of wounded brought there. Conditions were primitive, as men lay on tarpaulins on the ground, with a blanket, but otherwise completely without shelter. Adrian Knox, an Australian Red Cross commissioner and future Chief Justice, in August went to Egypt from where he described to Lady Munro Ferguson the arrival of wounded from the recent battle. 'I am afraid I shall be a long time getting used to seeing the poor fellows arrive here—even if not badly wounded they are trench weary and generally knocked out and with their ragged uniforms and dilapidated appearance afford a pitiable sight. This has been the worst week yet, I believe, for Australians and New Zealanders.' A nurse, Nellie Imlay, noticed that the lads did not talk about the war much. 'Many of them are nervous wrecks poor boys,' she remarked. The hundreds pouring in 'need all the attention we can give them, and more'. One of these wounded men told his wife and daughter that all were cheerful 'as long as we can get back to the firing line'.[8]

In London the coalition government responded to some persistent parliamentary questioning by denying that sick and wounded from the Dardanelles were being treated badly. Tennant, Undersecretary for War, claimed that on the whole the wounded 'were exceedingly well looked after' on the ships, while there were always ample beds in Egypt. But General Maxwell confided to Hamilton that he was 'having great struggles about the wounded etc. Australia, New Zealand, England in a lesser degree, have all got it into their heads that the arrangements are awful.' Godley read in a letter from his wife: 'I had such a visit from old Lady Carnarvon. . . . She was full of woe and wails about everything, thought everybody was killed or wounded, the hospital ships no good, no ships to take anyone anywhere, and no comforts or clothes.'[9]

After shipping wounded from the August battles, the Anzac medical authorities' next priority was to combat a resurgence of disease. Ill soldiers had fought, under the stimulus of the hoped-for breakout. Following military failure, the sick rate soared. Flies were at their worst at Anzac in August and September, when evacuation of men with infectious diseases reached its peak. Hamilton told Kitchener on 29 September the gist of the findings of a medical investigation into pulse rates, breathing irregularities, skin sores and cases of diarrhoea which confirmed that the incidence of poor health was much higher among seven battalions that had been at Anzac since the landing than it was among the recently arrived troops of the Australian 2nd Division. Hamilton explained that this showed the effect on top-class men of being in trenches under continuous shell and musketry fire for eighteen to twenty weeks. It also showed that sanitary arrangements at Anzac were defective, partly because of the crowded ground.[10]

The men kept their trenches meticulously clean. They 'would have made a dainty and clean suburban back yard look dirty—not even a dead match to be seen on the daily inspection, and all food was covered and no scraps left exposed'. But this good work was nullified because the Australians could not solve the problem of latrine sanitation. The space in Monash Valley which was not under Turkish fire was very limited, so it was very difficult to get sites for latrines. Attempts were made to introduce the pan system, but it was not possible to obtain enough pans. Nor, until near the end of the campaign, was there enough wood or tin to help make fly-proof latrines. So ordinary open latrines had to suffice. In most places pits about nine feet deep, ten feet long and two feet wide were used. With such handicaps it was impossible to reduce the fly problem, and diarrhoea and dysentery continued to be very bad.[11]

The 2nd Division succumbed to disease more quickly than the 1st, and the

stream of sick and wounded continued, further straining Britain's medical facilities in the Mediterranean. To reduce that congestion, from early in the campaign some hospital cases were taken to England. The first Australians arrived there in May, and much greater numbers followed from June to August, reaching a total of twelve thousand by the end of 1915. At one stage they were scattered through about thirty hospitals, although attempts were made to concentrate them. The convalescent hospital for Australians at Harefield steadily expanded, having eight hundred beds by the end of 1915. When Lieutenant-Colonel Fetherson visited England in November, he found administrative arrangements were confused. He recommended that Colonel Williams be appointed Deputy Director of Medical Services, AIF, in England, with direct responsibility to Brigadier-General Sir Newton J. Moore, a former Western Australian premier, who in December 1915 was placed in command of AIF troops in Britain. The War Office rejected Fetherston's proposal and instead placed Williams directly under its own control.[12]

Much information about Australian wounded in England appeared in the Australian press. Some women calling themselves the Committee of Australian Women in London circulated a letter complaining about the treatment accorded sick Australians in England. Seven Australian soldiers who heard of this wrote to the High Commissioner's office praising their treatment at Edgbaston. Sir George Reid, the High Commissioner, instituted inquiries, then issued a detailed statement refuting the women's complaints. There seems no reason to doubt Reid's assessment. It is likely that most of the twelve thousand Australians shipped to England were very well treated. One Australian commented on the great good luck of officers at Anzac who got slightly wounded, or a little sick, and had a trip to England on a hospital ship. They were better by the time they reached England. Army hospitals in England were better than those in Australia, where various shortcomings were apparent. Fetherston found them 'far more comfortable' than he ever 'imagined was necessary for temporary War Hospitals . . . far better than a great many' Australian public hospitals.[13]

George Mitchell, who spent some months in Netley Hospital, thirteen kilometres from Southampton, did not seem to suffer too much. The patients' rough horseplay brought 'complaints from the sisters that the row last night kept them awake', and the ruses to obtain leave passes were soon detected. But for Mitchell the present was very pleasant compared with the past and the doubtful long-term future. One night in mid-October he dreamt that he was in his original No. 9 Platoon. 'We were charging at a terrific pace in perfect alignment. Poor old Charlie Hunt was at my left elbow, and Byrnie [Lieutenant Byrne, his greatly admired officer who was killed on 25 April] was leading us with his same old laugh.' In nearby Red Cross hospitals there were some Japanese nurses and doctors. They were 'merry little things and well liked by patients and confreres. All the worse for us when der Tag No 2 arrives.'[14]

It was Australian policy that those whose wounds or illnesses made them unfit for further army service should return to Australia as soon as they were well enough for the voyage. By the end of 1915, 2,429 wounded men had been returned, together with 3,755 sick and the 1,354 'venereals' already mentioned.[15]

By mid-December thousands of Australians were among the Gallipoli veterans who now constituted a hospital population of twenty-one thousand in Egypt, fourteen thousand in Malta and twelve thousand in Mudros and on the peninsula. This Mediterranean tide of suffering had prompted Hamilton to issue a printed circular to counter a morale problem. It was addressed to medical personnel on ships that carried his troops. Doctors and nurses, he wrote, had allowed themselves to become too seriously impressed by the stories of young casualties they tended. 'It is natural that contact with so much suffering should incline the listeners to sympathy,' he continued; 'but it is certain also that . . . such enervating influences should be resisted. All . . . medical staff must make it a point of honour to maintain a hearty tone of optimism calculated to raise rather than to lower the confidence and courage of the fighting men who have been temporarily committed to their charge.'[16]

Meanwhile, on 31 August Fetherston left Fremantle to carry out his investigation; he reached Egypt on 21 September. He arrived believing that total absorption of the Australians into the British service was essential to overcome the problems that had alarmed the Defence Department. He soon changed his mind, cabling Pearce to explain that the medical services were in a complicated position and warning that big reforms were needed. After two weeks in Egypt Fetherston left on 9 October for the Dardanelles, spending three days at Anzac (17th–19th), and one at Suvla; he visited Mudros and Imbros before returning to Egypt on 22 October. He did not see Birdwood but met Howse, who favourably impressed him. After four days in Egypt, Fetherston left for England.[17]

By this time he had become convinced—partly because of Howse's strong advocacy—that the only satisfactory solution to the AIF's medical problems was to appoint an Australian officer as its Director of Medical Services. That officer, under Britain's Principal Director of Medical Services, should control all AIF medical services. He told Pearce that Birdwood supported him in recommending Howse for the post. Fetherston began efforts to persuade British authorities to accept his suggestion. In England, as we have seen, he urged upon Sir Alfred Keogh the same principle of an Australian in charge of all AIF medical services, which led to the compromise of Williams's appointment. The War Office was reluctant to give Fetherston all he wanted, and in turn he did not accept its suggestion that Howse should become a deputy-director of medical services for the AIF, on Babtie's staff. Fetherston persisted and, back in Cairo, advocated his solution in meetings with Maxwell and Ford on 29 November. The problem was complicated by Fetherston's well-founded belief that Howse was much more able than his formal superior, Williams, who still received some War Office support. It took some time for British and Australian authorities to agree fully on this issue, because the

War Office wanted general medical arrangements for Australians to conform as nearly as possible to British procedures. Fetherston 'provisionally' appointed Howse as Director of Medical Services, AIF, but the Defence Department in Melbourne did not confirm this until January 1916, following Fetherston's return to Australia.[18]

While fighting this battle, Fetherston was busy on his report, completed in England on 15 November. He covered many of the issues discussed in this and the preceding chapter. While he deplored the medical problems arising from the confused and unsatisfactory Anglo-Australian relationship, he praised the help he got from authorities in Egypt. However, he was not happy with the state of Australian hospitals there. He described his steps to have an Australian hospital set up at Alexandria. He also discussed the long-standing administrative problem of arranging the prompt return to active service of men invalided from Anzac who had regained their health. He returned to Australia before the end of December, and Pearce promptly read his report. Munro Ferguson sent a copy to England, where the Army Council in July 1916 took issue with a few points, although it generally praised the work of Australian medical officers.[19]

While Fetherston was in the Mediterranean theatre, the forceful, forthright Howse helped modify his views, although the two men had little opportunity to meet. Howse had strong opinions derived from observing the Gallipoli medical muddle. Two years later, in answer to a question by Andrew Fisher, he was to give the Dardanelles Commission his views on how Australian troops could best be protected, comforted and fed in future operations. Bitter experience, he said, had led to a great deal of feeling against the Imperial authorities among the medical corps and the combatants. He had heard officers of some rank declare that the fighting was murder. He agreed with those he heard saying that 'under no conceivable conditions would they advise . . . Australia to enter again upon any war where they were entirely placed under the authority of British headquarters'. Howse went on, 'I personally will recommend my Government when this war is over, that under no conceivable conditions ought they ever to trust to the medical arrangements that may be made by Imperial authorities for the care of their sick and wounded.'[20]

While Fetherston was overseas, the Melbourne *Age* made the first public exposé in Australia of the treatment of the wounded at the April landing. Journalist Philip Schuler wrote a series of articles on that tragic story. He depicted 'pitiful' scenes like those later described to the Dardanelles Commission. Schuler was sure these revelations would come to Australians 'as a great shock'. He thought the blame rested more on Imperial than Australian shoulders, although Australians might wonder what their own high-ranking medical officers were doing to protect the troops from the catastrophe. Although written in mid-July, the articles were delayed by the censors and did not appear in the *Age* until mid-October, when they were given great prominence under headlines proclaiming 'cases of neglect and carelessness, provisions absolutely inadequate, overcrowded and understaffed hospitals'.

Although Schuler's picture agrees with other evidence, he told one story not elsewhere corroborated. When a transport used as a hospital ship reached Alexandria one afternoon, he claimed, English disembarkation staff refused to begin to take off the sick and instead went to a race meeting. He said the officer concerned bore 'a family name honoured by His Majesty'. The story is scarcely believable, and it was deleted from his articles and not published in this ardently pro-Imperial newspaper.

Schuler also criticised some Australian officers, recommended specific improvements, warned that 'Australia might ask questions' and ended with a series of

(9) REST GULLY SHEWING 5ᵗʰ AUST. FIELD AMBULANCE
COPYRIGHT

*The 5th Australian Field Ambulance in Rest Gully is very exposed in comparison to dugouts on the hillside above it. Though nowhere at Anzac was safe, the enemy generally respected red cross markings.*

critical queries, the last one being: 'Is there any connection between these gross blunders and the heavy casualty list of "died of wounds"?' The articles were followed by brief rejoinders, sent by the censor from medical authorities in Egypt, which sought to explain away deficiencies.[21]

As we have seen, these mistakes changed the attitude of officers close to the event, such as Howse and Fetherston. However, although publicity about them appeared about the time Hamilton was recalled and Carson resigned, these revelations seem to have had little immediate impact on Australian attitudes and government policy. There was very little echo in parliament of the medical fiasco at Gallipoli. Under different circumstances these accounts would have produced immense controversy and could have seriously strained Australian-British relations.

No doubt shortcomings diminished in the campaign's last months as the fighting became less intense, as cooler weather came, reducing the number of flies and, one might hope, as more effective procedures and better facilities came into operation. But dealing with the Anzac wounded seems to have been difficult to the campaign's end. Disadvantages of the cramped beachhead could never be solved. On 30 November a soldier was on cook's fatigue when a shell came through the cookhouse tunnel, slightly wounding him and killing several near by. 'The concussion was awful—everything went black, and the next thing I knew was the smiling face of Sergeant Ford who reassured me by saying that I'd only got a little crack.' After having the 'surplus surface splinters' taken from his left leg and face at a light horse ambulance, he was soon on board ship, bound for Malta. He was luckier than the wounded lying in the 16th Casualty Clearing Hospital a few days later when shells hit it. Sick and wounded men were blown to pieces while waiting to board a hospital ship. As an onlooker wrote, 'It was an awful sight to see legs and arms all over the place.' Even in Cairo as late as 16 December wounded could still suffer from muddle. A veteran described wounded being shunted from one hospital to another for two days. 'It is a crying shame to see men . . . who have been broken in their country's service treated as we poor devils were for those 48 hours. Apparently, while you are fit and able to stand between the enemy and their object you are at least a soldier, but if you have the misfortune to fall out after having given of your best . . . you become so much junk, and are in everybody's road.'[22]

Doubtless, such men must have been in the mind of Eric Bogle, a Scottish migrant, when in the 1970s—with noteworthy historical inaccuracy—he wrote the following stanza for the song, 'And The Band Played Waltzing Matilda':

> They collected the wounded, the crippled, the maimed,
> And sent us all back to Australia—
> The armless, the legless, the blind, the insane—
> Those proud wounded heroes of Suvla.[23]

So the sad story of the treatment of the AIF's sick and wounded continued to the end of the Anzac campaign. The consequences, of course, continued for years, as the wounded and debilitated struggled to regain their health, sometimes in the bosom of a loving family, sometimes in a repatriation hospital. The story is one of astounding incompetence but at the same time one of outstanding soldierly courage and stoicism under the most trying conditions.

*The 6th Field Ambulance at Brighton Beach. After the August battles, the chief priority of Anzac medical authorities was to combat disease.*

*Arrangements to move wounded from the beach to ship proved inadequate throughout the Anzac battles. The strain tells on the face of Major J. Gordon, one of the few doctors to remain at Anzac from beginning to end. He is seen standing in front of the beach casualty clearing station, which is protected by sandbags and iron roof.*

# CHAPTER 33

# PRISONERS OF THE TURKS

NEITHER SIDE captured many prisoners at Anzac, and Turkey took many fewer than the Allies. On New Year's Eve 1915 the *West Australian* published the then official list of Australian prisoners of war, obtained through United States authorities in Constantinople. There were only thirty-eight names, including eight AIF who had died in captivity during the year and also three navy men from the RAN submarine *AE2*, sunk on 30 April during a daring raid through the Dardanelles into the Sea of Marmara. The list of Australian POWs in Turkey grew longer as the whereabouts of other prisoners became known and as the Gallipoli campaign was succeeded by hostilities in Sinai, Mesopotamia and later Palestine. By March 1918, 135 officers and men of the AIF had been reported as captured by the Turks, of whom 31 had died. In 1943, A. G. Butler, author of the medical services volumes of Australia's official history of the war, gave 70 as the official figure for AIF taken in 1915 at the Dardanelles, 126 for those taken in Egypt and Palestine, and said there were no exact statistics for Australians who served in Mesopotamia.[1] This chapter, strictly speaking, is concerned only with the AIF captured during the Gallipoli campaign, but the issues raised apply to all Australians who became prisoners of war in Turkey.

Compared with other aspects of war, prisoners traditionally receive relatively little public attention. Australia's Gallipoli POWs have received less than most, confined largely to a small library of personal accounts published fairly soon after the event. Their experience beyond Australia's front line is outside the scope of the official history, outside the Anzac tradition,[2] and in conflict with the AIF tradition of respect for the Turk as a fighter. Considered against some 3,800 captured by Germany from 1916 to 1918, and the 22,000 captured by the Japanese early in 1942, the numbers of men involved were minuscule. Nevertheless, the Gallipoli episode constituted Australia's first real acquaintance with this facet of war.

It was partly the confined AIF position at Gallipoli which militated against capture. The taking of prisoners occurs more often in fluid, confused fighting where command has disintegrated and soldiers, especially the wounded, are cut off, as was more likely to happen later on the Western Front. The proud tradition of bringing in the wounded reduced the chances of capture, and willingness to become, or for the enemy to take, prisoners was also relevant. Prisoners can be a source of labour and of information but a liability to feed and maintain.[3]

Aboard ship off Lemnos before the landing, 5th Battalion troops were exhorted not to leave their wounded because the enemy would mutilate them. One Brigade was told: 'Take no prisoners—let them all go—but not too far.' Willie Harris declared, 'We did not take prisoners for the first fortnight, after we found out what sort of enemy we were up against.' Accounts of Turks at Gallipoli bayoneting the wounded were not uncommon, but war historian Robert Rhodes James suggests the charges of mutilation were probably unfounded.[4] Giving quarter in the heat of battle was another matter, for Turk and Australian alike.

For Australians who surrendered and survived on the battlefield, the experience of capture and powerlessness was traumatic but not always brutal. Turks asked Captain R. T. A. McDonald, senior officer in a group of three 16th Battalion soldiers captured on 25 April, why Australia was fighting Turkey. McDonald replied: 'Australians [are] part of the Empire and [fight] for it.' According to McDonald, Essad Pasha, the Anzac zone commander, 'promised to send word of our capture and see that we were well treated'. Two individuals were picked up in early May, and in late June several injured 9th Battalion men were captured south of Lone Pine. Over fifty Australians from the 4th Brigade, more than half of them wounded, were captured during confused fighting at Anafarta on 8 August. Essad Pasha, keen to elicit information, had offered a reward of five pounds per head for captured prisoners. Australian experience in Turkish forward positions embraced to a greater or lesser degree risk of injury from action by their own forces, the stress of going without food and water, and the humiliation—perhaps particularly galling to military personnel—of losing items of uniform as well as personal possessions and food to captors who themselves were often poorly equipped. Some prisoners were 'introduced' to the bayonet and met hostility; Driver R. W. Griffiths, for example, was threatened with shooting and flogging. Private P. O'Connor recalled the 'barbarous brutality' of Turkish soldiers following his capture and then the gentle ministrations of the Turkish Red Crescent; a number reported wounds 'dressed properly' at the field hospital and offers of cigarettes and coffee. A march to the Dardanelles (or a bumpy and painful cart trip for the wounded), boat to Constantinople and installation into a barracks prison—or hospital—followed capture. Sergeant W. Bailey and Private R. F. Lushington, at this first acquaintance with social stratification in the sprawling and diverse Turkish state, noticed crude hostility from the 'common soldier' and 'Turkish Irregulars' and the courtesy of some Turkish and German officers, without whose intercession some AIF captured in August would have been killed. This whole experience, quite benign for some, was a foretaste of the unpleasant captivity to follow.[5]

Few knew what was happening to Australian captives. On the field of battle as late as October 1915 Monash was satisfied that the only men from his brigade who had become prisoners were 'two officers captured by a ruse on 25 April'.[6]

Likewise in Australia, apart from capture of the *AE2* crew, known from relatively early in the campaign, there was little information. The Fisher government soon recognised its new responsibility to establish who had been captured and to do what it could for them. But it was difficult enough for powerful governments with diplomatic muscle to ensure that the Hague Regulations for the treatment of captives were faithfully honoured. Australia lacked even a diplomatic service. Relying on the Imperial government to make representations to Turkey was its only feasible recourse at that time. This, however, lengthened the chain of responsibility. It also exposed Australia to British policy priorities for conduct of the war—a situation Australia had largely accepted all along. The consequent difficulties were complicated by some divergence in Australian and British attitudes on certain social issues and by London's concern to avoid any adverse Australian reaction to disturbing news from Turkey. There were complications, too, stemming from the doctrine of the diplomatic unity of the Empire. Reciprocity had its advantages in helping protect one's nationals held by the enemy, but ill-treatment of Germans by Australia could also have dangerous implications for British subjects held by the Central Powers. Berlin's representations to London about conditions for Germans held in Australia provided a backdrop for Melbourne's concerns about its own POWs. Following capture of German New Guinea, Colonel Holmes had had some

German offenders publicly flogged in Rabaul. Munro Ferguson realised that such 'follies' would 'not be understood in Europe'. One or two instances during 1915 of German internees in Australia being flogged and of an escapee being shot also caused him 'much anxiety' and necessitated considerable British and American diplomatic activity.[7]

A request by Andrew Fisher led the Colonial Office on 15 June 1915 to ask the Foreign Office to obtain information on Australian and New Zealand prisoners in Turkey. The answer came back that a Turkish Prisoners of War Information Bureau, corresponding to a similar British organisation, would forward the relevant information which Turkey agreed to provide, but because this process would be so slow the Foreign Office would ask the United States Embassy in Constantinople for help. This, then, was the extended and attenuated channel of communication on which the Australian government had to rely for information about prisoners.[8]

At first the Foreign Office thought only of tracing the fate of officers, but the Colonial Office pointed out that such a restriction would 'not be agreeable' to Australia and New Zealand. Accordingly the Foreign Office sought information on other ranks too. By mid-July some 9th Battalion men, together with a few other wounded Empire prisoners, were located in hospital in Constantinople 'doing well'. Embassy officials, including Ambassador Henry Morgenthau, were permitted to visit regularly and dispense comforts, as were American Red Cross women. Two American journalists also visited. Charles Bean at Anzac, disgusted at 'caddish' treatment of Turkish prisoners by some 'Australians and Britishers', noted on 8 August, 'So far as we know . . . [the Turks] have treated our captured men and officers excellently.' Morgenthau undertook to search for other prisoners, and a Colonial Office official minuted that there was 'no reason for thinking . . . our prisoners in Turkey are more to be pitied than those in Germany'.[9]

Payments to supplement host-country provision for POWs were permitted under the Hague Regulations, and the Commonwealth had quickly requested that arrangements made for a British POW allowance also cover 'members of Australian contingents'.[10] But officials of the United States Embassy, permitted to visit *AE2* officers and men in Anatolia, discovered they were in rags, worked hard and had received no money in three months since capture on 30 April.[11] Moreover,

*Constantinople, the fabled city on the Bosphorus. Ironically, the only men of the AIF to reach Constantinople during the war were prisoners of war.*

although the Fisher government generally wanted Australian prisoners treated on a similar basis to British prisoners, Australian authorities were more generous than the British in their notion of the proper level of financial relief for its POWs, which complicated the matter of the *AE2* prisoners because about half the men were Royal Navy, not RAN. The Defence Department proposed paying them three pounds a month, and High Commissioner Reid had already been in contact with Sir Edward Grey at the Foreign Office about having the arrangement for POWs in Germany extended to those in Turkey. The Foreign Office insisted on applying the principle that 'colonial' forces serving with other British forces should not receive preferential treatment. This was perhaps not unreasonable, given the need to maintain the morale of Empire POWs as a whole, but the clash of attitudes added to the difficulty of getting funds raised by Australians to the intended recipients. In November 1915 the Foreign Office stated that the thousand pounds sent by Lady Helen Munro Ferguson, president of the Australian Red Cross Society, should be distributed to British POWs generally.[12]

Britain's approach to the payment of POWs prevailed: the *AE2* men would receive an initial allowance of six pounds each for two months (forwarded through the United States Ambassador) and would then come under a general arrangement for British POWs held in Turkey.[13] Negotiated towards the end of November 1915 in keeping with the Hague Conventions, this agreement provided that Turkey would pay officer POWs (three shillings a day for lieutenants, five shillings for captains and above), and they would buy their own food and clothing; other ranks would be fed, clothed and housed by the Turkish government.[14]

Having an agreement in place was not the end of the matter. Shortly afterwards, Ambassador Morgenthau was refused entry to the Constantinople hospital holding wounded POWs captured in the August offensives.[15] Enver Pasha had declared Turkey would exact reprisals for claimed maltreatment of its POWs held in Egypt, and Allied POWs were told they were going to 'suffer'. And suffer they did. The wounded were consigned to much inferior Constantinople hospitals and, among other things, denied reading matter. Other prisoners were moved to squalid lice- and bug-ridden barracks out of public—or American—view. Here they were startled by a Turkish custom of communal eating from a huge bowl set on the floor. Private D. B. Creedon soon began thinking bitterly: 'Promises with the Turks are like pie-crust. Their promises are cruelty worked up to a fine art.'[16]

By late October Morgenthau was cabling, 'I experience much difficulty in arranging...for payments to prisoners. I now find [others]...in the interior ...in much need of funds and clothing.' He estimated Turkey held no more than 450 prisoners from Britain and the dominions. Reid received a copy of some of Morgenthau's reports, and Australia was invited to suggest any further action it wanted taken.[17] As yet there were very few names.

It was to the 'interior'—Anatolia in Asia Minor—that most Gallipoli prisoners were being progressively dispatched, entrained with other Allied prisoners to centres such as Afion Kara Hissar, a rail junction on the Berlin-Baghdad railway, and, north-east from there, Angora (modern-day Ankara). It is difficult to generalise about the experience on which they were now embarked. Conditions varied greatly according to rank and race, the front where the prisoners were captured, the place where they were held and the stage reached in the war. Chances of survival were worst for those captured on the Mesopotamian front, from where they were forced on a 'death march' to prison camp.[18] Indian prisoners were more harshly treated than whites. One Australian, Private J. Beattie, thought that 'two Maoris and one Australian half caste', whom he did not see again, had been 'done in' by the Turks.[19]

Many officer prisoners had a comfortable captivity. A notable example was

Major-General Charles Townshend. His small Anglo-Indian striking force in Mesopotamia overreached itself and surrendered at Kut el Amara on the Tigris in April 1916. While his men suffered at Turkish hands, Townshend accepted the hospitality of enemy officers and responded in kind with stylish dinners at big Constantinople hotels, all expenses met by the Turkish government. Abraham Elkus, Morgenthau's successor as American ambassador to Turkey, considered Townshend's behaviour 'ill-advised'.[20]

Generally, officer prisoners were conveyed and accommodated separately from other ranks. At Afion Kara Hissar, they lived with other Allied officer POWs in housing that was 'good for Turkey'. Separated from their men, officers faced the problems of constant struggle to exist on limited funds in face of inflation and food shortages and of managing the boredom and frustration of confinement. No wonder those making escape attempts characteristically were officers rather than the men.[21]

Other ranks, in accordance with 'instinctive social differentiation',[22] and as allowed under the Hague Conventions, were accommodated less commodiously—and required to work. Along with other Allied POWs, most Australian men were employed by private contractors to the government, remaining under a military camp commandant for discipline. They were frequently moved, often on foot, among camps in perhaps twenty locations in that rugged, remote interior. Conditions differed from camp to camp, with non-commissioned officers at times having privileges and discipline responsibilities. Many were assigned to a German construction company for the pressing work of completing three gaps in the great Berlin-Baghdad railway. Until the summer of 1917, they were concentrated on the two sections requiring tunnels through the Taurus and the Amanus mountains. They worked ten to twelve hours a day quarrying, drilling tunnels, felling timber, laying track, blacksmithing and maintaining power stations. After completion of the mountain works, some Allied POWs moved east to work on the third and last Mosul link, while others were employed on a light rail link east out of Angora. Later in 1918, as the British advanced into Palestine, they tended to be concentrated at Afion Kara Hissar. A trial train went through from Constantinople to Aleppo in October of that year.[23]

Apart from railway construction, government work for other ranks included navvying on roads, wharf labouring, and orderly duty—even for their own Australian officers.[24] Work in the agricultural sector appears to have been the exception.

International conventions permitted the employment of POWs, provided there was no immediate connection with the operations of war. At Anzac, some Turkish POW work parties were organised, like this one in Headquarters Gully.

Conditions were harsh. Morgenthau's staff told the Colonial Office that POWs received treatment similar to that given Turkish soldiers,[25] but the Turkish fighting man in 1915 had to be hardy to survive. Furthermore, the Turkish administration, chronically inefficient and overstressed, seemed constitutionally incapable of planning ahead. It was 'inefficiency not malice', said Lieutenant S. L. Stormonth. Such 'inefficiency', of course, had far greater impact on other-ranks prisoners than on officers. A report to the House of Commons in 1918 summed up the Turkish attitude: 'It can matter very little what becomes of the ordinary mass . . .'.[26]

Men generally arrived from the front with very little clothing, and this deficiency was rarely made good by Turkey, whose own soldiers were often very ill-clothed, sometimes having no better footwear than rawhide sandals. POWs could expect to share their captors' meagre and nutritionally very restricted diet. The government ration consisted of small quantities of coarse bread and boiled wheat with a few lentils or hard white peas ('shrapnel', as the prisoners called them), generally innocent of any meat. Quality apart, the ration quantity was inadequate. POW accounts constantly mention hunger. Accommodation was mostly cramped, bug-infested and with minimal bedding. Wages (if paid) were low and usually only for output, with costs of keep deducted—a 'no work, no bread' regime, although some manoeuvring towards a 'no bread, no work' rule occurred. Allowance payments, arriving irregularly, enabled limited purchases of local fresh food at the inflated prices that greeted the arrival of prisoner parties. There was not enough money left over for clothing. The solicitude of American consuls at Mersina and Aleppo helped.[27]

At Afion Kara Hissar, officers could sometimes intercede on behalf of their men in the nearby camp, but much depended on individual initiative, on comrades' support and continued good health. The military camp system exerted few sanctions on commandants, among whom Maslum Bey at Afion Kara Hissar, a notorious 'proper savage', made 'some of the lives of his prisoners a ghastly nightmare by his acts of cruelty and beastliness'. 'Afion at the end of September, 1916 was a veritable hell.'[28]

Working conditions varied. The Baghdad Railway Construction Company, an example of aggressive German economic penetration of Turkey, was something of an outlet from the camp system and treated POWs 'very well in comparison'. Though it supplied food and clothing 'insufficiently', POWs were no different from other civilian employees ('only working . . . to escape conscription'), and a reasonable work regime had some benefits over the enforced inactivity endured by officers. At Belemidik camp, Private Lushington was impressed by the 'tremendous project' of blasting solid rock for a twenty-four-kilometre tunnel 'straight as a die'—'truly a great engineering feat'. Here, he said, 'with the rough open air life, good health was kept by all until the terrible summer of 1916 took its toll of so many of our lads with malarial fever'. At the same camp, Charles Suckling from the *AE2* was on tunnel drilling: 'rather dangerous, as it was a common thing to drill into an unexploded charge . . . the gang I was with was lucky—we had with us [an AIF] sergeant who had been an underground manager in a coal mine.'[29] Not all were so lucky: Private L. G. New was killed and his mate injured by a falling log at Belemidik.

The 1918 House of Commons report concluded that the work 'undoubtedly' was hard but that it was 'more tolerable to be a prisoner in Turkey under some sort of business-like rule, even a strict one, than to be exposed to the full carelessness of the Turk'. Taken broadly, Lushington might wholeheartedly have agreed. Turkish regulations provided only for those on government work to be paid. Volunteering for a work party, he found his German Jew employer did not pay wages and that workers suffered heavily from typhus, malaria and dysentery contracted in the execrable working and living quarters.[30]

POWs also told gruesome stories about health 'care'. Chaotic arrangements for AIF sick and wounded during the Gallipoli campaign (chapters 31 and 32) demonstrated the importance of administrative efficiency and compassion. These were both in short supply in Turkey, compounded by no doubt greater shortages of drugs and competent staff and by its own avalanche of wounded soldiers: between 22 and 26 August 1915 alone, Turkey brought back some twenty-six thousand wounded from the Gallipoli front.[31]

Good modern Constantinople hospitals had competent Turkish and German doctors and German nursing sisters. Sergeant Bailey in Tahappa Hospital thought it 'compared favourably with British hospitals'. But ordinary Turkish institutions were different. At Thash-Kishla Military Hospital—a 'dungeon'—Turkish military orderlies habitually offered brutality (less, some noticed, than to fellow-soldier patients). Sanitation was primitive, the usual boiled wheat with a little gritty bread served for food, and there was a constant shortage of drugs. At Thash-Kishla an Armenian doctor—'worse than an animal'—amputated Private P. O'Connor's leg (under chloroform) by sawing the bone half-way through and then breaking off the rest, an amputation considered avoidable by another competent doctor. Private W. Williams, who succumbed to the malaria sweeping Belemidik camp in the summer of 1916, ended up in the Turkish hospital at Afion Kara Hissar. 'I got out in four days as I thought I could do better outside,' he said. Apart from shortages of medicine, sheer want of food caused deaths. Officers were better treated than other ranks, who believed that in these hospitals 'if you lingered too long they would help you on your way'. Others may have fared even worse than Allied POWs. At Belemidik Private H. Foxcroft noticed Turks and Russians had the 'heaviest death roll' from malaria.[32]

The appalling conditions experienced by Australia's POWs could be understood only imperfectly by the outside world. Allied press censorship effectively muzzled publicity which might provoke reprisals, and no doubt the larger numbers of POWs taken on the Western Front overshadowed the small contingent in Turkey. Moreover, notwithstanding its chaotic and corrupt administration, Turkey was successful in limiting the flow of information and Britain could exert very little leverage. In December 1915 Turkey decreed that prisoners could write only one letter of four lines each week and that a like restriction applied to incoming letters. Britain imposed a similar regimen on all Ottoman prisoners of war in the British Empire—'a very ineffective reprisal as the average Ottoman prisoner is entirely illiterate', commented someone in the Colonial Office. Enlisting American aid to protest at what would cause 'so much needless hardship and anxiety to their prisoners and their relatives' yielded only slight relaxation of restrictions by Turkey in April 1916, which Britain reciprocated.[33]

The picture was sufficiently clear by January 1916 for Grey at the Foreign Office in London to become increasingly concerned. Australia received copies of Foreign Office correspondence on the subject with Morgenthau and with W. H. Page, the United States ambassador in London. Grey complained of 'the shocking and callous indifference displayed by the [Sublime] Porte to the dictates of ordinary humanity'. Turkey now agreed to reciprocal visits by neutral observers to prisoner-of-war camps holding Turks and Britons. Morgenthau reported improved procedures for distributing money and supplies to British prisoners, but this was offset by the Turkish practice of moving them from place to place, making it very hard to maintain contact.[34]

In May the War Office was able to provide the names of Empire POWs to the Colonial Office and, on request shortly afterwards, specific lists of Australians held in Turkey. The list showed fifty-seven AIF men and thirty-one 'RAN' but did not indicate how many had already died.[35]

The urgency attaching to the Empire's POW problem in Turkey greatly increased from mid-1916. Townshend's surrender at Kut el Amara in April 1916 poured thousands more British POWs—over ten thousand Indians and three thousand Britons—into the ramshackle Turkish polity. Negotiations with Turkey conducted by the British and American governments bore fruit in September 1916 when the Turkish government offered to allow neutral vessels carrying parcels to unload at Mersina, on the southern coast of Asia Minor east of the Taurus Mountains. The American Embassy reported in January 1917 that Enver Pasha had agreed to transport the goods by military train and that as far as was known, all 'British' POWs in Asia Minor had received outfits of winter clothing.[36] Agreement was also reached permitting sick Allied prisoners to be treated by American and British doctors concentrated in one or two camps. Sergeant Maurice Delpratt noticed a marked improvement in late 1916 at Hadji-Kiri camp in the Taurus Mountains after a British doctor arrived.[37]

With British and American diplomacy spearheading moves to assist prisoners, Australia's main role *vis-à-vis* its men in Turkish hands was one of endeavouring to ensure the actual arrival of supplies of money, food and clothing against the rigours of captivity and the bitter winters. Sergeant A. J. Rawlings of the 2nd Battalion received nothing from his government during seven months. Andrew Fisher, now High Commissioner, wrote with some concern in May 1916 to the Colonial Office seeking assurance that the three shillings a week allowance for other ranks was actually paid and asking to be advised 'from time to time' of the expenditure. A slight increase in the payment, not favoured by the British Army Council because it meant differentiating between British soldiers and those from the overseas Empire, appears to have been conceded; also, arrangements were made to distribute a hundred pounds contributed by the Citizens' War Chest in Sydney to Australian POWs. Within the Colonial Office it came to be recognised that the 'Australian organisation was keeping much closer touch with its people in Turkey than our own'.[38]

But the most visible form of Australian support was organised extra-governmental assistance. It did not take effect until after mid-1916. Until then, private support had simply been a matter for the interested public, whose parcels London eventually agreed could go to the International Red Cross Committee in Geneva stating the prisoner's last known address. When Germany began taking prisoners on the Western Front, the Australian Red Cross Society formed a discrete unit to care for POWs. This activity plainly impinged on Allied blockade measures against the Central Powers, and the society worked under the War Office, which by the end of 1916 had acted to regulate the amount of food and clothing being sent by specifying individual prisoner quotas.[39] Many Red Cross 'comfort' parcels would fail to arrive, subject as they were to 'censoring' in Constantinople and depredations by the likes of Maslum Bey, but the program improved morale and increased the chances of survival. Corporal W. Cliffe described these parcels as 'the maintenance of our lives'.[40]

Australia's support for its POWs within the framework of Empire diplomacy and high war policy accorded with Britain's approach to the matter, and London wanted it to stay that way. By September 1917, Walter Long, Secretary of State for the Colonies in Lloyd George's government, was becoming increasingly worried about the 'most serious effect' in Australia and New Zealand as news of the 'most appalling' facts about the treatment of British men in Turkish hands, half of whom had died, became more widely known.[41] London responded to Australia's unease by further judicious pruning of information passed on to Melbourne. It does not appear to have accepted Prime Minister Hughes's proposal to boost recruiting by publishing a dispatch from Long about POW treatment.[42]

Similarly, the important matter of which country should be entrusted to act as 'protecting power' in respect of Empire prisoners in Turkey was one for Britain alone. This role of 'protecting power' had by the First World War become well established as a pillar of the Hague Conventions. Britain wanted the American government, as the only neutral great power and as a country also acting for the Central Powers (and no doubt for other high war policy reasons), to act on its behalf; visits by 'international agencies' would not be an adequate substitute. Without disagreeing, the Australian High Commission early in 1917 expressed concern that American reports said little about Australians and asked could Spanish authorities be approached to provide more details. The Colonial Office thought this a most unwise suggestion, as no one could get more information than the Americans.[43]

Shortly afterwards, in April 1917, America's entry into the war ended its role as 'protecting power' for prisoners in Turkey, and Britain turned to the Netherlands, although unsure that the work could be done as satisfactorily by the Dutch. Some Australian POWs would have agreed. One said that the 'Netherlands Ambassador did not trouble about us at all', and another that, unlike American supplies, Dutch clothing was poor. The Spanish government also played a minor part in assisting POWs in Turkey during the latter months of the war.[44] Britain does not appear to have asked Australia to contribute to the decision on the change in the 'protecting power', and there is no sign that Australia could have done anything useful in the matter.

Turkey meanwhile continued to closely control contact with POW camps. In 1915, Enver released one *AE2* officer who had a link to the Vatican, and two Roman Catholic priests sent by the papal nuncio were later permitted to visit POW camps. Following international publicity given to the 'death march' of prisoners from Kut el Amara in 1916, Turkey also allowed the International Red Cross Committee based at Geneva to visit prisoner-of-war camps. Dr Adolphe Vischer, on the Swiss commission to inspect British prisoners in Turkish camps, with Alfred Boissier, presented a sixty-page printed report following a visit from October 1916 to January 1917. A copy was forwarded to Australia. The report had to be circumspect because criticism could lead Turkey to veto further inquiries. Australian cases mentioned were but a very small proportion of total Empire prisoners. The great majority were Indian, whose terrible march from Kut, well known by early December 1916 to have given the participants an 'extremely hard time', claimed the lives of two-thirds of the Indians and one-third of whites.[45]

Moderate though his report had been, Vischer's inspection process had some effect. In early 1917 Turkey, 'under pressure', replaced Maslum Bey, whose abuses had included brutal neglect of Kut survivors. Afion Kara Hissar camp improved in ensuing months, and one inmate described conditions there in September 1918 as 'good'.[46] But Turkey ignored later requests for International Red Cross Committee visits to POW camps. As the war closed, the House of Commons report pointed to 'the remarkably sustained effort . . . by which the Turkish Government has tried to conceal the results of its neglect'.[47]

In keeping with difficulties over access to POW camps, Britain made only limited progress on the question of prisoner exchange. From 1915 Australia was kept fully informed on the seemingly interminable negotiations with Turkey, perceived as 'extremely obstructive' and largely indifferent to the fate of its nationals in Allied hands. Britain suggested exchange of five hundred invalid prisoners, and negotiations were conducted over exchange of civilian internees. Australia held only about a hundred Turkish internees in camps or under surveillance (Canada had the significant Empire holdings of Turkish internees), but the many thousands of captured Turkish soldiers (including over forty thousand taken by light-horsemen in the Sinai) far exceeded Empire POWs held by Turkey.[48] The Berne Agreement, reached finally in December 1917, provided for exchanges of civilian internees and of invalid combatants; but little advantage could be taken of this in 1918, partly because Germany opposed its application. Britain's proposal in August 1918 of a three-for-two exchange of combatant prisoners was overtaken by the end of the war.[49]

During 1918, the struggle continued to get food and clothes to Empire POWs in Turkey. A prisoner support group formed in Britain by a senior British officer escapee from Turkey assisted by marshalling influential public pressure on the Turkish POW issue and contesting the restrictive War Office approach to pro-vision of help.[50] Understandably British attention focused most on the fate of the Kut 'death march' survivors. Fisher in London had to remind British authorities, who were not always accurately informed, of the need to alleviate Australian anxiety that their men also were being maltreated. Following arrival in London of two repatriated invalid AIF soldiers, a brief report of their experience in Turkey appeared in the *Sydney Morning Herald* headed 'Always Inhuman'.[51]

It seems clear that the fortunes of war brought improving conditions for POWs in 1918. Mails were freer, and people were asking, 'When are the English coming?' One Australian prisoner commented, 'Towards the finish I would much rather have been a British prisoner of war in Turkey than a German soldier, the people showing their hatred of the German in many ways.' Lieutenant Elston thought they were being 'well-treated according to Turkish ideas.'[52]

However, this was not universal. During 1918, Private Lushington endured his 'last hell in Turkey'. In San Stefano, a suburb of Constantinople, Serbians doing the same government work as he were 'dying in hundreds'; he was kept alive by parcels from the Netherlands Embassy.[53] By late October 1918, when the armis-tice with Turkey opened the Dardanelles and the Allies speedily occupied Con-stantinople, Red Cross records told a stark tale: only thirty-three men captured at Anzac were still on their books.[54] Overall, Australian POWs in Turkey, according to official figures, had a death rate of some 30 per cent compared with 9 per cent for those held in Germany. Furthermore, whereas in Germany under 2 per cent died of other than battle wounds, nearly 20 per cent did so in Turkey. Deaths among Anzac other ranks appear to have been heavier than among officers, unlike on the Gallipoli battlefield, where officers, needing to been seen and heard and to set an example, appear to have suffered more severely than their men.[55]

In a real sense there could be no satisfactory resolution of the prisoner-of-war problem short of conclusion to the war. Turkey itself suffered widespread food shortages and was fighting a battle against invasion. POW experience in Turkey reflected the captor nation's prevailing social attitudes and economic conditions, compounded by administrative inefficiency. Countless other thousands of POWs on the Eastern front during the Great War endured similar or worse distress,[56] and so did captives in Asia during the Second World War.

In many ways, Australians captured by Japan in 1942 were to repeat the experi-ence of the small band taken by Turkey in 1915.[57] They also suffered from the sheer indifference and brutality of captors whose culture placed less value on the sanctity of human life, as well as from the failures of an overburdened administra-tive structure. The privations were similar—appalling shortages of food, inad-equate medical care and forced labour. But this last element, which under the Japanese immeasurably burdened the hapless prisoner, in Turkey under the Bagh-dad Railway Construction Company tended to ameliorate his circumstances. And on the whole, Turkey was marginally less restrictive than the Japanese. The Otto-

mans allowed Red Cross supplies to be distributed, were more liberal in allowing correspondence between prisoners and relatives at home, and furnished Allied nations with a nominal roll of prisoners held. Indeed, POWs did not carry the same stigma of dishonour as in Japan, and representations by a powerful neutral and other international agencies had some influence with the élite of a country having a foot in Europe and historic involvement in the European political system.

In 1919, the Australian Defence Department published extracts from debrief statements of POWs captured by Germany. This was not done in respect of Turkey. T. W. White, an Australian Flying Corps officer captured in Mesopotamia and later a minister in the Lyons and Menzies governments, wrote in 1928 that German treatment of POWs 'soon became common knowledge' but the 'heavy mortality among prisoners of war in Turkey is not generally known, and the reputation . . . the Turk earned on Gallipoli as a stubborn foe and clean fighter biased the British public in his favour'.[58] Charles Suckling declared, 'We are nothing more than living skeletons [after our] sorry existence.' The need to tell this unfortunate story helps explain why the few Australians captured by Turkey produced a very substantial proportion of Australia's POW writing on the Great War.

*George Lambert*, Gallipoli from the Chanak side, *1919 (oil on wood panel, 23.7 × 35.6 cm). The ineffable beauty of the Dardanelles, swiftly opened by the Allies at the end of October 1918, impressed Lambert as it did many of the AIF.*

# AUSTRALIA AND THE DARDANELLES COMMISSION

$I$T IS NOT NORMAL to hold a large-scale parliamentary inquiry into a major military failure while a war is still raging, but the frequent criticism of the Asquith government for its handling of the Dardanelles campaign was associated with pressure for an inquiry, or for publication of the government papers explaining the campaign's inception. So, although the fate of the British Empire was to be decided by the battles in France and Flanders, the Gallipoli venture remained an active issue in British politics. In time, these initiatives would oblige Australians to decide whether or not they wished to criticise the political and strategic management of the operation. The Australian reaction was polite and moderate, to the great relief and surprise of Asquith and some of his ministers. Partly this was because the Australian psyche was so British-oriented. The Australians were in the war to see that the Empire won, and saw little point in launching furious criticism against the 'home country'. Given Australia's lack of experience in matters of strategy and diplomacy, and its lack of a foreign service, and the great distance from the Dardanelles, it was not unreasonable for Australians to take the attitude 'that Britain knew best'. As well, the government wished to do nothing that might harm recruiting, and there were fears that a full-scale investigation of the reasons for the Gallipoli fiasco might weaken sympathy for the Empire.

As early as April 1915 Lord Charles Beresford predicted that at 'some future time an inquiry would have to be made' into the campaign's origins. A group of British parliamentarians fruitlessly asked for one in June. The government refused to give Sir Henry Dalziel a chance to debate the Dardanelles 'scandals' in the House of Commons. Early in November Lord Morley was one of several lords asking for an inquiry. As one said, 'The terrible story of [Hamilton's] force will have to be known by the British public some day or another.' One of Asquith's ministers, perhaps unwisely, agreed: Lord Crewe on 3 November left the door open for an inquiry at the appropriate time.[1]

Many of Hamilton's troops remembered their famous shared experience with no sense of failure and were uninterested in inquiries into mismanagement. On New Year's Eve Hamilton went unexpectedly to the King George and Queen Mary Club for Overseas Forces, in Regency Street, Westminster—'the big Australian and New Zealand Club,' he called it, appropriately that evening, as Anzacs were holding a celebratory concert. Next day he told Braithwaite that he had 'had a really outstanding reception'. He went on: 'All of a sudden some of the men spotted me. There was great shouting of my name and then yells for a speech. I tried to resist, but was practically dragged on to the platform. . . . they were all very enthusiastic, especially when I said that we could have won through had we been properly supported.'[2] The *Daily Mail's* account of this incident agreed with Hamilton's.

Nonetheless, Hamilton's critics remained active. One of the fiercest was the war correspondent Ellis Ashmead-Bartlett, who condemned Hamilton's handling of operations in publications which in 1928 were to be consolidated in *The Uncensored Dardanelles*. By early 1916 he was attacking conduct of the campaign along the lines that 'brave Australians' had 'been sacrificed by [the] incompetence of English officers'. An example was a newspaper article of 1 February denouncing Hamilton's official report of the campaign. The general, wrote Ashmead-Bartlett, 'may attempt to deceive the general public, but he cannot deceive those who were on the spot and in the know'. 'Why were 2,500 of the First Australian Division sent to their doom to acquire a perfectly useless position . . . of Lone Pine? Why were thousands more lives thrown away in useless attacks from Quinn's, Pope's and Courtney's posts, which had nothing to do with the main operations?' He blamed the government for having given Hamilton the command.[3]

The Asquith government thought that Ashmead-Bartlett had 'done much harm' on his recent United States tour (undertaken because he needed the money) through his strong criticism of British military authorities. Still needing money, Ashmead-Bartlett arranged with entertainment entrepreneurs J. and N. Tait to tour Australia and New Zealand, to the alarm of both the British and Australian governments. Bonar Law and others would have preferred the correspondent not to visit Australia, but the British accepted that this was for Australia to decide. At Bonar Law's suggestion, the Hughes government readily agreed to the visitor's speeches being censored before delivery, as was also to be done in New Zealand.[4]

Ashmead-Bartlett reached Sydney on 11 February 1916. He was immediately in touch with the censor, who could find nothing objectionable in his planned address. He asked men to enlist, and naturally spoke of Australian bravery in the most glowing terms. He featured the 'extraordinary gallantry' shown by the light horse on 7 August: 'These men deliberately made attacks under conditions which made the Charge of the Light Brigade hardly worth the mention.' There was no mention of mistakes and military incompetence, although of course it was open for people to wonder why soldiers had to make hopeless charges.

The visitor told Munro Ferguson that he would be discreet, and gave ample profession of his patriotic aims, but spoke regretfully of the severity of Australian censorship. The Governor-General replied that 'it had necessarily been made strict and would be applied to anybody'. Pearce also had a 'straight talk' with Ashmead-Bartlett and defended the strict censorship by stating bluntly that the British censor should never have allowed publication of the journalist's critical statements. Ashmead-Bartlett was said to have agreed.[5] The Hughes government was mainly worried that trenchant criticism of Britain's military leaders might prejudice recruiting. There was probably also a feeling that in Australia criticism of British leaders might threaten the Imperial link, whereas similar criticism in Britain could easily be perceived as a normal part of the domestic political debate.

Australian authorities did not trust Ashmead-Bartlett, and a censor attended his lectures to ensure he kept to his approved text. He gave his first Australian lecture in the Sydney Town Hall on the night of Saturday 12 February. He proved to be only a moderately skilled public speaker and later explained that he was nervous and hesitant because of the censor's presence. His reputation as a man who had 'done so much to make known the great fighting qualities of the Australian troops' and his title, 'With the Anzacs at the Dardanelles', ensured that the 'immense auditorium' would be packed to overflowing. The crowd was 'liberally besprinkled with khaki, and the attitude adopted was one of keenly sympathetic attention', although the 'feeling that . . . the loss of gallant lives [was] a sacred theme, subdued the house'. These people of Sydney had come to hear lavish praise of the 'sustained bravery of our own dear soldiers', but they applauded just as warmly when the speaker commended men of the Royal Navy. He knew the importance of state loyalties in Australia, and both here and in Melbourne he gave special attention to the exploits of the local units and officers. In this way he 'made good' with the audience. He claimed that the 'eastern enterprise' was not abandoned and that the Entente powers would not end the war until they held Constantinople.[6]

Ashmead-Bartlett's other public lectures were just as successful and were supported by illustrations of the Anzac landmarks whose names had become famous in Australia. He also spoke to journalists at a Sydney luncheon, where he declared himself surprised to discover he was 'handicapped here far more by the censorship than in England'. The journalists cheered his claim that Lord Northcliffe's papers, *The Times* and the *Daily Mail*, 'had done a distinct service to the Empire' by trying 'to wake the nation up' to the mistakes of its political and military leaders.[7]

After his four Sydney lectures, spread over eight evenings, Ashmead-Bartlett took the train to Melbourne, where he was met at Spencer Street station by a group of literati. He was welcomed at the Town Hall by the Lord Mayor, members of the City Council and its officers. His lectures repeated the Sydney pattern, replete with 'intense public interest'.[8]

The terrible conflict, he said, had brought one benefit in the greater awareness people had of the Empire. The English people had nothing but the greatest admiration and affection for Australians, and this feeling had increased since it was known how the Australian people had accepted the inevitable evacuation of Gallipoli after so great a cost of life. He was not divulging any secret now when he said that the Imperial government had been terrified about the effect the evacuation would have on Australia. Any fears that costly blunders at Gallipoli might have led Australia to withdraw help quickly vanished. Australia's 'willingness to help and shoulder her responsibility was all the more remarkable because here [were] no indications of the horrors perpetrated by the enemy. It was, therefore, all the more credit to Australia to raise such an army purely on the voluntary system, and to promise immediately after the Gallipoli campaign had failed, to raise an army of 300,000 men.' Ashmead-Bartlett visited every state except Western Australia before leaving for New Zealand on 7 April.[9]

Shortly before he reached Australia, another remarkable sequel of the Anzac campaign had occurred in Britain. The Scottish-born Sir George Reid, former premier of New South Wales and prime minister of Australia, after completing his term as high commissioner, entered the House of Commons on 11 January after a 'walkover' in the safest Conservative seat in London, St George's, Hanover Square. The local Unionist Committee accepted him, partly out of admiration for Australian patriotism and despite his store of venerable and tedious witticisms. He was selected as a 'great Imperialist'. In supporting his candidature, Walter Long, a minister in the coalition government, stressed the 'glorious achievements of the Australians at Gallipoli'.[10]

In Britain the Gallipoli campaign was not seen as a sacred national event. To many who were active in politics it was both a reason and an opportunity to work for the fall of Asquith, as this was a major wartime issue on which he was vulnerable. Even after the evacuation, he had to face constant political pressure over it. One member of the House of Commons, Henry Bentinck, declared in March that the expedition was 'a reckless gamble, conceived in a spirit of levity, and resulting in the most disastrous and lamentable waste of men'. The government's Balkans diplomacy of 1915 was denounced. Some complained, accurately, that the expedition had sought to secure Constantinople for Russia, which objected to Greece participating, as that would mean a rival claimant for the city. Members claimed that a lot of shipping had been tied up in an absolutely futile and disastrous expedition. Questions were asked about the responsibility for the Suvla fiasco. Again, the government was asked, by men such as Dalziel and Commander C. W. Bellairs, if there would be an inquiry. Privately, Major C. J. L. Allanson, one of the many officer-parliamentarians, thought Staff College students would be failed if their work was no better than that of the Gallipoli planners.[11]

Dalziel might have thought that Reid's advent in the House would have meant extra support for his pressure for an inquiry. He was disappointed in this, which prompted an irritable speech on 31 May immediately after one by Reid whose main burden was to lavish great praise on Kitchener. Dalziel complained that Australians were satisfied with everything about Gallipoli, with the object, the conduct of the campaign, and the medical and landing arrangements—'the whole of Australia is satisfied with it'.[12]

Although Dalziel got no help from Australia in his persistent campaign for a searching inquiry, there were many Britons who, for varying reasons, agreed with him. One was no less than the venture's main architect. With remarkable buoyancy, Churchill thought that his chances of achieving his ambition of returning to high office would be improved if the full story were revealed. Constant pressure eventually led to a government announcement, on 1 June, that documents relating to the Dardanelles would soon be laid before parliament. Churchill was delighted, as was the amazingly self-confident Hamilton, who thought 'the completest publicity' for all campaign documents would help his reputation.[13]

Many people, then and since, thought it was a mistake to allow a wartime public scrutiny of the government's inner workings. Objections to such publicity were presented forcefully by Sir William Robertson, Chief of the Imperial General Staff. Disclosure, he pointed out, would call more attention to a story that brought little credit to Britain's methods of conducting war and would harm Britain's prestige in the East. Another strong opponent of publication was Maurice Hankey, who sifted through the mass of papers and on 5 June gave Asquith a list of thirty-five that could be released without harming the public interest. He told Asquith that all Hamilton and Churchill wanted was to be 'whitewashed' in the public eye. He added that the government should do everything possible to suggest to the Turks that Britain meant to return to Gallipoli, in order to oblige them to retain their forces there, so restricting their freedom to reinforce the Caucasus.[14]

Asquith was under pressure to honour his commitment to the House, while releasing as little as possible, especially in view of the military leaders' strong objections to publication. Many members of parliament suspected him of backsliding, and from late June the government was frequently asked when it would honour its promise of 1 June. By mid-July Asquith did decide that his promise had been rash, and he told the House the papers would not be published. There was an angry reaction, fully voiced in a brief but spirited debate on 18 July.[15] Dalziel and Carson wanted the chance to debate the issues raised by the campaign, and Carson moved for an inquiry. The campaign's critics maintained their pressure for an inquiry, thinking that this parliamentary process would eventually bring the desired result as Asquith's resistance was steadily weakened. This duly happened, the government's stand being weakened by another military setback, this time in Mesopotamia, where General Townshend's force had been forced to surrender at Kut el Amara.

Parliamentary and public disquiet over this second defeat inflicted by the Turks greatly strengthened the case of Asquith's opponents. After more vacillation on 20 July, he announced inquiries into both the Mesopotamian and Dardanelles campaigns, though with procedures that would prevent the publication of the major papers.[16] He hoped thereby to avoid some embarrassing disclosures. Among those angry at this decision was Churchill, who thought his reputation would suffer more under an inquiry than through the publication of the papers. Another was Hankey, who regarded the decision as 'sheer cowardice' and one from which, he later believed, the Asquith government 'never recovered'. A later scholar, John Grigg, biographer of Lloyd George, aptly calls Asquith's decision an 'act of self-mutilation'.[17] Many men still in central positions in the government were to have their dealings with Gallipoli investigated, and Hankey was given much extra work preparing their cases to present to the inquiry. The government was to be protected partly by holding the inquiry in secret, but its report was to be published. Nevertheless, publication of the original papers, as promised on 1 June, might have involved Asquith in more immediate embarrassment.

The two inquiries were set up under the same act—the Special Commissions (Dardanelles and Mesopotamia) Act. The composition of the Dardanelles Special Commission was very important. In a move that could be viewed as adroit, honest, courageous, or possibly foolhardy, the government first asked Lord Milner, a severe critic of the campaign and of the coalition government, to be chairman. The result might have been a searching inquiry and a hard-hitting report. But Milner, who had other important public tasks to perform, promptly declined.[18] The government then turned to an older, no less famous servant of Empire, the deeply conservative Earl of Cromer, a pre-war political opponent of Asquith. Aged seventy-five, Cromer had been critically ill in 1915. Many objected that he was too old for the post. He took the attitude: 'Young men are giving their lives for their country, so why should not I who am old?' In December an attack of influenza prevented him from chairing sessions, and when his health briefly improved the commission sometimes met at his home. He probably was largely responsible for the interim report, signing it in January 1917; but he died on the 29th, before it was released and with most of the commission's work still to be done.[19]

Among Asquith's first four selections as ordinary members of the commission were Andrew Fisher[20] and Sir Thomas Mackenzie, the two high commissioners from the antipodes. Both were born in Scotland, the former in 1862, the latter in Edinburgh in 1854. As soon as Hamilton suspected that Fisher would be a commissioner, he wrote to Asquith about 'a certain disability under which he seems to labour'. Because Fisher was a friend of Murdoch's, Hamilton feared Fisher might be prejudiced against both him and the British part of the force. Asquith had already considered this point, but as the Australian government had 'behaved very well in the matter of Murdoch's report',[21] and as both Asquith and Hamilton agreed that Fisher was an honourable and sincere man, the Prime Minister did not fear that Murdoch's views would prejudice Fisher's assessment of the evidence to be presented before him. Fisher accepted the position subject to the approval of his government.[21]

It soon became even clearer that Hamilton's fears of an indignant colonial inquisition were completely groundless. The news from London reached Australia as the *Euripides*, carrying Hughes on his return journey from England, was a few days out of Fremantle. Pearce, the acting prime minister, no doubt determined the Commonwealth government's response. It allowed Fisher to accept the seat, but not having been consulted on the appointment or scope of the inquiry,[22] it took no other part in the commission's work. Asquith confirmed the appointment on the basis that Fisher was a nominee of the home government and did not represent Australia. Munro Ferguson told Bonar Law that he thought the Australian government did not approve of an inquiry.[23] He was right. Pearce told Fisher, 'I think it a foolish blunder and displaying great weakness on the part of Govt.' Such excessive loyalty towards Britain was characteristic of the Australian-born Pearce. Although hard-working, effective in a quasi-administrative role, and active in promoting Australian command of its own troops, he was an unimaginative minister and lacked a grasp of many wider issues. Doubtless he spoke for most Australians, including probably a majority of Labor supporters, in his response to Fisher's appointment. Certainly this had no direct relationship to the 1916 conscription campaign in Australia. The government told London what it had decided a month before Hughes launched that campaign, and it was completed five months before the Dardanelles Commission published its interim report.

The government of W. F. Massey in New Zealand emphatically protested against the Asquith government's procedure. Annoyed that Mackenzie had been appointed without consulting them, it thought that there should be no inquiry until victory, lest evidence and report provoke bitter controversy. Bonar Law replied with a mollifying cable, explaining how Asquith's hand had been forced by parliamentary pressure. The two high commissioners were not regarded as representing their respective governments, but the home government had felt it desirable to have an Australian and a New Zealander on the inquiry. It would take evidence in secret and would not report for a long time. The government hoped this delay would mean trouble would be avoided.[24]

The other two of Asquith's initial selections as commissioners were Sir Frederick Cawley and J. A. Clyde, KC, both members of the House of Commons. To both, Asquith seemed intent on 'self-mutilation'. Clyde, a highly reputed lawyer, was a Scottish Unionist. Cawley, although a Liberal, was a leader of a small group, the Liberal War Committee, whose aim was 'a more vigorous prosecution of the war'. His fellows in the group included two of the most consistent critics of the Dardanelles venture, Markham and Dalziel.[25] Aged sixty-six, Cawley had already lost two of his four sons in the war, one killed at Gallipoli. A third was to be killed in France in August 1918. With Clyde he was to join Lloyd George's government, formed in December 1916, ample indication of their attitude towards Asquith.

Cromer initially had wanted a small commission, but during the bill's journey through parliament five men were added, to cater for special needs. Perhaps this also indicated that Asquith was losing command of the situation. There had been controversy in Ireland over the role of the 10th (Irish) Division at Suvla, so it was deemed appropriate that Captain Stephen Gwynn, an Irish Nationalist MP who served in France with the 16th (Irish) Division from 1915 to 1917, should join the inquiry. This left Wales unrepresented, although thousands of Welsh soldiers had served at Gallipoli. Asquith then allowed a free vote on Dalziel's successful motion to add a Welsh MP, Walter Roch, to the list. Roch, a lawyer, who was member for Pembrokeshire, had been the first man in the Commons to suggest there should be an inquiry along the lines now adopted by the government. In supporting Dalziel's move, Llewelyn Williams mentioned the 'grave anxiety' felt all over Wales at the 'great disaster' befalling its division at Suvla. This had 'caused great searchings of heart in Wales in the parts from which those battalions were drawn'. Others who voted with Dalziel were prompted by a wish that at least one member of the commission should be appointed by the House, to reduce fears of a 'whitewash'.

Asquith then agreed, without a division, that an army and a naval representative should be added. As one admiral in the House put it, admirals and generals were to be on trial in the commission and needed representation. As well, the commission needed military expertise.[26] The service members had to be drawn from the retired list. Those selected were Field Marshal Lord Nicholson, who had been on Lord Roberts's staff during the Boer War before becoming Chief of Imperial General Staff from 1908 to 1912, and Admiral of the Fleet Sir William May, who from 1909 to 1911 had commanded the Home Fleet. Cromer was anxious to have someone 'of large judicial and legal experience' on the commission. He was very satisfied with the government's eventual choice, Sir William Pickford, one of the Lord Justices of Appeal. The secretary was E. Grimwood Mears, a man experienced in this type of work who agreed to accept the job in return for a knighthood, duly conferred in mid-1917.

Five of the ten commissioners were aged over sixty-five. Much the youngest was Roch, aged thirty-seven. Neither Dalziel nor Markham nor any other prominent critic of the Gallipoli venture was on the commission. Many observers, no doubt unaware of the approach to Milner, declared the inquiry was intended as a whitewash. This view persisted, but it was unfair. Not one of Asquith's original selections was particularly close to him politically. All were potential critics of his Dardanelles policy, as were four of the men added by parliament. Roch had already criticised the handling of the campaign. Dalziel, probably the most consistent critic of the Dardanelles gamble, was decent enough to admit he was agreeably surprised at the government's proposals. He said they were very fair and that Asquith had tried 'very hard to meet the views expressed in various parts of the House'.[27]

Other general issues were canvassed in the debate on the bill. Opponents of a wartime inquiry were outspoken. An Irish member, A. A. Lynch, however, speaking also for others, approved 'piercing to the bottom the reason why the lives of thousands of soldiers were needlessly sacrificed'. Another Irish member, T. M. Healy, thought the basic idea of the Dardanelles campaign, which he had followed in great detail, 'was a proper act of war', but he was very angry that the Dublin and Munster Fusiliers (part of the 29th Division) did not receive the praise they deserved. He thought that resentment over this largely helped to explain the Sinn Fein troubles in Ireland.[28]

There was dispute over whether Australia wanted an inquiry. Some members stressed the official Australian opposition to involvement. Dalziel, however, insisted that, given an opportunity to express their views, Australians would prefer an inquiry. That inquiry, he asserted, was wanted promptly, while the major participants were still alive, and with details relatively fresh in their memories. Carson spoke even more forcefully along these lines; but Colonel Aubrey Herbert, a Gallipoli veteran, disagreed, claiming: 'We know what the live people in Australia think. They want to get on with the work, and they do not want to go back on their past mistakes, and we know what the Australians who are dead and the New Zealanders thought.'[29]

Much evidence suggests that Herbert, not Dalziel, correctly read the Australian psyche. The Ansteys, the Brennans, the Maloneys, and the other Labor men who were Hughes's opponents on conscription made no parliamentary reference to the high-level British inquiry into its handling of the 1915 campaign. The *Age* and *Argus* severely criticised the appointment of the commission and the government's decision to allow Fisher to sit on it. The *Age* on 31 July stated that apparently in Britain some public opinion was dangerously misinformed about Australian purposes and sentiment. The Catholic Melbourne *Advocate* assumed that it now was widely recognised that the expedition had been a mistake, but it did not welcome the commission and was aware of the political reasons motivating many of those in Britain who had pressed for an inquiry. The Hobart *Daily Post*, which gave one of the most thorough coverages in Australia of the commission's establishment, stressed the need for an inquiry although it found its terms unsatisfactory, as it appeared it would not be probing in sufficient detail. This complaint was echoed by the *Australian Worker*, which thought that the inquiry would be unsatisfactory from a dominion point of view unless it included Australian representation—for example, Pearce. The *Daily Post* claimed that many Australians would want to know why the expedition was launched at all. It added, 'It seems strange that a nation that has warred from time immemorial should make such blunders.' The anti-conscriptionist Perth *Truth* later agreed that however much the Northcliffe press might regret it, no demand 'ever came from Australia for an inquiry into the Gallipoli failure'.[30]

*Truth's* comment was not strictly true. Although most small-circulation anti-capitalist journals, like *Direct Action* and *Ross's Magazine*, did not mention the commission's establishment, an occasional voice asked for the punishment of those responsible for the 'ghastly ghoulish "gamble"' at Gallipoli. *The Woman Voter*, a Melbourne pacifist journal, described how the Women's Peace Army asked for a woman representative on the commission. 'This was done on behalf of the mothers of Australia whose sons' lives were gambled with so recklessly at Gallipoli.'

In the House of Commons Sir George Reid, more conservative than Hughes and Pearce, showed no animus in his speech on the bill. He saw that the Empire, especially in the East (including Australasia), might be weakened by revelations of incapacity on the part of 'high Imperial officials', and he hoped that the commission would 'reassure the public mind' by discovering extenuating circumstances to explain the glaring mistakes which admittedly had occurred. Meanwhile, he thought 'one of the brightest passages in the history of this War is the attitude of Australia in connection with the loss of so many thousands of her gallant sons in the Dardanelles. While she bowed her head with profound grief at the loss of so many of her sons, she, suspecting all sorts of mistakes, offered up the sacrifice of her grief and resignation to leave to those at the centre of the Empire the duty of either ordering, or refraining from ordering, an inquiry into these matters.'[31]

Apart from the addition of extra commissioners, some other minor amendments were made to the bill during its passage through parliament. It received royal assent in mid-August. There were several parliamentary references to the Roebuck Committee, set up during the Crimean War, the most recent previous occasion of the House appointing a committee during war to investigate the conduct of operations. But this special commission had no exact precedent. It included members of both houses of parliament, men who were not parliamentarians, and two who were employees of other governments. After some early uncertainty about rules of procedure, it adopted a flexible attitude. It had the option of sitting in private or in public, although in the event it always sat in private. It could require men to appear as witnesses and hear others at their own request. It required preliminary written submissions from some witnesses and allowed others to present such documents. It allowed witnesses to make supplementary submissions (or to be re-examined) to reply to adverse comments by other witnesses. Churchill probably viewed the commission as his own private vehicle to vindicate his role in the whole episode, and the commission seems to have been generous in allowing him wide scope to present his case. He wrote several hundred pages of notes for his evidence, some of which he later incorporated into *The World Crisis*.[32]

Churchill's opportunity was Hankey's torment. This key official, at a crucial stage of the war, had to spend an inordinate amount of time—some two hundred hours—analysing the mass of relevant documents in order to help defend the government. He 'was flooded with letters from or visits by the principal witnesses seeking his advice on those aspects which particularly concerned themselves'.[33] The great majority of these submissions relate directly to British rather than Australian history: an investigation of these recriminations between British officers is not relevant to the present study.

The commission also stimulated much other activity. Leading Gallipoli actors, 'on trial' before the commission, prepared to vindicate themselves. Naturally, generals resented politicians inquiring into their actions. Maxwell complained to Hamilton, 'All the mistakes are the work of politicians, they dart off into enterprises without any preparation or consultation with the general staff.'[34]

With so much apprehension on the part of those with reputations at stake, collusion was inevitable. Churchill advised some (for example, Admiral Sir Henry Oliver, Chief of the Admiralty War Staff) on how to give their evidence. Hamilton had a voluminous correspondence with and about witnesses appearing before the commission.[35] He discussed with Birdwood how best to protect their reputations, assuring 'Birdie' that he would not say a word which would 'in any tiniest respect reflect on' Birdwood or his 'views or actions'. 'No matter how cunningly questions may be framed', he assured Birdwood, 'you may feel quite safe of my replies.' He went on to give Birdwood hints on how to make his 'proposed line of defence . . . fairly safe'. He told Birdwood on 23 May 1917, 'I am still being tormented by this devilish Commission.'[36] Birdwood's two-page initial submission to the commission in December 1916 was insultingly brief considering the status of the inquiry and the number of soldiers under his command who had been killed. Godley sent Hamilton a copy of his statement, adding, 'I have tried to say as little as possible.' He promised to keep in touch with Hamilton if asked to appear before the commission, which he hoped would not happen, although inevitably it did.[37]

On the other hand, generals sometimes fell out. Perhaps it is surprising there was not more recrimination. Hamilton and Stopford were to disagree before the commission about the reasons for failure at Suvla. On 21 June 1917 Birdwood told Hamilton he had heard from Mackenzie 'that Nick [Nicholson] was apparently out to do all he could to whitewash Stopford.' Birdwood thought it 'scandalous' that 'Nick' should listen attentively to Ashmead-Bartlett's evidence. Godley 'had it out with' Allanson about what Allanson 'had said to the Commission about the attack on Sari Bair'.[38] No doubt there were other quarrels between officers over rival versions of various battles.

The commission's task was to inquire into 'the origin, inception and conduct of operations' in the campaign, 'including . . . the provision for the sick and wounded'. It divided its work into two main goals and set out to report on the campaign's inception before dealing with the later issues.

On 23 August 1916, while it was absorbing the voluminous initial written submissions,[39] the commission, with seven members present, examined its first witness, General Monro, who was about to sail to India. The commission next met on 19 September, to question Hankey. It then worked consistently until early November, normally meeting in a House of Lords committee room, to question all those most closely involved in the highest planning for the expedition—although not, of course, Kitchener, who had lost his life when the cruiser *Hampshire* sank in the North Sea in June. Churchill did not have a free hand to blame Kitchener for everything that had gone wrong, because the dead field marshal was defended before the commission by some, including Sir George Arthur, his former private secretary and future biographer. Churchill's bitter refutation of Arthur's version of Kitchener's role was one of the many cross-currents provoked by the commission's work.[40]

The first stage of inquiries was conducted as Asquith's hold on the prime ministership steadily weakened. He was forced to resign on 5 December, to be succeeded by Lloyd George. This reduced somewhat the political significance of the commission's work, as Asquith never again held ministerial office and Churchill, to his surprise, was not offered a ministerial post by his former colleague. The two members of the commission given posts in the new government—Cawley, who became Chancellor of the Duchy of Lancaster, and Clyde, who became Lord Advocate— both consequently resigned from the commission and were not replaced. After Cromer's death, Pickford became the new chairman.

The interim report, Cromer's last work for the Empire, was presented to the government on 2 February 1917, when the commission had already examined many witnesses involved in the conduct of operations at Gallipoli. This initial report covered the period from 6 August 1914 until 23 March 1915. It began by discussing the higher organisation of the government's machinery for running the war: the War Council, the Board of Admiralty and the War Staff Group. The junior Sea Lords resented being placed in an inferior position: not one had been consulted about the Dardanelles expedition. Similarly, the commission criticised Kitchener for giving orders without consulting subordinates. The bulk of the report then gave a digest of events, divided into fifteen sections and a summary. Churchill's role was clearly specified. The commission thought there was an obligation on Churchill, Asquith and the rest of the War Council to obtain the views of the naval advisers. By mid-January the military advisers, also, should have been fully involved in the planning. On the War Council decision of 13 January to use ships alone to 'take the Gallipoli peninsula, with Constantinople as its objective', the commission pronounced, 'A surprise amphibious attack on the Gallipoli Peninsula offered such great military and political advantages that it was . . . ill-advised to sacrifice this possibility by hastily deciding to undertake a purely naval attack which from its nature could not attain completely the objects set out.' Worse perhaps, Kitchener's delay of three weeks, without telling Churchill, in sending the 29th Division, gravely compromised the probability of success for the initial land attack. However, the commission did think that the decision to abandon the naval attack after 18 March was inevitable. Asquith was seriously remiss in not calling a meeting of the War Council between 19 March and 14 May, the period of the initial, crucial land battles on Gallipoli. In sum, the commissioners did not think the expedition was a complete failure, as it achieved one of its aims, to create a diversion in favour of the Russians and immobilise a large force of Turks which might have been better used in other war theatres.[41]

Although its criticisms were very serious, the report was couched in relatively staid language. Roch's minority memorandum was much more trenchant. It criticised both the War Council and Churchill quite severely. He strongly urged that military and naval staff should be heavily involved in the planning of future amphibious operations of a similar kind. This proposition would have seemed axiomatic to any strategist involved in the Second World War. Newspapers seized on the commission's strictures, but their language, naturally, was far more inflammatory.

The commission had a respite from its questioning in April and June, and finished this part of its work on 5 September 1917. It had sat on eighty-nine days and questioned two women and 166 men, many several times, at a total cost of about £4,850. Ninety-three of the witnesses had also given preliminary statements. The most important custodians of Empire headed the list, including three present or former prime ministers, leading cabinet ministers, heads of service departments and service chiefs. Witnesses included forty-eight army officers of the rank of major-general or above, fifteen brigadier-generals and eleven admirals. Most of the MEF's divisional commanders appeared, as did many knights, about a dozen lords and one future governor-general of Australia, Lieutenant-Colonel Hore-Ruthven (later Lord Gowrie). Many middle-ranking and junior army and navy officers were questioned, as were three non-commissioned officers, four clergymen, several journalists and some other civilians. In its closing stages, the commission paid much attention to the treatment of the MEF's sick and wounded and to shortcomings in providing the troops with basic services, such as an efficient postal service.

Members of the House of Commons pressed for the interim report to be tabled and debated. Lloyd George refused to publish the evidence but was forced to respond to the strong resentment when it emerged that certain passages in the report, given confidentially to leaders of all political parties in the House, were to be excised from the version later tabled. Reasons of national interest were given— accurately, because these deletions involved the names of spies and like matters. As a compromise, the government on 19 March released a one-page supplementary report giving the gist of the deleted passages.[42]

As with so much associated with the campaign itself, this decision to release the report was controversial, particularly as the outcome of the war was very much in doubt and many young soldiers were doomed to die before peace came. 'Our prestige in the Orient must be safeguarded,' Sir George Reid said. 'The report gives the enemy a multitude of texts of which it will readily take advantage. We have washed our national linen in public to Germany's delight.' Prince Louis Alexander of Battenberg, the former First Sea Lord, exclaimed, 'How delighted the Huns will be when they read it.' Lewis Harcourt thought the release 'an outrageous thing to have done at this time and in the absence of some of the evidence and necessary suppression of many of the material facts'. He thought it would make Hughes's task in Australia harder and probably harm recruiting.[43]

Amid speculation on why the report was released—apart from the fact that setting up the inquiry implied its findings should be made public—the most likely explanation was that it was meant to be 'a nail in the coffin of the old gang'.[44] It contained less damaging information on Lloyd George than on Asquith and Churchill, the latter complaining that it treated him unfairly by not referring to some 'evidence' which, he claimed, vindicated his policy.[45] It certainly was in Lloyd George's interest further to discredit Asquith and Churchill and thereby strengthen his hold on the prime ministership.

In the *Evening News* and the *Daily Mail* Northcliffe assailed Asquith's 'old gang' and asked, 'When will they be prosecuted?' The *Daily Mail*'s headlines were: 'Asquith Wobbled, Kitchener did not realise the facts and ignored his staff, Churchill misled everybody, Lord Fisher and other experts sat mum—weeks of muddle and delay'. It went on: 'The report proves they threw away the lives of 40,000 men of our race, wasted £300,000,000 of the Treasure, alienated possible allies, and brought on our arms the greatest disaster which those arms ever suffered, through their reckless folly, dereliction of duty, and negligence. . . . Are politicians whose blunders cost the lives of thousands to escape scotfree?'[46]

Some New Zealand press comment was even sharper in its castigations. One Christchurch newspaper said the report proved what many had long suspected, that the campaign would be remembered 'as one of the most shocking examples of official blundering and malfeasance on the part of British politicians aspiring to the name and rank of statesmen'.[47]

A précis of the report prepared by the Australian Cable Association was printed in major Australian newspapers on 10 March. It was not comforting; a *West Australian* headline was 'Disagreeable Revelations'. The précis concentrated on defects in the machinery for running the war and on other faults in procedure, including some in the service departments. Kitchener was properly criticised for his highly centralised and secretive methods. These were suitable for a limited campaign, like the Sudan in 1898, it was observed, but not for running a great war from London. Churchill, and to a lesser extent his colleagues, were blamed for not adequately consulting their senior service advisers who, in turn, were criticised for not having been more forthright in telling the War Council of their objections to the Dardanelles plan.

'The Commission was convinced', Australians read, 'that had the naval members of the board been regularly and collectively consulted on large questions of war policy during the present naval campaign, some, at least, of the events which the Empire was now bitterly deploring would not have happened.' Further on, the précis stated: 'It is impossible to read all the evidence and papers without being struck by the atmosphere of vagueness and want of precision which characterised the War Council's proceeding. It is almost inconceivable that anyone, whether military, naval, or civilian, should have imagined that Constantinople could be captured without military help on a somewhat large scale.' When Hamilton took over command of the MEF 'no scheme had been drawn up, no water supply arrangements had been made, and there was a great want of staff preparation'.

During the week beginning 10 March Australian press comment on the report—and on the steps leading to its release—was extensive. This commentary lacked the virulence of much of the British press, partly because the reputations of Australian political leaders and parties were not at stake. Moreover, the general reluctance to condemn Britain's conduct of the war still operated. A strong strand of opinion remained opposed to any debate on the report's findings. However, British leaders could not be entirely exonerated, even by the most Empire-minded of Australian editors and journalists. Most such criticism was recorded in a mood more of sorrow than of anger—sorrow that Titans like Kitchener failed to measure up to the demands of running a great war. Most critics of the 'grave defects' of Asquith's administration were adamant that Australia should fight on until victory was assured. Better results were hoped for under the new Lloyd George government.

This was a 'time for action', not for disputes, claimed the *Sydney Morning Herald*. Much opinion still thought the strategy basically wise and of benefit to the Allied cause. The *Newcastle Morning Herald* thought that the report apparently gave inadequate consideration to the expedition's value 'at a critical period of the war'. It compelled the Turks to retain strong forces near their capital when they were challenging their Russian enemies and when they had been hoping to threaten Britain in Egypt, and it barred their exit to the sea. 'The expedition was a great conception.' The *Sydney Morning Herald* also thought that the expedition 'was needed by Russia'. So did the Adelaide *Advertiser*, endorsing the report's view that a 'sudden onslaught by sea and land offered . . . enormous advantages', and frankly admitting it 'would be painful to reflect that the heroes of Gallipoli had shed their blood in vain'. The 'expedition held up a great body of the best Turkish troops who would otherwise have been operating against the British or the Russians, [while] the attempt to force the gates enclosing Russia has united us to that Power, and doubtless contributed to baulk the enemy intrigues to beguile her into a separate peace'. Australian newspapers also acknowledged that the chance of taking Constantinople was foredoomed to failure by mistakes made before the landing on the peninsula. Even the Hobart *Daily Post*, which was sure that reinforcements 'would most certainly have saved the position . . . and probably enabled the Allied troops to reach Constantinople', still saw the campaign as 'a matter of bungle almost from beginning to end'.[48]

Churchill was vigorously criticised, the *Newcastle Morning Herald* specifying how the report revealed lies in his resignation speech of November 1915. The *West Australian* was equally to the point. Under Churchill, 'there was a proposal to subdue Turkey, but no scheme'. 'Like a new Joshua, he would sound his trumpet, and the walls of Jericho would collapse.' The *Sydney Morning Herald* thought that Churchill's failure was a rare 'example of the rashness of an amateur in risking great issues on the strength of his opinion on highly technical subjects'. He was so possessed by 'self-confidence' that he 'would be guided by no advice, however expert'. 'No system would have assured . . . even the First Sea Lord [his] proper share of authority under such a Minister as Mr. Churchill.' He was, wrote the pro-Labor *Daily Standard*, 'always a showman-politician, who liked fame' and as minister 'in control of the greatest navy in the world, decided on the big hazard of making a grab for' Constantinople.[49]

Australians were so well-informed on the raging controversy in England fuelled by the interim report that, despite any public protestations to the contrary, they must have formed a low opinion of the abilities of the Empire's war leaders, an opinion encouraged by reading the magisterial judgement in *The Times* that Churchill was 'a dangerous enthusiast' and Asquith 'utterly lacking in leadership qualities'. The Ballarat *Evening Echo*, edited by J. H. Scullin, noting 'the severity with which [the report] criticises all the chief directors of the war policy of the Empire', remarked that they could not wholly subordinate their own ambitions 'to the supreme interests of the nation'.[50]

Australia's own reputation did not suffer. The report's appearance gave local newspapers another opportunity to assert that one beneficial result of Churchill's foolish campaign was 'that it proved to the whole world the indomitable bravery and the splendid fighting qualities of the soldiers of Australasia'. One of the most interesting expressions of this viewpoint was made in *Soldier*, the 'Journal of Australian Patriotism', an organ of the Returned Sailors' and Soldiers' Imperial League of Australia (later the Returned Services League, or RSL), which asked if dead heroes buried at Gallipoli would benefit if the blame for the 'muddling and blundering' was apportioned correctly. Had Germany undertaken such a task, wrote *Soldier*, it would have thoroughly prepared an overwhelming force which would have 'smashed into Constantinople like an avalanche'. *Soldier* thought Britain should improve its military efficiency instead of investigating past disasters.[51]

Other comment expounded on the military feasibility of the expedition. The Adelaide *Advertiser*, forgetting the exploit of Admiral Duckworth's squadron in 1807, claimed that 'since the Turks captured Constantinople in the fifteenth century no enemy fleet had ever battered its way through the Straits. The question of their impregnability seems to have come as a novelty to the [British] authorities', even though experts had long considered this question. 'The cardinal mistake', it added, 'was in treating as feasible an attack by ships alone.' The *West Australian* printed some of the fiercest criticism, commenting on the 'lamentable. . . story of incompetent politicians'. Even if the way through the Dardanelles had been opened, 'the ships having got into the Sea of Marmora, would quickly have had to get out again because of the lack of land supports'.

Roch's minority report, which critically summarised the War Council's planning failures along lines followed by later historians, was featured in Australia, even, for example, in the modest regional daily, the Ballarat *Evening Echo*. As well, Andrew Fisher was taken to task for his dissenting opinion that the naval authorities should not have expressed their views to the War Council. He asserted that responsibility had to be borne by the ministers alone. He thought it would seal the fate of responsible government if state servants shared the responsibility of ministers. The *West Australian* said this comment came from a man 'imbued with a deep sense of the importance of politicians', and asserted that it was the duty not of politicians but of experts to decide whether policy can be carried out. Mackenzie sided with Fisher on this point, but more significantly disagreed with the other commissioners who claimed that the expedition was a complete failure. On the contrary, he wrote, it was 'fairly successful' in its basic aim of creating a 'diversion in favour of the Russians'.

Substantial fundamental criticism of the Gallipoli 'tragedy' was made by the Brisbane *Daily Standard*, which had links with the Brisbane *Worker*. 'From the antimilitarist viewpoint,' it wrote, the report had 'no redeeming features' except that it exposed 'the hideousness of war and how easily the masses can be duped and led by a handful of men with political power. 'The memory of the tens of thousands of lost lives, thrown away on this dreadful gamble, cannot be wiped out. Shattered bodies, wrecked lives, broken hearts, ruined homes, are too common now. . . to allow the horror of the Dardanelles to be forgotten here or elsewhere.' It regretted 'the staggering fact. . . that two or three men were able to and did gamble with the lives and patriotism of scores of thousands of men. . . . Australia has a very real grievance, not only against [Britain's war leaders], but also against those of her own leaders who misled her.' It was censorship by 'our so-called national leaders', aided by the 'jingo press', which distorted the truth and allowed the army to expand. A week later this paper published a letter from 'Jack Cade', denouncing 'British military imperialists' and 'their servile Australian followers'.[52]

This line of reasoning could have been pursued by socialist, trade union, left-wing and anti-capitalist journals. But most prominent ones were silent on the interim report, perhaps owing to censorship, but more likely because their journalists and editors, by and large, thought they lacked the expertise and resources to compete with the major newspapers on such issues. Similarly, they were largely to ignore the final report, released in 1919.

The Australian press had great matters to report on during March 1917, in addition to the fighting on the Western Front. Federal parliament was dissolved on the 16th for an early election. The long campaign was a crucial one, in which Hughes sought electoral approval for the new Nationalist 'Win the War' party he had formed from former Liberals and Labor conscriptionists. Australians were also reading astounding news from Russia, of the Tsar abdicating during the Russian Revolution.

Despite this competition for print space, Australian newspapers kept their readers well informed of the sequel in Britain to the interim report's appearance. Many summarised the brief supplementary report. The Lloyd George government refused Asquith's request to publish the evidence but kept its promise to allow a debate on the interim report. The House was crowded for the occasion, when thirteen members spoke on the afternoon of 20 March. Australian newspapers, in their extensive accounts, concentrated on the speeches by Asquith and Churchill, the latter's being very long and made with few interjections. The next speaker, J. A. Clyde, the former commissioner now Lord Advocate in the new government, said that, as the House probably guessed, he had already heard Churchill's 'vigorous able and persistent speech' in the commission itself. For all his forceful eloquence in defending his decisions against strictures in the report, Churchill failed to persuade his critics, one of whom condemned his poor judgement in military affairs and declared that he came out of the report very poorly.[53]

The other eleven speakers, including many officers, several of whom had fought on the peninsula, gave a wide range of opinion, some asserting that the report should not have been published, others that its authors were carefully chosen to exonerate Asquith. Some, apart from Churchill, defended the concept of the expedition, claiming 'the nucleus of the Turkish army was practically destroyed at the Dardanelles' and that Hamilton's force was of great importance in helping to relieve pressure on the Russians. Their opinions were reported in Australia. For example, the *Evening Echo* summarised the views of Sir Mark Sykes, the able, witty linguist, soldier, and Conservative member of the Commons throughout the war, a Catholic who favoured the Arabs yet became popular with Zionist leaders, and whose great niche in history was his part in the Sykes-Picot agreement of May 1916. He thought the operations on Gallipoli were worth the blood and treasure, as they prevented the Turks from running over Persia and opening the road to India.

Of the several officers who praised the Australians, the most eloquent was Lieutenant-Colonel Sir Matthew Wilson, who spoke of 'the imperishable glory of . . . our comrades in arms, whose valour has written for them at their first trial in Europe a shining page of history'. The Australians and English, as Captain G. C. Tryon said, were 'all of one race and of one Empire'. For a few minutes Colonel Aubrey Herbert focused the heart of the Empire on an old Turkish post which he briefly shared with sixty New Zealanders, remnants of a battalion. At night they would argue over whether the expedition was a mistake. They concluded that in a gigantic war there must be gigantic mistakes. They had decided 'to come and fight for freedom' and thought it 'relatively unimportant' whether they were killed at Gallipoli or in France.

Sir George Reid had an opportunity to protest at faulty British decision-making which had led to so much Australian suffering. Instead, like so many others, he opposed publication of the report and thought the commission had reflected unfairly on 'the powers of the greatest figures in the history of this country'. He claimed that the dominions did not want 'excursions into [such] controversial matters'. He explained, 'Nothing offends Colonial sentiment more, after the Colonies have sent their boys by . . . tens of thousands to give their lives for the Empire, than to see, as if this awful conflagration was not enough, new fires started in this House upon controversial questions.' Reid's opinions seemed to be borne out by the comparative lack of Australian controversy on the report. Most of his speech was a passionate defence of Kitchener, whom he praised lavishly.[54]

As the report was being debated, the public in both Britain and Australia was aware that the commission was examining more witnesses. The first Australian, Keith Murdoch, was questioned on 5 February 1917. The six other Australians examined were Isaac Unsworth, a colonel in the Salvation Army, four medical officers who testified in July (Surgeon-General Sir Neville Howse, Lieutenant-Colonels John Corbin and Charles Ryan and Major Wilfrid Kent Hughes), and Captain Albert Jacka, the first Australian to win a Victoria Cross in the war. Murdoch was the only Australian witness who did not deal mainly with the medical arrangements for Australian sick and wounded. These were strongly criticised by most of the Australians, who sometimes spoke with nationalist fervour. Such evidence was considered in chapter 31.

There were many AIF men of various ranks, including men convalescing in England, who no doubt could have testified. They spurned the opportunity to speak on the conduct of the campaign, perhaps as it was widely known that the Australian government did not want to be involved in controversy with Britain over the issue. There is no evidence of obstacles of any sort being placed in the way of a man wanting to be a witness, although such pressure from senior officers is not inconceivable.

By inviting Fisher to join the commission, Asquith had given Australia a superb opportunity to pursue a nationalist line of inquiry, critical of British command. Fisher eschewed any such approach. His role conformed with his government's policy of coolness towards the inquiry. Birdwood commented to Hamilton in June 1917 that the Australian government did not wish to convey the impression that it had grievances it wanted investigated. Fisher's complaisance might also have been consistent with his abilities as a high commissioner. Early in May 1916 one English observer wrote, 'I don't think Fisher has done any great service since he came here . . . either for Australia or the Empire, and, of course, during Hughes' visit he is entirely thrown into the shade.'[55]

Fisher attended only thirty-seven of the commission's eighty-nine sittings, half as many as Mackenzie. Fisher was absent when Birdwood was questioned and on most days when Churchill was in the witness chair. When other key witnesses appeared, frequently he either was absent or raised only minor issues. Mackenzie was generally more assiduous in questioning the Empire giants who planned Gallipoli. Fisher several times referred to himself as a novice in military and naval matters, and the only occasion when he showed flair in persistent questioning on a strategic theme was when he pressed Lord Fisher and Admiral de Robeck about the practicability of forcing the Dardanelles by ships alone and the likely results of such a success.[56]

Enough evidence came before the Dardanelles Commission to provide fuel for a heated argument between Australian and English witnesses and commissioners. A

*Bungled medical arrangements at Gallipoli were the chief focus of evidence by Australians at the Dardanelles Commission. The shortage of proper transport to evacuate wounded could force barges like these carrying the wounded to go from one ship to another, trying to find space. Sometimes the barges had last been used by horses or mules.*

number of Fisher's remarks suggested he felt keenly the incompetence of many of those running the campaign, but he rarely pursued this issue to any extent. Mackenzie was more active in this type of questioning and more willing to condemn tactics used in the land fighting, and to stress the horrific, generally useless results of frontal attacks. Once he complained about the 'butchery' involved.[57]

The commission's work was well advanced before Fisher for the first time voiced his worry that the campaign had been mishandled by Britain. During the examination of Reginald McKenna, a member of both of Asquith's governments in 1915, he observed that the best advice available should have been sought and given on 'a matter of big policy that concerned not only immediately the Mother Country but all the Dominions'. Much later, in a sentence of homespun simplicity, he told Carson, in the witness chair, 'I am in the unhappy position of having been Prime Minister of a Dominion which sent men [to Gallipoli], and we relied upon your knowing better about things than we did and being able to look after things with which you could not entrust us.' Carson replied, 'I felt all along that we ought to know a good deal more than we did.'

Fisher asked several witnesses about postal arrangements at Gallipoli and probed another about water supply deficiencies at the Suvla landing, strongly implying that such problems should have been foreseen.[58]

Proceedings assumed an 'Australia versus England' tone while Surgeon-General Birrell was being examined. As noted in chapter 31, he defended himself against harsh criticisms by Australian medical officers of his handling of medical arrangements at Gallipoli. But many of the English involved were also ready to damn Birrell, including one admiral who had come 'to blows with him for not taking steps to provide necessities'.[59]

The most likely flashpoint for an Anglo-Australian row was Keith Murdoch, fierce critic of English generals. Fisher and Mackenzie were present when Murdoch appeared on 5 February, and much of the exchange took on an 'England versus Australia' flavour. Murdoch named six Australian officers who had told him in September 1915 that the situation on the peninsula was parlous and not receiving adequate attention in London. Half of Murdoch's questions came from Pickford, the chairman, who was distinctly unsympathetic towards the young journalist. It might have been easy to become annoyed at Murdoch's demeanour, but Fisher praised him. 'I would give you a letter of introduction to the King if necessary, knowing you as I knew you.'[60]

Questions to Murdoch concentrated on the alleged impropriety of his methods. Pickford assured him that the commission would not be influenced by the many unsupported 'hearsay statements' he had made. As Pickford seemed too unfriendly, Fisher came to Murdoch's support, openly differing from the chairman before the witness and stressing Australia's 'separateness' from Britain. He suggested to Murdoch that he was carrying a mandate from one self-governing dominion, 'directly concerned with the Gallipoli campaign', to give his 'best impression' of what he saw. As the disagreement continued between Pickford and Fisher, the latter suggested that Murdoch felt he had a duty to his native country to report truthfully his assessment of the situation on the peninsula. Fisher stressed this and said, 'I think that this is a sufficient answer to the allegation of misbehaviour.' That ended Pickford's series of questions on this issue, but naturally there were many harsh words said about Murdoch by other witnesses whom he had impugned. British participants in the planning for Gallipoli did much dissecting of Murdoch's evidence. Hankey and Hamilton were only two who found fault with his testimony. Hamilton complained that no soldier, 'unless in the full tide of victory', could long withstand the type of 'backstairs influence' Murdoch had brought to bear against him.[61]

Murdoch's claim during questioning that appointments to the British army's general staff were made from motives of friendship and social influence was objected to by Field Marshal Nicholson, who pointed out that he had had more experience and responsibility than any one else in appointing officers of the general staff. The tense exchange ended with Murdoch still obdurate. 'I would not like to have the task of proving the statement here and now, but it is still my strong opinion that the rigid caste system and favouritism in the army is a great weakness to the British Army, and also slightly to our Australian Army, although ours is a very much more democratic Army than the British Army.'[62] These exchanges marked the height of Anglo-Australian tension in the commission.

The last evidence was taken on 5 September 1917. The commissioners continued working with their customary dedication, their final report going through at least twelve revisions before it was signed—by six commissioners, including Mackenzie but not Fisher—on 4 December 1917. In its published form it traced in 186 pages the history of the campaign and dealt with specific problems like postal and medical arrangements and water supply. It was restrained and courteous in its criticisms of the ministers and commanders responsible for the disaster. Churchill could scarcely have hoped for kinder treatment.[63]

This was the most prestigious official judgement ever passed on the campaign. The commissioners thought it was doomed from the outset, unless Britain had diverted more of its resources there from the Western Front. This finding implicated Churchill, but no strictures were specifically levelled against him in the report's general review and conclusions. Instead, Hamilton was admonished for his continually sanguine, uncritical attitude, which had led him to fail completely in assessing the arguments for and against continuing the campaign.

The commissioners thought the plan for the August offensive 'was open to criticism . . . as too little importance was attached to natural difficulties', especially as 'no complete preliminary reconnaissance . . . could have been made'. The need to make a night advance through 'very difficult country' to Sari Bair greatly increased 'the risk of misdirection and failure'. The report did not mention the Nek attack but commented generally that it was unreasonable to expect to maintain stringent timetables in such rugged terrain.

The report extensively reviewed the Suvla operations because of the controversy they generated in Britain. The commissioners thought 'that the absence of the artillery and horses available at Alexandria and Mudros must have materially contributed' to this failure. Hamilton, Stopford, Sir Frederick Hammersley (commanding the 11th Division), and Brigadier-General W.H. Sitwell (34th Brigade) were dispraised, the report thus confirming past decisions, as all had been relieved of their commands, the three last-named in August 1915.[64]

In a change of mind since the interim report, the commissioners were now not impressed by the argument that the campaign could have been justified because it contained a Turkish force on the peninsula. They quoted Kitchener's estimate that the Turks allocated nearly 300,000 troops to the defence, whereas the Entente powers committed 385,000 to Hamilton's force, which sustained casualties totalling 119,846, including 31,389 killed and 9,708 missing, losses they thought outweighed any alleged gains.

In five terse sentences in a separate minute, Fisher explained that he did not feel justified in signing the report because the demands of other duties had prevented him from adequately assessing the evidence.[65] No doubt it suited the Hughes government that its High Commissioner should express no formal opinion on the vast amount of evidence available.

Mackenzie was forthright, providing a short supplementary report in which he commented intelligently on some reasons for 'the Gallipoli disaster'. He thought that Hunter-Weston and Hamilton had sacrificed human lives in frontal assaults at Helles because of a shortage of artillery and ammunition. He stressed the shortcomings in the treatment of the wounded, holding Birrell largely responsible. He nominated Birdwood as the outstanding figure of the campaign. He thought that 'the haphazard, uncertain methods [had] largely disappeared and a good deal of the inefficiency which formerly prevailed [had] been swept away', and wrote optimistically that the British army had learnt some of the lessons of 1915.[66]

For the time being the report was not made public, although it was announced that it had been presented, and it was shown to some of the witnesses. It was so gentle in its wording that Hamilton thought it had exonerated him. Ever the optimist, he therefore wanted it published during the war, as he saw 'a chance of bringing into play the results of [his] life time of experience and study'.[67]

Others, for different reasons, wanted the commission's proceedings published. The Lloyd George government responded to such requests in 1918 by telling the House of Commons that the War Cabinet had accepted advice from the chiefs of staff that publication would give valuable information to the enemy. No doubt it would; but an equally telling reason for suppressing the final report perhaps was that Churchill had joined the cabinet in July 1917, and Lloyd George obviously did not want another embarrassing row over Churchill's role in the Gallipoli campaign. For whatever reason, the government refused to release the report during the war, and there seems to have been little further complaint about this in 1918.

Perhaps most private members agreed with the government and with the attitude of Lieutenant-Colonel M. Archer-Shee, who in July 1917 had asked if ministers knew of any public report by the German government on a failure of its arms to gain a military objective. One of the Dardanelles Commissioners, Lord Nicholson, died on 13 September 1918, the day after Sir George Reid. Both were buried in London on the afternoon of the 17th, *The Times* reports of their funerals being next to each other.[68]

After the Armistice in 1918, strong pressure developed for release of the commission's proceedings. Was the government intent on shielding individuals? The public was gravely suspicious. Bonar Law responded in February 1919, saying the government had 'minutely considered' the question and had decided against publishing the evidence, at least before the peace treaty was signed. However, it would consider the later release of the final report.

In Australia some interest was shown in the suppressed report. In 1919 Senator Pearce, for the second time, asked Britain for a copy as soon as possible. The relevant British ministers, Bonar Law and Milner, agreed that copies should be sent confidentially to Australia and New Zealand. On 11 July 1919 F. G. Tudor, who had succeeded W. M. Hughes as leader of the Australian Labor Party after the conscription split of 1916, asked W. A. Watt, the acting prime minister, if he would have the report printed and made public. Watt replied tersely that the government could not do this, but he did not mention the approach to London.[69]

A few days later Australians saw parades of former AIF men as part of the joyful celebrations of Peace Day throughout the British Empire, to mark the signing of the Treaty of Versailles on 28 June 1919. This was another formal occasion when Australians especially remembered their war dead and thanked the soldiers for their part in saving them from the horrors of defeat at the hands of a ruthless foe. The signing of the treaty also opened the way for the publication of the final report of the Dardanelles Commission. The decision was announced on 7 August 1919. Printing was delayed because of the need to provide maps. The report was expected to be 'of exceptional interest', although nothing 'of a really sensational character' was foreseen.[70]

Meanwhile, some of its findings were mentioned in the British and Australian press. *The Times* printed a well-informed selection. The *Argus* presented a skilful thumbnail summary of the AIF's fighting at Anzac and claimed that history would 'not hastily write "failure" against the account of the Gallipoli campaign'. Citing as its authority Henry Morgenthau, the United States Ambassador to Constantinople from 1913 to 1916, the *Argus* proclaimed that the Turks had been 'in despair' and 'were devoutly thankful and profoundly surprised when they found that our troops had silently stolen away'.

The Lloyd George government eventually released the report in mid-November. On the 18th and 19th *The Times* summarised it and commented on it over several pages. Its 'Correspondent on War' sensibly wondered why 'after lying in the cupboard for nearly two years' it was made public 'precisely at this moment'. Was it to divert attention from some current political difficulty?

The Australian Cable Association prepared a summary of the report's findings which appeared in major Australian and some provincial dailies on 20 or 21 November. The association's employees wrote a skilful précis which, like *The Times*'s summary, pointed up the mistakes and the ineptitude in the Gallipoli story. It repeated evidence to support the conclusion that 'from the outset the risks of the failure of the expedition outweighed its chances of success'. The syndicated summary contained much that would not have surprised those who had carefully read the press coverage on the interim report, but some of its material was new. It quoted Howse's warning against Australians ever again trusting 'the Imperial

authorities with medical arrangements for care of Australian sick and wounded'; thus, this aspect of Anglo-Australian tension was brought to the notice of virtually every Australian interested in the issue. The *World* (formerly *Daily Post*) of Hobart featured Howse's statement in its lengthy report headlined 'The Appalling Tragedy of Gallipoli', and the *Daily Herald* (Adelaide) and the *Daily Standard* mentioned it in their short items on the 'Gallipoli Disaster' and the 'Great Bungle'.

The report's appearance in Australia coincided with political controversy. Federal parliament was dissolved on 24 October for the general election of 13 December, which was won by Hughes's National Party. Concentration on the election campaign, and the passage of time since the Anzac fighting, together no doubt explain why much less press attention was paid to the final report than to its predecessor. Major dailies in Brisbane, Adelaide, Sydney and Melbourne ran no leading article on it.

As usual, most left-wing journals ignored it, although the *Australian Worker* (Sydney) commented sensibly on Kitchener's ruined reputation. Various newspapers reprinted an article by Lieutenant-Colonel Repington in the London *Morning Post*, stating that it 'was an act of supreme folly' to attack such a highly important objective as the Dardanelles while the Allies were outnumbered in France. *Soldier*, in an article not uncharacteristic of its general attitude, bitterly drew far-reaching conclusions from the report. Fundamentally, the disaster stemmed from the 'years of stubborn, autocratic, pig-headedness' in the British army which 'prevented competency coming to the front'. Promotion from the ranks was the solution. These new men must 'travel the world and learn the strategical positions for themselves'. *Soldier* hoped that the Gallipoli failure would ensure that Australia learnt the lesson 'that our men's lives are never again entrusted to the care of those who are ready to gamble with them'.

Among major newspapers, the *West Australian* complained that it had taken nearly four years for the Empire to be told of the bungles that had caused the

*Men of the 6th Field Battery on water-carrying fatigues stop for a rest and a smoke. This classic photograph conveyed an Anzac image to readers of Phillip Schuler's book,* Australia at Arms, *in 1916.*

243

failure of 'that great enterprise'. The paper found that, in general, the report showed 'that there was a continuous series of shortcomings and misapprehensions among the military, naval and even political authorities'. It reminded its readers of Churchill's ill-advised warnings to the enemy of November 1914 and February 1915. The newspaper that strongly urged conscription in 1916 and 1917, in the only state to vote strongly twice for that policy, here presented a clear statement of what has become the standard view of Anzac—a combination of bungling Imperial leadership and Australasian valour.

In a long survey of the campaign, it showed that the first impressions had not dimmed after the passage of four years. 'The great assault [of 25 April], the superlatively gallant attack, was delivered in defiance of apparent impracticabilities, and was delivered successfully, through the dauntless intrepidity and resolute dash of the Anzacs. . . . How that handful of troops held and extended their position, on the desolate little strip of country swept ceaselessly by shell and rifle fire, seems even now incredible. Yet it was held . . . by heroic Australians for eight months. The cost, to the people of the Commonwealth of this endurance may be gauged by the graves of Gallipoli, and the honour lists of the dead which are in evidence in every town and almost every village in Australia. . . . amid all the dangers, privations, and risks of their position, the Gallipoli troops held on tenaciously to the shell-swept beaches and sand ridges they had won.' Although Australians 'must sorely regret that the gallant soldiers of Gallipoli were deprived of . . . victory, through official ineptitude, hesitancy and disagreements, [the campaign] at all events stands among the glorious failures of British warfare.'[71]

The evidence was never publicised and for decades was closed to scholars. Even in the British services there was, by the 1920s, little knowledge of its contents. Few copies of the complete evidence were bound. By the 1920s only six seem to have been available, massive volumes, running to 1,687 double-column foolscap printed pages. In 1926 or early 1927 the Australian government asked for a copy. This request raised such sensitive issues that it was considered by the Committee of Imperial Defence's Subcommittee for the Control of Official Histories, and by Stanley Baldwin's Conservative cabinet. Despite ample evidence of Australian governmental refusal to criticise Britain over Gallipoli, Hankey, at the subcommittee's meeting on 11 February 1927, strongly opposed Australia's request. He pointed out that he had given much evidence to the commission based on War Council minutes and other secret documents. To accede to Australia's request would be to invite other dominions to ask for copies of these privileged documents. The issue went to cabinet, which decided to send Australia only the evidence on the medical arrangements.[72] For decades no complete copy of the evidence was available in Australia. Fisher kept less than 10 per cent of it. In 1965 it was opened to scholars using the Public Record Office in England; many years later a microfilm copy became available in Australia.

To sum up, in 1916 and 1917 most Australians in a position to inquire into the mistakes at Gallipoli consistently refused to do so. Some did not wish to subject themselves excessively to the pain of admitting pointless slaughter. Others were 'Imperial-minded' and were wary of 'disagreeable revelations' which could adversely affect recruiting. Some probably were reluctant to criticise a campaign in which Australian soldiers first won fame. Many no doubt believed that the Anzacs came very close to victory, and that they had done much to weaken Turkey's army, a contention that has some merit. Many accepted that mistakes were inevitable in war and concentrated more on final victory than on recriminations over previous errors. For these various reasons, and no doubt for others, the campaign never became the subject of a violent, widespread Australian controversy of the type seen in 1944–45 or during the Vietnam War.

# CHAPTER 35

# *'GALLIPOLI NEVER DIES'*

$T$HE DARDANELLES CAMPAIGN gave rise to an extensive 'Gallipoli industry' which shows no sign of decline, embracing as it does parades, memorials, pilgrimages, books, the popular press, plays, films and television documentaries. Of most significance for Australians generally was the emergence of 25 April as a national day of commemoration for those who have served and died in Australia's wars. This chapter looks at how Anzac Day was formally enshrined in Australia's national calendar and at the continuing link with Gallipoli.

In 1916, as the first anniversary of the landing drew closer, Australians in many different places decided that it should be commemorated. In England, fourteen soldiers at Monte Video camp for AIF convalescents and invalids at Weymouth, west of Southampton, addressed a laudatory letter to Hamilton in which they said: 'The day draws near that marks Australia's Birthday. With you on the 25th of April last year we laid firmly the foundation of our Military History, and in a few days we hope to celebrate a glorious anniversary. Anzac is a topic still much discussed among us . . . you could have led us to Constantinople, if those responsible in London could have got interested enough to provide you with the means.'[1]

Andrew Fisher told editors of major British newspapers: 'Their Majesties, the King and Queen of England, [W.M.] Hughes, and others will attend a service at Westminster Abbey . . . and over 2,000 Australian and New Zealand troops will be there. There will be a luncheon at the Hotel Cecil for 1,000 Australians. The day is being celebrated far and wide in Australia.'[2] Britain's quality press duly noted the coming event.

On the day itself, Australian veterans marched from the Strand through Whitehall to Westminster Abbey in the proud display envisaged by Kitchener in August 1914. Inside the Abbey, wrote an Australian patriot, 'statues of Pitt, Canning, Gladstone and Disraeli, timorous builders of a wider Empire, looked down upon the men whose heroism has given cohesion and unity to the statesmen's work.' The wounded were not forgotten: the day before, Birdwood visited convalescing soldiers at Harefield hospital.[3]

Closer to the former battlefield, in Egypt thousands of other Australian soldiers celebrated Anzac Day in distinctive fashion. Monash described how he turned out his whole brigade for a dignified service, followed by sports and later 'many comic items . . . including a skit on the memorable landing by a freak destroyer manned by a lot of corked blackfellows hauling ashore a number of tiny tin boats full of tiny tin soldiers'. There were mess dinners 'everywhere' that evening, and band concerts as the soldiers rejoiced on 'this famous day—*Our Day*'.[4]

People across Australia also marked the catharsis of 1915. Church services and public ceremonies in state capitals and country centres were well attended. Newspapers devoted much space to the commemorations. Pride mingled with sadness: 'Though the record of Anzac is written in letters of gold, the page is yet wet with tears.' There were ceremonial plantings of native trees whose longevity seemed a

*On the first anniversary of Anzac Day in 1916, men visited and laid wreaths at the old Cairo cemetery, where many comrades were buried.*

fitting memorial for the dead. The contribution of Anzac to Australian nationalism was a common theme, and some people used the occasion to promote recruiting.

In Victoria, celebrations 'of Anzac's pride and inspiration' lasted over a fortnight, beginning with 'Anzac Week'. On Tuesday 25 April, memorial services were held in St Paul's Cathedral, Scots Church and Wesley Church (a requiem at St Patrick's Roman Catholic Cathedral would follow on Sunday afternoon). At St Paul's, the Anglican archbishop said: 'Before the war Australia was looked upon as a distant settlement in the Southern seas, but now we are known as a real part of the Empire. . . . We [have] been reborn and henceforth [will] have our place and our destiny.' The midday service was followed by dinner for returned soldiers. At a large afternoon public meeting in Melbourne Town Hall arranged by the City Council, and attended by federal and state politicians including the acting prime minister, speakers stressed Anzac's contribution to Australian nationhood and to increased influence in Imperial destinies. George Elmslie, leader of the Victorian state Labor opposition and strong supporter of Empire war aims, said: 'In the past we [have] gloried in boys of the bull dog breed. Now we [have] boys of the Anzac breed. . . . Anzac should be a sacred spot to all Australians, and when the war [is] over . . . that part of Gallipoli [should be] handed over to us for our future care. (Loud cheers.)' Sir William Irvine, a federal MP, and others took the opportunity to advocate conscription. That night, fireworks at the Melbourne Cricket Ground began a carnival in aid of the Discharged Soldiers' Fund. The *Age* on 25 April ran a long résumé of the Anzac campaign and next day a patriotic editorial. 'Had the Anzacs numbered hundreds where they numbered scores,' it asserted, the Allies would swiftly have seized the peninsula and opened the way to Constantinople.[5]

At 9 a.m on 25 April 1916 Adelaide came to standstill: train and tram traffic stopped for two minutes and whistles sounded in factories as work briefly ceased to honour the Anzacs and cheer the King and Empire. Crawford Vaughan, the Labor Premier, said: 'Anzac day would ever be to Australia what Trafalgar Day was to

England.' Perth mounted a parade followed by luncheon for soldiers who had landed at Gallipoli.[6]

The public will to celebrate the anniversary overtook more customary reserve. Some eight years later in the New South Wales parliament the seventy-year-old George Black, Labor stalwart for a quarter-century before leaving the party over conscription, recalled that first anniversary: sixty thousand to a hundred thousand people packed the Sydney Domain, and when four thousand returned Gallipoli men marched in 'the emotion . . . was such that I shall never forget it. It was as though the crowd was swayed by a great wind, and sobs and sighs went up on every hand. Then suddenly somebody . . . began to sing "Abide with me, fast falls the even tide" and the great crowd took it up. . . . it was one of the most emotional moments of my life.'[7]

The infant New South Wales Returned Soldiers Association brought out a book, *Anzac Memorial*, aimed at recording the names and deeds of soldiers and sailors of the AIF from New South Wales. This tribute prefigured the role soon taken on by the federal returned servicemen's association—the RSL, as it was to become—custodian of the Anzac tradition.[8] Much more writing about Anzacs would follow, including in due course by official historian Charles Bean.

This overwhelmingly spontaneous Anzac Day activity had largely bypassed the Governor-General, thereby precipitating a behind-the-scenes vice-regal skirmish. Queensland's Labor government, led by T. J. Ryan, had approached London direct for an Anzac Day message from the King. The Colonial Office draft—described by one official as 'rather garrulous, but the Dominions seem to like it'—proclaimed that Gallipoli had brought the two peoples 'more closely together and added strength and glory to the Empire'. Release of the King's message for Australia and New Zealand to the New South Wales press through Sir Gerald Strickland, Governor of New South Wales, fuelled conflict between him and the Governor-General. Munro Ferguson contested Strickland's assertion of state governors' right to correspond directly with Imperial authorities. The dispute, which one senior Colonial office administrator deemed 'quite . . . intolerable . . . in war time', lasted for months.[9]

There was principle involved, but in pursuing his contention Munro Ferguson was perhaps also attempting to repair an oversight. He had not recognised the depth of Anzac sentiment. Unaware how the Gallipoli landing was to be marked when London inquired a week before 25 April, he had hurriedly consulted each state. The information he gave to Bonar Law, Secretary of State for the Colonies, was that a parade in Perth would be followed by luncheon for men present at the landing and church services in the evening, some other states would hold parades, and Victoria would mark the day in state schools only.[10]

Of course there were many more commemorative services and functions throughout Australia than his information suggested. But in one sense Munro Ferguson was right. Little of the activity had been *formally* organised by federal or state governments. Queensland had tried unsuccessfully to co-ordinate a state-government approach, and at federal level Acting Prime Minister Pearce marked the occasion officially only by naming 25 April 'Anzac Day'.

Following this first Gallipoli commemoration, amidst talk of proclaiming 25 April a national day, Pearce remained cautious during Hughes's absence overseas. He felt it better to decide after the war which AIF event was most worthy of remembrance.[11] With the Anzac concept already sacrosanct, however, he was prepared to ban use of the term *Anzac* by private individuals or for 'trade, business, calling or profession'. Regulations were promulgated under the War Precautions Act, and Pearce asked that the United Kingdom also ban use of the term for commerce.

London responded carefully. The English company that named a locomotive 'Anzac' was using an 'honorific' rather than seeking to bring traffic to its line, and Bonar Law would only request the Board of Trade to 'do all they can'.[12] Further instances of affront eventually provoked a British ban in December 1916.

Anzac Day 1917 fell midway between the first and second conscription campaigns. The federal government, with Hughes back at the helm, contributed on this second anniversary to the inception of that enduring Anzac Day feature, the public march. Pearce, as Defence Minister, approved parades of all available AIF troops in each capital city in formal celebration of the Gallipoli landing on the morning of 25 April. Accompanied by bands, returned soldiers would head columns including mounted light horse, artillery with guns, and militia. Provincial centres would have similar parades.[13]

Despite Hughes's enthusiasm for another royal message, and Munro Ferguson's satisfaction that this time it would be conveyed through his office, London decided against it, at that distance still so unaware of the power of Anzac in the antipodes as to believe repetition might detract from the previous year's message. Not until 1921 would another Anzac Day royal message be sent.[14] Munro Ferguson, invited to speak at the Brisbane Exhibition Hall on Anzac Day, conveyed the Imperial viewpoint: while acknowledging Australia's contribution at Gallipoli, he skilfully dwelt on the part played there by other members of the Empire and the need to maintain the war effort. In hearty support, Queensland Premier T. J. Ryan praised Australia's reponse to the call for arms in the 'great, free, and enlightened Empire'.[15] For though Anzac Day signified a flowering of pride in Australian identity, that identity resided within the Imperial bond. Munro Ferguson had been wanted by several capitals. State governors took salutes. Ceremonies, which as in 1916 extended over several days, were often linked to recruiting meetings or collections for returned soldiers. Editorials were as patriotic as ever.

The third anniversary coincided with the crisis on the Western Front following vast and damaging German offensives, and with disappointingly low recruitment rates. Munro Ferguson was one who used the anniversary to help boost enlistments: 'Celebration will be an empty ceremony unworthy of the deeds we commemorate if unattended by a great improvement in recruiting whereby . . . the Australian army [is] made fit to take as glorious a part in the last as it did in the first phase of the War.'[16] Recruitment rates improved fairly consistently for the rest of the war, although still well below 1915 figures.

In 1918 the AIF achieved meritorious victories, perhaps far worthier of celebration than any feat at Anzac. The stirring and successful recapture of Villers-Bretonneux occurred on 25 April, a victory Monash held to be the real turning-point of the war.[17] But there could be no return to Pearce's idea of assessing all AIF battles before selecting a day to commemorate. Similarly, although Armistice Day on 11 November would become a day of great significance for the post-war generation, as an Allied and not distinctly Australian landmark it lacked the personal and national identification commanded by the Gallipoli landing at Anzac.

Hughes was in London for 25 April 1919, the first peacetime Anzac Day. He insisted that—separate from and in addition to the dominions' march in early May—on 'The Day We Celebrate', five thousand AIF soldiers headed by Monash would march through streets at the heart of Empire in symbolic assertion that Australia had 'gained for herself a place among the fighting nations of the earth'. Within the War Office the view was that Australians had 'behaved rather badly'.[18]

The momentum gathered by Anzac Day ensured some special post-war status, but the road to pre-eminence as a national event had yet to be charted. While the idea of gazetting it as a public holiday had quite widespread support, some people disliked the implied invitation to public revelry and instead preferred solemn commemoration on the nearest Sunday. Others wanted to avoid disruption to business life. At that time, apart from the central Christian festivals, a 'holiday' usually applied only to public servants or to banks and/or some other single section of the community; business and industry were not compelled to close. If they did, the ordinary worker stood to lose a day's wages unless provided for in the relevant court award. Australia's cumbersome federal system confines Commonwealth powers over holidays to its Public Service and the territories; holidays are largely a state matter. The ensuing Anzac Day debate would reflect adversarial politics operating across seven parliaments.

The touchstone was public opinion, and whose views were more relevant than those of the returned men themselves? The RSL had by 1919 achieved ascendancy in volatile 'digger' politics and reached a post-war peak membership of 150,000. Hughes's National Party government, valuing RSL political and administrative support for repatriation policies, recognised it as the 'official representative body' for returned soldiers. As early as 1917 the RSL (to no avail) requested that the Commonwealth declare 25 April a public holiday, at that stage primarily so returned soldiers could participate in ceremonies. RSL policy soon crystallised: Anzac Day must retain a special status, not only for commemoration but also for reminding Australians of obligations to returned men. As influential lobbyist for returned men in a favourable post-war political environment, the RSL would constantly press—and itself organise—to ensure Anzac Day was observed on the day it fell and in a distinctive manner.[19]

Western Australia, Pearce's home state, which had contributed a disproportionately high percentage of men to the AIF, was the only state to support conscription twice and was 'sympathetic' towards returnees, accorded official recognition to Anzac Day in 1919. Nationalist Hal Colebatch, state premier for just one month, agreed that returned soldiers employed by the state should have the day off on full pay. So too did the Commonwealth, lobbied by the RSL, which had in 1918 adopted a resolution that Anzac Day be a public holiday throughout Australia. The newly launched populist newspaper *Smith's Weekly* declared that gratitude and pride for these men 'must burn forever . . . in the heart of our new nation . . . tempered with a divine sadness for those who will never return'.[20]

Later that year, Western Australia also became the first state to establish Anzac Day as a statutory public holiday. In October 1919 James Mitchell's National–Country Party coalition government introduced a bill providing for gazettal of 25 April as a Public Service and bank holiday. Debate highlighted heroism and national identity. Attorney-General T. H. Draper held that 'tradition . . . plays a great part in the moulding of any nation', and by creating a public holiday future generations would be more likely to remember 'those glorious deeds of which we are all so proud'. Opposition Labor leader Philip Collier heartily endorsed the bill, saying that every man in the AIF 'participated in the glory of Anzac'; the word was 'world famous, and undoubtedly [would] live for all time'. W. C. Angwin, Labor member for East Fremantle, strongly supported the bill. In committee, some Labor members favoured dropping one of the other state holidays to compensate for Anzac Day, because many wage-earners did not get a paid holiday, but the bill quickly passed through the lower house. In the Legislative Council Hal Colebatch, now Minister for Education and Health, said one reason to celebrate Anzac Day was for the sake of children and to develop 'a healthy Australian sentiment'. Armistice Day was shared with all Allied nations, so he preferred celebration of Anzac Day as the distinctively Australian event, a 'baptism of fire . . . [that] brought Australia . . . into prominence in the minds of the people of the world such as it had never before received'. It was agreed that when 25 April fell on Sunday (as in 1915) state government offices and banks would take the holiday on

*George Lambert,*
Anzac, the landing,
*1918–22 (oil on canvas, 190.5 × 350.55
cm). Subjects chosen by
war artists reflected the
focus of Australian interest.*

Monday. After very brief discussion, this most uncontroversial of bills passed quickly into the statute books.[21]

Western Australia's act was a first step only. The measure simply *facilitated* commemoration. It prescribed neither the day nor the form of observance. Shops were not compelled to close, nor was racing banned.[22]

Anzac Day 1920 fell on Sunday, and there was much public uncertainty. Was 'Sunday observance'—no work, no public entertainment and no selling of liquor— the right way to mark the day? Although New South Wales declared the Monday a full holiday to celebrate Anzac under the Banks and Bank Holidays Act, large retail stores stayed open; in Melbourne the Commonwealth government observed Friday 23 April, because Monday 26 April in Victoria was Eight Hour day.[23]

Wide celebration of Anzac Day on 25 April 1921 manifested public support for special ceremony on the calender day and also community division over what form that should take. The Governor-General reported that all states declared a public holiday—all, that is, except for New South Wales, whose government, under Labor Premier John Storey, took the view that a public holiday would not be conducive to solemn observance. Some states set the tone by prohibiting races and public sports. The Commonwealth, lobbied by the RSL, for the first time declared a Public Service holiday and agreed also to pay casual workers in the Works and Railways Department. August 1921 found differing community views vigorously debated at the RSL national conference. The meeting resolved the issue with a two-part formula reminiscent of 1916 celebrations in Cairo: a morning solemn with compulsory military force parades including children, and an afternoon reserved for 'sports and celebrations as become Australia's National Day'.[24] The RSL approach—consistent with its sympathies, some would say—contained a prescriptive element (soon dropped) but was otherwise in harmony with broader community attitudes.

E. G. Theodore's Queensland Labor government legislated in the spring session for a 'national holiday' on 25 April, at the request of Canon O. J. Garland's Anzac Day Committee (headed by the Premier) and supported by the state RSL and the affiliated (Queensland) Returned Soldiers' Association. The legislation, based on a New Zealand model already in place, did not go as far as 'Sunday observance'; however, all liquor outlets would be closed and racing banned (thereby curtailing also the associated gambling), and Monday would be a holiday when 25 April fell on a Sunday. As in Western Australia, parliamentary debate was brief, indicating strong support. 'The Anzacs are the real saints', declared E. W. Fowles, member for Toowong.[25]

The federal government also took up the question. Hughes had ensured that, after repeal of the War Precautions Act in 1921, Defence Regulation Act statutory rules would continue to prevent misuse of the term *Anzac*, which would be reserved for formal public use and only with the Governor-General's permission. At the Premiers' Conference in October 1921 Hughes secured agreement that Anzac Day would be observed on 25 April, irrespective of the day of the week on which it fell, as a holiday uniform throughout the country. At the same time, on the vexed issue of holidays in general, he proposed including Anzac Day in a standard nine days, the fewest observed by any one state.[26] Recognising where consensus already lay, the Commonwealth later invited the states and leading religious bodies to co-operate in a fitting observance of Anzac Day 1922 with memorial services in the morning. They 'generally complied'.[27]

But there was no stampede by the states to implement the premiers' agreement. Queensland's Labor government had added another to its existing fourteen public holidays, which included four saints' days. Elsewhere, employer groups were reluctant to proliferate holidays for which under many awards workers would have to be paid.

South Australia had generally celebrated Anzac Day on the nearest Sunday. In November 1922 Sir Henry Barwell's conservative government essayed a reduction of public holidays from eleven to nine (jettisoning the Prince of Wales's Birthday and the King's Accession Day), but such was the weight of public opinion that his proposal inadvertently opened the door to an Anzac Day holiday. William J. Denny, a prominent Catholic lawyer and pre-war Labor state minister who had been severely wounded and won the Military Cross at Ypres in September 1917, now argued: 'We make a greater declaration of loyalty in Australia than they do in Great Britain. . . . [We] observe the King's Accession Day and the Prince of Wales' Birthday [but] Anzac Day is not a holiday. . . . I don't think Anzac Day should be regarded as a day of piety. The spirit of the Anzacs did not run in that direction. . . . Holidays should . . . chiefly . . . commemorat[e] great Australian events.' During committee stages, a telegram from 'General Monash', pressure from the local RSL branch backed by South Australian church groups and information that Hughes was a 'sympathetic helper' clinched the matter. 'Against the vote of the Government', South Australia would now have ten statutory holidays, including Anzac Day.[28]

The most populous and pluralist states, Victoria and New South Wales, together with Tasmania, had not yet reached the political consensus for a statutory Anzac holiday, but public support was consolidating. C. W. Oakes, acting New South Wales premier, perceived that in 1923 'throughout Australia, particularly in New South Wales and Queensland, [there] was a far better recognition of the spirit of Anzac Day than any previous celebration'. His government had inched towards the issue by amending legislation to empower the state to close hotels.[29]

In mid-1923 at another Commonwealth/state conference, Prime Minister S. M. Bruce, leader of the Nationalist–Country Party coalition, observed that whether commemoration should be on 25 April or the nearest Sunday had been the subject of 'divergent representations ... from manufacturers in one State from in another ... and ... division of opinion is evident in all classes of the community ... [but] the preponderance of representations made to me is certainly in favour of observance on the 25th April'. By now the RSL was calling also for a ban on trading, industry and gambling similar to that on Sundays, though only until one o'clock. Some state leaders feared that 'sentiment attached to the occasion [was] diminishing'. They all saw a need to impress the lessons of Anzac on young people. This time, going further than in 1921, they agreed that Anzac Day should be 'Australia's national day' and uniformly observed, the morning devoted to religious and memorial services and the afternoon not to the sports wanted by the RSL but to suitable addresses, notably for instilling in children's minds awareness of the day's significance. At the same time, state leaders insisted that the proposed core group of common holidays be increased to ten with up to another four at the governments' discretion.[30]

Again, however, despite the premiers' resolve, Anzac Day 1924 was not uniformly observed. Though it was widely celebrated throughout Australia as a 'public holiday', many commercial enterprises remained open, some conceding a few minutes silence at 11 a.m.[31]

Sir George Fuller's non-Labor government in New South Wales began moves in August 1924 to legislate for a bank holiday on 25 April; the Prince of Wales's Birthday holiday (taken on Monday when it fell on Sunday) would be abandoned. But this provoked anger from an unusual alliance of loyal monarchists and industrial workers. The former ranged from those objecting to 'gratuitous affront to the eldest son of the King' to those simply uneasy that celebrating Anzac Day was disloyal to the 'Old Country'.[32] Mark Davidson, a radical bush worker from the far western electorate of Sturt, expressed the other viewpoint: 'I do not think there are sufficient holidays. I do not mind whether a holiday is called Anzac Day or Prince of Wales' holiday, so long as it is a holiday.... we want to set aside a universal [recognised industrial] holiday for all workers in the Commonwealth.' Carlo Lazzarini, a moderate Labor man, strongly objected to loss of the Prince of Wales's Birthday but agreed that an Anzac Day holiday would commemorate 'the great day that will ever reflect honor on this country'. Many still wanted Anzac Day celebrated on the Sunday nearest 25 April. This issue, and that of retaining the Prince of Wales's Birthday holiday, on which cabinet was divided, were keenly fought in upper-house debates, and moves in committee stages to reinstate the Prince of Wales's Birthday failed only narrowly. The bill became law in November 1924.[33]

During debate, the form of Anzac Day observance had been much canvassed. Some, like James Dooley, the Catholic, Irish-born former Labor premier, wanted Anzac Day to be 'a holy day in the strictest sense of the term' with the same ban on public entertainment as on Good Friday and Christmas Day. So did C. H. Murphy, an ex-AIF Labor backbencher active in the RSL: 'Anzac Day is slowly but surely ceasing to be observed in the sacred way it was observed eight or nine years ago.... Many of the rising generation do not know anything about Anzac Day.'[34] The government obliged, bringing in a bill that would close hotels and prohibit racing. But it provoked marked division. Frank Burke, Labor member for the inner Sydney electorate of Botany, did not want a day of mourning. Nor did the leader of the conservative Progressive Party, Lieutenant-Colonel M. F. Bruxner, who had been wounded at Gallipoli. He wanted people free to celebrate Anzac Day as they wished,[35] and so did many other returned men. The existing practice of keeping hotels closed until 'dinner time' (1 p.m.) and having the co-operation of racing authorities achieved suitable solemnity. The 'most bitter opponents' of the bill were the state RSL and the affiliated state Returned Soldiers' Association, which did not want an Anzac Day like Good Friday. Because of their opposition, the bill did not go through the Legislative Council.[36]

Labor under J. T. Lang won the elections of May 1925. In September Lang incited intense anger by a bill providing that when Anzac Day fell on Sunday (which would happen in 1926) the following day would be a bank holiday (as in Western Australia, South Australia and Queensland). Carlo Lazzarini, now Colonial Secretary, affirmed that Fuller had 'robbed the workers of the State of a holiday when it transferred the Prince of Wales' Birthday holiday to Anzac Day'. Objections flared briefly. Lang was denounced for attempts 'to degrade the name of Anzac'. Bruxner was irate, and John Lee, a Nationalist wounded while in the AIF, claimed the 'Government apparently [was] determined to destroy every phase of loyalty and regard for the memory of those who laid down their lives'. Sir Thomas Henley, a minister in the Fuller government, condemned the 'insult to those who regard Anzac Day as a sacred day'. Lazzarini joined battle, observing that the Returned Soldiers' Association executive regarded the amendment as 'a measure of justice'.[37] The bill became law on 2 December 1925.

In Melbourne, seat of the federal government, the *Age* on 17 April 1925 lamented that, each Anzac Day, 'bitter discord . . . made a mockery of the solemn ceremony' on what should be 'Australia's national day'. In the event, the tenth anniversary of Anzac Day, in Victoria as elsewhere, was more impressive than ever. On this Saturday, parades held for the first time in all capital cities established this as a permanent feature of the occasion.

Victoria's march, the first of returned men rather than regular troops, was headed by Sir John Monash and had been organised by the RSL's Anzac Day Commemoration Council. An *Age* leading article commented: 'The ceremonies . . . were beautifully appropriate. . . . Anzac Day is now forever memorable in our national calendar, successfully established as a national holy day.'[38]

Under public pressure the Country-National coalition government led by John Allan promised to legislate for a solemn public holiday. Victoria's particular difficulty was that Eight Hour Day usually fell in the same week, causing a 'complete upset of business',[39] but Chief Secretary Stanley Argyle, with memories of AIF in Cairo hospitals, believed it was time Victorians made up their minds. A bill introduced in September 1925, backed by the Anzac Day Commemoration Council, which Monash now chaired, and by the RSL, had bipartisan support for establishing a solemn and 'close' Anzac public holiday: newspapers, shops, factories and theatres would not operate, nor would hotels (except for travellers over twenty miles), and races would be banned; a Monday holiday in lieu of Sunday was provided.[40] Debate produced expositions of the Anzac ethos but also exposed continuing differences of view. Arthur Hughes, the member for Grenville, who had fought at Pozières, did not want Anzac Day singled out, because he thought Australian soldiers had shown even greater courage in several battles on the Western Front. Some were concerned about militarism: Gordon Webber, later a minister without portfolio in three state Labor governments, wanted to commemorate the day peace was declared rather than Anzac Day, which he feared would celebrate war; he also wanted commemoration on Sunday so workers would not lose a day's pay.[41] Argument whether workers should be paid for the holiday provoked the government to list state Wages Board decisions (and also Commonwealth awards) already including this provision. A move to observe Anzac Day on the fourth Sunday in April, predominantly reflecting business interests, was defeated on the voices after long debate. In acrimonious crossfire between those who had volunteered and those who had not, justification by the latter on grounds of advanced years was met by taunts about not volunteering for the Boer War. Returned soldiers in the lower house were divided on the form the holiday should take, and a free vote was allowed.[42] The bill became law in November 1925, providing for the nation's strictest Anzac Day observance in a state with a long record of powerful Protestant influence on public policy.

Shortly afterwards, Tasmania, where the significance of the Gallipoli landing took on a more Imperial tinge,[43] also passed Anzac Day legislation. By this stage in Tasmania, as elsewhere across the country, Australia's 'national day' had eclipsed continued loyal observance of the officially inspired annual celebration of patriotic spirit—Empire Day, 24 May, an occasion originated by a British peer and introduced to Australia in 1905. The Hobart *Mercury* thought the city had probably never seen a more 'impressive parade and service than the inspiring ceremony' on Anzac Day 1925. The words of a Charles Dickens character, Sydney Carton—'I shall hold a sanctuary in all their hearts'—expressed the nation's regard for 'one of the most cherished sentiments in Australian experience', the 'glorious tradition of Gallipoli'. Following this tenth anniversary, public sentiment overrode the Chamber of Commerce, which for years had wanted observance on the nearest Sunday, to provide in the Shops Act of December 1925 for closure of retail outlets on Anzac Day. An amendment of the Banks Holidays Act in 1927 reflected the new equilibrium in public sympathies: the business community, opposed to increasing the number of statutory holidays, was prepared to displace the King's Birthday in favour of Anzac Day.[44]

State parliamentary debates in the first half of the 1920s confirmed the profound significance of Anzac. Everywhere this 'national day' had become a statutory holiday, the 'one day of the year' honouring all Australian soldiers who died during the war, not only those lost at Gallipoli. Everywhere the form of observance drew a distinction between this day and the central Christian religious holidays, sacred in a different way. The ritual of national celebration differed little from state to state—marches to war memorials, silences and speeches at ecumenical services, reunions and hearty drinking with comrades, editorials and broadcasts. Special ceremonies for schoolchildren etched the minds of the 'rising generation'. A new element adopted widely by the early thirties, and inaugurated at Sydney's cenotaph in 1927,[45] was the moving 'dawn service' marking the very time of the landing.

Inevitably some features of early Anzac celebrations could not survive. In 1923 six hundred thronged the federal Government House ballroom, where Lady Chauvel presided at Lady Rachel Forster's 'usual gathering of Bereaved Mothers and Widows'. Monash enriched Victoria's activities in the early 1920s. On Anzac Day 1923, in a 'stirring address' in Wilson Hall to over a thousand members of the University of Melbourne, he pointed out that while the landing as a military feat did not compare with what was done later in the war, 'the landing was the keynote . . . a tangible inspiration during dark moments in 1917', memorable because it founded AIF tradition and first put Australia on 'the stage of history'. He offered the judgement that raising an overseas expeditionary force of 330,000 would have been impossible but for the drama of the landing which stirred people to their 'utmost efforts'.[46]

But twenty-three years after the first anniversary there was little sign of waning public sentiment. Western Australia in 1939 was typical, continuing to celebrate Imperial ties on Empire Day with a twenty-one-gun salute but otherwise largely at private functions, whereas Anzac Day was the major public and national event. Record crowds watched the Perth march. Fifty-four thousand attended the main service on the Esplanade, and over ten thousand people participated in the sacred dawn service. All shops and other business houses, including hotels, were closed all day. Picture theatres and motor service stations opened at noon. Flags flown at half mast in the morning were raised to the masthead at 11.03 a.m. after two

*Horace Moore-Jones, The man with the donkey, 1917 (water-colour, 102.6 × 75.3 cm). Moore-Jones painted this in New Zealand from a photo-graph taken at Galli-poli of the man who stepped into Simpson's shoes after his death on 19 May 1915. Young Australians became very familiar with the story about this man of compassion from their school magazines.*

minutes silence in the service at the state memorial in King's Park. In 1939 the day corresponded with a threatening international crisis. 'Should our worst fears be realised,' stated the *West Australian*, 'young Australians of today [might] be invited to follow the example of the men of Anzac and enrol for service overseas'; Anzac Day, 'comparable in some respects' to 14 July for France and 4 July for the United States, reminded Australia of 'the combination of idealism and self-sacrifice, an essential attribute of democratic nationhood'. The paper predicted it would 'still be commemorated . . . when there [were no Anzacs] left to march on the parade ground'.

Certainly returned men themselves remembered dead comrades and the fighting. They also had a proud volunteer and strongly egalitarian and masculine military tradition to celebrate.[47] Experiences could be shared at the precious Anzac Day ritual and at a multitude of other Gallipoli reunions. At an RSL club in country New South Wales or the Army and Navy Club in London's West End, the mistakes and 'lost opportunities' of a campaign against 'the flower of the Turkish army' would be recalled and debated. Australian veterans were not the only ones to remember: over many years on the anniversary of 'Gallipoli Day', the British 29th Division, which had fought other severe battles on the Western Front, held a parade and dinner. Gallipoli naval and military commanders often attended. They, together with political leaders, also contributed to remembrance with many books and addresses defending their role in the tragedy. Hamilton missed few opportunities to vindicate his role as commander-in-chief of the Mediterranean Expeditionary Force. But his critics included one who thought he needed 'a hide tougher than a rhinoceros' to go round post-war England unveiling Anzac memorials and, in 1927, Sir Thomas Mackenzie, the wartime New Zealand High Commissioner, who deplored talk about the Gallipoli campaign: the 'arch enemies to success . . . [had been] the many incompetent men' involved.[48] In 1929 the federal RSL did not pursue a suggestion that Hamilton be invited to visit Australia.

Australians thinking about the campaign have until recent times focused strongly on the national deeds of their own men to the exclusion of wider military and political questions, as reflected in 1926 when the RSL president flatly rejected a notion originating in Britain that Australia's celebration be renamed 'Gallipoli Day'.[49] Nevertheless, being the source of the Anzac ethos, Gallipoli as a place was always very important. There are 7,247 Australian war graves on the peninsula. The War Graves Imperial Commission had already begun work there in 1919, when the *Argus* reported: 'Trenches have become overgrown with shrubs and flowers. It is hoped . . . next spring everything will be in readiness for those able to . . . make a pilgrimage to Gallipoli.'[50] Visiting the old familiar sites became a tradition for British ex-servicemen as well as for Australians seeking in particular to be present for Anzac Day. Notable Australian visits occurred on the fortieth and fiftieth anniversaries. T. S. Louch, a corporal at the Anzac landing and a brigadier in the Second World War, thought the beachhead—with some obvious exceptions—looked very much in 1955 as in 1915. His 'memory of what happened at Anzac [was] far more vivid than of any experiences later on in that war, or even the second war'. In the decades since then, with veterans themselves unable to make this journey, civilians as well as soldiers are maintaining the tradition of visiting that barren, isolated cove virtually destitute of population but wreathed with memorials to events and deeds of national importance.

Turkey's benign reception of Australian visits has supported the tradition of

*The tradition of visiting Anzac has maintained a physical link with Gallipoli. At this early service in Anzac Cove on 25 April 1923 there were many diggers in uniform and even one of the horses brought from Australia in 1914 by the 6th Light Horse.*

respect for the Ottoman soldier carried away from Gallipoli by the AIF.[51] So too have awareness that the dogged foe at Anzac was commanded by the founder of modern Turkey, Mustafa Kemal, and Turkey's subsequent unambiguous Western alignment. But only lately has 'the landing' been recognised more clearly in Australia also as an 'invasion' whose defeat by Turkey, its first of a European power in living memory,[52] is part of its own national tradition. Turkey fought five major campaigns during the Great War and eventually lost them all except for Gallipoli. Annual commemoration of the Gallipoli conflict, especially victory over the British and French navies at Çanakkale in March 1915, relives for Turkey an episode in war among the great powers which precipitated nation building.[53]

Recently AIF and Turkish traditions have been eloquently intertwined. Mustafa Kemal's tribute in 1934 to dead opponents on the peninsula recorded at Quinn's Post was inscribed on a plaque at Brisbane's Gallipoli Fountains of Honour opened in 1978. 'Those heroes that shed their blood and lost their lives . . . You are now lying in the soil of a friendly country. Therefore rest in peace. There is no difference between the Johnnies and the Mehmets to us where they lie side by side here in this country of ours. . . .' The Fountains Appeal Committee chairman, Alan Campbell, himself a Gallipoli light-horseman, wrote to the director of the Turkish Historical Society, Ulug Igdemir: 'We always held your soldiers in high respect and admired their great courage. On Gallipoli we could not understand how [they] survived the very heavy bombardments by the English naval guns.' Later, at the suggestion of the Australian League of Gallipoli Veterans, Australia agreed with Turkey that the unnamed bay where Anzacs landed in 1915 should officially become Anzac Cove and in return that the entry to Albany harbour and part of Canberra's Lake Burley Griffin foreshore be named Ataturk Entrance and Gallipoli Reach respectively. A memorial stone at Anzac Cove and a monument in Ataturk Memorial Gardens near the Australian War Memorial in Canberra unveiled on the seventieth Anzac Day each carry Atatürk's words.[54] Nothing similar has been done for other former Australian enemies, Germany and Japan.

Charles Bean recognised in 1941 that AIF traditions laid down at Gallipoli could fade with changing conditions. But he, like other observers before and since, would acknowledge the persistent grip of Anzac on the public imagination. In a letter to a fellow historian in 1962 he wrote, 'Gallipoli never dies.'[55] Certainly there was continuing controversy over strategy and leadership of the campaign, particularly in Britain, but also there was the palpable phenomenon of Anzac celebration. In Australia, loss of life carved deeply, the maimed being a living reminder. Some fifty thousand members of the AIF, from a population of less than five million, served at Anzac. About the same number served over some ten years in Vietnam, but deaths in the entire Vietnam conflict were almost certainly exceeded by Australian losses on the first day at Anzac. The Gallipoli campaign itself was a distinctive experience for all who served there, particularly for Australians. The constant fighting—the sniping and often ferocious hand-bomb exchanges—was geographically confined in terrain overlooked by the enemy; there was scope for individual enterprise with victory seeming 'so tantalisingly close', for informal army life and for strong mateship, but not for proper leave from a battleground of incessant conflict and wasting disease.[56] Beginning, unusually, as an amphibious assault, the action on the small beachhead was soon thought of as a unique military operation. No forgotten sideshow, that remote battlefield devoid of civilians earned high Imperial praise for Australian men-at-arms in national contingents. For Australia, recently created from a congeries of separate colonies, the 'baptism' of 25 April aroused pride in national identity among its participants and among the Australian public at large, pride perhaps the more exhilarating for a sense of 'rebirth' from a divided colonial past and mute shame about convict origins.[57]

*Another well-known photograph from the Gallipoli campaign which has often been used to depict the image of Anzac. It shows 1st Brigade men in Turkish Lone Pine trenches.*

Ken Inglis in an elegant discussion has traced evolution of the Anzac military tradition down the decades—through the questioning articulated in Alan Seymour's 1960s play, *The One Day of the Year*, and symbolised in 1987 when Vietnam veterans, who included conscripts and who had long felt they had been denied public honour, for the first time led Anzac Day marches. Vietnam was no glorious crusade within an Imperial framework but 'a messy Australian implication in a huge American failure'.[58] Australia's Vietnam commitment could be seen as impugning rather than defining the national identity recognised in 1915.

Indeed, the Gallipoli element in the Anzac Day of the multicultural and more feminised 1980s seems fainter. It is still a truly national day but without the same rush of patriotic spirit. The style of observance also shows the impact of change. In Victoria no less than elsewhere, prohibitions have given way before more liberal social attitudes. Yet although the hold of Anzac on the Australian psyche is not as profound now as in years gone by, a vigorous 'Gallipoli industry' in print and on film and television shows the episode continues to have relevance for a much later generation. Anzac Day itself, Australia-wide, maintains the duality of the earliest anniversaries with a solemn morning ceremony and afternoon camaraderie, and annually in schools the tradition of the Gallipoli landing is seeded afresh in the minds of Australian children. Distilled as the essence of Australia's reaction to the landing so many years before, Anzac Day remains the 'one day of the year' for commemoration of service and sacrifice in the nation's conflicts, in no present danger of being displaced from the national calendar.

# CHAPTER 36

# WAS IT WORTH WHILE?

*T*HE NOTION that the 'Anzac legend' was 'created' by Charles Bean or was a figment of his imagination seems to be becoming fashionable among a younger generation of historians. The evidence in this book shows conclusively that this attitude does not accord with the facts. Eliminate Bean's writing from the story, and the same picture emerges of bravery, recklessness, a cynical or disrespectful attitude towards authority outside battle, stern discipline under fire, and so on.

The creators of the Anzac legend were, of course, the men themselves. A wide variety of observers cited in this book, who perhaps never heard of Bean or had not known of him when they wrote, expressed high respect for Australians at Gallipoli. Bean was important as the main transmitter, particularly to Australian civilians, of the Anzac legend. Even here Bean was not alone, as several books considered in the appendix show. Private British sources also provide very persuasive evidence of most of the normally accepted features of the Anzac legend. War naturally promotes hyperbole, but so many observers wrote about Australian skill and bravery in battle that their views cannot be dismissed. They were supported by some of their former opponents, including Dr Harry Stuermer.[1]

One wonders what qualifies people who have never experienced the rigours of campaigning or the terrifying savagery of battle to belittle the valour of those who have. Australians in 1915 were anxious to make a mark on the world and so were very receptive to the views of Ashmead-Bartlett, Masefield and others of like mind. With remarkable rapidity Australians enshrined these views in their national psyche. But it cannot be said that they exaggerated or misled each other. They simply drew inspiration from what had happened on the battlefield.

Of the various features of the Anzac legend, three merit special mention here. One is mateship. Friction must be expected to develop when many men are forced to live together in cramped ship accommodation or in what were rudimentary training camps which, though less cramped than ships, allowed men little privacy. It was amazing that friction was largely contained. Rough men learned to live together and to tolerate others, such as the sensitive but nonetheless soldierly Ellis Silas. Arrangements at Mena were more tolerable, for by that time, with tent accommodation giving more privacy, small group friendships had a chance to mature. As well, incompatible colleagues could be avoided. At Anzac men were again very cramped, but there were opportunities for friends to stay together, as portrayed in Peter Weir's poignant film *Gallipoli*. Moreover, heroic acts by a disliked fellow soldier naturally weakened antipathies. Battlefield dangers encouraged mateship. Monash even declared that the bonds of mateship virtually stamped out all possibility of cowardice, and Leonard Mann's novel *Flesh in Armour* has exemplified this perhaps extravagant claim.[2] Nonetheless, this mateship was real, and it continued in post-war gatherings and commemorations.

*Sidney Nolan*, Young Soldier *(above), and* Head *(right), 1977 (acrylic on hardboard, 122 × 91.5 cm). Sidney Nolan once commented: 'You grew up with Anzac, not so much a fact of life; it was just part of one's existence.' During his stay on the Greek island of Hydra in 1955–56 he began working on a series of Gallipoli paintings. He was inspired by Homeric legend, but he also visited the actual battlefields and used contemporary photographs for his paintings.*

Next to consider are the attitudes of other ranks towards officers. There is no evidence in the letters and diaries of a generalised dislike or distrust of officers. Despite some sarcasm and irreverence about some of Birdwood's public statements, this English general was popular with the AIF. His popularity with the troops was helped by his modest headquarters on Gallipoli being so close to the front and exposed to enemy fire, and by his frequent visits to the firing line. It has been said that Birdwood never returned from these visits with an accurate account of the location of each company in the front line, perhaps indicating that the visits were primarily public relations exercises by a general whose military skills have yet to be impartially assessed. Other generals have been criticised for being aloof, whereas Birdwood was accepted—irrespective of the professional military dimension—for being pleasant, considerate, forthcoming and cheerful. The tumultuous reception he received in Australia during a six-month 'tour of splendid memory' in 1919–20, along with other evidence, testifies to that.[3]

Similarly, junior and medium-ranking officers were accepted on their merits. A brave, cheerful, competent and compassionate officer was greatly admired by those he commanded. Particular officers attracted criticism; others were highly praised. As early as June, Private Richards of the Australian Army Medical Service analysed two broad types. Those who took 'the high and mighty disciplinarian stand', he thought, were wrong. The men were volunteers who had proved themselves so easy to handle and willing to work, whether on fatigues or in battle, that officers could best exercise authority by kindness and homeliness among these free and easy warriors.[4] Of course, this is not to say that there were no incompetent officers at Anzac. Antill and Hughes were obvious examples. There were others, but many of these, fortunately, were removed from the battlefield before they could do much harm.

Much of this book relates to the third of the Anzac legend themes, its inspiring effect on the steady development of Australian nationalism and the subtle changes in its intricate relationship with Empire loyalty. Letters of the time amply show growing awareness of Australian self-reliance and confidence amounting to a sense of nationhood. Statements by public figures that Australia became a nation on the shores of Gallipoli are of course on the plane of symbolism but relate to a national identity felt and generated by the deeds of a force genuinely representative of Australia. A community does not become a nation on a single day but through steady growth on a wide variety of fronts over a long time. Nonetheless, some single days can legitimately be regarded as more important than others in spurring national self-awareness and self-esteem. Whether other days, such as 8 August 1918, or brief periods such as February 1942 (the fall of Singapore) or August–September 1942 (the Kokoda campaign) are inherently more important is in a sense irrelevant. Anzac Day has pride of place because it is the first of these and because it saw a highly meritorious military achievement. Its symbolic and substantial significance did *not* primarily stem from the tragic loss of life, as some current-day moralists declare. It arose because for the first time Australians made a spectacular and praiseworthy contribution, recognised as such by some great powers, to the course of world history—and that in a conflict of surpassing importance rather than in some insignificant human pursuit.

Australian self-reliance naturally affected the complex relationship with the British Empire, despite the strong Imperial sentiments expressed by many Australians after the first Anzac Day. Thus the *Newcastle Morning Herald* on 26 November 1915 began an editorial rejoicing that 'one great result of the war will be to cement the whole of the British Empire in firmer bonds'. Empire Day and Trafalgar Day remained important occasions for celebration, and Australian achievements in battle were seen as a rebirth of the spirit of Marlborough, Wellington, Drake and Nelson. Some people in Britain saw it the same way, declaring, 'We of the old country proudly recognise that the stock bred under the Southern Cross are the true sons' of Britons who fought bravely and successfully in earlier wars.[5]

Both Empire loyalists and Australian nationalists tried to appropriate the Anzac legend to their side—seen, for example, in speeches during Birdwood's tour in 1919–20. Probably most Australians in the immediate post-war years saw no incompatibility between Empire loyalty and Australian nationalism. The latter could live comfortably within the Imperial ambit. Nonetheless, there was a spectrum of feeling ranging from those who definitely adhered to anti-British aspects of the Anzac legend, to the great bulk who saw little or no tension and regarded Australia as a special case within the British Empire, and those who had strong, if not prime, loyalties to the Empire which they usually interpreted to mean Great Britain. With the passage of decades, of course, and as the Empire disappeared, the first ethos steadily overtook the other two.

It was noteworthy that the lack of respect felt by Australians for so many English soldiers and officers did not have a devastating effect on their loyalty to Empire. Australians were intelligent enough, or else so conditioned by their upbringing, to distinguish between the entity of Empire and the unworthiness of so many of its sons. To an extent, Australian soldiers showed meritorious freedom from prejudice in their attitudes towards Britons, generally assessing them as individuals to be commended or denounced according to their qualities. Not the only instance of this, but the most notable, was the attitude towards Birdwood. To some in 1914 he could have seemed destined for an uneasy relationship with his 'wild colonial corps'. The subsequent harmonious relationship reflected credit both on

Birdwood's relaxed personality and good sense and on Australian readiness to accept a man on his merits, whatever his origins. Indeed, in this case the general's merits were exaggerated by the soldiers. His empathy with the troops was strikingly evidenced by the astounding welcome he received from returned men on his Australian tour. For all the complexity of the relationship, there was not the slightest doubt that Anzac Day, reinforced by other events of the war, set Australian nationalism on a new course, which after that steadily diverged from Empire loyalties, with no significant reversal of the trend.

To move from the world of sentiment to that of actualities, a major result of a growing sense of nationhood was the Australian government's attempts to make the AIF organisation and command more independent of Britain. We have seen that attempt in the case of medical services, but in other areas of the AIF similar moves were made to have its tasks planned and controlled by Australian officers directly and unequivocally responsible to the Australian government. Complaints about important AIF field commands going to British officers instead of to allegedly more capable Australians became common from 1915 and persisted for decades in the Australian armed forces.

Regarding the campaign itself, in military terms was the Australian heroism and sacrifice at Gallipoli worth while? In the simplest sense, the result indicates that it was not. But there is no doubt that, as an ally of Germany and a potential threat to the Empire's interests in Egypt, particularly the Suez Canal, Turkey was a legitimate target for an attack by the Empire's forces. So the wisdom of conducting such an enterprise remains a reasonable question.

It has to be recognised that even if faultlessly planned, the peninsula campaign may not have been worth while. The Turks, stiffened by Germans, could still have barred the way to Constantinople, aided by topography and a war technology favourable to the defensive. As it was, the ground chosen by the attackers greatly assisted the enemy.

Apologists for the campaign make several claims for it, the main ones being that it came close to success, that had an English fleet pushed through the Dardanelles it would have overawed Turkey into suing for peace, that a Balkan front could have been established, and that the campaign so weakened the Turkish army as to contribute to the Ottoman Empire's eventual defeat.

Despite Churchill's claims about the 'terrible ifs', and opportunities missed by British commanders in August, there is no real evidence that the Allied forces came close to breaking the Turkish lines and moving on to Constantinople. The Allied advance would have been aided had the British fleet steamed relatively unscathed through the straits and reached the Golden Horn, but Turkey might not have collapsed. Certainly, the fleet could have destroyed Turkey's only munitions works on the coast near Constantinople, ending resistance in European Turkey, but fighting quite likely would have continued in the Ottoman Empire's much larger Asiatic territories. Although Turkey could have been hampered by inadequate munitions supplies, a campaign would still have had to be fought there to ensure its defeat.

As to the chimera of the Balkan Alliance, there is no doubt that several states in the region were desperately anxious to join the winning side and participate in the spoils of war. But to ensure they joined the Entente, not only the Gallipoli campaign but more importantly Russian campaigns on the Eastern Front, to which Balkan states looked, also needed to be successful. In the event, setbacks to the Russian campaigns encouraged Bulgaria to enter the war on Germany's side—with disastrous consequences for Serbia. Besides, a solid Balkan military alliance would always have been problematic given the hatreds existing between the various Balkan nations and their competition for territorial gain.

Of all the apologists' claims, the most credible is that the Gallipoli campaign contributed to the eventual weakening and defeat of the Ottoman army. Liman von Sanders' 5th Turkish Army has been judged probably the best the Ottomans ever put into the field. Yet it suffered more casualties than its opponents. The Yildirim (Lightning) army later organised in Asiatic Turkey was thought to be inferior to the 5th Army, and there is no reason to doubt this, although General Townshend's fiasco in Mesopotamia in 1916 indicates that the Turks retained the capacity to profit from their opponents' mistakes. Some enemy assessments agreed with the apologists' attitude, as can be seen in the appendix, and T. E. Lawrence, who could have no vested interest in exaggerating the importance of the Dardanelles campaign, gave support to the view that 'the remaining Ottoman first-line army was destroyed' in the Gallipoli 'slaughterhouse', which made it easier for the Arabian revolt to register victories.[6]

The apologists do not explore whether the flower of the Turkish army could have been more easily destroyed had the attackers chosen a campaigning area which did not give such great advantage to the defenders. An alternative approach, along the lines considered by the CID paper of 1906, could have been through Sinai and Palestine, based on the Suez Canal. This approach may have provided better opportunity for enterprise, initiative, deception and the use of a modicum of intelligence in creating a war of manoeuvre than was possible on the cramped, rugged Gallipoli Peninsula. It also would have allowed closer liaison with Lawrence and the Arabs and permitted better use of the Australian light horse, instead of its being squandered on stupid infantry assaults. No doubt Hamilton would have been better suited in a more traditional, less unfamiliar, war of manoeuvre, although this is not to suggest that he could have been as successful as General Allenby in 1917–18. However, had Turkey not been decisively defeated in Syria, the problems presented by a campaign through the Amanus and Taurus mountains in Anatolia would probably have ruled this out.

Casualty figures for the forces on Gallipoli are not precise, and there is now no chance of obtaining complete accuracy. Kannengiesser claims that the Ottomans committed 310,000 men (probably an underestimate) to the campaign and the Allies 539,000 (most likely an overestimate). By far the greater proportion of these were contributed by the British Empire—468,987, according to one source. Several thousand Germans also participated in the campaign or manned the Dardanelles forts or gave logistic support of some kind.[7] One Turkish estimate is that its Gallipoli army suffered 289,000 casualties (killed, wounded, ill, missing and prisoners), but this figure seems excessively high, at over 90 per cent of the total committed, if Kannengiesser's figure is accepted. A more official—although not necessarily more accurate—Turkish estimate still puts the total loss at well over half, 186,829 men, of whom 100,177 were wounded and 21,498 died from illness. The Anzac, or Ari Burnu, front accounted for somewhat under one-third of those killed, wounded and missing. Turkish losses in the August battles were about 50,000, compared with 58,000 in the series of slaughters at Helles from April to July.[8]

Thousands of Allied soldiers had illnesses, but only an infinitesimal number died as a result, compared with the heavy Turkish death-rate. Turkish official accounts grossly exaggerate the Allied losses, at 216,000 British and 115,000 French.[9] A more reliable figure is that 5,053 British Empire officers and 114,676 men were killed, wounded or taken prisoner, a casualty rate of about 25 per cent. Of this, the numbers (probably quite an accurate estimate) for Australian losses are 7,594 dead (compared with 2,431 New Zealanders), and total casualties of 27,594. About 50,000 is the commonly accepted figure for the number of AIF personnel who served on Gallipoli. Thus over half were casualties—many of them lightly wounded or sick—while just over 15 per cent died. If the above figures are correct, the AIF suffered a casualty rate twice that of British Empire forces as a whole. This could be partly explained by the average Australian's more active fighting role, and partly by the fact that cramped Anzac was more dangerous and unhealthy than the comparatively spacious Helles and Suvla beachheads. French losses amounted to some 27,000, of whom 3,706 died, heavily concentrated in the first three weeks of the fighting. About 79,000 men served at Gallipoli in French units, so their death rate was about one-third that of the Australians.

If the Gallipoli campaign was not worth while in military terms, was it equally pointless to make a great sacrifice to ensure that the proud and powerful, aggressive, militarist and intolerant Germany of the early twentieth century did not win the war? Some Australians now tend to believe that Australia's national interests did not justify participation in the war. This belief is induced perhaps more by feelings of revulsion at the deplorable diplomacy which precipitated the war and at the horrors of the fighting than by sensible assessment of the penalties of defeat. Such views are probably advanced by those who know little of the writings and influence of Heinrich von Treitschke or General Friedrich von Bernhardi, although presumably they are aware of Friedrich Nietzsche. All three wrote against a background of venerable German tradition. Carl von Clausewitz, the early nineteenth-century military theorist, still 'supreme' as an analyst of war and an important reference for scholars and practitioners, wrote in his text *On War*: 'A people and nation can hope for a strong position in the world only if national character and familiarity with war fortify each other by continual interaction.'[10]

Treitschke, a member of the Reichstag from 1871 and professor of history in Berlin from 1874, did more than anyone else to shape the minds of the rising generation of his countrymen. Even Prince von Bulow, German Chancellor from 1900 to 1909, privately enthused about Treitschke's patriotic writings before he entered high office, where he pursued an aggressive foreign policy in various areas, including the Balkans, the Ottoman Empire and the Pacific. A strong advocate of colonial expansion, a bitter enemy of Great Britain, and a supporter of attacks on Jews which began in 1878, Treitschke violently denounced all opinions and parties that hindered the growth of German power. As an influential patriotic historian, he was largely responsible for the bitter anti-British feeling of German chauvinism in the last years of the nineteenth century. He always insisted that Germany's 'final reckoning' would be with Britain.[10]

Treitschke's attitudes gained support of a kind from the teaching of the philosopher Friedrich Nietzsche, who became world famous in the late 1890s. Nietzsche argued that all human behaviour could be reduced to a single basic drive, the will to power. Some Germans held that this political philosophy justified Germany's growth and striving for European and even world dominance.[11]

Von Bernhardi's military writings also provoked much anti-British feeling in the years just before the Great War. He held that a European war was inevitable and that Germany must win or go under; so he advocated maximum possible rearmament. His *Germany and the Next War* (1911) was translated into English and widely read in the English-speaking world, where it helped persuade many of Germany's aggressive intent and indicated what England could expect if defeated. It provoked so much anti-German feeling in Britain that later General Ludendorff said it would have been better had the book never been written. There followed *How Germany Makes War* (1914). Bernhardi believed that war was 'a biological necessity', that 'might is right' and that 'war is the father of all things'. His views influenced Germans in positions of authority, supporting the build-up of that nation's army and navy which began before the turn of the century.

The great controversy in the 1960s between the eminent German historians

Fritz Fischer and Gerhardt Ritter, and their respective disciples, over Germany's war aims in the Great War threw up further evidence, if that were needed, to support Fischer's view that there was an essential continuity in German foreign policy from pre-1914 to the Nazi era. Fischer held that a victorious Germany in, say, 1918, would have been intent on profiting from the war at the expense of its victims.[13]

Australians professedly were fighting for high ideals in 1914–18. Most, even those who declined to enlist, would have believed in the lofty principles enunciated from time to time by their leaders and other public figures. They fought for defence of national freedom and integrity, way of life, standard of living and the well-being of their families and friends, as well as for the liberation of Belgium and France.

Even today scholars can legitimately doubt whether the world would have been a better place had Germany won the Great War. Granted Britain's war role was besmirched by the 'evils of secret diplomacy', but once the struggle had progressed for a few weeks or months it became important to win, for Australia's sake as much as for any Allied belligerent. The penalties for losing that war were great. Of the four defeated Central Powers, two lost their empires. Germany had to pay an indemnity, it lost its navy, its overseas empire, and some of its European territory. Foreign troops were stationed on its soil, and it was plunged into social turmoil and economic troubles which eventually led to even greater disaster. Under the Treaty of Neuilly (signed on 27 November 1919) Bulgaria was disarmed and compelled to pay a heavy indemnity; the Allied Reparations Commission had the power to control the nation's finances. Bulgaria also lost three hundred thousand of its population as some of its territory went to Greece, Romania and Yugoslavia, including the slice that had provided access to the Aegean Sea.

The harsh terms initially imposed on the Ottoman Empire were later moderated only as a result of the effectiveness of Kemal's nationalist movement. Under the Treaty of Sèvres in August 1920 France and Britain ensured that Turkey lost all its

*Totally unexpected cliffs: the ridge culminating in the Sphinx, the most distinctive landmark at Anzac. Photographed by John Robertson in 1986.*

Arab territories. As well, Turkey had to renounce its shadowy claim to suzerainty of many of its territories, including Egypt and Cyprus; and Greece was to assume control of parts of both European and Asiatic Turkey. The Allies sought to protect the lands and political freedoms of Turkish minorities such as Armenians and Kurds and to establish international control of the Dardanelles. The Turkish navy was severely reduced, the air force suppressed, and the army reduced to fifty thousand. Allied commercial interests were to be given a privileged position. Of particular concern to Australians, including those living today and still to be born, were the special provisions for the care of Allied war graves on Gallipoli.

The revitalised Turkish nationalist movement led by Kemal, who was outraged by the Treaty of Sèvres, crushingly defeated invading Greek forces in 1921 and 1922 and won more favourable terms under the Treaty of Lausanne signed in July 1923. This treaty, recognising Turkey's recovery and military victories, allowed it to retain some of its territory—relatively close to Constantinople and Angora—and demilitarised the Dardanelles without internationalising them. But Turkey essentially ceased to be the centre of an empire, because its Arab territory and subject races were not restored.

If the Allied powers, influenced by President Woodrow Wilson and French Premier Georges Clemenceau, imposed severe penalties on the vanquished, there is nothing to suggest that Germany and its allies would have been more liberal had *they* won the war. The harsh peace Prussia imposed upon France in 1871 and Germany upon Russia by the Treaty of Brest-Litovsk in March 1918, and the severe treatment of occupied Belgium and Poland from 1914 to 1918, strongly suggest that a victorious Germany would have imposed a punitive peace on the Entente powers. It is difficult to imagine a victorious Germany in 1918 offering a magnanimous treaty.

It would be possible, using much space, to run through a series of scenarios for differing degrees of success by Germany, but here it is necessary merely to consider briefly the implications for Australia of a German victory similar to that actually achieved by the Allies. The most obvious penalty would have been the destruction of the British Imperial system and disappearance of the Royal Navy, Australia's shield since the first settlement. Germany might not have spared the troops for occupation, but other penalties would have been imposed. It would have extracted reparations, not only for itself, but for its allies. Before the war, Bulgaria and the Ottoman Empire had much lower living standards than Australia, and those powers would have used all their influence to exact as much as possible from their relatively wealthy victim. Australia's standard of living would have fallen considerably. Most likely, trading restrictions inimical to Australian interests would have been applied and the control exercised by German firms before the war over Australia's metals industry would have been reinstated—without the pre-war legislative protection. The terms of a peace treaty might have geared Australia's economy to the needs of German industry and controlled other aspects of national policy, such as defence and immigration. Germany would certainly have resumed possession of its scattered island empire in the western and southwestern Pacific and would probably have acquired Australian New Guinea as well, localities of great strategic importance to Australia. Germany would have had one of the most powerful navies in the world, and Australia's security and development would have been at its mercy. If challenged by Japan, the way would have been open for eventual accommodation between Germany and Japan at Australia's expense. Anyone who thinks Australia could be indifferent to the issue of whether it was better to rely on Britain's help or to be an incident in German-Japanese great power rivalry is not qualified to think sensibly on Australian defence and foreign policy.

Those who declare that Australia's interests were not at stake in the Great War are victims of a strange amnesia. They cannot be actuated by an understanding of the issues or by any awareness of the fate of defeated countries. The men who served in the AIF were under no such illusions. They knew they were fighting an important struggle that had to be won to avoid disastrous consequences. These men sacrificed much for what they rightly considered a noble cause. It is sadly ironic that a later generation has doubted the value of their cause.

*A group of Anzacs at Gallipoli, June 1915.*

# GALLIPOLI: CONTINUING HISTORICAL CONTROVERSY

$C$ONTROVERSY OVER GALLIPOLI was far from over when the last British troops left in January 1916. Much of the lengthy argument has been conducted across the publisher's desk. Even before the war ended, patriotic encomiums and memoirs by fighting men and by lower-ranking officers appeared; after 1918, unofficial accounts from the trivial to the excellent followed—by politicians and military leaders, by Americans, and by Turkish, French and German participants. Official histories began to emerge in 1921. The flow of material that began in 1915 has not stopped since.

Readers of this literary plethora have a choice of approaches. The Australian predilection for focus on heroism and manly qualities (despite a reaction from younger scholars) contrasts with the central British interest—the enduring strategic argument which enthralls historians, military leaders and others. And the role of individual leaders has been matter for endless dispute. Churchill's unique role in the imbroglio was, of course, vigorously to promote the campaign, whereas Asquith and Kitchener merely declined to oppose it. It is remarkable that Asquith and Kitchener have been comparatively unscathed by this controversy; both, perhaps more in a passive sense than active sense, bear much responsibility for the Gallipoli venture. Asquith as prime minister could have vetoed it. Indeed he was ultimately culpable for any disaster befalling Britain's war policy. Kitchener could have refused to allow use of British troops. Nonetheless, Churchill figures in the literary battle somewhat more prominently than warranted even by his decisiveness and belief in his own judgement. A commanding, colourful personality and spectacularly successful later career saw to that.

The following survey does not deal with the high-quality scholarship on the diplomacy surrounding Turkey's entry into and participation in the war but concentrates on works by the generation that endured Gallipoli and on themes most germane to those covered in this book, seeking to expose the central controversy and guide the reader through material available. I follow established custom in allowing Churchill a prominence denied Asquith and Kitchener. We shall see what information was available to those wanting to know what 'really happened' at Gallipoli.

Granville Fortescue, an American former soldier and then London *Daily Telegraph* special correspondent, was first to publish with two books in 1915. *Russia, the Balkans and the Dardanelles* emphasised rival national interests in the Balkan imbroglio. Having spent time in Constantinople and the Dardanelles, Fortescue was much better informed and more sensible than Churchill with his pipe-dreams. His stylish, intelligent essay, *What of the Dardanelles? An Analysis*, trenchantly denounced elementary mistakes in Allied Dardanelles strategy. He was convinced that the Turks, helped by German expertise, had made the strait impregnable to any naval attack conceivable in 1915 or the immediate future.

Before the war ended, several Australians published memoirs or accounts of the campaign. They tended to romanticise. E. C. Buley had completed the manuscript for *Glorious Deeds of Australians in the Great War* as early as October 1915, having interviewed hundreds of soldiers in London hospitals. Buley portrayed the AIF as a 'democratic army', close to physical perfection, with officers chosen on ability, not social status. He identified units, dates and names used—including a Private Hogarth who averred, 'War is a great game, and I wouldn't have missed our scrap for all the tea in China.'[1]

Oliver Hogue landed at Gallipoli as a lieutenant in the 2nd Light Horse Brigade. *Trooper Bluegum at the Dardanelles* (1916), based on his regular *Sydney Morning Herald* articles, largely echoed Buley's sentiments. He could write 'all war is hell', yet glorify the 7th Battalion charge at Helles. He also displayed a paradoxical Australian love for the Empire alongside mild antagonism. Caustic references to 'the fool English' interlarding his appraisal of Australian valour against British courage suggest Australians at war building national identity and also self-esteem towards expunging a hated 'convict stain'. He claimed the British treated the campaign very seriously, whereas for Australians it was a great adventure. In *Love Letters of an Anzac*, also published in 1916, Hogue light-heartedly described the 'grandly picturesque entry' of Australians into a war theatre hallowed by heroes of antiquity. He wrote of mutual respect between Australian and Indian troops, who often called themselves 'the Black Australians', and had no particular animus towards Turks, although he was disturbed by the Armenian massacres. By October he had tired of a campaign without the exciting manoeuvres light-horsemen craved. 'Poor old Australia', he wrote of the heavy losses, 'is paying the price.'

Queenslander Captain R. Hugh Knyvett also wrote in heroic vein. *'Over There', with the Australians*

(1918) presented Gallipoli as 'the adventure of youth' and Australians 'eager to prove their country was a breeder of men'. The *Southland* incident had 'written letters of gold on the pages of Australia's history'.

Hector Dinning, writing in 1917, was an exception in judging the campaign an 'ill-starred venture'. He had served at Anzac and, unlike Knyvett, did not glamorise war. *By-ways on Service*, published in 1918, praised Australians but observed: 'War isn't fun. A good deal of drivel is spoken and written about the ennobling effects of warfare.' Men after four months at the beachhead were 'in great part, pasty-faced ghosts, with nerves on raw edge'.[2] Another Australian, Ion Idriess, who enlisted in the 5th Light Horse Brigade as a trooper in 1914 and who from 1927 published forty-seven books for popular audiences, waited until 1932 before bringing out *The Desert Column*. This jaunty but realistic memoir covering his experience at Gallipoli from late August as a sniper accurately conveyed the matter-of-fact attitude assumed by men in the front line.

Philip Schuler's *Australia in Arms* (1916) was the first full-scale narrative of the Anzac campaign. In Australia in 1914, Ian Hamilton had thought Schuler a 'highly intelligent young fellow', and he allowed him as Melbourne *Age* special correspondent 'to go anywhere and see everything' on arrival at Gallipoli on 10 July. Schuler felt 'intense pride' at the 'instantaneous response made by the young manhood of Australia' to the first signs of danger to Empire, approved of 'drum and bugle' recruiting and described AIF excitement in the Suez Canal at seeing foreign soldiers, manifestations of Entente power. He wrote good contemporary history, marred by some important distortions of the truth. Portraying Australian valour at Anzac, he said the first three days there were terrible. He admitted 'appallingly heavy' casualties in the May attack at Helles, instancing one officer, himself injured, saying he would never forget wounded Victorians calling for help and water. But he claimed these Victorians were satisfied, thinking the Turks had fled. His descriptions of terrain, tactical points and daily routine at Anzac were clear and unembroidered. Light-horsemen who charged on 7 August 'won deathless glory . . . and formed the traditions on which the splendour of the young Army was built', but he did not say the August offensive failed; instead he listed alleged gains—heavier Turkish losses than British, and expansion of the Anzac beachhead from three hundred acres to about eight square miles. Also, he claimed Hill 60 was captured. Nevertheless, his account of Lone Pine was accurate. He saw after only one day's fighting men 'covered with blood; unrecognizable in the dirt . . . scattered over them; . . . lean and haggard from want of sleep'. He also several times stressed the great bravery, good physique and soldierly qualities of the Turkish enemy. There was much Schuler did not, or could not, discuss, but he gave Australians a clear impression of what the fighting entailed.[3]

A similar ethos pervaded *Gallipoli*, by the future poet laureate John Masefield. Also a product of 1916, this book is well known in Australia if only for its famous encomium, taken for Anzacs but including also the Royal Naval Division: 'They were . . . the finest body of young men ever brought together in modern times. For physical beauty and nobility of bearing they surpassed any men I have ever seen; they walked and looked like the kings in old poems.' As an account of the campaign, Masefield's book cannot compare with modern scholarship. It is very general and quite uncritical, even of the Suvla fiasco. The August defeat is simply 'a gallant failure'. Masefield claimed the campaign achieved much politically, and even something militarily, patriotism understandable in a wartime account. His book, enriched by much acute reasoning, was about as good as one could expect so soon after the event, although it lacked the detail to be found in Hamilton's published dispatches.[4]

While it had little if any impact in Australia, a contemporary German memoir lent support to Bean's stress on democratic values. Dr Harry Stuermer published *Deux Ans de Guerre à Constantinople* in Paris in 1917. As war correspondent in Turkey for a leading German newspaper, the *Cologne Gazette*, he reached Turkey in the northern spring of 1915 with great good will, thinking its rulers better than Abdul Hamid and sympathising in the struggle against Britain, but became convinced that, by instigating the war, Germany had committed an atrocious crime against humanity. What he saw at Anzac—the Ari Burnu front in his (and the Turkish) lexicon—soon rent his soul in grave conflict. He admired the heroic stoicism of the Turkish soldier and simple Anatolian peasant defending native soil, but were not his sympathies with those on the beach below constantly throwing themselves against almost impregnable Turkish positions to be cruelly cut down? He noticed the different values put on human sacrifice: on the one hand brave, brutish, dirty Anatolians, and on the other colonial sportsmen of superior race and high living standards, coming from afar to defend not merely Britain but also liberty and humanity. On his second visit to the Ari Burnu front, he no longer saw the invaders as enemies but as magnificent troops of rare quality, sacrificing themselves in a last vain, heroic assault.[5]

Stuermer's impressionistic account had important themes in common with two other contemporary memoirs by foreigners in Turkey—disillusion over despotic rule and abhorrence of the Armenian massacres. Lewis Einstein, a young anglophile United States diplomat, served briefly in Constantinople during Abdul Hamid's rule and returned as second secretary from 1913 to September 1915. His *Inside Constantinople: A Diplomatist's Diary During the Dardanelles Expedition, April–September 1915* appeared in London in 1917. The following year Henry Morgenthau, his German-born pro-Allied ambassador, published *Secrets of the Bosphorus: Constantinople 1913–1916*, robustly criticising the Young Turks and the German envoy, Baron von Wangenheim. Morgenthau saw Enver as he 'really was—a savage, bloodthirsty Turk'. Horrified at the Armenian massacres ordered by the Young Turks and German concurrence in the atrocities, he left early from Constantinople in February 1916. Returning home by way of Berlin, he found the Foreign Minister, von Jagow, indifferent to—even supporting—von Wangenheim's attitude and concluded that official Germany bore a large responsibility. Einstein's book, just as critical of the Ottoman regime, also comments adversely on Enver. His views on the Young Turks and their savagery and the folly of the Dardanelles venture had not changed some forty years later.[6]

Djemal, former governor of Constantinople, navy minister, and commander of the 4th Army in Sinai, Palestine and Syria, in 1922 had a translation of his *Memories of a Turkish Statesman, 1913–1914*, published in London. A forthright denunciation of Morgenthau's opinions,[7] it persuasively, if not convincingly, defended the Young Turks' diplomacy which brought the Ottoman Empire into the war on Germany's side.

Amongst enjoyable English memoirs, those of the 'remarkable' Aubrey Herbert, interpreter on Godley's staff, are well worth reading. Born in 1880, educated at Eton and Balliol and with some diplomatic experience, Herbert travelled extensively in the Turkish provinces from 1905 and was a Conservative member in the House of Commons from 1911 until his death in 1923. *Mons, Anzac and Kut* (1919) is uncontroversial and anecdotal in style. Its choice vignettes include tension between Australian medical authorities and the Royal Army Medical Corps, whose callousness contrasted with the devotion of English nurses at Alexandria.[8]

From Germany came some unemotional critical analyses of the Gallipoli campaign. An early example was *Der Kampf um die Dardanellen* (1916) by von Sanders' adjutant, Major E. R. Prigge. Generally accurate, sensible and intelligent, it was a straightforward story of the operation and no literary creation full of impressionistic images of Turkish demigods. Prigge was able to place the campaign in the wider context, seeing its most significant result in the adverse impact on England's status as a world power. The German reader was well served by this book, a more realistic appreciation of strategy than those by Australian authors.[9] Between 1917 and 1921 the prolific writer Hermann Stegemann produced a four-volume history of Germany in the Great War. Two decades later another German account, competent like Prigge though in more heroic style, was Walter von Schoen's *Die Hölle von Gallipoli: Der Heldenkampf an den Dardanellen* (1937).[10]

The first Australian accounts no doubt encouraged the general tendency in Australia to focus on Anzac heroism rather than strategic issues. By contrast in Britain, while Australian valour continued to attract praise, controversy about campaign strategy blazed. In 1916, Sydney A. Moseley's title for his scrappy, superficial book, *The Truth About the Dardanelles*, was a shameless misnomer for what amounted to an apologia for defeat. Moseley, one of the MEF's official correspondents, was kind towards Hamilton, saw little wrong in the treatment of the wounded, vigorously denounced critics such as the 'jaundiced' Ashmead-Bartlett and Granville Fortescue of the United States, criticised General Monro at some length as 'quite fresh to the situation at Gallipoli', and claimed that an advance of 'even a couple of miles at Anzac' in the August battle would have been 'fatal for the Turkish Empire'. He took the Hamilton-Keyes line, reasoning that Gallipoli was a 'tragic failure' because it lacked resolute London support: after the abortive naval attack of 18 March, 'crabbers mobilised and did their worst'. He was, however, no Churchill sycophant. In his view, the 'soldier-politician is a dangerous creation of the civilian. He does not exist outside England.'[11]

A much finer analytical study followed Moseley's, one that gave a far better idea of what really happened at Gallipoli and which for years had strong claims to being adjudged the standard general history—although many would have disagreed with its strong defence of Churchillian strategy. Henry W. Nevinson, a prolific author since 1895 and a war correspondent with extensive warfare experience in many parts of the world, including the Balkans, did not reach Gallipoli until the Suvla landing, by which time the War Office had accredited him as press representative for the *Manchester Guardian* and for lesser provincial newspapers. His book, *The Dardanelles Campaign*, published in 1918, fully conveyed 'the tragic splendour of the theme'. He claimed Churchill's 'brilliant' concept properly implemented could have brought victory and peace, and he regretted that London policy-makers, including Kitchener, refused to divert resources from the Western Front. This he saw as the ultimate cause of failure, premature naval bombardment being merely one of several subsidiary reasons. He had known Hamilton in South Africa and provided a sympathetic 'thumbnail' biography but expressed doubt about his ability as commander: April landings concentrated on Suvla Bay or just north of Ari Burnu would have achieved better results than dispersion; similarly, the August attack was handicapped by the night-time break-out and dispersion under too complicated a plan. Bean perhaps encouraged him to regret being unable to go below battalion level in describing battles. 'Men are the actual units in war as in the State,' declared Nevinson. His praise for the Anzacs would have satisfied his friend and colleague.[12]

The end of the fighting war brought fresh impetus to the war on paper about Gallipoli. The most important engagements would be fought in Britain, with interventions from Germany, Turkey, Australia and France. Planners and commanders had their say, beginning in 1919 with Major-General Callwell's *The Dardanelles* and Admiral Fisher's *Memories* and virtually ending in 1941 with books by Birdwood and Keyes. Fisher's memoirs, like the man, were idiosyncratic. He stressed that the Royal Navy had to remain predominant in the main theatre of war and termed the Gallipoli plan a disaster, caused by a 'miasma' floating like a cloud of poisonous gas above cabinet. He quoted the Nelsonian dictum that 'any sailor who attacked a fort was a fool'. Fisher has been the subject of several biographies and other works which do not change one's assessment of his role in the Dardanelles imbroglio.[13]

In the immediate post-war years Sir Charles Callwell, Director of Military Operations in 1915, wrote three memoirs, *The Dardanelles* containing by far his most substantial post-mortem on Gallipoli.[14] He had worked on the question as a staff problem in 1906 and in 1915, and in retirement found it far easier to devise tactical solutions to his satisfaction that when dealing with an overbearing Churchill in the heat of the fray. Something of a time-server in his relationship with the 'great man', he was now sure that in 1914–15 a meeting of three senior naval officers and three senior army officers, with no cabinet minister present, would have rejected the idea of an operation against the Dardanelles. But if there had to be a campaign, in hindsight he thought Helles should have been avoided and the whole thrust made north of Gaba Tepe. The action of 25 April on the Gallipoli Peninsula was 'the most interesting and illuminating day's fighting that took place during the greatest of all wars'. He reckoned that from about 8 a.m. the defenders at Anzac were always stronger than the attackers. He emphasised the need for comprehensive planning of future amphibious operations, that many more boats were needed to land many more men quickly for full tactical surprise and to secure a large area immediately, and noted the value of portable artillery. The book considered tactical options and drew useful conclusions. This text of quality by a methodical and conscientious former staff officer, though careful to offend no one and circumspect in passing no judgement on Hamilton's recall,[15] nevertheless by implication criticised Churchill—as Fisher had openly done.

Beaten to the bookstores by Callwell and Fisher, Hamilton had begun dictating his version to his devoted personal assistant, Mrs Mary Shield, in 1916. It was published in 1920 in two volumes as *Gallipoli Diary*, misleading many people by its format into thinking Hamilton actually wrote it at the time. It was pro-Churchill and anti-Kitchener and splenetic in tone only when dealing with Keith Murdoch. Elegant but lightweight, Hamilton's study lacked incisiveness compared with Callwell's. The stylish and gracious recalled force commander, in great demand as an after-dinner speaker, at times did radio book reviews, no doubt thereby also helping promote his own book, high in self-justification. He probably did not succeed in rehabilitating himself, but among congratulatory letters he received a sympathetic one from Godley; Maxwell criticised him for strictures on Kitchener, and Andrew Fisher, still High Commissioner, said the book would be controversial, which was preferable to it not being published. Indeed, the Australian press in May 1920 carried Murdoch's angry retort to a book which attracted considerable attention in Australia.[16]

Also in 1920 the sixty-year old General Sir George Arthur, Kitchener's private secretary from 1914 to 1916, brought out his three-volume life of the dead ex-minister. The third volume trenchantly defended Kitchener's role regarding Gallipoli, deriding criticism by the Dardanelles Commission. To vindicate Kitchener, Arthur had to see merit in the campaign and so found it 'politically well conceived' and 'far from barren of eventual effect'; he joined those claiming it 'had broken the spine of Turkish military power'. Arthur described Kitchener's mission to Gallipoli and notorious vacillation without suggesting his indecision was hampering Britain's war policy and that he was losing the confidence of cabinet colleagues. If Kitchener were guilty of any error of judgement, it was in accepting Churchill's views on the power of naval ordnance. Rather shallow, the book contributed usefully to debate by printing long extracts from important documents. It also helped undermine Churchill's reputation. Some forty years later Philip Magnus, who strongly supported Churchill's campaign concept, damned Kitchener in his valuable biography. Kitchener's constant shilly-shallying about evacuation was 'the act of a passenger in a feeble team', proving his 'unfitness to remain the Government's principal adviser upon strategy'.[17]

By the end of 1922 the weight of published personal accounts was on balance unfavourable to Churchill. Young and ambitious, with a long political career still ahead, Churchill more than anyone needed to defend himself. He produced by far the most famous autobiographical vindication. The second volume of his *The World Crisis*, dealing with 1915, ran to a reprint in the month of its publication, October 1923. It was long, magnificent and influential. In 1925 Sir William McPherson, Victoria's Nationalist premier in 1928–29, told parliament this book completely rehabilitated Churchill as one of the Empire's leading statesmen.

Churchill criticised the dead Kitchener, affirmed his opposition to attacking Turkey at a place other than Gallipoli (being 'unswervingly set upon the main enterprise'), mentioned the 'impression of inconceivable majesty and crisis' during the attack of 18 March, claimed that attack left the defenders short of ammunition, dismissed the General Staff–Admiralty paper of December 1906 and its endorsement in February 1907 by the Committee of Imperial Defence as 'a confession of complete impotence', and repeated his wartime arguments on the advantage of victory at the Dardanelles. He was not vitriolic in his assessments of the generals and troops who wrecked the Suvla operation; instead, he tended to admonish London for slow dispatch of adequate reinforcements. His tendentious story has been rigorously analysed by Robin Prior in *Churchill's 'World Crisis' as History*, and it would be an act of supererogation to attempt to further summarise his argument here.[18]

Another strong advocate of the Gallipoli strategy published his version in 1924. Admiral Wester Wemyss, who reached Lemnos in mid-February 1915 and in November succeeded de Robeck as naval commander, restated his views of 1915 in *The Navy in the Dardanelles Campaign*. He criticised aspects of Churchill's role and War Council deliberations, blamed Admiral Fisher for his planning failures, and ascribed 'the tragedy' to premature naval attack before land forces were ready.[19]

As if influenced by *The World Crisis*, three German accounts available by 1927 accepted Churchill's strategy as a real threat to the Ottoman Empire. All three writers had personal interest in highlighting the importance of a campaign in which they personally had fought. Hamilton's adversary, Liman von Sanders, architect of one of Turkey's few great victories of the war, expatiated on the superior merit of his plans over Enver's for defending the peninsula and stated that Australian losses on 19 May roughly equalled Turkish casualties. He complained about British naval bombardment and destruction of Maidos and other small Turkish towns. He held that success of Hamilton's plans in August would have been decisive and that consequences of defeat included loss of the Dardanelles forts, a Russian landing aimed at Constantinople with dire consequences for the capital, and a dramatic improvement of the Allies' position in the Balkans.[20]

The English translation of von Sanders' book appeared in 1927 about the same time as books by two of his officers, Captain Muhlmann and Colonel Kannengiesser. C. Muhlmann's *Der Kampf um die Dardanellen* is a straightforward account of operations against the hated British. He admitted that in early August they had been close to victory for forty-eight hours, but 'unpredictable factors and the boldness of the Turks had defeated them at the very moment when [British] victory seemed assured'. He described the Turks' utter amazement when the English at Suvla, opposed only by inferior forces, remained inert for a day or so; von Sanders looked down from surrounding hills at 'a very peaceful picture. It was like being out on manoeuvres. The entire plain was full of life. The movement on the beach was like the high season of a fashionable seaside resort.'[21]

A memoir by Hans Kannengiesser, who temporarily commanded Turkey's 9th Division, was translated into English in 1927 as *The Campaign in Gallipoli*. Stressing the shortage of equipment for defending the peninsula, he said Australians on 25 April approached Sari Bair 'in a manner which caused us the greatest anxiety'. He praised Kemal's decisiveness and also, not surprisingly, that of von Sanders, upon whose shoulders hung 'the success of the whole campaign, the existence of the whole Empire'.[22]

In 1929 Compton Mackenzie, on Hamilton's staff in 1915, published *Gallipoli Memories*, in which he claimed that opinion was gradually veering around to belief in the value of the expedition. Keen to have all Turks ejected from Europe even if that meant using the sword, Mackenzie thought the change in opinion was helped by continued survival of most of the campaign's 1915 advocates, whereas opponents who had allegedly caused the attack to fail were dying off.[23]

But Ashmead-Bartlett's powerful polemic, *The Uncensored Dardanelles*, had appeared in 1928. While it pronounced Churchill's Dardanelles scheme a brilliant strategic concept and did not hold him responsible for things going wrong after the naval attack of 18 March, it exonerated Churchill mainly by blaming others, especially Hamilton. This very experienced war correspondent was sure that with a better plan the fleet could have got through the strait in March 1915. He admired Keyes, the enthusiast for continuous naval attacks on the Dardanelles, but claimed he had thought as early as 22 April 1915 that Hamilton's methods were 'almost certainly doomed to failure'. Much of his book is a forceful denunciation of 'all the faults and weaknesses of that commander's plans'. Ashmead-Bartlett was furious at Hamilton's ill-based optimism after the April landings failed to achieve their objectives and by May was sure 'the whole Expedition [was] doomed to failure'. His relations with Hamilton's staff soon became strained. Hearing frank conversation in senior messes, Ashmead-Bartlett in July reflected, 'Never have I known an army which has quite such a poor opinion of its chief.' He judged that Hamilton's headquarters set impossible tasks for its forces, the August offensive capping them all. After careful analysis of the means, the objectives and the battlefield's formidable terrain, he concluded, 'So much for the assiduously asserted fiction that only a hair's-breadth separated us from victory at Anzac.' However, he did think that the Anzac Corps, if landed at Suvla, could have gained the stipulated objectives. His final break with Hamilton soon followed. 'Never have I known such a collection of unsuitable people to whom to entrust a great campaign, the lives of their countrymen, and the safety of the Empire,' the embittered journalist summed up. 'Their muddles, mismanagement, and ignorance of the strategy and tactics of modern war have brought about the greatest disaster in English history.'[24]

*The World Crisis* had not silenced Churchill's critics. In 1931 something of a literary counter-attack developed, although without Ashmead-Bartlett's ferocity. In that year Sir George de Symons Barrow published *The Life of General Sir Charles Monro*. Barrow saw no redeeming merit in the 'unrelieved disaster' of Gallipoli and made a robust attack on the views of Churchill, Keyes and Wemyss, forcefully defending the acumen of Monro, under whom he served when Monro commanded the Third British Army on the Western Front. Barrow cited Wolseley's landing in Egypt in 1882 as a good example of the 'method, order and foresight' so conspicuously lacking in the MEF landing on Gallipoli.

In 1931 there also appeared a short, highly intelligent critique by Lieutenant-Colonel . O. Head, *A Glance at Gallipoli*. Head was not on Gallipoli during the campaign but visited the old battlefield after the war. He stressed that possession by Australians of the Sari Bair heights would not of itself have been much use, for troops on that exposed hill would have been good targets for the Turks. (Kannengiesser says exactly the opposite: 'the occupier of [Sari Bair] is master of the whole surrounding country'.) Head judiciously assessed the choice of landing beaches, the significance of German machine-guns and similar details of campaign strategy, tactics, achievements and opportunities. His language was worlds apart from violent diatribe, but his measured judgement on the difficulties inherent in Churchill's pipe-dream of an offensive through the Balkans is still today quite devastating.[25]

French writers joined the campaign's critics. Edmund Delage's *Tragedy of the Dardanelles* appeared in English translation in 1932. It denounced Hamilton as 'a superb example of insular obstinacy. He was like a bull that had rushed headlong against a door and had already damaged its horns, but immediately resumed its onslaught.' He was a 'veritable incarnation of British obstinacy', closing his eyes to errors and instigating one futile massacre after another. Suvla 'displayed the full extent of his incapacity'. Stopford and his divisional generals were found equally wanting, being termed 'incapables who had made such havoc of the extremely hazardous plans of the Commander-in-Chief'. Astoundingly, Hamilton wrote an introduction to this book, remarking that he did not like its argument. However, the book dealt with the battles in reasonably adequate detail and quickly ran through fifteen editions in France and was widely discussed. It included praise for Australasian troops.

Delage's best-seller amply indicated French interest in a British-led campaign in which comparatively few white Frenchmen from metropolitan France participated. More French memoirs appeared. Henri Feuille, in his *Face aux Turcs: Gallipoli 1915* (1934), was as critical as anyone of the Suvla fiasco. Hamilton, he wrote, made a practice of conducting at a distance operations which required his presence among his troops. Feuille adjudged him '*le mauvais génie de la tragédie des Dardanelles*'.[26]

E. Keble Chatterton in *Dardanelles Dilemma: The Story of the Naval Operations* (1935) justifiably claimed to have written 'an independent history'. He would have agreed with Head. His theme was that on 3 November Carden's squadron, in bombarding the ancient fortress of Sedd-el-Bahr, on orders from London, 'took the first step towards that series of disasters which were to be the logical conclusion of false premises'.[27]

APPENDIX

Independent assessments were, however, still outnumbered and overshadowed by accounts from the viewpoint of participants. And during the 1930s other former campaign leaders, some now retired, entered the lists propounding views both for and against Churchill. In 1932 Sir George Arthur's biography of Sir John Maxwell gave that contender a voice: from first to last Maxwell had not favoured a landing on Gallipoli. In 1934 the fiery Keyes supported Churchill in a long, powerful account, *The Naval Memoirs of Admiral of the Fleet*. Keyes argued as fiercely as ever that forcing the Dardanelles 'would have shortened the war by two years, and spared literally millions of lives'. A few old British battleships 'might have won imperishable glory for the Navy'. The crucial failure was the refusal to provide an efficient mine-sweeping force before the naval attack of 18 March. He also thought the change of emphasis from naval to military attack 'an unhappy decision'. He was not surprised that the 4th AIF Brigade lost its way on the night of 6–7 August and described his 'fever of resentment at these leisurely proceedings [of Stopford's Corps at Suvla]'; he extolled the skills of von Sanders and Kemal, criticised Monro as seeing little of the peninsula, and lavished praise on Churchill. Keyes's life-long regret about the supposed lost opportunities led him in 1941 to recapitulate virtually word for word in *The Fight for Gallipoli*. His praise for Churchill had led to a very friendly although not enduring relationship, reflected in Keyes's appointment, past his prime, as first director of the Combined Operations Command in July 1940 and his removal in October 1941. Substantial publications on Keyes include Cecil Aspinall-Oglander's biography in 1951, which criticised his life-long obstinacy in believing a naval attack late in 1915 could have brought the Royal Navy through the strait without army help. Keyes's papers, published in 1972, contain much material on the Dardanelles.[28]

Godley, surprisingly—and most unusually for a general—was willing to admit professional mistakes. His competent *Life of an Irish Soldier* (1939) acknowledged that his planned 'left hook' on the night of 6–7 August 1915 had been too ambitious. In planning the Sari Bair assault again, he would do it very differently. For instance, he now thought the Australian light horse sacrificed at the Nek could have been better used in the main advance. In self-defence, however, he claimed the Nek charge had drawn Turks away from the main attack; and he did not criticise the Gallipoli venture generally, clinging to the view that it destroyed the flower of the Turkish army.[29]

Another powerful indictment of Churchill appeared in 1939 when Vice-Admiral K. G. B. Dewar published *The Navy from Within*, which strongly criticised the Dardanelles operations, Asquith's ministers and the RN's high command. Dewar, commanding the battleship *Prince of Wales* from 1913, conveyed men of the 10th Battalion to Anzac Cove. He thought the 'whole affair was a desperate and unjustifiable gamble', an unprecedented task, giving the soldiers little chance of success. There was 'something a little ludicrous in the scope and variety' of Churchill's plans: he had 'an ardent temperament and a superficial mind', undisciplined by criticism or study. And he denounced Fisher. 'Certainly', he wrote, 'there is little in that campaign on which [the RN] can look back with pride.' The March attacks on the forts showed 'an extraordinary lack of vigour and determination'. He criticised the mine-sweeping methods, instancing analysis in Julian Corbett's official history of the Russo-Japanese War which showed the danger of mines and that forts pitted against ships were practically invulnerable.[30]

Birdwood's breezy *Khaki and Gown* (1941) was favoured with a foreword by Churchill—despite many more pressing duties at the time—endorsing the author's view. Birdwood blamed failure on the 9th Corp's inexcusable lack of urgency after landing: but for that, he had always felt, 'the whole Force would have won through to the Dardanelles'. Nonetheless, Birdwood admitted that the task given Godley's troops on the night of 6–7 August was more difficult than he realised at the time, and that he (Birdwood) had overestimated the men's physical fitness. He had the decency to admit he had little to do with planning the evacuation, praising plans by other officers and the 'unspeakably firm discipline shown by every man in that great force'.[31]

Among independent assessments written during the 1930s, according to literary critics Major John North's *Gallipoli, the Fading Vision* (1936) towers above all others. However, the book, which is a full-blooded disagreement with the views of Chatterton, Head and Ashmead-Bartlett, has been greatly overrated. North, a barrister who served in France and Belgium as a subaltern and later wrote various works of fiction, vigorously defended Churchill and his 'brilliantly conceived' campaign. Much of his book echoed Churchill's thoughts. North denounced Churchill's critics, joining issue on specific criticisms and berating them for 'prejudice'. He claimed the campaign was lost not through inadequate preparation but on the peninsula. He strongly criticised Kitchener and the War Office, was sympathetic towards Hamilton without exonerating him, and took up some issues with Bean. His attacks on de Robeck and the Royal Navy provoked Aspinall-Oglander into angry rejoinder in the *Observer* of 22 March 1936.

Although fluently written and making few demands on the reader, North's book is chaotically disorganised and added little to what an informed reader of 1936 would have known of Gallipoli. However, he had many influential contacts in Britain's literary circles and was able to arrange favourable reviews. No doubt this was not the sole reason why the book was widely and sympathetically reviewed. Perhaps it appealed to writers of fiction; historically speaking it was lightweight. A reviewer in the Australian journal *Reveille* summed up North's book as 'an epic of human endurance and of sacrifice'. 'Page after page records its relentless indictment of gross mismanagement, of appalling ignorance, of amazing indifference. . . . horror is piled on horror. [We have] the stark record of what I can describe only as human stupidity, folly, and even wickedness without parallel in the history of our race.' Authorities in London did not 'seem to have cared a damn for the men on Gallipoli'. The long and laudatory Australian reviews included one on the *Bulletin*'s 'Red Page', terming it fine literature recommended without reservation. North's favourable reception in Australia probably arose from delight in strong criticism of British officers contrasted with the superb bravery of ordinary soldiers. This, of course, sat easily with the Anzac legend; but Bean, alleged 'creator' of the legend, thought so little of North's book that his *Sydney Morning Herald* review said little about it, instead dwelling learnedly on a few crucial tactical issues.[32]

While private individuals produced a substantial Gallipoli literature, governments sponsored the major scholarly work in the same area. Most of the relevant books had appeared by 1932. Less saleable than some private ventures, they made valuable contributions to the long argument, relatively sober if not always authoritative. The stated purpose varied; Britain's Chancellor of the Exchequer in 1922, heading off complaint in the House of Commons about the cost of producing the official history, stressed the value of the lessons of history; Australia's history was a memorial as well as record.[33]

Official histories of the campaign began to appear in 1921 with publication of Bean's first volume and Sir Julian Corbett's second volume in Britain's series, *Naval Operations*, concerning the Dardanelles campaign from inception to May 1915. Corbett, a former Royal Naval College lecturer and prolific naval historian, now director of the Historical Section of the Committee of Imperial Defence, drew on a confidential joint services report of 1919 assessing campaign operational lessons,[34] along with all the Dardanelles Commission material. Very conscious of the difficulties inherent in amphibious operations, Corbett admitted Royal Navy mistakes such as arriving at the wrong place—Anzac Cove—although in defence he claimed this showed the service right to oppose a night landing. Significantly he was very circumspect in assessing the wisdom of the venture and Churchill's role. In volume 3 Corbett completed his story of the Dardanelles venture, but his attitude had changed. The book appeared late in 1923, at the same time as volume 2 of Churchill's *The World Crisis*. Corbett now strongly defended Churchill's strategy, characterising Hamilton's front as 'the decisive point of the war' and quoting the senior German commander, General E. Falkenhayn, in support. As for the navy's landings of April and August, 'nothing quite equal to it, either in conception, difficulty or magnitude, had ever been attempted before'. Corbett's terse description of the attack on Sari Bair tallied with Bean's view: 'By a display of leadership, hard fighting and endurance that nothing in the war surpassed, the two assaulting columns had never ceased to grope their way forward up the scrub-filled ravines and over the tortuous ridges. No wire was too thick, no trenches too well held, no scarps too precipitous to stop them. Higher and higher they fought their way, and the stubborn Turkish resistance melted before them like the shadows of the night.'[35]

Corbett's volumes were subject to specific cabinet approval before publication. The official history of army operations by Cecil F. Aspinall-Oglander, Hamilton's former staff officer writing under his new name, did not appear until 1929–32, and only after creation of a mechanism to handle politicians' desire for 'balance'. Controversy, including fall-out from concerns expressed by Churchill and other ministers about Corbett's draft first volume, led to cabinet establishing a CID subcommitte: Control of Official Histories. This subcommittee met yearly until the Second World War, probably its most lively meeting being in 1928 when Churchill, Chancellor of the Exchequer in Stanley Baldwin's government, energetically intervened against proposed War Office amendments to the draft first army volume on Gallipoli. Brigadier-General Sir James Edmonds, supervising the army histories within the CID, thought Aspinall-Oglander a little too hard on some generals: it was often sufficient to state the facts, without rubbing them in. Aspinall-Oglander protested that his book was not a General Staff publication. Churchill, in support, declared it would be 'an atrocious falsification' if the War Office had its way and censored six pages early in the volume. The committee was sensitive to Australian views and wanted criticism of Anzac Corps officers—Birdwood, Bridges, Godley and White—for 'losing heart on the Beach' on the night of 25–26 April balanced by reference to Australians in the field digging in and making a second line. In the event, the committee compromised: three sections would be revised, less than the War Office wanted.[36]

Not surprisingly, Aspinall-Oglander's volumes—while risking controversy on some issues—are mostly very cautious. For example, bland discussion of the Suvla fiasco terms 8 August 'a wasted day' and mildly criticises Hamilton for being too gentle with Stopford in the aftermath. There is little criticism of Australians; on the contrary. his volumes contained fewer strictures on individual Australians than Bean's. His subject was the whole campaign and concerned a level higher than Australian command decisions. Aspinall-Oglander subscribed fully to the Anzac epic, writing of the landing: 'The predominant feeling, which that astounding battlefield must always arouse in the military student who visits it, will be a sense of unstinted admiration for those untried battalions who did so exceedingly well. The magnificent physique, the reckless daring, and the fine enthusiasm of the Dominion troops on their first day of trial went far to counteract anything they lacked in training and war experience.' As for the 4th Brigade's failure to take Hill 971, the assault was an impossible task, post-war knowledge revealing it was twice as difficult as imagined at the time.[37]

Aspinall-Oglander's military background, the scale of his subject and the official hand in his work all differed from the official history produced by Charles Bean. Oglander's volumes were traditional in concentrating on planning, strategy and the role of commanders. They rarely went far down the chain of command to say much about individual front-line warriors. Many thought this an advantage over Bean's highly detailed accounts of small actions and found the gracefully written British overview much easier reading.

Bean's masterly account of the Australians at Anzac, his second volume appearing in 1924, was too long for many busy readers. Nevertheless, this level of detail is necessary for tactical problems to be properly examined and a satisfying story to be told of events in a campaign full of incident. This approach was not replicated by New Zealand.[38] Bean, uniquely, insisted as a condition of his writing that it not be censored. Probably his most quoted sentence in Britain was forthright criticism of Churchill's impetuosity as a cause of 'the tragedy of Gallipoli'. Churchill's response in *The World Crisis* was:

'It is my hope that the Australian people, towards whom I have always felt a solemn responsibility, will not rest content with so crude, so inaccurate, so incomplete and so prejudiced a judgement, but will study the facts for themselves.'[39]

Bean is most spoken of in Australia, however, not for his many and significant assessments of strategy and command, in which Australians had less interest, but for his democratic outlook, which gave full weight to the men at the 'cutting edge' who actually did the fighting. His work, based on meticulous personal as well as official records and a return to Turkey in 1919 which encouraged his positive attitude to the former enemy, attracted favourable overseas attention. Scholars greatly admired his new standards for the writing of military history, standards scarcely bettered in this genre in Australian historiography. The comparatively small scale of Australia's contribution to the campaign—some fifty thousand men—the confined battlefield, and virtual absence of Australians from strategic planning lent themselves to Bean's 'grass roots' approach, which resulted in a literary masterpiece and a superb record of a great national event. Bean was disappointed in its impact. He once lamented he had rarely met a university historian who had read his volumes, a sad reflection on the state of the profession; and at a time of great crisis in Australia's history, May 1942, he remarked to John North, fellow writer on Gallipoli, that he did not think the official history had had much influence on conduct of the nation's war effort. 'Most of the old mistakes had been made over again.' He was consoled by the thought that the series could have helped indirectly 'in keeping up the Anzac tradition', while Arthur Butler's medical volumes were receiving 'a good deal of attention'.[40]

The German official history understandably provided only a brief account of the main operations of the Gallipoli campaign. The relevant volume, no. 9, *Die Operation des Jahres 1915*, was published by the Reichsarchiv in Berlin in 1933. Despite its comparative brevity, it stressed the campaign's importance, in effect largely agreeing with Churchill's assessments of the advantages for the Entente of a Dardanelles victory. It also agreed with Churchill's 'terrible ifs' theory (of alleged great opportunities narrowly missed), asserting that the campaign 'often rested on a razor's edge', with the situation saved only by Turkish courage and the cool-headedness of von Sanders.[41]

Both the Turkish and French official histories of the campaign were quite brief. A version of the former, translated into French by M. Larcher in 1924, could scarcely have been more different from Bean's epic. In some ninety pages it discussed the campaign's major strategic and tactical moves, with only brief mention of the Turkish 5th Army's stoic and grand achievement and its resounding success in the trenches. Nor did this book have much to say about wider strategic and political implications of the Dardanelles campaign and its impact in helping rejuvenate Turkish nationalism and self-esteem. The French official history, more expansive on Dardanelles fighting, naturally had relatively little to say about Australians, because the two allies fought in different areas.[42] This was true even of the fleeting and disastrous Australasian encounter with Turks at Helles, for the French were on the Allied right, whereas the Anzacs advanced on the left.

The Second World War marked a new era in Gallipoli historiography. Recourse to print by commanders and planners tailed off, though some memoirs by younger men—of lower rank in 1915—still appeared. An illustrious French veteran, Jerome Carcopino, a member of the Académie française, wrote thirty-three books before *Souvenirs de la Guerre en Orient 1915–1917* (1970), which contains a slight personal memoir and a brief campaign analysis. He served on Gallipoli as a subaltern in a colonial regiment. Although his zouaves had loudly disparaged Hamilton's habitual avoidance of the battlefield, he was reasonably sympathetic to the disgraced general and did not regard this orator and man of letters as out of place in the army. Carcopino was more inclined to explain the campaign's failure by Kitchener's stubbornness and refusal to give Hamilton adequate freedom of strategic manoeuvre: it was not Hamilton's fault that he was ordered to attack a peninsula perhaps impossible to conquer, and the August offensive to take the enemy in the rear made sense. Overall Carcopino's judgement was sombre—a campaign entangled from the start in contradictions between French and English warlords and crowned by the supreme injustice that if it had been successful all the sacrifice would merely have led to Russia getting the conquered territory under the secret agreement of March 1915.[43]

In 1956, twenty years after John North's book, another celebrated and significant popular history of the campaign, *Gallipoli*, was published by the expatriate Australian writer and British war correspondent Alan Moorehead. Its favourable reviewers included Compton Mackenzie and the former British Labour prime minister, Clement Attlee, who had served on Gallipoli. Using archives in London and Ankara and interviews with many participants, Moorehead, in flowing prose, subscribes to the Anzac legend and condemns British handling of the Suvla operation. But as for precisely what happened on Gallipoli, he is too general and scarcely any improvement on Masefield or North. For example, units are not identified, and the Nek is not named despite a brief reference to the charge. His book usefully depicts the Turkish view but is marred by errors and lacks incisiveness. Indeed, Moorehead's account is less perceptive than Masefield's book of forty years standing. The epilogue ignores the historiography, claiming 'no serious student now questioned the wisdom of the Allies going to the Dardanelles', Churchill having been the first to restore the campaign's reputation as the 'most imaginative conception of the war'.[44]

But other works of excellent historical scholarship examining political and military aspects of the campaign have wrought a striking change in the Gallipoli library—an example of the historiographical process, as large collections of papers, including public records, become available to scholars and as the passage of time assists objectivity. Even so, passions engendered by the campaign still sometimes inform the scholarly approach. Hankey's *The Supreme Command*, volume 1 (1961), and Stephen Roskill's *Hankey*, volume 1 (1970), added valuably to public knowledge of the 'inside story'. Hankey, secretary to the CID and later of the War Council and the Dardanelles Committee, had no executive authority but was shrewd, articulate and friendly with Asquith and exercised considerable influence. His contemporary and later writing analysed the desperate need for co-ordination at Allied, ministerial and operational levels in the Dardanelles campaign.

Other recent works of literary and scholarly quality offer a rewarding entry for anyone wanting to adopt the biographical approach to the higher planning of the campaign. George H. Cassar's sympathetic portrait of Kitchener, *Kitchener: Architect of Victory* (1977), does not absolve him of a 'tragic mistake' but identifies Asquith's leadership shortcomings and finds that Churchill 'must shoulder a large portion of the blame' for the Dardanelles operation, 'a classic example in war of wanting the ends without providing the means'. Martin Gilbert's vast biography of Churchill is of great value for its detail. Two companion volumes of documents to the biography contain a wealth of excellent reading on the Dardanelles campaign. Among modern scholars' contribution, A. J. Marder's *From the Dreadnought to Scapa Flow*, volume 2 (1965), is unsurpassable; American writer Trumbull Higgins's *Winston Churchill and the Dardanelles* (1964) says Bean's famous indictment should be paraphrased using cabinet, not Churchill, as the arch-villain; Roskill's *Churchill and the Admirals* (1977) succinctly discusses the Churchill/Admiral Fisher relationship; Peter Fraser's *Lord Esher* (1973) closely analyses military policy-making; M. S. Anderson's *The Eastern Question* looks at broad strategic issues; and George Cassar's *The French and the Dardanelles* (1971) throws perspective on the alliance, as does David French's *British Strategy and War Aims 1914–16* (1986).[45]

To these English and American books must be added excellent studies of Anzac battles by the contemporary Australian masters on Monash, Geoffrey Serle and Peter Pedersen. These men used material not available to Bean. Pedersen especially, focusing on command rather than the front-line soldier (or romanticised heroism), gives improved critical insight to weaknesses in the way those battles were conducted. He shows the command failings of Birdwood and Godley, and Monash making mistakes but 'learning fast'. He agrees with many Bean judgements on Monash but concludes, like Serle, that Bean was ambivalent about a man he did not understand. C. Coulthard-Clark in *A Heritage of Spirit* (1979) convincingly argues that Bridges' outlook tended to be more Imperial than Bean allowed. Complementing these works and A. J. Hill's *Chauvel* (1981), New Zealander Christopher Pugsley's fine *Gallipoli* (1984) concludes: 'On Gallipoli Godley lost the trust' of his men.[46]

The best general history of the entire Gallipoli campaign, by British scholar Robert Rhodes James, appeared in its golden jubilee. Mary Shield, Hamilton's secretary, thought it 'a marvel of research' but 'marred by far too much trivia and gloom'. The quality of James's account, including his characterisation of the 'drift to the Dardanelles' propelled by Churchill and lacking co-ordination, can be measured by the attention other historians give to particular judgements.[47]

While numerous recent slight publications have added nothing to our knowledge of the campaign, some more substantial books, such as Eric Bush's *Gallipoli* (1975) and Peter Liddle's *Men of Gallipoli* (1976), have been more useful in covering certain of its aspects, the former concentrating on naval tactics and the latter on the 'personal experience' of men in the front line. Since Rhodes James's book, most of the best writing on Gallipoli has been in individual chapters or short passages of books dealing with wider issues, such as wartime diplomacy, but these contributions are too brief and numerous to consider here. Most of these writers denounce the strategy and tactics employed by the Allies.

Taken altogether, the extensive and excellent scholarship in the last two decades has provided us with comprehensive critical narrative accounts of the campaign. There are now enough studies on British politico-military decision-making to allow one to state with some confidence that in terms of grand strategy the operation was ill-conceived and would have yielded meagre results even if successful. Other aspects of the campaign are less well served. There are no modern studies of the British commanders at Gallipoli—Hamilton, Birdwood and Hunter-Weston. There is a similar hiatus in matters of logistics and of infantry and artillery tactics. In short, notwithstanding the extensive literature on Gallipoli, the campaign can still provide a fruitful field for historical research.

Of the existing historiography, it is apparent that some of the finest writing and best scholarship concerning Gallipoli is to be found in official histories, notably in Bean's volumes. Nevertheless, private memoirs and histories have attracted much wider attention and have probably had a bigger impact on general public understanding of the campaign.

Since Bean, until very recently the writings of non-Australians, overall, have been far more significant than those of Australians. The dearth of substantial Australian historical writing about what happened at Gallipoli is only partly explained by the existence before 1972 of a fifty-year rule for the opening of Australian official documents to public scrutiny. Bean's formidable achievement, and, as suggested in this survey of the literature, the aura cast by the Anzac legend itself, have both had an influence. But one might also seek explanation in a long-standing reluctance of some circles in Australia to recognise in war experience a fit subject for historical inquiry.

# NOTES

Where a date consists of day and month only, the year is 1915. See also Biographical Notes for further information on sources of soldiers' letters, diaries, etc.

## ABBREVIATIONS

| | |
|---|---|
| AA | Australian Archives, Canberra (also Melbourne) |
| *ADB* | *Australian Dictionary of Biography* |
| AIF | Australian Imperial Force |
| AP | Allanson Papers, Imperial War Museum, London |
| AWM | Australian War Memorial, Canberra |
| BLP | Bonar Law Papers, House of Lords Record Office, London |
| Bod. | Bodleian Library, Oxford |
| BP | Bush Papers, Imperial War Museum, London |
| Cab | Cabinet Office record in Public Record Office, London |
| CCAC | Churchill College, Cambridge |
| CID | Committee of Imperial Defence |
| CO | Colonial Office |
| CP | Curzon Papers, India Office, London |
| *CPD* | *Commonwealth Parliamentary Debates* |
| DaP | Dawnay Papers, Imperial War Museum, London |
| DC | Dardanelles Commission |
| deRP | de Robeck Papers, Churchill College, Cambridge |
| DMS | Director of Medical Services |
| DNI | Director of Naval Intelligence |
| DP | Davidson Papers, House of Lords Record Office, London |
| FO | Foreign Office, London |
| FP | Andrew Fisher Papers, National Library of Australia, Canberra |
| *GBPP* | *Great Britain Parliamentary Papers* |
| GP | Godley Papers, Old War Office Library, London |
| *HCPD* | *House of Commons Parliamentary Debates* |
| *HLPD* | *House of Lords Parliamentary Debates* |
| HLRO | House of Lords Record Office, London |
| HMS | Harcourt Manuscripts, Bodleian Library, Oxford |
| HP | Hamilton Papers, Liddell Hart Centre for Military Archives, King's College, University of London |
| HuP | Hutton Papers, British Library, London |
| HWP | Hunter-Weston Papers, British Library |
| IO | India Office, London |
| KiP | Kiggell Papers, Liddell Hart Centre for Military Archives, King's College, University of London |
| KP | Keyes Papers, Churchill College, Cambridge |
| LGP | Lloyd George Papers, House of Lords Record Office, London |
| LH | Liddell Hart Centre for Military Archives, King's College, University of London |
| MaP | Maurice Papers, Liddell Hart Centre for Military Archives, King's College, University of London |
| MEF | Mediterranean Expeditionary Force |
| MiP | Milligan Papers, Imperial War Museum, London |
| MMS | Milner Manuscripts, Bodleian Library, Oxford |
| MP | Monash Papers, National Library of Australia, Canberra, and Australian War Memorial, Canberra |
| NLA | National Library of Australia, Canberra |
| NMM | National Maritime Museum, Greenwich |
| NP | Natusch Papers, Imperial War Museum, London |
| OWO | Old War Office Library, London |
| PaP | Paris Papers, Imperial War Museum, London |
| PLA | The Liddle Collection, Leeds University Library |
| PoP | Porter Papers, National Maritime Museum, Greenwich |
| *PP* | *Parliamentary Papers* |
| PP | Pearce Papers, Australian War Memorial, Canberra |
| PRO | Public Record Office, London |
| RSLP | RSL Papers, National Library of Australia, Canberra |
| S | Prisoner-of-war statement |
| *SMH* | *Sydney Morning Herald* |
| WO | War Office, London |

## CHAPTER 1. SOLDIERS FOR EMPIRE

1. Arthur, *Life of Lord Kitchener* 1: 318–19.
2. Wallace, *Australians at the Boer War*, 264; Elands River: *ibid.*, 257–74 and Field, *Forgotten War*, 153–55.
3. Tilby, *English People Overseas* 5: v, 441; Lewin *Oxford Survey*, 310.
4. 'Fervent belief': Hill, *Chauvel*, 22; Hamilton to Hutton, 13 Jan. 1902, Hutton to Hamilton, 4 Nov. 1902, HuP, Add MS 50086.
5. Hamilton to Hutton, 4 June 1903, ibid.
6. Hamilton to Hutton, 25 Dec. 1903, Hutton to Hamilton, 2 Feb. 1904, ibid.
7. Hill, *Chauvel*, 38.
8. Nish, *Anglo-Japanese Alliance* and *Alliance in Decline*.
9. Hill, *Chauvel*, 39–40; Meaney, *Search for Security*, 197–98; Coulthard-Clark, 'Formation of the Australian Armed Services'; Kitchener's 'visitation': Souter, *Lion and Kangaroo*, 150–52, Arthur, *Kitchener* 2: 289–95.
10. Haldane to Kitchener, PRO 30/57/39 TT13.
11. Kitchener to Ward, 2 Mar. 1910, PRO 30/57/39 TT14.
12. Compulsory training scheme: Barrett, *Falling In*.
13. Meaney, *Search for Security*, 201, 228–29; Crowley, *Modern Australia in Documents* 1: 200–202.
14. Hamilton to wife, 2 Feb. 1914, HP 25/12/2/9; *West Australian*, 4, 5 Feb. 1914.
15. 'Epoch making': Hamilton to wife, 6 Apr. 1914, HP 25/12/2/2; *Argus*, 23 Apr.
16. *Argus*, 20, 22, 25 May 1914.
17. Cunneen, *Kings' Men*, 109.
18. Munro Ferguson to Pringle, 10 July 1914, papers of W. M. R. Pringle, HLRO 226.
19. Newspapers of mainland state capitals, 27 July–4 Aug. 1914.
20. Turner, *The First World War*; Steiner, *Foreign Office and Foreign Policy*.

## CHAPTER 2. A SMALL EMPIRE EASILY WON

1. Meaney, *Search for Security*, 276–77; Jose, *Royal Australian Navy*, 475.
2. Australian offer: CO 616/1, 55; Admiralty: CO 616/10, 23; cf Boer War, in which nearly all Australia's costs were met by Imperial funds: CO 616/45, 325, 501.
3. Public servant: 10 May 1917, AA CP78/21.
4. Hughes, *Splendid Adventure*, 42. Hughes told PM Lloyd George on 10 Mar 1916 that Britain had no definite plan to win the war (Riddell, *War Diary*, 161).
5. Cab 22/1/1. Note: the War Council met first on 25 Nov. 1914.
6. CO 616/15, 321.
7. Munro Ferguson to Harcourt, 6 Aug. 1914, HMS box 479.
8. Harcourt to Kitchener, 11 Sept. 1914, Kitchener to Harcourt, 14 Sept. 1914, CO 616/16, 245–46.
9. Gellibrand diary, 7 Aug. 1914, AWM 3 DRL 8050; Richards diary, 30 Oct. 1914.
10. R. Antill to parents, 3 Aug. 1914; recruiting fever: see, e.g., Robson, *First A.I.F.*, chap. 2.
11. Francis Beggs to White, 7 Sept. 1914, White Papers, NLA, folder 58; copy of recruiting leaflet in Walker Papers.
12. Lowe, *Great Britain and Japan*, 216–17; Louis, *Great Britain and Germany's Lost Colonies*, 37.
13. CO 616/1, 113.
14. AA AIF 112/2/218 B539.
15. Grey to Greene, 6 Aug. 1914, Gooch and Temperley, *British Documents* 2: 823; Lowe, *Great Britain and Japan*, 202–4, 214–15; Gilbert, *Winston S. Churchill* 3: 42–44.
16. Nish, *Alliance in Decline*, 115–27; Lowe, *Great Britain and Japan*, 186–93.
17. CO 616/10, 69–71.
18. CO 616/10, 427, 429 (22 Dec. 1914).
19. Jose, *Royal Australian Navy*, 47–51; Macandie, *Genesis of the Royal Australian Navy*, and Hyslop, *Australian Naval Administration*, 189.
20. *Age* leader, 12 Aug. 1914, cited in Thompson, *Australian Imperialism in the Pacific*, 203.
21. 'Imperialist': Thompson, *Australian Imperialism in the Pacific*, 204; Holmes report, 6 Sept. 1914, p 7, AA A2 1914/4181/44.
22. CO 616/7, 241–76, 516–25, 556–68; New Guinea capture and after: Mackenzie, *Australians at Rabaul*, Rowley, *Australians in German New Guinea*, Piggott, 'Stonewalling in German New Guinea'.
23. Fitzhardinge, *William Morris Hughes* 1.
24. Coulthard-Clark, *Heritage of Spirit*, 117–18; Army Council: Cassar, *Kitchener: Architect of Victory*, 183; Fraser, *Lord Esher*, 88–89, 160–64.
25. CO 616/3, 89 (14 Sept. 1914).
26. MacLaurin report *c.* early Oct. 1914, WO 95/4341.
27. CO 616/5, 506; CO 616/14, 354A.
28. WO to CO, 1 Sept. 1914, CO 616/14, 155.

## CHAPTER 3. ISLANDS FOR JAPAN; SOLDIERS FOR EUROPE

1. CO 616/16, 197.
2. CO 616/12, 148
3. CO 616/10, 303–5, 307–8; CO 616/12, 326, 341, 356.

4. Naval Board Minutes, AA A2585/2.
5. Fitzhardinge, 'Australia, Japan and Great Britain'.
6. CO 616/13, 230.
7. See Louis, 'Australia and the German Colonies in the Pacific'.
8. Message of thanks: AA 1915/3777; Creswell to Pearce and Fisher to Munro Ferguson, 23 Feb., AA A1 1920/7685; naval co-operation: *SMH*, 1 Jan., Fisher to Pearce, 15 Jan., PP bundle 7, no. 87. See also Thornton, 'Invaluable Ally or Imminent Aggressor?'.
9. *SMH*, 18 Jan., 22 Apr. (leader).
10. British High Commissioner in Fiji to Munro Ferguson, AA A1 1920/7685; Australian reaction: (handwritten) minute, 23 Mar., AA A1 1920/7685, CO 418/143, 358.
11. See Fitzhardinge, 'Australia, Japan and Great Britain'.
12. Pearce, Legge, Irvine: Munro Ferguson to Harcourt, 13 May, HMS box 479.
13. George V: CO 616/4, 203–4; Harcourt to Munro Ferguson, 24 Sept. 1914, CO 616/4, 424–25.
14. Admiralty to CO, 5 Oct. 1914, CO 616/10, 249; CO 616/5, 805.
15. Munro Ferguson's message dated 15 Nov. 1914, cited in Jose, *Royal Australian Navy*, 111.
16. Robson, *First A. I. F.*, Gammage, *Broken Years*, White, 'Motives for Joining Up'.
17. 'Godsend': Pte J. M. Aitken to mother, 27 Jan.; Antill to parents, 17 Nov. 1914; Fowler memoir re Sept. 1914; Blows memoir, n.d., IWM.
18. Silas diary, Aug.–Dec. 1914.
19. Pte V. Finch to Marjorie Stoddart, 7 Sept. 1914; Sutton diary, 19 Sept. 1914.
20. Mitchell diary, 20 Oct. 1914; 2 Lt H. J. F. Coe to parents, 29 Oct. 1914.
21. Sutton diary, 30 Oct. 1914.
22. Munro Ferguson to Harcourt, 29 Oct. 1914, HMS box 479.
23. Munro Ferguson to Harcourt, 3 Nov. 1914, ibid.
24. Mitchell diary, 28, 31 Oct. 1914.
25. Sutton diary, 30 Oct. 1914; Mitchell diary, 1 Nov. 1914.
26. *CPD* 1914, 75: 109 (Bakhap, 14 Oct.), 473 (Mathews, 11 Nov.), 147–49 (Anstey, 14 Oct.).
27. See Scott, *Australia During the War*.
28. Harcourt to Munro Ferguson, 19 Sept. 1914, AA CP 78/23 14/89/38.

### CHAPTER 4. THE VOYAGE

1. Aitken to mother, 7 Nov. 1914.
2. Sutton diary, 9, 10, 15 Nov. 1914; patriot: Frederick Arthur Robinson Great War TS diary, 22 Oct. 1914 (p. 47), 10 Nov. (p. 70) 1914, IWM; *CPD* 1914, 75: 468 (Fisher, 11 Nov.); Gov.-Gen. to Harcourt, 15 Nov. 1914, HMS box 479.
3. Sutton diary, 13, 17, 26 Nov. 1914; Richards diary, 18 Nov. 1914; Coe to parents, 22 Nov. 1914.
4. Hagan diary, 28 Nov. 1914; Sutton diary, 28 Nov. 1914; Coe to parents, 29 Nov. 1914. It has not been possible to locate Dawkins papers.
5. AA AIF 79/1/98 B539; Hill, *Chauvel*, 45.
6. Blamey to wife, 6 Dec. 1914, AWM PR 85/355, item 2.
7. Sgt W.W. B. Allen to mother, 27 Dec. 1914.
8. AA AIF 112/2/292 B539 for origin of the decision about change in destination. See also AA A2 1914/4179/169, CO 616/15, 102–4, and Brugger, *Australians and Egypt*, 18–20.
9. *CPD* 1914, 75: 1268.
10. Sutton diary, 2 Dec. 1914; Copp diary, 30 Nov. 1914; 'cheering': Hagan diary, 5 Dec. 1914.
11. Animal noises: D. W. Lechte recollection; Aitken to mother, 8 Dec. 1914.
12. Aitken to mother, 8 Dec. 1914; A.E. Joyce diary, 6 Dec. 1914; Copp diary, 2 Dec. 1914.

### CHAPTER 5. THE AIF BUILD-UP IN EGYPT

1. Leading Egyptian newspaper *Misi*, cited by Bean in message to 'Australia', 20 Dec. 1914, AA A2 1915/3625. Bean was a *SMH* leader-writer before being appointed official war correspondent by the Fisher government.
2. Cab 22/1/3.
3. Strength in Egypt: War Council, 19 Feb. 1915, Cab 22/1/14; Reid cable to Australia, 25 Nov. 1914, AA AIF 79/1/98 B539.
4. Orlo C. Williams diary, pt 1, 21 Mar. 1915, IWM; Birdwood, *Khaki and Gown*, 124, 239–40.
5. 'Kitchener man': Orlo Williams diary, pt 1, 18 Apr. 1915, IWM; Birdwood to Rawlinson, 15 Dec. 1914, MaP 3/4/5/; Birdwood, *Khaki and Gown*, 123–24, 238.
6. Birdwood to Kitchener, 25 Dec. 1914, PRO 30/57 64 WL 138, p.2.
7. Birdwood to Kitchener, 13 Jan. 1915, PRO 30/57 61 WL1.
8. Munro Ferguson to Pearce, 10 Nov. 1914, PP bundle 1, folder 2, no. 63; Munro Ferguson to Hamilton, 25 Dec. 1914, HP 1/2/2.
9. Harcourt to Munro Ferguson, 7 Dec. 1914, AA A2 1914/4179/200; Bridges despatch no. 8, Mena, AA AIF 116/2/43 B539.
10. Munro Ferguson to Harcourt, 25 Jan. 1915, CO 616/45, 277–79.
11. Fowler memoir, 26 Nov. 1914; Silas diary, 22, 23 Dec. 1914, 3 Jan. 1915.
12. Maj. I. G. Mackay diary, 15 Jan. 1915, AWM 3 DRL 6850; Capt. P. H. Auld diary, 17, 21 Jan. 1915; route march: Pte D. G. Alexander to mother, 8 Apr. 1915.

13. Comfortable (on *Ceramic* with 3,000 troops): Fowler memoir, pp 60–61 and Harris diary, 21 Jan. 1915; 'greatness': Pte Alfred Moon diary, 29 Jan. 1915; Mackay diary, 29 Jan. 1915.
14. Natusch TS diary, Dec. 1914, NP.
15. Col.V.C.M. Sellheim's despatch no. 9, 24 Jan. 1916, AA AIF 112/6/27 B539.
16. In the 1st Division, 'Protestant' and Catholic were 86 per cent to 15 per cent respectively, with proportionately fewer officers than men being Roman Catholic—only 6 per cent, reflecting concentration at that time of this religious group in less well-to-do levels of society. Figures for 1 Div. and 1 ALH calculated from Bridges' Divisional Order no. 43, Mena, 27 Jan. 1915, copy in Gellibrand Papers, AWM.
17. The best statistical analysis of the AIF is Robson, 'Origin and Character of the First A.I.F.'. Robson sampled two thousand attestation papers of the 417,000 volunteers. The First AIF Project, begun in 1986 in the Department of History of the University of New South Wales, at the Australian Defence Force Academy, Canberra, is compiling from First World War AIF records a computerised database amenable to sophisticated computer analysis (see Gilbert, Robertson and Russell, 'Computing Military History').
18. 'National command', 'Imperial': Coulthard-Clark, in Horner, ed.,*The Commanders*, see also Bean, *Story of Anzac* 1: 36; London plans inapplicable: Bridges' despatch no. 5, 7 Dec. 1914, CO, 616/4, 23; Godley to Rawlinson, 23 July 1915, MaP, 3/4/6.
19. Legge's appointment: Hamilton to Kitchener, 19, 27 May 1915, PRO, 30/57 61 WL/43, 45, Hamilton to Munro Ferguson, 6 Oct., HP, 3/26; also PRO, 30/57 61 WL/60 62, copy of Fisher to Munro Ferguson, 16 Sep. 1915, CO, 616/29, 496–97, and CO, 616/48, 81–88, and Coulthard-Clark, *No Australian Need Apply*, chap. 6; Birdwood's officer appointments: Pearce to Birdwood, 4 Feb. 1916, PP, Pearce-Birdwood Corres., bundle 5.
20. Birdwood GOC AIF: Bean, *Story of Anzac* 1: 417–8; Australians for command: e.g., Pearce to Birdwood, 4 Feb. 1916, PP, Pearce-Birdwood Corres., bundle 5; Shedden in his draft manuscript, chap. 53, Shedden Papers, AA A5954, box 1270.
21. Maxwell: Lt-Col. R. J. H. Fetherston to Sec. for Defence (Melbourne), 29 Sep. 1915, AA AIF 239/8/181 B539. For Sellheim, *ADB* 10, also AA AIF 323/3/21 B539.

## CHAPTER 6. 'PAINTING CAIRO VERY RED'

1. Mitchell diary, 9 Dec. 1914; Hagan diary, 18 Dec. 1914.
2. Above paragraphs: Bridges' Mena despatches no. 5, 7 Dec. 1914, AIF 116/2/43, no. 6, 19 Dec., AIF 112/6/143 B539, no. 7, 8 Jan. 1915, AIF 112/2/341 B539, no. 8, 27 Feb., AIF 116/2/43 B539, all at AA. See also Coulthard-Clark, *Heritage of Spirit*.
3. Storrs to Fitzgerald, 5 Dec. 1914, PRO, 30/57 45 00/69, 1; Maxwell to Fitzgerald, 23 Dec. 1914, ibid., 00/72; Birdwood to Bridges, 27 Dec. 1914, printed, HMS, box 470.
4. Birdwood to Kitchener, 25 Dec. 1914, PRO 30/57 64 WL 138, 2.
5. Maxwell to Fitzgerald, 11 Jan. 1915, PRO 30/57 47 QQ, p.2; Casey diary, 26 Jan. 1915, MS 6150, ser. 4, box 16, NLA.
6. *SMH*, 21 Apr. 1915.
7. Aitken to mother, 13 Dec. 1914; Coe to parents, 26 Dec. 1914.
8. Cpl H. T. McKern diary, 5 Dec. 1914.
9. Pte D. J. C. Anderson letter, 15 Dec. 1914; Monash diary, 23 Apr., 13 Feb.1915, MP box 130, folder 955, NLA.
10. McKern diary, 9 Jan. 1915.
11. Hagan diary, 12 Dec. 1914; Copp diary, 14 Dec. 1914.
12. Hagan diary, 25, 26 Dec. 1914.
13. D. J. C. Anderson letter, Dec. 1914.
14. Mitchell diary, 26 Dec. 1914.
15. Coe to parents, 26 Dec. 1914.
16. Sutton diary, 31 Dec. 1914; Aitken to mother, 31 Dec. 1914; Hagan diary, 31 Dec. 1914.
17. Reaction to Bean articles: e.g., letters to editor *Argus*, 25 Jan. 1915, Pte R. L. Donkin diary, 12 Mar. 1915; Schuler, *Australia at Arms*, 67–68; Aitken to mother, 19 Jan. 1915.
18. Fowler memoir; Copp diary, 14 Dec. 1914; Sutton diary, 31 Dec. 1914.
19. Birdwood to Kitchener, 25 Dec. 1914, PRO 30/57 64 WL 138, 2; Birdwood to Kitchener, 13 Jan. 1915, ibid., 61 WL 1.
20. Reid to WO, 3 Dec., and WO to Reid, 20 Dec. 1914, AA AIF 112/2/322 B539; Aitken to mother, 2 Jan. 1915.
21. Mitchell diary, 1 Jan. 1915; Reid speech: Schuler, *Australia in Arms*, 350–53.
22. Copp diary, 1 Jan., J. Gellibrand to brother, 14 Mar., Gellibrand Papers, AWM.
23. Aitken to mother, 7 Jan., 11 and 18 Feb.
24. Pearce: *Argus*, 25 Jan.; Hagan diary, 3 Feb.
25. *Kyarra* reaches Melbourne: *Argus*, 12, 13 Mar.; Bridges' Mena despatch no. 8, 27 Feb., AA AIF 116/2/43 B539; Pearce to Bridges, 10 Feb., PP bundle 3, folder 1, no. 10; disciplinary cases: *Brisbane Courier*, 15 Mar. *Argus*, 22 Apr.; Green: *SMH*, 3 Apr.; 'level best': letter to editor *Argus*, 22 Apr.
26. Pfeifer diary, 13 Feb., Morrish: Capt. H. G. Carter to Cmdr Gibson, 26 Apr., Rear-Adm. I. W. Gibson Papers, IWM.
27. Fairbairn to mother, 21 Mar., Fairbairn Papers, IWM; Lady Godley to husband, 11 Aug., GP.
28. Joyce diary, 23, 24 Jan.

29. Natusch to father, 15 Mar., NP; Rickard, *H. B. Higgins*, 218–19; Higgins, *In Europe 1914–15*.
30. 'Galloping Major': McKern diary; Hagan diary, 12, 19 Jan.
31. Bridges' Mena despatch no. 8, 27 Feb., AA AIF 116/2/43; McKern diary, 15 Jan.
32. Joyce diary, 29 Jan., Feb.; Aitken to mother, 18, 21 Feb.
33. Donkin diary, 24 Feb.
34. *Argus*, 15 Apr.
35. Mena operational order, e.g., 12 Mar.: Gellibrand Papers, AWM; Monash diary, 13, 18 Feb., MP, box 130, folder 955, NLA.
36. Joyce diary, 1 Feb., 25 Jan.; 'flaming desert': Edward Augustus Sampson memoir, n.d., PLA; Silas diary, 26 Feb.
37. 'Mess': Joyce diary, 17 Feb.; 'toffs': Hagan diary, 26 Feb.
38. Joyce diary, 17 Feb.; Bridges' Mena despatch no. 8, 27 Feb., AA AIF 116/2/43 B539; Birdwood to Kitchener, 23 Jan., and Birdwood to Fitzgerald, 2 Feb., PRO 30/57 61 WL1; ready for war: Hagan diary, 16 Feb., Capt. H. G. Carter diary, 12–16 Feb.
39. Hagan diary, 28 Dec. 1914.
40. Hagan diary, 3 Feb. 1915; Birdwood to Kitchener, 14 Feb., PRO 30/57 61 WL4; lengthy TS account of this engagement, PP bundle 3, folder, 1, no. 12.
41. Hagan diary, 27 Jan.
42. Joyce diary, Feb.; 'brawls': Hagan diary, 26 Feb., 1 and 3 Mar.; H. G. Carter diary, 7 Feb.
43. Bean (26 Mar.), *SMH*, 21 Apr.; Pte. V. Finch to Marjorie Stoddart, 23 Feb.
44. 'Keen': Sutton diary, 27 Jan.; Birdwood to Kitchener, 6 Apr., PRO 30/57 WL 17; *Queenslander*: W.W.B. Allen to sister, 14 Feb.
45. Aitken to mother, 27 Jan.
46. Birdwood to FitzGerald, 2 Feb., PRO 30/57 61 WL 3.

## CHAPTER 7. THE GALLIPOLI ENTERPRISE

1. Jabotinsky, *Turkey and the War*, 152, 158–59, 168–84. European powers' designs were an open topic in Constantinople diplomatic circles (Morgenthau, *All in a Lifetime*, 183–84).
2. Djemal, *Memories*, 66–69.
3. Listed in Kannengiesser, *The Campaign in Gallipoli*, 1. For a useful introduction to the Turks' campaign, see Larcher, *La Guerre turque*, pt 1.
4. Djemal, *Memories*, 97–115, 'iron claws', 106. For a discussion of the German-Ottoman coalition, see Trumpener, *Germany and the Ottoman Empire*, and Trumpener's chapter in *Coalition Warfare*, ed. Nelson and Prete.
5. Emin, *Turkey in the World War*, 66–71. During the war Dr Emin was Professor of Statistics in Constantinople University and later war correspondent with links to the ruling Turkish politicians.
6. General staff memo (copy), 19 Dec. 1906, and DNI advice in Cab 17/184. See also Roskill, *Hankey: Man of Secrets* 1: 85, and Gilbert, *Churchill* 3: 294.
7. C. E. Callwell, Director of Military Operations, memo 3 Sept. 1914, Cab 17/132.
8. Anderson, *Eastern Question*, 315.
9. Among numerous British accounts, see especially the very detailed description of Churchill's role in Gilbert, *Churchill*, vol. 3, James, *Gallipoli*, and Prior, *Churchill's 'World Crisis' as History* for analysis of Churchill's version.
10. Churchill to Kitchener, 24 Nov. 1914, WO 106/1469. Many key Gallipoli planning documents, including Churchill submissions, are in Cab 17/123.
11. Cited in Gilbert, *Churchill* 3: 331.
12. Anderson, *Eastern Question*, 322–26.
13. Kitchener cable to Maxwell, 24 Feb., cited in Cassar, *Kitchener*, 296.
14. Morgenthau, *Ambassador Morgenthau's Story*, 191–95. Representative of support for his view amongst eminent historians is that of Anderson (*Eastern Question*, 322, 326); Delage (*Tragedy of the Dardanelles*, 94) took a similar approach.
15. 'Account and comment on Gallipoli landings by Lt-Col. R. H. Williams, American Military Attaché with the Turkish forces at Gallipoli', comments recorded 3 June 1928, Cab 45/223. Williams was at the Suvla fighting with Liman von Sanders.
16. Morgenthau, *Ambassador Morgenthau's Story*, 201; for Turks fleeing Constantinople, Morgenthau, *Secrets of the Bosphorus*, 121–22.
17. Gilbert, *Churchill* 3: 288; Bean, *Story of Anzac* 1: 183.
18. Bean, *Story of Anzac* 1: 191; Cassar, *French and the Dardanelles*, 71–79.
19. Gilbert, *Churchill* 3: 303.
20. Cab 22/1/15–16.
21. Having some familiarity with British and Australian Second World War records of cabinet discussions and strategic analyses, I was amazed to read the amateurish, imprecise War Council discussions 'planning' the Dardanelles venture.
22. Military Board Special Order 15 Dec. 1914, copy in MP, AWM.
23. Gilbert, *Churchill* 3: 332.
24. Birdwood to Kitchener, 10 Mar., PRO 30/57 61 WL 12, p. 8.
25. Charles à Court Repington in *Morning Post*, reported in *Newcastle Morning Herald* (NSW), 25 Nov. 1919. Repington, on Kitchener's staff in 1898, military correspondent for *The Times* from 1904 to 1918 and later for the *Daily Telegraph*, became a prominent critic of the Dardanelles campaign.

## CHAPTER 8. 'THE WILD COLONIAL CORPS HAS LEFT CAIRO'

1. Copp diary, 21 Feb.; Sutton diary, 21 Feb.; Aitken to mother, 21, 22 Feb.; 'probably France': Fred Biddle to mother, 28 Feb.
2. Casey diary, 1 Mar., MS 6150, ser. 4, box 16, NLA; Monash diary, 4 Mar., MP box 130, folder 955, NLA.
3. Joyce diary, 28 Feb.; Hagan diary, 28 Feb.; Mitchell diary, 28 Feb.; Aitken to mother, 2 Mar.
4. 'Sardined': Joyce diary, 28 Feb.; Finch to Stoddart, 4 Mar.
5. Joyce diary, 8 Mar.
6. Lotbinière statement to DC, 9 Dec. 1916, Cab 19/20, 601.
7. RN officer: Oliver Backhouse diary, IWM; Sutton diary, 17 Mar.
8. 'Convicts': Joyce diary, 29 Mar.; 'monotonous', 'want to be a soldier', likely casualties: Mitchell diary, 16, 17, 14 Mar.; rope ladders: Maj. A. J. Aspinall, AAMC report 1923, AWM 41 [1/3.8]; Sutton diary, 31 Mar.; Aitken to mother, 10 Mar.; 'seagulls': Finch to Stoddart, 7 Apr.
9. Sutton diary, 15, 28 Mar. The 1st Division of the Corps Expéditionnaire d'Orient contained many colonial troops.
10.* De Robeck memo 'Queen Elizabeth', and 'Turkey, Bombardment of the Dardanelles', US Army War College Report, 13 Apr., copies in KP; Kannengiesser, *Campaign in Gallipoli*, 56–58; German numbers: Trumpener (Nelson and Prete, *Coalition Warfare*, 35) estimates there were 10,000 in Turkey by mid-1916, 25,000 in 1918. See also Larcher, *La Guerre turque*, pt 1.
11. Limpus, 'Notes on Situation inside Dardanelles' (n.d. but *c.* late 1914/early 1915), KP.
12. 'Disaster': Cmdr I. W. Gibson on *Albion*, diary, 18 Mar. 1915, Gibson Papers, IWM; gunner: T. Moore diary, 19 Mar., IWM.
13. Prior, *Churchill's 'World Crisis'*, 97–99.
14. The heroic role of the old mine-layer *Nusrat* is featured in Chanak's military museum. A new poster commemorating defeat of the Allied fleet adorned the wall of the waiting room for the Chanak bus in the Topkapi bus station, Istanbul, in June 1986.
15. Hamilton to Kitchener, 18 Mar., HP 5/1.
16. 'Report on Landing Facilities between Gaba Tepe and Cape Helles', 12 Apr., KP.
17. 3rd Bde: Joyce diary, 29 Mar.; Hamilton to Asquith, 25 Mar., Asquith MS, vol. 14, p. 21a, Bod.; Hamilton to Kitchener, 30 Mar., PRO 30/57 61 WL 14; Bridges Mena dispatch no. 10, 6 Apr. AA AIF 112/2/489 B539.
18. Casey diary 17 Mar. 1915, Ms 6150, ser. 4, box 16, NLA; Bridges diary, 1 Mar., AWM.
19. Health: P. Callary to family, 28 Mar.; R. E. Antill to mother, 11 Mar.; training in Egypt: Capt. A. G. Carne, memoir p. 26; Pedersen, *Monash as Military Commander*, 54.
20. Bridges Mena dispatch no. 8, 27 Feb., AA AIF 116/2/43 B539; Military Order 279, 1915; Monash diary, 27 Feb., MP box 130, folder 955, NLA.
21. Col. J. B. Maher to A. G. Butler, 20 Mar. 1923, AWM 41 [3/10.8].
22. Gellibrand to brother 8 Mar. AWM 3 DRL 8050; *Argus*, 1 Mar.
23. *CPD* 1915, 76: 2653 (Anstey, 28 Apr.); Capt. K. M. Gresson (NZ) diary, 10 Mar., IWM.
24. Donkin diary, 12, 18 Mar.; D. J. C. Anderson letter, 26 Mar.; Silas diary, 15 Mar.
25. Silas diary, 10 Mar.; R. E. Antill to parents, 4 Mar., 1 Apr.; Coe to father, 5 Apr.
26. Rumours: e.g., reports in *The Times* 16, 30 Mar.; 'smack': W. Fairbairn (NZ artillery) to mother, 4 Apr., IWM.
27. Hunter-Weston, extracts from letter, 3 Apr., HWP; Paris to C. Kinstone Pilkington, 10 Apr., PaP.
28. Natusch to mother, 4 Apr., NP; Fairbairn to mother, 4 Apr., IWM; Clennett to mother, 4 Apr.
29. S. S. Argyle diary, 4 Apr.; 'disgusted': Carter diary, 2 Apr.; 'disgraceful': G. S. Cox diary, 2 Apr.; Aitken to mother, 10 Apr. On the riot, see also Brugger, *Australians and Egypt*, chap. 2.
30. Cpl T. Valentine, British 243G Company Band, diary 2, 3 Apr., IWM.
31. Sellheim despatch no. 2; Intermediate Base, Cairo, 14 June, AA AIF 112/6/43 B539.
32. *SMH*, 21 Apr.; Clennett to mother, 4 Apr.
33. Officer: Carter diary, 3 Apr.; Copp diary, Apr.; Paris to C. Kinstone Pilkington, 10 Apr., PaP.
34. E. Rochdale diary, late Jan., 8 Apr., letter to grandmother, 5 May, IWM.
35. Orlo Williams diary, 7 Apr., IWM; Carter diary, 4 Apr.; 'blackhole': Corbin diary, 7 Apr.
36. Fowler memoir, 14 Apr.; Valentine diary, 7 Apr., IWM; Harris diary, 11 Apr.
37. Fowler memoir, 14 Apr.

## CHAPTER 9. PREPARING FOR A LANDING

1. Harris diary, 15 Apr.; Aitken to mother, 17 Apr.; 'covered with ships': Sutton diary, 8 Apr., on *Canada*, 4 Apr.
2. Birdwood to Kitchener, 11 Apr., PRO 30/57 61 WL 22.
3. Hunter-Weston to Wigram, 22 Apr., HWP 48364; G. Dawnay to wife, 4 Apr., DaP 69/21/1. Glasfurd helped to train Bridges's division, and Dawnay was on Hamilton's staff.
4. Scott, RN, to family, 4 Apr., IWM; Drage diary, 18 Apr., IWM; Ashmead-Bartlett, *Uncensored Dardanelles*, 30.
5. Callwell to Robertson, 1 Mar., Robertson Papers I/8/11a, LH.
6. Woods evidence to DC, 6 Feb. 1917, Cab 19/33, 150–64.
7. Maxwell evidence, 22 Feb. 1917, ibid, 975–76.
8. Ryan evidence, ibid, 1569.
9. WO 106/1472.

10. Gilbert, *Churchill* 3: 279.
11. Hamilton to Kitchener, 18 Mar., HP 5/1, 1–2.
12. Hankey's memo of 30 June 1916 for CID, Cab 17/132, p. 25.
13. Kitchener to Churchill, 13 Mar. Cab 17/132; notes by Henry Wilson of a meeting at Chantilly, 29 Mar., WO 159/7.
14. Hamilton to Kitchener, 30 Mar., and Birdwood to Kitchener, 3 Mar., PRO 30/59 61 WL/16, 3; intelligence summary of Anzac HQ, 23 Mar., WO 157/667; 'knock': Herbert, *Mons, Anzac and Kut*, 77.
15. 'Appreciation on situation to 25 March', copy in HWP 48356.
16. NZ and A Div. War Diary, 14 Apr., AWM 4; 'a lot of Australians': Maj.-Gen. Sir Stewart Hare Papers, Gallipoli diary, IWM; Bridges diary, 14 Apr., AWM.
17. Birdwood to Kitchener, 6 Apr., PRO, 30/57 61 WC/17; Callwell to Gwynne, 7 Apr., Gwynne Papers, box 17, Bod.; Gwynne to Asquith, 22 Apr., Asquith MS, vol. 27, 100–6, Bod.; on Beresford: Ashmead-Bartlett, *Uncensored Dardanelles*, 253.
18. Hamilton to Kitchener, 30 Mar., PRO 30/59 61 WL/16, 3; scale: Callwell, *The Dardanelles*, 336, and Corbett, *Naval Operations* 3: 84; beaches: Capt. D. J. Claris, RN, (OC *Queen Elizabeth* in 1915) diary, p. 16, IWM; Rylands (navigating officer on *Ark Royal* at Gallipoli) memoir, p. 9, IWM.
19. PRO 30/57 61 for Birdwood to Kitchener letter, 14 Feb. WL22, 3 Mar. WL5 p. 5, 11 Apr. WL22; Birdwood's pessimism: Godley to wife, 15 Apr., GP.
20. Carter diary, 11 Apr.; Corbin diary, 17 Apr.; Herbert, *Mons Anzac and Kut*, 77; Harris diary, 20 Apr.; Silas diary, 10 Mar.
21. Blamey to mother, 21 Apr., AWM, corres. item 1; Monash diary, 25 Mar., MP, box 130, folder 955, NLA; Casey diary, 11 Apr., MS 6150, ser. 4, box 16, NLA.
22. Mitchell diary, 23 Apr.; Biddle to mother, 5 Apr.; Copp diary, 24 Apr.
23. Recollections of Capt. W. Maxwell, Cab 19/33, 978; Chambers memoir, p. 2; Birdwood to Kitchener, 19 Apr., PRO 30/57 61 WL/24, also 22 Apr.; ibid, WL/26.
24. Harris diary, 24 Apr.; Corbin diary, 24 Apr.; Monash diary, MP box 130, folder 955, NLA.
25. Coe to father, 23 Apr.; Lawless diary; Bean: Fewster, *Gallipoli Correspondent*, 57.
26. British diarist: G. Barsley (*Southland* crew member but not when it was torpedoed) diary, 24 Apr., p. 6, IWM; Ashmead-Bartlett, *Uncensored Dardanelles*, 36–37.
27. Bean diary: Fewster, *Gallipoli Correspondent*, 56; Silas and Mitchell diaries, 25 Apr. For the approach by 3rd Brigade to the landing, see Bean, *Story of Anzac* 1: 245–55.

## CHAPTER 10. 'THE REAL MEANING OF WAR'

1. 'Grim': Sgt D. J. Anderson, 8 Bn, to father n.d. (early May?); Beevor memoir (1930), p. 5; Smith to father, 14 May. Winter, 'The Anzac landing,' argues there was a last-minute change of plan to switch the landing-place to a spot about two kilometres further north of Gaba Tepe. Of the scores of writers on this subject, no one else has suggested such a remarkable recipe for chaos. The best recent explanation for the mistake is in Eric Bush's *Gallipoli*, which blames not the northward current but an inability, in the dark, to identify the correct headland. For an excellent 'nutshell' account of the Gallipoli landings, see Pedersen, *Monash*, 54–55.
2. Beevor memoir, p. 12.
3. Casey diary, 30 Apr., AWM 3 DRL 2030; Birdwood, *Khaki and Gown*, 257; others: e.g., Capt. D. Hearder TS memoir, n.d., Aitken to mother, 5 May.
4. Lt Aubrey Darnell letter, 12 June, AWM.
5. Nicholas, account written shortly after the landing; Mitchell diary, 25 Apr.; Keast diary, 25 Apr.; Hearder memoir; Clark diary, n.d.
6. Aitken to mother, 25 Apr.; Cheney memoir, n.d.; Sig. D.A. Redmond to Perth friend, *Sunday Times*, 25 July, AWM.
7. 'Mule, goat and lion': Lt B. W. Champion diary, 13 Nov.; 'scrambling': Alwynne diary, 25 Apr.
8. Mitchell diary, 25 Apr.
9. Aitken to mother, 29 Apr.
10. Hamilton to Birdwood, 26 Apr.; Bean, *Story of Anzac* 1: 461.
11. Diary in Gibson papers, IWM; veteran's comments reported in Henry Stead (in Melbourne) to Harcourt, 11 Aug., HMS box 445.
12. Misc. 309, IWM.
13. Newspaper cutting, AA AIF 112/2/628 B539.
14. Carter diary, 25 Apr.; Baker to Vera Johns, 5 May (Brisbane *Courier Mail*, 25 Apr. 1981); Mitchell diary, 25 Apr.
15. Alwynne diary, 25 Apr.; Donkin diary, 26 Apr.; Baker to Johns, 5 May.
16. Mitchell diary, 25 Apr.
17. Hagan diary, 25 Apr.
18. Skinner postcard to Gert, 8 May 1916; McCowan diary, 27 Apr.; Smythe memoir; Duke memoir TS, n.d., p. 75.
19. A. R. [M.?] Andrews memoir (*c.* June 1915); Mitchell diary, 29 Apr.; Pte F. Robson diary, 28, 29 Apr.
20. Mitchell diary, 28 Apr.; Richards diary, 28 Apr.; Harris Diary, 27 Apr.; Silas diary, 26 Apr.; Copp diary, 26 Apr.
21. Needing artillery: Sapper G. C. Grove diary, 26 Apr.; Capt. W. T. Yates (8 Bn) diary, 26, 28 Apr.,

AWM; Corbin diary, 28 Apr.; Aitken to mother, 29 Apr.; Maidos: Liman von Sanders, *Five Years in Turkey*, 72.

22. Copp diary, 28 Apr.
23. Richards diary, 25 Apr.
24. Keyes, *Naval Memoirs* 1: 380.
25. Silas diary, 25 Apr.
26. 'Camouflaged': Cpl O. S. Blows diary, n.d.
27. Bennett diary, 26 Apr., NMM JOD/106/1. Wilkinson to brother-in-law, 3 Apr.–8 June, IWM; Drage diary, 25, 27 Apr., IWM.
28. Gresson diary, 25 Apr., IWM; Dawnay to wife 29 Apr., DaP 69/21/1; Bennett diary, 26, 29 Apr., NMM JOD/106/1; Brampton diary, 28 Apr., IWM 77/45/1; NZ view: Pugsley, *Gallipoli*, 115; Natusch to family, 2 May, NP.
29. Birdwood to Kitchener, 4 May; Arthur, *Kitchener* 3: 133–36; Bridges divisional order, 28 Apr., WO 95/4344; Hamilton to Kitchener, 30 Apr., PRO 30/57 61 WL/31; Godley to wife, 29 Apr., GP.
30. Thursby's report, 28 Apr., p. 5, and de Robeck's report, 25/26 Apr., p. 20, in Adm. 116/1434; Vice-Adm, Eastern Mediterranean cable to Admiralty, 28 Apr., copy in NMM OLV/5; Lady Richmond diary, 28 Apr. NMM RIC/1/17.
31. WO to CO, 28 Apr., CO 616/45, 509; Harcourt to Munro Ferguson, 28 Apr., CO 418/143, 221; *HCPD* question, 5 May, in CO 418/142, 333; Ashmead-Bartlett, *Uncensored Dardanelles*, 253.
32. Bean in Australian papers, 14 May; Fewster, *Gallipoli Correspondent*, 134.
33. Pearce to Bridges, 16 May, PP bundle 3, folder 1, no. 6.
34. Monash diary, 7 June, MP box 130, folder 956, NLA.
35. Amery to Milner, 27 May, MMS vol. 350.
36. Birdwood to Kitchener, 11 May, PRO 30/57 61 WL/37; Hamilton to Kitchener, 30 Apr., PRO 30/57 61 WL/31; Kitchener in War Council, 14 May, Cab 22/1/21, 4; Kitchener to Maxwell, 8 May, WO 158/574.
37. *SMH*, 30 Apr.

## CHAPTER 11. 'THIS NEWLY DISCOVERED SEASIDE RESORT'

1. For discussion of why commanders favoured the offensive, see M. Howard in Miller, ed., *Military Strategy*; Skinner to Gert, 14 May; Richards diary, 27 Apr.
2. 'Anzac Cove': Casey diary, 5 May, AWM 3 DRL 2030, Birdwood to Hankey, 15 Sept., Cab 17/124.
3. 'Knife edge': F. W. Johnston diary, 30 Apr., IWM; Casey diary, 5 and 6 May, AWM 3 DRL 2030; Quinn's: Godley to wife, 4 June, GP; 'no back' to trenches: Capt. B. L. Moore TS on tour of battlefields with Hamilton, Keyes and Aspinall, IWM.
4. Godley to wife, 6 June, GP.
5. Keyes, *Naval Memoirs* 1: 373–75.
6. Hamilton to Kitchener, 3 June, PRO 30/57 62 WL/48.
7. 'Cheesebite': Godley to Rawlinson, 23 July, MaP 3/4/6; trenches: Carne memoir; 'rather slack': Baker to Vera Johns, 5 May; Coe diary, 2 May.
8. Braund: Alwynne diary, 3 (sic) May; Grove diary, 12 May; 'cover for himself': McCowan diary, 8 May; 'cur': Mitchell diary, May.
9. 'Field of vision': Carne memoir; Alwynne diary, 3 May.
10. F.W. Johnston diary, 30 Apr., IWM; Aitken to mother, 29 Apr.; Godley to wife, 29 Apr., GP.
11. Bean, *Story of Anzac* 1: 281.
12. Finch to Stoddart, 27 May; Sutton diary, 7 May; Hamilton to Kitchener, 3 June, PRO 30/57 62 WL/48; Mitchell diary, 13 May; Corbin diary, 7 May, 16 June.
13. Frankcombe diary, 1 May; F. W. Johnston diary 1, 5, 11 May, IWM.
14. Silas diary, 2 May.
15. Skinner to Gert, 13 July.
16. Silas diary, 3 May.
17. Bean, *Story of Anzac* 1: 582–98 for the full story of the attack; Lawless diary, 2 May; *Campaign des Dardanelles*, 37.
18. Report on Action of May 2/3, MP letter book, box 128, folder 940, NLA.
19. McKern diary, 3–6 May; Alwynne diary, 8, 9 May.
20. Moor letter, 9 May; Aitken to mother, 12 May.
21. Grove diary, 11 May.
22. Lawless diary.
23. 'Standstill': Mitchell diary, 13 May; also Sutton diary, 10 May; Casey diary 9, 27 May, AWM 3 DRL 2030. By 30 May, Casey could not see what good small individual attacks could do.
24. Hamilton to Kitchener, 5 May, HP 5/13; Richards diary, 26 May; Gellibrand to Walter, 28 May, AWM 3 DRL 8050.
25. Bean, *Story of Anzac* 2, chap. 1; R. W. Chambers memoir, 7 May; McCowan diary, 9 May; 'cobbers': Gutteridge memoir, p. 4; Max [?] (7 Bn) to father, 4 Oct., in AWM 3 DRL 6489.
26. McCowan diary, May.

## CHAPTER 12. 'BEARING THEIR GRIEF NOBLY'

1. Pound and Harmsworth, *Northcliffe*, 479, 482.
2. *HCPD*, 5th ser., vol. 71 (1915), col. 1273 (Asquith, 6 May), col. 1794 (Outhwaite, 13 May); *HLPD*, 5th ser., vol. 18 (1915), cols. 969–70 (Lansdowne, 11 May), col. 1020 (Kitchener, 18 May);

Monash letter, 18 July, MP box 130, folder 956, NLA.

3. Munro Ferguson to Harcourt, 13 May, HMS box 479; WO to CO, 13 May, CO 616/45, 561; Godley to Lord Kilbracken, 9 May, cited in Godley, *Life of an Irish Soldier*, 16.

4. CO 418/133, 32; Munro Ferguson to Bonar Law, 30 June, DP box 1914–1918.

5. Asquith's statement: CO 616/48, 4–6; Pearce message, *SMH* 3 May.

6. Agitation: Fisher to Harcourt in Munro Ferguson to CO, 6 May, AA AIF 112/2/424 B539; Munro Ferguson to Harcourt 13 May, HMS box 479.

7. Fate of privates: Godley to Pearce, 7 May, PP bundle 6, no. 51; Monash diary, 27, 20 May, MP box 130, folder 955, NLA; casualties 25 Apr., e.g., Birdwood, *Khaki and Gown*, 259.

8. Roth to Monash, 19 May, MP box 13, folder 113, NLA.

9. Fisher, 19 June, AA CP 78/23 14/89/101; Collins to Pearce, PP bundle 7, no. 115; Pearce to Godley, PP bundle 6, no. 51; Pearce to Bridges, 16 May, PP bundle 3, folder 1, no. 6.

10. Weymss to Limpus, 17 May, Limpus Papers, NMM; Paris to Mrs Pilkington, 28 May, PaP; Brodrick (Dardanelles) to Curzon, 21 May, CP MSS EUR F 112–59; Hamilton to friend, 29 May, HP 1/3/2.

11. Political crisis: Hankey, *Supreme Command* 1: 335; Roskill, *Hankey* 1: 176; 'blow': Hamilton, *Gallipoli Diary* 1: 240, 242; Godley to wife, 21 May, GP; Hamilton to Churchill, 26 May, HP 5/13.

## CHAPTER 13. 'A VERITABLE INFERNO'

1. 'Charges': Fowler memoir, p. 75; Lennie diary, 12 May; Silas diary, 11 May; Casey diary 10, 16 May, AWM 3 DRL 2030.

2. 'Horrible': Lt Charles G. J. Stinson diary, 18 May, AWM; Sutton diary, 11 May.

3. Aitken to mother, 13 May; R. E Antill to parents, 14 May; 'safe': Pte D. Alexander to mother, 15 May; Chaplain E. N. Merrington (AIF, returned to Australia 8 Apr. 1919) diary, p. 6, AWM; Simpson: Gallishaw, *Trenching at Gallipoli*, 83–84; see also Benson, *Man with the Donkey*.

4. Robson diary, 12 May; 'dabster': Sutton diary, 13 May; trenches: Casey diary, 18 May, AWM 3 DRL 2030; Aitken to mother 15, 17 May.

5. POW: Lawless diary, 14 May; Stinson diary, 8 May, AWM; Robson diary, 14 May; 'sweating': Pte D. J. C. Anderson letter, 28 May.

6. Silas diary, 14, 16, 17 May.

7. *Campaign des Dardanelles*, 44; Einstein, *Inside Constantinople*, 53; Birdwood, *Khaki and Gown*, 265; AIF VCs: Wigmore, *They Dared Mightily*.

8. 'Sport': 2 Bn War Diary, 19 May, WO 95/4341; 'wallaby drive': J. L. Merivale to father, 31 May; 'veritable inferno' Aitken to mother, 19 May.

9. W. W. Paterson to brother, 12 July PLA; Ashmead-Bartlett memo to Asquith during campaign, printed, Cab 19/33, 712; Monash diary, 19 July, MP box 134, folder 1033, NLA.

10. Misc. 1172, IWM.

11. Grove diary, 24 May; 'Dante's Inferno': McCowan diary, 24 May.

12. Cpl F. C. W. Wright (1st LH) diary, 29 May, AWM.

13. Butler memoirs, IWM PP/MCR/107.

14. Owen diary (Anzac) and other papers, Cab 45/246; Scott to family, 10 May, IWM.

15. Birdwood circular memo, 28 Apr., WO 95/4280, and to Kitchener, 4 June, PRO 30/57 62 WL/49; Hamilton cables to Kitchener, 28, 30 Apr., Cab 17/123.

## CHAPTER 14. 'AN ANTHEAP OF KHAKI ANTS'

1. Hamilton to Kitchener, 27 June, PRO 30/57 62 WL/62; Ashmead-Bartlett memo, 12 June, Cab 22/2/2.

2. Orlo Williams diary, pt 1, 24 May, IWM.

3. Hamilton to Kitchener, 19 June, PRO 30/57 62 WL/60, 8; McCowan diary, 22 June; Mackenzie, *Gallipoli Memories*, 83; Allanson, 5 Aug., photostat, p. 5, BP 75/65/3; Hankey to Asquith, 28 July, Hankey, *Supreme Command*, 379, and to wife, 28 July, Roskill, *Hankey* 1: 194–95.

4. Birdwood to Fitzgerald, 20 June, PRO 30/57 62 WC/61; 'diggers' at Anzac, e.g. Lt-Col. J. S. Millar TS, p. 27, IWM: discussion in Butler, *The Digger*; visitor: Kisch, *Australian Landfall*, 172 cited by K. S. Inglis in 'ANZAC and the Australian Military Tradition', 7.

5. Entombed: Grove diary, 29 June; Birdwood to Kitchener, 16 June, PRO 30/57 62 WL59; 'terrible': A. W. Skinner reminiscences, p. 24, n.d., IWM.

6. Liman von Sanders, *Five Years*, 71–72; Hamilton to Kitchener, 2 July, PRO 30/57 62 WL/64; Dawnay to wife, 10 June, DaP 69/21/1.

7. Rev. John D. D. de Vitre to mother, TS p. 11, n.d., NMM DEV/1; Liman von Sanders, *Five Years*, 75; Keyes to wife, 17 July, KP.

8. 'Not funny': Hearder memoir TS, n.d. (*c.* May); 'leisure': 3 LH Brigade Feb–May TS, Misc. 77, item 1172, IWM; Clennett to mother, 2 July.

9. Maj.-Gen. S. S. Butler memoirs, IWM PP/MCR/107; 'biscuits': Godley to wife, 8 June, GP; kettle: Casey diary, 7 June, AWM 3DRL 2030.

10. Hamilton to Kitchener, 3 June, PRO 30/57 62 WL/48; on canteen, 30 Aug., PRO 30/57 63 WL/93; Keyes to wife, 30 July, KP; Ashmead-Bartlett, *New York Times*, 6 Aug.; de Vitre TS p. 12, NMM DEV/1; Dr Mayo-Robson DC evidence, Cab 19/33, 927.

11. 'Tin-openers': W. E. English to sister Nurse English, 19 July, *Kalgoorlie Miner*, 5 Oct.; Monash letter in MP box 130, folder 956, NLA.

12. McCowan diary, 17 June.

13. Birdwood to Kitchener, 9 June, PRO 30/57 62 WL/51; Hamilton to Kitchener, 24 Aug., PRO 30/57/62 WL 59; Birdwood to Hamilton, 25 Aug. HP 5/10; Hogue, *Trooper Bluegum*, 191–93; Idriess, *Desert Column*.

14. A. W. Skinner reminiscences, p. 25, IWM; Smythe memoir, n. d., Clennett diary, 4 June; Radnell diary, 28 June, PLA.

15. Godley to wife, 19 May, GP; Howitt MS Dec. 1915, IWM; Paterson to brother, 12 July, p. 160.

16. Monash diary, 18 July, MP box 130, folder 956, 31 May, folder 955, 8 June, folder 956, NLA; letter book, 30 June, MP box 128, folder 941, and 27 July, box 139, folder 1033 NLA; Hamilton to WO on C. P. Smith, 12 Oct., Cab 19/30 19/2/82.

17. Richards diary, 11 June; F. D. Howitt, 31 July, in MS Dec. 1915, IWM; Allanson diary, 23 July, AP CJA1, and Aug. 1915 photostat, BP; 'want of care': Allanson to brother, 23 Sept., AP CJA2; Keyes, 30 July, KP1, pt 2, p. 168.

18. Godley to wife, 4 June, GP; drunkeness: I. T. Birtwhistle diary, 17 July, CO 418/143, 170, 194; asleep on duty: Lt-Col. Lord Rochdale (42 Div.) re Helles in Sept., Cab 19/30, 353; self-inflicted wounds: Butler, *Medical Services* 3: 79–80, and Bean, *Story of Anzac* 2: 425 n.

19. Birdwood to Kitchener, 4 June, PRO 30/57 62 WL/49.

20. Hamilton to Kitchener, 2 July, PRO 30/57 62 WL/64 p. 1, 7 June, WL/50, p. 1.

21. Hamilton to Kitchener, 7 June, PRO 30/57 62 WL/50, to French, 17 June, copy in BP 75/65/4; Turkish strength: Kitchener, 28 May, Cab 19/30, 353; Hamilton to Kitchener, 3 June, PRO 30/57 62 WL/48, 7 June, WL/50; Birdwood to Kitchener, 4 and 29 June, PRO 30/57 62 WL/49; Godley to wife, 18 July, GP.

22. Italy 'in the argument': McCowan diary, 23 May; ruses: Birdwood to Kitchener, 9 and 4 June, PRO 30/57 62 WL/51, WL/48; 'chances': Hamilton to Asquith, 2 Aug., PRO 30/57 63 WL179, 5.

23. White to Hutton, 19 June, HuP add. MS 50089; Hamilton to Asquith, 2 Aug., PRO 30/57 63 WL/79; Godley to wife, 6 June, GP, and to Rawlinson, 23 July, MaP 3/4/6; Barton to Fisher, 8 July, FP 2919/1/111, 112.

## CHAPTER 15. REINFORCEMENTS FROM AUSTRALIA

1. Munro Ferguson to Bonar Law, 12 July, CO 418/133, 143A, cable, 14 July, (copy 'Peninsula Press', 16 July, no. 57) HP 17/5/6; J. A. Raws to father, 12 July.

2. To Monash: R. Taylor, 4 Aug., folder 114, Lt F. Monash Behrend, 28 Aug., folder 113, and 28 Aug., folder 115, L. Roth, 20 Nov., folder 118, and 17 Sept., folder 114, all MP box 13, NLA.

3. Army Council request and outcome: AA AIF 190/1/81 B539.

4. Munro Ferguson to Bonar Law, 28 May, 30 June, 13 July, DP box 1914–1918; Dodds: Bean, *Story of Anzac* 2: 804, n. 16; rifles: Munro Ferguson cable to Bonar Law, 10 July, CO 418/133, 123.

5. Munitions production: *CPD* 77: 4095–4101 (Fisher and Cook, 17 June), also *CPD* 78: 5713; training: AA AIF 264/1/28.

6. Wounded: F. Tate (Melbourne) to Monash, 26 July, MP box 13, folder 113, NLA.

7. Australia's resolve: *CPD* 78: 5538 (Fisher), *SMH*, 5 Aug.; Seelenmayer to Monash, 30 June, MP box 13, folder 113, NLA.

8. Stead to Harcourt, 11 Aug., HMS box 445.

9. Munro Ferguson to Hamilton, 23 Aug., HP 3/26, to Bonar Law, 13 July, DP box 1914–1918.

10. Debate: *HCPD*, 5th ser., vol. 72, cols. 1895–1907; Rochdale: Cab 19/30, 351–53.

11. Northcliffe to Lloyd George, 15 June, LGP D/18/1/14; Hamilton to Kitchener, 9 June, PRO 30/57 62 WL/50; Birdwood to Kitchener, 9 June, PRO 30/57 62 WL/51, 1.

12. Orlo Williams diary, pt 1, 30 June, IWM; Allanson diary, 23 July, AP CJA1; Capt. M. Ralston-Kennedy, 9 June, PRO 30/57 62 WL/66, 3 July, PRO 30/57/62 WL/65; Birdwood to Fitzgerald, 20 June, PRO 30/57 62 WL/61.

13. 'Magnificent': Monash diary, 30 May, MP box 130, folder 958, NLA; 'enchanted': Nevinson, *Dardanelles Campaign*, 210–12; Lady Godley to husband, 4 June, 16 Sept., 20 Oct., GP; subaltern: Capt. A. M. McGrigor diary, 14 Jan. 1916, pp. 265–67, IWM.

14. AA CP 78/23 14/89/97.

15. Reinforcements: Munro Ferguson to Bonar Law, 9 July, CO 616/26, 339; Military Board proceedings, 14 July, agenda, 10 June (note p. 314), Recommendations of Military Board 1915, pp. 80–81, all at AA A2653.

16. Sellheim dispatch no. 4, Intermediate Base, Cairo, 12 Aug., AA AIF 112/6/43 B539.

17. Mêlée: Alcock to brother, 14 June; 'naughty': Aram to mother, 4 July.

18. Cairo heat: W. H. Bertwistle diary, July; Brind to mother, 20 June; Alcock to brother, 14 June.

19. Aram to mother, 3 Aug.

20. Maxwell to Hamilton, 18 and 4 Aug., HP 5/12; Bertwistle diary, 31 July; R. Raws to family, 4 Aug.

21. Sellheim dispatch no. 4, Intermediate Base, Cairo, 12 Aug., AA AIF 112/6/43 B539; Collins to Pearce, 18 Aug. PP bundle 7, no. 116; Maxwell to Hamilton, 4 Aug., HP 5/12.

22. Aram to mother, 20 July; Mitchell diary, 10 July; 'rout': Corbin diary, 11 July.

## CHAPTER 16. 'ON THE BRINK OF THE UNKNOWN'

1. Selborne to Bonar Law 7, July, BLP 51/1/10; 'rising': Gilbert, *Churchill*, 432.

2. Robert Rhodes James, ed., *Winston S. Churchill: His Complete Speeches 1897–1963*, 8 vols (New York, 1974), 2378–84.

3. Bonar Law to Selborne, 8 June, DP box 1914–1918, Dardanelles folder, to Selborne, 7 July (draft),

BLP 53/6/31, to H. Wilson, 15 July, BLP 53/6/33; Gen. Sir T. Morland to Hutton, 6 July, HuP Add. MSS 50099, Hunter-Weston to Callwell, 15 July, HWP 48356; Haig to Kiggell, 1 July, KiP 11/2; Wilson to Bonar Law, 12 July, BLP 51/1/15; sapper: R. Carnell diary, AWM.

4. 'Furore': J. Midleton to Curzon, 3 Aug., CP EUR F112/115; Godley to Rawlinson, 23 July, MaP 3/4/6; Allanson diary, AP DS/MISC/69 CJA1; Hamilton to de Robeck, 21 July, deRP 4/40.

5. Birdwood on 'next big push . . . into Anzac, not Helles': to Fitzgerald, 20 June, PRO 30/57 62 WL/61, 3, and *Khaki and Gown*, 268; Bean, *Story of Anzac* 2: 433–39; 'waking or . . .': Dawnay to wife, 9 Aug., DaP 69/21/1; Casey diary, June, AWM 3 DRL 2030.

6. For 'major feint' and excellent summary of August offensive plan, see Pedersen, *Monash*, 83.

7. Monash diary, July–Aug., MP box 139, folder 133, NLA.

8. Stopford: Prior, 'Suvla Bay Tea-Party', 26–27; Birdwood to Kitchener, 29 June, PRO 30/57 62 WL 63, 9 July, PRO 30/57 62 WL/69.

9. Godley to Rawlinson, 23 July, MaP, 3/4/6; Hankey to Kitchener, 28 July, Cab 17/123; Shaw diary, 6 Aug., IWM; Allanson diary, 2 Aug., BP 75/65/3; Hamilton to Asquith, 5 Aug., PRO 30/57 63 WL/81; 'non-communicative': Sir James Porter, Principal Hospital Transport Officer 'Some Memories of the Dardanelles July to Dec. 1915' n.d. (hand-written in old age) PoP PTR/8/1/2; Birdwood to de Robeck, 6 Aug., deRP 4/42.

10. Ashmead-Bartlett, *Uncensored Dardanelles*, 151; Mackenzie, *Gallipoli Memories*, 52–53; Hamilton, *Gallipoli Diary* 2: 306.

11. 2 Bn War Diary, 5 Aug., WO 95/4041; instruction (copy) War Diary General Staff NZ & A Div., WO 95/4344; Birdwood to Keyes, 6 Aug., KP; S.S. Argyle diary, 22 July.

## CHAPTER 17. 'WE FELT LIFE WILD BEASTS'

1. Turkish strength at Anzac, 1 Aug. 1915: Lt-Col. F. A. Rayfield Papers, IWM 69/61/3.

2. Godley to wife, 31 Aug., GP.

3. Drewry to father, 28 Sept., Drewry Papers, IWM.

4. Aitken to mother, 7 Aug.

5. Lt J. W. McPherson (non-combatant medical aide) diary, pp. 1007–8, IWM 80/25/1.

6. Drewry to father, 7 Oct., Drewry Papers, IWM.

7. De Vine diary, 6 Aug.

8. Letter (anon), 18 Aug., Merivale Papers; Dowse to cousin Gladys, 19 Sept.

9. Cpl J. Neal (Lemnos) letters, n.d.; Gammage diary, n.d.

10. Jury (St George's Hospital, Malta) to mother, n.d.; R. E. Antill (Alexandria) to parents, 15 Aug. and (London) 30 Aug.

11. Mychael to sister Mary, 19 Aug.; Max [?] 7 Bn (Lemnos) to father, 4 Oct., in Sgt E. W. Pinder Papers, AWM 3 DRL 6489.

12. 2 Bn War Diary, WO 95/4341.

13. Gammage diary, 8–9 Aug.; de Vine diary, 8 Aug.; Donkin diary, 11 and 14 Aug., and Pte. R. Anderson to Donkin's aunt, 15 Dec., AWM 2 DRL 69.

14. Gammage diary, 8–9 Aug.; de Vine diary, 8 Aug.; Bennett to mother, 14 Jan. 1916; 'sang froid': copy of letter (anon), 18 Aug., Merivale Papers; 'Fighting': Carter diary, 11 Aug.; Ashmead-Bartlett, *Uncensored Dardanelles*, 202.

15. De Vine diary, 10 Aug.

16. Kitson memoir.

17. Allanson photostat, 6 Aug., p. 8, BP 75/65/3.

18. J. R. Bell to mother, 10 Aug.; dispatch rider: Cpl H. A. J. Lamb (Royal Engineers) diary notes, 7–11 Aug., Lamb Papers, IWM.

19. Pedersen, *Monash*, 106; Dawnay to wife, 15 Aug., DaP 69/21/1.

20. Keyes to wife, 16 Aug., KP.

21. Godley to wife, 12 Aug., GP; Keyes to wife, 24 Aug., KP; Godley to Pearce, 14 Aug., PP bundle 6, item 51; Hamilton to Callwell, 13 Sept., HP 5/11. Ashmead-Bartlett dispatch, 19 Aug., *Kalgoorlie Miner*, 4 Sept.; Bonar Law to Munro Ferguson, 13 Aug., DP 1914–1918 box; Birdwood to de Robeck, 30 Aug., deRP; Lt McPherson Letters, p. 1028 n.d., IWM.

## CHAPTER 18. THE NEK ATTACK: SOME CONFLICTING VERSIONS

1. See, e.g., Kemal Ataturk memoir TS, p. 17, IWM; Hill, *Chauvel*, 60; Liddle, *Men of Gallipoli*, 201–2; Bean, *Story of Anzac* 2: 622–24.

2. Skeen and Braithwaite orders of 5 Aug., copy in War Diary of Gen Staff NZ & A Div., WO 95/4349; 'hopeless': Bean, *Story of Anzac* 2: 464.

3. Hankey to Curzon, 26 Oct., CP EUR F112/60.

4. 8 LH and 10 LH war diaries (also 9 LH War Diary), 7 Aug., WO 95/4288; Lt-Col. N. M. Brazier diary, 7 Aug.; see also Olden, *Westralian Cavalry in the War*.

5. HQ 3 Aust LH Bde War Diary, WO 95/4280.

6. Godley: quotes from 'Report on Operations Against Sari Bair position 6–10/8/15' signed A. J. Godley, WO 158/600; his other reports: 'Short Preliminary Account of the Attack on Sari Bair 6/8–10/8/15', n.d., WO 158/600, 'Operations against Sari Bair position 6–10/8/15' in War Diary Gen. Staff NZ & A Div., WO 95/4349; Birdwood, *Khaki and Gown*, 275; 2 LH: Chauvel report, 10 Aug., War Diary HQ Aust. Div. LH Bde, WO 95/4354; 'wise': Godley report, WO 158/600, 11–12.

7. Hamilton cable to Kitchener, 8 Aug., WO Tels vol. 2, Cab 19/31, report of 11 Dec. in *London*

*Gazette*, 6 Jan. 1916, and *The Times* 7 Jan. 1916, supplement p. 18; Hamilton, *Gallipoli Diary* 2: 55–57.

8. Bean, *Story of Anzac* 2: 617 and f.n. 36; Maj. Love letters to Lt-Col. Brazier, July, AWM 1 DRL 147.
9. Military Board Proceedings 1915, Agenda pp. 179–84, AA A2653; 'pitiful' and 'right through': J. M. Antill to Hutton, 4 Feb. 1916, HuP Add MS 50089; 'piffling': J. M. Antill war diary, 20 Oct., AWM 3 DRL 6458; 'incompetent': Munro Ferguson to Hamilton 23 Aug., HP 3/26. Birdwood praised Antill to Hutton, 30 Sept. 1916, HuP Add MS 50089.
10. Bean's account of 15 Aug. in *Kalgoorlie Miner*, 28 Sept., and *New York Times*, 4 Oct.
11. Weir, *Gallipoli: The Screenplay*, 144; a copy of Brazier's report is in J. M. Antill Papers, AWM 3 DRL 6458.
12. 'Turkey is paying': P. I. Callary to family, 14 Aug.; 'nothing can compare': W. M. Cameron diary, 18 Aug.; skeletons: McGrigor diary, 22 Nov. AWM.
13. Walker to parents, 8 Dec.
14. Nevinson, *Dardanelles Campaign*, 242–46; Ashmead-Bartlett, *Uncensored Dardanelles*, 232. Ashmead-Bartlett in *The Times*, 29 Sept., was 'good and quite accurate', wrote C. J. to H. Allanson, AP CJA2.

## CHAPTER 19. 'STORIES . . . UTTERLY FALSE AND MISLEADING'

1. *Argus*, Aug., including 'Devils for Fighting', 28 Aug.
2. Ibid.
3. *New York Times*, 23 Apr., reported Churchill discussing with the French the best way of forcing the Dardanelles. Hankey likened the March 1915 naval bombardment to 'an American Cinema Show', meaning the wide advertisement before anything happened (Blake, ed., *Private Papers of Douglas Haig*, 90); some soldiers expressed anger: e.g., Corbin diary, 5 May. For censorship, see Fewster, 'Expression and Suppression', and Sarina Lee, 'The British Press and the Gallipoli Campaign', BA Hons thesis University of Adelaide, 1985.
4. Examples are legion: e.g., Sutton diary, March.
5. By 30 Dec. the *West Australian* was publishing the 128th list of casualties; also, each hospital ship reaching Fremantle was noted.

## CHAPTER 20. 'THAT SUVLA BUSINESS'

1. Pedersen *Monash*, 113.
2. Keyes to wife, 16 Aug., KP; *The Times*, 3 Sept.
3. H. T. England (commanding destroyer HMS *Chelmer* during Dardanelles campaign) TS, n.d., and DC submission, 14 Dec. 1916, R-Adm. H. T. England Papers, IWM; Lotbinière DC statement, 9 Dec. 1916, Cab 19/29.
4. Sir Ivone Kirkpatrick (commanded a platoon [?] in 10 Div. at the Suvla landing) memoir 1, 18, IWM; Ashmead-Bartlett at DC, Cab 19/33, 1424; water supply arrangements: report tabled 11 Dec., *HLPD*, 5th ser., vol 20, col. 485.
5. 'Do a lot': Allanson at DC, Cab 19/26 q. 11784; see James, *Gallipoli*, 245–47, also Prior's judicious defence of Stopford in 'The Suvla Bay Tea-Party'.
6. Natusch to mother, 26 Aug., NP; Australians rating themselves highly: e.g., Richards diary, 19 Dec., Aram to mother, 15 Sept., Gellibrand to Walter (on English officers), 17 Oct.
7. Keyes to wife, 22 Aug., KP; Victorian: R. Raws to family 4, 5 Dec., also Capt. H. E. Armitage to parents, 14 Dec.; criticism in Australia of Suvla troops: Munro Ferguson to Bonar Law, 30 Nov., DP box 1914–1918.
8. McPherson diary *c*. 10 Aug. IWM; Moore diary, 8 Aug., 10 Oct.; Rettie diary n.d. [*c*. Aug.], p. 28, IWM. Rettie commanded the British 59 Bde (11 Div.) at Gallipoli.
9. Monash diary, 18 Aug., 20 and 26 Sept., 24 Oct., MP box 130, folder 956, NLA.
10. Orlo Williams diary, pt 1, 10 Aug., IWM; Keyes to wife, 16 Aug., 13 Sept., KP; Lady Godley to husband, 23 Oct., GP; Hamilton to Kitchener, 19 Aug., PRO 30/57 63 WL/88; Divs 10 and 11: Backhouse diary, 9 Aug., IWM; Sclater at DC, Cab/33, 48.
11. Hankey's letters, 28 July, 5 and 12 Aug., largely reprinted in his *Supreme Command* 1: 378–88, 390–402; Asquith to Kitchener, 20 Aug., PRO 30/57 63 WL/87; Sanders (RN Devon Hussars MEF) to Talbot, 14 Nov., BLP p 51/5/25; Einstein, *Inside Constantinople*, 283.
12. Correspondence Jan. 1931, Cab 45/241. Aspinall-Oglander was formerly Maj. C. F. Aspinall, a Hamilton staffer at Gallipoli.
13. Callwell, *The Dardanelles*, 252–53.
14. Hamilton to Kitchener, 11 Aug., WO Tels vol. 3, 2, Cab 19/3; Birdwood to Rintoul, 12 Sept., IWM WRB/1, also Birdwood to Hankey, 10 Aug., Cab 17/124; 'spirit . . . Colonials': Brig.-Gen. H. Mends to Hutton, 19 Oct., HuP Add MS 50099; Keyes to wife, 22 Aug., KP; *The Times*, 3 Sep.
15. Hankey memo, 30 Aug., Cab 19/29.
16. Maxwell to Hamilton, 28 Aug., HP 5/12; Birdwood to de Robeck, 30 Aug., deRP 4/42.

## CHAPTER 21. THE 2ND DIVISION REACHES ANZAC

1. 5th Bde: Aram to mother, 15 Aug.; bayonet: 18 Bn soldier (anon) Heliopolis, 6 Aug., AWM PR 82/8(1), D. R. Argyle diary, 17 Aug.; 'sacrifice': Sister M. Aitken MS, AWM 41.
2. Monash diary, 27 and 30 Aug., MP box 139, folder 1033 , NLA; Einstein, *Inside Constantinople*, 264.
3. 'Whole story': Howitt MS, Dec., IWM; Allanson, 23 Aug., photostat, BP 75/65/3.
4. Walker to siblings, 12 Oct., and to parents, 13 Oct.

5. Hamilton to Kitchener, 31 Aug., WO Tels 3, 15, Cab 19/31.
6. R. Raws to family, 2 Jan. 1916.
7. Curnow to Frank, 17 Aug.; R. Raws to family, 21 Aug.
8. Aram to mother and Aram diary, 2 Sept., also Capt. C. E. Benson (4 Bn, Gallipoli) letter, 24 Sept. (extract); 'rush of stokers': HQ 6 Aust. inf. Bde War Diary, WO 95/4348; War Diary Gen. Staff 2 Aust. Div., WO 95/4345.
9. CO 616/29, 446–47; CO 616/46, 546; Munro Ferguson to Bonar Law, 4 Nov., CO 616/31, 557; Pearce to Birdwood, 16 Nov., PP, Pearce-Birdwood corres.
10. Sgt G. S. Laslett, of landing 28 Aug., memoir.
11. 'Radiant': J. E. G. Stevenson memoir, 6 Sept.; Hamilton to Kitchener, 21 Sept., PRO 30/57 WL/102; Birdwood to Kitchener, 6 Sept., PRO 30/57 WL/94.
12. 'Brave lads': Cpl O. Bruce diary, 13 Sept.; Argyle diary, 20, 22 and 25 Aug., 1 Sept.; Coen to mother, 26 Aug.
13. Walker to parents, 30 Aug.; Leane to mother, 22 Aug.
14. Aram to mother, 19, 20 and 21 Sept.; D. W. Caldwell to mother, 12 Sept.
15. 'Shrapnel buzzing': Bertwistle diary, 20 Oct., PLA; 'dark day': Blows diary, 22 Sept.; Clennett to mother, Sept–Oct.
16. 'Decent spell': Aitken to mother, 13 Sept.; 'air blue': de Vine diary, 12 Sept.
17. Dowse to Gladys, 19 Sept.; Daniels diary, 19 Sept.; Aitken to mother, 4 Oct.
18. Sleeping in mud: de Vine diary, 16 Sept.; indigestion: Stevenson memoir, Sept.; Fitzmaurice diary, 7 Aug., 13 and 16 Nov.; Anzac familiar: N. Hart to mother, 27 Nov., Hart Papers, IWM.

## CHAPTER 22. 'WAITING FOR THE TURKS TO GROW TOO OLD TO FIGHT'

1. Allanson to H. L. L. Allanson, 8 Sept., AP CJA2; Monash diary, 5 Sept., MP box 130, folder 956, 9 Sept., box 131, folder 1033, NLA.
2. Silence: Aram to mother, 2 Oct.; 'Turks to grow too old': Turnley diary, 17–19 Sept., AWM 2 DRL 543; 'sit down': Curnow to Frank; 'Abdul': F. W. Bennett letter, 14 Jan. 1916.
3. 'Hot knife': Biddle to mother, 14 Oct.; optimism: Caldwell to mother, 19 Sept.; D. R. Argyle diary, 1 Oct.; Birdwood to Kitchener, 6 Sept., PRO 30/57 63 WL 120, 22 Oct., PRO 30/57 64 WL 120; R. Raws to family 13 Sept. 1915.
4. 'Sit down' warfare: Brind to mother, 22 Sept., to relative, 18 Sept.; Abbott diary, 23 Sept., 14 Nov.; P. W. Chapman diary, 26 Nov.
5. British subaltern: McGrigor diary, 25 Sept., AWM.; Aitken to mother, 23 Aug.
6. Allanson to brother, 8 Sept., AP CJA2; British press: Capt. C. E. W. Brayley letter, 23 Sept., IWM.
7. Lady Godley to husband, 14 Sept., GP; artillery officer: Harrison to aunt, 17 Sept., IWM; difference between Suvla and Anzac: McGrigor diary, 10 Oct., AWM.
8. Blows diary, 14 and 15 Sept.; Clennett to mother, Sept., 10 Oct.
9. Fildes to mother, Sept.; Angus to Nance, 19 Sept.; Edgerton diary, 9 Dec; D. R. Argyle diary, 1 and 7 Oct.
10. Paull diary, 26 Sept.
11. Aram to mother, 27 Sept., 12 Oct.; 'tucker': Worland diary, 6 Sept.
12. Birdwood to Hamilton, 20 Aug., Cab 17/124; sickness rate: Corbin to Birdwood, 19 Aug. 1915.
13. Brodrick to Lord Midleton, 6 Sept., CP EUR F112/54.
14. Birdwood to Kitchener, 6 Sept., PRO 30/57 63 WL/94, 3; A/DDMS 6 Oct., WO 95/4285.
15. Paull diary, 29 Oct.
16. Blankets: Sapper R. Carnell (3rd Field Coy RAE) diary, 29 Aug., AWM. Aitken to mother, 8 Oct.; complaints: J. M. Antill diary, 12 Oct., AWM 3 DRL 6458.
17. 'Cheeriness': McGrigor diary, 6 Dec., AWM; Allanson to brother, 21 Oct., AP CJA2; Paris to Mrs Pilkington, 26 Sept., PaP; Birdwood to Hankey, 15 Sept., Cab 17/124.
18. Aram to mother 5 Oct., 30 Sept.; Alabaster to family, c. Oct.; Ryrie to wife, 10 Oct., AWM PR 84/193.
19. D. R. Argyle diary, 2 Sept.; R. Raws to nephew, 10 Oct.; Coen to family, 8 Sept.
20. 'Johnny Turk': AIF man No. 19 Gen. Hospital letter, 1 Sept., AWM PR 82/8 (1); Bradley to family, 29 Sept.
21. Aitken to mother, 29 Aug. (cited in Gammage, Broken Years, 88) and 6 Sept.
22. Birdwood to Kitchener, 6 and 29 Sept., PRO 30/57 63 WL/94 and WL/105.
23. Scott to father, 29 Sept., Scott Papers, IWM.
24. Bonar Law to Munro Ferguson, 17 Sept., DP box 1914–1918. England to Patrick Acheson, RN, 9 Sept., H. T. England Papers, IWM.
25. Altham to Hamilton, 26 Sept., HP 25/12/2/21b; Hamilton to Stamfordham 12 Oct., HP 5/9.
26. 'Scandalous': Hugh Buxton (54 Div.) to Violet Buxton, 18 Oct., Howell Papers, LH V/C/4/5; stealing: Redmond Buxton (Gallipoli) to home, n.d., LH V/C/4/9; Dawnay to wife, 5 Nov., DaP 69/21/1; de Vitre memoir, pp. 7–8, NMM DEV/1; British army officer: E. F. Lawson to Uncle Harry (Lord Burnham), 19 Sept., Misc 1172, IWM.

## CHAPTER 23. LONDON STALEMATE; BALKANS DISASTER

1. Orlo Williams diary, pt 2, 2 Sept., IWM.
2. Dawnay to wife, 21 Dec. (re conversation 13 Aug.), DaP 69/21/1; Porter to wife, 6 Oct., PoP PTR 8/1(4).

3. Kitchener, 20 Aug., Cab 22/2/8,3; Churchill, 19 Aug., Cab 22/2/7,2; Churchill to Kitchener, 23 Aug., PRO 30/57 62 WL/55; Keyes memo, 17 Aug., and, on de Robeck, to wife, 22 Aug., KP.
4. Hankey memo, 30 Aug., Cab 19/29; Gilbert, *Churchill* 3: 525; Roskill, *Hankey* 1: 206–12: Carson to Bonar Law, 5 and 7 Sept., BLP 51/3/5,7.
5. Cab 17/128.
6. Letter, n.d. (possibly from an Irish source), received by Hankey, Cab 17/124.
7. Dawnay visit: James, *Gallipoli*, 316; Capt W. H. Deedes (Intelligence officer with 29 Div.) diary, pp. 218–23, IWM; Gilbert, *Churchill* 3: 539–41.
8. Admiralty and War Office studies in Cab 17/124 and 17/128; Corbin diary, 19 Aug.; Godley to wife, 17 Sept., GP.
9. *HCPD*, 5th ser., vol. 74 (1915), col. 65 (Dalziel, 15 Sept.), col. 479 (Markham, 22 Sept.).
10. Ferdinand: Hamilton to Kitchener, 21 Sept., PRO 30/57 63 WL/102, 11; Cassar, *French and the Dardanelles*, 201–2, 223.
11. 'Balkan tangle': Birdwood to Kitchener, 22 Oct., PRO 30/57 64 WL/120, 5; Balkans diplomacy: Wallace (Lancashire) to Curzon, 12 Oct., CP, EUR F112/110; Carson to Bonar Law, 23 Oct., BLP 51/4/26; Munro Ferguson to Bonar Law, 29 Oct., DP 1914–1918 box.
12. Germany's Balkan strategy: Cassar, *French and the Dardanelles*, 196, Gilbert, *Churchill* 3: 550.
13. Ibid., 549.

## CHAPTER 24. KEITH MURDOCH'S LETTER

1. 'Dear George': e.g., Murdoch to Pearce, 4 Nov., PP, bundle 8, no. 46; Fewster, *Gallipoli Correspondent*, 10. Various accounts of the Murdoch episode include those in Hamilton, *Gallipoli Diary* 2, Moorehead, *Gallipoli*, 307–12, and Zwar, *In Search of Keith Murdoch*.
2. Complaints about mail: *CPD* 1915, 77: 4619–28 (7 May); Murdoch to Pearce, 13 Sept. PP bundle 7, no. 48.
3. Lloyd George: Fewster, 'Expression and Suppression', 87; Fisher's instructions to Murdoch in Murdoch to Hamilton, 17 Aug., Cab 19/30, 163–6; Hamilton, *Gallipoli Diary* 2: 266–67.
4. Examination of Murdoch at DC: copy in BP 75/65/3; Fisher, Cab 19/33, 1175. For the Ashmead-Bartlett incident, see Knightley, *First Casualty of War*, 100–103.
5. Murdoch's letter, copy in Murdoch Papers, NLA MS 2823/17, and Cab 19/30, 133–47 (supporting correspondence at Cab 19/30, 163–6), selections in Zwar, *Murdoch*, chap. 4; Lloyd George on letter, LGP D/17/8/8; Carson at Cab 19/33, 1172; Dardanelles Committee, 6 Oct.: Cab 22/2/17, 5.
6. Copies of related correspondence by Hamilton, Hankey, Callwell and Curzon, 14 Oct.–2 Dec., are in BP 75/65/3; Hamilton memo, 26 Nov., Cab 19/29, 112 ff; Hamilton to Kitchener, 14 Oct., HP 5/1.
7. Lloyd George to Bonar Law, 25 Sept., BLP 51/3/21. Lloyd George, Hankey's report: Dardanelles Committee, 6 Oct., Cab 22/2/17, 5; Asquith to Dawnay, 2 Oct., DaP 69/12/1.
8. Munro Ferguson to Harcourt, 15 Nov., CO 616/32, 156. Major Australian newspapers were consulted and none had details of Murdoch's letter.

## CHAPTER 25. HOME FRONT

1. Pearce to Godley, 11 Sept., PP bundle 6, no. 51.
2. *HLPD*, 5th ser., vol. 19 (1915), col. 815 (Kitchener).
3. Legge to Pearce, 18 Sept., PP bundle 7, no. 119, 28 Sept. and 4 Oct., PP bundle 7, nos. 120–21; Birdwood to Pearce, 8 Nov., PP, Pearce-Birdwood corres., bundle 3; Munro Ferguson to Bonar Law, 4 Oct., DP 1914–1918 box.
4. Collins to Pearce, 23 Sept., 14 and 21 Oct., PP bundle 6, no. 34, bundle 7, nos. 117, 33.
5. See, e.g., Cassar, *French and the Dardanelles*, 171–73, 177–79, 185–86; *SMH* leader, 27 Sept., article 25 Sept.
6. Gallant 'Servians': *Age*, 14 Oct.; Gilgandra march arrives Molong, NSW: *SMH*, 23 Oct.; Neyland brothers: *Argus*, 20 Oct.; army strength: Munro Ferguson, 18 Nov., CO 418/134, 191.
7. War census cards: *Age*, 23 Aug.; *SMH* leader, 18 Sept.; labour problems: *SMH*, 16 Sept., *Age*, 20 Oct.
8. *CPD* 77: 4923–26 (Bakhap, 15 July); Universal Service League: *SMH*, 11 Sept., leader, 13 Sept., Fisher's view, *SMH*, 25 Sept. See also Robson, *First A.I.F.*, 70, and McKernan, *Australian People and the Great War*, 35.
9. *CPD* 78: 6149, 6195–97 (Brennan, Fisher, 26 Aug.).
10. Harris diary, Aug./Sept.
11. *Barrier Miner* leader, 21 Oct.
12. Dunstan: *Age*, 18 and 19 Oct.
13. Scott to Hamilton, 12 Oct., HP 1/3/7.
14. Correspondence in MP box 13, folder 115, NLA; Cook in *Brisbane Courier*, 3 Nov.
15. *West Australian* leader, 21 Oct.; Arabic: *Age* leader, 23 Aug; 'bloodiest outrage': *Argus*, 22 Oct.; 'unspeakable': Robinson dairy, 12 Oct., p. 434, referring to article in *The Times*, IWM; 'Neither chivalry . . .': letter to *Argus*, 21 Oct.; Cavell: e.g., *Argus*, 23 Oct.; CO 616/49, 573–603.
16. *Argus*, e.g., 24 July, 8 Aug., 28 Sept., Bryce appeal, 22 Sept.; Einstein, *Inside Constantinople*, 159, 175; Morgenthau, *Secrets of the Bosphorus*, 215–53, and *Ambassador's Morgenthau's Story*, 322. Djemal Pasha, *Memories*, estimates 600,000 deaths; Emin, *Turkey in the World War*, chap. 18; for a review of the Armenian issue, see Dyer, 'Turkish "Falsifiers" and Armenian "Deceivers"'.
17. Bean, *Argus*, 2 Dec.; *Age* leader, 16 Oct.

## CHAPTER 26. 'A CHOICE OF DISASTERS'

1. *SMH*, 23 Oct.
2. Carson: Bonar Law to Asquith, 15 Oct., BLP 53/6/44; *HLPD*, 5th ser., vol. 19, cols. 1061–62 (Ribblesdale), col. 1055 (Milner); British press: *Age*, 10 Oct.
3. Hankey to Asquith, 15 Oct., Cab 17/125; MMS vol. 351, p. 67 (correspondent, 17 Oct.), p. 58 (Sydenham), p. 46–48 (schoolmaster).
4. Maxse to Bonar Law, 15 Oct., BLP 51/4/12.
5. CO 616/49, 703.
6. Difficulties for a democracy: *Argus* leader, 20 Oct.; leaders *SMH*, 23 Oct., *Daily Telegraph*, 20 Oct., *Advertiser*, 21 Oct.
7. *Age* leader, 22 Oct.
8. New vigour: report in *West Australian*, 21 Oct.
9. 'Bombshell', Braithwaite's capacity: Orlo Williams diary, pt 2, 16 Oct., IWM; Godley to wife, 16 and 25 Oct., GP, and to de Robeck, 21 Oct., deRP 4/79; Paris to Mrs Pilkington, 19 Oct., PaP; Murdoch, 5 Feb. 1917 at DC, Cab 19/33 q. 16479.
10. Midleton to FitzGerald, 12 Oct., FitzGerald Papers, IWM; heavy artillery: Lt-Gen. F. M. Byng (at Suvla) to Howell (commanding 10th Corps, Third Army), 29 Oct., Howell Papers, LH IV/C/2/183; Aspinall appreciation, 22 Oct., WO 158/575 (15 pp. TS copy, BP 75/65/4).
11. Mends to Hutton, 19 Oct., HuP Add MS 50099.
12. *West Australian* leader, 9 Dec.; *Argus*, leader, 30 Oct.
13. *Newcastle Morning Herald*, 20 Oct., leader, p. 7; howitzers: *Argus*, 20 Oct.
14. *Ballarat Courier* leader, 19 Oct., report on Carruthers, 22 Oct.
15. Munro Ferguson cable to Bonar Law, 29 Oct., CO 418/134, 76; Munro Ferguson to Bonar Law, 8 Nov. ('asset'), 14 Oct. (on Reid), 22 Dec., all in DP 1914–1918 box; visit Gallipoli: Pearce to Fisher, 9 Dec., FP 2919/1/186.
16. AA CP 78/23 89/148/1, 296 and CP 78/22, 296.
17. *Kalgoorlie Miner*, 29 Oct. (Bartlett lecture), 30 Oct. (Brassey).
18. *CPD* 1915, 79: 7022 (Hughes); Bonar Law to Munro Ferguson, 9 Nov., DP 1914–1918 box.
19. Pearce to Birdwood, 16 Nov., PP, Pearce-Birdwood corres.
20. Monro to Kitchener, 28 and 31 Oct., WO Tels, vol. 3, 30, 31, Cab 19/31; Pelling, *Winston Churchill*, 333.
21. *HCPD*, 5th ser. vol. 75, col. 511 (Asquith), col. 552 (Barnes: Churchill responsible).
22. Ibid., cols. 575–77 (Beresford), col. 564 (Dalziel), col. 531 (Carson).
23. *HLPD*, 5th ser., vol. 20, cols. 121, 192, 196; *HCPD*, 5th ser., vol. 75, cols. 1454–55 (Ponsonby); *Brisbane Courier*: Milner, 10 Nov., leader, 4 Nov.
24. Hart to mother, 18 Nov., Hart Papers, IWM; Capt. Basil Holmes (17 Bn, at Quinn's Post) to woman in NSW, 29 Oct., PLA.
25. Hart to mother, 27 Nov., Hart Papers, IWM.
26. View in cabinet: Magnus, *Kitchener*, 366; War Committee: Roskill, *Hankey* 1: 22.
27. Callwell (on Birdwood 'through the Turks') to Robertson, 23 Oct., Robertson Papers 1/8/306, LH; Keyes and Wemyss: Magnus, *Kitchener*, 361; Godley to wife, 7 Nov., GP; Hankey to Bonar Law, 6 Nov., BLP 51/5/14; Chamberlain to Bonar Law, 7 Nov., BLP 117/1/23.
28. Balfour to Bonar Law, 7 Nov., BLP 51/5/15; Asquith (undertaking to call cabinet) to Bonar Law, 5 Nov., BLP 51/5/7; Maxse to Balfour, 9 Nov., BLP 51/5/19; Bonar Law to Asquith, 8 Nov., BLP 53/6/47.
29. Bonar Law to Munro Ferguson, 9 Nov., BLP 51/5/8; Wilson to Bonar Law, 20 Nov., BLP 51/5/38; Bentinck to Bonar Law, 23 Nov., BLP 51/5/42.
30. *Argus* leaders, 8 Nov.; CO cable, 15 Nov., CO 616/49; Kitchener cable to Asquith, 15 Nov., WO Tels, vol. 3, 40 Cab 19/31, and Ashmead-Bartlett, *Uncensored Dardanelles*, 263–64; *HLPD*, 5th ser., vol. 20, col. 409 (Ribblesdale, 18 Nov.); anger: e.g., Robinson diary, pp. 481–82, IWM.
31. *HCPD*, 5th ser., vol. 75, cols. 1499–1521 (Churchill, 15 Nov.), cols. 1505–18 (Gallipoli campaign); *Age* leader, 15 Nov.; Ashmead-Bartlett letter, *The Times*, 24 Nov.
32. Birdwood: Keyes to wife, 2 Dec., KP; 'villain': Keyes letter-diary, Oct.–Nov., p. 2, KP; views on evacuation: Godley to wife, 20 Dec., GP.

## CHAPTER 27. 'NOT DEAD YOU SEE'

1. Gellibrand to Walter, 4 Nov., AWM 3DRL 8050; Aram to mother, 2 Oct.
2. Raws to family, 19 Oct.; 27 Nov.; Burgess to Dora, 17 Oct.; Aram to mother, 28 Oct.
3. McGrigor diary, 3, 4, 6, 9 Nov., AWM; Chambers to parents, 26 Oct.; Caldwell to mother, 22 Nov.
4. Burgess to family, 18 Oct.; R. Raws to family, 19 Oct.; suspicions: Aram to mother, 11 Nov., 28 Oct; WO2 E. W. Baker to family, 22 Oct., AWM 1 DRL 83.
5. Burgess to family, 22 Oct.; mail lost: Sgt L. S. Horder diary, 23 Nov.; Keith Chambers to parents, 19 Nov.
6. Letter from 17-year-old: 5 Nov. AWM PR 82/8(1); Cavanagh to family, late Oct.; R. Raws to family, 6 Nov.; Biddle to mother, 31 Oct.; Aitken to mother 31 and 29 Oct.
7. Champion diary, 1 and 9 Nov.
8. Names on hats: Burgess to Dora, 17 Oct.; 'as dirty': Champion diary, 9 Nov.; 'insect hunt': Blows diary, 25 Oct.

9. Aitken to mother, 17, 14, 21 Nov.; Arnold to father (UK), 31 Oct.; Lt.-Col. R. W. Chambers, 1st Bde, memoir.
10. Walker to parents, 26 Oct.; Aram to mother, 23 Oct.
11. Shell noises: Aram to mother, 2 Nov.; Cavanagh to family, late Oct.
12. Gas: circular memo, 5 July, A&NZAC HQ, copy in Gellibrand Papers, AWM; Champion diary, 10 Nov.; Horder diary, 17 Oct.
13. Aram to mother, 20 Oct., 2 Nov.; Walker to parents, 26 Oct.; 'bravest': P. W. Chapman diary, 26 Nov.
14. Shellfire and Hill 971 attack: returned private (Sydney) in *Ballarat Courier*, 23 Oct.; 'no one . . . afraid': *Argus*, 23 Oct.; Dinning to Maj. J. A. J. Ferguson, *Brisbane Courier*, 9 Nov.
15. *Argus* leader, 30 Oct.; King's message: CO 616/49, 605; recruiting: *Brisbane Courier*, 8–13 Nov. (clever argument in support, 10 Nov.).
16. *CPD* 79: 7484 (Fenton, 11 Nov.); Ada Krakowski (friend in Subiaco, WA) to Monash, 14 Oct., MP box 13, folder 115, NLA.
17. For marches, see also Robson, *First A.I.F.*, 57–58.
18. War census, Hughes's appeal: Robson, *First A.I.F.*, 62–66; passports: *Argus*, 26 Nov.
19. AA AIF 24/7/2 B539.
20. Hughes (Qld) to Pearce, 4 Dec., and Pearce to Hughes, 15 Dec., PP bundle 3, no. 25 .
21. Call to Arms: *West Australian*, 15 Dec; leader in support, 17 Dec.

## CHAPTER 28. ANZAC-SUVLA TO BE ABANDONED

1. Aram to mother, 11 Nov.
2. Blows diary, 19 Oct.; Monash diary, 10 Nov., MP box 130, folder 957, NLA; English officer: Lt-Col. C. C. Aston (8 Bn Welsh Regt, 13 Div.) to mother, 23 Nov., Aston Papers, IWM; Champion diary, 14 Nov. (slippery), and McGrigor diary, 17 Nov., AWM.
3. Birdwood to Kitchener, 27 Nov., PRO 30/57 64 WL127; R. Raws to family, 26 Nov.
4. McGrigor diary, 28 Nov., AWM; frozen bedding: Cpl H. A. J. Lamb (13 Div.), Lamb Papers, IWM; comparison with Flanders: Brayley, 5 Dec., Brayley letters, IWM; Moscow: Aston to mother, 8 Dec., Aston Papers, IWM; statistics: GOC cable to Kitchener, 4 Dec., WO 62/68; Suvla worst: Birdwood to Kitchener,2 Dec., PRO 30/57 64 WL 129; Ryrie to F. Fleming, Hunter's Hill, NSW, 4 Dec., AWM PR 82/8(2); thirst: Gammage diary, 27 Oct. [*sic* for Nov.]; snowballing: Cavanagh to mother, 2 Dec.; 'ugliness of war': Notes by Maj. Cole, AWM 41[1/5.12].
5. Government vacillation: Roskill, *Hankey* 1: 235; silence 'did not mean . . .': Bean, *Story of Anzac* 2: 843; Horder diary, 25 Nov.; Champion diary, p. 30.
6. Ahern diary, 29 Nov.; Aram to mother, 29 Nov.
7. Exchange of cables, CO 616/50, 782, 783–84, 792.
8. For a good short account, see Woodward, *Great Britain and the War of 1914–1918*, 86–94. Curzon's paper and a Hankey paper of 29 Nov. opposing evacuation: Roskill, *Hankey* 1: 235–36; Williams's article: Maxse's *The National Review*, no. 443 (June 1920); Ashmead-Bartlett, *Uncensored Dardanelles*, 265–66; Hamilton to Curzon, 6 Dec., CP EUR F112/160; Keyes to de Robeck, 2 Dec., deRP 4/78; Keyes letter-diary, Oct./Nov., 'fury': Keyes to Admiral Oliver, 29 Nov., Keyes to wife, 26 Mar. 1917, KP.
9. Curzon memos, 30 Nov., p 4, 25 Nov., p. 5, copies for DC in Cab 19/28, and see Cassar, *Kitchener*, 430.
10. Rumours 'buzzing': Gilbert, *Churchill* 3: 589; Bonar Law to Munro Ferguson, 1 Dec., CO 616/50, 792; Hughes's reaction: Munro Ferguson to Bonar Law, 13 Dec., DP 1914–1918 box; Bonar Law response, 16 Dec., CO 616/50, 795.
11. Risks of evacuation: Keyes letter diary, Oct./Nov., KP; Kitchener's report, PRO 30/57 66 WM/7; expected casualties: R. W. Williamson, RN, to brother-in-law, 10 Jan. 1916. IWM.
12. Cab 41/36/54 and see Jenkins, *Asquith*, 385 and Cassar, *French and the Dardanelles*, 229–234; dominions told, 14 Dec., CO 616/50, 793.
13. Bourke to father, 8 Dec.; Page to E. Page, 5 Dec.; R. Raws to family, 5 Dec.
14. Wary: Brind to mother, 2 Dec.

## CHAPTER 29. 'THE TURKS HAVE BEATEN US. WE HAD TO GO'

1. R. W. Chambers memoir, 19 Nov.; Hart to mother, 21 Dec., Hart Papers, IWM; Bertwistle diary, 25 Nov. PLA; Aram to mother, 25 Dec.; East, ed., *Gallipoli Diary of Sergeant Lawrence*, 127; Billings TS memoir, 15 Dec., IWM; Monash diary, 10 and 12 Dec., MP box 128, folder 57, NLA.
2. East, *Diary of Sergeant Lawrence*, 126; R. Raws to family, 11 Dec., and Aitken to mother 12 Dec.
3. Armitage to parents, 19 Dec.; Richards diary, 18 Dec.; P. W. Chapman diary, 15 Dec.; Walker to parents, 13 Dec.; Moody letter, 19 Dec.; de Vine diary, 20 Dec.; Coen diary, 17 and 19–20 Dec.
4. C. J. to H. L. L. Allanson, 27 Jan. 1916, AP CJA2; sheer lunacy: H. V. Howe to E. Bush, 25 Nov. 1968, BP 75/65/3.
5. Planning by Keyes, KP; Monash diary, 12 Dec., MP box 130, folder 957, NLA; casualties: R. W. Chambers memoir, 19 Nov.; MEF to Surg.-Gen. W. Babtie, 9 Dec., WO 162/68.
6. Birdwood to Hamilton, 12 Dec., HP 5/10.
7. Message: War Diary Gen Staff 2 Aust. Div., WO 95/4345; Coen diary, 13 Dec.
8. Ryrie, 23 Dec., AWM PR 84/193; P. W. Chapman diary, p. 40.
9. Capt. S. L. Milligan TS on evacuation, AIF General file, MiP.

10. Ibid.; Lechte recollection.

11. Aram to mother, 25 Dec.; Lechte recollection; P. W. Chapman diary, p. 40.

12. Billings diary, 29 Dec., AWM 3 DRL 6060 (also tape script); de Vine diary, 19 Dec.

13. Aram to mother, 25 Dec.; Monash diary, report on last days at Anzac, 20 Dec., MP Letter Book, box 128, folder 943, NLA; Dawnay to wife, 23 Dec., DaP 69/21/1; Milligan TS, MiP.

14. Tent down: P. H. Luke (6 Inf. Bde HQ) diary, 20 Dec., AWM PR 83/44; Brownell diary, 22 Dec.; 'rabble': Brisco diary, Dec.[?]; Monash, 23 Dec. MP Letter Book, box 128, folder 943, NLA.

15. Aram to mother, 25 Dec.; Lechte recollection; R. Raws to family, 31 Dec.; Armitage to parents, 21 Dec.

16. Donkey rides: Aram to mother, 26 Dec.; Aitken to mother, 27 Dec.; Sarpi art: Armitage to parents, 19 Dec.

17. Lennie diary, 24 Dec.; Coen to mother, 28 Jan. 1916; Allardyce to father, 1 Jan. 1916; Aitken (from WA; billy from Bendigo, Vic.) to mother, 25 Dec.; kangaroo: Lechte recollection.

18. Aitken to mother on New Year's Eve, 1 Jan. 1916; Aram to mother re mail, 28 Dec.

19. Armitage to parents, 19 and 25 Dec.

## CHAPTER 30. 'ANZAC IS NOW FAMOUS THROUGHOUT THE EMPIRE'

1. *West Australian*: Fortescue, 15 Dec., Keenan, 16 Dec., and howitzers, 13 Dec.

2. WO worries: Dardanelles Army HQ to WO, 18 Dec., WO 158/580; need for censorship: Bonar Law to Munro Ferguson, 21 Dec., CO 616/50, 666.

3. Hughes's statement: *Age*, 22 Dec., Munro Ferguson to Bonar Law, 22 Dec., DP 1914–1918 box.

4. *HCPD*, 5th ser., vol. 77, col. 394 (Dalziel), col. 417 (Markham), col. 241 (Carson); *New York Times Magazine*, 26 Dec., p. 1273; *The Times*, 21 Dec.

5. Haig to Kitchener, 20 Dec., PRO 30/57 53 WD11; Milner diary, 20 Dec., MMS vol. 86; Dawnay to wife, 2 Jan. 1916, DaP 69/221/1; Birdwood to Rintoul, 28 Dec., IWM WRB/1.

6. Birdwood to Pearce, 20 Feb. 1916, PP, Pearce-Birdwood corres., no 6.

7. Pearce to Godley, 15 Jan. 1916, and Godley to Pearce, 16 Mar. 1916, PP bundle 6, item 51.

8. Contemporary parlance: Bill Gammage, 'The Crucible: The Establishment of the Anzac Tradition', in McKernan and Browne, *Australia Two Centuries of War and Peace*.

## CHAPTER 31. 'THE SUFFERINGS OF THE SICK AND WOUNDED': APRIL–JULY 1915

1. Promise: Butler, *Medical Services* 1: 87; 'medical problems': ibid., 102.

2. Fetherston report, AA Dept of Defence Correspondence files 1914–1917 239/8/181 B539; Mackenzie, *Gallipoli Memories*, 370–71; Ashmead-Bartlett, *Uncensored Dardanelles*, 48.

3. Butler, *Medical Services* 1, 22; Monash diary, 13 Feb., MP box 130, folder 955, NLA.

4. S. S. Argyle diary, 20 and 22 Jan.; ambulances: Butler, *Medical Services* 1: 106, 401.

5. Butler, *Medical Services* 1: 102–3, 199, and Barrett and Deane, *Medical Corps in Egypt*, 38; S. S. Argyle diary; Monash, 10 Sept., MP Letter Book, box 128, folder 942, NLA.

6. Canadians: Butler, *Medical Services* 1: 77 fn; AIF disease statistics Jan. 1915–Mar. 1916, ibid., 426.

7. S. S. Argyle diary, 11 Mar.; Munro Ferguson to Pearce, 2 Apr., PP bundle 1, folder 2, no. 78.

8. *CPD* 76: 2641–53, also 2294 (Mathews).

9. Birrell 18 and 24 Apr.: Butler, *Medical Services* 1: 124, 129; 'entirely inadequate': Wemyss to Adm. Limpus, 17 May, Limpus Papers, NMM; Howse, Cab 19/33, 1517–8.

10. Medical planning: Butler, *Medical Services* 1: 117–23, 172; orders re dispostion of wounded: Thursby, 19 Apr., copy in KP; Godley to wife, 22 Apr., GP.

11. Clark TS EBC/1 P27OT, Bidder Clark Papers, IWM; '600 yards': Corbin, Cab 19/33, 1557; 'uncomplaining': C. C. MacMillan to Butler, 31 Dec. 1923, AWM 41 [3./10.9].

12. Corbin diary, 28 Apr.; Capt. C. K. Brampton, RN, diary, 29 Apr., IWM 77/45/1; Cab 19/33, 1558; Drage diary, 27 Apr., IWM.

13. Ashmead-Bartlett, Cab 19/33, 1405–1613; horses, Cab 19/33, 1587; Drage diary, 28 Apr., IWM.

14. Howse evidence, Cab 19/33, 1507–9, 1517.

15. No surgical aid: Howse, Cab 19/33, 1509; Ashmead-Bartlett, Cab 19/33, 1405; barges seeking space: Col. B. J. Neumarch memoir, *c.* 1919, AWM 41 [3/11.5]; Fenwick, 29 Aug. 1917, Cab 19/33, 1612; Ryan to Butler, 14 Mar. 1919, AWM 41 [3/11.5]; bully beef: Lt-Col. J. R. Muirhead about the *Aragon*, memoir, n.d., AWM 41 [3/110.24]; *Itonus*: Neumarch memoir, AWM 41 [3/11.5]; S. S. Argyle diary, 12 May. See also Hamilton, *Gallipoli Diary* 1: 216–17.

16. Corbin, Cab 19/33, 1555–65 and note 1565 (Birdwood emerged from discussion of his role in having improvements made for transporting wounded from the beaches with his reputation enhanced); Corbin diary, 31 May (also 6 Aug. on his attempts to get more tows and his eventual success in persuading Birdwood).

17. Jacka, Cab 19/33, 1589–91; Cairns and May, Cab 19/33, 1591–93.

18. Birrell, Cab 19/33, 1658.

19. Carnarvon, Cab 19/33, 871, 877, 1601 and also her statement Cab 19/28.

20. Ryan, Cab 19/33, 1568–9; Begg, Cab 19/33, 1587; deaths en route to Alexandria: Butler, *Medical Services* 1: 180–81.

21. 'Appalling numbers': Barrett and Deane, *Medical Corps in Egypt*, 43; Cuthbert narrative, AWM 41.

22. Lady Godley to husband on WO, on HQ, Australian and NZ medicos in Egypt: 5, 16 May, 21 June, 7, 9, 18 May, and 9 June, GP.

23. Harris diary, May; Gellibrand to Walter, 28 May, AWM 3 DRL 8050.

24. Fowler memoir, pp. 78, 85.
25. D. R. Baker diary; Cairenes: Carnarvon statement, Cab 19/28, 6.
26. Capt. (later Maj.) A. J. Aspinall (1st Fld Amb.) diary, 25 May, AWM 41 [1/3.8]; S. S. Argyle diary, 12 May.
27. Disease: Butler, *Medical Services* 1, chap. 12; trench sanitation: Birrell, Cab 19/33, 498; blankets to latrines: a New Zealander, Cab 19/33, 1147,
28. Birrell to Keogh (DG Army Medical Services in Britain), 10 June, WO 162/67; see also claims by Gen. Maxwell in Arthur, *General Sir John Maxwell*, 182–83.
29. *HCPD*, 5th ser., vol. 73, col. 1288 (Tennant); *Saturnia* voyage: Cab 19/33, 1608, 1610, 1681; NZ MO, Cab 19/33, 1687; Treves: Lady Godley to husband, 29 July, 3 Aug., GP and Cab 19/33, 1533–4.
30. Lady Godley to husband, 16 July, GP; Unsworth, Cab 19/33, 896. For the press articles, see below, chap. 32, pp. 210–11.
31. Bridges and Williams: Coulthard-Clark, *Heritage of Spirit*, 139.
32. Pearce statement on reasons for recall, *CPD* 78: 6127–28 (20 Aug.). A precis of relevant cables is in PP bundle 1, folder 2, no. 102, and see also no. 90. The report of the WO inquiry and a 135-page TS of minutes of evidence is in AA AIF 239/8/78 B539. For the imbroglio in No. 1 AGH, amidst an extensive literature see Butler, *Medical Services* 1: 257–60, 405, and Roe, *Nine Australian Progressives*, 72–84.
33. Johnston's letters, 28 May and 4 and 6 June, AA CP 78/23 14/89 136.
34. For this correspondence, AA CP 78/23 14/89 136, also AA AIF 239/2/1191 B539.
35. Maxwell to Pearce, 29 June, AA CP 78/23 14/89 136; Army Council inquiry: WO to CO, 5 Apr. 1916, and Maxwell to Sec WO, 1 Mar. 1916, CO 616/63, 308–11; Harris diary, July 1915.
36. WO to Hamilton, 5 July, WO 162/67.
37. On Porter: Cab 19/33, 1517, 1660; praise for Babtie: Cab 19/33, 1584–5, recovery record at Australian hospitals in Cairo: Butler, *Medical Services* 1: 200–201, 271; Maxwell to Kitchener, 19 July, and Babtie to Keogh, 21 July, WO 162/66.
38. Munro Ferguson exchange with Col. Sec., 10 and 15 Aug., AA CP 78/23 14/89/101; WO Tels, vol. 3, p. 3, Cab 19/31.
39. Butler, *Medical Services* 1: 275–76, 516; *Argus* leaders, 26 Aug., 2 Sept.

CHAPTER 32. THE AIF'S SICK AND WOUNDED: AUGUST–DECEMBER 1915

1. Hamilton to WO, 13 July, WO to Hamilton, 20 July, WO 162/66.
2. Howse to Birdwood: Butler, *Medical Services* 1: 289–90; casualties moved: ibid., 323; Porter to wife, 19 Aug., PoP PTR 8/1/4.
3. 'Outcry': Orlo Williams diary, pt 1, 7 Aug., IWM; Godley to wife, 12 Aug., GP; Ryan, Cab 19/33, 1568.
4. Comparing the landings: Corbin diary, 6 Aug., also at DC, Cab 19/33, 1558–60; Edney Moore diary, 6–7 Aug.
5. Admiralty record: Graeme Thompson (Director of Transports under the Admiralty), Cab 19/33, 1208; *Clan MacGillivray*: Lt-Col. A. W. Mayo-Robson, Cab 19/33, 923; May, Cab 19/33, 972; *Delta*: V. E. Upton diary, IWM.
6. Jottings of medical officer, Lieut. Norman King Wilson, copy in BP 75/65/3.
7. Porter to wife, 14 and 12 Aug., PoP PTR 8/1/4; Cab 19/33, 961–74; Porter (in old age) 'Some Memories of the Dardanelles July to August 1915', PoP PTR 8/1/2.
8. Lemnos: Butler, *Medical Services* 1: 334–38; Knox to Lady Munro Ferguson, 16 Aug., copy in PP bundle 1, folder 2, no. 94; Imlay to mother, 8 Aug., AWM PR 84/133; wounded man: Ernie Lorentzen of Kensington, NSW, AWM PR 82/8 (1).
9. *HCPD*, 5th ser. vol. 75, col. 1544 (Tennant, 15 Nov.); Maxwell to Hamilton, 18 Aug., HP 5/12; Lady Godley to husband, 30 Aug., GP.
10. Hamilton to Kitchener, 29 Sept., PRO 30/57 63, pp. 2–3, WL/104.
11. Trenches: Lt-Col. R. M. Bowman account, 18 Mar. 1919, AWM 41 [1/4.12]; latrines: Capt. T. R. Ritchie (NZ medical officer at Anzac) to DC, Cab 19/33, 1066–67, and Howse, Cab 19/33, 1511, and Lt-Col. H. K. Fry's memoirs, pt 3, AWM 41 [2/7.15].
12. Fetherston to Defence (Melbourne), 10 Nov., AA AIF 239/8/19 B539, to Keogh, 10 Nov., AA AIF 239/8/58 B539, and to Defence, 27 Nov., AA AIF 239/8/29 B539; Butler, *Medical Services* 1: 508.
13. Women's complaints; AA AIF 239/8/40 B539; Reid statement (printed) AA CP 78/23 14/89/136; 'good luck': K. Chambers to parents, 29 Oct.; Fetherston report, p. 26, AA AIF 239/8/181 B539.
14. Mitchell diary 15 and 18 Oct., 5 and 15 Nov.
15. Returned to Australia: Butler, *Medical Services* 1: 426, 3: 745, 903; Australian policy, ibid., 1: 503 and Fetherston minute, 8 Nov., AA AIF 239/8/58 B539.
16. Hospital population: Babtie to War Office WO 162/68; circular memo, 5 Oct., copy in PoP PTR 8/1.
17. Fetherston views on reaching Egypt: Butler, *Medical Services* 1: 433; Fetherston cable to Pearce, 29 Sept., AA AIF 239/8/4 B539, and letter to Babtie, 25 Oct., AWM 41 [2/7.4].
18. WO on need for uniformity: cables Dec. 1915–Mar. 1916, AA AIF 239/8/87 B539; Fetherston on Howse to Defence, Melbourne, cables, 29 Nov., AA AIF 239/8/31, and 3 Dec., AA AIF 239/8/32 B539; Fetherston to Sec. for Defence, 8 Jan. 1916, AA AIF 239/8/72 B 539.
19. Fetherston report, AA AIF 239/8/181 B539; Munro Ferguson to Bonar Law, 7 Apr. 1916, CO 616/53, 679–83; Army Council, 4 July 1916, CO 616/63, 480–83. Other material on Fetherston's

visit: Birdwood to Pearce, 20 Oct. 1915, PP, Pearce-Birdwood corres., no. 2, and AWM 41 [2/7.14].

20. Howse, Cab 19/33, 1511.

21. *Age*, 15 and 16 Oct.; for deletion, AWM 41 [4/12.1].

22. 'Cook's fatigue': Champion diary, 30 Nov.; onlooker: Lennie diary, 5 Dec.; A. E. Leane to mother, 16 Dec.

23. Eric Bogle, *And the Band Played Waltzing Matilda*, (Epping, NSW: Larrikin Music, 1977).

## CHAPTER 33. PRISONERS OF THE TURKS

1. Fisher to Long, 12 Mar. 1918, CO 693/8; Butler, *Medical Services* 3: 896. Sellheim's dispatch no. 9, 24 Jan. 1916, gave 58 POWs, AA AIF 112/6/27; 'less than 100': Bean, *Anzac to Amiens*, 181.

2. Gerster, *Big-Noting*, 20, 143–5.

3. By late August some 3,200 Turks had been captured at Gallipoli: WO monthly return, Aug. 1915, WO 157/648. For capture of Australians by Turkey: Brackenbury, 'Becoming Guests of the Unspeakable'; cf. Noble, 'Raising the White Flag'.

4. Off Lemnos: Copp diary, 24 Apr.; brigade order: L/Cpl W. E. Rhodes to parents, 28 Apr. (location of Rhodes's material unknown); Pte W. R. Felton (1039, 13 Bn, returned to Australia 19 Feb. 1919) to aunt and uncle, 11 Oct., AWM PR 82/8 (1); on mutilation, James, *Gallipoli*, 176.

5. Capture: Brackenbury, 'Becoming Guests of the Unspeakable', 19 (wounded) and app. 1; AIF POW debrief statements 1918/19 at AWM30: McDonald S, Griffiths (meeting bayonet) S, O'Connor S; Bailey S; Lushington, *Prisoner with the Turks*, 5; Essad Pasha: Bean, *Story of Anzac* 2: 524, also Einstein, *Inside Constantinople*, 229 and on pro-British Turkish upper class, 74.

6. Monash diary, 24 Oct., MP box 130, folder 956, NLA.

7. 1899 and 1907 Hague conventions had provisions for POWs and, though technically not applicable, had been ratified by Turkey and Britain. See Beaumont, 'Rank, privilege and prisoners of war', 70. Munro Ferguson to Pearce, 21 Oct. 1915, 21 Jan. 1916, PP bundle 1, folder 2, no. 161, bundle 1, folder 1, no. 2; diplomatic activity: e.g., CO 418/141, 360–73; CO 418/145, 676–707.

8. CO advice, 19 June, AA CP 78/23 14/89/101.

9. CO 616/39, 51, 53, 183, 215, 227 and 367, official's comment, 180; visitors: Pte D. B. Creedon (re July 1915) diary, *c.* Aug., Einstein, *Inside Constantinople*, 236–37; Bean: Fewster, *Gallipoli Correspondent*, 149.

10. Munro Ferguson cable, 16 June, AA CP 78/23 14/89/58/54.

11. Leading-stoker J. Keiran to uncle O. McGrail (Newtown, Sydney), *SMH*, 21 Oct.; C. Suckling, RAN (submariner *AE2*), narrative *c.* 1940, AWM 3 DRL 6226.

12. FO to CO, 3 Nov., CO 616/41, 404.

13. CO 616/36, 77, 133, 136–39, CO 616/46, 197–200. The *AE2* crew comprised three officers and twenty-nine ratings.

14. WO to CO, 29 Nov., CO 616/50, 481.

15. Creedon diary, *c.* 19 Aug.

16. Pte L. D. Lightfoot S; 2 Lt L. Stormonth S; two RN officers (one from the *AE2*) were put in solitary confinement (Stoker, *Straws in the Wind*, 239); eating: Pte J. Beattie S: Creedon diary, Oct.

17. Morgenthau cable to W. H. Page, US Ambassador London, 27 Oct., CO 616/41, 403–18, and to FO, 28 Oct., 345–47.

18. For a first-hand account, see *Black Bread and Barbed Wire: Prisoners in the First World War*.

19. Beattie S.

20. Townshend, *My Campaign in Mesopotamia*, 364; interview with A. I. Elkus, 20 June, dated 2 July 1917, CO 693/3.

21. McDonald S. For officer experience, see also White, *Guests of the Unspeakable*, Stoker, *Straws in the Wind*, and Foster, *Two-and-a-Half Years a Prisoner*.

22. Beaumont 'Rank, privilege and prisoners of war', 69.

23. NCOs: Lushington, *Prisoner with the Turks*, 31, Bailey S, Foxcroft S; GBPP 1918, vol. 26, Cd 208, *Report on the Treatment of British Prisoners of War in Turkey* (Cd 9208 *Report*), 11–13.

24. Pte W. Williams S, Pte J. Pasmore S.

25. US Embassy, 5 Aug., CO 616/39, 449.

26. Cd 9208 *Report*, 2.

27. Stormonth S; Beattie on 'shrapnel' S.

28. 'Savage': Beattie S; Lushington, *Prisoner with the Turks*, 63.

29. Griffiths on German company S, also Pte P. O'Connor S, Beattie on civilians S; Lushington, *Prisoner with the Turks*, 35; Suckling narrative.

30. Cd 9208 *Report*, 11, 13; Lushington, *Prisoner with the Turks*, 67.

31. Turkey's wounded: Liman von Sanders, *Five Years in Turkey*, 90.

32. Bailey S; O'Connor S; Williams S; 'lingered': Pte H. N. Brown S; on Turkish hospitals: Pte A. Carpenter S, also Lt J. McGelligott AFC and Pte D.S. Armstrong, 4th LH (both captured Palestine) S, AWM 30 B3.3; Foxcroft S; officer experience: McDonald S.

33. Col. Sec. cable to Munro Ferguson, 23 Dec., AA CP 78/23 14/89/58/197a; action in Apr. 1916, CO 616/60, 80; Turkish soldiers illiterate: Kannengiesser, *Campaign in Gallipoli*, 146–49, 266.

34. Grey to Page, 25 Jan. 1916, CO 616/59, 237; also ibid., 235–75, 421–28.

35. AA CP 78/24 16/89/58; CO 616/59, 237, 235–75. The WO list did not distinguish between *AE2* RN and RAN men and included two AFC officers captured 1916, CO 616/58, 423–27 (25 NZ names at CO 616/58, 399–400).

36. Sept. 1916, CO 616/58; US Embassy letter, 23 Jan. 1917, CO 693/2.
37. CO 693/2; Delpratt S.
38. Fisher to CO, CO 616/58, 391–92; CO 616/60, 86, 88–91; CO letter to (British) POW Dept (created late 1916), 10 Oct. 1917, CO 693/4.
39. Munro Ferguson cable, 22 Nov. 1915, Col. Sec. reply, 15 Jan. 1916, AA CP 78/24 16/89/58; Red Cross: Chomley, 'Final Report' (copy in AWM), Butler, *Medical Services* 3: 990–91, Scott, *Australia During the War*, 705–7.
40. Beattie S; O'Connor S; Cliffe S; Suckling narrative.
41. CO letter to POW Dept, 10 Oct. 1917, CO 693/4.
42. Munro Ferguson to CO, 23 Jan. 1918, CO 693/6.
43. POW Dept to CO, 9 Jan. 1917, and High Commission to CO, 20 Feb. 1917, CO 693/2.
44. Netherlands role: CO 693/3; POWs' views: Cpl D. Boyle S, Brown S; on Spain, Beattie S.
45. *AE2* officer: Stoker *Straws in the Wind*, 250, 256, Morgenthau, *Secrets of the Bosphorus*, 171–72; Military Attaché Berne to WO, 15 Jan. 1917, CO 693/2; Vischer report, 6 Mar. 1917, ibid.; US Embassy, Constantinople, memo, 4 Dec. 1916, on Kut, ibid.
46. Cd 9208 *Report*, p. 11; Armstrong S, AWM30 B3.3.
47. Correspondence copied to Australia and NZ, July 1917, CO 693/3.
48. Proposed civilian exchanges: AA CP 78/23 14/89/58/191, 192; POW exchange: AA CP 78/24 16/89/58, also CO official minute, 31 July 1918, CO 693/8; perception of Turkey: e.g, CO minute, 13 Jan. 1917, CO 693/2, and Sir H. Rumbold to FO, 18 Sept. 1918, CO 693/8.
49. *GBPP* 1918, vol. 26, *Agreement between the British and Ottoman Governments respecting Prisoners of War and Civilians*; CO official minute, 31 July 1918, CO 693/8; POW Dept Report, Sept. 1918, CO 693/9.
50. CO minute, 14 Mar. 1918, CO 693/8; Chomley 'Final Report'.
51. Fisher to CO, 12 Mar. 1918, CO 693/8; Ptes J. Davern, O'Connor, *SMH*, 25 Feb. 1918.
52. Turkish attitudes: Lightfoot S, AWM 30 B1.19; Armstrong S, AWM B3.3, Bailey S, Lt W. E. Elston S; mail: Pte B. J. Dunne, AWM 30 B1.2.
53. Lushington, *Prisoner with the Turks*, 90.
54. Chomley 'Final Report'. A few men had already been repatriated.
55. Statistics are not precise. Figures in Butler, *Medical Services* 3: 896 and 901, relate to all AIF POWs in Turkey. Battlefield casualty rate: preliminary indications from data relating to the 1st Brigade compiled by the first AIF Project. See above, chap. 5, fn 17.
56. *Essays on World War 1: Origins and Prisoners of War*, Barker, *Behind Barbed Wire*.
57. See Nelson, *P.O.W Prisoners of War*.
58. Dept of Defence, 'How the Germans treated Australian prisoners of war; extracts from statements made by repatriated Australian prisoners of war . . . with a copy of a report to the German Government from the Acting Consul for Switzerland . . . on the German concentration camp at Holdsworthy in Australia' (Melbourne, 1919); White, *Guests of the Unspeakable*, 95; Suckling narrative.

## CHAPTER 34. AUSTRALIA AND THE DARDANELLES COMMISSION

1. *HCPD*, 5th ser., vol. 71 (1915), col. 969 (Beresford, 4 May); *HLPD*, 5th ser., vol. 20, cols. 131–32 (Morley, 3 Nov., 'terrible story'), col. 121 (Lord Willoughby de Broke), cols. 140, 131 (Crewe).
2. Hamilton to Braithwaite, 1 Jan. 1916 HP 17/7/16/6.
3. Ashmead-Bartlett in *The World*, 1 Feb. 1916, p. 779.
4. Munro Ferguson to Bonar Law exchanges, Feb. 1916, CO 616/53, 202–17, CO 616/59, 294, 296; Ashmead-Bartlett, *Uncensored Dardanelles*, 260.
5. Munro Ferguson to Bonar Law, 22 Feb. 1916, CO 616/53, 341, and 7 Mar. 1916, DP 1914–1918 box.
6. *SMH*, 14 Feb. 1916; copy of lecture in CO 616/53, 317–40.
7. *SMH*, 16 Feb. 1916.
8. *Argus*, 22 and 23 Feb. 1916; 'intense': *Age*, 23 Feb. 1916.
9. For Ashmead-Bartlett's tour, see also Fewster, 'Expression and Suppression', 118–26, and 'Ellis Ashmead-Bartlett'.
10. Long: *The Times*, 12 Jan. 1916.
11. *HCPD* 5th ser., vol. 80 (1916), col. 2190 (Cavendish-Bentinck, 15 Mar.); Constantinople: ibid., col. 553 (Outhwaite); ibid, vol. 84 col. 1747 (Dalziel, 26 July); C. J. to H. L. L. Allanson, 21 Jan. 1916, AP CJA2.
12. *HCPD*, 5th ser., vol. 82 (1916), cols. 2843–46 (Reid, 31 May), col. 2847 (Dalziel).
13. Pelling, *Churchill*, 218; Hamilton to Hankey, 28 June 1916, Cab 17/132.
14. Robertson, 9 July 1916, Cab 17/184; Hankey to Asquith 5 June, 11 July 1916, Cab 17/132.
15. *HCPD*, 5th ser., vol. 84 (1916), col. 850–60 (Asquith, 18 July).
16. Ibid., col. 1236 ff. (Asquith statement), cols. 1242–91, (debate, 27 and 30 July).
17. Grigg, *Lloyd George*, 435–36, for formation of the Dardanelles Commission and its place in the 1916 British political crisis; Hankey note, 11 Aug. 1916, ADM 116/3491.
18. 'An Act to constitute a Special Commission to inquire into the origin, inception and conduct of Operations of War in the Dardanelles and Gallipoli . . .', no. 34, *Public General Acts* (London, 1916); Gollin, *Proconsul in Politics*, 349–50, 604–5.
19. Zetland, *Lord Cromer*, 344; *The Times*, 8 Dec. 1917.
20. Australian representation suggested: *HCPD*, 5th ser., vol. 84 (1916), col. 1262 (Col. Norton Griffiths, 30 July).
21. 'Disability': Hamilton to Asquith, 21 July 1916, HP 17/6/26; Asquith's view: M. Bonham Carter

(Asquith's private sec.) to Hamilton, 24 July 1916, Cab 19/32, 76(2); Fisher's accepts: cable to Pearce (acting PM), 22 July 1916, FP 2919/7/5.

22. Decision not to consult Dominions: CO minute, CO 616/55, 216; Pearce cable to Fisher, 24 July 1916, FP 2919/7/3.

23. 'Foolish blunder': Pearce to Fisher, 26 July 1916, FP 2919/1/217; Munro Ferguson to Bonar Law, 27 July 1916, CO 616/55, 215.

24. CO 616/55, 217–18.

25. Hazelhurst, *Politicians at War*, 292.

26. Cromer, House of Lords, 3 Aug. 1916, FO 633/33, 115; *HCPD*, 5th ser., vol. 84 (1916) col. 1897 (Dalziel, 27 July), cols. 1908–9 (Williams), cols. 1911–12 (Adm. of the Fleet Sir H. Meux on 'whitewash' and need for service representation).

27. *HCPD*, 5th ser., vol. 75 (1915), cols. 1278–80 (Roch, 10 Nov.), vol. 85 (1916), col. 1708ff., (Dalziel, 26 July).

28. Ibid., vol. 84 (1916), col. 1908 (Lynch, 27 July), cols. 1721–22 (Healy, 26 July).

29. Ibid., vol. 85 (1916), col. 88 (Herbert, 1 Aug.), col. 115 (Dalziel).

30. CO minute, 22 Sept. 1916, on *Age* and *Argus* reports 31 July forwarded by Munro Ferguson, CO 616/55, 267–69; *Age* leader, 31 July 1916; *Australian Worker*, 15 Mar. 1917, *Truth* leader, 17 Mar. 1917.

31. *HCPD*, 5th ser., vol. 84 (1916), col. 1744 (Reid, 26 July).

32. No exact precedent: *HCPD*, 5th ser., vol. 91 (1917), col. 1809 (Clyde, 20 Mar.); Gilbert, *Churchill* 3: 790.

33. Roskill, *Hankey* 1: 294.

34. Maxwell to Hamilton, 8 Dec. 1916, HP 17/3/1/26.

35. HP 17/3/1–143, 17/3/2/1–80.

36. Hamilton to Birdwood, 8 Dec. 1916, HP 17/3/1/25, and 23 May 1917 ('tormented'), HP 17/4/2/63.

37. Birdwood's statement, Cab 19/28; Godley to Hamilton, 4 Dec. 1916, HP 17/3/1/15.

38. Stopford statement on 9 Aug. 1915 operations and memo *c.* July 1916 criticising Hamilton's version, Cab 19/31, 24–38; Birdwood to Hamilton, 21 June 1917, HP 17/4/2/106; Godley to wife, 18 Feb. 1917, GP.

39. The DC Report of Proceedings, Cab 19/33, contains about seventeen hundred foolscap pages of evidence; see also Cab 17/184 submissions and evidence and Cab 19/29 (some printed statements are at AWM 51/102, some evidence at AWM 51/103).

40. Gilbert, *Churchill* 3: 817–19.

41. Interim Report, Cmd 8490 (edited version of 1916 Secret Report), *HCPP*, vol. 10, p. 42 'amphibious attack').

42. Cost: *HCPD*, 5th ser., vol. 112 (1919), col. 1372 (Baldwin, 24 Feb.); pressure: ibid., vol. 90 (1917), cols. 2150–52 (Dalziel, 1 Mar.); supplementary report, Cmd 8502, *HCPP*, vol. 10; Cab 17/132 for discussion of papers to be published in Hankey's memo on War Council, Dardanelles Committee and War Committee proceedings.

43. Battenberg to G. J. Aston, 11 Mar. 1917, Aston Papers 6/15, IWM; Harcourt to Munro Ferguson, 14 Mar. 1917. HMS box 479.

44. London cable service in *New York Times*, 10 Mar. 1917.

45. Cab 17/84.

46. *Daily Mail*, 9 Mar. 1917.

47. *The Press*, 10 Mar. 1917, and other cuttings, HP 17/1/6.

48. *SMH* and *Advertiser* leaders, 10 Mar. 1917, articles in *Newcastle Morning Herald and Advocate*, 10 and 17 Mar. 1917; *Daily Post*, 10 and 23 Mar. 1917.

49. *West Australian* leader, 12 Mar. 1917; *Daily Standard*, 12 Mar. 1917.

50. *Evening Echo* leader, 14 Mar. 1917.

51. *Soldier*, 16 Mar. 1917.

52. *Daily Standard*, 12 and 19 Mar. 1917.

53. *SMH*, 22 Mar. 1917; *HCPD*, 5th ser., vol. 91 (1917), cols. 1807–8 (Clyde), cols. 1807–8 (Churchill).

54. *HCPD*, 5th ser., vol. 91 (1917), col. 1785 (Wilson), col. 1830 (Tryon), col. 1822 (Herbert), cols. 1780–81 (Reid).

55. Birdwood to Hamilton, 21 June 1917, HP 17/4/2/106; observer: Hannon to S. Eardley-Wilmot, 2 May 1916, Hannon Papers, box 2, folder 3, HLRO.

56. Fisher, 5 Oct. 1916, Cab 19/33, 171.

57. Mackenzie on 'butchery': Cab 19/33, 1074.

58. Fisher: 'big policy', Cab 19/33, 361; 'unhappy', 1170; postal arrangements, 848/9, 898–902, 1021; water supply, 1021, 1050.

59. Birrell's defence, 26 and 28 Aug. 1917: Cab 19/32, 9(2), 11 (2), 13, 25–26; C-in-C East Indies and Egypt to Porter, 30 April [1917?] PoP PTR 8/1/4.

60. Fisher, Cab 19/33 q. 16478.

61. Questions of Murdoch: Cab 19/33 qq. 16418–54; Hamilton, Cab 19/32, 77.

62. Murdoch, Cab 19/33 q. 16537.

63. Final Report, Cmd 371, *HCPP* 1919, vol. 13 (appendixes include Hamilton dispatches, 20 May, 26 Aug. and 11 Dec. 1915, Anzac/Suvla August attack operational orders), 12th revise, 12 Dec. 1917, copy NMM, MAY/6; judgement, cf. Roskill, *Churchill and the Admirals*, 63: 'grotesquely biased conclusions'.

64. Final Report, 86–88.

65. Final Report, 92.
66. Mackenzie's supplementary report in Final Report, 93–96.
67. Hamilton to Keyes, 25 Jan. 1918, KP.
68. General Staff advice: *HCPD*, 5th ser., vol. 101 (1918), cols. 308–9 (Bonar Law, 16 Jan.); ibid., vol. 96 (1917), col. 1441 (Archer-Shee).
69. *HPCD*, 5th ser., vol. 112 (1919), col. 268 (Bonar Law, 13 Feb.), copies to Australia: Fisher to Bonar Law, 2 July, BLP 97/5/2; Hankey to Bonar Law, 23 July 1919, BLP 97/5/21.
70. *The Times*, 20 Aug. 1919.
71. *West Australian* leader, 21 Nov. 1919.
72. Cab 16/52 (20) 5, also Cab 45/238; preceding CID discussion, Cab 16/53; medical evidence and statements, AWM 51/102, 103.

## CHAPTER 35. GALLIPOLI NEVER DIES

1. Bombardier B. A. Clarke, AFA, to Hamilton, n.d., HP.
2. Fisher circular letter, 18 Apr. 1916, FP 2919/1/2026.
3. *Age* reports 25 and 26 Apr. 1916.
4. Serle, *Monash*, 261; Sekuless and Rees, *Lest We Forget*, 46.
5. *Age*, 25 and 26 Apr. 1916, *Catholic Advocate* 19 Apr. 1916. 'Boys of the Bull Dog Breed' was a popular song.
6. *Age*, 26 Apr. 1916.
7. *NSWPD* 1924, 98 (2nd ser.): 2761.
8. *Anzac Memorial*, with a foreword by Pearce, contains Hamilton's 20 May, 26 Aug. and 11 Nov. 1915 dispatches, tributes in prose and verse from such writers as Dorothea Mackellar, Nettie and Vance Palmer, Christopher Brennan, Mary Gilmore, Hugh McCrae and J. le Gay Brereton, and copious advertising by Sydney business houses. The RSL, known First as the Returned Sailors' and Soldiers' Imperial League of Australia (later Airmen was added), was formed Australia-wide from state Returned Soldiers' Associations affiliated with a central body.
9. Qld cable, 8 Mar. 1916, and CO comment, CO 418/151, 368, 369; dispute, CO 418/144, CO 418/145, also AA CP 78/21, 380.
10. Munro Ferguson cable, 18 Apr. 1916, and follow-up, AA CP 78/21, 379.
11. Pearce to Fisher, 15 Apr. 1916 FP 2919/1/202.
12. Munro Ferguson to Bonar Law, 27 May 1916, and later action, CO 418/144, 615ff.
13. Munro Ferguson to state governors, 17 Apr. 1917, cable to Qld governor, AA CP 78/21, 381.
14. Munro Ferguson to Col. Sec., 4 Apr. 1917, AA CP 78/21, 381; Anzac Day royal messages 1916–26, AA CP 78/21, 390.
15. *Brisbane Courier*, 26 Apr. 1917.
16. Munro Ferguson Anzac Day message, AA CP 78/21, 382.
17. Serle, *Monash*, 317.
18. 'The Day': *SMH* leader, 25 Apr. 1919; minute by CO official, CO 616/82, 556.
19. Kristianson, *Politics of Patriotism*, 12–14; Marilyn Lake, 'The Power of Anzac', in McKernan and Browne, *Two Centuries of War and Peace*, 200–206; Sekuless and Rees, *Lest We Forget*, 47; state sec., WA, to gen. sec., RSL, 29 May 1926, RSLP 2622B.
20. WA and AIF: Welborn, *Lords of Death*, 4, chap. 9; 'sympathetic': Kristianson, *Politics of Patriotism*, 11; federal pay for ex-AIF in 1919, RSL resolution: RSLP 303 and box 96 (Records of Minutes of National Conferences 1917–30); *Smith's Weekly*, 26 Apr. 1919, p. 9. *Smith's Weekly* circulation reached 150,000 in 1923.
21. *WAPD*, new ser., vol. 60 (1919), 798–800 (7 Oct.), 869–70 (15 Oct.)
22. Amendments to relevant WA acts closed shops on Anzac Day from 1920 and closed hotels and banned racing from 1923.
23. *SMH*, 20 Apr. 1920; *CPD* 1920, 91: 1488 (Hughes, 23 Apr.)
24. *CPD* 1921, 95: 7593–94 (Hughes); Munro Ferguson to Col. Sec., 17 May 1921, AA CP 78/21, 383; RSLP box 96. NSW RSL at 1923 national conference wanted sports proscribed and hotels closed (RSLP 178B).
25. *QPD* 1921, 138: 886–88, 1094–95, 1480. A 1930 amendment to the act closed all shops, factories, theatres and newspapers on Anzac Day.
26. *1921 Premiers' Conference, CPP* 1920–21, vol. 4, no. 156, p. 2. In 1922, 'to insure Anzac Day shall be observed on its due date', the Commonwealth removed provision from the Public Service Act for a Monday Anzac Day holiday in lieu of Sunday (*CPD* 1922, 101: 3274).
27. *Conference of Commonwealth and State Ministers, Melbourne May–June 1923, CPP* 1923–24, 2: 493.
28. *SAPD* 1922, 2: 1803–4, 2305–6; SA Treasurer W. Hague, *CPP* 1923–24, 2: 494. For Barwell (and SA political alignments), see *ADB* 7.
29. Oakes, *CPP* 1923–24, 2: 493.
30. Ibid., 493–96; RSL view: RSLP box 6.
31. Gov.-Gen. Lord Forster to Col. Sec., 27 May 1924, AA CP78/21, 386.
32. *NSWPD*, 2nd ser., vol. 98, Legislative Council (1924), 3372–73 (5 Nov.).
33. Ibid., vol. 96 (1924), 1369 (Davidson, 21 Aug.), 1367 (Lazzarini); ibid., vol. 98, Legislative Council (1924), 3765–84 (5–6 Nov.).
34. Ibid., vol. 96 (1924), 1370 (Dooley, 21 Aug.), 1365 (C. H. Murphy). NSW seems to have been later than Vic. in initiating Anzac Day school programs.
35. *NSWPD*, 2nd ser., vol. 98 (1924), 3547 (Burke, 11 Nov.), vol. 96 (1924), 1372 (Bruxner, 21 Aug.).

36. Ibid., vol. 103 (1925), 1562 (Lazzarini, 14 Oct.), 1563 (Oakes); NSW Undersec. to RSL state sec., 15 May 1925, RSLP 2925B.
37. *NSWPD*, 2nd ser., vol. 102 (1925), 919–21 (22 Sept.), vol. 103 (1925), 1564 (Lazzarini, 14 Oct.).
38. Sekuless and Rees, *Lest We Forget*, 48; Serle, *Monash*, 469–70.
39. Acting Premier Sir W. McPherson, *CPP* 1923–24, 2: 496.
40. *VPD* 1925, 169: 992–96.
41. Ibid., 1284–86 (Hughes), 1265–67 (Webber).
42. Ibid., 1574–93.
43. Ely, 'First Anzac Day', 50.
44. *Mercury*, 25, 27 Apr. and 22, 23 May 1925; Premier J. B. Hayes, *CPP* 1923–24, 2: 496; acting premier Tasmania to gen. sec. RSL, 1 Dec. 1926, RSLP 2926B. Amendment (after consulting London) of the Bank Holidays Act dropped the King's Birthday holiday provision for a Monday holiday in lieu of Sunday. In 1923, King's Birthday had been one of the holidays uniformly precribed by the states and Commonwealth.
45. Sekuless and Rees, *Lest We Forget*, 49.
46. Rachel Forster to Starling, 11 Apr. 1923, AA CP 78/21, 388; *Argus*, 26 Apr. 1923.
47. Historiography of the Anzac tradition began with Inglis, 'Anzac Tradition', and Serle, 'Digger Tradition and Australian Nationalism'; a useful recent discussion of C.E.W. Bean, most famous interpreter of the Anzac tradition, is Barrett, 'No Straw Man'.
48. T. Mackenzie letter to Wellington *Dominion*, reprinted in Bournemouth *Echo*, 17 Nov. 1927.
49. Suggested Hamilton visit: RSLP box 96; *Herald* (Melbourne), 4 Sept. 1926, cited in Inglis, 'ANZAC and the Australian Military Tradition', 8.
50. *Argus*, 1 Dec. 1919. Royal Charter, 21 May 1917, established the War Graves Imperial Commission; Peninsula graves (includes identified graves and names on memorials): Commonwealth War Graves Commission to Australian High Commissioner, London, 18 May 1988.
51. *Official History* team visit 1919: Bean, *Gallipoli Mission*; lavish Turkish arrangements 1955: RSLP 4225c/1, 4225; ex-AIF visit 1965: Inglis, 'Return to Gallipoli'.
52. Kinross, *Ataturk*, 113.
53. Fewster, Basarin, and Basarin, *Turkish View of Gallipoli*, chap. 1.
54. A. J. Campbell to U. Igdemir, 17 May 1978, Igdemir, *Ataturk ve Anzaklar*, 50; Australian Embassy, Ankara, 'ANZAC Day 1985'.
55. Bean to J. North, 10 Mar. 1962, North Papers, LH I/3/88; Bean, *AIF in France 1918*, 1093.
56. Liddle, 'Distinctive Nature of the Gallipoli Experience'.
57. Cf. Hughes, *Fatal Shore*, xii. The influence of the convict past is also a central theme of Noel McLachlan in *Waiting for the Revolution*.
58. Inglis, 'ANZAC and the Australian military tradition', 13.

## CHAPTER 36. WAS IT WORTH WHILE?

1. Fewster, 'Ellis Ashmead-Bartlett'; for discussion of Masefield, *Gallipoli*, Hogue, *Trooper Bluegum*, and 'opponents' such as Dr Harry Stuermer, see Appendix.
2. Monash diary MP box 130, folder 958.
3. 'Splendid memory': Adelaide *Advertiser*, 5 Mar. 1920.
4. Richards diary, 11 June 1915.
5. *The Standard*, referring to 'the men of Albuera and Badajoz', cited *Kalgoorlie Miner*, 6 Oct. 1915.
6. Lawrence, *Seven Pillars of Wisdom*, 51.
7. Kannengiesser, *Campaign in Gallipoli*, 259.
8. First estimate: Murphy, *Soldiers of the Prophet*, 151; *Campaign des Dardanelles*, 76; losses at Anzac front: Larcher, *La Guerre turque*, 242.
9. *Campaign des Dardanelles*, 77; French losses: *Les Armées françaises*, 549.
10. Clausewitz, *On War*, 192; 'supreme': Smith, 'Clausewitz and War', 1.
11. For a brief exposition of Treitschke's views see Kennedy, *Rise of the Anglo-German Antagonism*, 68–69.
12. On Neitzche, see Stern, *Hitler*, chap. 5.
13. Fischer, *War of Illusions* and *Germany's Aims in the First World War*; Ritter, *Sword and the Sceptre*. For an Australian interpretation of Fischer, see Moses, *Politics of Illusion*.

## APPENDIX. GALLIPOLI: CONTINUING HISTORICAL CONTROVERSY

1. E. C. Buley papers, AWM 1 DRL 221; Hogarth: Buley, *Glorious Deeds*, 161.
2. Hogue, *Trooper Bluegum*, 157 ('war is hell'), *Love Letters of an Anzac*, 93, 158; Knyvett, *'Over There'*, 95, 97, 122; Dinning, *By-ways*, viii, 87.
3. Hamilton, *Gallipoli Diary* 2: 21; Schuler, *Australia in Arms*, 15, 25, 155–56, 244, 270–71, 277, chap. 22. Schuler travelled with the first convoy messing with 5 Bn officers, joined the AIF in Apr. 1916, and was killed in action in June 1917.
4. Masefield, *Gallipoli*, 19.
5. Stuermer, *Deux Ans de Guerre*, Preface, 35, 72–74.
6. Morgenthau, *Secrets of the Bosphorus*, 267; Einstein, *Inside Constantinople*, 130–31, and *A Diplomat Looks Back*, 140–41.
7. Djemal, *Memories*, 68–69 (Morgenthau), chap 3 (Young Turk diplomacy).
8. 'Remarkable': Bush, *Gallipoli*, 181; Herbert, *Mons, Anzac and Kut*, 195–96.
9. Realistic strategic thinking: Prigge, *Der Kampf um die Dardanellen*, 35–39.

10. *The Hell of Gallipoli. The Heroes' Battle at the Dardanelles.*

11. Moseley, *Truth about the Dardanelles*, 93–122 (wounded), 148–62 (RAMC), 197 (attacks critics), 215 (Monro), 232 ('tragic failure'), 261 ('crabbers'), 266 ('soldier politician').

12. Nevinson, *The Dardanelles Campaign*, 23 ('brilliant'), 408 (failure), 65–67 (Hamilton), xi ('actual units'), 72–73 (Anzacs).

13. Fisher, *Memories*, 74 (main theatre of war), 50 etc. (miasma), 71 (Nelsonian dictum).

14. Callwell, *The Dardanelles, Experiences of a Dug-out*, and *Stray Recollections*.

15. Callwell, *Dug-out*, 92–93 (senior officers' views); *The Dardanelles*, 127–31 (better to attack at Helles), 105 ('illuminating'), 102 (Turks stronger), 342–44 (planning) 267 (Hamilton's recall).

16. Godley to Hamilton, 25 May 1920, HP 18/5/26; Murdoch letter, *Morning Bulletin* (Rockhampton), 19 May 1920; *SMH*, 17 May 1920. The Aust. Press Assoc. had early publication rights.

17. Arthur, *Kitchener* 3: 210 ('politically well conceived'); Magnus, *Kitchener*, 369.

18. *VPD* 1925, 169: 1278 (McPherson on *World Crisis*).

19. Wemyss, *Navy in the Dardanelles Campaign*, 275–78 (Fisher), 264–66 (bad planning).

20. Liman von Sanders, *Five Years*, 89–90 (August offensive).

21. Muhlmann, *Der Kampf um die Dardanellen*, 150–51 (private translation).

22. Kannengiesser, *Campaign in Gallipoli*, 259–70.

23. Mackenzie, *Gallipoli Memories*, 153.

24. *Uncensored Dardanelles*, 39 (Keyes), 38 ('doomed to failure'), 162 ('poor opinion'), 218–20 (August plans), 225 ('assiduously asserted fiction'), 229 (Anzacs for Suvla), 247–48 ('unsuitable people' and 'muddles').

25. Barrow, *Life of Munro*, 63, 60–61; Head, *Glance at Gallipoli*, 152–53 (Sari Bair), 94–96 (Balkans offensive).

26. Delage, *Tragedy of the Dardanelles*, 150, 218–19, 223; Feuille, *Face aux Turcs*, 216.

27. Chatterton, *Dardanelles Dilemma*, 54.

28. Arthur, *Maxwell*, 173, and Maxwell to Hamilton, 25 Apr. 1915, HP 5/12; Keyes, *Memoirs* 1: 253 (save lives), 343 ('glory'), 273 (minesweepers); Halpern, ed., *Naval Memoirs of Admiral of the Fleet Sir Roger Keyes*.

29. Godley, *Life of an Irish Soldier*, 202.

30. Dewar, *Navy From Within*, 175 ('gamble'), 190 (Corbett's analysis).

31. Birdwood, *Khaki and Gown* 275, 276, 274.

32. North, *Gallipoli*, 54–61 (defence of Churchill), 214–15 (Anzacs), 318 and chap. 7 generally (Hamilton), 335 (Kitchener), 82 (Bean). Copies of about fifty reviews are in North Papers, LHI/4a, including Lt-Col. Graham Seton Hutchinson in *Reveille*, 1 April 1936, *Bulletin's* comment and Bean's *SMH* review of 8 May 1936.

33. *HCPD*, 5th ser., vol. 155 (1922) cols. 278–87 (13 June). Bean recommended both Australia's official history and the establishment of the AWM as a monument to the AIF (Inglis, *C.E.W. Bean*, 19–20). A desire in Australia for public record is also reflected in, e.g., Tasmania's publication of *Tasmania's War Record*, ed. L. Broinowski, a narrative and 'Muster Roll' of all Tasmanians in the First World War, including nurses and those enlisted in other states and NZ.

34. The 'Mitchell' committee, established by the Admiralty in March 1919, chaired by Commodore F. H. Mitchell and including five naval, four army and two airforce members, visited Turkey and reported on campaign operational aspects (copy of Mitchell Report at AWM 51 No 39). James, *Gallipoli*, 351, suggests it did not much advance joint-service aspects of amphibious doctrine.

35. Corbett, *Naval Operations* 2: 321–23 (RN mistake), 106–9, 151–56, 201–4, 410 (Churchill's role); 3: 40 ('decisive') 147 (Falkenhayn), 84, 97 (April and August).

36. Wilson, *Cabinet Office to 1945*, 122–23; CID Sub-committee meeting, 9 Mar. 1928, PRO Cab 16/53. Corbett's vol. 2 was published only after cabinet was satisfied that 'reception [of vol. 1] was all that could be desired'. With creation of the CID subcommittee, drafts usually were circulated to departments and officers who had participated; one went to 799 recipients.

37. Aspinall-Oglander, *Gallipoli* 2: chap. 20 ('wasted day'), 325–27 (Stopford); 1: 200 ('predominant feeling').

38. Waite, *New Zealanders at Gallipoli* (forewords provided by Hamilton and Birdwood); Inglis, *C.E.W. Bean*, 22–23.

39. Bean, 'Writing of the Australian Official History', 86; Bean, *Story of Anzac* 1: 201; Churchill, *World Crisis*, 122.

40. Bean, *Gallipoli Mission*; Bean to North, 28 May 1942, North Papers LH I/3/86; the writing of Butler's volumes: O'Keefe, 'Butler's Medical Histories'.

41. *Der Weltkrieg*, 192–93 (private translation).

42. *Historique des Opérations Ottomans dans la Guerre Mondiale Campaign des Dardanelles* (Paris 1924), French translation of official Turkish history by Commandant M. Larcher (1922); *Les Armées Françaises dans La Guerre*, Tome VIII, Premier Volume (Ministère de la Guerre, Paris, 1923).

43. Carcopino, *Souvenirs*, 62–69.

44. Moorehead, *Gallipoli*, 140 (Turkish view, e.g.), 365 ('serious student').

45. Cassar, *Kitchener*, 440–41, 439; Marder, *Dreadnought to Scapa Flow*, 262–63; Higgins, *Winston Churchill*, 87.

46. Pedersen, *Monash*, 113–114 (Birdwood and Godley), 68 (Monash 'learning'), 216, 297 (Bean, e.g.); Serle, *Monash*, 397–98 (Bean); Pugsley, *Gallipoli*, 348–49 (Godley).

47. E.g., Prior, *Churchill's 'World Crisis'*, 49; Pedersen, *Monash*, 105.

# SOURCES

THE FOLLOWING NOTES comprise private papers and material relating to individuals cited in this book (other than for those men listed in the Biographical Notes), plus a select bibliography. Official government record series used at Australian Archives, the Australian War Memorial or the Public Record Office, London, are cited in the endnotes.

## PRIVATE PAPERS AND MATERIAL RELATING TO INDIVIDUALS

AUSTRALIAN WAR MEMORIAL, NATIONAL LIBRARY OF AUSTRALIA, AND AUSTRALIAN ARCHIVES, CANBERRA

Aitken, Sister M. Memoir AWM 41
Antill, Brigadier-General J. M. Papers AWM 3 DRL 6458
Armstrong, Private D. S. POW statement AWM 30 B3.3
Aspinall, Major A. J. Papers AWM 41 [1/3.8]
Baker, Warrant-Officer E. W. Papers AWM 1 DRL 83
Bean, C. E. W. Diaries AWM 3 DRL 606
Bean, Major J. W. B. Diary AWM
Blamey, Field-Marshal Sir Thomas. AWM PR 85/355
Bowman, Lieutenant-Colonel R. M. AWM 41 [1/4.12]
Bridges, Major-General W. T. AWM 2 DRL 469 [copy of diary in IWM]
Buley, E. C. Papers AWM 1 DRL 221
Butler, A. G. Papers of the Official Historian AWM 41
Carnell, Sapper R. Diary AWM PR 83/87
Carpenter, Private A. POW statement AWM 30 B3.3
Cole, Major G. E. Papers AWM 41 [1/5.12]
Darnell, Major Aubrey. Papers AWM PR 82/175
Dunne, Private B. J. POW statement AWM 30 B 1.2
Felton, Private William Robert. Letter AWM PR 82/8(1)
Fetherston, Major-General R. H. J. Extracts from reports, etc. AWM 41 [2/7.4]
Fisher, Andrew. Papers NLA Ms 2919
Fry, Lieutenant-Colonel H. K. Memoirs AWM 41 [2/7.15]
Gellibrand, Major-General W. Papers AWM 3 DRL 8050
Imlay, Sister Nellie. Letters AWM PR 84/133
Lorentzen, Ernie. Letter AWM PR 82/8(1)
Luke, P. H. Diary AWM PR 83/44

MacMillan C. C. Memoir AWM [3/10.9]
McGelligott, Lieutenant J. POW statement AWM 30 B3.3
McGrigor, Captain A. M. Diary AWM 3 DRL 4152 (copy in IWM)
Maher, Colonel J. B. Memoir AWM 41 [3/10.8]
Merrington, Chaplain E. N. AWM 1 DRL 496
Mackay, Major-General Sir Iven. Papers AWM 3 DRL 6850
Monash, General Sir John. Papers NLA Ms 1884; AWM 3 DRL 2316
Muirhead, Lieutenant-Colonel J. R. AWM 41 [3/110.24]
Murdoch, Sir Keith. NLA Ms 2823
Neumarch, Colonel B. J. Memoir AWM 41 [3/11.5]
Pearce, Sir George Foster. Papers; AWM 2 DRL 970
Redmond, Signaller D. A. Papers AWM 3 DRL 7247
Returned Services League of Australia. Papers NLA Ms 6609
Ryan, Major-General Sir Charles S. AWM 41 [3/11.5]
Ryrie, Major-General Sir G. L. Papers AWM PR 84/193; AWM PR 82/8(2)
Shedden, Sir Frederick. Manuscript AA A 5954 Box 1270
Stinson, Lieutenant G. J. Diary AWM PR 84/66
White, Major-General Sir C. B. Papers NLA Ms J172; AWM 3 DRL 1400
Wright, Corporal F. C. W. Papers AWM PR 83/103
Yates, Captain W. T. Diary AWM 3 DRL 7219a

BODLEIAN LIBRARY, OXFORD UNIVERSITY, UK

Asquith, Herbert Henry, 1st Earl of Oxford and Asquith. Papers
Gwynne, Howell Arthur. Papers
Harcourt, Viscount Sir Lewis. Papers
Milner, Viscount Sir Alfred. Manuscripts

BRITISH LIBRARY, LONDON

Cromer, 1st Earl of, Sir Evelyn Baring. Papers
Hunter-Weston, Lieutenant-General Sir Aylmer. Papers
Hutton, Sir Edward T. H. Papers
Keyes, Admiral of the Fleet Sir Roger. Papers

CHURCHILL COLLEGE CAMBRIDGE ARCHIVES CENTRE, UK

Fisher, Admiral of the Fleet and Baron John Arbuthnot. Papers
Hankey, Sir Maurice. Papers

de Robeck, Vice-Admiral and Baron John Michael. Papers

HOUSE OF LORDS RECORD OFFICE, LONDON

Davidson, J. C. C. Papers
Hannon, Sir Patrick. Papers
Law, Andrew Bonar. Papers
Lloyd George, David, Earl Lloyd-George of Dwyfor. Papers
Pringle, W. M. R. Papers

IMPERIAL WAR MUSEUM, LONDON

Allanson, Colonel C. J. L. Diaries and Papers
Aston, Lieutenant-Colonel C. C. Papers
Ataturk, Mustapha Kemal. 'Memoirs of the Anafartalar Battles'
Bachtold, Capt H. Papers
Backhouse, Admiral Oliver RN. Diaries
Barsley, G., RN. Diary
Bennett, Lieutenant Harry T., RN. Diaries
Bidder Clark, Commander E., RN. Papers
Birdwood, Field Marshal Sir William. Papers, Correspondence with Col. D. Rintoul
Blows, O. S. Diary
Brampton, Captain C. K., RN. Diary
Brayley, Captain C. E. W., RN. Letters
Bush, Eric. Papers
Butler, Major-General S. S. Papers
Claris, Captain D. J. RN. Diary
Dawnay, Major-General G. P. Papers
Drage, Commander Charles H., RN. Diary
Drewry, Lieutenant G. L., RN. Papers
England, Rear-Admiral H. T. Papers
Fairbairn, W. Papers
Fitzgerald, Lieutenant-Colonel B. Diary and letters
Gibson, Rear-Admiral I. W. Papers
Gresson, Captain K. M. Diary
Hare, Major-General Sir Stewart W. Papers
Harrison, Lieutenant-Colonel W. R. E. Papers
Hart, Colonel N. B. Papers
Howitt, Lieutenant F. D. Manuscript
Hunter-Weston, Major-General Sir Aylmer. Papers
Johnston, Chief Petty Officer F. W. Diaries
Kirkpatrick, Sir Ivone. Papers
Lamb, Corporal H. A. J. Papers
Lowry, Commander R. G. Papers
McGrigor, Captain A. M. Diary (copy)
McPherson, Lieutenant J. W. Diary
Millar, Lieutenant-Colonel J. S. Gallipoli Memoir

Milligan, Captain S. L. Papers
Miscellaneous 77, 309, 1172
Moore, Captain B. L. Diary
Moore, Gunner T. Diary
Natusch, Stanley. Papers
Owen, Brigadier-General Cunliffe. Papers
Paris, Major-General Archibald. Papers
Rayfield, Lieutenant-Colonel F. A. Papers
Robinson, Frederick Arthur. Diary (3,473 pp typed)
Rochdale, Lady Elizabeth. Diary and letters
Rochdale, Colonel Lord. Papers
Rettie, Lieutenant-Colonel W. J. K. Diary
Rylands, Lieutenant-Commander G. K. Memoir
Scott, Reverend W. F. Memoirs
Shaw, Lieutenant-General Sir Frederick C. Letters
Skinner, Private A. W. Reminiscences
Upton, V. E. Diary
Valentine, Corporal T. Reminiscences
Wedgwood, Lieutenant-Commander Josiah C., RN. Diary
Wilkinson, Lieutenant-Commander R. W., RN. Letters
Williams, Dr Orlo C. Diaries
Williamson, R. W., RN. Letters

INDIA OFFICE LIBRARY, LONDON
Curzon, Marquess George Nathaniel. Manuscripts

LIDDELL HART CENTRE FOR MILITARY ARCHIVES, KING'S COLLEGE, UNIVERSITY OF LONDON
Hamilton, General Sir Ian. Diary and Papers, 1900–1917
Howell Papers
Kiggell, Lieutenant-General Sir L. E. Papers
Maurice, F. W. Papers
North, John. Papers, including correspondence with C. E. W. Bean and General Hamilton
Robertson, Field-Marshal Sir William. Papers

NATIONAL MARITIME MUSEUM, GREENWICH, UK
Bennett, Harry T. Diaries kept on HMS Canopus 1914–16
Limpus, Rear-Admiral Sir Arthur Henry. Papers
May, Admiral of the Fleet Sir William Henry. Papers
Oliver, Admiral of the Fleet Sir Henry Francis. Papers
Porter, Vice-Admiral Sir James. Papers
Richmond, Lady. Diary
de Vitre, Reverend J. H. Transcripts of letters to his mother 1915
Wyld, Commander H. W. Papers

OLD WAR OFFICE LIBRARY, LONDON
Godley, Sir Alexander and Lady Godley. Letters and Papers

THE LIDDLE COLLECTION, LEEDS UNIVERSITY LIBRARY
Holmes, Captain Basil
Note: For the many other papers consulted at the Peter Liddle Archives, see the Biographical Notes.

## BOOKS, ARTICLES, THESES.

Anderson, M. S. The Eastern Question 1774–1923: A Study in International Relations. London, 1966.
Anzac Memorial. Returned Soldiers Association, Sydney, 1916.
Arthur, Sir George. Life of Lord Kitchener. 3 vols. London, 1920.
———. General Sir John Maxwell. London, 1932.
Ashmead-Bartlett, Ellis. The Uncensored Dardanelles. London, nd [1928].
Aspinall-Oglander, C. F. Military Operations: Gallipoli. Vols 1 and 2 of Britain's official History of the Great War. London, 1929–32.
———. Roger Keyes. London, 1951.
Australia. Parliament. 1921 Premiers' Conference. CPP 1920–21, vol. 4, no. 156.
———. Conference of Commonwealth and State Ministers, Melbourne, May–June 1923. CPP 1923–24, vol. 2.
Australian Embassy, Ankara. 'Anzac Day 1985: Naming of Anzac Cove'. Australian Foreign Affairs Record, April 1985, pp. 290–92.
Barker, A. J. Behind Barbed Wire. London, 1974.
Barrett, James W., and Lt P. E. Deane. The Australian Army Medical Corps in Egypt. London, 1918.
Barrett, John. Falling In. Sydney, 1979
———. 'No Straw Man: C. E. W. Bean and Some Critics'. Australian Historical Studies 23, no. 90 (April 1988): 102–114
Barrow, Sir George de Symons. The Life of General Sir Charles Monro. London, 1931.
Bean, C. E. W. The Story of Anzac. Vols 1 and 2 of Official History of Australia in the War of 1914–1918. Sydney, 1921, 1924.
———. 'The Writing of the Australian Official History of the Great War—Sources, Methods and Some Conclusions'. Royal Australian Historical Society Journal and Proceedings 24 (1938), pt 2.
———. The Australian Imperial Force in France, 1918. Vol 6 of Official History of Australia in the War of 1914–1918. Sydney, 1942.
———. Anzac to Amiens. Canberra, 1946.
———. Gallipoli Mission. Canberra, 1948.
Beaumont, Joan. 'Rank, Privilege and Prisoners of War'. War and Society 1, no. 1 (May 1983): 67–94.

Benson, Sir Irving. The Man with the Donkey. London, 1965.
Bernhardi, General Friedrich von. Germany and the Next War. Translated by Allen H. Powles. London, 1912.
———. How Germany Makes War. Translated by Karl von Donat. London, 1914.
Birdwood, William. Khaki and Gown. London, 1941.
Black Bread and Barbed Wire: Prisoners in the First World War. New York, 1978.
Blake, Robert, ed. The Private Papers of Douglas Haig 1914–1919. London, 1952.
Brackenbury, Noel. 'Becoming Guests of the Unspeakable'. BA Hons thesis, Macquarie University, Sydney, 1983. (Copy at AWM MS 975)
Broinowski, L., ed. Tasmania's War Record. Hobart, 1921.
Brugger, Suzanne, Australians and Egypt 1914–1919. Melbourne, 1980.
Buley, E. C. Glorious Deeds of Australians in the Great War. London, 1915.
Bush, Captain Eric Wheler. Gallipoli. London, 1975.
Butler, A. G. Special Problems and Services. Official History of the Australian Army Medical Services in the War of 1914–1918. Vol 1 Melbourne, 1938; Vol 3 Melbourne, 1943.
———. The Digger. Sydney, 1945.
Callwell, C. E. The Dardanelles. London, 1919.
———. Experiences of a Dug-out, London, 1920.
———. Stray Recollections. London, 1923.
Campagne des Dardanelles. Turkish Official History translated by M. E. Larcher. Paris, 1924.
Carcopino, Jerome. Souvenirs de la Guerre en Orient 1915–1917. Paris, 1970.
Cassar, George H. The French and the Dardanelles. London, 1971.
———. Kitchener: Architect of Victory. London, 1977.
Chatterton, E. Keble. Dardanelles Dilemma: The Story of the Naval Operations. London, 1935.
Chomley, M. E. 'Final Report on the Prisoners of War Department of the Australian Red Cross Society', ts, nd.
Churchill, Winston S. The World Crisis. 2 vols. London, 1923.
Clausewitz, Carl von. On War (Vom Kriege, 3 vols, 1832–37), ed. and trans. by M. Howard and P. Paret. Princeton, 1976.
Corbett, Julian. Naval Operations. 5 vols of Britain's official History of the Great War. London, 1920–31.
Coulthard-Clark, C. D. A Heritage of Spirit. Melbourne, 1979.
———. 'Major-General Sir William Bridges: Australia's First Field Commander'. In The Commanders, ed. D. M. Horner. Sydney, 1984.

————. *No Australian Need Apply*. Sydney, 1988.

————. 'Formation of the Australian Armed Services, 1901–14'. In *Australia: Two Centuries of War and Peace*, ed. Michael McKernan and Margaret Browne. Canberra, 1988.

Crowley, F. K. *Modern Australia in Documents*. Vol 1. Melbourne, 1973.

Cunneen, Christopher. *Kings' Men*. Sydney, 1983.

Delage, Edmund. *Tragedy of the Dardanelles*. Trans. by W. Ray Hamilton. London, 1932.

*Der Weltkrieg* (German official history of the war). Vol 9, *Die Operation des Jahres 1915*. Berlin, 1933.

Dewar, Vice-Admiral K. G. B. *The Navy from Within*. London, 1939.

Dinning, Hector. *By-ways on Service*. London, 1918.

Djemal Pasha. *Memories of a Turkish Statesman, 1913–1914*. London, 1922.

Dyer, Gwynne. 'Turkish "Falsifiers" and Armenian "Deceivers": Historiography and the Armenian Massacres', *Middle Eastern Studies* 12 (1976): 99–107.

East, Sir Ronald, ed. *The Gallipoli Diary of Sergeant Lawrence*. Melbourne, 1981.

Einstein, Lewis. *Inside Constantinople: A Diplomatist's Diary during the Dardanelles Expedition, April–September 1915*. London, 1917.

————. *A Diplomat Looks Back*. London, 1968.

Ely, Richard. 'The First Anzac Day: Invented or Discovered?' *Journal of Australian Studies* 17 (Nov. 1985): 50.

*Essays on World War I: Origins and Prisoners of War*. New York, 1983.

Emin, A. *Turkey in the World War*. New Haven, 1930.

Feuille, Henri. *Face aux Turcs: Gallipoli 1915*. Paris, 1934.

Fewster, Kevin, ed. *Gallipoli Correspondent: The Frontline Diary of C. E. W. Bean*. London, 1983.

————. 'Ellis Ashmead-Bartlett and the Making of the Anzac Legend'. *Journal of Australian Studies* 10 (June 1982): 17–30.

————. 'Expression and Suppression: Aspects of Military Censorship in Australia during the Great War'. PhD thesis, University of New South Wales, 1980.

Fewster, Kevin, Vecihi Basarin, and Hatice Hurmuz Basarin. *A Turkish View of Gallipoli. Canakkale*. Richmond, Vic, n.d. [1985].

Field, L. M. *The Forgotten War. Australian Involvement in the South African Conflict of 1899–1902*. Melbourne, 1979.

Fischer, Fritz. *Germany's Aims in the First World War*. Trans. James Joll. London, 1967.

————. *War of Illusions: German Policies*

*from 1911 to 1914*. Trans. Marian Jackson. London, 1975.

Fisher, Admiral Sir John. *Memories*. London, 1919.

Fitzhardinge, L. F. *William Morris Hughes: A Political Biography*. Vol. 1, *That Fiery Particle, 1862–1914*. Sydney, 1964.

————. 'Australia, Japan and Great Britain, 1914–18: A Study in Triangular Diplomacy' *Historical Studies* 14 (1970): 250–59.

Fortescue, Granville. *Russia, the Balkans and the Dardanelles*. London, 1915.

————. *What of the Dardanelles? An Analysis*. London, 1915.

Foster, J. R. *Two-and-a-Half Years a Prisoner of War in Turkey*, related by Trooper G. W. Handsley, 2nd Light Horse Regiment. Brisbane, n.d.

Fraser, Peter. *Lord Esher*. London, 1973.

French, David. *British Strategy and War Aims 1914–16*. London, 1986.

Gallishaw, John. *Trenching at Gallipoli*. New York, 1916.

Gammage, Bill. *The Broken Years: Australian Soldiers in the Great War*. Canberra, 1974.

Gerster, Robin. *Big-Noting: The Heroic Theme in Australian Writing*. Melbourne, 1987.

Gilbert, Alan D., John Robertson, and Roslyn Russell. 'Computing Military History: A Research Report on the First AIF Project'. *War and Society* 7, no. 1 (May 1989): 106–13.

Gilbert, Martin. *Winston S. Churchill*. Vol. 3, *1914–1916*. London, 1971.

Godley, Sir Alexander. *Life of an Irish Soldier*. London, 1939.

Gollin, Alfred M. *Proconsul in Politics: A Study of Lord Milner*. London, 1964.

Gooch, G. P., and H. V. Temperley, eds. *British Documents on the Origin of the War, 1898–1914*. 11 vols. London, 1925–38.

Great Britain. *House of Commons Papers 1918 Vol 26. Agreement between the British and Ottoman Governments Respecting Prisoners of War and Civilians.*

————. *Parliamentary Papers 1918 Report on the Treatment of British Prisoners of War in Turkey*. Cmd 9208.

Grigg, John. *Lloyd George*. London, 1978.

de Groot, Maria. 'Aborigines in the Australian Armed Forces in the Great War and the Second World War'. BA Hons thesis, University of Adelaide, Adelaide, 1979.

Halpern, Paul G., ed. *The Naval Memoirs of Admiral of the Fleet Sir Roger Keyes*. Navy Records Society, Florida State University, 1972.

Hamilton, General Sir Ian. *Gallipoli Diary*. 2 vols. London, 1920.

Hankey, Lord Maurice. *The Supreme Command, 1914–1918*. 2 vols. London, 1961.

Hazelhurst, Cameron. *Politicians at War July 1914 to May 1915*. London, 1971.

Head, C. O. *A Glance at Gallipoli*. London, 1931.

Herbert, Aubrey. *Mons, Anzac and Kut, by an M. P*. London, 1919.

Higgins, H. B. *In Europe 1914–15*. Melbourne, 1917.

Higgins, Trumbull. *Winston Churchill and the Dardanelles*. London, 1964.

Hill, A. J. *Chauvel of the Light Horse*. Melbourne, 1978.

Hogue, Oliver. *Trooper Bluegum at the Dardanelles*. London, 1916.

————. *Love Letters of an Anzac*. London, 1916.

Horner, D. M., ed. *The Commanders*. Sydney, 1984.

Hughes, Robert. *The Fatal Shore*. London, 1987.

Hughes, W. M. *The Splendid Adventure*. London, 1929.

Hyslop, Robert. *Australian Naval Administration, 1900–1939*. Melbourne, 1973.

Idriess, Ion L. *The Desert Column*. Sydney, 1932.

Igdemir, Ulug. *Atatürk ve Anzaklar (Atatürk and the Anzacs)*. Ankara, 1978.

Inglis, K. S. 'The Anzac Tradition'. *Meanjin Quarterly* 24(1965), no. 100: 25–44.

————. 'Return to Gallipoli'. *ANU Historical Journal*, No.3 (Oct. 1966): 1–10.

————. *C. E. W. Bean: Australian Historian*. John Murtagh Macrossan Lecture. Brisbane, 1970.

————. 'Anzac and the Australian Military Tradition'. *Current Affairs Bulletin*, April 1988, pp. 4–15.

Jabotinsky, Vladimir. *Turkey and the War*. London, 1917.

James, Robert Rhodes. *Gallipoli*. London, 1965.

Jenkins, Roy. *Asquith*. London, 1964.

Jose, A. W. *The Royal Australian Navy 1914–1918*. Vol 9 of *Official History of Australia in the War of 1914–1918*. Sydney, 1928.

Kannengiesser, Hans. *The Campaign in Gallipoli*. Translated by Major C. J. P. Ball. London, 1927.

Keyes, Roger. *The Naval Memoirs of Admiral of the Fleet Sir Roger Keyes: The Narrow Seas to the Dardanelles 1910–1915*. London, 1934.

————. *The Fight for Gallipoli*. London, 1941.

Kennedy, Paul M. *The Rise of the Anglo-German Antagonism 1860–1914*. London, 1980.

Kinross, Lord. *Ataturk*. New York, 1965.

Knightley, Phillip. *The First Casualty of War from the Crimea to Vietnam*, New York, 1975.

Knyvett, R. Hugh. *'Over There', with the Australians*. London, 1918.

Kristianson, G. L. *The Politics of Patriotism*. Canberra, 1966.

Larcher, Commandant M. *La Guerre turque dans la Guerre Mondiale*. 1926.

Lawrence, T. E. *The Seven Pillars of Wisdom* (1926). London, 1935.

*Les Armées françaises dans la Guerre* (French official war history). Vol. 8, pt 1. Paris, 1923.

Lewin, P. Evans. *The Oxford Survey of the British Empire*. London, 1914.

Liddle, Peter, *Men of Gallipoli*. London, 1976.

———. 'The Distinctive Nature of the Gallipoli Experience'. *Journal of the Royal United Services Institute* 122, no. 2 (June 1977): 51–56.

Liman von Sanders, Otto. *Five Years in Turkey*. Annapolis, 1927.

Louis, W. Roger. *Great Britain and Germany's Lost Colonies 1914–1919*. Oxford 1967.

Louis, W. Roger. 'Australia and the German Colonies in the Pacific 1914–1919'. *Journal of Modern History* 37 (1966): 407–21.

———. *Great Britain and Germany's Lost Colonies 1914–1919*. London, 1967.

Lowe, Peter. *Great Britain and Japan 1911–1915*. Glasgow, 1969.

Lushington, R. F. *A Prisoner with the Turks 1915–1918*. London, 1923.

Macandie, G. L. *The Genesis of the Royal Australian Navy*. Sydney 1949.

Mackenzie, Edward Montagu Compton. *Gallipoli Memories*. London, 1929.

Mackenzie, S. S. *The Australians at Rabaul*. Vol. 10 of *Official History of Australia in the War of 1914–1918*. Sydney, 1927.

McKernan, Michael. *The Australian People and the Great War*. Melbourne, 1980.

McKernan, Michael, and Margaret Browne. *Australia: Two Centuries of War & Peace*. Canberra, 1988.

McLachlan, Noel. *Waiting for the Revolution: A History of Australian Nationalism*. Ringwood, Vic, 1989.

Magnus, Sir Philip. *Kitchener: Portrait of an Imperialist*. London, 1958.

Mann, Leonard. *Flesh in Armour*. London, 1932.

Marder, Arthur J. *Fear God and Dread Nought: The Correspondence of Admiral of the Fleet Lord Fisher of Kilverstone*. 3 vols. London, 1952–59.

———. *From the Dreadnought to Scapa Flow: The Royal Navy—the Fisher Era, 1904–19*. 5 vols. London, 1961–70.

Masefield, John. *Gallipoli*. London, 1916.

Meaney, Neville. *A History of Australian Defence and Foreign Policy 1901–23*. Vol. 1, *The Search for Security—the Pacific, 1901–14*. Sydney, 1976.

Miller, Steven E., ed. *Military Strategy and the Origins of the First World War*. Princeton, 1985.

Moorehead, Alan. *Gallipoli*. London, 1956.

Morgenthau, Henry. *Ambassador Morgenthau's Story*. Garden City, NY, 1918.

———. *Secrets of the Bosphorus: Constantinople 1913–1916*. London, 1918.

———. *All in a Lifetime*. New York, 1922.

Moseley, Sydney A. *The Truth about the Dardanelles*. London, 1916.

Moses, John A. *The Politics of Illusion*. Brisbane, 1975.

Muhlmann, C. *Der Kampf um die Dardanellen*. Berlin, 1927.

Murphy, Lt.-Col. C. C. R. *Soldiers of the Prophet*. London, 1921.

Nelson, Hank. *P. O. W., Prisoners of War: Australians under Nippon*. Sydney, 1985.

Nelson, Keith, and Roy A. Prete, eds. *Coalition Warfare: an Uneasy Accord*. Waterloo, Ontario, 1983.

Nevinson, Henry W. *The Dardanelles Campaign*. London, 1918.

Nish, Ian H. *The Anglo-Japanese Alliance: The Diplomacy of Two Island Empires, 1894–1907*. London, 1966.

———. *Alliance in Decline: A Study in Anglo Japanese Relations, 1908–23*. London, 1972.

Noble, Lt R. J. H. 'Raising the White Flag: The Surrender of Australian Soldiers in France during the Great War'. BA Hons thesis, University of New South Wales at the Australian Defence Force Academy, Canberra, 1988.

North, John. *Gallipoli: The Fading Vision*. London, 1934.

'Notes on the Turkish Army' (MS, 113 pp.).

O'Keefe, B. 'Butler's Medical Histories'. *Journal of the Australian War Memorial*, no. 12 (April 1988): 25–34.

Olden, A. C. N. *Westralian Cavalry in the War*. Melbourne, 1921.

*Oxford Survey of the British Empire*. London, 1914.

Pedersen, P. A. *Monash as Military Commander*. Melbourne, 1985.

Pelling, Henry. *Winston Churchill*. London, 1974.

Piggott, Michael. 'Stonewalling in German New Guinea'. *Journal of the Australian War Memorial*, no. 12 (April 1988): 3–15.

Pound, Reginald, and Geoffrey Harmsworth. *Northcliffe*. London 1959.

Prigge, E. R. *Der Kampf um die Dardanellen*. Weimar, 1916.

Prior, Robin. *Churchill's 'World Crisis' as History*. London, 1983.

———. 'The Suvla Bay Tea-party: A Reassessment'. *Journal of the Australian War Memorial*, No 7 (Oct 1985): 25–33.

Pugsley, Christopher. *Gallipoli: The New Zealand Story*. Auckland, 1984.

Rickard, John. *H. B. Higgins*. Sydney, 1984.

Riddell, G. A. *War Diary 1914–1918*. London, 1933.

Ritter, G. *The Sword and the Sceptre*. 4 vols. London, 1969.

Robson, L. L. *The First A. I. F.: A Study of Its Recruitment 1914–1918* Melbourne, 1970.

———. 'The Origin and Character of the First A. I. F., 1914–1918: Some Statistical Evidence'. *Historical Studies* 15, no. 61 (Oct. 1973): 737–49.

Roe, Michael. *Nine Australian Progressives: Vitalism in Bourgeois Social Thought 1890–1960*. St Lucia, 1984.

Roskill, Stephen Wentworth. *Hankey: Man of Secrets*. 2 vols. London, 1970.

———. *Churchill and the Admirals*. London, 1977.

Rowley, C. D. *The Australians in German New Guinea 1914–1921*. Carlton, Vic., 1958.

Schoen, Walter von. *Die Hölle von Gallipoli: Der Heldenkampf an den Dardanellen*. Berlin, 1937.

Schuler, Philip. *Australia in Arms*. London, 1916.

Scott, Ernest. *Australia during the War*. Vol. 11 of *Official History of Australia in the War of 1914–1918*. Sydney, 1937.

Sekuless, Peter, and Jacqueline Rees. *Lest We Forget: The History of the Returned Services League, 1916–1986*. Sydney, 1986.

Serle, Geoffrey. *John Monash: A Biography*. Carlton Vic, 1982.

———. 'The Digger Tradition and Australian Nationalism'. *Meanjin Quarterly*, No 101, Vol 24/2 (1965): 149–158.

Smith, Hugh. 'Clausewitz and War: The Contribution of *On War* to the Analysis of War', Department of Politics, University of New South Wales, Australian Defence Force Academy, Canberra [1988].

Souter, Gavin. *Lion and Kangaroo. Australia: 1901–1914*. Sydney, 1976.

Stegemann, Hermann. *Geschichte des Krieges*. 4 vols. Berlin, 1917–21.

Steiner, Zara S. *The Foreign Office and Foreign Policy 1898–1914*. Cambridge, 1969.

Stern, J. P. *Hitler: The Fuhrer and the People*. London, 1975.

Stoker, Commander H. *Straws in the Wind*. London, 1925.

Stuermer, Dr. Harry. *Deux Ans de Guerre à Constantinople*. Paris, 1917.

Thompson, Roger C. *Australian Imperialism in the Pacific: The Expansionist Era, 1820–1920*. Carlton, Vic., 1980.

Thornton, Robert. 'Invaluable Ally or Imminent Aggressor? Australian and Japanese Naval Assistance 1914–1918'. *Journal of Australian Studies*, 12 June 1983, pp. 5–20.

Tilby, A Wyatt. *The English People Overseas.* Vol. 5, *Australasia 1688–1911.* London, 1912.

Townshend, Sir Charles V. F. T. *My Campaign in Mesopotamia.* London, 1920.

Treitschke, Heinrich von. *Deutsche Geschichte im 19 Jahrhundert* (History of Germany in the Nineteenth Century). 5 vols, 1879–94.

Trumpener, Ulrich. *Germany and the Ottoman Empire, 1914–1918.* Princeton, 1968.

Turner, L. C. F. *The First World War.* Melbourne, 1967.

Waite, Major Fred. *The New Zealanders at Gallipoli.* Vol 11 of the New Zealand Popular History Series. Auckland, 1921.

Wallace, R. L. *The Australians at the Boer War.* Canberra, 1976.

Weir, Peter. *Gallipoli—The Screenplay.* Ringwood Vic, 1981.

Welborn, Suzanne. *Lords of Death*: *a people a place a legend.* Fremantle, 1982.

Wemyss, Lord Wester-. *The Navy in the Dardanelles Campaign.* London, n.d. [1923].

White, R. J. 'Motives for joining up. Self Sacrifice, self-interest and social class, 1914–1918.' *Journal of the Australian War Memorial,* no. 9 (Oct 1986): 3–16.

White, T. W. *Guests of the Unspeakable.* London, 1928.

Wigmore, Lionel. *They Dared Mightily.* Canberra, 1963.

Wilson, S. S. *The Cabinet Office to 1945.* London, 1975.

Winter, Denis. 'The Anzac landing—the great gamble?' *Journal of the Australian War Memorial,* no. 4 (Apr 1984).

Woodward, Sir Llewellyn. *Great Britain and the War of 1914–1918.* London, 1967.

Zetland, Lord. *Lord Cromer.* London, 1932.

Zwar, Desmond. *In Search of Keith Murdoch.* Melbourne, 1980.

# BIOGRAPHICAL NOTES

Included are most AIF members mentioned up to colonel rank who are in the text and who served during the Gallipoli campaign. Ranks shown are those at death or discharge from the AIF.

| | | | | | |
|---|---|---|---|---|---|
| AA | Australian Archives | DAC | Divisional Ammunition | MG | Machine-gun |
| AAMC | Australian Army Medical | | Column | MID | Mentioned in dispatches |
| | Corps | DCM | Distinguished Conduct | MM | Military Medal |
| AASC | Australian Army Service | | Medal | MO | Medical Officer |
| | Corps | DOD | Died of disease | NLA | National Library of |
| ADC | Aide-de-camp | DOI | Died of illness | | Australia, Canberra |
| AFA | Australian Field Artillery | DOW | Died of Wounds | n.o.k. | next of kin |
| AFC | Australian Flying Corps | DSO | Distinguished Service | PLA | The Liddle Collection, |
| AGH | Australian General | | Order | | Leeds University Library |
| | Hospital | Dvr | Driver | PO | Petty Officer |
| AN&MEF | Australian Naval and | FAB | Field Artillery Brigade | POW | Prisoner of War |
| | Military Expeditionary | FCE | Field Corps of Engineers | PSL | Paymaster Sub-Lieutenant |
| | Force | Fld Amb. | Field Ambulance | Pte | Private |
| ASH | Australian Stationary | Gnr | Gunner | QMS | Quartermaster-Sergeant |
| | Hospital | GOC | General Officer | RAN | Royal Australian Navy |
| AWM | Australian War Memorial | | Commanding | RFC | Royal Flying Corps |
| Bde | Brigade | HQ | Headquarters | Rfmts | Reinforcements |
| Bdr | Bombardier | IWM | Imperial War Museum | RN | Royal Navy |
| Bn | Battalion | KIA | Killed in Action | RSM | Regimental Sergeant- |
| Capt. | Captain | L/Cpl | Lance-Corporal | | Major |
| CCS | Casualty Clearing Station | LHB | Light Horse Brigade | RTA | Returned to Australia |
| CO | Commanding officer | LHR | Light Horse Regiment | Sgt | Sergeant |
| Col. | Colonel | L/Sgt | Lance-Sergeant | Spr | Sapper |
| Cpl | Corporal | Lt | Lieutenant | S/Sgt | Staff-Sergeant |
| CQMS | Company Quartermaster- | Lt-Col. | Lieutenant-Colonel | VD | Volunteer Decoration |
| | Sergeant | Maj. | Major | WO | Warrant Officer |
| CSM | Company Sergeant-Major | MC | Military Cross | 2 Lt | Second Lieutenant |

Pte H. H. Abbott, 1138, 24 Bn, of Victoria Park, East Perth, WA. Enlisted 8/3/15. KIA 29/11/15. AWM 3 DRL 3817.

Sgt H. A. Affleck, 871, 1 FAB, of Malvern, Vic. Enlisted 19/8/14. Sick, left Anzac for Mudros 15/9/15, returned to Anzac 5/10/15, left Anzac sick 10/12/15. KIA 17/8/17, aged 26. Buried Reninghelst new military cemetery, Belgium. AWM 1 DRL 12.

Lt T. P. Ahern, 54 Bn, wood-turner, of Northcote, Vic. Enlisted as Sgt, 24 Bn, 29/5/15. KIA Fromelles, 20/7/16, aged 22. Buried Anzac Cemetery, Sailly-Sur-La-Lays, France. AWM 1 DRL 12a.

Lt J. M. Aitken, MC, 11 Bn, accountant, of Kalgoorlie, WA, b. Bendigo, Vic. 1891. Enlisted 4/9/14, aged 23. Company Observer Dec. 1914 (Pte), L/Cpl 17 July 15, Cpl 18/8/15 (in charge of section), QMS 1/9/15, Lt in early 1916. KIA France, 10/8/18. Buried Villers-Bretonneux, France. AWM 1 DRL 13.

Pte H. T. C. Alcock, 484, 23 Bn, of

Toorak, Vic. Enlisted 24/2/15. DOD (appendicitis) 14/2/16, aged 20. Buried Chatby War Memorial Cemetery, Alexandria, Egypt. AWM 1 DRL 17.

Cpl A. G. Alderdice, 2 Bn, woolscourer, of Chatswood, NSW, native of Beechworth, Vic. Enlisted 23/4/15. Wounded Fleurbaix, France. DOW Wandsworth Hospital, UK, 15/8/16, aged 35. Buried Wandsworth Cemetery, UK.

L/Sgt C. Alwynne, 481, 2 Bn, labourer, of Narrabri, NSW. Enlisted 3/9/14 aged 26, Cpl April 1915. RTA 10/8/18. AWM 3 DRL 3854.

Sgt W. Alabaster, MM, 45 Bn, native of Westcliff-on-Sea, Essex, UK. Enlisted 29/10/14. DOW France 5/4/18, aged 27. Buried Doullens Communal Cemetery Extension, France. AWM 1 DRL 16.

Pte D. G. Alexander, 1509, 13 Bn, of Sydney, NSW. Enlisted 21/12/14. DOW Gallipoli 15/8/15. Buried Lone Pine Memorial, Gallipoli. AWM 1 DRL 20.

Sgt W. W. B. Allen, 236, 9 Bn, native of Hamilton, Vic. KIA Gallipoli 25/4/15, aged 29. AWM 2 DRL 284.

Lt G. G. Allardyce, 4 Bn, undergraduate, Trinity College, Dublin, of Melbourne, Vic. Enlisted 11/11/14. Wounded Anzac 25 August, went to Lemnos. Wounded France, DOW Oxford, UK, 18/5/16, aged 23. AWM 1 DRL 24.

2 Lt H. Allen, 3 Bn, bookkeeper, native of Fenton, Staffordshire, UK. Enlisted 28/8/14. Wounded 7/8/15, Lone Pine, Gallipoli. DOW 7–9/8/15, aged 39.

Sgt D. J. Anderson, 1175, 8 Bn, pharmaceutical student, of Bendigo, Vic. b. 30/7/1896. Enlisted 10/9/14. KIA Shrapnel Valley, Gallipoli 16/6/15, aged 18. AWM 2 DRL 142.

Pte D. J. C. Anderson, 1040, 2 Bn, clerk, of Lindisfarne, Tas. KIA 17/8/16, aged 23. AWM 2 DRL 165.

Pte A. R. [M?] Andrews, 1 Bn, grocer, of Gosford, NSW. Enlisted 22/8/15. KIA 5/11/16, Ypres, Belgium, aged 29. AWM 1 DRL 42.

Pte J. C. Angus, 591, 28 Bn, of Pingelly, WA (parents North Shields, England). Enlisted 10/3/15. DOW 6/7/16, aged 24. Buried Etaples Military Cemetery, France. AWM 1 DRL 45.

Cpl R. E. Antill, 1228, 14 Bn, cabinetmaker, of Windsor, Vic. (parents Harringay, London, UK). Enlisted 12/10/14. KIA Belgium 5/7/17, aged 20. AWM 1 DRL 47.

Capt. T. H. Aram, 57 Bn, accountant, of St Kilda East, Vic. Lt at Gallipoli. KIA 25/9/17, aged 30. Buried Menin Gate Memorial, Ypres, Belgium. AWM PR 84/87.

Pte D. R. Argyle, 4562, 6 Bn, farmer, of Kerang, Vic. Enlisted 8/3/15. KIA Passchendaele 20/10/17, aged 24. AWM 1 DRL 50.

Lt-Col. Sir Stanley S. Argyle, AAMC, No. 1 Australian General Hospital, Cairo. Enlisted 1914, Maj. in 1915. RTA 22/2/17. AWM 2 DRL 1014.

Capt. H. E. S. Armitage, MID, 10 Bn at Anzac, 50 Bn, student, of Millicent, SA. Enlisted as 2 Lt, 10 Bn, 5th Rfmts, 25/3/15. KIA 3/4/17, aged 22. AWM 1 DRL 53.

Pte G. H. Arnold, 1131, 2 Bn, of Coolamon, NSW. Enlisted 28/11/14. KIA 26/4/17, aged 28. AWM 1 DRL 61.

Bdr A. E. Attwell, 875, 2 FAB, of Hawkesdale, Vic. Enlisted 20/8/14. KIA 11/10/17, aged 27.

Capt. P. H. Auld, MC. PSL Enlisted 4/11/14. RTA 25/3/19. AWM 2 DRL 72.

Sgt W. Bailey, 1901, 15 Bn, carpenter, of Bulimba, Qld. Enlisted as Pte on 23/1/15, aged 21. POW, captured 8/8/15 during advance on Hill 971. RTA 1/8/19. AWM 30 B1.2.

Sgt D. R. Baker, MM, 692, 1 MG Bn. Enlisted 20/8/14 as Pte. Wounded at Gallipoli, hospital Malta May 1915, effective abroad 1919. AWM 3 DRL 7852.

CSM B. B. Barnes, 324, 21 Bn, motor mechanic, of Geelong, Vic. b.1895. Enlisted 15/1/15. KIA 4/10/17. AWM 2 DRL 4.

Pte J. I. Beattie, 1827, 15 Bn, miner, of Townsville, Qld. Enlisted 11/3/15, aged 25. POW, captured 8/8/15 during attack on Hill 971. RTA 31/12/18. AWM 30 B1.3.

Lt-Col. M. F. Beevor, 10 Bn, accountant, of Unley, SA. Enlisted as Maj. 19/8/14, aged 31. RTA 11/10/16. AWM 3 DRL 3911.

Lt J. R. Bell, 12 Bn reinforcement, pilot, AFC. RTA 17/3/19. PLA.

Pte T. G. Bell, 905, 6 Bn, telephonist, of Cunninghame, Vic., b. 1895. Enlisted 20/8/14. KIA 25/4/15, aged 22. AWM 2 DRL 177.

Pte F. W. Bennett, 6 Fld Amb., AAMC. Enlisted 13/2/15, embarked 8/5/15. RTA 22/4/19, discharged 21/6/19. Served on Gallipoli, in

Middle East, England, France and Belgium with AFA. AWM 3 DRL 7507.

Lt S. J. Bennie, 21 Bn, of Lauriston, Vic. Enlisted 7/5/15. KIA 5/10/18, aged 27. AWM 2 DRL 330.

Capt. C. E. Benson, DCM, 9 Bn, clerk, of Townsville, Qld (Ryde, NSW, father). Enlisted 20/8/14, as Sgt, 874. KIA 2/7/16, aged 26. AWM 1 DRL 112.

Sgt W. N. Berg, 1132, 18 Bn. Enlisted 10/2/15. RTA 15/4/18. AWM 2 DRL 442.

2 Lt W. H. Bertwistle, 27 Bn and 7 MG Coy b. 1895. Enlisted 2/3/15, commissioned 14 Nov 1915. RTA 13/2/17. Diary PLA, TS copy of diary AWM 2 DRL 428.

Gnr R. W. Betts, 3604, 2 FAB, of Mildura, Vic. Enlisted 7/12/14. DOW 20/4/17, aged 30. AWM 1 DRL 115.

L/Sgt R. S. Beveridge, 165, 20 Bn, of Randwick, NSW. Enlisted 15/3/15. KIA 12/11/16, aged 22. AWM 2DRL 325.

Maj. F. L. Biddle, DSO, 2 FAB, of Melbourne, Vic. DOW 17/8/17, aged 31. AWM 1 DRL 119.

Cpl H. D. Billings, 14, 1 LHB, 1st Signal Troop. Enlisted 19/8/14. RTA 3/12/18. AWM 3 DRL 6060 (also IWM).

L/Cpl I. T. Birtwhistle, 730, 22 Bn, journalist, of Subiaco, WA. Enlisted 13/2/15, aged 23. RTA 22/2/17. Diary in PLA.

Cpl O. S. Blows, 229, 28 Bn. Enlisted 4/3/15, ill and evacuated 19/11/15. RTA 3/9/19. IWM.

Lt J. J. Bourke, 1 MG Bn, farmer, of Wangaratta, Vic. Enlisted 17/8/14. KIA 20/9/17 at Passchendaele, Belgium aged 26. AWM 1DRL 140.

PO H. L. Bowden, 1 RAN Naval Bridging Train. Assisted in evacuation of Anzac. RTA 29/5/17. AWM 3 DRL 7597.

Cpl D. Boyle, 296, 14 Bn, carpenter, of Warrnambool, Vic. Enlisted as L/Cpl 10/9/14, aged 22. POW, captured 9/8/15 during attack on Hill 971. RTA 15/11/18. AWM 30 B1.4.

Sgt A. W. Bradley, 1656, 22 Bn, clerk, of Moonee Ponds. Enlisted 19/5/15. KIA Pozières, France, 5/8/16, aged 19. AWM 3 DRL 3418.

Lt-Col. G. F. Braund, VD, MID, 2 Bn HQ, general merchant and MLA for Armidale, NSW, of Neutral Bay, NSW. Enlisted 15/8/14. KIA 4/5/15, aged 49.

Lt-Col. N. M. Brazier, CO, 10 LHR, pastoralist, of Capeldene, Kirup, WA. Enlisted 2/10/14, aged 48. Wounded 28/8/15, appointment terminated 14/5/16, reappointed AIF 19/12/16, appointment terminated June 1917. AWM 1 DRL 147.

Lt T. Brew, DCM, 2 Bn, wool sorter,

of Ballarat, b. Southport, Lancs. Enlisted August 1914. KIA Polygon Wood, Belgium, 4/10/17, aged 21. AWM 2 DRL 140/276.

Major E. T. Brind, 23 Bn, distiller, of Ballarat, Vic. KIA Pozières, France, 28/7/16, aged 32. AWM 1 DRL 153.

L/Cpl G. H. H. Brisco, 28 Bn, farmer, of Babakine, WA. Enlisted 27/3/15. KIA Pozières, France, 29/7/16, aged 21. AWM 1 DRL 154.

Dvr E. A. Brown, 48, 1 Sig. Troop, 1 LHB. Enlisted 19/8/14, RTA 13/10/18. AWM 2 DRL 1285.

Pte H. N. Brown, 1333, 14 Bn, farm hand, n.o.k. address Manchester, UK. Enlisted 28/9/14, aged 19. POW. RTA 9/2/19. AWM 30 B1.15.

2 Lt R. J. Brownell, MM, RFC (gunner 2058 in first contingent), of Claremont. WA, but a Tasmanian. Enlisted 12/9/14. Discharged 16/3/17. PLA.

Cpl O. Bruce, 4 FCE, mining surveyor, of Kahibah, NSW. Enlisted 16/3/15. KIA Longueval, France, 18/12/16, aged 23. AWM 2 DRL 294.

Gnr E. Burgess, 1674, 5 FAB, clerk, of Geelong, Vic. Enlisted 17/5/15. Wounded 21/11/15, to hospital in Malta. KIA Passchendaele, Belgium, 4/10/17, aged 22. AWM 1 DRL 162.

Pte P. R. Burns (P. R. Bunny), 7 Bn, labourer, of Ascot Vale, Vic. Enlisted 16/9/14. KIA Gallipoli, 8–9/8/15, aged 26, AWM 2 DRL 479.

Lt A. G. McL. Burns, MC, 4 Div Sig. Coy, of Katoomba, NSW. Enlisted 17/8/14. RTA 9/3/19. AWM 2 DRL 738.

Capt C. C. Burton, 7 Bn, fire loss adjuster, of Sandringham, Vic. DOI in London, 14/12/18, aged 35. AWM 1 DRL 167.

2 Lt F. J. Burton, 4 LHR, soldier, of Minyip, Vic. Enlisted 22/8/14. KIA Beersheba, 31/10/17, aged 23. AWM 1 DRL 168.

Lt A. J. Byrne, 10 Bn, electrician, of Broken Hill, NSW. Enlisted 19/8/14, aged 24. KIA 25/4/15.

2 Lt D. W. Caldwell, 27 Bn, carpenter, of Semaphore, SA. Enlisted 26/1/15, Sgt at Gallipoli. KIA Harlencourt, France, 2/3/17, aged 24. AWM 1 DRL 176.

Capt. P. I. Callary, 9 LHR, storekeeper, of Peterborough, SA. Appointed 2 Lt AIF 1/11/14, Lt 16/1/15, promoted to Capt. 1/6/15. KIA 29/8/15 in attack on Hill 60, aged 29. AWM 1 DRL 178.

2 Lt W. M. Cameron, 9 LHR, of Rushworth, Vic. Enlisted 23/9/14, promoted to 2 Lt 25/8/15. KIA 4/9/15. AWM 1 DRL 185.

Capt. A. G. Carne, MC, 6 Bn, student, of Malvern, SA, b. 1888. Enlisted as Pte 71, 18/8/14, aged 26. AIF appointment terminated 27/1/20. AWM 2 DRL 13.

Pte A. A. Carpenter, 1926, 15 Bn, labourer, of Brisbane, Qld. Enlisted 18/1/15, aged 20. POW. RTA 9/2/19. AWM 30 B1.6.

Capt. H. G. Carter, 1 Bn, electrical engineer, of Darling Point, NSW. Enlisted as Lt, 3/9/14, aged 29. AWM 3 DRL 6418.

Maj. R. G. Casey, DSO, MC, 3 Inf. Bde (General List). Discharged 10/6/19. AWM 3 DRL 2030, 3 DRL 3267; NLA MS 6150.

Lt E. R. Cavanagh, DCM, 23 Bn, later AFC, b. 1892. Enlisted 9/2/15. RTA 1919. AWM 2 DRL 131.

S/Sgt B. M. Challen, 669, Dental Corps. Enlisted 19/10/14. RTA 2/1/19. AWM 1 DRL 195.

Capt. L. Keith Chambers, 17 Bn, of Mosman, NSW. 2 Lt AN & MEF 19/8/14; Lt 1/1/15; joined AIF 7/5/15 as Lt (17 Bn), promoted to Captain 23/7/16, Adjutant 8/10/15–31/3/16. KIA Pozières, France, 29/7/16. AWM 2 DRL 49.

Lt-Col. R. W. Chambers, DSO, AAMC, medical practitioner, of Sandringham, Vic., b. Melbourne, 1/1/1890. Capt. 2nd Fld Amb. March 1915. Commanded detachment at Helles 5–8 May 1915. Effective abroad 1919. AWM 41 [1/5.7].

Lt B. W. Champion, 1 Bn, dental apprentice, Wahroonga, NSW. Enlisted 21/5/15, aged 18. RTA 30/6/18. AWM 2 DRL 512.

Lt-Col. C. L. Chapman, DSO, AAMC. Effective abroad 1919. AWM 2 DRL 1228.

Pte J. Chapman, 1167, 15Bn, railway porter, of Hobart, Tas. Enlisted 22/9/14, aged 23. KIA Gallipoli 9–10/5/15. Buried Quinn's Post Cemetery, Gallipoli.

Capt. P. W. Chapman, 55 Bn, of Goulburn, NSW. Enlisted 9/3/15, as Pte, promoted Lt December 1915 at Gallipoli. KIA 12/3/17, aged 30. AWM 1 DRL 198.

Sgt H. A. Cheney, 50 Bn, clerk, of Mitcham, SA, b. Northallerton, Yorks. Enlisted 28/8/14 as 806, 10 Bn; served at Gallipoli; transferred to 50 Bn in UK in 1916. KIA 2/4/17, aged 26. AWM 1 DRL 199.

Pte W. M. Clark, 1126, 10 Bn, labourer, of Kalangadoo, SA. Enlisted 24/8/14, aged 26. RTA 15/8/15. PLA.

Cpl A. J. Clennett, MM, 3309, 10 FAB, of Tas. Enlisted 23/9/14. RTA 8/10/18. Papers in PLA.

Gnr J. H. Clennett, MM, 3 (Army) FAB, of Tas. Enlisted 12/9/14. RTA 31/3/19. Papers in PLA.

Cpl W. Cliffe, 482, 4 Bn, coachman, of Port Hacking, NSW. Enlisted 24/8/14 aged 32. POW, captured during reconnaissance raid on Turkish tren-

ches on Johnston's Jolly, opposite MacLaurin's Hill, while escorting wounded comrade back to trenches. RTA 5/3/19. AWM 30 B1.8.

Maj. H. J. F. Coe, 2 Dvn Art, 12 FAB. 2 Lt 18/8/14, Lt 25/6/15, Capt. 21/1/17, Maj. 12/1/18; Adjutant 12th AFA 1916/17. RTA 10/5/19. AWM 2 DRL 491.

Capt. F. Coen, 18 Bn, of Yass, NSW. KIA 28/7/16, aged 33. AWM 1 DRL 203.

Sgt R. M. Collins, 697, 23 Bn. Enlisted 1/3/15. RTA 9/2/16. PLA.

Lt C. H. Copp, AFC. Enlisted 17/8/14 as Pte, L/Cpl 2/5/15. Wounded 9/5/15, sent to Suez; left Suez 29/7/15. RTA 19/6/19. AWM 3 DRL 7055.

Lt-Col. John Corbin, AAMC. No. 1 ASH. Capt. March 1915. RTA 22/7/17. AWM 41 [1/5.18].

S/Sgt G. S. Cox, 1360, 2 AGH. Enlisted 2/11/14. RTA 16/10/18. AWM 3 DRL 6234.

Pte D. B. Creedon, 589, 9 Bn, clerk, of Maryborough, Qld. Enlisted 19/8/14, aged 21. POW. DOI 27/2/17, aged 23. Buried Baghdad (North Gate) War Cemetery. Diary AWM 1 DRL 223.

Capt. H. F. Curnow, 22 Bn, clerk, of South Melbourne, Vic. Enlisted as 2 Lt aged 22, in C Coy, which embarked 10/5/15. KIA 5/8/16. AWM 1 DRL 229.

Cpl H. Daniels, 46, 16 Bn, fireman, of Midland Junction, WA. Enlisted 7/9/14, Pte at Gallipoli. RTA 21/7/18. AWM 3 DRL 7605.

Pte J. Davern, 2474, 16 Bn, labourer, of Carnamah, WA. Enlisted 2/6/15, aged 27. POW. RTA 17/6/18.

Lt W. H. Dawkins, 2 Field Coy Div. HQ, Aust. Engineers, of Fern Tree Gully, Vic., parents Camberwell, Vic. KIA 20/5/15, aged 22. Location of papers unknown.

Sgt Maurice Delpratt, 636, 5 LHR. Enlisted 15/11/14. POW. RTA 3/7/19. AWM 30 B2.1.

Dvr G. W. Dennis, 3432, 1 DAC. Enlisted 14/9/14. RTA 31/10/17. AWM 3 DRL 7507.

Sgt A. L. de Vine, 330, 4 BN, electrical engineer, of Waverley, NSW. Enlisted as Pte 19/8/14, aged 28. RTA 16/6/19. AWM 1 DRL 240.

CSM S. C. Dewey, 1342, 56 Bn. Enlisted 6/11/14. RTA 12/5/18. AWM 3 DRL 6620.

Sgt H. W. Dinning, AASC, journalist, of Qld. RTA 3/7/19. Wrote By-ways on Service.

Pte R. L. Donkin, 817, 1 Bn, labourer, of East Maitland, NSW. Enlisted 31/8/14. KIA 15/8/15, aged 24. AWM 2 DRL 69.

Pte A. E. Dowse, 734, 2 Bn, G Coy, fireman, of Manning River, NSW. Enlisted 22/8/14, aged 25. Effective

abroad 1919. AWM PR 82/8(2).

Capt. C. R. Duke, MC, enlisted as Pte 963, 4 Bn, B Coy, architect, of Dunedin, New Zealand. Enlisted 2/9/14, aged 25. RTA 18/7/19. PLA.

Lt E. D. H. Edgerton, DSO, MM & Bar, 24 Bn, of Elsternwick, Vic. Enlisted 14/4/15. KIA 11/8/18, aged 21. AWM 1 DRL 257, 3 DRL 6582.

Lt H. T. Elder, 5 Bn HQ, salesman, of East Prahran, Vic. Enlisted 28/8/14, signal instructor aged 23. Promoted Lt 1/2/15. DOW at sea after second battle of Krithia, 9/5/15. AWM1 DRL 259.

Capt. W. E. Elston, 16 Bn. Lt at Gallipoli. POW. RTA 15/11/18. AWM 30 B1.13.

Pte H. A. Fildes, 675, 12 Bn, clerk, of Croydon, SA. Enlisted 3/9/14, aged 19. RTA 3/12/18. Papers in PLA.

Pte V. Finch, 429, 1st FCE. Enlisted 8/9/14. RTA 3/9/19. AWM PR 84/58.

Cpl J. Fitzmaurice, DCM, 30, 10 LHR, stockman, father's address Liverpool, U.K. Enlisted 6/12/14, aged 23. RTA 6/9/19. Diary in PLA.

CQMS W. L. Fowler, 137, 15 Bn, bank accountant, of Innisfail, Qld. Enlisted 26/9/14 (L/Cpl). KIA Polygon Wood 27/2/17. AWM 3 DRL 6135.

Pte H. Foxcroft, 1720, 14 Bn, father's address Manchester, U.K. Enlisted 2/12/14. POW, captured during advance on Hill 971 on 8/8/15. RTA 12/5/19. AWM 30 B1.15.

Pte V. E. Frankcombe, 1036, 15 Bn, overseer, of Beulah, Tas. Enlisted 19/9/14, landed Anzac 25/4/15. KIA 13/5/15, aged 24. PLA.

L/Cpl John Gammage, 1764, 1 Bn, baker, of Cootamundra, NSW. Enlisted as Pte 27/1/15. RTA 2/8/19. AWM PR 83/117.

Capt.-Chaplain A. Gillison, MID, 13 Bn, 4 Bde, Presbyterian clergyman, of East St Kilda, Vic. DOW 22/8/15, aged 47. AWM 3 DRL 6277.

Lt J. J. Greatorex, MID, 1 LHB MG Sqn. Enlisted 14/9/14, Lt 1/2/18. RTA 16/3/19. AWM 3 DRL 6776.

Dvr R. W. Griffiths, 266, 1 DAC (attached to HQ 1 AFA Bde). POW, captured 7/8/15 during counterattack by Turks at Cape Helles. RTA 23/12/18. AWM 30 B1.16.

Lt G. C. Grove, 2nd Pioneers, of St Kilda, Vic. Enlisted as Sapper, 23/10/14. RTA 19/2/19. PLA.

Capt. E. W. Gutteridge, medical officer, 7 Bn HQ, physician and surgeon, of Collins Street, Melbourne, Vic. Enlisted 20/9/14, aged 26. Invalided to Australia 2/1/16. AWM 41 [2/8.8].

Sgt J. S. Hagan, 1343, 3 Bn & 206, 1 Div Sig. Sqn, telegraphist, of Mittagong, NSW. Enlisted 29/8/14, aged

25. RTA 21/1/16. AWM PR 84/188.

Pte William Harris, 1045, 16 Bn, insurance inspector, of North Adelaide, SA. Enlisted 11/9/14, aged 24. RTA 15/8/15. AWM 3 DRL 7285.

Maj. Dixon Hearder, 11 Bn, solicitor, n.o.k. wife, Carmarthen, U.K. Enlisted as Capt. 1914, aged 35. RTA 25/8/17. AWM 3 DRL 7140 (& IWM).

Maj. Oliver Hogue, 14 LHR, journalist, of Sydney, NSW. Enlisted 16/9/14. DOD (influenza) 3/3/19. Buried Brookwood Military Cemetery, Surrey, UK.

Sgt L. S. Horder, 1050, 1 LHB MGS. Enlisted 13/4/15, arrived Anzac 28/9/15. RTA 6/9/19. AWM 3 DRL 6595.

L/Cpl G. Irving, 2094, 3 Bn, motor driver, native of Annan, Scotland. Enlisted 26/3/15, aged 31. RTA 19/6/19. AWM 3 DRL 6547.

Pte A. E. Joyce, 2175, 9 Bn and AFC. Enlisted 22/8/14. RTA 7/7/19. PLA.

Pte S. G. Jury, 458, 4 Bn, butcher, of Ashfield, NSW. Enlisted 24/8/14, aged 19. RTA 23/10/18. AWM PR 82/8 (1).

Pte J. R. T. Keast, 967, 11 Bn and 4 Aust. Motor Transport Coy, carpenter, of Popanyinning, WA. Enlisted 7/9/14 aged 23. RTA 3/12/18. PLA.

Trooper P. F. Keenan, 427, 10 LHR, timber worker, of Albany, WA. Enlisted 27/10/14, aged 22. RTA 22/7/19.

Cpl E. H. Kitson 1067, 4 Fld Amb. Enlisted 26/10/14. RTA 13/2/17. AWM 41 [3/9.14].

Sgt G. S. Laslett, 773, 11 LHR MGS. Enlisted 5/1/15, S/Sgt by 22/8/15. RTA 6/7/19. AWM 3 DRL 6590.

L/Cpl C. J. Lawless, 1375, 12 Fld Amb. Enlisted as Pte 27/10/14. RTA 8/10/18. PLA 1375.

Lt C. Lawrence, 1 Div. Engineers. Sgt at Gallipoli. RTA 24/1/19.

Capt, A. E. Leane, 48 Bn, of Adelaide, SA. Enlisted 22/4/15. DOW 2/5/17, aged 23. Buried Villers-Bretonneux, France. AWM 1 DRL 411.

Pte D. W. Lechte, 848, 22 Bn, orchardist, of Mt Waverley, Vic. Enlisted 15/2/15, aged 19. RTA 9/3/19. AWM 3 DRL 7178.

Pte J. C. Lennie, B Section, 4th Fld Amb., AAMC. Enlisted 2/10/14. RTA, 12/11/16. AWM 3 DRL 7681.

Pte L. D. Lightfoot, 2378, 16 Bn, clerk, mother's address Finsbury Park, London, U.K. Enlisted 22/4/15 aged 20. POW. RTA 17/3/19. AWM 30 B1.19.

Maj. A. J. Love, 10 LHB, accountant, of Mount Lawley, Perth, W.A. Enlisted 28/10/14. RTA 13/2/19. See Brazier papers AWM 1 DRL 147.

Pte R. F. Lushington, 507, 16 Bn, farmer, of Upper Swan, WA. Enlisted

24/9/14, aged 23. POW. RTA 25/12/18.

Pte I. A. McCowan, 407, 5 Bn, C Coy, seaman, of South Melbourne, Vic. Enlisted 24/8/14. In 8 Bn at Quinn's Post, June 1915, but died in 5 Bn. KIA 14/7/15, aged 32. Buried Shrapel Valley Cemetery, Anzac. IWM.

Capt. R. T. A. McDonald, 16 Bn, A Coy HQ (Adjutant). Captured 25/4/15, Pope's Hill, Gallipoli. POW. RTA 23/9/19. AWM 30 B1.22.

Cpl H. T. McKern, 454, 4 Bn, farmer, of Wentworth, NSW. Enlisted 23/8/14, aged 21. DOW 16/8/15 AWM 3 DRL 3906.

2 Lt J. L. Merivale, 4 Bn. Enlisted 21/10/14. KIA Gallipoli 6–9/8/15, aged 28. Buried Lone Pine Cemetery. AWM 3 DRL 3961.

Lt O. F. Metcher, 5 Div. Sig. Coy. Enlisted 22/8/14, RTA 5/3/19. AWM 3 DRL 6187(2).

Lt-Col. S. L. Milligan, DSO, CMG, 4 Bn, survey draughtsman, of Chatswood, NSW. Enlisted as 2 Lt 27/8/14, aged 27. Effective abroad, 1919. Milligan Papers, IWM.

Lt G. D. Mitchell, DCM, MC, 48 Bn, clerk, of Thebarton, SA. Enlisted as Cpl (1014, 10 Bn) 5/9/14. Evacuated Gallipoli September 1915; in Netley Hospital, England, until January 1916. RTA 5/4/19. AWM 2 DRL 928.

Lt H. E. Moody, 3 FAB, solicitor, of Yorketown, SA, native of Adelaide, SA. DOW 27/8/16. Buried Puchevillers British Cemetery, France. AWM 1 DRL 504.

Pte A. A. Moon, 3861, 6 Bn, carpenter, of Port Melbourne, Vic. Enlisted 26/7/15, aged 45. RTA 17/3/17. Diary in AA AIF 112/2/382 B 539.

Pte E. A. Moor, 1502, 16 Bn, of Bunbury, WA (parents Subiaco, WA), native of Croydon, England. KIA 9/5/15, aged 27. AWM PR 82/8(2).

Sgt E. P. Moore, 1427, 1 CCS, AAMC. Enlisted 19/9/14. RTA 12/3/18. PLA.

L/Cpl E. W. Moorhead, 557, 5 Bn, clerk, of Malvern. Vic. Enlisted 17/8/14, aged 24. RTA 21/7/17. AWM 3 DRL 7253.

Pte F. Morrish, 549, 1 Bn, B Coy, station hand, of Neutral Bay, NSW (mother Stoke, Devonport, England). Enlisted 7/9/14, aged 23. KIA 25/4/15. Letter from Capt. H. G. Carter in Rear-Adm. I. W. Gibson Papers, IWM.

Dvr A. J. Mychael, 146, 1 LHR, of Moonan Flat, Scone, NSW. Enlisted 27/8/14. KIA 7/8/15. AWM 3 DRL 6051.

Cpl J. Neal, 1505, 2 Bn, 3rd Rfmts, bricklayer, of Carlton, NSW. Enlisted 17/11/14, aged 24. RTA 6/11/

18. AWM PR 82/8(1).

Pte H. F. Nelson, 1599, 9 Bn, dentist, of Buderim, Qld. Enlisted 14/12/14, aged 27. RTA 19/1/16.

Pte L. G. New, 2181, 15 Bn, labourer, of Brisbane, Qld. Enlisted 14/3/15, aged 21. POW. Accidentally killed, Turkey, 7/5/16. Buried Baghdad (North Gate) War Cemetery.

Pte P. O'Connor, 1568, 14 Bn, farmer, of Monbulk, Vic. Enlisted 21/12/14 (as 1659, 14 Bn, 3rd Rfmts), aged 22. POW, captured 8/8/15 during attack on Hill 971. RTA 18/1/19. AWM 30 B1.27.

Maj. H. H. Page, MC, DSO, 25 Bn. RTA 16/3/19. AWM 3 DRL 6910.

Pte J. Pasmore, 486, 14 Bn, labourer, of Pyramid Hill, Vic. Enlisted 15/9/14, aged 22. POW, captured 8/8/15 during attack on Hill 971. RTA 9/2/19. AWM 30 B1.28.

Pte W. W. Paterson, 337, 11 Bn, blacksmith, of Springwood, NSW. Enlisted 22/8/14, aged 34. RTA 31/8/15. PLA, AWM PR 82/8(1).

Pte H. Paull, 2546, HMT. Coy. Enlisted 27/8/14. Discharged 22/4/19. IWM.

L/Cpl A. E. Pfeifer, 333, 15 Bn, farm labourer, no address (mother Kent Town, London, England). Enlisted 25/9/14, aged 18. Wounded Gallipoli late May 1915. RTA 4/6/19. Diary 79/46/1, IWM.

Sgt G. A. Radnell, DCM, 1182, 8 Bn, grocer's assistant, of Tarnagulla, Vic. Enlisted 16/9/14, aged 23. RTA 8/10/18 as 1126, 1 MG Bn. PLA.

Sgt A. J. Rawlings, 890, 2 Bn, blacksmith, of North Fitzroy, Vic. Enlisted 20/8/14, aged 29. POW. DOW 3/5/17.

Lt J. A. Raws, 11th Rfmts, 22 Bn, journalist, of Spring Street, Melbourne, Vic. (father Rev. J. G. Raws, Malvern, Adelaide, SA), b. Manchester, UK. Enlisted 24/7/15. Camp Seymour 21/7/15. 2 Lt Jan. 1916. Embarked 28/3/16. KIA 22/8/16, aged 33. Buried Villers-Bretonneux, France. AWM 2 DRL 481.

Lt R. G. Raws, 23 Bn, warehouseman of Adelaide, SA, b. Manchester, UK. Enlisted Melbourne Jan. 1915, 2 Lt 24/3/15, embarked 8/5/15, Lt 26/8/15, arrived Gallipoli 3/9/15, France 29/3/16. Reported missing July 1916, presumed KIA 28/7/16, aged 30. Buried Villers-Bretonneux, France. AWM 2 DRL 481.

L/Cpl W. E. Rhodes, 270, 9 Bn, grocer, of Kangaroo Point, Brisbane, Qld. (father Bradford, UK). Enlisted 21/8/14, aged 31. Wounded Gallipoli. RTA 15/8/15. AWM?

Lt J. T. Richards, MC, 1 Bn, commercial traveller, of Charters Towers, Qld, b. Emmaville, NSW, 8/4/1883. Enlisted as Pte 26/8/14. RTA 6/8/

18. AWM 2 DRL 786.

Pte F. Robson, 339, 15 Bn, butcher, of Rockhampton, Qld. Enlisted 20/9/14. KIA 18/5/15, aged 26. Buried Lone Pine Memorial Cemetery. AWM PR 84/172.

Pte Harold Rush, 152, 10 LHR, farmhand, of York, WA, native of Witnesham, Ipswich, UK. Enlisted 6/10/14. KIA 7/8/15, aged 23. Buried Walker's Ridge Cemetery, Gallipoli.

Pte E. C. Skinner, 1662, 16 Bn, wire worker, of East Perth, WA. Enlisted 12/1/15, aged 30. RTA 14/2/18. PLA.

Pte Ellis Silas, 634, 16 Bn, artist, of Cliff Terrace, Perth, WA. Enlisted 28/9/14, aged 30. Discharged 17/8/16. AWM 1 DRL 566.

Capt. V. E. Smythe, MC and Bar, 3 Bn, clerk, of Narrandera, NSW. Enlisted as Pte aged 20 (1174, 3 Bn), 2 Lt May 1915. RTA 8/1/19. PLA.

2 Lt G. H. Henderson Smith, 11 Bn, clerk, of Perth, WA. Enlisted as Pte (618, 11 Bn) 10/9/14, aged 19, 2 Lt 22/5/15. KIA 25/5/15. AWM 3 DRL 7247.

Capt. J. E. G. Stevenson, MC, 1 FCE. Enlisted 14/12/14. RTA 28/3/19. AWM 3 DRL 2995.

2 Lt S. L. Stormonth, C Coy, 15 Bn, clerk, of Toowoomba, Qld. Enlisted as L/Cpl E Coy, 15 Bn, 3/10/14, aged 26. POW, captured 8/8/15 in attack on Hill 971. AWM 30 B1.30.

Charles Suckling, RAN, Submariner, AE2. POW, captured in Sea of Marmara. AWM 3 DRL 6226.

Lt-Col. A. Sutton, CB, CMG. CO 3rd A. Fld Amb., of Brisbane, Qld. Left Anzac 26/7/15 for posting in 2nd Aust. Div. AWM 2 DRL 1227.

Cpl W. E. Turnley, 84, 1 FCE. Enlisted 20/8/14. RTA 10/6/16. AWM 2 DRL 543 and 863.

Maj. J. J. Walker, 19 Bn. RTA 23/9/18. Papers AWM 3 DRL 6395.

Lt-Col. A. H. White, MID, 8 LHR, maltster, of Ballarat, Vic. KIA 7/8/15 aged 33.

Dvr A. J. Williams, 2148, 6 Bn at Gallipoli 14 AFA. Enlisted 23/9/14. RTA 20/11/18. AWM 2 DRL 862.

Pte W. W. Williams, 1195, 14 Bn, farm hand (father's address Rotherhithe, London, UK). Enlisted 12/9/14, aged 20. POW, captured 8/8/15 during attack on Hill 971. RTA 5/3/19. AWM 30 B1.32.

Pte V. O. Worland, No. 2 Fld Amb., 1 Aust. Div. Enlisted 18/8/14. RTA 11/5/16. AWM 3 DRL 3904.

# SOURCES OF ILLUSTRATIONS

ABBREVIATIONS

AWM Australian War Memorial; *Gal. Gallipoli*, by Alan Moorehead (Macmillan Australia, 1989); JR John Robertson

Front jacket background *Anzac Cove, looking towards Achi Baba*, H. Moore-Jones, AWM, top AWM PS1576, bottom AWM H10350; p.1 AWM PS1514; p. 2–3 AWM; p.6 AWM; p.18 AWM P69/01/01; p.19 AWM P117/64/53; p.27 AWM A3116; p.32 AWM P117/64/16; p.35 AWM G761; p.41 AWM P113/01/01; p.52 *Gal.* p.37; p.53 AWM A2647; p.54 AWM H10350; p.56 AWM PS1447; p.66 AWM C1654; p.67 AWM PWDJ157; p.69 top JR T147, bottom JR T39; p.70 AWM P35/01/01; p.72 AWM J5577; p.74 AWM G933; p.75 AWM G916; p.77 AWM; p.80 AWM G377; p.82 C958; p.84 AWM A3088; p.86 AWM PWDJ160; p.89 AWM C1808; p.90 AWM; p.91 AWM A2023; p.94 AWM; p.96 top AWM G991, bottom AWM A1413; p.97 JR T89; p.98 AWM G1016; p.100 AWM A1520; p.101 AWM P252/03/01; p.103 AWM G268; p.104 AWM P600/02/01; p.105 AWM A1037; p.108 AWM C3686; p.109 AWM P188/22/08; p.112 AWM P188/22/10; p.114 AWM A5295; p.115 AWM; p.117 AWM A1006; p.122 AWM G1126; p.124 AWM C1685; p.125 AWM A2025; p.127 AWM; p.128 JR T69; p.133 *Gal.* p.256; p.136 JR T71; p.137 AWM J2391; p.140 AWM; p.141 AWM A2336; p.142 AWM H3931; p.143 AWM C1471; p.144 AWM C4407; p.147 AWM PWDJ163; p.149 AWM P591/29/04; p.152 AWM H3448; p.153 AWM A2011; p.155 *Gal.* p.257; p.156 AWM A5384; p.157 AWM A5401; p.161 AWM A3770; p.165 AWM G531; p.169 AWM G573c; p.173 AWM P188/22/14; p.174 AWM PWDJ142; p.175 AWM H3557; p.176 AWM A910; p.178 AWM PWDJ127; p.179 AWM C5238; p.183 AWM C2315; p.184 AWM A5298; p.189 AWM G1534; p.190 top AWM, bottom AWM P177/64/22; p.195 AWM PS1659; p.196 AWM C1602; p.199 AWM C4015; p.203 AWM H18510; p.204 AWM; p.208 AWM C660; p.211 AWM P61/14/07; p.212 top AWM P176/20/1, bottom AWM A2024; p.215 *Gal.* p.12; p.217 AWM P166/25/22; p.223 AWM; p.239 AWM A1798; p.243 AWM PS1576; p.246 AWM C4022; p.250 AWM; p.255 AWM; p.256 AWM H12952; p.258 AWM PS1514; p.260 left and right AWM; p.265 JR T139; p.267 AWM H15538.

# INDEX

Numbers in italics refer to illustrations. Ranks given are those last referred to in the narrative.

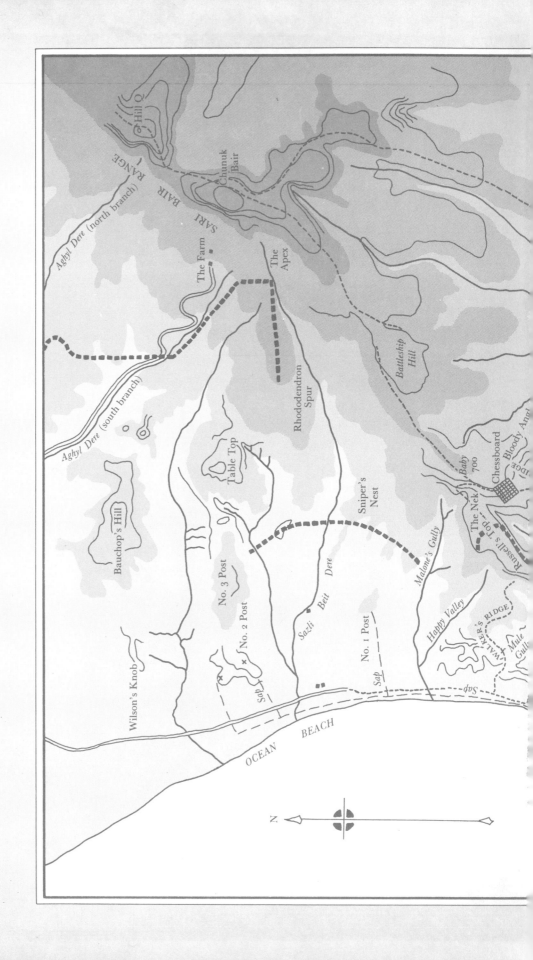